TOWARD JOY

TOWARD JOY

New Frameworks for American Art

Stephanie Sparling Williams

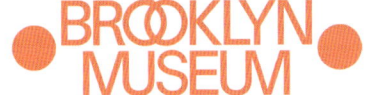

Contents

6   Director's Foreword
Anne Pasternak, Shelby White and Leon Levy Director

8   Acknowledgments
Stephanie Sparling Williams, Andrew W. Mellon Curator of American Art

10   New Frameworks for American Art
Stephanie Sparling Williams

30   Through Gimlet Holes: New Visions for American Art

      32   EXPLORING THE SHOALS
           Leigh Raiford

      33   [FROM A PLACE OF LOVE]
           Leslie Wilson

      33   SOWING SEEDS, LAYING GROUND
           Kelli Morgan

      34   A BLACK MIRROR
           Brittany Webb

      35   A BLACK FEMINIST FRAMEWORK FOR THE DECORATIVE ARTS
           Tiffany Momon

      36   LOOK AGAIN
           Jonathan Michael Square

      38   BRAIN LOVE
           Xiao Situ

      39   UNTITLED
           Sará Yafah King

40   Framework: Trouble the Water

      62   CRITICAL SHORT: TROUBLED WATERS AND CURRENTS OF RESTORATION
           Caroline Gillaspie, Assistant Curator of American Art

66   Thanksgiving Address: Greetings to the Natural World

68 Framework: Radical Care
- **103 CRITICAL SHORT: FRAMING THE WORLD THROUGH GRATITUDE**
  Dare Turner, Curator of Indigenous Art

104 Framework: To Give Flowers
- **124 CRITICAL SHORT: FROM OUR MOTHERS' GARDENS**
  Grace Billingslea, Curatorial Assistant, Arts of the Americas and American Art

126 Framework: Counterparts
- **156 CRITICAL SHORT: IN DIALOGUE**
  Camille Bacon and Leslie Wilson

158 Framework: Surface Tension
- **178 CRITICAL SHORT: THE DORSAL VIEW**
  Stephanie Sparling Williams with Sena Amuzu and Madeleine Levinsohn

180 Framework: Several Seats
- **204 CRITICAL SHORT: TO BE REAL!**
  Caroline Gillaspie

206 Framework: A Quiet Place
- **225 CRITICAL SHORT: *REST LIFE***
  Tricia Hersey

226 Framework: Witness
- **250 CRITICAL SHORT: SHOWING OUR WORK**
  Stephanie Sparling Williams

253 Contributor Biographies

255 Photography and Copyright Credits

Director's Foreword

We are proud to share *Toward Joy: New Frameworks for American Art*. This first major American art collection installation at the Brooklyn Museum since 2016 furthers our commitment to creating a more inclusive history of art.

The Brooklyn Museum is home to one of the oldest and most extensive collections of American art in the world, as collecting began in 1855, with commissions of paintings from two of New York's celebrated artists, Asher Brown Durand and Daniel Huntington. Even in the mid-nineteenth century, the Brooklyn Museum was committed to presenting contemporary artists and telling stories relevant to its audiences. Blazing trails, the Museum's curators have a long history of bridging diverse perspectives and building the collection with works made by underrepresented individuals and communities that have expanded the art historical canon. Today, as it has since our founding, the collection allows the Museum's curators to explore the depth and breadth of human creativity, draw rich connections between cultures, and examine multiple perspectives and truths through innovative programming for visitors.

Toward Joy is a timely rethinking of American art displays and brings together an impressive array of artworks spanning 2,000 years of creative excellence in the Western Hemisphere. In addition to American painting, sculpture, and works on paper, the galleries and this publication brim with artworks and belongings from the Arts of the Americas, Decorative Arts and Design, Modern and Contemporary Art, and Photography collections.

Chronological, stylistic, and thematic installations are common, even traditional, in collection installations and dominate most museum presentations of historical art. But *Toward Joy* goes further and is daring for its interpretative strategies and creative design. Led by the vision of Stephanie Sparling Williams, Andrew W. Mellon Curator of American Art, and shaped with multiple Brooklyn Museum curators as well as a roundtable of experts, the installation is experiential, intellectual, and bold as it expands representation and prioritizes belonging. And while most contemporary installations are about the "stories" objects can tell, here the team cultivates something akin to a collection of symphonic or tone poems for American art, to borrow an incisive observation from Trustee Tracey Riese, inviting audiences to encounter each cross-section of the collection in radically new contexts. Truly, it is a breakthrough.

Toward Joy exemplifies the importance and potential of polyvocality, contributing myriad viewpoints on some of the Brooklyn Museum's most noted works, including Mesoamerican ceramics and Indigenous beadwork, colonial-era and nineteenth-century portraiture, nineteenth-century landscape painting, and twentieth-century urban realism and abstraction. Each work in the gallery installation and the book have been researched, reimagined, and interrogated to elucidate new narratives and stories that focus on the theme of joy, and Black joy in particular. This is exactly right for Brooklyn, our city, and our nation in these increasingly divisive times. And as cities at large continue to be the most vibrant and diverse places as a result of mass migrations, the urgency to build understanding with one another—across the street and around the world—is all the more urgent.

It takes a scholarly, smart, creative, courageous, and hard-working team to pull off such a project. I wish to thank Stephanie Sparling Williams for her vision and deep dedication to this work as she is exemplary of these qualities. So too are the many colleagues who joined her on this journey. I want to thank the entire staff for their dedication to our mission and to this groundbreaking installation and book.

This exhibition is made possible through support from the Terra Foundation for American Art. Leadership support is provided by Tracey and Phillip Riese. Major support is provided by American International Group, Inc.; Saundra Williams-Cornwell and W. Don Cornwell; Pfizer, Inc.; and the Brooklyn Museum Council for African American Art. Generous support is provided by Lizanne Fontaine and Robert Buckholz, the Hasso Philanthropic Foundation, the National Endowment for the Humanities, and Nkonye Okoh. Additional support is provided by Barbara Madsen Smith, Barbara F. and Richard W. Moore, Ruthard C. Murphy II, and Ellie Meek Tweedy and David Tweedy.

For their ongoing support, we extend special gratitude to Barbara Vogelstein, Chairman, and every member of the Brooklyn Museum's Board of Trustees. The openness of our trustees and donors to risk-taking allows us to champion innovation in our work. We are blessed to have such a team at the Brooklyn Museum.

Anne Pasternak
Shelby White and Leon Levy Director
Brooklyn Museum

Acknowledgments

On the occasion of the Brooklyn Museum's two hundredth anniversary, we celebrate the institution's long commitment to presenting art to the public. This catalog commemorates the trailblazing approaches to research and collection display that respond to the concerns and curiosities of our contemporary visitors.

We are deeply grateful to Anne Pasternak, the Shelby White and Leon Levy Director of the Brooklyn Museum, for her early and steadfast support of this initiative. Her bold leadership set the tone for a groundbreaking transformation of the American galleries. Further, Anne's advocacy has resulted in important acquisitions of artworks by Black American, Asian American, and women artists that have bolstered the breadth and depth of the American art collection.

We are fortunate to have received generous funding for the reinstallation. The Terra Foundation for American Art's visionary sponsorship across several key aspects, including planning and implementation phase support, conservation treatments to care for collection works, and this publication, were essential to the success of the project. This backing reflects the Foundation's commitment to the field of American art and their forward-thinking and holistic funding models.

The National Endowment for the Humanities supported the convening of an advisory committee essential for establishing and refining our early goals and concepts. We are indebted to Glenn Adamson, Tahnee Ahtone, Tatiana Flores, Turry Flucker, Tiffany Momon, Anya Montiel, Kelli Morgan, Polly Nordstrand, Catherine Whalen, and Adriana Zavala. To each of you: thank you for your generous engagement and guidance.

The project also benefited from an experimental review in the form of the Black Feminist Roundtable, sponsored by the Terra Foundation. We are eternally grateful to the individuals who participated: Camille Bacon, Gregory Childs, Andrea Chung, Jennifer DeClue, Ryan Dennis, Martina Dodd, Treva Ellison, Taj Frazier, Sará Yafah King, Tiffany Momon, Kelli Morgan, Leigh Raiford, Harmonia Rosales, Xiao Situ, Jonathan Square, Brittany Webb, and Leslie Wilson. Your love and intellect have touched this project in profound ways and we are overwhelmed with gratitude.

The reinstallation and this catalog were collaborative efforts. We express our sincere thanks to all of the many colleagues across the institution and beyond who supported our work from soup to nuts. Many contributed their expertise and tremendous energy to ensure the success of *Toward*

Joy. Project managers Gwen Arriaga and Jocelyn Mosquera and curatorial assistant Grace Billingslea have been true partners in coordinating all aspects of this reinstallation. Our talented exhibition designer, Melinda Zoephel, worked with the curatorial team through countless design drafts to showcase the collection and provide the best experience for our visitors.

The Museum's exceptional conservation department went above and beyond preparing artworks and belongings for display, and our colleagues in the registrar's office managed the arrival of new acquisitions and several strategic loans. Jennifer Lu, our brilliant and tireless editor, read hundreds of wall texts, many of which became the foundations for writing in this volume. The Museum's in-house team of graphic designers skillfully generated the in-gallery graphics, while the wonderful Katty Huertas produced a truly stunning treatment for the Haudenosaunee Thanksgiving Address. We are also grateful for the skillfulness of the Museum's painters, carpenters, electricians, and art handlers who brought our plans to life. Installation and individual artwork photography, as well as image licensing, was completed by our talented colleagues in digital collections and services.

Dolores Farrell, the director of exhibition planning, provided expert guidance on this catalog's production. Reinstallation team members Grace Billingslea, Caroline Gillaspie, and Dare Turner contributed smart and timely insights that bookend several frameworks. Cross-departmental curatorial colleagues also generously wrote for this volume amid their departments' many ongoing projects, and several interns supported our efforts. Erin Barnett edited all written content, and did so with warmth, patience, and encouragement. Anjali Pala designed a dazzling book with input from the Museum's in-house team. We are grateful to Jennifer Norman and the entire Scala team for showing early and enthusiastic interest in the book proposal, and great collegiality and support as the book took shape and came into fruition.

We have been tremendously fortunate to work with a vibrant community of external thought partners who surrounded this work. We thank those who contributed to the in-gallery experience and to this catalog. Our Brooklyn Botanic Gardens neighbors—Jesse Brody, Kathy Crosby, Chelsea Forgenie, Ellen McCarthy, and Karen Wylie— penned insightful labels and entries on works featuring florals. Five fierce and talented New York–based drag and ballroom artists drafted incisive "reads" of sitters in some of our historic portraits: Chiquitita, Emi Grate, Miss Peppermint, Miz Cracker, and Victoria Von Blaque. Scholars of decorative arts and Native and Indigenous art, as well as community members contributed their expertise to wall labels: SGidGang.Xaal (Shoshannah Greene), Marissa A. Gutiérrez-Vicario, Jorge Lizarazo, Melissa Peter-Paul, Diana Cristina Rose, and Cheryl Simon. Several members of the Black Feminist Roundtable contributed critical texts to this catalog, which offer new ways of thinking about American art: Camille Bacon, Sará Yafah King, Tiffany Momon, Kelli Morgan, Leigh Raiford, Xiao Situ, Jonathan Square, Brittany Webb, and Leslie Wilson.

There were a handful of lenders to this unique collection presentation to whom we are indebted. The African American Museum in Philadelphia generously allowed us to fabricate an area rug from a hand-painted carpet design swatch by artist and designer Anna Russell Jones, whose archives are in their care. Similarly, the Smithsonian American Art Museum granted us permission to reproduce artist and designer Loïs Mailou Jones's design for Cretonne in their collection as an in-gallery wallpaper. While primarily a collection display, the installation was amplified by loans from Mr. and Mrs. Jack Buchanek, Georgia and Michael de Havenon, the Gochman Family Collection, Warren and Charlynn Goins, Edward J. Guarino, The Rita and Alex Hillman Foundation, Aisha Hinds, Ralph Julius and Kenneth Nelson, Carla Shen, Hong Gyu Shin (Shin Gallery), Rose M. Singer Center, and the artists Bisa Butler, Andrea Chung, Adama Delphine Fawundu, and Chester Higgins, Jr.

This project has truly brought much joy to the American art department, and the team is eternally grateful for the support, collaboration, and generosity of colleagues, thought partners, donors, and lenders. We look forward to sharing *Toward Joy* with our audiences here in Brooklyn and beyond.

Stephanie Sparling Williams
Andrew W. Mellon Curator of American Art
Brooklyn Museum

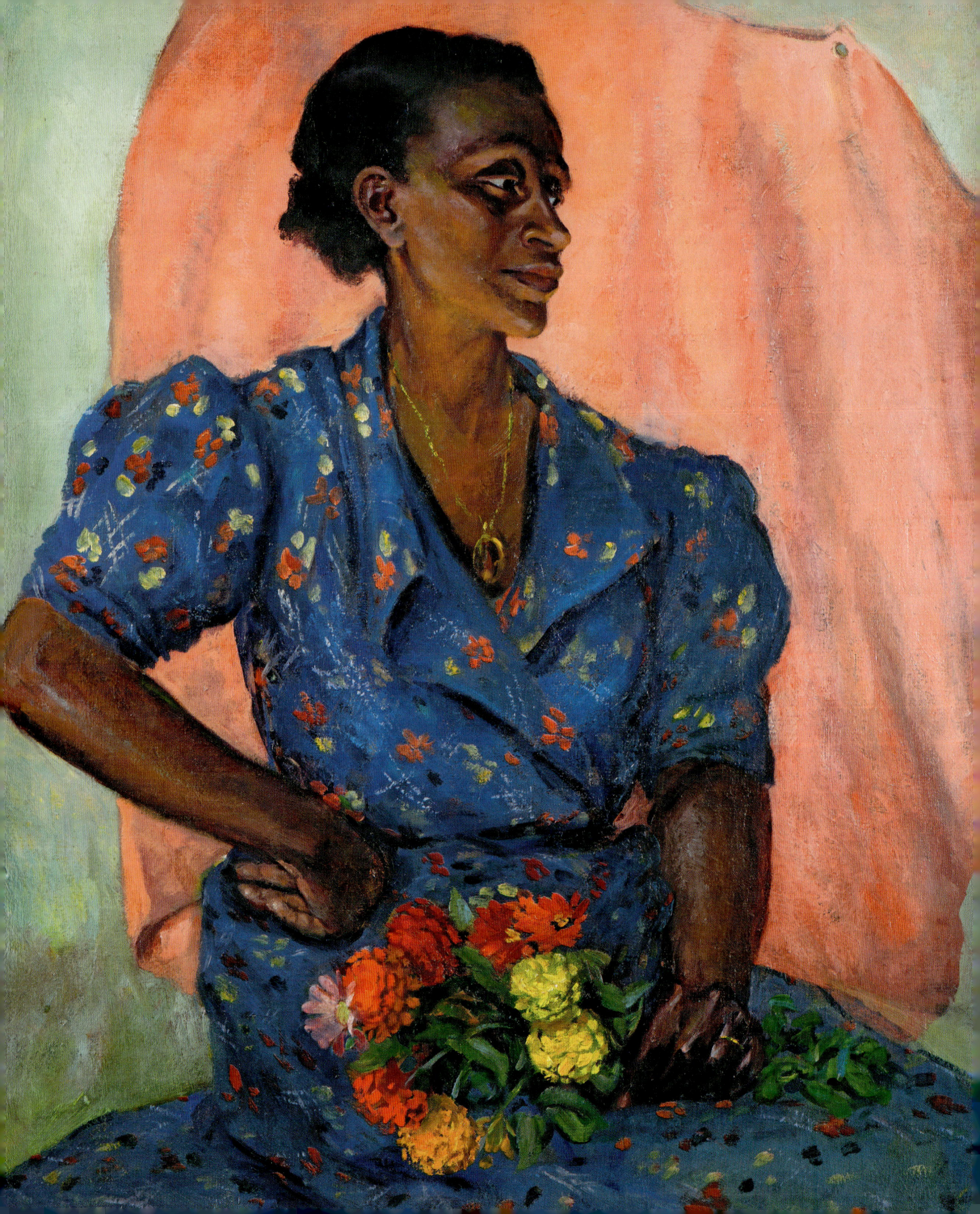

New Frameworks for American Art

**Stephanie Sparling Williams,
Andrew W. Mellon Curator of American Art**

Dabs of paint form the tightly clustered petals of freshly picked red, orange, and yellow zinnias, their dark green leaves frame each blossom and cling to the lengths of their sturdy stems. The bouquet has been given to, and is held lightly in the left hand of, a poised and pensive Black woman, the subject of Laura Wheeler Waring's painting *Woman with Bouquet* (1940). The bundle rests in the woman's lap, which is covered by her blue dress printed with a pattern containing its own red, orange, and yellow flowers.

Hand on hip, the woman sits upright and gazes off to her left, out of the composition's frame. Her expression is multitudinous, and there is a calm, quiet dignity that exudes from her pose. Is she relaxed? Content? Zinnias are dazzling technicolored flowers rich with their own symbolism, yet their beauty cannot hold the woman's attention. Waring seems to capture her in a state of time travel, she is miles, perhaps even years, away. Is it a sense of longing that Waring's paint and brushes document?

Regardless of where she is looking, where her mind has wandered, or what she is feeling, I want to advance an argument that what we see represented when looking into Waring's moving portrait is something akin to joy . . . Black joy.

In Search of Feeling: A Method, Map, Toolkit

As a cultural worker who belongs to an oppressed people my job is to make revolution irresistible.[1]

—Toni Cade Bambara

One core aspect of all curatorial work is asking what time it is.[2] However, as a field, we less often acknowledge or move temporally *toward* the museum audiences we invite to spend time with historical collections. Instead, museums typically expect visitors to bend, formulate, fashion, or socialize themselves into and around existing institutional structures, which are perceived as fixed and unchanging. But what time is it here, today, in the moment our audiences are navigating? What might it look like for an institution to hold time lightly, to hold traditions lightly, or to put them down for a while to pick up other things?[3]

Toward Joy: New Frameworks for American Art is the accompanying catalog to the Brooklyn Museum's trailblazing presentation of its American art collection that imagines how historic collections might be experienced anew. Bringing together extraordinary artworks and belongings that span 2,000 years, including over 120 pieces that have never been on view in our galleries, this reinstallation project offers fresh encounters with art and material culture from across the Western Hemisphere. Simply put, the goal of this undertaking is to transform how Brooklyn Museum audiences experience the American Art Galleries, focusing on responsive encounters with the collection that are engaged with contemporary concerns and curiosities. Here, we pose the urgent questions: How might American art be experienced at *this* moment? And, how can the American Art Galleries be a place of belonging for everyone who enters?

As a Black feminist curator, one of my core concerns is how the collections and galleries within my purview and care might be a place of enjoyment and belonging for Black women specifically. Recognizing that museums are vehicles of social belonging, everything from how information is presented, how spaces are staged, and how artworks are installed within specific parameters of style and taste are all acts of power that set the terms of social belonging.[4] It is from this understanding that each redesigned space offers a unique alternative to traditional displays of American art, together charting new paths forward in research, interpretation, and care for collections that are inspired by the ways previously marginalized communities see and experience the world. This catalog provides a companion on this journey, serving simultaneously as a compass and a map of possibilities, and at other points a bridge over rough, murky, deep, or otherwise uncharted waters.

I often find myself in the galleries with brilliant people who are disenchanted with displays of historic American art. They accurately sense in their bones the disconnect between the artworks on view in museums and what is being represented as the history and cultural landscape of the United States and the larger hemisphere. At times those feelings of disenchantment are actually the physical effects of alienation or being made to feel less than—less than knowledgeable, less than equipped, less than cultured, stupid.

These are sentiments my own mother would often articulate as I dragged her from museum to museum while I was in graduate school. Her bafflement and dispassion irritated me. She has a collection of degrees to her name, and I would watch her wander apathetically by art considered by many to be national treasures. "You just have to *look* at it," was often my exasperated response, "there is nothing particular you have to *understand*, just enjoy it, just look!" She would amble aimlessly, humoring me, but also brushing it all off, this "art thing" was simply "not for her."[5]

A decade or so later, I now know so intimately what I could not recognize then: my mother, like innumerable others, was not responding to the art itself. Glowy Hudson River School paintings and Neoclassical sculptures were not making her feel stupid, less than, or disinterested. Rather, what she was responding to and continues to respond to is how white supremacy is imbricated in the museum ritual. Everything about her experience—from the building architecture and design of the galleries to the curatorial framing and interpretation—communicated to her that she was not the intended audience, that she did not belong.

Historically, American art collections have been complicit in upholding white supremacy. They have privileged the perspectives and cultural contributions of white men and have marginalized or omitted everyone else. Where forced migration, genocide, and mass enslavement characterized much of early American history, exclusion and erasure have come to define the study and presentation of American art. Indeed, the field still struggles to acknowledge that many of the practices we as art historians, curators, and scholars of the visual have been trained in and accordingly inculcate future generations are violent. These practices continue traditions of rendering different forms of knowledge and people invisible or invaluable.[6]

Yet, for centuries, scholars, artists, and educators have challenged erasure and exclusion, while understanding the role that museums and art institutions play in creating social belonging. In recent decades, museums have made important strides toward greater and more meaningful inclusion with targeted acquisition initiatives, through collection assessments and reinstallations to build more expansive histories, and by instating advisory committees and institution-wide structures for inclusion and accountability. These efforts make apparent the complex and troubling intricacies of collection formation and development. Due to the slow nature of this work, it often takes lifetimes to realize incremental shifts in collection makeup and institutional cultures.

Today, an increasing number of American art curators are charting new visions for the research and display of historical American art. This transformation at the Brooklyn Museum seeks to orient a collection of American art toward new understandings and frameworks, offering fresh encounters with historic art that might reshape our collective futures. To present a more expansive definition of American art, we exhibit art from collections traditionally excluded from the American art canon: art of the ancient Americas, decorative arts, contemporary art, Indigenous art, and photography. We unflinchingly take up the collections we have, pushing the boundaries of representation by framing a largely white and canonical American art collection through the cultural contributions, lenses, and critical sensibilities of non-white communities, rather than the other way around.

The Black feminist lenses and frameworks applied in the installation are not limited to the gallery walls, however. Additionally, and largely behind-the-scenes, our curatorial and institutional work necessarily extends beyond display, revealing the depth of how coloniality and white supremacy are inherent to the systems through which we work as collection stewards. Collections, databases, display, wayfinding, and other in-gallery experiences continue to be categorized, codified, standardized, simplified, and labeled, much like the colonial impulses to organize people and entire cultures into taxonomies for the purpose of classification and the establishment of hierarchies. This is why it is no longer sufficient for exhibitions and collection displays to "add and stir" previously omitted artworks into existing organizing schemas, or simply exhibit or elevate underrecognized histories by juxtaposing pieces by contemporary artists. Our tools must fit the task at hand.

The approach advanced here offers a complete rethinking of how permanent collections are managed and their spaces are experienced by diverse audiences. Framing and interpretive focus is placed on African diaspora and Indigenous ways of seeing and knowing, as these perspectives have been categorically undermined, exploited, and erased in the process and aftermath of the nation's formation, and have historically served as a foil, and indeed a justification, for white supremacy. Where the gaze, frameworks, and analysis offered through Black feminist approaches to care, liberation, and space-making are employed and modeled throughout the installation and this publication, equally important is that the same ethics shape the work that is not directly experienced by museum visitors. Notably, what is presented here is not a "set it and forget it" or "one and done" special exhibition or book. Instead, the American art department at the Brooklyn Museum is building a new foundation and exploring and experimenting with fresh starting points from which to develop rigorous transdisciplinary curatorial work into the future.

Much like the installation itself with each gallery dedicated to frameworks, each chapter in this catalog addresses the aforementioned questions, namely: How might American art be experienced at *this* moment? Building on the rich contributions of thinkers and cultural producers who identify as Black or persons of color, the framework model offers a way to boldly experiment with and richly layer representation in the galleries, to explore innovative curatorial ideas and actions, and to systematically center more voices and perspectives, as we pursue equity across the collection. As an art museum, the Brooklyn Museum is a site for celebrating beauty. But what does one do when beautiful artworks are entangled in ugly and often violent histories?

These pages invite you to trace alternative relational contours for American art—the strictures and possibilities—through more inclusive lenses. However, like all U.S.-based collections, the gaps and omissions borne out across time and institutional collecting practices have produced and perpetuated overwhelming cultural erasure. This is America and the history of American art, too.

"Brooklyn Feeling": A Destination, a Vibe, a Collection

The Brooklyn Museum's history can be traced to the founding of the Brooklyn Apprentices' Library in 1823 by Augustus Graham (1775–1851), a businessman and philanthropist, and one of early Brooklyn's most important civic leaders, who was eager to promote literacy and culture by "forming a [free] repository of books, maps, pictures, drawing apparatus, models of machinery, tools and implements, all collected for enlarging knowledge in literature, science and art."[7] It was out of this charter that the fine art collections were later established in the mid-nineteenth century, and further catalyzed by Graham's vision—"art in service of social improvement."[8]

The American art collection was among the first of its kind, driven by an initiative to support living American artists, and fueled by Graham's ethos of art for the people of Brooklyn.[9] Today, the American art department collectively dreams deeper into this radical notion of art for social improvement, and toward a shift in what is now the field of American art, namely by generating more capacious models for how American art is stewarded in collections, studied, written about, and exhibited. We reach further into social, cultural, and intellectual realities defined by improvisation and experimentation, where there might be room to breathe different air.[10] But how might we dream, think, and act beyond this so-called moment of social and cultural reckoning? What can be learned from historic liberation struggles and also our collective future-oriented move toward alternative, simulated, and metaversal realities, where the terms of social existence are in flux? How might a historical ethos of social improvement translate to the Museum's local, national, and global audiences today?

The late 1840s were the heyday of the early Brooklyn Institute and the founding commitment to education and—here I want to emphasize the language used at the time—*enjoyment* of the working classes was further championed. Exhibitions and classes were complemented by a progressive lecture series. The increasingly popular annual loan show—where artists, institutions, and private collectors lent work for display—for example, started in 1843 and ran through 1849, and as this momentous event in the Brooklyn social calendar gained early traction, another parallel phenomenon emerged into the cultural landscape, and that was "the Brooklyn feeling." By 1847, the widely attended annual exhibition drew both praise from the Brooklyn community and local press, and also accolades of a writer for the exclusive New York journal *The Literary World*, who lauded his neighbors for "a very commendable spirit in relations to the Fine Arts, and . . . an earnest desire to . . . distinguish themselves as separate and distinct from this whirlpool of a city."[11] The author particularly praised the Institute's "social spirit," adding, "art belongs to the people—it is no luxury for the favored few—it is a boon to all mankind, and may be enjoyed . . . by all those who have eyes to see it."[12]

In the second half of the nineteenth century this curious phrase—Brooklyn feeling—emerged from the review pages of the *Brooklyn Daily Eagle*. Commonly invoked alongside statements of Brooklyn pride and exemplars of Brooklyn exceptionalism, it is apparent across these early references that the borough enlivened a uniquely democratic, class-defying, progressive ethos, filled with family-oriented everyman-types, and the "feeling" seemed to have encompassed this prevailing ethos—this way of being in New York, at the time.

Regarding the Brooklyn feeling, one reviewer wrote effusively about the 1845 opening festivities:

> We visited the rooms of the Institute last evening and were exceedingly gratified, not only with the entertainment . . . but also with the very large throng of citizens . . . that we found in attendance . . . Had the intrinsic merits of the exhibition proper been less than they were it would still have been an ample reward for the trouble of visiting it to witness . . . so much of that subtle element called *Brooklyn feeling*.[13]

Indeed, this "Brooklyn feeling," a sense of wonderment, cultural pride, and progressive inclusivity, is something the institution is still lauded for in the contemporary moment. Today, in addition to the best monthly art party in New York, the Museum also serves as a polling site and offers its restrooms for those attending free speech enactments, pickets, protests, and parades, amplifying and expounding Graham's vision for the institution's civil function.

It was during this same period in the late 1840s that Graham's founding endowment was established to support the acquisition of work by living American artists, a radical notion at a time when institutions in New York, Boston, and Philadelphia were focused nearly exclusively on exploring European styles and traditions, and exhibiting European masters. It was this gift of American art that inaugurated the permanent collection at the Brooklyn Institute. The institution's first purchases with the funds were commissioned works by Daniel Huntington (1816–1906) and Hudson River School painter Asher Brown Durand (1796–1886), whose 1855 painting *The First Harvest in the Wilderness* represents both a landscape allegory of progress and a tribute to Graham's efforts as a cultural pioneer. Then described as "ardent, radical, and progressive," and under the pervasive influence of the social reform and cultural uplift movements that swept through the United States for much of the antebellum period, Graham's bequest would fund works by living American painters for the new public galleries.[14]

What often goes undetected by general audiences to museums are the ways collection building and display are inextricably linked to institutional vision, and the individual interests and priorities of each successive curator, and of course this moment is no different. Indeed, this historical overview serves to situate the ongoing work of the American art department and its current curators within the radical lineage of the collection and its display. The emergence of the Brooklyn feeling in concert with the museum's early exhibition program, and the innovation of its installations over time, are historically aligned with the bold initiatives that center the welcome and delight of Brooklyn audiences that are being pursued today. In the last 130 years, there have been just over 30 curators dedicated to stewarding the American paintings and sculpture collection, and this overview glosses their accomplishments to demonstrate the ways the current work of the department builds on and departs from their foundational efforts.

The American collection began to grow more vigorously after 1900. The work of artists such as John Singer Sargent (1856–1925) and Winslow Homer (1836–1910) were early collecting pillars across several curatorial tenures, with the first acquisitions happening in 1909 under William Henry Goodyear. Through the teens and twenties, the Museum maintained a dual interest in early American painting and the more recent art of the Gilded Age (the late 1870s to the late 1890s) and the early twentieth century. Through a series of evolving priorities in acquisition and display, the Brooklyn Institute and later the Brooklyn Museum (not unlike the larger museum field) saw several transformational shifts that would shape how Brooklynites and the institution's wider audiences would come to experience American art. First, the Museum's early twentieth-century directors such as Philip Newell Youtz concentrated on making the Museum a leading *fine art* institution by encouraging the acquisition of American paintings and sculpture.[15] With this change, the institution would no longer be seen as an eclectic library and science/art museum but as a serious—and bona fide—art museum. Youtz was also passionate about offering the public a superior education in the arts and reinstalled the Museum collections "so that the contents of the Museum will be presented to the public in an organic and orderly panorama of the various fields the collection represents."[16] As one of the earliest proponents of a progressive social sciences education for adult learners, Youtz believed that audiences

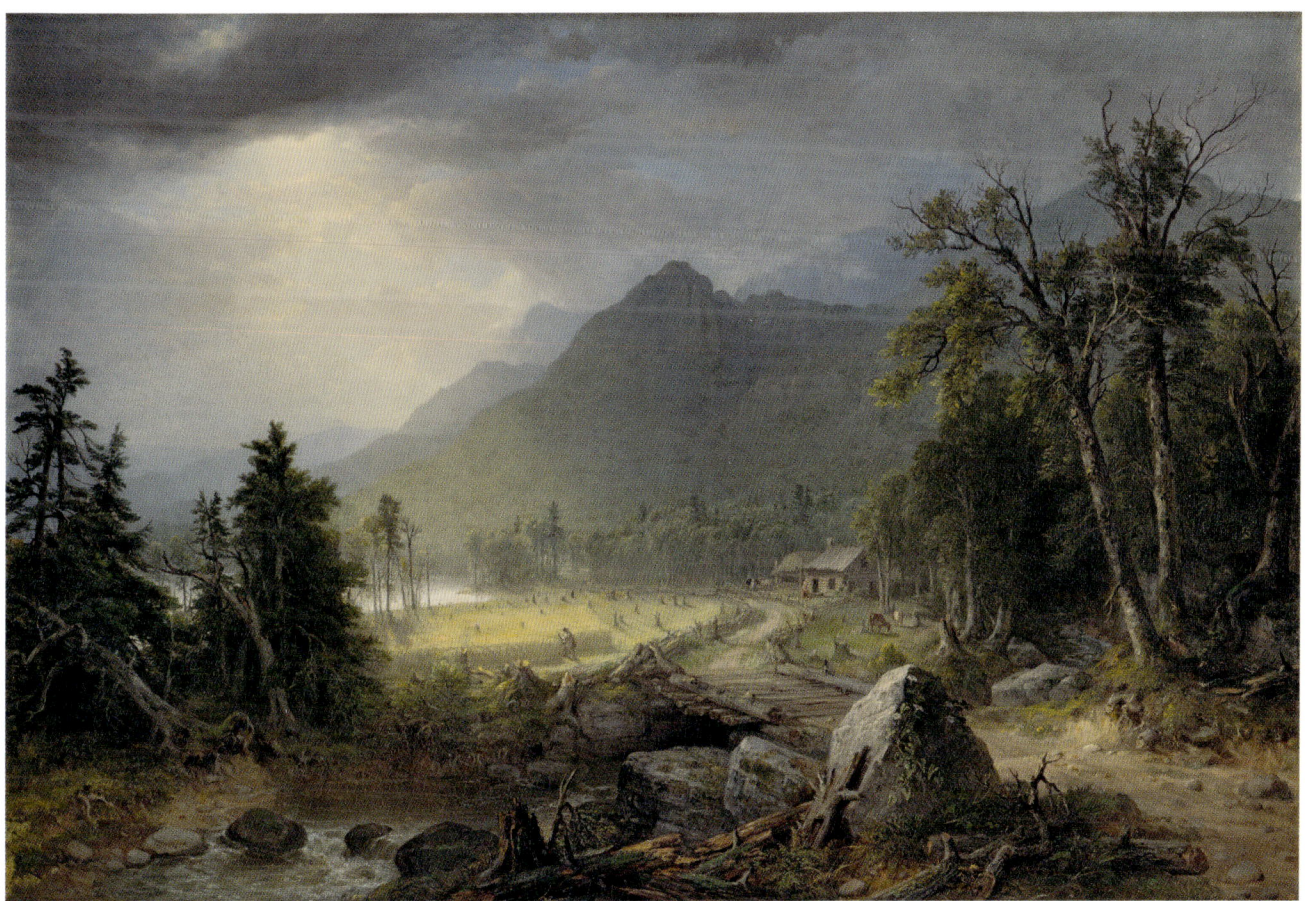

Asher Brown Durand (American, 1795–1886). *The First Harvest in the Wilderness*, 1855.

New Frameworks for American Art

would be engaged by and understand the social history of art, rather than aesthetics or a more formal art historical approach.

Second, curators continued to rearrange gallery spaces throughout the 1930s. For example, a general reinstallation of the Museum's contemporary paintings and sculpture separated the various schools and periods more clearly. And in another iteration, sculptures were reinstalled chronologically, and American oil paintings were reorganized with separate sections created for the Impressionists and for the Munich school. This was quite radical at a time when American painting and sculpture was often lumped together, at times with European art. Brooklyn Museum's curators saw American art as worthy of its own distinct space. This education-driven shift also impacted the audiences' experiences as it was less reliant on extensive knowledge of art history. While these shifts appear most quotidian and unremarkable to contemporary audiences, curators at the time, just as they are today, were experimenting with the very organizational logics for which we have come to encounter the Museum's wide-ranging collections.[17]

Under his curatorial leadership from 1936 to 1952, John I. H. Baur strengthened the American art collection through key acquisitions in eighteenth- and nineteenth-century North American painting and sculpture. Baur also organized well-received thematic exhibitions of nineteenth- and early twentieth-century artists and installed extensive surveys in American art such as *AMERICA: 1744–1944* in 1944, and an ambitious show covering fifty years of American painting, titled *Revolution and Tradition*, on view from 1951 to 1952. In a progressive departure from most permanent collection installations, *AMERICA: 1744–1944* drew from the Museum's holdings to include paintings, sculpture, prints and drawings, furniture, decorative arts, costumes and accessories, books and fashion illustrations and sketches—blurring the lines between fine art and popular culture and enlivening the visitor engagement through immersive displays.

During his tenure as curator in the 1960s, Axel von Saldern, like many of his predecessors, emphasized American art in his collecting policy.[18] He noted that the great strength of the museum's holdings lies in its collection of American paintings, and in his assessment, "it was through the judicious selection of previous administrations that it ranks among the best in this country." Von Saldern also invested in the improvement of the collection galleries to enhance the *experience* for visitors. Chief among the changes was a new labeling system, whereby in addition to individual identification labels, the gallery walls featured—for the very first time—introductory panels describing the context and often the historic periodization of groupings of artworks.

Innovations to in-gallery experiences in the late 1960s included a new "Study Storage Gallery" on the fifth floor, which allowed visitors to view a large selection of the painting collection on moving racks. Furthermore, the groundbreaking exhibition titled *Listening to Pictures* in 1968 provided greater context and accessibility around the modern art coming into the collection. Headphones were provided in front of each artwork, and audiences could experience the work while listening to interpretations from the artists themselves, a cutting-edge archival resource that lives on to this day in the Museum's special collections.

The late 1960s and early 1970s was a time of social and political upheaval in American society. At the Museum, a forward-thinking orientation toward previously unrepresented and marginalized communities aided in the expansion

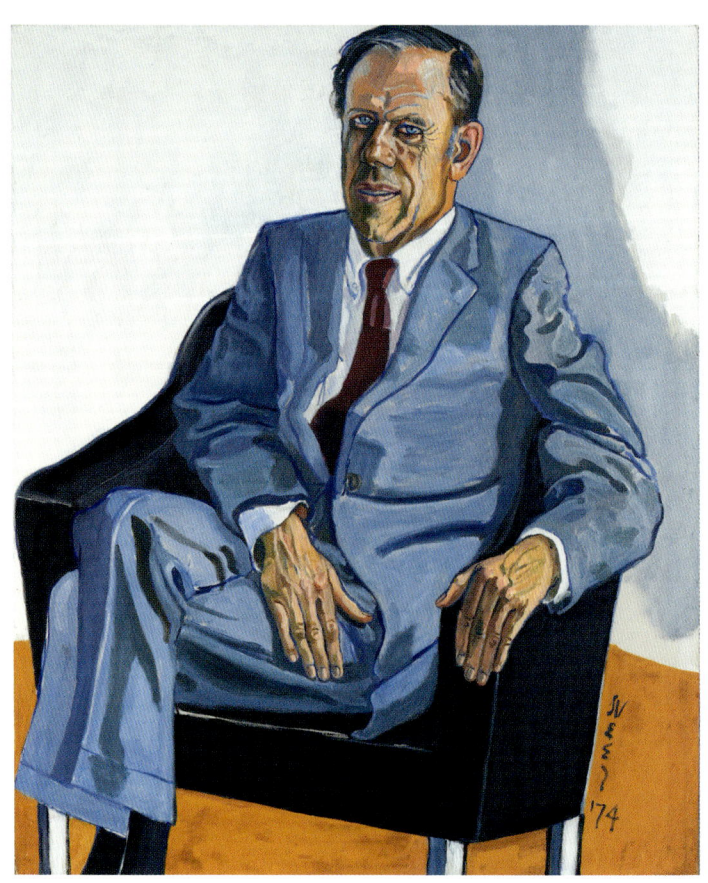

Alice Neel (American, 1900–1984). *John I. H. Baur*, 1974.

of subjects and themes deemed acceptable for exhibition, and at times, acquisition. In 1969, the same year the Metropolitan Museum of Art opened its controversial exhibition *"Harlem on My Mind": The Cultural Capital of Black America, 1900-1968*, which did not include any paintings or sculptures by Black artists, the Brooklyn Museum hosted the Harlem Cultural Council's exhibition *New Black Artists*, which exposed visitors to an entirely new group of living artists. In acknowledging the cultural significance of recognizing these American artists and the value of their work, curator Edward K. Taylor described the show as "really only a beginning, a hint of uncovered ground and a new area of exploration."[19]

In the years to follow, more shows featuring Black artists and the interpretation of works with African American themes came to or were curated by the Museum. These included *Two Centuries of Black American Art* (1977), *Black Folk Art in America* (1982), *Facing History: The Black Image in American Art, 1710-1940* (1990), *Alone in a Crowd: Prints of the 1930s and 1940s by African American Artists* (1996), and *Committed to the Image: Contemporary Black Photographers* (2001). Like Black American artists, women artists went largely underrepresented across the museum world, and their absence was also reflected in Brooklyn's early collecting practices. Despite this lack of visibility, the National Association of Women Painters and Sculptors exhibited at the Brooklyn Museum as early as 1928, and a very small number of women were featured in one-artist shows: Bessie Potter Vonnoh in 1913 and Dorothea Dreier in 1925.

In the 1970s, and with the help of several notable donations, including Edith and Milton Lowenthal's gift of Georgia O'Keeffe's painting *Ram's Head, White Hollyhock-Hills (Ram's Head and White Hollyhock, New Mexico)*, the Museum encouraged a more serious evaluation of women artists. To that end, the retrospective *Women Artists: 1550-1950*, organized by the Los Angeles County Museum of Art, traveled to the Museum in 1977.[20] During this time, the American art department also organized a large reinstallation project in the fifth-floor galleries in order to show the Museum's rich collection of American paintings from the mid-eighteenth- to the mid-nineteenth centuries with an updated educational approach. The installation was arranged chronologically, with works grouped by topic and style.

The department continued to devote increasing attention to overlooked developments in American art in the 1970s and 1980s. Since that time, it has also been at the forefront of efforts to reimagine the canon through the acquisition of works by Black American artists and by women, which remains central to collecting efforts today, and has been expanded to include the art and cultural production of Indigenous Americans, Mesoamericans, Asian Americans, and Pacific Islanders, all of whom were making a life in the Americas during the nineteenth and twentieth centuries.

From the late 1980s onward, the department continued to expand its collections, renovate gallery space, and offer important and original exhibitions. It experienced a dramatic shift away from its legacy of male leadership and saw the rise of successive women heads of the department, such as Sarah Faunce, Linda Ferber, Barbara Millstein, and later Barbara

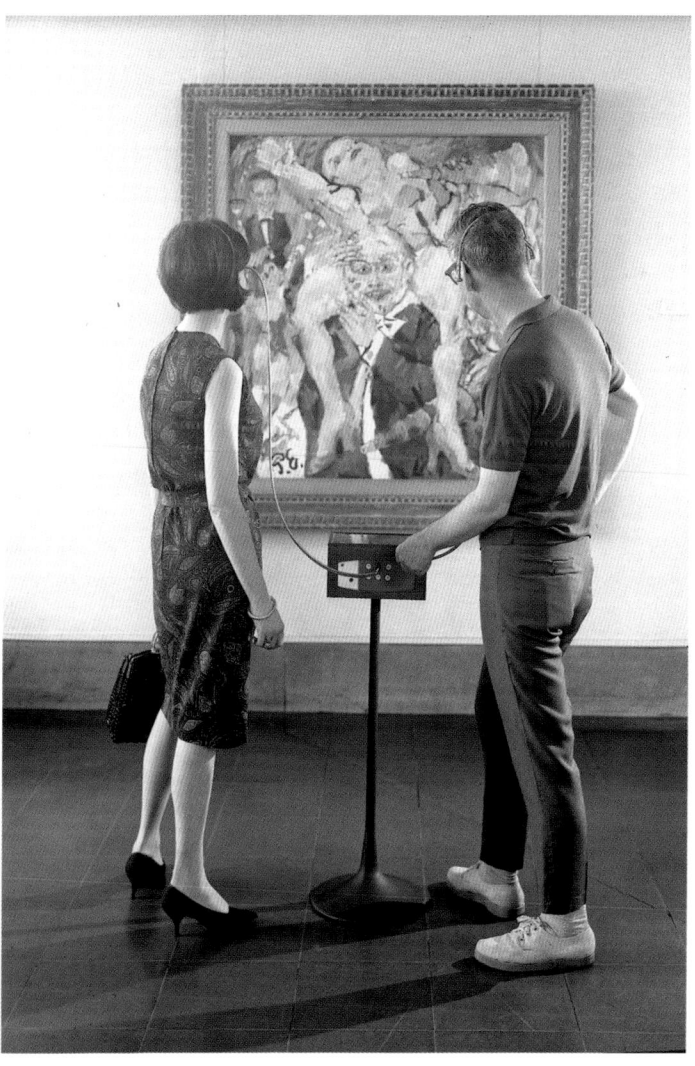

Installation view, *Listening to Pictures,* Brooklyn Museum, April 28, 1968-73.

Gallati and Teresa Carbone. Coincidently, the department has since been steered exclusively by women, their leadership coinciding with the rise of Black members to the Museum and the Board of Trustees in the 1990s and early 2000s. In 2010, a group of Trustees led by Charlynn Goins, Tracey Reise, and Saundra Williams-Cornwell established the Fund for African American Art, which supported the collection and preservation of historic art made by Black Americans. The Fund, eventually renamed the Council for African American Art, brought in dozens of important pieces by artists such as Edward Mitchell Bannister (1828–1901), Grafton Tyler Brown (1841–1918), Robert Seldon Duncanson (1821–1972), Loïs Mailou Jones (1905–1998), Charles Ethan Porter (1847–1923), Nancy Elizabeth Prophet (1890–1960), Laura Wheeler Waring (1887–1948), and Hale Woodruff (1900–1980).

In the 1990s, the Kress Foundation granted the department a significant award to conduct research and perform technical examinations on all the museum's American paintings, over 700 in total. This led to the impressive two-volume *American Paintings* catalog, edited by Teresa Carbone, and published in 2006, with support from a Luce Foundation granting initiative that was launched in the 1980s to address the dearth of collection catalogues at nearly all major institutions. Throughout the early 2000s, director Arnold Lehman reconceived the structure of the Museum's administrative staff, including the curatorial team. As part of his new vision, individual departments were dissolved and working groups intended to stimulate collaboration were established.[21] These shifts had an immediate impact on the Museum's exhibition program, which saw an uptick in collaboration on collection-based projects and initiatives.

While the American galleries have been reinstalled repeatedly over the last century, of particular note is Teresa Carbone and Barry Harwood's milestone installation, *American Identities: A New Look*, which opened in September 2001 and moved beyond traditional collection boundaries and constraints of chronology and medium. The installation was composed of eight galleries—some based on time periods and others on more general subjects. The gallery wall colors and large text panels signaled each new theme, some of which also offered quotations from artists and historical figures. Comfortable living room-style seating was provided in each corner gallery of the American art wing, breaking up the lengthy journey around the architecture of the Museum's center Beaux Art court.

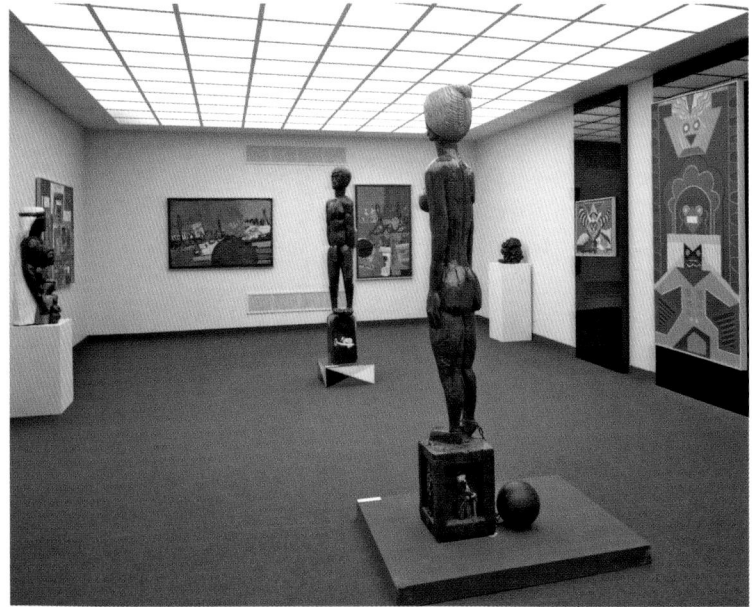

Installation view, *New Black Artists*, Brooklyn Museum, October 7, 1969–November 10, 1969.

Additionally, the Museum's American art curators continued to shape the field at large with projects such as *Youth and Beauty* (2011), which examined the surge in American realism prior to the Great Depression and coincided with the acquisition of works by Luigi Lucioni (1900–1988), Paul Manship (1885–1966), and Richard Bruce Nugent (1906–1987). In 2012, Carbone went on to facilitate, with Lehman, the purchase of an impressive Black Arts Movement collection from David Lusenhop, which included several suits by Jae Jarrell, including *Revolutionary Suit* (2010), a two-piece salt-and-pepper wool tweed ensemble with a faux bullet bandolier trim; this is the work that won the Board's approval and catalyzed the sale.

For the fiftieth anniversary of the Civil Rights Act, Carbone organized an exhibition commemorating the occasion and celebrating the recent acquisition. Cocurated with art historian Kellie Jones, and with the assistance of research associate Connie Choi and assistant curator of American art Dalila Scruggs, *Witness: Art and Civil Rights in the Sixties* opened in 2014.[22] The exhibition, which coincided with the end of Lehman's tenure, reflected the director's rigorous push for diversity at the Museum—in its collecting and display—and was amplified through robust public program offerings that sparked a surge of intergenerational audiences from around the five boroughs.

The Brooklyn Museum's current director, Anne Pasternak—the first woman to lead one of New York City's largest collecting institutions—continues to build on the work of her predecessors. Guided by a bold new vision for the museum to serve as a center for art and civic activity in the community and beyond, Pasternak has championed social justice initiatives in the institution's artistic, education, and curatorial programs. In 2016, the fifth-floor galleries were once again completely overhauled, this time within six months and organized by Choi, returning the spaces to a largely chronological display that explored themes related to American history and nationhood.

Today the American collection, foundational to the Brooklyn Museum and its history, ranks among one of the leading surveys of American art in the world. The collection consists of over 1,200 paintings, 250 sculptures, and approximately 6,000 works on paper, which provide an impressive, albeit traditional, overview of American art from 1720 to 1960. Responsive to historic trends, current sensibilities, and the language of political demand shaping the contemporary cultural landscape, The American Art Galleries once again underwent complete transformation in October 2024, and likewise reflect a collaboration between collections, moving beyond geopolitical boundaries to look at American art hemispherically as well as cross-temporally. There is a renewed effort to provide comfort and care to audiences within the installation through the creation of inviting spaces rich in texture and color, ample seating, and accessible texts, and finally—like Carbone and Harwood's presentation—the new reinstallation returns to bold design with the aim of welcoming and delighting visitors.

Nearly two hundred years ago, the Brooklyn Museum's art collection was catalyzed by an initiative to support living American artists and founded on the ethos of "art for social improvement."[23] Historically, the institution has championed innovations in the field and has been unafraid to exhibit artworks or experiment with displays considered nontraditional or risky. With renewed focus on experiences rooted in belonging and in pursuit of a distinctly Brooklyn feeling, the American art department today takes up the radical notion of rigorous joy, dreaming more capaciously still of a shift in what is now the field of American art.

Toward Joy

Joy is such a human madness.[24]

—Zadie Smith

Care is the antidote to violence.[25]

—Saidiya Hartman

In what direction do we move when we turn away from white supremacy in our collections and their display?

The answer posited here is toward joy . . . Black joy.

When asserting joy as one possible direction, one set of coordinates, in the department's continued migration away from histories of exclusion and violence, there is likely some resulting discomfort. I get the sense that this tension largely stems from an understanding of joy as unserious, or even frivolous. The joy I am referring to, however, is accessible to everyone, and is not merely sentiment, but ontology, no thin theoretical valence, but rigorous and tried methodology. Consider Eldzier Cortor's 1944–45 painting titled *Southern Landscape (Southern Flood)*.

Barefoot and outstretched on a blanket, a couple lounge casually in the foreground of a disturbing scene. Flood waters, just beyond their figures, carry entire buildings, telephone poles, and other debris off the edges of the composition. Bonnet and shoes cast aside, the woman studies one of nearly a dozen recently plucked flowers while her companion pensively gazes in the direction of a dilapidated church, its crumbling arches, stained glass windows, and abandoned crucifix stand dismally amid the chaos.

Cortor was a master of tensions, cultivating with brush and pigment complex microcosms of Black life. In the catalog entry for the painting (p. 59), Caroline Gillaspie highlights the compounded adverse effects of environmental disasters, such as flooding, and the building of hydroelectric dams, both occurring alongside the dust bowl conditions that characterized the Great Depression. Gillaspie interprets Cortor's painting through the lens of environmental racism, the reality that the burden of environmental disaster falls heaviest on Black and impoverished communities. Often described as surreal, what is captured in *Southern Landscape* is the affecting luminescence of Black interiority. Despite the devastating impact on Black communities proximate to

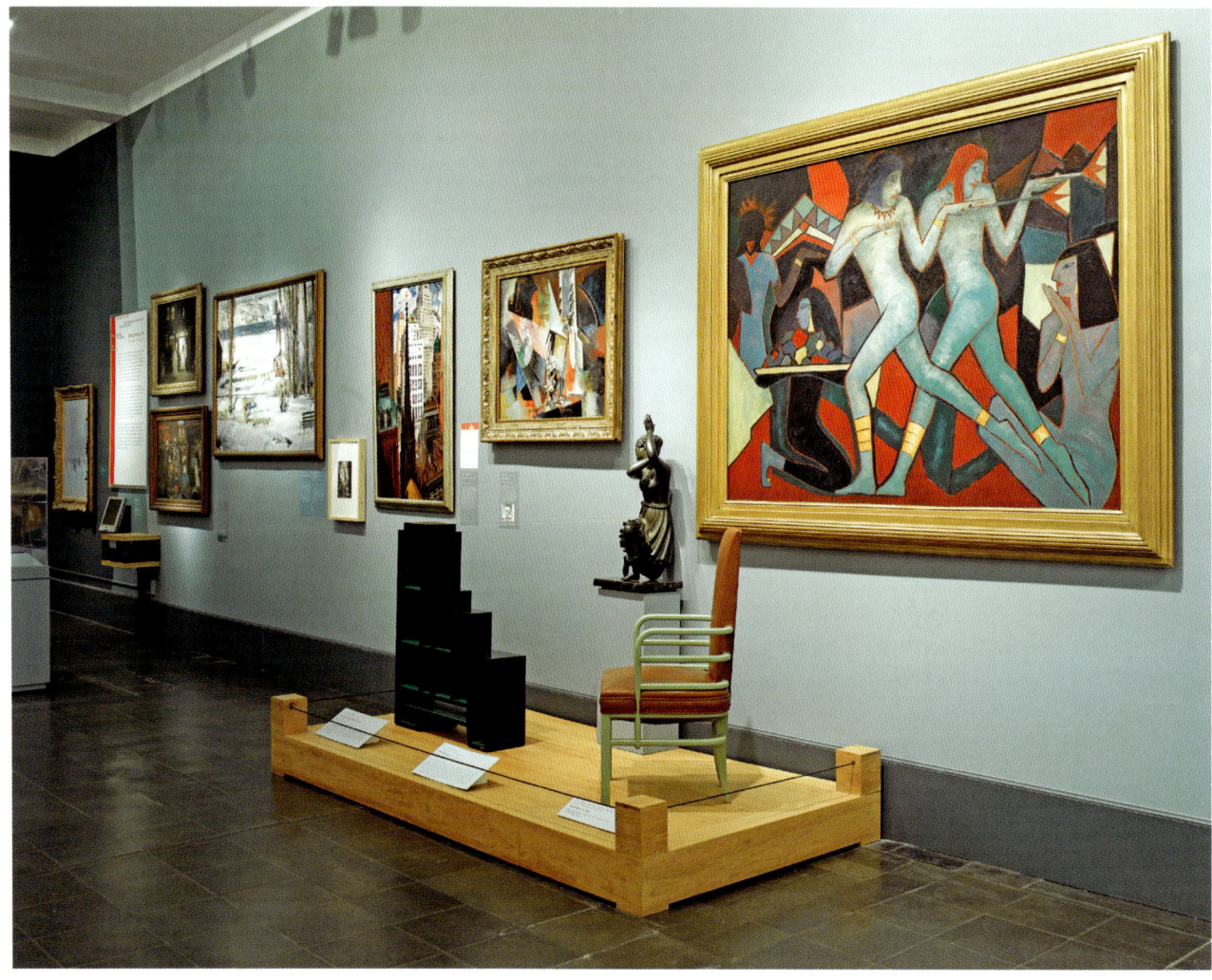

Installation view, *American Identities: A New Look*, Brooklyn Museum, September 12, 2001–February 28, 2016.

environmental destruction, Cortor's figures are dignified, self-assured, and caught in states of tranquility, a master class in narrative tension. Cortor's paintings manifest Black peace and Black joy as both beauty and resistance, against a harrowing backdrop.

Settler colonialism, global imperialism, genocide, enslavement, and environmental degradation are heavy realities to confront when stewarding an art collection reflective of this nation's complex and violent history. The archive attests, and Cortor confirms, that nothing is too weighty for Black joy.[26] Rather than an absence of seriousness, however, or the pursuit of frivolous escapism, poet and essayist Ross Gay puts it this way: "joy is what emerges when we care for each other through our pain and suffering . . . instead of refuge or relief from heartbreak, [joy] is what efflorescences from us when we help each other carry our heartbreaks."[27]

Indeed, joy and pain are entangled much like violence and care must also be in our attending to the art and audiences we are privileged to serve. Our curatorial contributions to this moment are both theoretical and practical, the goal being to hold in regenerative tension the joys and pains of this collection of American art, and to apply an ethos of rigorous and radical care that we might realize greater structural change in the department, across the Museum, and into the field.

In working with collections, care is a framework that propels a desire for a radically different order. Saidiya

Hartman asks through her scholarship: What would it mean to not have a social political order that's founded on settler colonialism (the erasure of Indigenous people, history, and culture), and slavery, racism, and anti-Blackness? The American art department is asking a similar set of questions of our display practices. In an interview with Thora Siemsen, Hartman elaborates that caring for ourselves and others is partly the way we destroy *this* social order and make another. "We help each other inhabit what is an otherwise uninhabitable and brutal social context."[28] And here I am thinking with Hartman of the daily lived experience of the most vulnerable people in our society—those whose proximity to physical violence and premature death is something they carry, marked on their body—and these people, if we are lucky, enter the museum.[29]

To advance the argument that the American art department moves *toward joy* is to propose an extension of and advanced modes for curatorial care. What might it mean to care for audiences (people) as much as we care about (and for) art, historical artists, and their supposed histories? Ultimately, a movement toward joy is to step out in speculation, and with a desire for new and alternative experiences and realities within museums, ones not centered around trauma and oppression but healing, liberation, and possibility. Thus, this audacious project is really an ode to Black feminist space-making in the key of Black joy and pursued through wayward improvisation and radical care.[30] These are the new terms that ground and orient the work behind the transformation of Brooklyn Museum's historic American art collection, and its display.

Black Feminisms for American Art

When I arrived at the Brooklyn Museum in December 2021, the compulsion toward change was palpable. The desire of audiences, staff, and leadership to shed traditions and to step out boldly were impassioned mandates. Audience surveys and focus group reports were thrust into my hands, social action priorities were presented, and a myriad of staff members welcomed me with sincere pleas for a new direction.[31] It was in this context of urgency that I began, in earnest, to scale the work I had been pursuing for the previous decade. I thought about "the gestures, feelings, and ethics that make up a Black feminist art history," and how Black women in particular, and strategically marginalized audiences more broadly, might come to feel more "at home," safe and affirmed within galleries dedicated to American art.[32]

What became clear was a need to rethink how we understand representation, how we see American art, and what it means to cultivate experiences of recognition and belonging in communities previously excluded from the history of art and its display. Rather than alienation, disenchantment, and disinterest, our aim is to manifest a sense of joy, wonderment, and curiosity in all audiences. It is out of this priority that we reframe the Brooklyn Museum's American art collection through bold experiments in representation and evermore expansive and creative applications of Black feminist theories and methodologies.

Central to the shifts being pursued within the American art department at the Brooklyn Museum is a methodological approach that hinges on the traditions, theoretical contributions, and modalities emerging from Black feminist thought.[33] Part of what makes this conceptual work and practice so innovative is the way they draw upon the lived experiences of the most marginalized to inform and chart new possibilities that uplift and support those very individuals.[34] Black feminist application or methodology is not only about centering people who identify as Black women though. Black feminist praxis imagines and articulates a just world where everyone has a place and what is needed to thrive, where one's intellectual and creative contributions are explored and amplified. Black feminism encourages us to be creative about what we decide to accept or not. In fact, interpretation is always an ongoing project, and we can and should introduce different terms. In doing so, this work creates galleries, institutions, cultures, and worlds.[35] These practices must be inherently interdisciplinary, ever-growing, and evolving to meet the just demands of previously excluded or underserved audiences, specifically. Moreover, Black feminist approaches to the transformation of Brooklyn's American Art Galleries are characterized by a theoretical and practical orientation toward the curatorial work itself, and a human and care-centered orientation toward our audiences.

Regarding this powerful reorientation in the realm of representation, sustainability, and field-relevancy, curators Janet Dees and Alisa Swindell articulate a shared investment in:

exploring what it means to proliferate an abundance of Black feminist ideas and aesthetics into the institutional fabric of art history and museums. Might these institutions feel less obsolete if we accept the work of Black feminism as an urgent task: not just increased representation of Black women in museums, but a fundamental shift of material circumstances?[36]

Museums have historically lagged behind intellectual output and pedagogical innovations, much like scholarship. They trail the daily practices and the social and cultural conversations taking place in real time. For decades visionary thought leaders have been charting new paths, while also applying pressure to the field of art history and museums, calling on institutions to assess themselves transparently and make changes that align with their stated missions and visions of diversity, equity, and inclusion. Kinshasha Holman Conwill, Valerie Cassel Oliver, Gwendolyn DuBois Shaw, Kelli Jones, Samella S. Lewis, Lowery Stokes Sims, Sharon Patton, Deb Willis, and many others have introduced us to new artists, new subjects, new art histories, and helped us build new institutions. Adrienne Childs, Cheryl Finley, bell hooks, Charmaine Nelson, Leigh Raiford, and Judith Wilson brought to the field new ways to think about American art and its histories, and Rhea Combes, Lisa Farrington, Thelma Golden, Sarah Lewis, and Nell Painter gave and continue to give us new tools for the research, interpretation, teaching, and display of an ever-widening range of art and visual culture. Building on these legacies, Adrienne Edwards, Melanee Harvey, Rujecko Hockley, Ashley James, Kelli Morgan, Legacy Russell, Rebecca VanDiver, Brittany Webb, and Leslie Wilson continue to research, write, exhibit, and teach art and Blackness, in bold and visionary ways, into our collective futures. And of course, where would any of us be without the artists who, like Edmonia Lewis (1844–1907), Alma Thomas (1891–1978), Minnie Evans (1892–1987), Loïs Mailou Jones (1905–1998), and Elizabeth Catlett (1915–2012), create beauty out of madness, pioneer and shape-shift form and material, and inspire us to look more lovingly and studiously at ourselves?

In Practice

Building on this inheritance of scholarly and curatorial practice, the American art department at the Brooklyn Museum is applying the tools of Black feminisms in service of the Museum's significant American art collection. It is an application that has shape-shifted the material conditions around the department's work. For example, Black feminist values of coalition building, representation, and accountability called for the restructuring of an existing advisory committee assembled for the reinstallation planning phase. This included the addition of two Latinx luminaries working at the intersections of Latin American art, Latinx art histories, and contemporary cultural theory and practice: Tatiana Flores and Adriana Zavala. It also called for inviting the field's most incisive and critical voices, including American art scholar and curator Kelli Morgan, who focuses on anti-racist approaches to work within museums, and Kiowa artist and curator Tahnee Ahtone, whose work opens spaces for Indigenous artists to engage with the colonial legacies of museums.

Black feminist values also inspired the timely development of a term-based senior fellow position in the American art department focused on Asian American Art, and supported by the Terra Foundation for American Art. This position was held by ShiPu Wang, professor of art history at the University of California, Merced, whose collection research and partnership led to the department's first ever Collection Development Plan for the acquisition of art made by Asian Americans. Additionally, and in alignment with this new strategic vision, the department accessioned thirty-five artworks by Japanese American artists, including works by Chiura Obata (1885–1975); Kyohei Inukai (1886–1954); Yasuo Kuniyoshi (1889–1953); Bumpei Usui (1898–1994) Hisako Hibi (1907–1991), the American art collection's first by an Asian American woman; and Kyohei Inukai (the younger; 1913–1985).

Through the practices of collectivity, interdisciplinary thought-partnership, and resource sharing, the department is building an environment within which to conduct cutting-edge research at the intersections of art history, American studies, and myriad related disciplines. Attracting and supporting an impressive number of fellows, interns, scholars, and curators within this new model, the department has become a home for a wide array of research interests and projects beyond the reinstallation. The department's past and current staff are contributing innovative scholarship on topics ranging from ecocritical examinations of the coffee trade through the depictions of artists working in the Americas to the study of fashion and clothing in American art in their construction and proliferation of ideas around race and gender; from new research on John Singer Sargent as well as the art and material culture of the Viceroyalty of Peru to explorations into Black body politics in early American paintings and photography, queer art histories, and finally, a focus on museum theory and practice. Additionally, this transformation of our gallery spaces has prompted the massive assessment and treatment of hundreds of artworks by the Museum's team of art conservators. Over one hundred never-before-exhibited artworks have been made ready for installation, and in several instances, daring curatorial moves—together with imaginative conservation tactics—have been employed to give audiences novel access to masterworks in the collections. These efforts can be seen as scaffolding the newly installed galleries and this publication, and with time will continue to expand and deepen. Other projects will also come to fruition in the future. We have created a context for learning and unlearning how to speak and write about art in the collection and in the field more broadly, and this list offers a small sample of our ongoing efforts and what is to come.

The application of Black feminist approaches to this work also asks the field what spaces oriented toward the social, emotional, and cultural thriving of strategically marginalized communities might look and feel like, and how they might function. This means dismantling and rebuilding the many aspects of American art museums and collections which have been designed nearly exclusively for white European American social, emotional, and cultural thriving. To that end, what we are moving toward in the American art department is the use of frameworks. While thematic displays typically involve a grouping of artworks that are brought together under a particular topic or focus, our use of frameworks is distinctly about what is done *with* the objects once they are brought together. Frameworks are about ideas and actions. Through frameworks, we are building the space, structure, and home in which our curatorial thought and care work with the collection can flourish. A space from which we might "learn to see." We are building display structures that give us room to boldly experiment with representation, to practice radical care, and to be attentive to the language of political demand, ultimately creating those much-needed bridges between contemporary audiences and our historic collections.

Frameworks
. . . a way to organize ideas and actions.

This is the story of a house. It has been lived in by many people. Our grandmother, Baba, made this house a living space. She was certain that the way we lived was shaped by objects, the way we looked at them, the way they were placed around us. She was certain that we were shaped by space. From her I learn about aesthetics, the yearning for beauty that she tells me is the predicament of heart that makes our passion real. A quiltmaker, she teaches me about color. Her house is a place where I am learning to look at things, where I am learning how to belong in space. In rooms full of objects, crowded with things, I am learning to recognize myself. She hands me a mirror, showing me how to look. The color of wine she has made in my cup, the beauty of the everyday. Surrounded by fields of tobacco, the leaves braided like hair, dried and hung, circles and circles of smoke fill the air. We string red peppers fiery hot, with thread that will not be seen. They will hang in front of a lace curtain to catch the sun. Look, she tells me, what the light does to color! Do you believe that space can give life, or take it away, that space has power? These are the questions she asks which frighten me. Baba dies an old woman, out of place. Her funeral is also a place to see things, to recognize myself. How can I be sad in the face of death, surrounded by so much beauty? Death, hidden in a field of tulips, wearing my face and calling my name. Baba in a swoon, tulips everywhere. Here a soul on fire with beauty burns and passes, a soul touched by flame. We see her leave. She has taught me how to look at the world and see beauty. She has taught me "we must learn to see."[37]

Toward Joy: New Frameworks for American Art establishes a set of tools—fresh ways of seeing that readers explore as they move through the book just as audiences move through the installation. This book's organization mirrors the frameworks that shape the in-gallery experience. Just as the galleries move away from traditional display, the text also departs from some of the formatting conventionally found in collection books, with each chapter offering a bird's-eye view of the operationalized thinking and actions therein. Fresh visions for the research and bold display of the collection in the twenty-first century are offered through installation images and a concise introduction at the onset of each section. Entries span from single object interpretations that highlight new or little-known perspectives inspired by the framework itself to multi-object conversations that deepen our engagement with artworks across disparate collecting areas.

Succinct essays and entries emerging from an abundance of voices from both inside and outside of the institution offer a set of accessible inroads to the collection and highlight and preview a selection of artworks and ideas. Rather than a venue for showcasing new or in-depth research for an audience of peer scholars and curators, this book was conceived with a wider, more casual, readership in mind. By design, entries and essays are not definitive or comprehensive. Instead, most texts fall between 200 and 600 words, a decision made in recognition of the various demands on readers' time and attention, and reflective of the ways we collectively seek out and receive information in shorter bursts that can be explored further at will.

Most of the 421 objects within the installation are featured within the installation photography, though only a selection are included as plates or in the interpretive conversations. The writing itself amplifies a range of voices and perspectives, including those of artists, curators, community members, and scholars, who teach us to see artworks in new ways. People outside of the institution bring different questions, expectations, and experiences to the work than scholars and curators, and our perspectives are shifted and our understanding of the collection is richer as a result. Each chapter concludes with a "Critical Short," where contributors build upon the interdisciplinary possibility of the framework model to extend and enrich our understanding of and appreciation for American art.

Readers are invited to pick up new ideas, strategies for looking, ways to read—much as they would in the galleries—and carry them throughout. In this context, while Black feminism is the very air, the "room to breathe" that Hartman imagines, readers will find that the experience starts in a framework that employs water for its powerful metaphor of flow—how one might move, go with or against currents, be cleansed, refreshed, or caught up and washed away.

In the Museum's fifth-floor American galleries, the elevator lobby is an essential starting point for audiences to experience the transformed spaces beyond. In collaboration with Brooklyn-based interior designers Jannah and Kiyanna Handy of BLK MKT Vintage, the first gallery serves

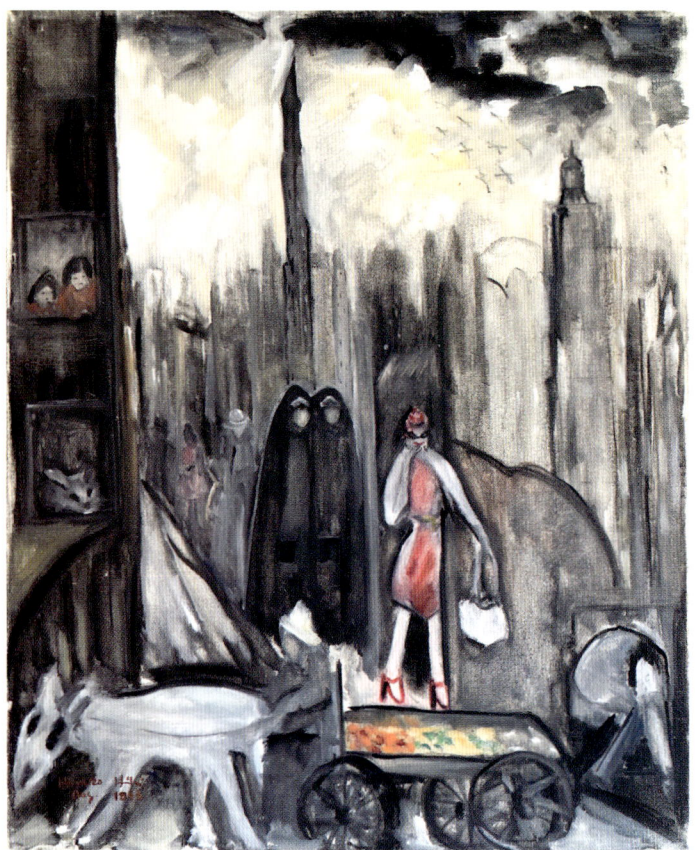

Hisako Hibi (American, born Japan, 1907–1991), *Frightful New York*, 1946.

as a vibrant reception area where audiences are warmly welcomed and invited to relax, get oriented, explore their own curiosities and rethink their expectations. With an eye toward maximalism, the designers created a comfortable space reminiscent of a Black living room across time, looking simultaneously to the fullness of the past as well as the promise of an Afrofuturist tomorrow for inspiration. The design sets the vibe/tone for the in-gallery experience to follow.

The second gallery and first framework, **Trouble the Water**, is guided by the nineteenth-century Black American spiritual "Wade in the Water." This section explores the powerful links between water and notions of freedom, life, spirituality, and progress in ancient pottery, Hodinöhsö:ni' beadwork, works on paper by Deng Ming-Dao (b. 1954) and Winslow Homer (1836–1910), and romantic and sublime landscapes by Eldzier Cortor (1916–2015), Thomas Moran (1837–1926), and Frederick Waugh (1861–1940). The artworks and their framing reveal legacies of colonialism, displacement, and the changing environment; the latter is the topic of this framework's "Critical Short: Troubled Waters and Currents of Restoration," written by Caroline Gillaspie, Assistant Curator of American Art at the Brooklyn Museum. Readers and in-gallery audiences alike are encouraged to move slowly, to traverse intentionally.

Opening with the Hodinöhsö:ni' Thanksgiving Address, or the "Words that Come Before All Else," **Radical Care** is a framework that explores modes of curatorial care—for artworks, belongings, and people—rooted in African diasporic and Indigenous ways of knowing. Dare Turner, Curator of Indigenous Art at the Brooklyn Museum, explores the power of thankfulness in our work with historic collections in the "Critical Short: Exploring the World Through Gratitude." Another core element of the conception and installation of Radical Care is the American (Art) Study; its form and function serve to acknowledge and enhance knowledge production that supports contemporary justice movements, calls to "decolonize" and diversify institutions, and combat dehumanizing representations of non-white people and cultures within museums. Part library, part laboratory, the Study places the ongoing project of learning—and unlearning—at the physical center of the conversation. This space in particular and entries within this chapter aim to meaningfully link our curatorial work with larger political struggles for more just futures. Both gallery space and catalog writing situate the American art department within a different set of histories and traditions than is typical within museums, and reorients and "shows" our work. The Radical Care framework, following scholar and curator Jami Powell, provides an opportunity to "think beyond decolonization and antiracism as separate methodological practices, but as part of larger movements that consider Indigenization and collective liberation."[38]

To Give Flowers meditates on the adage "to give someone their flowers." Emerging from Black American funerary and gospel traditions, the saying encourages listeners to

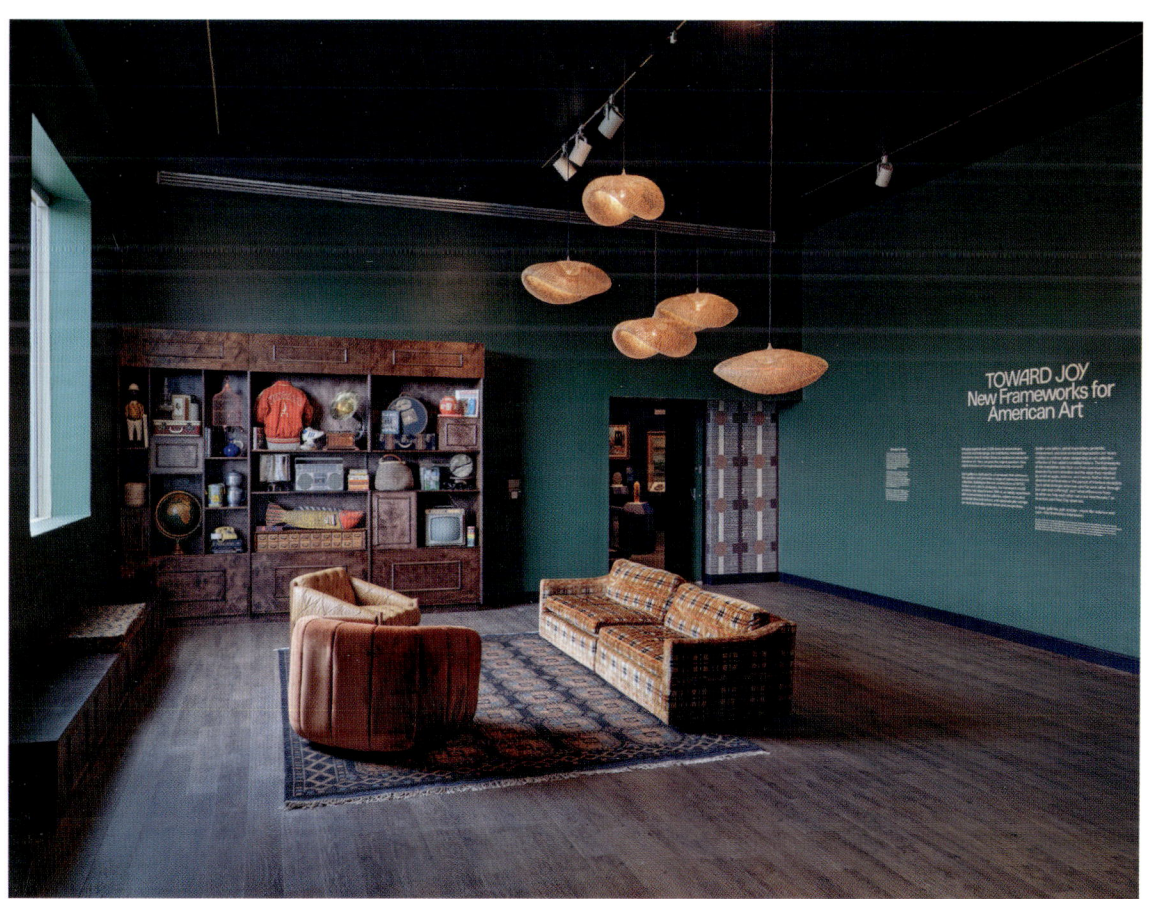

Installation view, *Toward Joy: New Frameworks for American Art*, Brooklyn Museum, October 2024.

"give flowers" while the recipient can "smell them," asserting the importance of giving people their due credit while they are alive to receive it. In the installation, the modern floral wallpaper of Loïs Mailou Jones (1905–1998) provides a vibrant and immersive backdrop for displaying underappreciated pieces in the collection, new acquisitions, and iconic favorites, all featuring floral motifs. In the book, readers can take a closer look at ornate silver work from Chile, an intricately beaded buckskin shirt, and art by Charles Ethan Porter (1847–1923), Georgia O'Keeffe (1887–1986), and Laura Wheeler Waring (1887–1948). Finally, the chapter closes on a critical short by Grace Billingslea, Curatorial Assistant for American Art and the Arts of the Americas at the Brooklyn Museum, which explores the recently acquired work of Hisako Hibi (1907–1991) and the intergenerational gardens cultivated out of dust.

Celebrating form and materiality, the framework **Counterparts** creates a space for daring conversations and dramatic discoveries in black and white. For example, the painting *Lady in Black* from 1901 by Emil Fuchs (1866–1929) is presented alongside *Untitled (Composition #104)* (1954–60) by Ad Reinhardt (1913–1967). Vessels by Earl Hooks (1927–2005), Helen Shupla (1928–1985), and a fifteenth-century Chimú-Inca artist speak to each other across centuries. Here, these shades are not opposite—but rather coequal and counterpart. This framework is inspired by two past exhibitions: the Black artist collective Spiral mounted *FIRST GROUP SHOWING (works in black & white)* in 1965 and Black feminist conceptual artist Lorraine O'Grady curated *The Black and White Show* in 1983. Black Feminist Roundtable members Camille Bacon and Leslie Wilson close this chapter by highlighting the ways this framework brings together typically segregated artwork in a display that heightens similarities and recontextualized differences.

In a time of heightened visibility and contentious control for human bodies, the framework **Surface Tension** celebrates the nude figure and highlights the Museum's impressive strength across multiple collections. Customs, religion, and society have always shaped how artists depict the human form—and dictated whose bodies are worthy of artistic study. This chapter illuminates masterpiece depictions of the human form and sets them in conversation with contemporary questions of power, agency, and embodiment. Much like the installation itself, the goal of this chapter is to empower audiences to examine the nude in productive tension with our most pressing contemporary concerns, and to engage anew with depictions of the human body as a transhistorical and transcultural form of art.

Several Seats examines two other strongholds in the American art and decorative arts collections—seated portraiture and historical seating—offering a lively context to engage with the questions and challenges their display within museums presents. Rather than remove these works from public view and disengage with them, this framework takes its cue from the expression "have several seats." Originating in Black and Latinx ballroom culture, the rebuke is directed at someone monopolizing space. Discussions of these artworks present critiques of art historical traditions that privilege white, wealthy individuals. Together, both collections—furniture and portraiture—prompt questions and discussions about individual wealth and privilege within societies built on displacement, colonialism, and enslavement. Further inspired by the expression "the T" or "my T"—first used by transgender actress and performer Lady Chablis to stand for her "truth" and often expressed as "the tea"—this section answers calls from visitors to present the "truth" about artworks in the collection and their sitters by inviting drag artists to provide readings of the collection's historic portraits. This chapter closes with the "Critical Short: To Be Real!" by Caroline Gillaspie. Citing drag performance as a rigorous form of creative self-fashioning and social critique, Gillaspie affirms the practice and positionality of drag artists as especially well-suited to examining the Museum's historic holdings afresh.

Prompted by the ways American artists have sought quietude through their art, **A Quiet Place** is a framework designed for reflection and rest. Together, images of leisure and sleep, peaceful reflections on the landscape, and belongings that promote restfulness capture experiences of silence, repose, tranquility, and spaciousness. The work of Black feminist creatives and cultural critics such as Tricia Hersey of the Nap Ministry and Cole Arthur Riley of Black Liturgies deeply inform this framework. Hersey and Riley call for individuals and communities to slow down, practice introspection, and move with intention through the world. Speaking to contemporary experiences of fatigue, including "museum fatigue," they foreground the need for care and rest-centered communion with the objects on view. In her work on African diaspora photography, art historian and cultural theorist Tina Campt entreats readers to "listen to images" that may not be fully discernible to the naked eye. She offers tools for mining the subtle ways artworks resist the oppressive forces around them. Building on Campt's approach, this publication invites visitors to engage the "lower frequencies" within the art through close looking.[39] The chapter concludes with Tricia Hersey's powerful meditation *Rest Life* to deepen this engagement.

Finally, the framework **Witness** is about seeing and being seen. Witnessing is distinct from merely looking. To bear witness means you are accountable to what you have seen. Whether in fast-paced, high-tech, high-consumption environments or a quiet gallery in a large art museum, we sometimes take the act of looking, and of witnessing culture, for granted. With its depictions of people and other beings with distinct and direct gazes, the artworks in this framework, largely portraits, formally bear witness to the present as contemporary audiences move through the gallery or turn pages in this book. Whether you choose to flip through quickly or pause for several moments to examine each image with care, your very presence activates the relationships embedded within this section, challenging and complicating who and what is being witnessed when we look at American art and how our looking impacts our collective seeing and understanding. The final "Critical Short: Showing Our Work," is dedicated to curatorial practice.

Commitment

Hope is a discipline.[40]

—Mariame Kaba

The installation and this catalog chart an American art display for this moment: today. And it is through this new model that curators within the department look forward to innovating further for the American art of tomorrow, and well into the future. As our audiences and sociocultural realities continue to expand and shift, we will lean in, listen, and especially hold these best laid plans—indeed time—lightly. We will make mistakes. Yet, we commit to experiment boldly here with the hope that our shortcomings create openings for colleagues across the institution and the field to join even more fearlessly in vital and ongoing transformation.

We hope this undertaking creates a novel and worthwhile experience for you: one that sparks curiosity, joy, and a renewed sense of wonder in historic art from across the Americas.

Notes

1. Toni Cade Bambara, *Conversations with Toni Cade Bambara* (Jackson: University of Mississippi Press, 2012).
2. Black feminist luminaries have been concerned with this question for decades. From the call and response of early organizers for anti-lynching and civil and human rights asking, "What time is it?" to the resounding answer: "Freedom Time!" There is social activist and philosopher Grace Lee Bogg's query: "What time is it on the clock of the world?" and curator and author Legacy Russell noting the time at the 2024 Black Radical Curation Symposium, held at Princeton University, April 11, 2024, https://arts.princeton.edu/news/2024/04/princeton-collaboratorium-presents-the-radical-practice-of-black-curation-a-symposium/.
3. Russell, ibid.
4. Interdisciplinary scholar Treva Ellison, in conversation with the author about social belonging.
5. Sarah Stefana Smith's work on bafflement is helpful for thinking through my mother's experiences within museums, and by extension my own work to disrupt widely held expectations for experiencing installations of American art. For scholar and visual artist Stefana Smith, bafflement is a space of pause, "a form of confusion, frustration, and disease and becomes the methodological and theoretical scaffolding" with which one might approach contemporary [curatorial] work. https://ideasonfire.net/96-sarah-stefana-smith/.
6. And this treatment—the erasure and devaluing—of people and different forms of knowledge is violent/violence. This discussion emerged from a conversation with art historian Leslie Wilson on April 8, 2024.
7. See Linda Ferber, "History of the Collections," in *Masterpieces in the Brooklyn Museum* (New York: Brooklyn Museum and Harry N. Abrams, 1988), 8–10.
8. Teresa A. Carbone, "The Making of a Collection: Part 1," in *American Paintings in the Brooklyn Museum: Artists Born by 1876*, Teresa A. Carbone, Barbara Dayer Gallati, and Linda S. Ferber (New York: Brooklyn Museum; London: D. Giles Limited, 2006), 13.
9. While Graham's civic charter is one we still see reflected in the museum's mission today, the audiences to which Graham was directed were working-class white, largely immigrant families. This vision has since expanded to encompass the museum's ever-changing audiences as the borough itself has evolved. For a summary of this evolution, see ibid.," 11–62.
10. Here I am inspired and motivated by Saidiya Hartman in her reflections on "waywardness": "Waywardness is a practice of possibility at a time when all roads, except the ones created by *smashing out*, are foreclosed. It obeys no rules and abides no authorities. It is unrepentant. It traffics in occult visions of other worlds and dreams of a different kind of life. Waywardness is an ongoing exploration of *what might be*; it is an improvisation with the terms of social existence, when the terms have already been dictated, when there is little room to breathe . . . " Saidiya Hartman, *Wayward Lives, Beautiful Experiments: Intimate Histories of Social Upheaval* (New York: W.W. Norton, 2019), 228.
11. In 1842, the Institute held its first of a series of important early loan exhibitions featuring impressive selections of paintings and sculpture as well as machinery, manufactured wares, and "specimens of any unusual, ornamental or curious works of Nature or Art." These displays were an impressive rival to the annual exhibition of the National Academy of Design in New York, and the art section of the 1843 exhibition was dominated by the works of American painters, including Thomas Cole, Asher Brown Durand, and William Sidney Mount. It was during the run of the 1846 annual that the trustees publicly

announced their intention to establish a permanent Gallery of Art, "at all times free to the public under proper restrictions, as a means for refining and elevating the taste for art culture," and to that end they invited donations of art. Carbone, "The Making of a Collection," 18.
12. Ibid.
13. Emphasis in the original text. Ibid., 16.
14. Teresa A. Carbone, "'Ardent, Radical, and Progressive': Augustus Graham, Walt Whitman, and American Art at the Brooklyn Museum," in *American Paintings at the Brooklyn Museum*, 11–25.
15. While this account focuses on the developments around the Museum's American art collection, the director Philip Youtz was also behind the long-term loan of the New-York Historical Society's Egyptian, Assyrian, ancient Americas, and Native American art collections. With the goal of presenting global artistic traditions to Brooklyn audiences. Youtz requested that Herbert Spinden, the curator of ethnology, engage the Mexican government in an exchange between the National Museum of Anthropology in Mexico City and the Brooklyn Museum. To learn more, see Nancy B. Rosoff, "Nineteenth Century Rambles in Mexico, an Itinerant Peruvian Textile, and Pan-American Cooperation at the Brooklyn Museum, 1930–1950," *Collecting the Other Americas: Ancient Americas Collections in American Art Museums*, ed. Victoria Lyall and Ellen Hoobler (Denver: Denver Art Museum, 2025).
16. Teresa A. Carbone, "American Art at the New Brooklyn Museum," in *American Paintings in the Brooklyn Museum*, 44–46.
17. Other directors such as William Henry Goodyear, who was a Yale-trained former Metropolitan Museum of Art curator in the department of paintings, and William Henry Fox, a lawyer and former director of the John Herron Institute (now the Indianapolis Museum of Art), had their own wide-ranging values and visions for the institution's priorities and function. Regarding display, these varied from densely packed triple-row installations of the museum's painting collections under Goodyear to the complete overhaul of the collection into spacious and "harmonious groupings" during Fox's tenure (Carbone, "American Art at the Brooklyn Museum," 35). For more on the shifts in mission, vision, and display in art and cultural institutions, see Andrew McClellan's thematic history in *The Art Museum from Boullée to Bilbao* (Berkeley: University of California Press, 2008).
18. Over its development, the departmental structure of the institution evolved as collections grew and new collecting areas were pursued. Beginning in 1890, there were two departments—Fine Arts and Natural History—which were joined by Ethnology in 1903. Curators at the time and in the following decades were broad, general collections stewards, rather than specialists. And each successive director played a pivotal role in the Museum's collection development and display, which included the nascent field of American art. Curators such as Herbert Tschudy, John Baur, John Jay Gordon, and Axel von Saldern were regarded as fine art curators, who were largely responsible the Museum's growing paintings collection, which included works spanning the Renaissance to the present. Specialized training in American art would further impact the museum world in the late 1960s and into the 1970s as an increasing number of Americanists entered the field. This, along with other field specialists in Egyptology and the decorative arts, saw the organic formation of divisions based on increased specificity, reaching its peak in the 1970s. Sometime in the 1960s, American paintings and sculpture became a department or division within the Fine Art department, which had remained as the institution's sole collecting department as its Natural History holdings were rehomed and the department of Natural History discontinued in the early 1930s. For more on the Museum's early collecting practices see Carbone, "The Making of a Collection," 11–62.
19. One of the earliest presentations of art by Black Americans took place in 1945 at the Brooklyn Museum with the exhibition *The Negro Artist Comes of Age*, organized by the Albany Institute of History and Art with the assistance of the artist Hale Woodruff (1900–1980). Teresa Carbone notes the exhibition in her essay on the development of the American art collections in *American Paintings in the Brooklyn Museum*, 50.
20. Thirty years later, the Museum would open the Elizabeth A. Sackler Center for Feminist Art in March 2007, the first and most significant exhibition and education facility of its kind dedicated entirely to feminist art of the past, present, and future.
21. These working groups included: "Arts of the Americas and Europe," "Contemporary," which included Prints and Drawings, "ECANEA—Egyptian, Classical, and Ancient Near Eastern Art."
22. Despite *Witness* opening nearly five years prior, when *Soul of a Nation: Art in the Age of Black Power* traveled to the Brooklyn Museum from the Tate Modern in 2018, the earlier exhibition was written out of the coverage surrounding the event, which was discussed as a first-of-its-kind installation. In reality, the Brooklyn Museum had been exhibiting Black American art for decades.
23. Carbone, "The Making of a Collection," 13.
24. Zadie Smith, *Feel Free: Essays* (New York: Penguin Press, 2018).
25. Saidiya Hartman, "In the Wake: A Salon in Honor of Christina Sharpe," Barnard Center for Research on Women (BCRW), February 2, 2017, https://bcrw.barnard.edu/videos/in-the-wake-a-salon-in-honor-of-christina-sharpe/.
26. According to author Tracey Michae'l Lewis-Giggetts, "Black joy is a strategy . . . It is a mechanism for resistance, a method of resilience, and a master plan for restoration." *Black Joy: Stories of Resistance, Resilience, and Restoration* (New York: Gallery Books, 2022), xx.
27. Ross Gay, "The First Encitement," in *Inciting Joy: Essays* (Chapel Hill, NC: Algonquin, 2022), pp. 1–10.
28. "In the Wake: A Salon in Honor of Christina Sharpe," Barnard Center for Research on Women (BCRW), February 2, 2017, https://bcrw.barnard.edu/videos/in-the-wake-a-salon-in-honor-of-christina-sharpe/; Saidiya Hartman in conversation with Thora Siemsen, "On Working with Archives," The Creative Independent, February 3, 2021, https://thecreativeindependent.com/people/saidiya-hartman-on-working-with-archives/.
29. Ruth Wilson, *Gilmore in Golden Gulag: Prisons, Surplus, Crisis, and Opposition in Globalizing California* (Berkeley: University of California Press, 2008). Art is often thought to exist outside of the body as an extension, or an entirely externalized expression of epistemology or ontology. However, the sciences reveal innumerable interconnections between art and the body. Neuroscientists in particular discuss how the art we encounter lives in and through us long after we have left its presence. See Marcus T. Pearce, Dahlia W. Zaidel, Oshin Vartanian, Martin Skov, Helmut Leder, Anjan Chatterjee, and Marcos Nadal, "Neuroaesthetics: The Cognitive Neuroscience of Aesthetic Experience," *Perspectives on Psychological Science* 11, no. 2 (2016): 265–79. "Art literally and figuratively moves and shapes us, including our relationships to intergenerational and transcultural phenomena, to a personal and collective past, and to longer arcs of historical experiences," neuroscientist Sará King, in conversation with the author.
30. See fn10.
31. When I arrived at the Brooklyn Museum, the institution had embarked on a series of social action frameworks or commitments that would inform the Museum's work over the next several years. This approach stemmed from the desire of staff and visitors alike, for the Museum to demonstrate and measurably track its social impact within the community and wider world. To do this, two issues were identified as long-term priorities—climate justice and mass

criminalization—and departments across the museum were encouraged to consider how their work might address these priorities directly and indirectly. The timing of these initiatives meant that climate justice and mass criminalization were top-of-mind in our planning for the reinstallation of the American art galleries. The successful result was the department's early exploration of ecocritical approaches to understanding our rich holdings, as well as our Asian American acquisition initiative to add works by Japanese American artists who were interned during World War II.

32. Janet Dees and Alisa Swindell, "A Site of Struggle, A Methodology of Accord," in *Reenvisioning Histories of American Art: Transforming Museum Practice*, ed. Jami C. Powell and Michael Hartman (Seattle: University of Washington Press, forthcoming).

33. This project exists at the junction of Black feminist thought and Black feminist practice. Black feminist thought, as articulated by social theorist Patricia Hill Collins, emerges from historic thought traditions in the empowerment of Black women, in particular. As a critical social theory outlined by Collins, it makes up a set of tools for combatting intersecting systems of oppression that Black women face, but that are not exclusive to Black women. As a critical social theory, Black feminist thought is designed for the purpose of dismantling systems of oppression and ending societal injustice. For Hill Collins, understanding Black feminist thought starts "from the assumption that African-American women have created independent, oppositional yet subjugated knowledges concerning our own subordination, contemporary U.S. Black women intellectuals are engaged in the struggle to reconceptualize all dimensions of the dialectic of oppression and activism as it applies to African-American women." Patricia Hill Collins, *Black Feminist Thought: Knowledge, Consciousness, and the Politics of Empowerment*, 2nd ed. (New York: Routledge, 2000), 13. Importantly, in her work, she emphasizes the connections between knowledge and power, which has been instructive in my intellectual and curatorial practices within academia and in fine art institutions. Finally, Hill Collins reminds us that there is always a political context for Black women's intellectual work, and here, that political context is the experience of Black women and other marginalized groups within American art museums. See ibid.

34. This is exemplified by the writing of bell hooks, where she coins terms like the oppositional gaze, which emerges from the ways Black people's sight/seeing was policed, disciplined, and weaponized, and transforms Black women's looking as a tool for empowerment and critical engagement within the sociopolitical and cultural landscape. When paired with Chela Sandoval's oppositional consciousness, which describes the thoughts, ideas, and sensibilities arising from an oppressed group, the goal of both oppositional gazing and oppositional consciousness becomes the disruption and dismantling of the oppressive systems that shape the very social realities undergirding exclusion, in museums specifically, establishing paths toward cultural recognition, agency, and meaningful inclusion. See bell hooks, "The Oppositional Gaze: Black Female Spectators," in *Black Looks: Race and Representation* (Boston: South End Press, 1992), and Chela Sandoval, "U.S. Third World Feminism: The Theory and Method of Oppositional Consciousness in the Postmodern World," *GENDERS* 10 (Spring 1991).

35. In 1977, the Combahee River Collective, a Black feminist queer socialist organization active in Boston, released their now canonical statement outlining their position, politics, and core coalition-building philosophies, ushering in a new wave of Black feminist and third world organizing. In it they assert that "if Black women were free, it would mean that everyone else would have to be free, since our freedom would necessitate the destruction of all systems of oppression." Nearly fifty years later, the authors of this powerful treatise reflect on their words in Marian Jones, "'If Black Women Were Free': An Oral History of the Combahee River Collective," *The Nation*, October 29, 2021, https://www.thenation.com/article/society/combahee-river-collective-oral-history/.

36. Janet Dees and Alisa Swindell, "A Site of Struggle, A Methodology of Accord."

37. bell hooks, "An Aesthetics of Blackness—Strange and Oppositional," *Lenox Avenue: A Journal of Interarts Inquiry* 1 (1995): 65.

38. Powell and Hartman, eds., *Reenvisioning Histories of American Art*.

39. Tina Campt, *Listening to Images* (Durham, NC: Duke University Press, 2017).

40. Activist and organizer Mariame Kaba has argued for hope to be understood as a discipline rather than an emotion, or even an optimism. For more on Kaba's understanding of hope as a commitment to think otherwise, a practice and a motion in the ongoing work toward all social justices, see "Hope is a Discipline: Mariame Kaba on Dismantling the Carceral State," *The Intercept,* March 17, 2021, https://theintercept.com/2021/03/17/intercepted-mariame-kaba-abolitionist-organizing/.

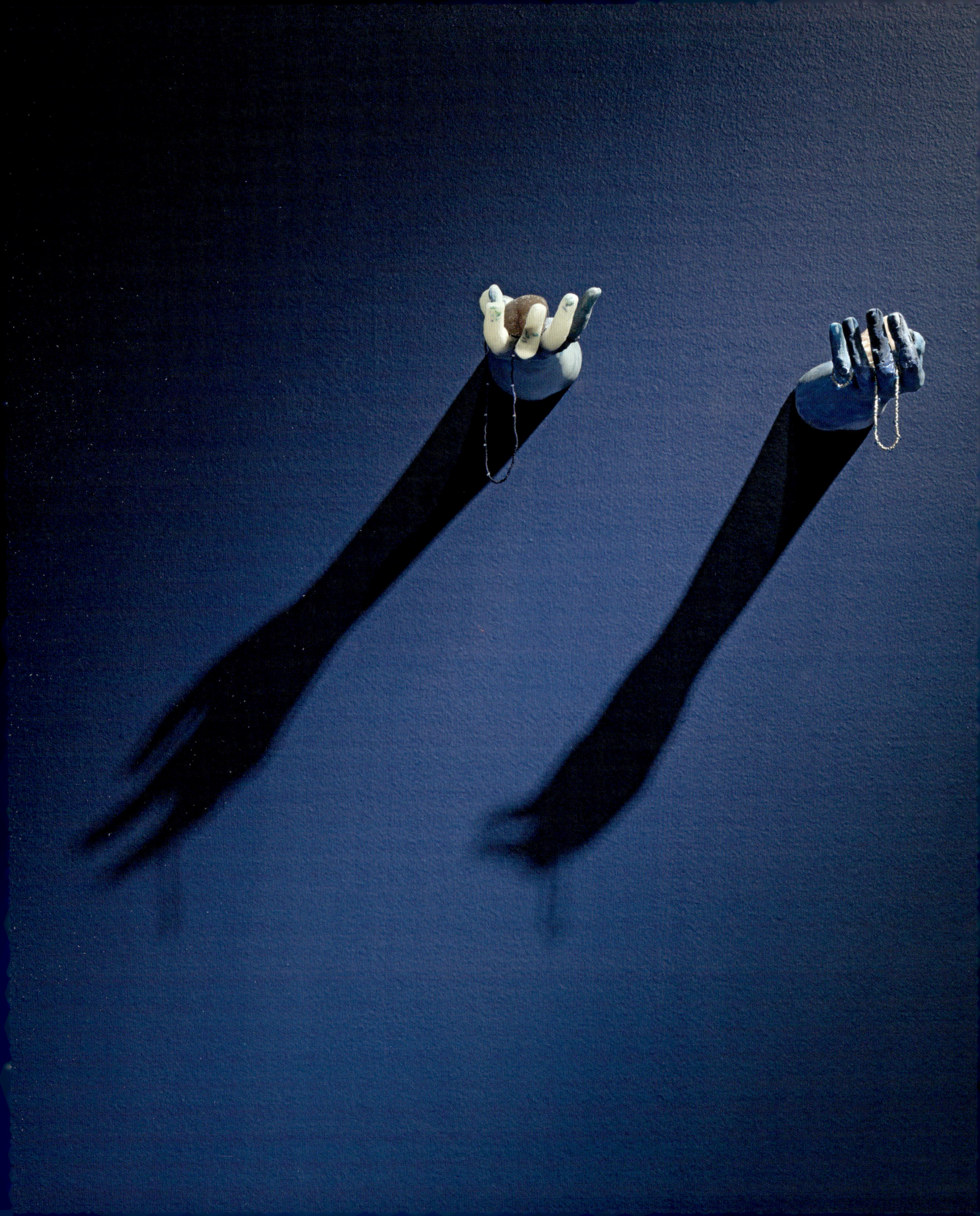

Through Gimlet Holes: New Visions for American Art

Jonathan Michael Square with Stephanie Sparling Williams

In 1861, a self-liberated Black woman named Harriet Jacobs published her autobiography, *Incidents in the Life of a Slave Girl*. In a pivotal moment in the book, Jacobs escapes from her enslaver and seeks refuge in her grandmother's garret, a space she refers to as her "loophole of retreat." Determined to remain close to her children, Jacobs spends seven years hidden in this crawl space, passing the time sewing and reading the Bible. Fortunately, she discovers a gimlet, a tool she uses to pierce the walls and floorboards, allowing her to see her children.

Jacobs's deployment of a gimlet to better see the world around her served as a powerful metaphor for the tools—and a catalyst for the conversations—that might be used to liberate museum practice from its own confinement. Less than two hundred years later, fifteen scholars, artists, curators, and freedom dreamers convened as the Black Feminist Roundtable to review and respond to the Brooklyn Museum's plans for their revamped American Art Galleries. The Roundtable gathered on Zoom for ninety minutes once a month to discuss a single gallery and framework. The group was sent materials in advance that included a floorplan, checklist, sample section and label texts, behind-the-scenes considerations, and in-progress designs. Additionally, the Roundtable was provided a concrete set of questions to guide their review and to help maximize feedback. The format for the virtual calls was straightforward: each month two different participants opened the session with a ten- to twenty-minute response to the materials in a style of their choice, before opening the floor to the rest of the Roundtable. The sessions were closed, and only members of the reinstallation team and a few key cross-departmental collaborators were permitted to attend, listen only, and take notes. The feedback offered by the Black Feminist Roundtable emphasized care and creative problem-solving, and foregrounded collective wisdom and lived experiences. Through a series of virtual discussions, the Roundtable inspired the reinstallation team toward even more capacious and rigorous engagement with the Brooklyn Museum's American art collections.

In the spirit of Jacobs, the following short essays are offered here as gimlet holes. Individually and collaboratively, these texts open fresh apertures onto American art and its display. Leigh Raiford meditates on Tiffany Lethabo King's formulation of the Black shoals as an instructive parallel project of spatialized becoming and highlights the importance of labeling Black and Indigenous epistemologies of care *as* curatorial modes for radical space-making. Leslie Wilson explores the brackets used by Alice Walker in her 1974 lodestar essay, "In Search of Our Mother's Garden," for their function of holding space. Kelli Morgan borrows Walker's metaphor of the garden from the same essay. Jonathan Square reflects on the juxtaposition of contemporary art within historic collection displays, and Brittany Webb turns to the Brooklyn Museum's collection, finding an instructive implement in Fred Wilson's piece *Iago's Mirror* (2009). Tiffany Momon brings Black craftspeople to the fore in the Black Craftspeople Digital Archive, which reveals the archive as a critical site for liberation practices in its focus on the lives and experiences of Black artisans. Xiao Situ offers a window into the transformative powers of rest on brain functioning and our dreams, while Sará Yafah King opens yet another portal of perception, pointing readers toward the stars.

Exploring new visions of American art, these short essays, and the pages throughout the publication—gimlets or gimlet holes—hint at the innumerable possibilities for thinking, experiencing, researching, and writing American art into the future of our museums and into the future of the field.

Exploring the Shoals
Leigh Raiford

What would it be to experience an installation of American art not organized around Eurocentric values of collection, display, and classification but arranged through modes of curatorial care rooted in African diasporic and Indigenous epistemologies (or ways of knowing)?

In her book *The Black Shoals*, scholar Tiffany Lethabo King stages a conversation between Black American and Native American communities, drawing on mutual but differently articulated concerns with violence, genocide, the afterlives of slavery, and the ongoingness of colonialism. Lethabo King takes up Black studies' concerns with water (blackness as ocean) and Native American studies' concerns with land (indigeneity as land or earth) and offers the shoals—an offshore geologic formation that is neither water nor land and at once water and land—as an organiz-

ing metaphor. The shoals are simultaneously beyond and between; they exist beyond national or more specifically nation-state formations. The shoals, in Lethabo King's study, require us to adjust, reimagine, shift our footing, embrace the unexpected, in order to create "a new space of becoming."[1]

This is the promise and the potential of the Brooklyn Museum's transformation of their American art galleries: to offer us—as curators, scholars, visitors, and citizens—new ways of understanding and moving through the museum, through curatorial practice, and through our relationship with the world and to each other by way of the objects our society has created to tell our stories. While offering a critique of institutional violence, a commitment to care is at the heart of the transformed galleries—and at the heart of this book. What does it mean for an institution and its curators to make place and build community with and through art? To hold space and engender a sense of belonging? And to develop, intervene in, or control a narrative?

When using "curatorial" here, I refer to the process of organizing, arranging, and looking after the items in a collection or a community: the early vocational meaning of the term. So too am I invoking the curatorial in its turn from the "vocational" iteration to the process of selection and "exhibition making practice." In this sense, I am also suggesting the necessity of collaborating with others, especially artists, to realize community and a space of belonging.

In these meanings, my use of curatorial returns the role of curator to its Latin root *curare*, as a practice and model of caretaking, and connects us to a Black feminist ethics of care, to an allegiance to gratitude and building consensus. Museum director and cultural space founder Koyo Kouoh offers a model when she describes her curatorial practice as follows: "to defend sites of criticality and dreaming, to care for the health and vitality of our society, [and to engage] with new and undervalued artistic practices."[2]

Take, for example, the inclusion of late Black American artist Beverly Buchanan's *Untitled (Fristula Series)*, a series of pigmented concrete block sculptures fashioned from milk cartons that in their quiet and constant transformation invoke memory, ruins, and the passage of time (p. 71). Take also the American (Art) Study (p. 69), a collection of books and syllabi placed in the center of the exhibition that provide tools to better understand the artwork in the space of the gallery and how might we carry that work beyond the museum walls. Here are two (of myriad) opportunities the galleries provide to connect us with the world beyond the museum, to force us to shift our footing (indeed to literally move around and with the work), and to hold space for our dreaming.

Naming Black and Indigenous epistemologies of care as "curatorial" proffers an invitation to situate the museum and its practices within a different set of histories and traditions, and a model for a museum that holds all of us in its regard.

Notes
1. Tiffany Lethabo King, *The Black Shoals: Offshore Formations of Black and Native Studies* (Durham, NC: Duke University Press, 2019), 3–4.
2. Koyo Kouoh, public talk, University of California, Berkeley, March 2, 2019. On contemporary definitions of the curatorial see also Hans Ulrich Obrist, "The Art of Curation": "Today, curating as a profession means at least four things. It means to preserve, in the sense of safeguarding the heritage of art. It means to be the selector of new work. It means to connect to art history. And it means displaying or arranging the work. But it's more than that. Before 1800, few people went to exhibitions. Now hundreds of millions of people visit them every year. It's a mass medium and a ritual. The curator sets it up so that it becomes an extraordinary experience and not just illustrations or spatialised books." "Hans Ulrich Obrist: The Art of Curation," *The Guardian*, March 23, 2014, https://www.theguardian.com/artanddesign/2014/mar/23/hans-ulrich-obrist-art-curator.

[From a Place of Love]
Leslie Wilson

People often preface the telling of hard truths by asserting that they're speaking, hand on heart, "from a place of love." They know that you might not want to hear what they have to say, but you need to. Speaking from a place of love makes space for critique.

Brackets can be used to make that kind of space. As punctuation, they are a gesture—a hand on heart—for placing language into existing text to clarify, expand, or correct what has already been said.

Alice Walker uses brackets in "In Search of Our Mothers' Gardens" (1974) to open and hold space for examining the ways Black women make art despite existing in environments that often refuse to acknowledge their humanity, let alone their creativity. Walker seeks out the myriad ways their creativity has been expressed, and so often overlooked, misunderstood, and foreclosed in everyday life. Through this exploration, including celebrating the artistry her mother expressed through cultivating her garden, she comes to understand her own creative lineage.

In that context, Walker applies brackets to quoted passages from Virginia Woolf's book *A Room of One's Own* (1929), offering another layer to Woolf's influential consideration of the conditions and circumstances necessary to foster women's creative lives.[1] For instance, to Woolf's claim, "Yet genius of a sort must have existed among women as it must have existed among the working class," Walker appends, "[Change this to 'slaves' and 'the wives and daughters of sharecroppers.']"[2] And where Woolf mentions Emily Brontë and Robert Burns, Walker adds, "[change this to 'a Zora Hurston or a Richard Wright.']" Walker invokes and intervenes in Woolf's discussion of overlooked creative talents to extend the frame of Woolf's insights about who has been left unaccounted for and unrecorded by official histories as well as far more personal relations.

Walker's brackets are devices for seeing further. In the many circumstances that Woolf identified in which talent was stifled or unacknowledged, there was yet more. The simplicity of the brackets is key to their power—they make space for people, ideas, possibilities. They make space for painful histories as well as overdue recognition of artistic contributions.

The Black Feminist Roundtable sought to open up that kind of space. In the Roundtable, our aim was to examine what else we can account for as we tell stories about American art—to make space for more now and more to follow. And we approached that new presentation of the American art collection critically—"from a place of love"—and, even, from a place of joy. And we did so in the full and emphatic spirit of our critical engagement with American art and its histories, not in spite of it.

Notes
1. Dianne Sadoff importantly observes that the brackets, however, do not offer symmetrical relationships between Walker's and Woolf's examples. Sadoff, "Black Matrilineage: The Case of Alice Walker and Zora Neale Hurston," *Signs* 11, no. 1 (Fall 1985): 11.
2. Alice Walker, "In Search of Our Mothers' Gardens," *Ms.* (May 1974): 70.

Sowing Seeds, Laying Ground
Kelli Morgan

The soil of American art has been tightly compacted for over a century, and I've dedicated my career to turning it over. From gallery interventions that read Black people back into historic works of art by Benjamin West (1738–1820), Charles Willson Peale (1741–1827), and John Singleton Copley (1738–1815), to complete gallery overhauls that utilized the establishment of Jim Crow segregation as a lens to understand the work of William McGregor Paxton (1869–1941) and Louis Comfort Tiffany (1848–1933) in relationship to Black political and economic disenfranchisement, I plowed my way through fields that felt unyielding. The institutions that employed me hired me with the expressed goal of broadening our collective understanding of the canon. Yet Black curators in particular are often blocked, undermined, and shamed for doing the very work they are brought in to do. This was my experience. Institutions want you to plant seeds without preparing the soil, want you to harvest evermore fruits without creating sustainable systems for cultivation.

This work took a tremendous toll on my emotional and psychological well-being. Though looking back, the stress and harm feels worth it, because my efforts have allowed other Black women to plant and harvest very ambitious gardens within the landscape of American art that will sustain our communities for years to come. This is an essential quality of Black feminism: loving oneself, one's art, one's voice, one's presence, and one's essence enough to use it to help others do the same. For that, I am forever grateful because the application of Black feminist principles to permanent collections of American art always seemed obvious to me.

In her 1974 essay, "In Search of Our Mothers' Gardens: The Creativity of Black Women in the South," Alice Walker muses over such topics as Jean Toomer's literary character Avey, Phillis Wheatley's poetry, Virginia Woolf's conceptualizations of what is needed to be a female artist, and her own mother's gardening. Walker does so to explain how African American women's artistic activities allowed them to withstand the severities of social, political, economic, and sexual oppression. In speaking about her mother's usage of creative skills to surmount the multifaceted dynamics of Black women's oppression Walker states, "[f]or her, so hindered and intruded upon in so many ways, being an artist has still been a daily part of her life. This ability to hold on, even in very simple ways, is work [B]lack women have done for a very long time."[1]

Walker's phrasing of her mother's "ability to hold on" deeply resonates. It articulates how a Black woman maintains her artistic acumen despite oppressions that very specifically obstruct the resources she needs to cultivate it. During and following my doctoral work, I had been immersed in curating American art through Black feminist frameworks at the Birmingham Museum of Art, PAFA, and the Indianapolis Museum of Art at Newfields. Like so many other Black women curators, I experienced resistance at each turn. However, as I think back to the beginning of my career, I now understand that Walker was not simply discussing Black women's resilience and I was not simply surviving the museum. Walker was illustrating the ways in which new life often springs from Black women's toil. In fact, that "ability to hold on" allows for the creation of life *and* the ability to make something out of nothing. It is a purposeful tilling and sowing of solid ground that eventually produces something new, and also more beautiful.

Thus, it is beyond an honor to witness Stephanie Sparling Williams bring that work to life in ways that will not only transform the field, but more importantly change the ways in which we view American art for years to come.

Note
1. Alice Walker, *In Search of Our Mothers' Gardens: Womanist Prose* (Boston, MA: Mariner Books: 2003), 242.

A Black Mirror
Brittany Webb

Iago's Mirror (2009) by Fred Wilson is a physically heavy and theoretically dense work of art, inspired by William Shakespeare's *Othello* and made in collaboration with glassmakers on the island of Murano in Venice, Italy. It is ornately detailed, consisting of layers of glass mirrors painted black and stacked on top of one another. In contrast to a traditionally silvered mirror, a viewer in front of *Iago's Mirror* may need to adjust their eyes as they gaze onto a surface that is both reflective and opaque: you might still see yourself in it, but not in the way you would expect.

Rather than presented as part of chronological or material considerations, *Iago's Mirror* is included in a gallery focused on chroma and inspired by two important artist-led curatorial projects: the Spiral collective's 1965 exhibition *FIRST GROUP SHOWING (works in black & white)* and Lorraine O'Grady's 1983 exhibition *The Black and White Show*. Its placement is emblematic of a curatorial practice

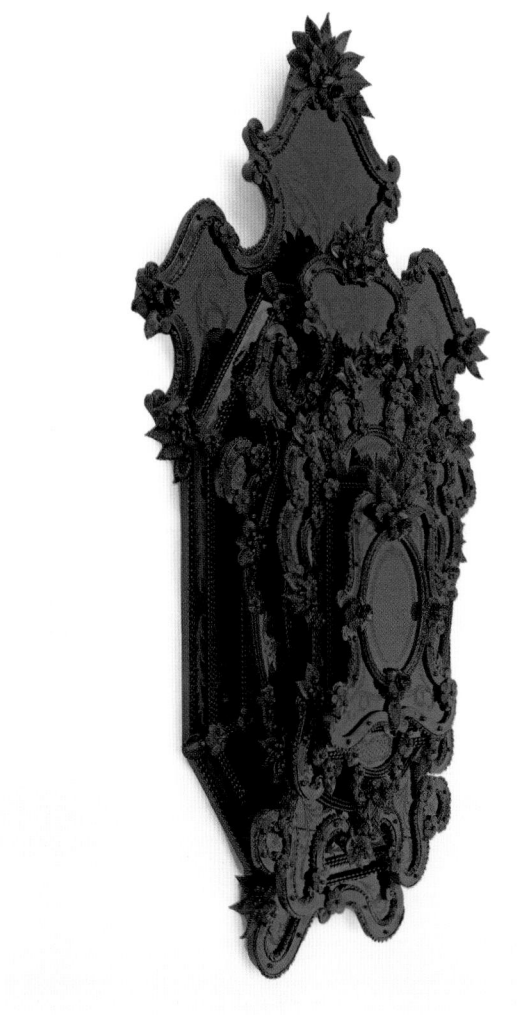

Fred Wilson (American, born 1954). *Iago's Mirror,* 2009.

that respects the beauty and rigor of the art, and engages in a citation politics recognizing the artists who came before as cultural and intellectual producers. This deceptively simple framing invites a different kind of looking. It also disrupts traditional art historical perspectives, a refreshing approach to museum work since, as art historian Faye Gleisser has recently pointed out, "It's really through art history's structural insistence on chronology, comparison, and classification that it reproduces anti-Black and colonial power structures."[1] The care with which Wilson's black mirror is treated theoretically is a front-stage extension of the behind-the-scenes Black Feminist Roundtable sessions that engaged in a peer-assessment of the new curatorial frameworks that guide this reinstallation and catalog.

Museum professionals often describe curatorial practice by grounding it in the etymology of the word curate and its Latin root, meaning "to take care of." Yet the version of curatorial care in the reinstallation is abundant. Attending closely to process, Stephanie Sparling Williams built a Black feminist room, a virtual kitchen table, and a garden at the center of her work with the Brooklyn Museum's collections, creating an infrastructure that made it possible for a team of professionals to think together out loud. This served as a Black feminist intellectual architecture that we worked within to see American art differently, think about new entry points into the history of the art of the Americas, and consider new meanings in existing contexts. The terms of engagement were set with care for everyone's time and labor. Art on the checklists was considered alongside a variety of texts that informed their selection: books, articles, audio lectures, films, music, memes. From a stated goal of galleries designed to "prioritize feelings of joy, wonder, and curiosity" to the pointed guide for feedback that included, "Where are the opportunities to make this experience even more meaningful and care-centered?" this backstage labor extended the history of Black feminist organizing into the museum, making possible new art historiographies as rich and layered as a brilliantly constructed mirror of black Murano glass.

Note

1. Huey Copeland, Sampada Aranke and Faye R. Gleisser, "Let's Ride: Art History after Black Studies," *Artforum*, October 2023, https://artforum.com/features/huey-copeland-art-history-after-black-studies-sampada-aranke-faye-raquel-gleisser-512513/.

A Black Feminist Framework for the Decorative Arts

Tiffany Momon

For far too long, Black craftspeople and artisans have been relegated to the margins of art history and the early American decorative arts, or ignored completely, with the field acknowledging their existence only when it cannot be avoided. This violent erasure not only rewrites history but also exposes the biases and weaknesses of archives rooted in white supremacy. This erasure calls for the creation of new archives that are invested in liberatory practice, such as the Black Craftspeople Digital Archive, which centers the lives and experiences of Black artisans and craftspeople because, in the words of artist Faith Ringgold, "You can't sit around and wait for somebody to say who you are. You need to write it and paint it and do it."[1]

Through the action of archiving histories connected to Black craftspeople and artisans, we must acknowledge the presence of Black women in the margins as the field has actively minimized their roles. We must be willing to create a Black feminist framework for the early American decorative arts that requires us to contend with the racialized and gendered stereotypes common in the lives of enslaved women, that demonstrates a dedication to critically recovering the silenced voices of women, and that sees Black women outside of subjects of the domestic sphere and sees them as the creators of art. Furthermore, we must define for ourselves an object study method that amplifies the narratives of individuals from African heritage throughout history, the present, and the future.[2]

A Black feminist framework for the early American decorative arts recognizes that not much has been written about Black women in the decorative arts, yet the documentary record fully records not only their presence and their contributions, but also their joy, pain, and resistance. Runaway advertisements document their craft, appearance, children and family, and reasons for their resistance. For sale notices highlight reasons for the impending sale of enslaved Black women including a note left by one enslaver who stated that the enslaved woman who he sought to sell wanted to be "sold at her own desire."[3] Private archival documents share the stories of Black enslaved women such as Crescent, who asked for and was given a new spinning wheel in 1816, and Sarah, who asked for and was given spectacles so that she could continue to create when her eyesight began to fail.[4] The experiences of these enslaved women highlight the complexities and varied experiences of being an enslaved artisan.

A Black feminist framework for the early American decorative arts serves as a window into a world of possibilities. It encourages us to ask new questions and empowers us to host exhibitions that center Black artisans. By using tools such as the Black Craftspeople Digital Archive, this framework emboldens us to recognize the experiences of Black women artisans and craftspeople and connect with them deeply. Black women are the archive, and it is through them that we say who we are, document who we are, and declare our significance for all to hear.

Notes
1. For more on the Black Craftspeople Digital Archive visit "Black Craftspeople Digital Archive," accessed April 15, 2024, https://blackcraftspeople.org/. Founded by Dr. Tiffany Momon in 2019, the BCDA seeks to tell a more inclusive story on the lives and experiences of Black craftspeople in the decorative arts through objects, primary sources, and place while emphasizing the need to fully understand the historical context of Black life in the Americas.
2. While there is value in the connoisseurship approaches to object study put forth by scholars such as Charles Montgomery, E. McClung Fleming, and Jules Prown, a Black people-centered approach is necessary. For more see E. McClung Fleming, "Artifact Study: A Proposed Model," *Winterthur Portfolio* 9 (1974); Jules David Prown, "Mind in Matter: An Introduction to Material Culture Theory and Method," in *Material Life in America, 1600–1800* (Boston, MA: Northeastern University Press, 1988); Charles Montgomery, "The Connoisseurship of Artifacts," in *Material Culture Studies in America* (Nashville, TN: American Association for State & Local History, 1982).
3. "For Sale," *The Evening Post*, April 13, 1808.
4. Charles Cotesworth Pinckney, "Pinckney Island Accounts (Account Book of Pinckney's)," 1816–1819, South Caroliniana Library, The University of South Carolina.

Look Again
Jonathan Michael Square

What are the duties and objectives of American art curators? How does the inclusion of contemporary art contribute to or detract from achieving those goals?

In my practice as an academic and occasional curator, I have often placed contemporary art in conversation with historical objects. But it is a practice that is the subject of ongoing debates because it presents a distinct set of challenges. Curators must skillfully juxtapose contemporary art with historical pieces to deepen comprehension without causing confusion. Moreover, one could argue that curators sometimes appropriate contemporary art to do their jobs, suggesting that relying solely on modern works may overlook thorough textual analysis, archival research, and formalist art historical methodologies. This is a delicate tightrope on which Stephanie Sparling Williams and the Brooklyn Museum's team have had to walk.

When Stephanie first shared her ideas for the reinstallation of the American wing, my first question was which contemporary artists she was including. To my surprise, she stressed that the project would prioritize the Brooklyn Museum's historic collections. Placing contemporary art in conversation with historical objects is an effective curatorial strategy, yet it is not a one that Stephanie has leaned on. Her aim is to encourage visitors to look again, i.e., engage in a closer, more critical examination of the museum's significant historical holdings.

Juxtaposing contemporary art with historic art and objects has become a popular tactic for sparking new conversations and disrupting visual normalcy in museum displays. In placing contemporary art in conversation with historical objects, curators delve into and illuminate nuances previously ignored in scholarship and museum curation. This approach boosts visitor engagement by attracting those who might otherwise find historical art less interesting or relevant. Indeed, contemporary art, with its range of mediums and themes that resonate with today's audiences, serves as one effective bridge to the past.

However, I suspect that this practice is motivated by the unspoken assumption that the past is less engaging than the present and that more captivating, innovative, and forward-thinking conversations are occurring today. This belief—intentional or not—results in a lack of meaningful engagement with history. Many of the ideas and movements we consider novel today were likely expressed in some form in the past. Therefore, curators must thoughtfully utilize and reinterpret their permanent collections at their museums to bridge the past and the present. I gained this valuable insight from Stephanie, who exemplifies this approach through her work in the reinstallation of the American wing.

Contemporary art has its place in the galleries, highlighted by contributions from Black Feminist Roundtable artist-members Andrea Chung and Harmonia Rosales. Yet, the way their work and others are integrated within the display feels like inclusion rather than an intervention. Here, artists are collaborators, and their work engages in dialogue—not just in contrast—with historical pieces. This strategy encourages audiences to look again, and more closely, at the work on view. It offers a methodological model for museum professionals aiming to deepen the relationship between past and present within their permanent collections.

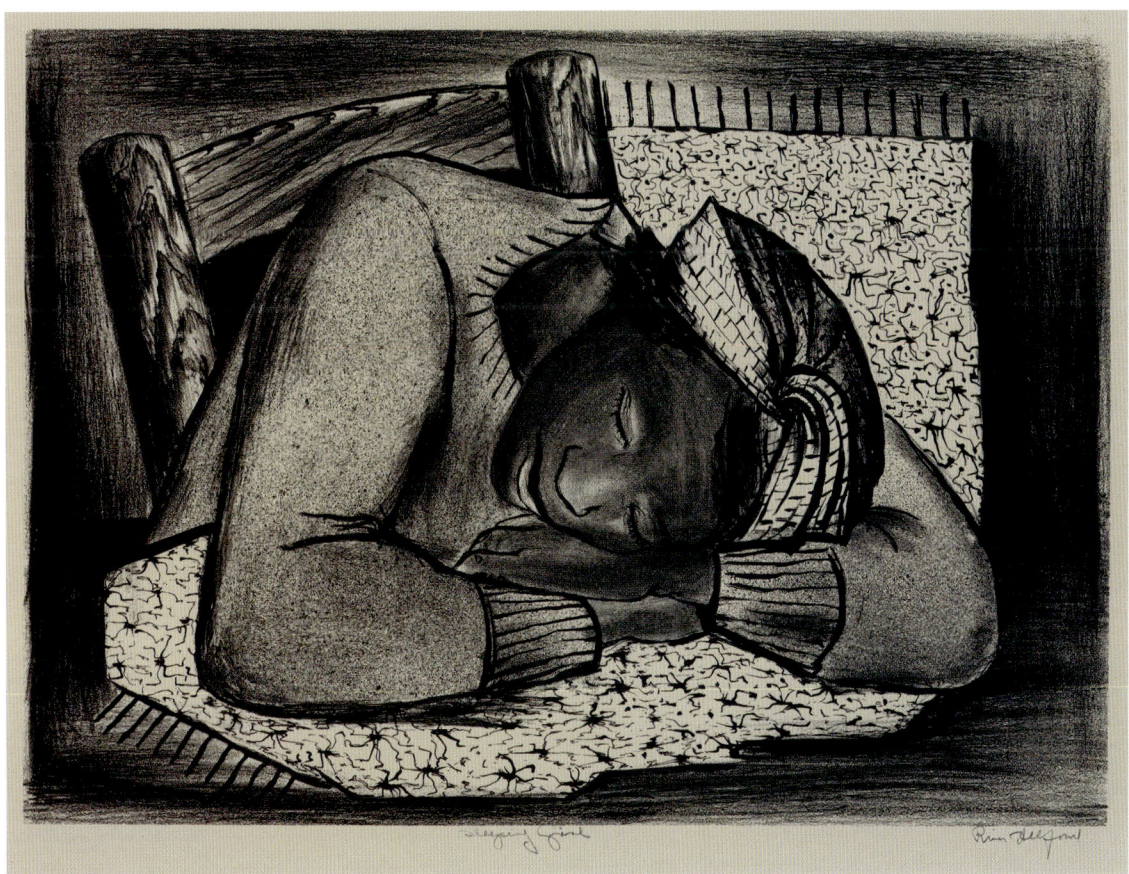

Riva Helfond (American, 1910–2002). *Sleeping Girl, Fatigued Black Woman,* ca. 1937.

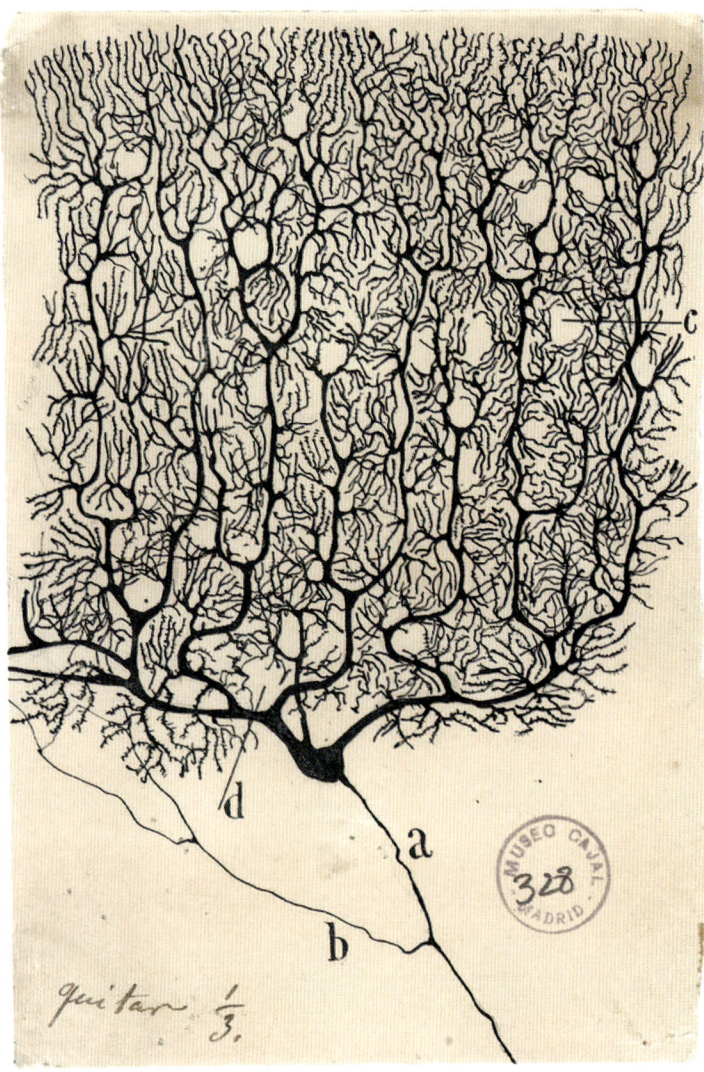

Santiago Ramón y Cajal (Spanish, 1852–1934). A Purkinje neuron from the human cerebellum, ca. 1900. Cajal Institute (CSIC), Madrid.

Brain Love

Xiao Situ

Created during the Great Depression, Riva Helfond's lithograph features a young woman seated at a table. Her eyes are closed and her head rests upon her crossed arms. Laid out on the surface of the table and up against the adjoining wall is a tasseled shawl. Helfond may have depicted this scene to underscore the heavy load of work and care she observed Black women performing—both professionally and in their own families and communities—during this period of economic struggle. The headscarf protecting the woman's hair and the impromptu layout of this corner of repose suggest that the woman is seizing some time for herself amid a long day of tasks.

Although this moment of rest might seem to be about a lack of activity, the design on the shawl suggests otherwise. The inky black splotches that branch out into quivering thin lines resemble a network of neurons engaged in synaptic messaging. The pattern is reminiscent of the drawings of renowned neuroscientist Santiago Ramón y Cajal, whose freehand renderings of brain cells and neural circuits pulsate with artistic verve.[1] Rather than drooping downward as the laws of gravity would predict, the tassels on the part of the woman's shawl leaning up against the wall paradoxically rise upward, taut—as if energized by the neurons' transmissions. We can interpret the shawl's design and tassels as a visual manifestation of the young woman's interior cosmos humming with life: collective connection and communal messaging is occurring even as she sleeps.

This image illustrates a core concept that Black Feminist theologian and artist Tricia Hersey uplifts in her work as founder of The Nap Ministry.[2] Hersey states that when she rests or sleeps, she enters a trans-chronological, trans-spatial realm called "DreamSpace." Here, she can commune with her Black Ancestors, especially her maternal grandmother Ora. The relationship is mutual and reciprocal: while her Ancestors infuse her with wisdom, inspiration, and intuition for how to resist the "cult of urgency and disconnection" promulgated by white supremacy culture and late-stage capitalism, the rest she engages in redeems the many hours of sleep and ease her Ancestors had lost as Black folks living in earlier eras of enslavement and Jim Crow. The rest is a form of reparations.[3]

Hersey describes the time spent in DreamSpace as rich in "brain love."[4] We can apply this term to the experience the woman is having in the print. The inky nodes and their wiry dendrites on the patterned shawl make visible the unseen relay in chemical and electrical messages of love and wisdom taking place between the napping woman and her Ancestors. The scene we witness here is not just of physical rest—it's spiritual revival, intergenerational reunion, and communal gathering.

Notes:
1. See Santiago Ramón y Cajal, *The Beautiful Brain: The Drawings of Santiago Ramón y Cajal*, ed. Eric A. Newman and Alfonso Araque (New York: Abrams, 2017).
2. To learn about and engage in the tenets and practices of The Nap Ministry, see Tricia Hersey, *Rest Is Resistance: A Manifesto* (New York: Little, Brown Spark, 2022).
3. Ibid., 17.
4. Ibid., 93.

Untitled

Sará Yafah King

We only perceive a fraction of the visible light which travels to us from the universe—and through this light we are given the gift of perceiving one another during the darkest of nights. As a neuroscientist, I have been taught that photons act as neurotransmitters inside of the human brain, producing the infrastructure for light-based communication and connectivity between neurons. As a lay person with a deep interest in astrophysics, I have an endless fascination with tracing the light inside our brains with its origin point—perhaps you could even say their ancestral origin—to the birth of stars themselves. When we look into the night sky and see stars winking at us, it is not that the star is producing an ebb and flow of brightness, but that we are seeing one star passing in front of its astral twin, temporarily blocking the light of the other in such a way that we perceive this motion as a twinkle. I had once seen stars as a metaphor for the stark human experience of being, a lone, suffering individual, effulgent from sheer will, luminous within the context of a cold environment hostile to life and all its forms. Sure, these stars existed in a constellation of others. But that togetherness, in my frame of mind, seemed constantly threatened by forces far greater than them which had been set in motion long before their existence. In some ways I felt this described an ontology of Blackness in the United States. A blend of cosmic fractal elements forged in the incandescent origin story of all of existence, light illuminating and refracting the wisdom of my ancestors. Most stars are caught within another's orbit, dancing around one another for billions of years in a kind of cosmic love cypher. When one of these stars dies, it slowly gives all of its matter to its twin, in a process called "mass transfer." One star literally gives its life force to the other. Billions of years later, this light hits our eyes, and we are blessed with the opportunity to gaze upon the countenance of our astral ancestors, our original forbearers.

Through the Black Feminist Roundtable, the collection of artworks forming the new American Art wing ceased to stand on their own within my imaginary, a monolithic statement of what America is, or ain't. Each of the fifteen contributors to the Roundtable process was like a star comprised of rich and complex elements which refracted every facet of American diversity of thought and creativity into the space, with Black feminist resonance forming a loving blanket of spacetime through which each person's expertise traveled, uniting us in the vast variability of our subject-matter expertise. Every painting, photo, piece of furniture, sculpture, was carefully considered by our members with deep intention within an infinite universe of representation. You might say that the previous iterations of American art exhibits have contributed their stellar mass to this project, and yet this exhibit has been infused with deliberations of collective liberation from every corner of the multiverse, as is represented by the contributions of my brilliant colleagues. The visual and felt narrative produced by the space is akin to riding an interdimensional drumbeat pulsing with the rhythm of the interdependence which Black feminism insists upon; a dizzying tapestry of bloodlines and genealogies calling and responding to one another; the deliberate dismantling of social hierarchies, and the usual boundaries between the physical, emotional, and psychic terrains that at one point sought to divide our nation united in a seamless and carefully considered flow of love. A mirror of the collective consciousness reflecting our own sacred starlight right back to us—reminding us of our full agency and responsibility to make of that reflection what we will.

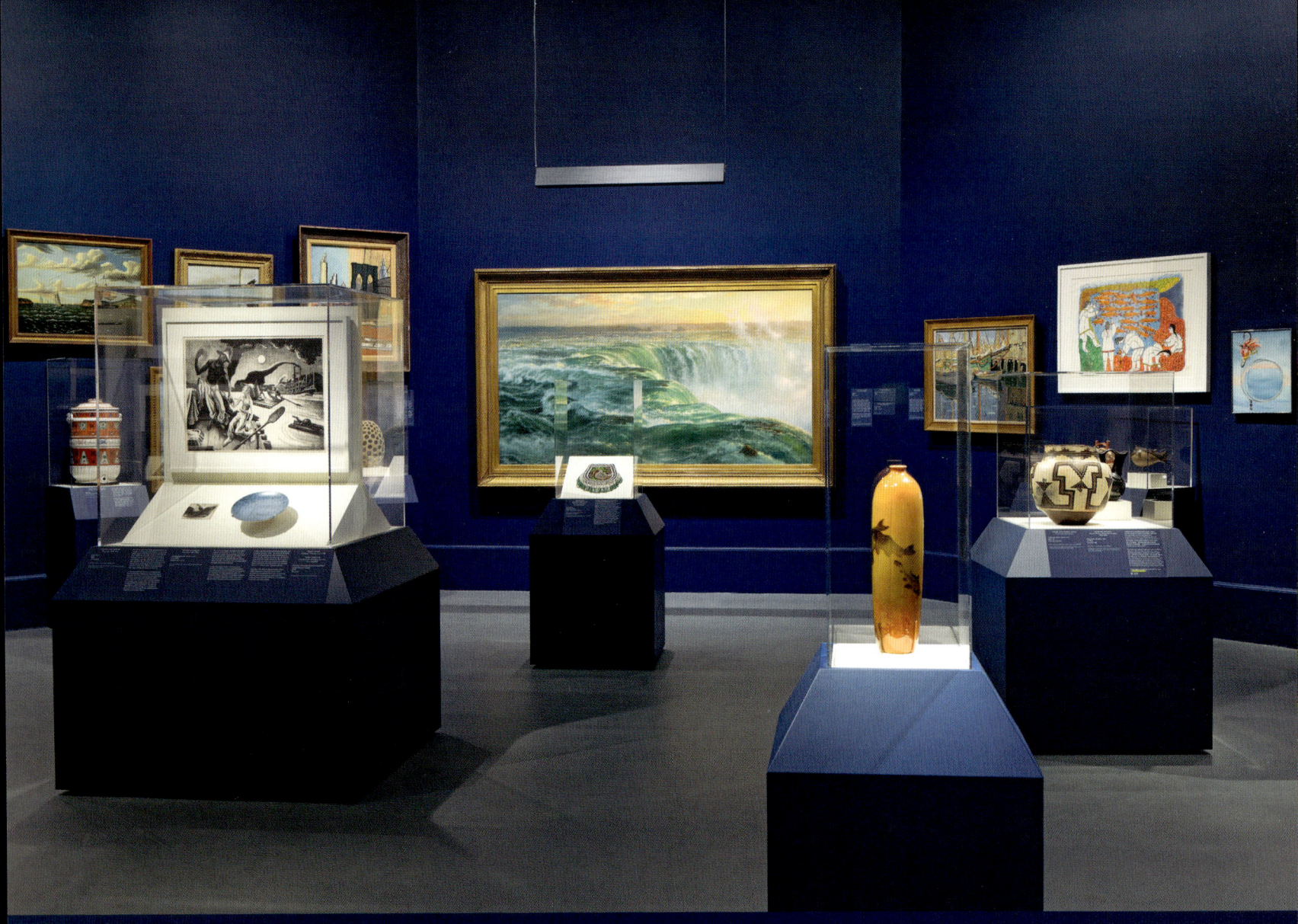

FRAMEWORK

Trouble the Water

Wade.

Guided by the nineteenth-century Black American spiritual "**Wade in the Water**," this framework explores the powerful links between water and notions of freedom, life, spirituality, and progress. Whether as subject, creative process, or theme, water connects the artworks on view in the galleries and here within this chapter, revealing legacies of colonialism, displacement, and the changing environment.

Swim with or against the flow. Float. Bathe. Drink.

From wading pools to waterfalls, seas to rivers, across millennia people have revered water for its power as a life-giving resource. In every form of artistic production, water is essential to the processing of clay, canvas, and pigments, to watercolor, printmaking, and photography. Honored in images on ancient Nasca pottery of Peru's south coast and stored in vessels made by Indigenous Pueblo women in the Southwest United States, water has shaped cultural production across time.

Water separates and binds.

Less than two hundred years ago, enslaved Africans manifested their own liberation. In coded instructional songs, they charted strategic paths through swamps, streams, and rivers to avoid recapture. At that same time, New York City waterways bustled with industry that was fueling rapid development across the tristate area. As wondrous as it is complex, water is inextricably woven within American histories of freedom and progress. It is the current carrying us into a new era.

Get clean. Get free.

The artworks featured within this section, together with the short essay, "Troubled Waters and Currents of Restoration" by Caroline Gillaspie, offer fresh perspectives on recent acquisitions, historic favorites, ongoing research, and forthcoming special projects. Here, we examine how the act of curating might trouble the waters of American history—and offer a bridge for safe crossing.

Wade . . .

SSW

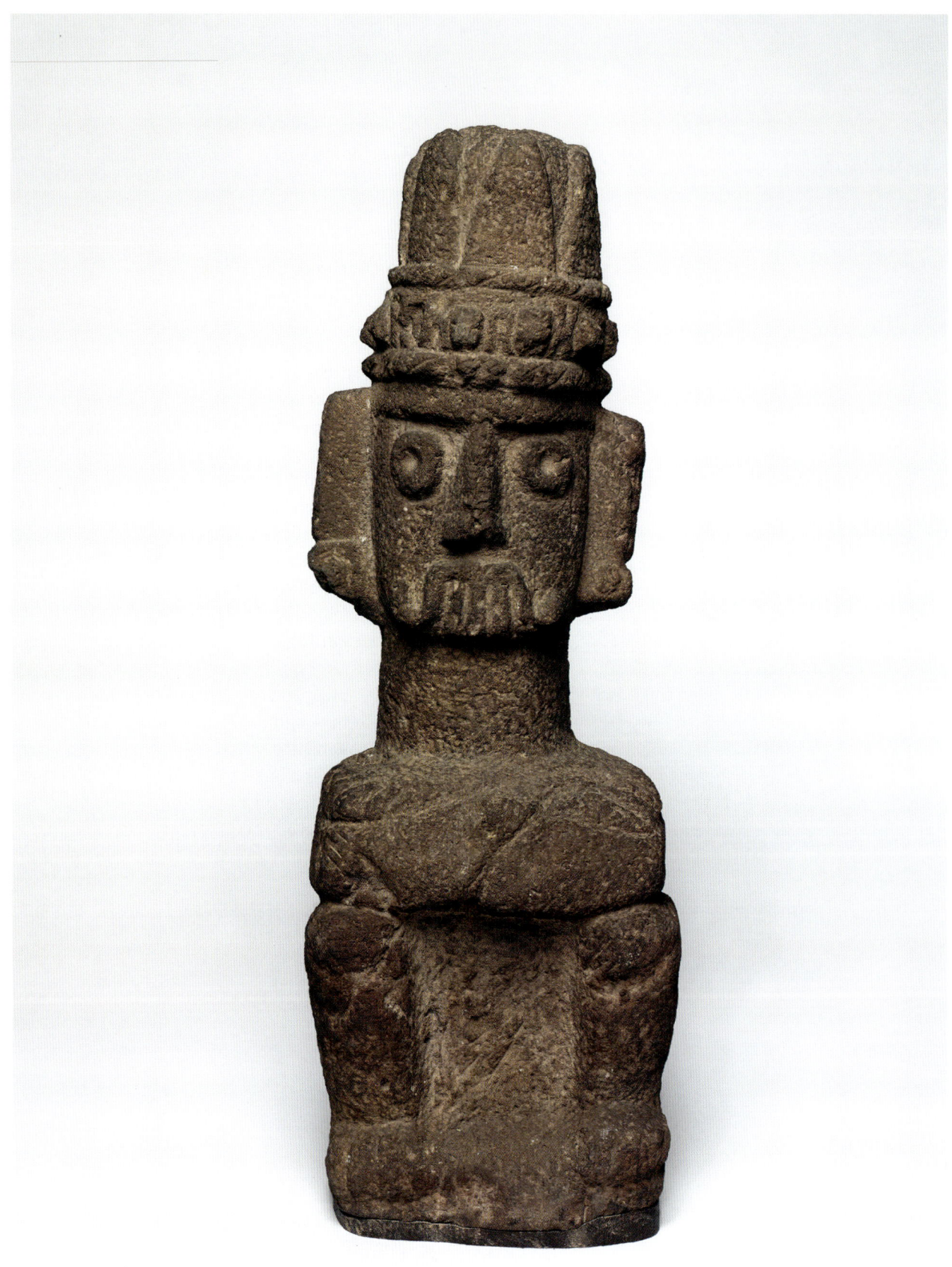

Mexica (Aztec) artist
Seated Figure of Tlaloc
Valley of Mexico, Mexico, ca. 1440–1521

Volcanic stone, 20½ × 6¹¹⁄₁₆ × 5⅛ in.
By exchange, 48.22.8
Provenance: Acquired by Museo Nacional de Antropología, Mexico City, Mexico, before 1948; purchased by the Brooklyn Museum, by exchange, 1948.

In this carved, volcanic-stone sculpture, Tlaloc, the god of water, rain, and fertility, sits with arms crossed over his knees. Often depicted as a human-like figure with jaguar teeth, a curled upper lip, and protruding, circular eyes, he wears circular ear ornaments and a tall headdress adorned with peaks that symbolize the mountain caves where he stores water.[1] The god was revered by the ancient Mexica people, who dedicated one of the twin temples atop the Templo Mayor in the capital of Tenochtitlán to this important deity. The Templo Mayor was the center of the ceremonial precinct and the heart of the Mexica's universe. The pyramid on which Tlaloc's temple stood symbolized the sacred mountain of Tonacatepetl, the Hill of Sustenance, which the Mexica believed contained maize and other foods provided to humans through successful harvests.

Tlaloc nurtured the earth and safeguarded agriculture. Together with his sister Chalchiuhtlicue, the goddess of seas, rivers, lakes, and springs, he presided over the *tlaloque*, the numerous lesser gods of rain, lightning, and other meteorological phenomena. Tlaloc demanded constant offerings, and the Mexica believed that failing to please him provoked his wrath and resulted in catastrophic events, such as droughts, floods, lightning storms, and hail. Offerings to him discovered at the Templo Mayor included large quantities of greenstone beads, conch shells, coral, sea urchins, seaweed, and the saws of sawfish.[2]

NR

1. Felipe Solís, ed., *The Aztec Empire* (New York: Guggenheim Museum, 2004), 460.
2. Juan Albero Román Berrelleza, "The Templo Mayor at Tenochtitlan," in *The Aztec Empire*, ed. Felipe Solís (New York: Guggenheim Museum, 2004), 148.

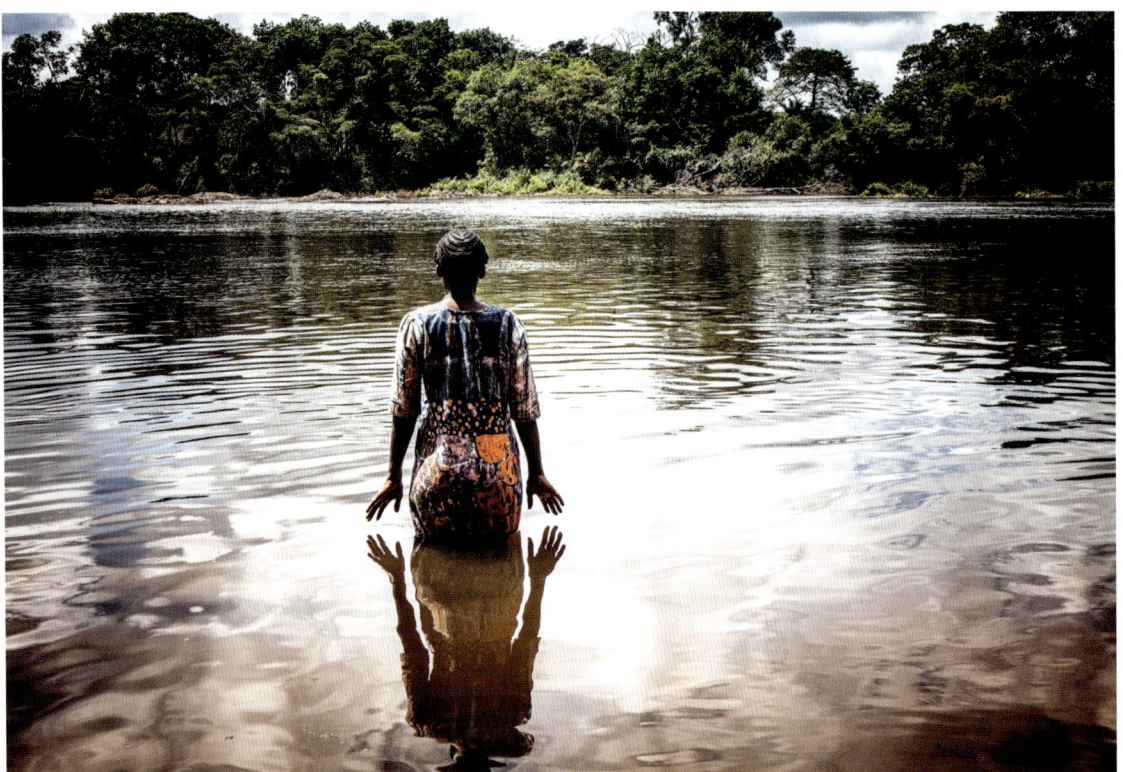

Adama Delphine Fawundu
(American, born 1971)
Mami Wata at Wajai River, Pujehun, Sierra Leone, 2017

Archival pigment print, 24 × 36 in.
Courtesy of the artist

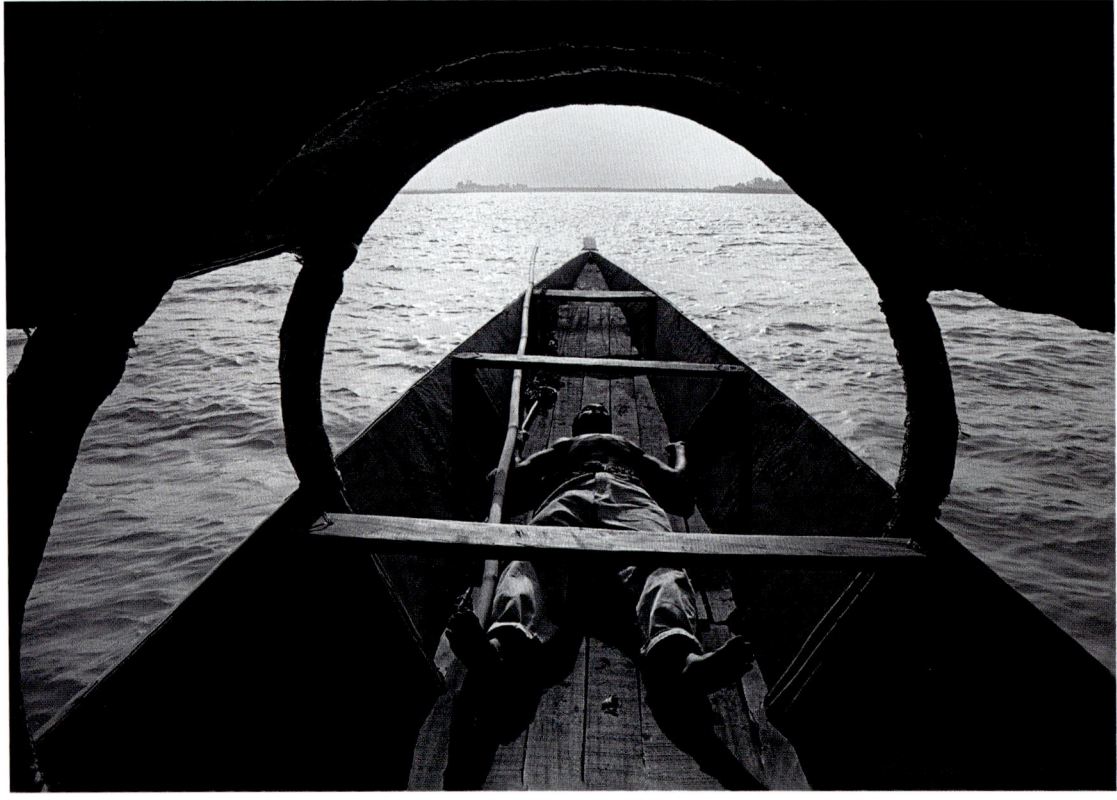

Chester Higgins, Jr.
(American, born 1946)
Voyage, 2001

Pigmented inkjet print, 20 × 30 in.
Courtesy of the artist and Bruce Silverstein Gallery

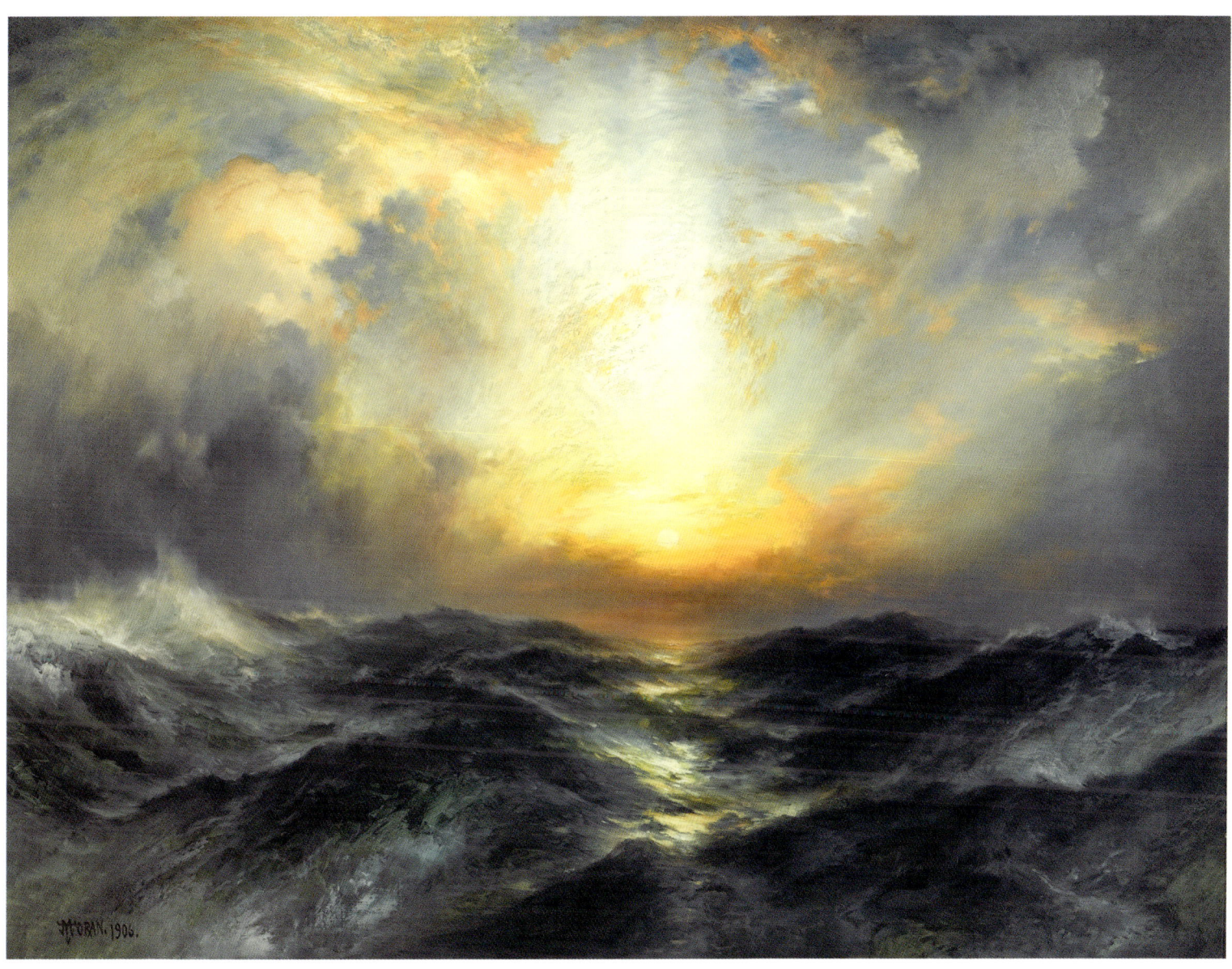

Thomas Moran
(American, born England, 1837–1926)
Sunset at Sea, 1906

Oil on canvas, 30 3/16 × 40 3/16 in.
Gift of the executors of the Estate of Colonel Michael Friedsam, 32.845
Provenance: Acquired from the artist by Benjamin Altman, 1907; acquired by Michael Friedsam, by 1913; donated by the estate of Michael Friedsam, October 25, 1932.

Water is the first thing in my imagination . . . All beginning in water, all ending in water. Turquoise, aquamarine, deep green, deep blue, ink blue, navy, blue-black cerulean water. . . . Water is the first thing in my memory. The sea sounded like a thousand secrets, all whispered at the same time. In the daytime it was indistinguishable to me from air. . . . The same substance that carried voices or smells, music or emotion.[1]

—Dionne Brand

A woman wades, thigh-deep, palms open, into calm, deep green waters of the Wajai River in Sierra Leone's Southern Province. Trees line the bank a short distance away on the opposite side. The cloudy blue sky is reflected along with the woman's body in the gently undulating surface, a vision, a return, a ritual captured by multisensory, native-Brooklyn artist, Adama Delphine Fawundu. Fawundu is known for her layered and immersive projects that deeply engage with themes emerging from the African diaspora, particularly the artist's own familial ties to Sierra Leone. In this context, water features most prominently as a conceptual and formal medium, a site through which the artist works. *Mami Wata at Wajai River, Pejuhun, Sierra Leone* introduces the ancient West African deity, Mami Wata, a frequent point of departure for Fawundu's creative engagement with her Mende heritage.

In her artworks that visually examine *wata bodis*, Krío for "water bodies," Fawundu weaves connections to her paternal grandmother by incorporating the designs of the hand-dyed and batik Gerra fabrics Mama Adama created as part of her successful textile business in Sierra Leone. In *Mami Wata at Wajai River*, the artist wades into the water wearing one of the last dresses her grandmother made for her. Often described in terms of magical realism, the arresting images Fawundu creates in and around the waters of Sierra Leone symbolize the horrific passages made through the transatlantic slave trade, and the journey made by the artist's parents when immigrating to the United States.

Voyages are often the subject of renowned photographer Chester Higgins, who traveled the globe for much of his career to photograph people of the African diaspora. First visiting Senegal in 1971, Higgins subsequently traveled to the African continent over fifty times, many visits occurring while on staff for the *New York Times* between 1975 and 2014. During this period, the photographer documented the beauty and complexity of Black people in over thirty countries in Africa, the Caribbean, Europe, and North and South America. Resulting in several books, notably, *Feeling the Spirit: Searching the World for the People of Africa* (1994), which reproduced 220 images from Higgins's travels.

In *Voyage*, Higgins captures a moving image of a Black man lying in the hull of a wooden pinasse as the boat lists on the Niger River. Typically, these pole-powered canoes are used for transportation along the river, and are often laden with goods and people. Staged from under the boat's canvas or wooden cover, the man is solitary in the empty boat, which appears just as alone on the river itself. The bow at the center of the composition points out onto tranquil water.

Framed only by roiling water and an opening in the heavens, Thomas Moran's *Sunset at Sea* precariously suspends viewers amid a ray of light. The sun sinks low over a windblown sea, as towering storm clouds tinged orange and yellow fade to lavender and blue, yielding to the impending night. Wispy brushstrokes transform the crests of waves into mist, while thick impasto reflects light on the rough surface of the gray-green ocean. Best known for his romanticized landscapes of the American West, Moran completed this painting after an Atlantic voyage to England in 1906, and meditates on the sublime qualities of the ocean.

The Atlantic Ocean is a subject at the heart of innumerable crossings and passages contained within the history of the United States, and certainly its art. From Fawundu's and Higgins's trips to the African continent—and of those individuals and communities to which their work speaks and represents—to Moran's travels to and from Europe. The ocean, its waters, contains depths and multitudes artists for centuries have been keen to reflect, including celebrated marine painter Frederick J. Waugh, who enjoyed early success in Europe in the late nineteenth century before serving as a ship camoufleur in World War I upon his return to the United States. He painted highly technical renderings of the sea onto maritime vessels to conceal them from enemy trackers.

The Great Deep (p. 48) highlights the artist's mastery of his inky ocean-blue palette. In 1909, Waugh reflected to students: "The sea itself is very subtle in color and ever changing. You must learn by heart these subtleties." With its roiling waves on the vast open sea, the painting is unique among Waugh's works, which predominantly feature waves framed by craggy rocks and churning surf as it meets the shore. As Waugh suggests, the sea itself is an unwieldy subject. Beyond its shape-shifting likeness, the ocean's imperceivable depths and expansive cultural connotations render it interpretively boundless. For viewers, *The Great Deep* may reveal a portal, a time capsule, dreams of freedom, a tomb—or...

SSW with CG

1. Dionne Brand, *A Map to the Door of No Return: Notes to Belonging* (Toronto: Doubleday Canada, 2001), 6–12.

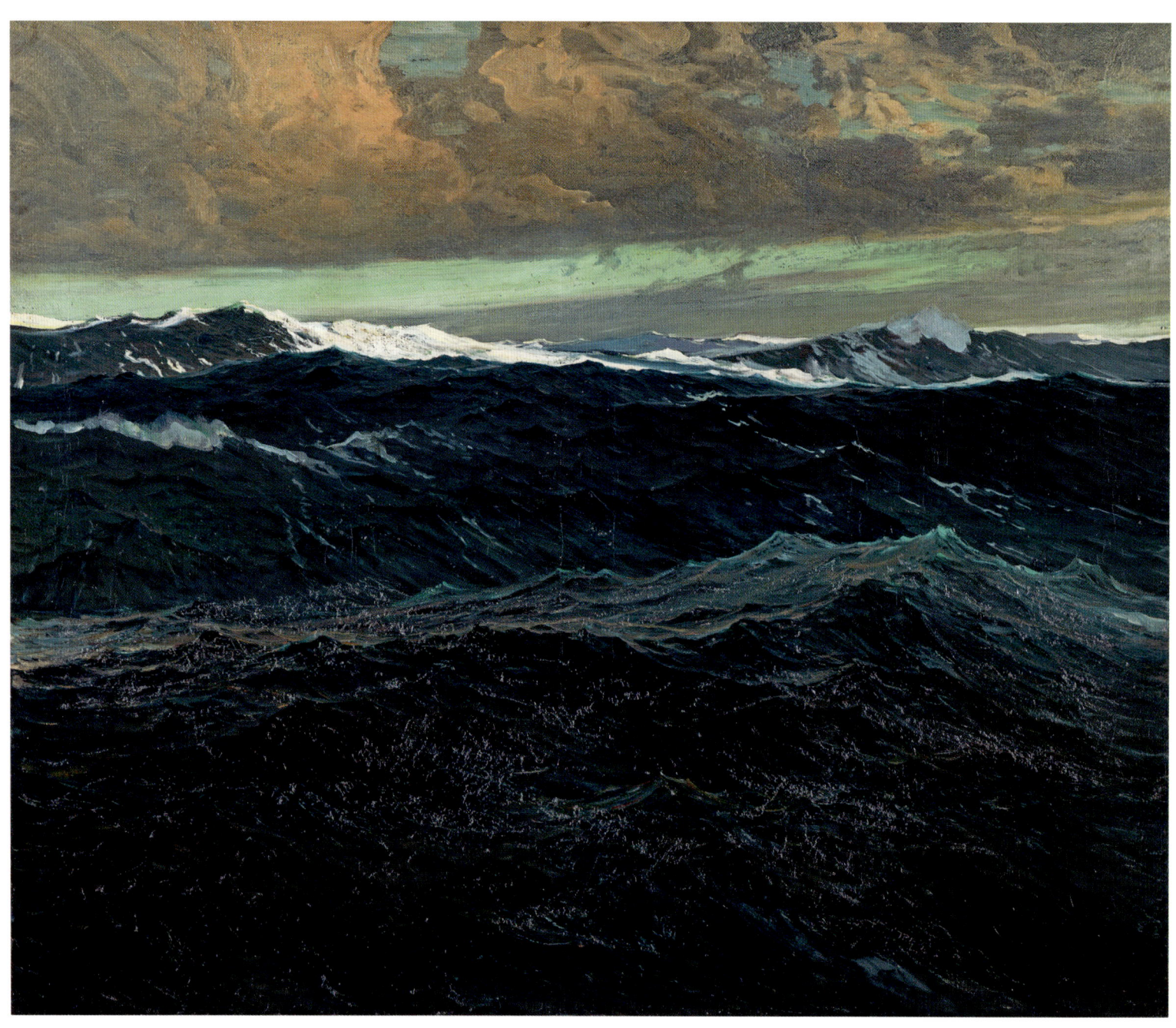

Frederick J. Waugh
(American, 1861–1940)
The Great Deep, 1909

Oil on canvas, 59⅞ × 71¹⁵⁄₁₆ in.
Anonymous gift, 42.44
Provenance: Acquired by Adolphus Lewisohn, before 1914; inherited by an anonymous individual, 1914; donated, 1942.

CONSERVATOR'S EYE: Thick and "painty" waves

. . . my best results are attained by impasto, thick painting, shadows and all, having all my picture of an even, rugged, ragged thickness all over, building up and dragging and so on until the surface is very painty.[1]

—Frederick J. Waugh

Frederick J. Waugh's *The Great Deep* is a tour de force, capturing the subtle effects of light passing through the rolling waves. The lower half has a puckered appearance that formed as the thick paint layers oxidized at different rates. Waugh may have encouraged this texture, known as drying wrinkles, in order to further the illusion of salt spray above the water. The sky has a dark underlayer applied using a wide brush and short strokes that run in all directions. These strokes create a stormy energy below the peach-colored clouds and acid green horizon.

As a paintings conservator, I appreciate Waugh's technical mastery of his craft. Despite his complex layering, the painting remains in excellent condition, with few cracks and no evidence of flaking between layers. The frame is original—small pieces of gilded gesso were found in the paint around the edges, indicating the painting was framed before it was fully dry.

LB

1. Frederick J. Waugh, "Some Words upon Sea Painting," *Palette and Bench*, November 1910.

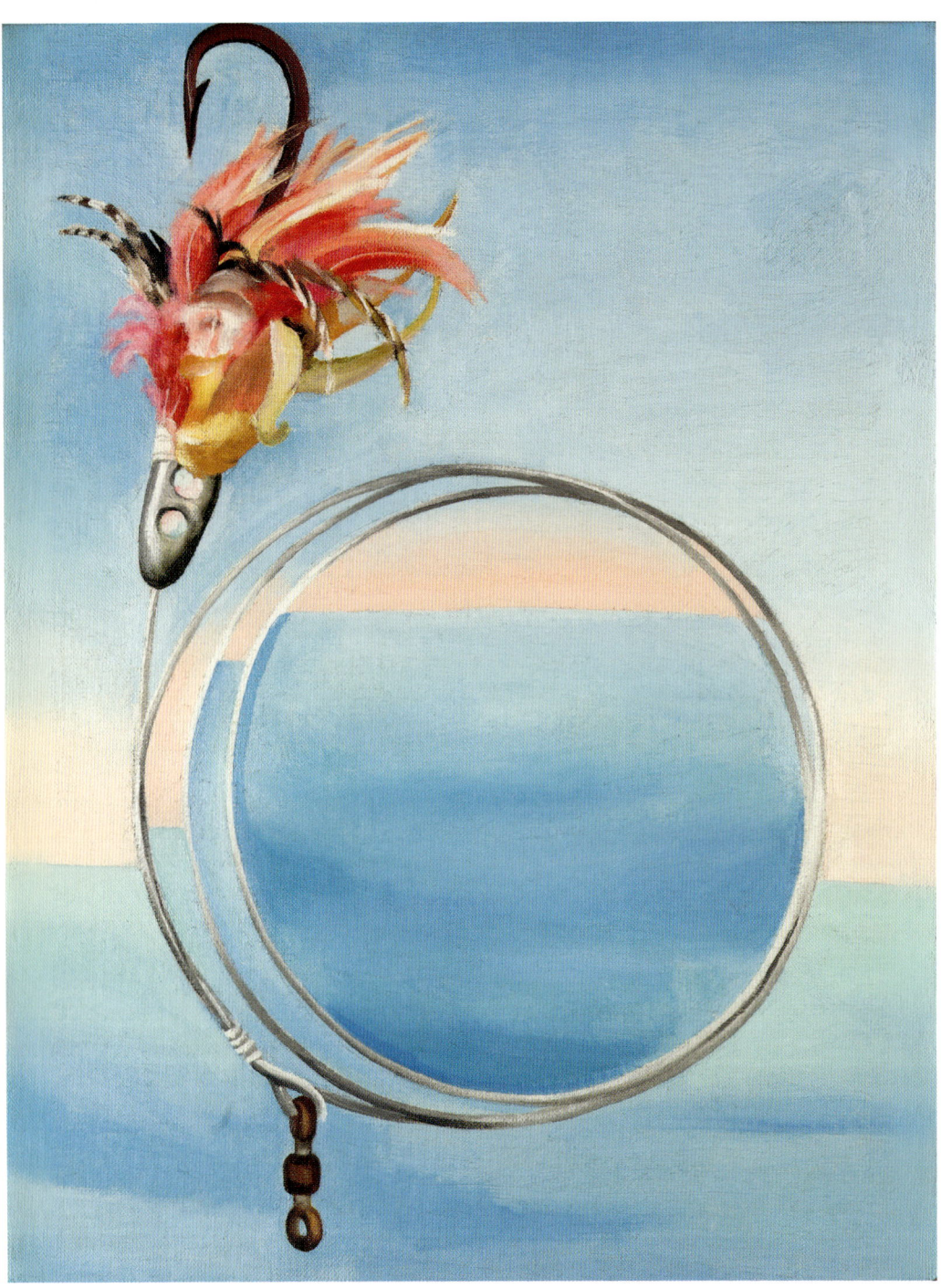

Georgia O'Keeffe
(American, 1887–1986)
Fishhook from Hawaii – No. I, 1939

Oil on canvas, 18 × 14 in.
Bequest of Georgia O'Keeffe, 87.136.2
Provenance: Bequeathed by the artist, October 29, 1987.

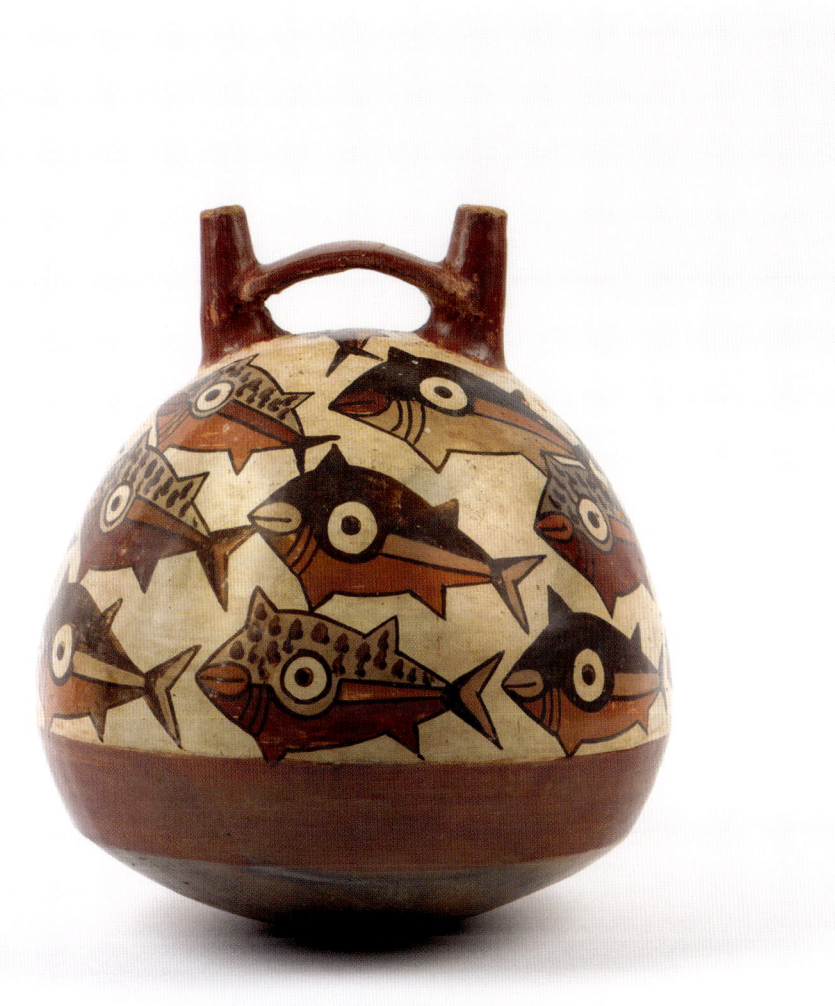

Nasca artist
Double-Spout Jar with Fish
Palpa, Peru, 150–300

Ceramic, polychrome slip, 9¾ × 9¼ × 9¼ in.
Henry L. Batterman Fund, 41.424
Provenance: Acquired by Good Neighbor Imports Inc., by 1941; purchased by the Brooklyn Museum, April 9, 1941.

This double-spout, bridge-handle jar features multicolored fish, which boldly contrast with the white background. The ancient Nasca people, who inhabited Peru's southern coast between 200 B.C.E. and 650 C.E., excelled at painted pottery, and images of fish are among their most repeated naturalistic subjects.[1]

The Nasca practiced intensive agriculture in river valleys, and also took advantage of the cold waters of the Pacific Ocean, hunting mammals such as seals and otters, using nets to catch a variety of fish, and collecting shellfish and mollusks. Cold waters rich in plankton attracted marine animals ranging in size from giant whales to small crustaceans.[2] Nasca iconography abounds with representations of this sea life, not just on pottery and textiles but also on monumental geoglyphs, more popularly known as the Nasca lines. Located in southern Peru, the geoglyphs are clearly visible from the air, adding to their mysterious quality.

In these diverse artforms, supernatural powers are indicated by the addition of human arms and hands onto depictions of powerful and intimidating sea creatures such as sharks and killer whales. The comingling of natural and supernatural elements reflects the Nasca belief that the spiritual world controls nature, but also keeps the world in balance. The wide-ranging representations of marine life show Nasca reverence and gratitude for the bounty of the sea.

NR

[1]. Donald A. Proulx, *A Sourcebook of Nasca Ceramic Iconography: Reading a Culture through Its Art* (Iowa City: University of Iowa Press, 2006), 150.
[2]. Ibid., 149.

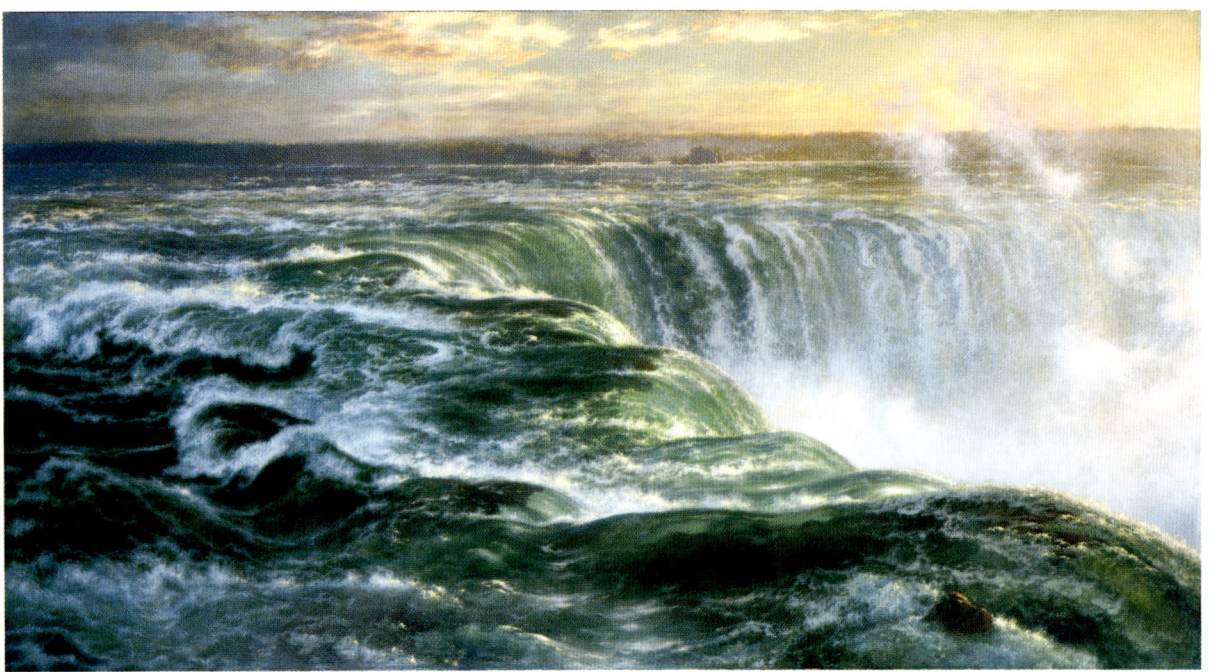

Louis Rémy Mignot
(American, 1831–1870)
Niagara, 1866

Oil on canvas, 48¾ × 91½ in.
Gift of Arthur S. Fairchild, 1993.118
Provenance: Acquired, possibly from the artist, by Fanny Harris, by 1872. Acquired by Horace Jones Fairchild, by 1884; inherited by Maria Stiles Fairchild (Mrs. Horace Jones Fairchild), 1900; transferred to Arthur Stiles Fairchild, September 25, 1913; donated, October 14, 1993.

Louis Rémy Mignot's sublime view of the rushing water and mist of Niagara Falls captures the terrifying power of nature over the viewer, who is situated precariously at the edge of the composition.[1] Mignot's vantage from Terrapin Tower on Goat Island on the U.S. side looks westward across the Horseshoe Falls toward Canada. A small waning crescent moon emerges in the sky as the setting sun casts raking light across the water, emphasizing the foamy whitecaps. The mist that rises from the torrent is tinged with lavender as day fades to night. Unlike typical nineteenth-century picturesque landscape images that employ a *repoussoir* (an object such as a tree placed in the foreground side of the composition), Mignot provides no framing device or grounding for the painting's viewer. The resulting suspended vantage point enhances the awe-inspiring effect of the churning water. One art critic commented favorably that "No one can complain of common-place, at any rate, in Mignot's remarkable illustration . . . placing the spectator on the brink, as it were, of the precipice over which these turbid heaps of water are about to discharge themselves, in a manner that is almost startling."[2]

Indigenous people inhabited the area surrounding Niagara Falls beginning nearly 13,000 years ago.[3] The site holds powerful meaning for Native Nations including the Hodinöhsö:ni', and the falls were believed to have healing and restorative qualities.[4] However, over the course of the eighteenth and nineteenth centuries, many communities were displaced from the region as Niagara Falls became a popular tourist destination, representative of America's natural beauty in the imaginations of European Americans.

CG

1. For further information about Mignot and this painting, see Teresa A. Carbone, "Louis Rémy Mignot," in *American Paintings in the Brooklyn Museum: Artists Born by 1876*, Teresa A. Carbone, Barbara Dayer Gallati, and Linda S. Ferber (New York: Brooklyn Museum; London: D. Giles Limited, 2006), 2: 789–93.
2. "Pictures by the Late L. R. Mignot," *The Builder* 34 (June 24, 1876): 607.
3. The name "Niagara" likely originated as an anglicized version of Onguiaahra, the name of an Indigenous tribe from the region.
4. "Cultural History," *Empathic Traditions: Niagara's Indigenous Legacy*, accessed May 6, 2024, https://empathictraditions.ca/about-the-collection/cultural-history/. This virtual exhibition brings together items and artworks from the Niagara Falls History Museum to understand the historical and present-day presence of Indigenous people in the Niagara region.

Hodinöhsö:ni' (Haudenosaunee) artist
Beaded Bag
New York, United States or Ontario, Canada, late 19th century

Velvet, glass beads, sequins, 13½ × ⅜ × 10½ in.
Gift of the Edward J. Guarino Collection in memory of Josephine M. Guarino, 2016.11.8
Provenance: Acquired by Crown & Eagle Antiques, by 2002; purchased by Edward J. Guarino, May 20, 2002; donated, October 27, 2016.

Did [Hodinöhsö:ni' beadworkers] know the beads would carry not only physical representations of our understanding of all living things on this earth, but also a message, a measure of time to adjust to the changes that whirl through our existence? It takes time to put thousands of tiny beads on cloth; it teaches you the patience to observe, the ability to see things as a whole or a multitude of parts. It is important to see how things are connected and what gives them life.[1]

—Jolene Rickard, Tuscarora artist and scholar

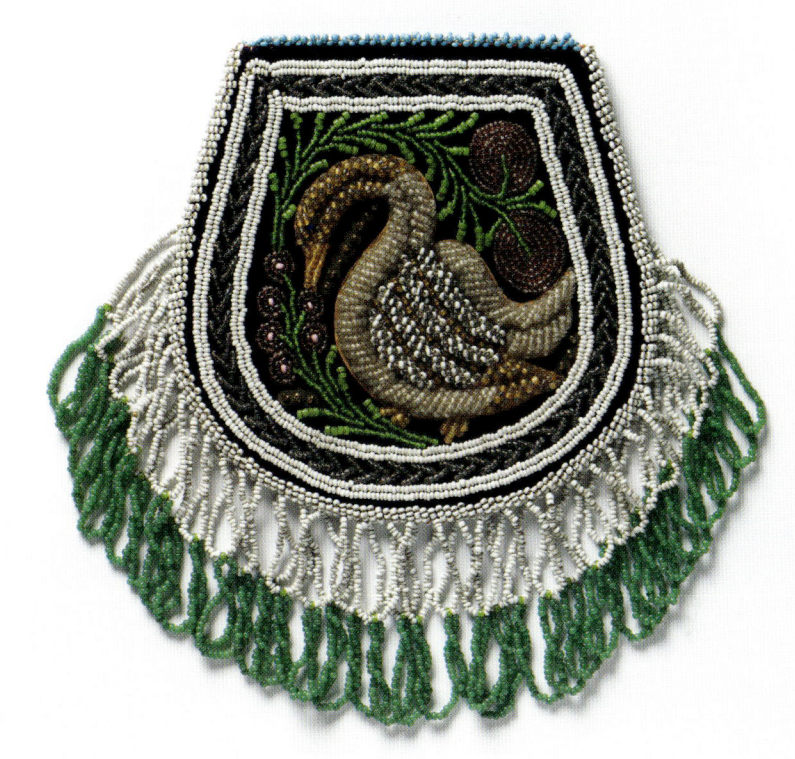

Crafted by a Hodinöhsö:ni' artist, this black-velvet bag blends the aesthetics of mid-nineteenth-century fashion and Indigenous art. As their communities' traditional lifeways were threatened, Hodinöhsö:ni' women began to sell beaded purses, pincushions, and whimsics to European Americans to provide income for their families. The rise of their beadwork industry tracks with the opening of the Erie Canal in 1825; historical documentation from 1827 indicates tens of thousands of tourists visited the region.[2] Such visitors avidly purchased beadwork from Native artists to commemorate their visit to the majestic falls.

During the last quarter of the nineteenth century, Hodinöhsö:ni' women—principally from the Tuscarora and Mohawk tribes—popularized raised beadwork, which creates a sculptural effect. Such pieces often utilized translucent and white beads whose appearance mimicked mist rising off the falls.[3] Once trivialized as tourist art, these art forms have now come to be seen as profoundly significant. Their beauty and inventiveness affirm the Hodinöhsö:ni' community's cultural identities, values, and beliefs, while also demonstrating artists' agency in the face of colonialism.

DT

1. Jolene Rickard, "Cew Ete Haw I Tih: The Bird that Carries Language Back to Another," in *Partial Recall: Photographs of Native North America*, ed. Lucy R. Lippard (New York: The New Press, 1992), 105–12.
2. "Haudenosaunee Beadwork: A History," PBS, Aired October 23, 2018, https://www.pbs.org/video/haudenosaunee-beadwork-history-eykeex/.
3. Ibid.

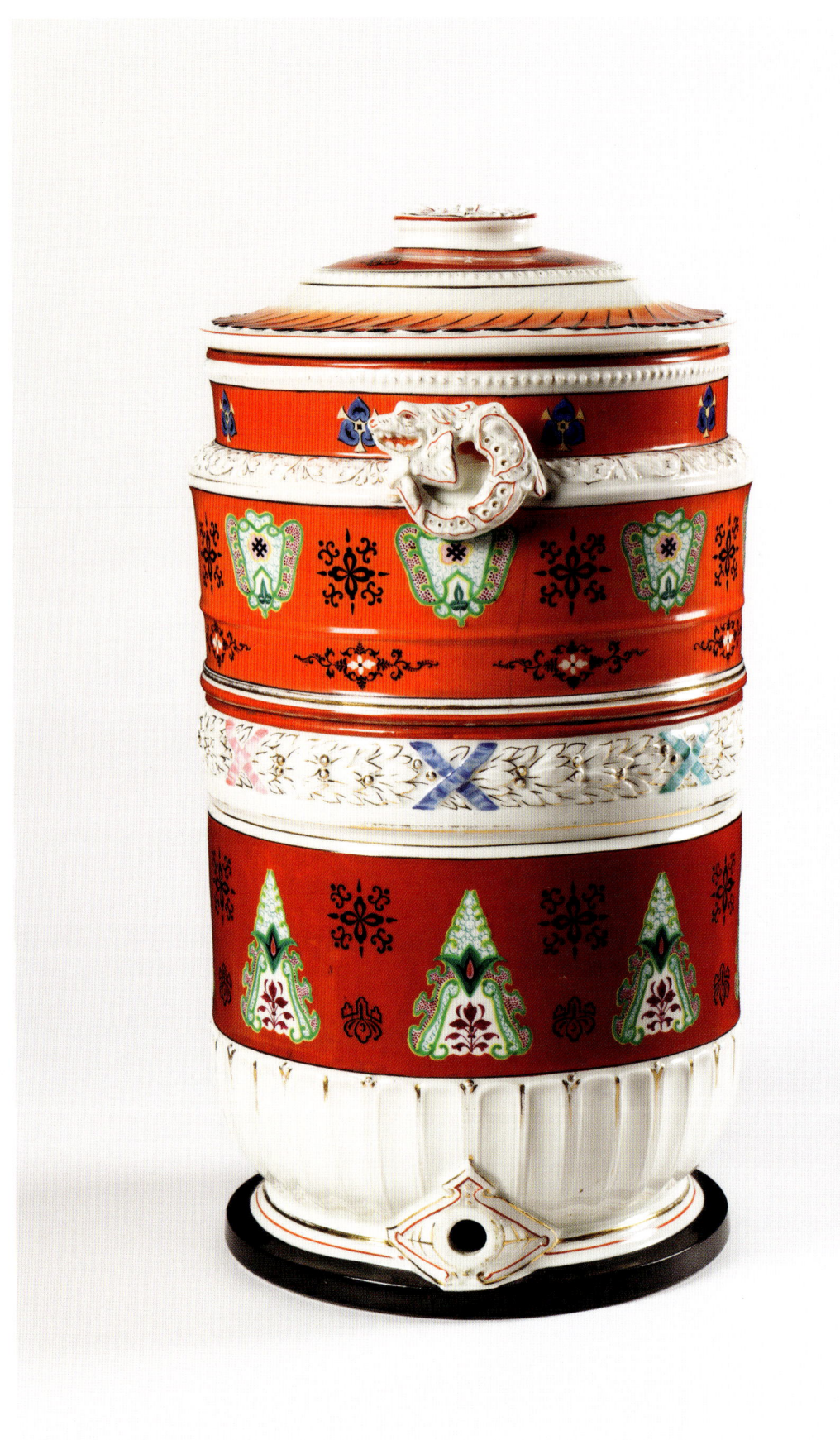

Union Porcelain Works
(Manufacturer, Brooklyn, New York, 1863–1922)
Water Filter, patented November 28, 1882

Porcelain, 20 × 12½ × 11½ in.
Bequest of Marie Bernice Bitzer, by exchange, 1995.143.1a-c
Provenance: Acquired by Florence I. Balasny-Barnes, by 1995; purchased by the Brooklyn Museum, December 14, 1995.

This Union Porcelain Works water filter is evidence of New Yorkers' need for and fascination with clean drinking water during the nineteenth century. Indeed, as public wells had become polluted, public health was a major concern for both citizens and the city's government. Beginning with the 1821 Commissioners' Plan, New York City administrators took action to regulate and systematize the city's infrastructure. First steps included establishing the metropolis's famous street grid, and then focus quickly turned to the pressing need for sanitary water. This eventually led to the opening of the Croton Waterworks on October 14, 1842, a massive water delivery system that flowed from the Croton River to present-day Bryant Park in Manhattan. By 1882, when this expensive and expertly crafted porcelain filter was made, most wealthy households had indoor plumbing and access to clean water. However, New York's large population and slums still generated anxiety about hygiene; elite New Yorkers were able to take measures for additional water purification. They frequently installed filters such as this example in their homes. Here the porcelain is elaborately ornamented, indicating that it was intended for use in formal dining interiors. Its Asian motifs, such as the dragon crest at the top, point to a widespread interest in Asian decorative arts, a result of the forced opening of China's and Japan's ports to international trade and the display of works from these countries at world's fairs.

LSG

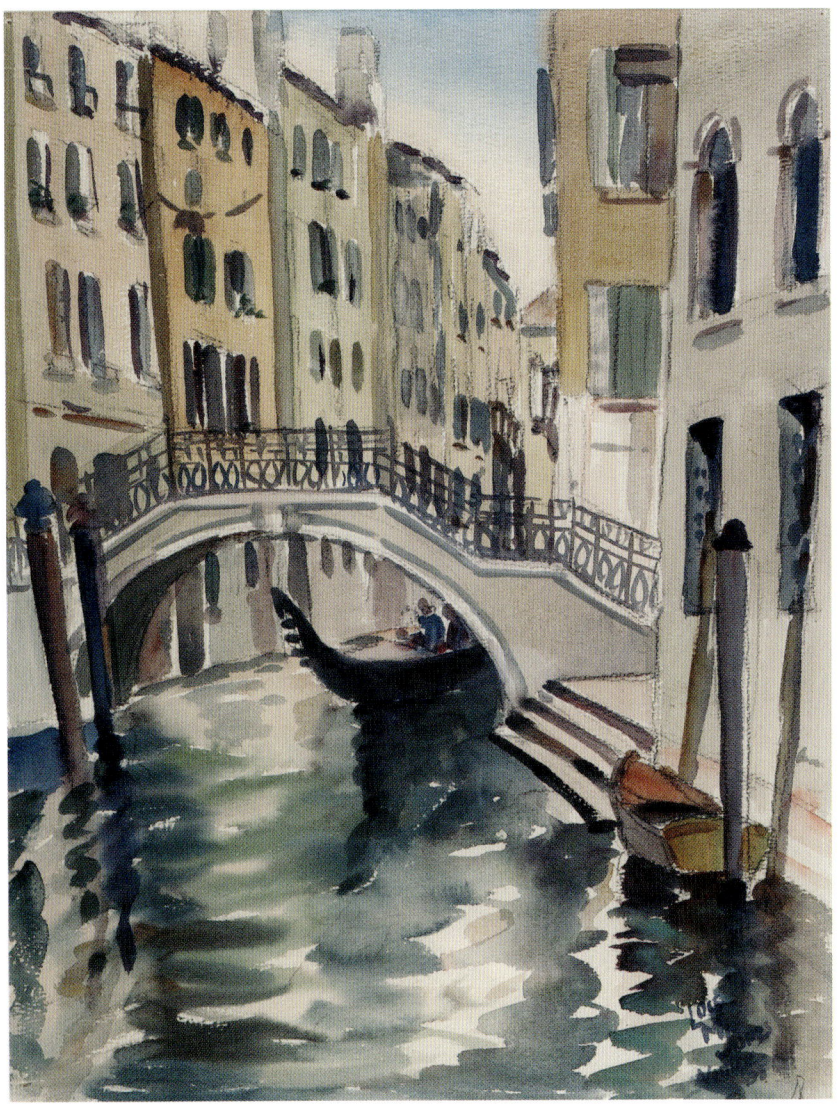

Loïs Mailou Jones
(American, 1905–1998)
The Bridge, 1938

Watercolor, graphite on paper, 19½ × 15½ in. Robert A. Levinson Fund, purchased in honor of Saundra Williams-Cornwell and Don Cornwell for their two decades of stalwart generosity and dedication to the Brooklyn Museum, 2022.8
Provenance: Acquired by an unidentified private collector, before 2022; acquired by Black Art Auction, by 2022; purchased by the Brooklyn Museum, April 5, 2022.

The Bridge, which depicts a Venetian canal, exemplifies Loïs Mailou Jones's substantial work in watercolor created while studying in France and Italy between 1937 and 1938. The work is typical of Jones's Impressionist painting style from her time at the Académie Julien in Paris. She first encountered the watercolors of American artists Winslow Homer and John Singer Sargent a decade prior, while studying at the School of the Museum of Fine Art in Boston. Jones stated their "explorations of nature reinforced [her] love of the landscape and ocean," and provided "great inspiration."[1] It is likely that watercolors such as Sargent's *Venice: Under the Rialto Bridge* (1909) shaped her desire to study abroad.

Like many Black Americans who found creative refuge in Europe, Jones returned several times during breaks from her position in the art department at Howard University to paint the countryside, quaint villages, and storied waterways. Sargent's "predilection for unusual vantage points and dramatic use of color" in his Venetian pictures likely informed Jones's own treatment of the city's architecture and channels.[2] These trips reflect Jones's shifting interest from the flickering light of Impressionism to the bold application of color of the Post-Impressionists. In this and other early paintings of Venice, Jones deftly handled watercolor to capture the subtle coloration and shifting light effects on the city's iconic and imperiled waterways.

SSW

1. As quoted in Rebecca VanDiver, *Designing a New Tradition: Loïs Mailou Jones and the Aesthetics of Blackness* (University Park: The Pennsylvania State University Press, 2020), 31; also see Loïs Mailou Jones, "Career of an African American Artist," in *Lives of Career Women*, ed. Frances Carpe (New York: Springer Science/Business Media, 1991), 43–54.
2. VanDiver, ibid.

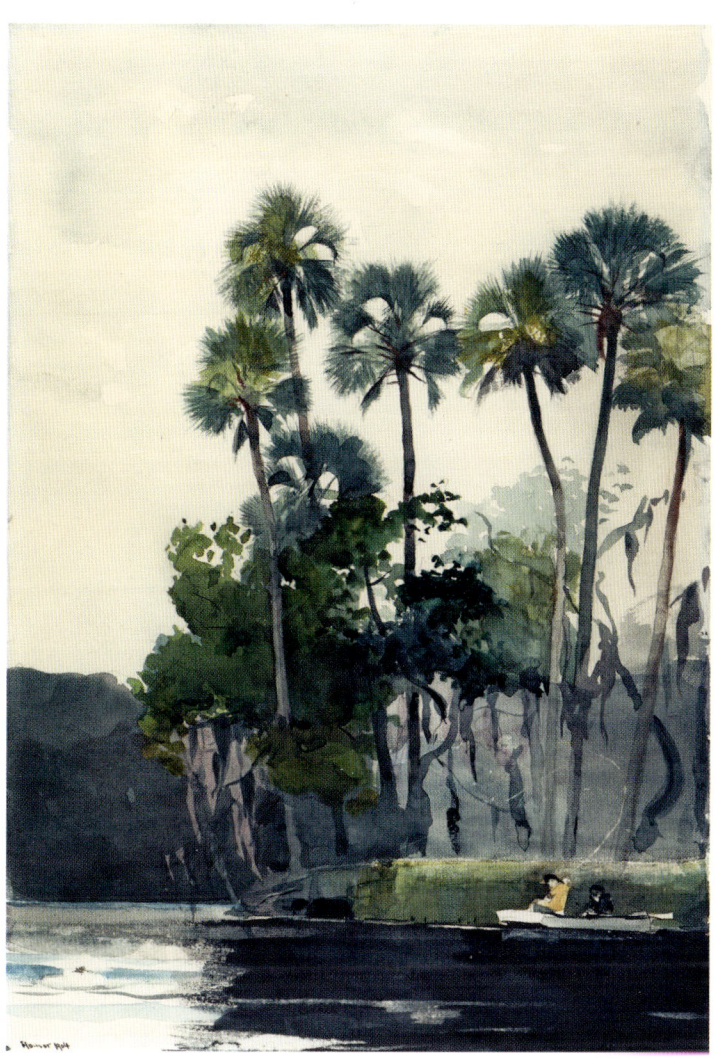

Winslow Homer
(American, 1836–1910)
Homosassa River, 1904

Watercolor with additions of gum over graphite on paper, 19¹¹⁄₁₆ × 13⅞ in.
Museum Collection Fund and Special Subscription, 11.542
Provenance: Acquired by M. Knoedler & Co., by 1922; purchased by the Brooklyn Museum, February 20, 1922.

During his first visit to Homosassa, Florida, in January 1904, Winslow Homer produced a group of twelve watercolors representing the region through scenes of fishing and game.[1] Employing primarily a "wet-on-wet" watercolor technique, Homer captured the lush and humid environment with dynamic tonal effects. The vertical format of this fishing scene, less common in Homer's watercolor works, emphasizes the towering palm trees against the gray skies. A stray water droplet in the lower left disrupts the layered pigment. Adding subtle drama to this scene, Homer deftly scraped away pigment, revealing paper, to indicate the sweeping arc of a fishing line cast from a small boat.[2] This tricky cast is captured in Homer's virtuosic handling of his aqueous paint while also himself sitting on the water in a fishing boat.[3]

Fishing is a popular subject in Homer's *oeuvre*. He was an avid angler himself, partaking in the sport during his time in Maine, visits to the Adirondacks, and winters in Florida.[4] During his 1904 trip to Homosassa, Homer wrote to his brother Arthur extolling the climate and bountiful game: "Delightful climate here about as cool as our September—Fishing the best in America so far as I can find."[5] Homer also included sketches of five fish species from the local waters, some of which were featured as enlarged subjects of watercolors from his visit. He submitted eight of the Florida watercolors to his New York gallery representative M. Knoedler & Co. in spring 1904, and Brooklyn Museum purchased this work from them in 1922, expanding the institution's impressive holdings of celebrated American watercolors.[6]

CG

[1] Abigail Booth Gerdts, ed., *Record of Words by Winslow Homer, vol. 5, 1890–1910* (New York: Spanierman Gallery, 2005), 349–60. Nicolai Cikovsky, *Winslow Homer Watercolors* (New York: Macmillan Pub. Co., 1991); Linda S. Ferber and Barbara Dayer Gallati, *Masters of Color and Light: Homer, Sargent, and the American Watercolor Movement* (Washington, DC: Smithsonian Institution Press, 1998); Martha Tedeschi and Kristi Dahm, *Watercolors by Winslow Homer: The Color of Light* (New Haven, CT: Yale University Press, 2008).
[2] Curatorial file for object 11.542, Brooklyn Museum.
[3] Theodore W. Barrow, "The Gilded Tropics: Winslow Homer and John Singer Sargent in Florida, 1886–1917" (PhD diss., The Graduate Center, CUNY, 2023), 87.
[4] Patricia A. Junker and Sarah Burns, *Winslow Homer: Artist and Angler* (Fort Worth, TX: Amon Carter Museum, 2002).
[5] Winslow Homer to Arthur B. Homer, January 1904, Gift of the Homer Family, Bowdoin College Museum of Art, 1964.69.105.a-.c.
[6] *Homosassa River* was acquired from Knoedler by exchanging another watercolor, *Palms, Florida* (n.d.), which the Museum had purchased in 1911 using the Museum Collection Fund supported by annual subscriptions—donations made by members of the public to support the institution's acquisition efforts. The "credit line" of the original watercolor was kept and applied to *Homosassa River* upon acquisition.

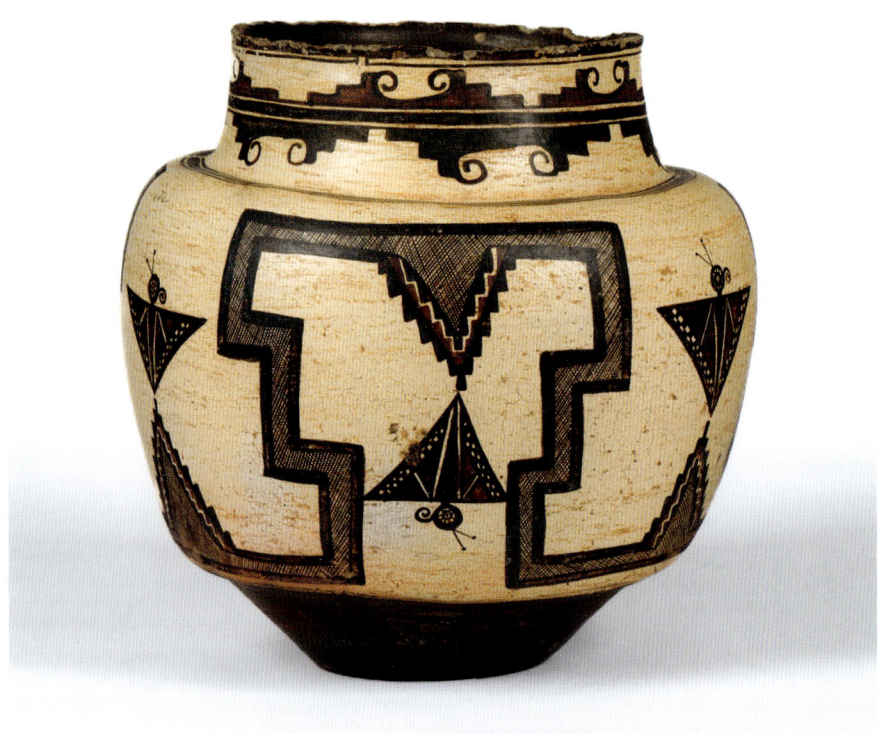

A:shiwi (Zuni Pueblo) artist
K'yabokya de'ele (Water Jar)
Pueblo of Zuni, New Mexico, 1825–1850

Ceramic, pigment, 12¾ × 12¾ in.
Museum Expedition 1903, Museum Collection Fund, 03.325.4723
Provenance: Acquired by Andrew Vanderwagen, by 1903; purchased in Zuni, NM by Stewart Culin for the Brooklyn Museum, 1903.

[Vessels are] a physical marker and a reminder of family.... Many, if not all, intact Pueblo jars in collections were used to store and serve water until the introduction, forced implementation, and subsequent growth of a colonial marketplace... In this reality, we are all vessels of water. Vessels with the potential for creating life. A gift given to us by Mother Earth. We return to Her after we have lived our best lives and ask that the pieces of ourselves that return, continue to inspire.[1]
—Monyssha Rose Trujillo; Cochiti, Santa Clara, Laguna, Jicarilla, Diné anthropologist and geographer

Created by an A:shiwi potter, this *K'yabokya De'ele* (Water Jar) highlights the artistic ingenuity among Pueblo women and honors water as a life-giving force for Indigenous communities across the American Southwest. Utilizing clay from A:shiwi people's ancestral homelands, the artist formed the vessel by layering long thin coils of clay, then smoothed it. She then applied mineral paints and slips to create the striking design, and fired the vessel. The imagery depicts architectural forms that support stylized butterflies, believed to represent "the beneficence of summer, when the country abounds in flowers and plants."[2] Beings who underwent radical physical transformation—like dragonflies, tadpoles, and butterflies—were common visual motifs on A:shiwi water jars.

Many Indigenous communities in that region live in Pueblos—permanent settlements that predate Spanish colonialism—and each group possesses a distinctive ceramic style. Water jars are ubiquitous forms that store the substance vital for agriculture and survival in the arid Southwestern climate.

DT

1. Monyssha Rose Trujillo, "Water Is Life," in *Grounded in Clay: The Spirit of Pueblo Pottery*, eds. Elysia Poon and Rick Kinsel (London: Merrell, 2022), 250.
2. Lois Sherr Dubin, *North American Indian Jewelry and Adornment from Prehistory to the Present* (New York: Harry N. Abrams, 1999), 508.

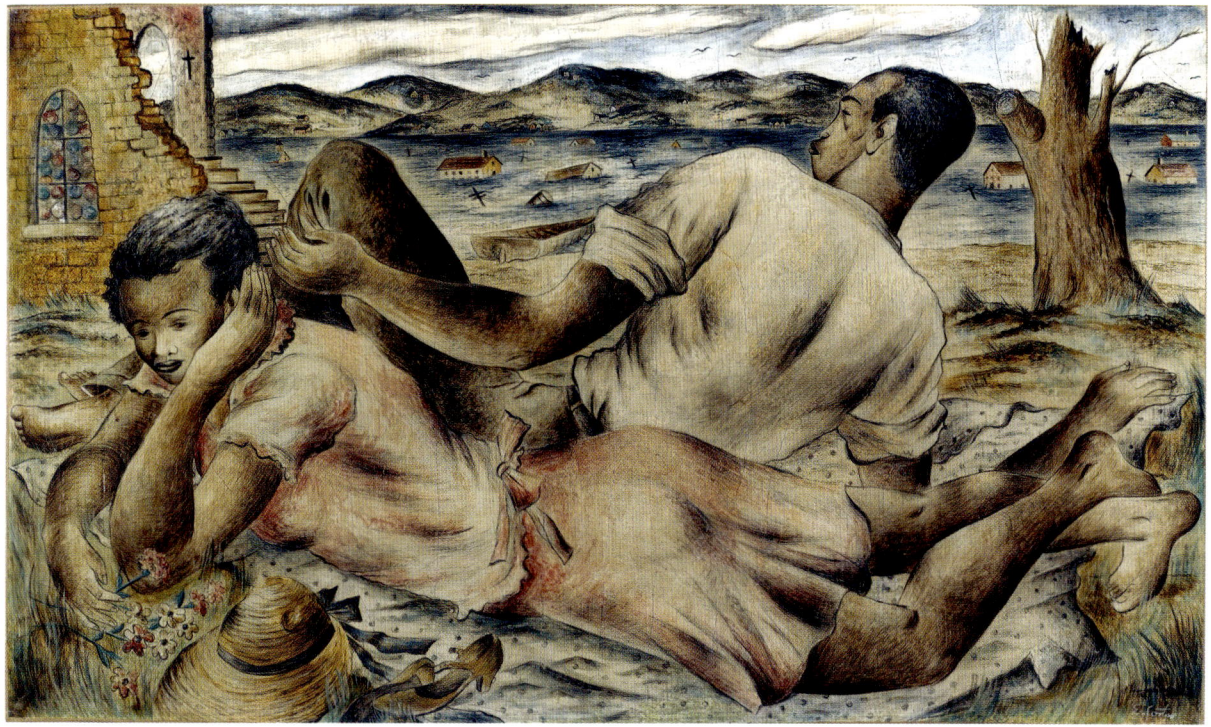

Eldzier Cortor
(American, 1916–2015)
Southern Landscape (Southern Flood), ca. 1944–45

Tempera on board, 20 × 34 in.
Gift of Mr. and Mrs. Abraham Adler and bequest of Laura L. Barnes, by exchange, 2006.2
Provenance: Acquired by Selden Rodman and Mrs. Selden Rodman (Hilda Clausen, Maia Wojciechowska, or Carole Cleaver), before 2002. Acquired by a private collector, by 2004; acquired by Robert Henry Adams Fine Art, by 2004; purchased by the Brooklyn Museum, April 6, 2006.

Eldzier Cortor's scene of a Black woman and man resting nonchalantly against a dystopian backdrop of buildings swept away in a flood is both surreal and mundane. The two lie on a polka-dotted blanket spread on the grassy shore; the man gazes out at the flood while the woman focuses on some picked wildflowers. Signs of devastation surround them, including the tree trunk that appears cut and decaying at the right and the dilapidated church building in the background on the left. The cross hanging on the crumbling wall is echoed in the shapes of electric wires floating in the flood waters alongside half-submerged houses. Drawing upon European modernisms and traditional African art forms, *Southern Landscape (Southern Flood)* exemplifies the artist's transition away from the realist style of his earlier paintings and toward elongated and distorted figures in dreamlike settings.

Southern Landscape presents an unsettling recollection of a devastating flood the artist witnessed in Kentucky. In a 2016 interview with Teresa Carbone, former Andrew W. Mellon Curator of American Art at the Brooklyn Museum, Cortor described witnessing this flood and the submerged houses.[1] Carbone and Cortor speculate that the flood was caused by the building of hydroelectric dams. A depiction of environmental racism, the painting reveals the reality that the burden of environmental disaster falls more heavily on Black communities and the poor. The 1930s and '40s were marked by a significant number of floods in the southern United States. Cortor reflects on these natural disasters, and relates them to more recent catastrophes, including Hurricane Sandy in 2012 after which he was trapped in his nineteenth-floor apartment in New York City for two weeks. Despite the devastation depicted in this composition, Cortor seeks to uplift the two individuals, and expressed that "the two figures represent youth with hope."[2]

CG

1. "An Oral History with Eldzier Cortor by Terry Carbone," *Bomb*, June 21, 2016, https://bombmagazine.org/articles/2016/06/21/eldzier-cortor/.
2. Ibid.

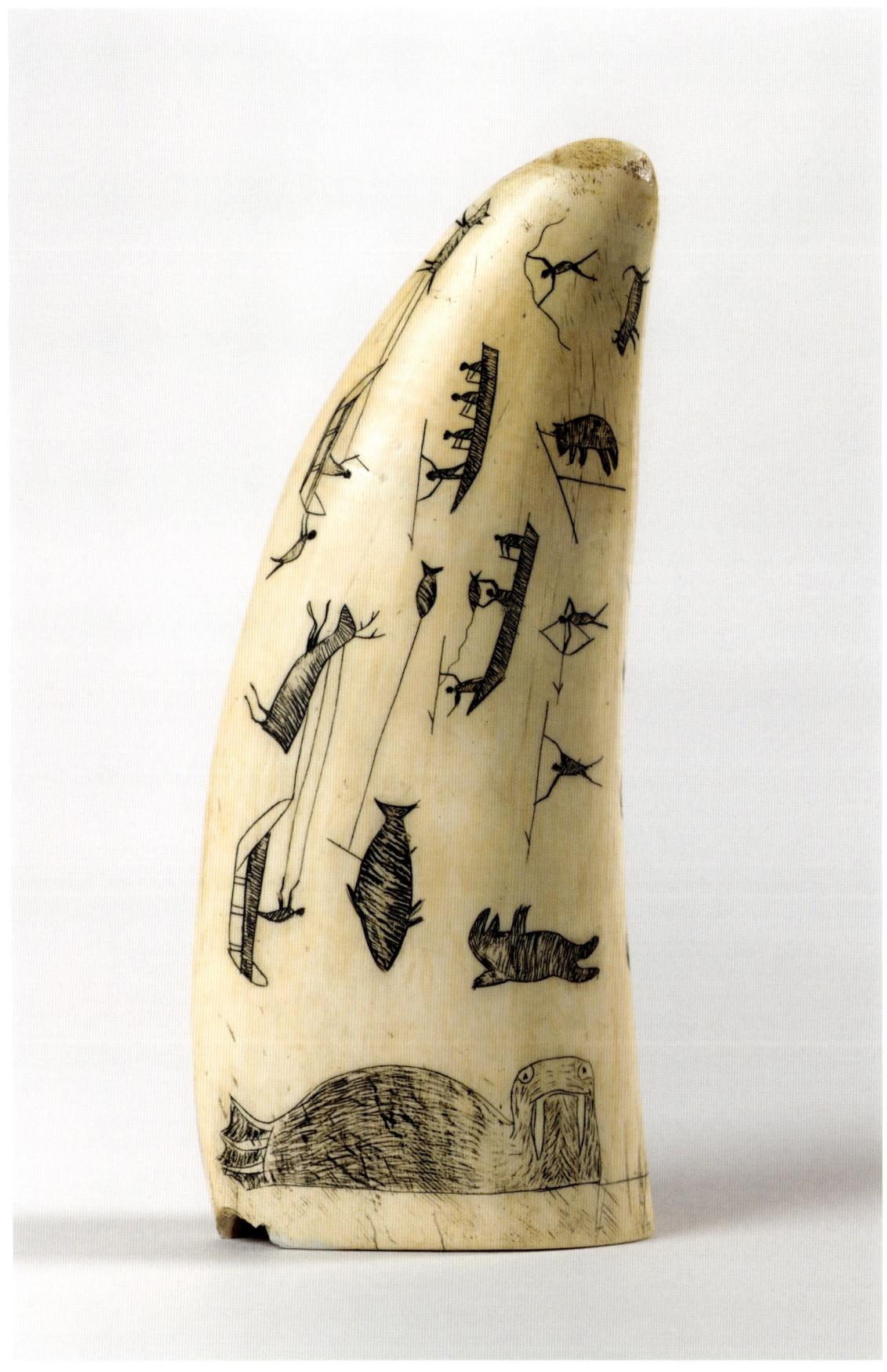

Yup'ik or Iñupiaq artist
Engraved Whale Tooth
Alaska, United States, late 19th century

Sperm whale tooth, black ash or graphite, oil,
6½ × 3 × 2 in.
Brooklyn Museum, Gift of Robert B. Woodward, 20.895
Provenance: Acquired by Robert Blackburne Woodward, by 1909; donated, 1909.

The camaraderie displayed by hunters forms bonds that are lifelong. The spirit of cooperation and sharing yields success and happiness to you, your family, and your community. ... There is a tremendous amount of respect for each other and for marine mammals...[1]
—George (Mangtaquli) Noongwook, a Yupik Elder and advocate for Indigenous whaling rights

This engraved whale tooth speaks to the critical importance of both the bodies of water and wildlife that allow Alaska Natives to flourish in the harshest of climates. The engravings present a variety of hunting scenes that honor the animals' sacrifice for the benefit of Native communities. These images depict hunters pursuing walrus and caribou, as well as a group of men in an umiak boat harpooning a whale. Artworks like this reflect a deep appreciation for the creatures with whom Indigenous communities shared their world.

Most Indigenous communities in the Arctic base themselves around coastal waters where sea mammals and fish can be found. Yup'ik and Iñupiaq people relied on these animals for both food and materials used to create everything from hunting implements to garments. The Iñupiaq knowledge keeper Beverly Faye Hugo described her community's relationship with whales: "We believe that a whale gives itself to a captain and crew who are worthy people, who have integrity—that is the gift of the whale. Caring for whales, even after you've caught them, is important."[2] The artist's treatment of the whale tooth here reflects relationships of reciprocity and respect between the hunter and hunted, and the land and sea, which nourish both humans and animals alike.

DT

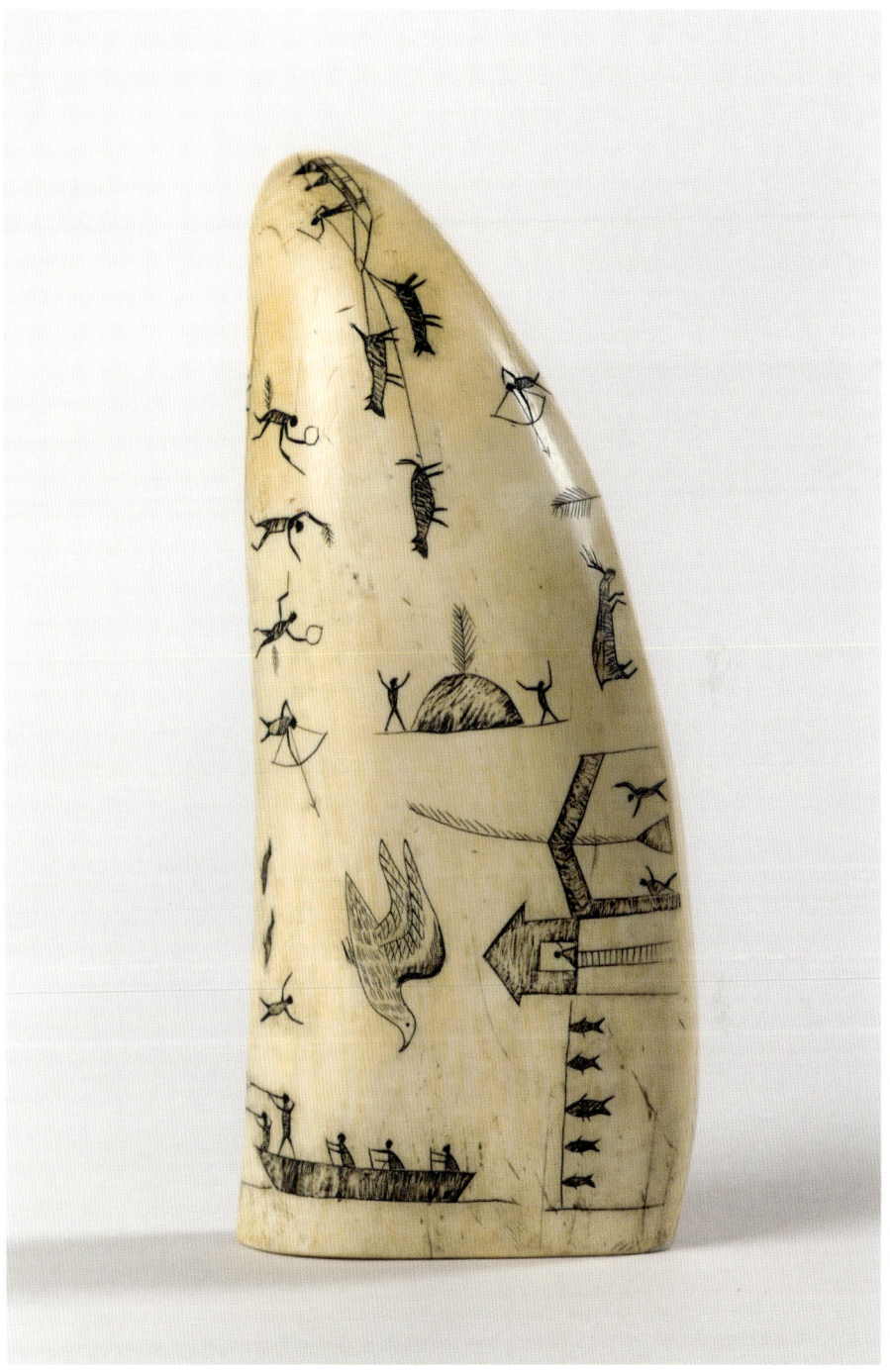

1. Henry Huntington, Hiroko Ikuta, and Igor Krupnik, "Yupik Elder Broke Ground in Whaling, Culture and Research," *ICT News*, December 13, 2023.

2. Beverly Faye Hugo, "Iñupiaq," in *Living Our Cultures, Sharing Our Heritage: The First Peoples of Alaska*, ed. Aron Crowell, Rosita Worl, Paul Ongtooguk, and Dawn Biddison (Washington, DC: Smithsonian Institution, 2010), 44–71.

CRITICAL SHORT

Troubled Waters and Currents of Restoration

Caroline Gillaspie

Would you swim in New York's East River or Brooklyn's Gowanus Canal? Would you eat an oyster from New York Harbor? Based on pollution reports, and New Yorkers' often cynical humor, you would be justified in answering "absolutely not." New York City's waterways—ocean, harbor, rivers, bays, creeks, and canals—have been significant points of connection and informed local development, often resulting in their contamination.[1] Beginning in the colonial period, the burgeoning port enriched the city but fundamentally damaged vital water systems. For centuries, New Yorkers have used these bodies of water for transportation, to power industrial buildings, and for dumping waste. In response to ecological damage, recent restoration projects have worked to counter shortsighted urban development.

The Brooklyn Museum's collection is rich in artworks that speak to the history of New York's waterways. Some artists documented the ways water shapes the environment and the experience of residents, while others illustrate the ways that Indigenous knowledge systems can address damage to water ecosystems.

During the nineteenth century, the dramatic expansion of industry along the East River impacted nearby living conditions and created the commercial architecture that defines John Koch's painting. A large smokestack frames the composition's right

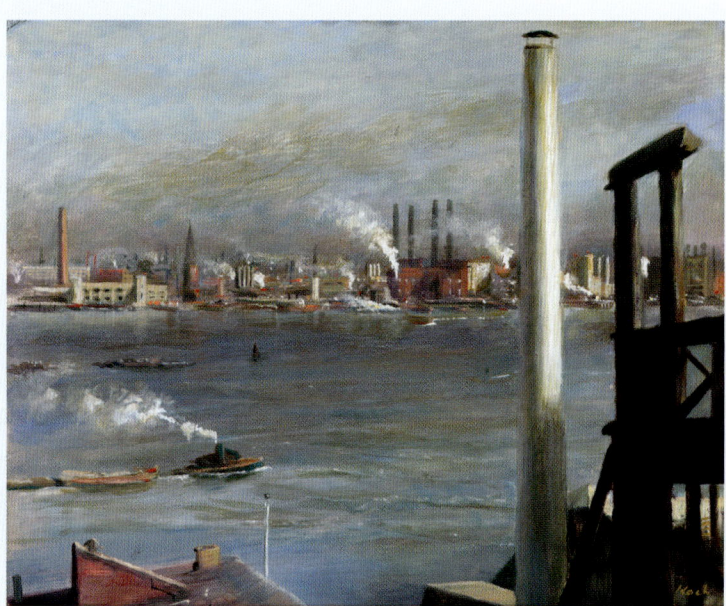

John Koch (American, 1909–1978). *East River,* ca. 1930.

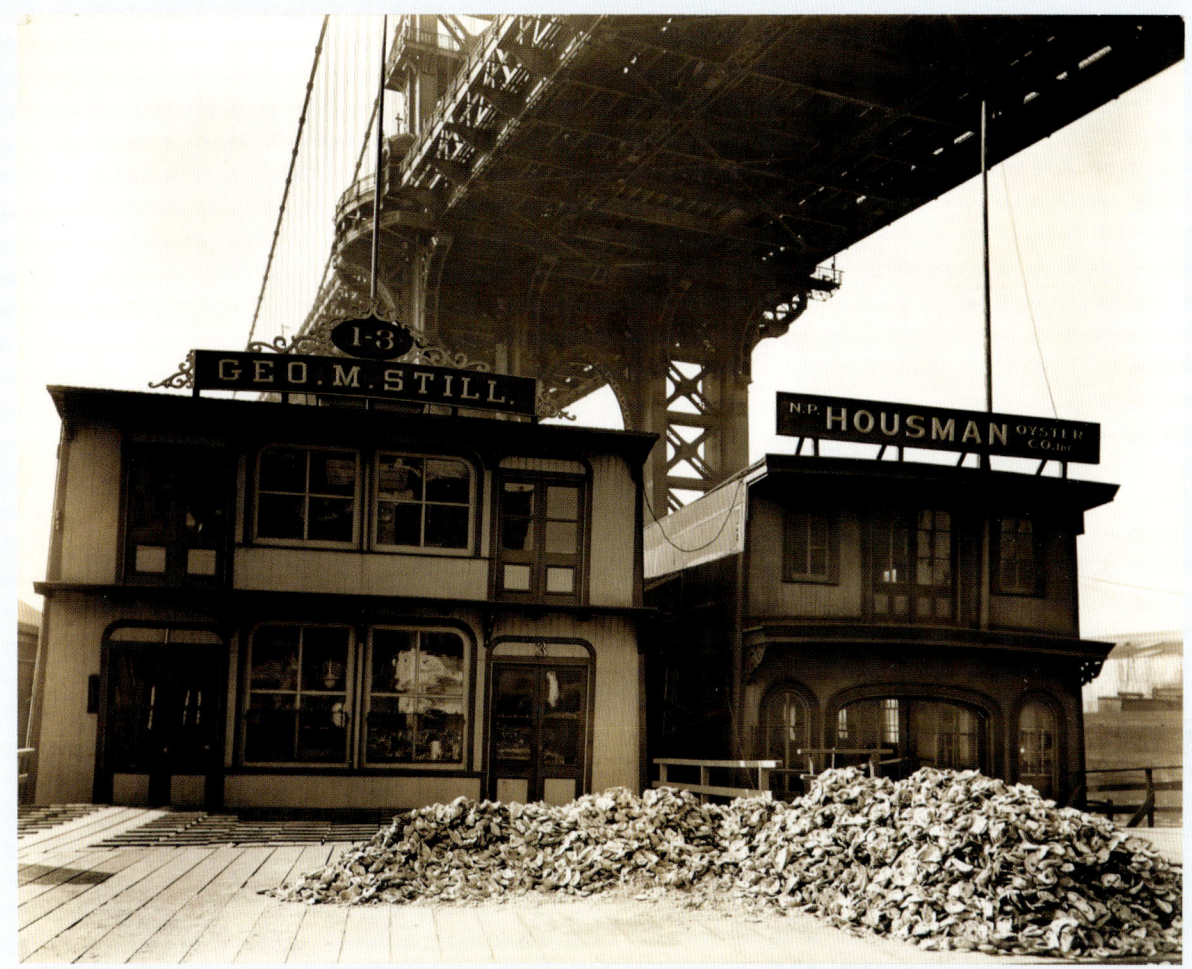

Berenice Abbott (American, 1898–1991). *Oyster Houses, South St. & Pike Slip,* April 1, 1937.

side, calling attention to the busy river scene. This industrialized stand-in for the weathered tree *repoussoir* that brackets traditional landscape paintings suggests urban development supplanting rural environments.[2] Beyond, a forest of smokestacks rises from the Queens cityscape, including those of the Long Island Power Station, built in 1906 to power the Long Island Rail Road. Painted from his Manhattan apartment on First Avenue and 48th Street, Koch's looser brushstrokes effectively mingle industrial pollution with hazy skies and murky water.

In Berenice Abbott's 1937 photograph, oyster barges dock on the East River where oysters were packed for shipping and sold directly to consumers as an affordable food staple.[3] While this appears a thoroughly modern scene, archaeological evidence of shell middens (heaps found along shorelines) indicate that local Native populations have harvested oysters for thousands of years. Dutch and English colonizers co-opted the practice, and a free Black community of oystermen at Sandy Ground on Staten Island flourished in the mid-1800s as the shellfish was avidly consumed by every class of New Yorker.[4] Simultaneously, oyster populations rapidly declined due to water pollution, overharvesting, and land reclamation to expand New York's shorelines, resulting in the closure of commercial oyster beds between 1921 and 1927.[5] The foregrounded midden in Abbott's photograph creates a misleading illusion of local abundance when in fact the oyster barges likely served shellfish from New England.

Just as European Americans radically transformed the East and Hudson Rivers, colonial settlement and extraction likewise impacted the Long Island coastline. For instance, seventeenth-century colonists established a port at Bellport, the ancestral homeland of the Unkechaug (Patchogue) Nation. Centuries later, the region experienced a tourist boom. William James Glackens painted several Bellport beach scenes between 1911 and 1916, including *Bathing at Bellport, Long Island*. He paints his wife and son holding hands at the center of this bright and bustling scene of

Trouble The Water

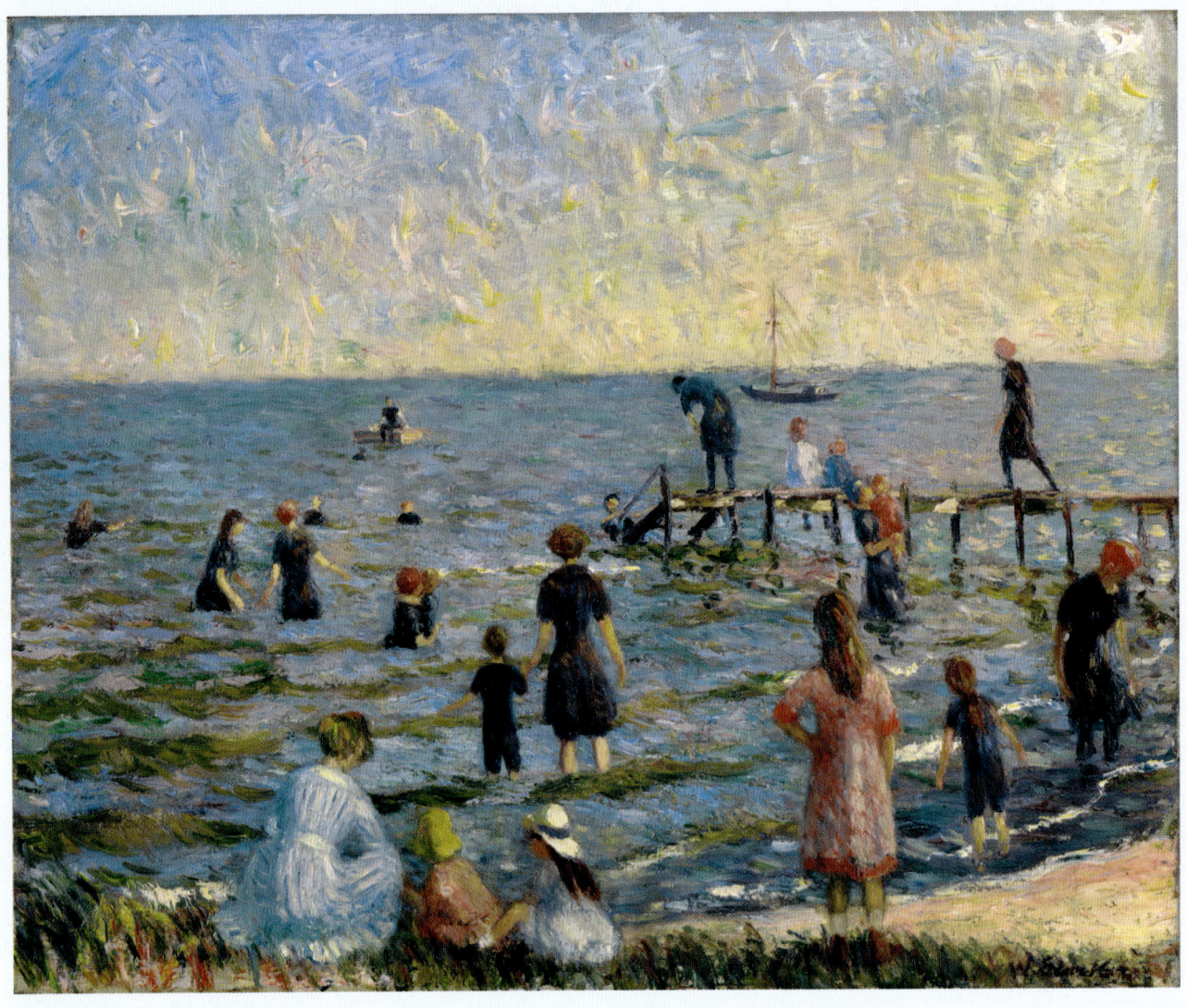

William James Glackens (American, 1870–1938). *Bathing at Bellport, Long Island*, 1912.

leisure. The painting underscores access afforded to tourists, yet obscures the impacts of tourism and development that followed the historic local seaport.

In the face of coastal degradation inflicted by centuries of colonization, Shinnecock artist Courtney M. Leonard's work engages her tribe's connection with water, whaling, and sustainability practices. ARTIFICE recalls the form of human-made reefs installed along Long Island shorelines to aid oyster bed growth and protect against storm surges. In other locations, concrete reefs have been used, but extracted sand required for their construction results in further erosion.[6] In response to shoreline erosion and rising waters due to climate change, the Shinnecock community's coastal-restoration project created reefs from calcified oyster shells and planted grasses to prevent sand erosion.[7] Collaborations between marine biologists and holders of Shinnecock traditional knowledge have resulted in sustainable solutions to colonial overharvesting, industry, and development. Other restoration projects also address historic damage amid advancing climate change.[8] From the Billion Oyster Project's restoration of New York oyster beds, to the dredging of contaminated sediment from the Gowanus Canal, to plans to restore wetland habitats in the Newtown Creek tributaries, care for our local waters is helping to reverse past harms. With the efforts of environmental advocates and artists alike, New Yorkers may strive for restored and sustainably managed waterways.

1. Kara Murphy Schlichting, *New York Recentered: Building the Metropolis from the Shore* (Chicago: University of Chicago Press, 2019).
2. A *repoussoir* is an object that is used as a framing device in the foreground of a composition that also helps create a sense of depth. See "Repoussoir," in Ian Chilvers, *The Oxford Dictionary of Art and Artists*, 4th ed. (Oxford: Oxford University Press, 2009), 524. The device is used, for example, in Thomas Cole's *A View of the Two Lakes and Mountain House, Catskill Mountains, Morning* (p. 218).
3. Berenice Abbott documented the transformations of New York City's urban environment in her 1930s photographic series "Changing New York."
4. Sandy Ground was established in 1833. See www.sandygroundny.com.
5. For more on the history of the oyster in New York City, including the decline of oyster beds, see Mark Kurlansky, *The Big Oyster: History on the Half Shell* (New York: Ballantine Books, 2006); Carmen Nigro, "History on the Half-Shell: The Story of New York City and its Oysters," *New York Public Library Blog*, June 2, 2011, https://www.nypl.org/blog/2011/06/01/history-half-shell-intertwined-story-new-york-city-and-its-oysters.
6. Information on the impacts of sand erosion on the coastline adapted from the writing and interdisciplinary marine biology research of the artist Courtney Leonard.
7. Anuradha Varanasi, "The Tribe that Brought a Damaged Shoreline Back to Life," *State of the Planet / Columbia Climate School*, September 18, 2019, https://news.climate.columbia.edu/2019/09/18/shinnecock-coastal-habitat-restoration-project/.
8. While New York City communities have worked toward environmental restoration, some are conscious of the impact of environmental gentrification (or "eco-gentrification"), in which neighborhoods gentrify after environmental conditions are improved. This presents an additional challenge for efforts to make the city healthy for all residents. See, for instance, Jeanne Haffner, "The Dangers of Eco-gentrification: What's the Best Way to Make a City Greener?," *The Guardian*, May 6, 2015, https://www.theguardian.com/cities/2015/may/06/dangers-ecogentrification-best-way-make-city-greener.

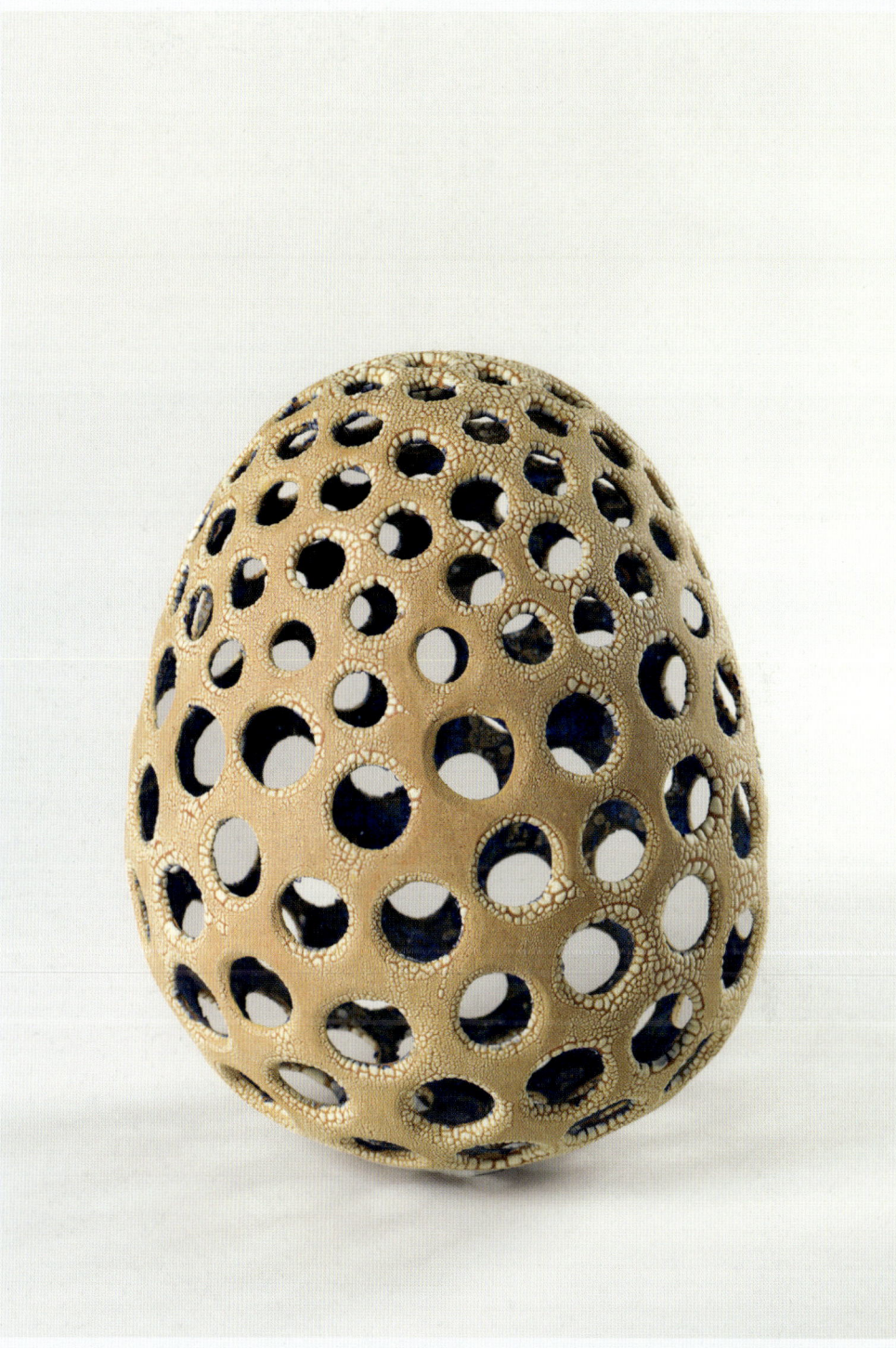

Courtney M. Leonard (Shinnecock, born 1980). *Artifice (Breach Series)*, 2016.

Thanksgiving Address: Greetings to the Natural World

Words That Come Before All Else

Spoken by members of the Hodinöhsö:ni' (Haudenosaunee) Confederacy since time immemorial, this text is known as the "Words That Come Before All Else," or Thanksgiving Address. The Hodinöhsö:ni' Confederacy includes six tribes who live in upstate New York and Canada: the Cayuga, Mohawk, Oneida, Onondaga, Seneca, and Tuscarora. The protocol of the address establishes gratitude as the highest priority and reminds us that everything in our world is subject to the same forces. The Thanksgiving Address statement exists in many forms. This translation of a Mohawk version of the Hodinöhsö:ni' Thanksgiving Address was developed and published in 1993, and provided, courtesy of Six Nations Indian Museum and the Tracking Project. All rights reserved.

The People
Today we have gathered and we see that the cycles of life continue. We have been given the duty to live in balance and harmony with each other and all living things. So now, we bring our minds together as one as we give greetings and thanks to each other as people.
Now our minds are one.

The Earth Mother
We are all thankful to our Mother, the Earth, for she gives us all that we need for life. She supports our feet as we walk about upon her. It gives us joy that she continues to care for us as she has from the beginning of time. To our mother, we send greetings and thanks.
Now our minds are one.

The Waters
We give thanks to all the waters of the world for quenching our thirst and providing us with strength. Water is life. We know its power in many forms—waterfalls and rain, mists and streams, rivers and oceans. With one mind, we send greetings and thanks to the spirit of Water.
Now our minds are one.

The Fish
We turn our minds to the all the Fish life in the water. They were instructed to cleanse and purify the water. They also give themselves to us as food. We are grateful that we can still find pure water. So, we turn now to the Fish and send our greetings and thanks.
Now our minds are one.

The Plants
Now we turn toward the vast fields of Plant life. As far as the eye can see, the Plants grow, working many wonders. They sustain many life forms. With our minds gathered together, we give thanks and look forward to seeing Plant life for many generations to come.
Now our minds are one.

The Food Plants
With one mind, we turn to honor and thank all the Food Plants we harvest from the garden. Since the beginning of time, the grains, vegetables, beans and berries have helped the people survive. Many other living things draw strength from them too. We gather all the Plant Foods together as one and send them a greeting of thanks.
Now our minds are one.

The Medicine Herbs
Now we turn to all the Medicine herbs of the world. From the beginning they were instructed to take away sickness. They are always waiting and ready to heal us. We are happy there are still among us those special few who remember how to use these plants for healing. With one mind, we send greetings and thanks to the Medicines and to the keepers of the Medicines.
Now our minds are one.

The Animals
We gather our minds together to send greetings and thanks to all the Animal life in the world. They have many things to teach us as people. We are honored by them when they give up their lives so we may use their bodies as food for our people. We see them near our homes and in the deep forests. We are glad they are still here and we hope that it will always be so.
Now our minds are one.

The Trees

We now turn our thoughts to the Trees. The Earth has many families of Trees who have their own instructions and uses. Some provide us with shelter and shade, others with fruit, beauty and other useful things. Many people of the world use a Tree as a symbol of peace and strength. With one mind, we greet and thank the Tree life.
Now our minds are one.

The Birds

We put our minds together as one and thank all the Birds who move and fly about over our heads. The Creator gave them beautiful songs. Each day they remind us to enjoy and appreciate life. The Eagle was chosen to be their leader. To all the Birds—from the smallest to the largest—we send our joyful greetings and thanks.
Now our minds are one.

The Four Winds

We are all thankful to the powers we know as the Four Winds. We hear their voices in the moving air as they refresh us and purify the air we breathe. They help us to bring the change of seasons. From the four directions they come, bringing us messages and giving us strength. With one mind, we send our greetings and thanks to the Four Winds.
Now our minds are one.

The Thunderers

Now we turn to the west where our grandfathers, the Thunder Beings, live. With lightning and thundering voices, they bring with them the water that renews life. We are thankful that they keep those evil things made by Okwiseres underground. We bring our minds together as one to send greetings and thanks to our Grandfathers, the Thunderers.
Now our minds are one.

The Sun

We now send greetings and thanks to our eldest Brother, the Sun. Each day without fail he travels the sky from east to west, bringing the light of a new day. He is the source of all the fires of life. With one mind, we send greetings and thanks to our Brother, the Sun.
Now our minds are one.

Grandmother Moon

We put our minds together to give thanks to our oldest Grandmother, the Moon, who lights the night-time sky. She is the leader of woman all over the world, and she governs the movement of the ocean tides. By her changing face we measure time, and it is the Moon who watches over the arrival of children here on Earth. With one mind, we send greetings and thanks to our Grandmother, the Moon.
Now our minds are one.

The Stars

We give thanks to the Stars who are spread across the sky like jewelry. We see them in the night, helping the Moon to light the darkness and bringing dew to the gardens and growing things. When we travel at night, they guide us home. With our minds gathered together as one, we send greetings and thanks to the Stars.
Now our minds are one.

The Enlightened Teachers

We gather our minds to greet and thank the enlightened Teachers who have come to help throughout the ages. When we forget how to live in harmony, they remind us of the way we were instructed to live as people. With one mind, we send greetings and thanks to these caring teachers.
Now our minds are one.

The Creator

Now we turn our thoughts to the Creator, or Great Spirit, and send greetings and thanks for all the gifts of Creation. Everything we need to live a good life is here on this Mother Earth. For all the love that is still around us, we gather our minds together as one and send our choicest words of greetings and thanks to the Creator.
Now our minds are one.

Closing Words

We have now arrived at the place where we end our words. Of all the things we have named, it was not our intention to leave anything out. If something was forgotten, we leave it to each individual to send such greetings and thanks in their own way.
Now our minds are one.

Originally published as: ***Thanksgiving Address: Greetings to the Natural World*** Copyright © 1993 Six Nations Indian Museum and The Tracking Project. ISBN 0-9643214-0-8. Reprinted by permission. "Thanksgiving Address: Greetings to the Natural World," English version: John Stokes and Kanawahienton (David Benedict, Turtle Clan/Mohawk); Mohawk version: Rokwaho (Dan Thompson, Wolf Clan/Mohawk); original inspiration: Tekaronianekon (Jake Swamp, Wolf Clan/Mohawk).

FRAMEWORK
Radical Care

Care is the antidote to violence.[1]

—Saidiya Hartman

This framework opens with the Hodinöhsö:ni' *Thanksgiving Address*, or "Words That Come Before All Else," which orients those gathered toward thanksgiving and unity ("now our minds are one"), while offering a material and scientific inventory of the natural world. It is from this ethic of fullness that the American art department and collaborators explore forms of curatorial care—for artworks, belongings, and people—rooted in African diasporic and Indigenous ways of knowing. **Sankofa** invites us to care for the past in order to care for the future. **Rematriation** asks us to consider our responsibilities and relationships to the land, our belongings, and each other. **Gratitude** reminds us that the abundance of our world provides everything we need.

In the works included here, artists illuminate the relationships between their subjects and the land—and those between and within communities, tribes, and nations. This is an invitation to consider the material histories and lives of the objects within the collection. Paintings by Benjamin West, Eastman Johnson, Francisco Oller, and Bumpei Usui encourage us to go back and retrieve through considering complex histories about the importance and precarity of place. Works by Robert Seldon Duncanson, John Biggers, and Carol Emarthle Douglas reflect on harmonious and restored relationships to places and people. And giving thanks for abundance is presented in all its forms by Arapaho and Haida makers and other artists like Hayden Haynes, Samantha Jacobs, and Lilly Martin Spencer.

At the heart of the in-gallery experience is the American (Art) Study, a purpose-built place for audiences to reflect on complex American histories. Part library, part laboratory, the experimental display and interpretation invite in-gallery viewers to take a closer, more critical look at the social, political, economic, and cultural histories that surround each artwork.

A public fervor for information and resources arose amid the Movement for Black Lives and the ongoing COVID-19 pandemic. In response, many Black scholars and educators publicly shared their syllabi and knowledge online, often as photos of book stacks as recommended reading. In the Brooklyn Museum's display, the Study brings together syllabi created by interdisciplinary scholars and educators in the stacked books on view, evoking their online counterparts. Embedded in the walls and related to nearby artworks, the additional books on view represent a range of disciplines, including American studies, Black studies, cultural theory, decolonial studies, ethnic studies, feminist theory, history, Indigenous studies, political science, and many others. These titles offer alternative lenses onto the collection and represent the scholarly foundations of our ongoing research and interpretation.

In addition to reorienting the collection, the Study also "shows" our work by reframing the American art department within different histories and traditions than is typical in museums. In creating this room for discourse, we place the ongoing project of learning—and unlearning—at the center of the conversation as we aim to link our curatorial work with larger political struggles for more just futures. This work is exemplified by Dare Turner in her essay "Framing the World through Gratitude," which positions gratitude and rematriation as curatorial modes. These practices consider how collections of belongings might be cared for and offer critical lenses for reexamining an entire art historical field and the artworks therein.

SSW

1. Saidiya Hartman, "In the Wake: A Salon in Honor of Christina Sharpe," Barnard Center for Research on Women (BCRW), February 2, 2017, https://bcrw.barnard.edu/videos/in-the-wake-a-salon-in-honor-of-christina-sharpe/.

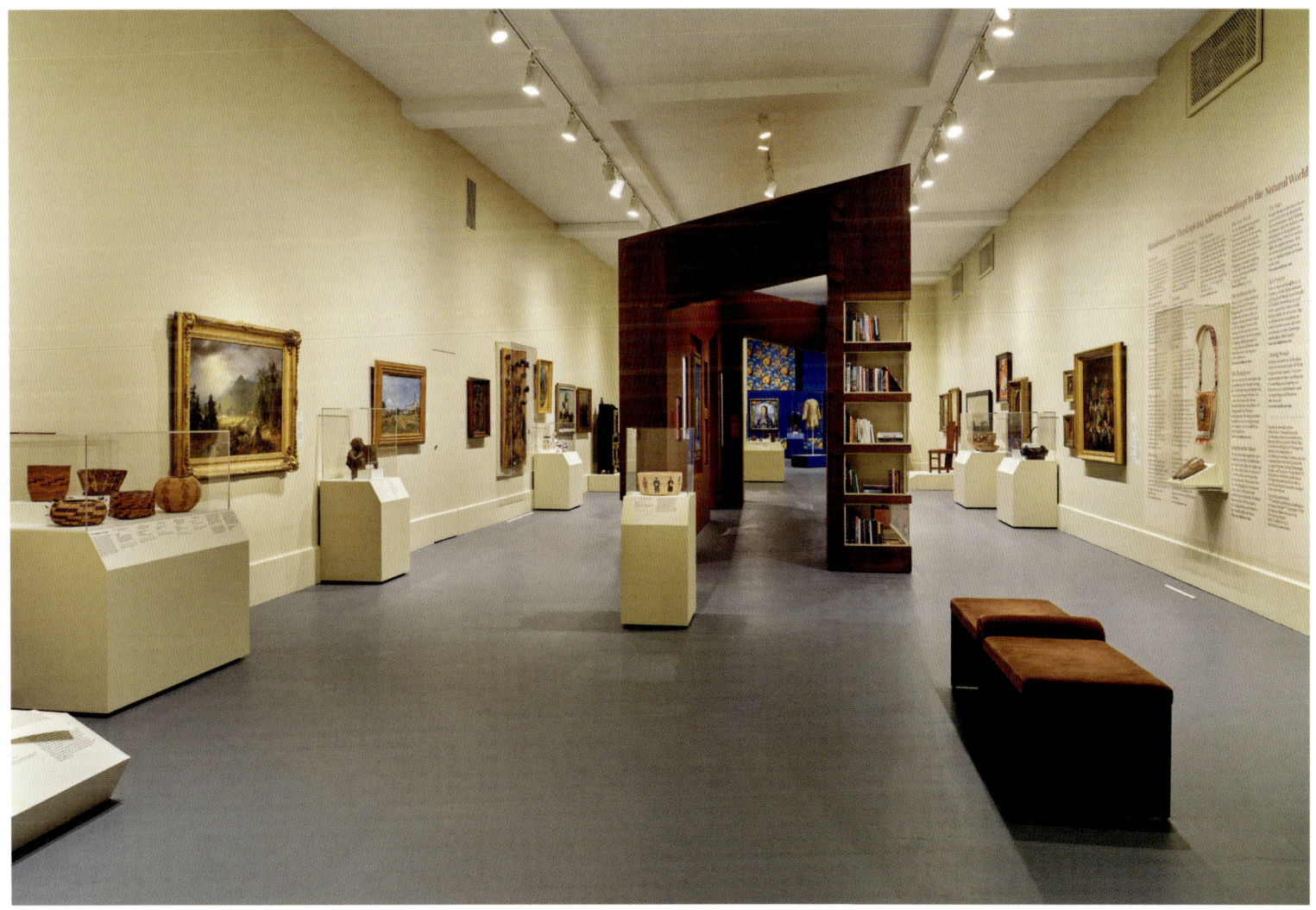

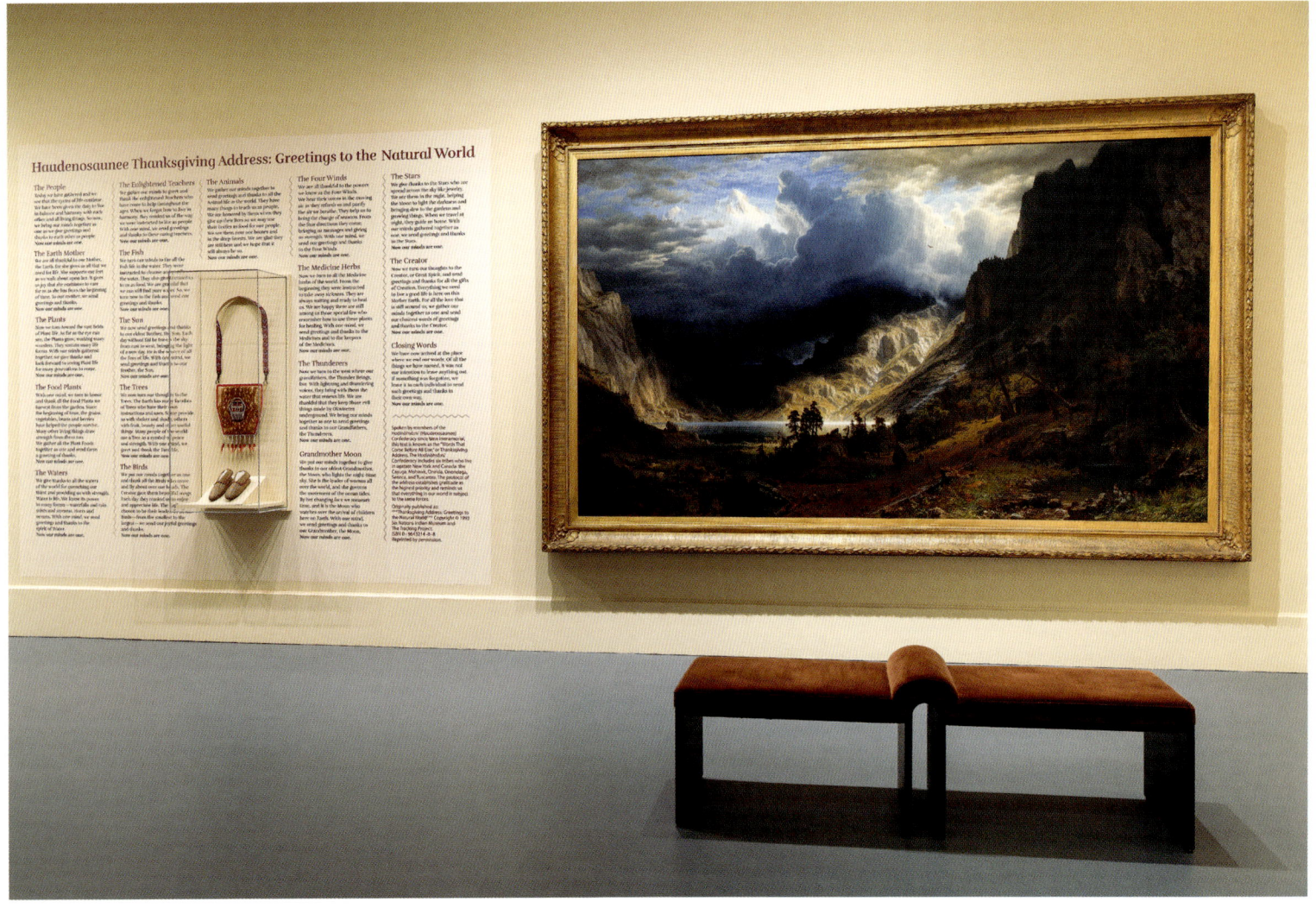

Rematriation is a process toward restoring right relationships to the land—it is a concept that emerges from Indigenous lifeways and sovereignty movements. A core tenant is the responsibility of humans to respect and care for nonhuman relations across the natural world, and to center reciprocity instead of extraction.

Rematriation offers a new way to see the land and our place in it.

Gratitude is a way of being in the world. Indigenous practices of gratitude remind us that everything needed to support life sustainably can be found in nature, and centers abundance rather than scarcity. The posture of gratitude challenges capitalist ideals and transactional interactions. Gratitude reveals our potential to reciprocally connect with things outside of ourselves and to build relationships rooted in abundance and contentment.

Gratitude is a revolutionary position.

Toward Joy

Sankofa is an important concept that resonates across the African diaspora, especially in Black American history and culture. Originating in Ghana, the word itself means to "go back" and "to retrieve." The popular symbol of the sankofa bird looking over its shoulder represents the necessity of examining the past in order to build one's future.

Sankofa is about knowledge transfer—about learning from the past.

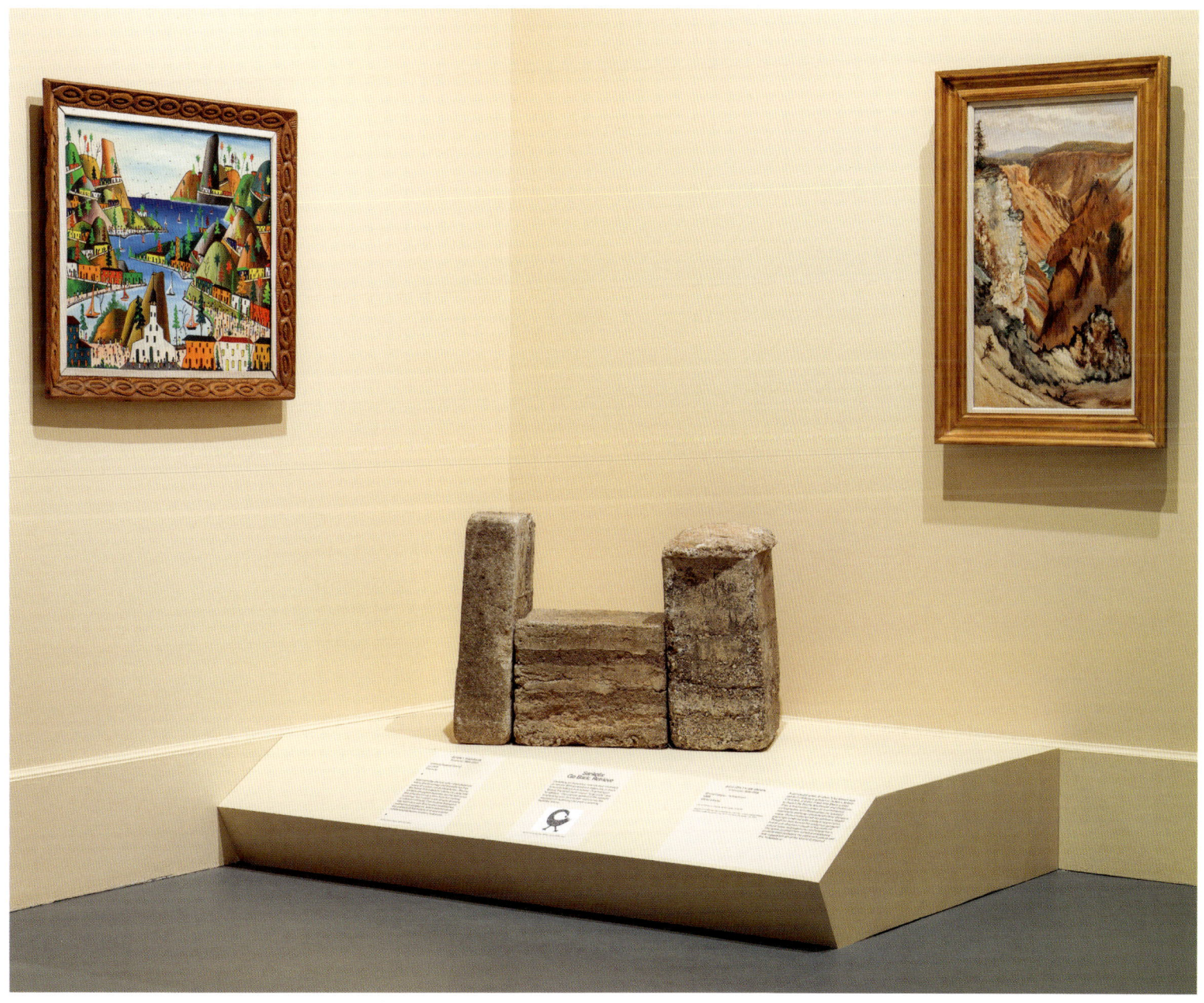

Radical Care

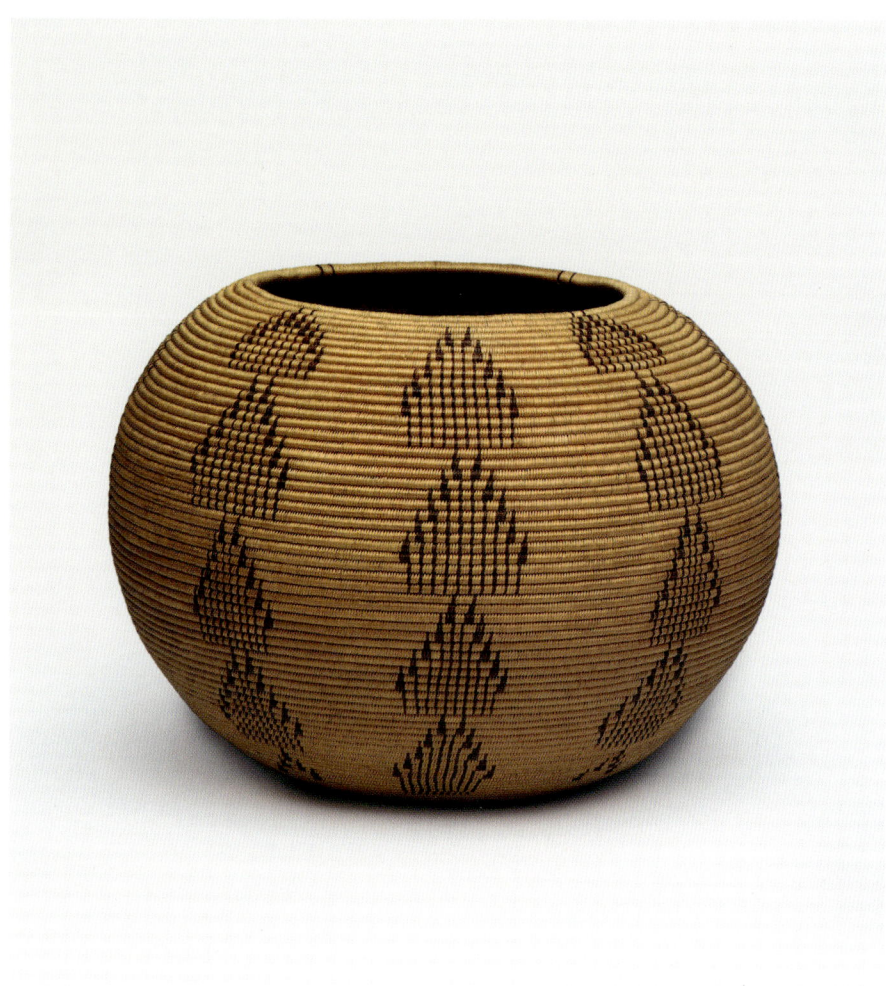

Louisa Keyser (Dat So La Lee)
(Washoe, 1850–1925)
Degikup Basket, 1900

Willow, bracken fern root, redbud, 8 × 10½ × 10½ in.
By exchange, 72.5.2
Provenance: Sold at The Emporium Company, December 20, 1900. Purchased at Sotheby's, New York, "Green Collection of American Indian Art" lot 137, by James Economos, November 19, 1971; purchased by the Brooklyn Museum, by exchange, January 18, 1972.

For longer than memory, Indigenous women have enacted and maintained cultural traditions through the creation of art. Many quintessential Native art forms exist firmly within the artistic domain of women. In fact, some estimates attribute up to 90 percent of Native American artworks in museum collections to female artists.[1] Art forms like basketry reflect the ways in which artists embraced and elaborated upon their people's creative traditions to manifest beauty in the world.

For countless generations, artists lived with, studied, and experimented with local plants to produce beautiful belongings. Through utilizing materials from the natural environment, Louisa Keyser (Washoe) pioneered the form of *degikup* baskets. Weaving from the bottom up, Keyser utilized a coiling technique in which she wrapped locally harvested willow threads around willow rods to create the item's tightly coiled circular form with its narrow base, wide center, and tapered top. Keyser used bracken fern root and redbud to create the decorative motif described as "hunting in the harvest time" in which the vertical shoots depict grain ready to be harvested, while the shapes at their tops represent arrow points.

Keyser created these sculptural baskets following a time of great cultural upheaval. While the Washoe community traditionally lived east of the Sierra Nevada mountains and near Lake Tahoe, the mid-nineteenth century discovery of gold and silver in that region led to an influx of non-Native settlers. Washoe people adapted to their changing circumstances; weavers like Keyser iterated on basketry traditions and created inventive pieces like this, which provided vital income and sustained artistic practices that may have otherwise been lost.

Basketry as an art form still thrives to this day. Contemporary artist Carol Emarthle Douglas's work *Gathering of Nations* builds upon the legacy of earlier generations of basket weavers. In this piece, women from eleven tribes offer both each other and the viewer baskets made from natural materials of their ancestral homelands. Each figure wears regalia emergent from her own tribal traditions and holds a basket crafted in the traditional style of her people. A technical marvel, four different basket weaving techniques appear in miniature—coiling, plaiting, twining, and plain weave. The artist says, "This basket is a tribute to our ancestors as weavers,

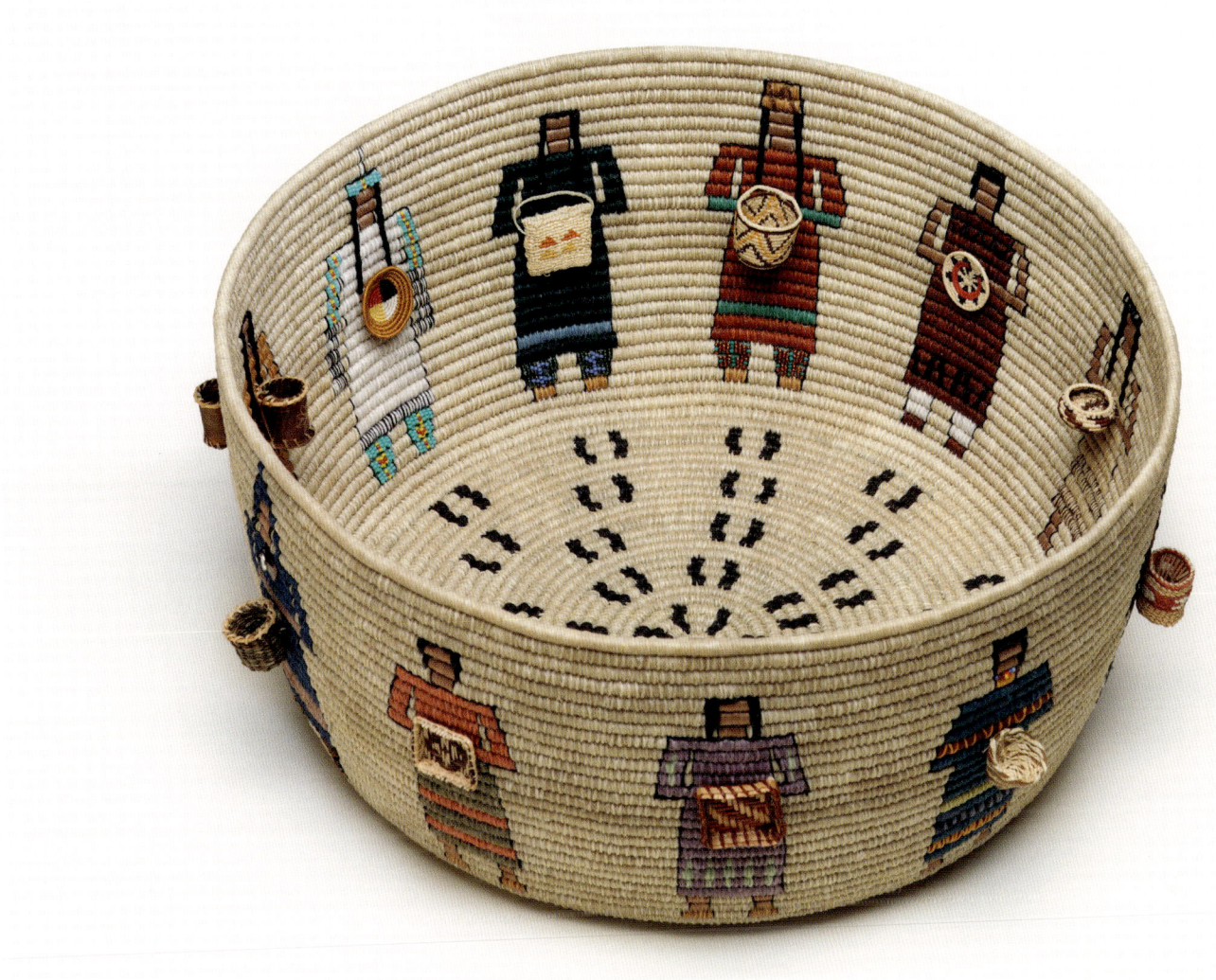

mothers, teachers, and culture carriers." *Gathering of Nations* embodies the concept of rematriation by acknowledging the crucial role of Native women as carriers of culture and illustrating what it means to have a positive and balanced relationship both with the natural world and with each other.

DT

1. This figure was ascertained by Jill Ahlberg Yohe, in conjunction with the 2019 exhibition *Hearts of Our People: Native Women Artists*, which she cocurated with Kiowa artist Teri Greeves. For additional context see Erica Cardwell, "The Undersung Art of Native American Women, Front and Center," *Hyperallergic*, August 15, 2019, https://hyperallergic.com/513465/hearts-of-our-people-native-women-artists/.

Carol Emarthle Douglas
(Northern Arapaho and Seminole, born 1959)
Gathering of Nations, 2010

Waxed linen thread, single-rod hemp core, red and yellow cedar, reed, raffia, sweetgrass, pine needles, silk thread, cherry bark, artificial sinew, 7 × 11½ × 11½ in.
Museum Collection Fund, 2011.5
Provenance: Purchased from the artist by the Brooklyn Museum, April 28, 2011.

Radical Care

A self-taught artist, Grafton Tyler Brown was the first landscape painter in Victoria, British Columbia, and one of the first African American artists to depict the American Pacific Northwest and California. Born in Harrisburg, Pennsylvania, Brown migrated to San Francisco when he was seventeen years old, and built a successful decades-long commercial cartography and lithography practice before selling his business to pursue landscape painting.[1] An intrepid outdoorsman, Brown traveled extensively to paint arresting canvases of iconic western vistas. By the time he completed these scenic views of Wyoming's Yellowstone National Park, Brown had lived and worked as a painter in Victoria, British Columbia, and Portland, Oregon, and had traveled to paint other well-known sites such as Yosemite in California.

Brown's luminous paintings, created in his studio, are rendered with clarity and precision. Despite maintaining the analytical perspective of a draftsman, he used a loose and expressive technique in *Grand Canyon, Yellowstone*. Here he applied varied and textured brushstrokes to depict the sulfur-rich yellow soil and rugged terrain.

Brown's Yellowstone canvases represent his longest sustained work—six years—within a particular environment. During this time the artist took advantage of local and tourist markets, engaging in a wide variety of advertising practices. For his Yellowstone paintings, Brown produced twenty-eight lithographic compositions of rugged terrain and breathtaking vistas, all rendered with boldness and authority. This painted-to-order menu allowed clients to select from vantages across the great river canyon and the western geyser belt. Using this approach—a counterpoint to widely acclaimed Hudson River School paintings made for East Coast patrons—Brown produced hundreds of paintings, each representing a unique combination of size, vista, support, and brushwork.

SSW

1. Robert J. Chandler, *San Francisco Lithographer: African American Artist Grafton Tyler Brown* (Norman, OK: University of Oklahoma Press, 2014).

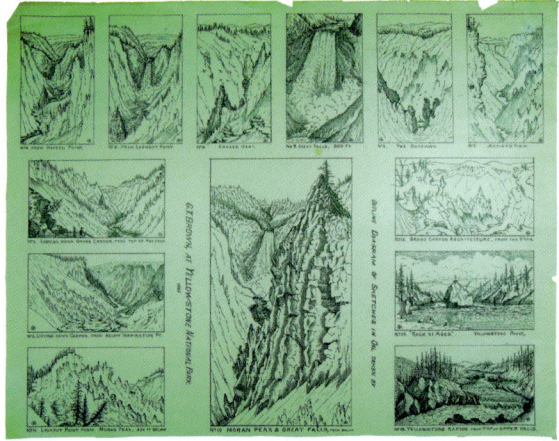

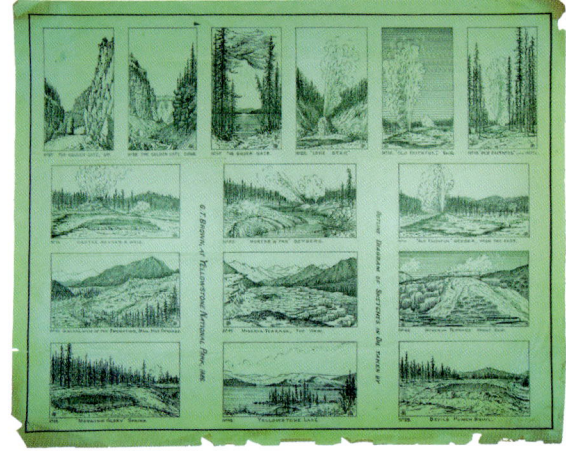

Outline Diagram of Sketches in Oil Taken by G. T. Brown, at Yellowstone National Park, 1886, reproduction of lithograph
Reprinted by permission of the publisher

THE CONSERVATOR'S EYE

In addition to its materials and painting techniques, an artwork's condition can also affect how it looks—and *Grand Canyon, Yellowstone* is a prime example. Conservation research revealed that a thin lead soap crust (a type of paint degradation) had formed on the surface and that the painting was abraded during cleaning prior to its acquisition by the Brooklyn Museum. The result is a cloudy, softened appearance to the artist's original brushwork.

Informed by a close study of comparative paintings by Brown, recent conservation treatment worked to restore the painting's clarity through careful cleaning, revarnishing, and retouching. This required addressing the impact of the aged paint while adhering to Brown's original vision. To bring out the artist's original brushstrokes, the conservator suppressed portions of the lead soap crust and knitted together areas of abrasion with tiny strokes of reversible paint.

EN

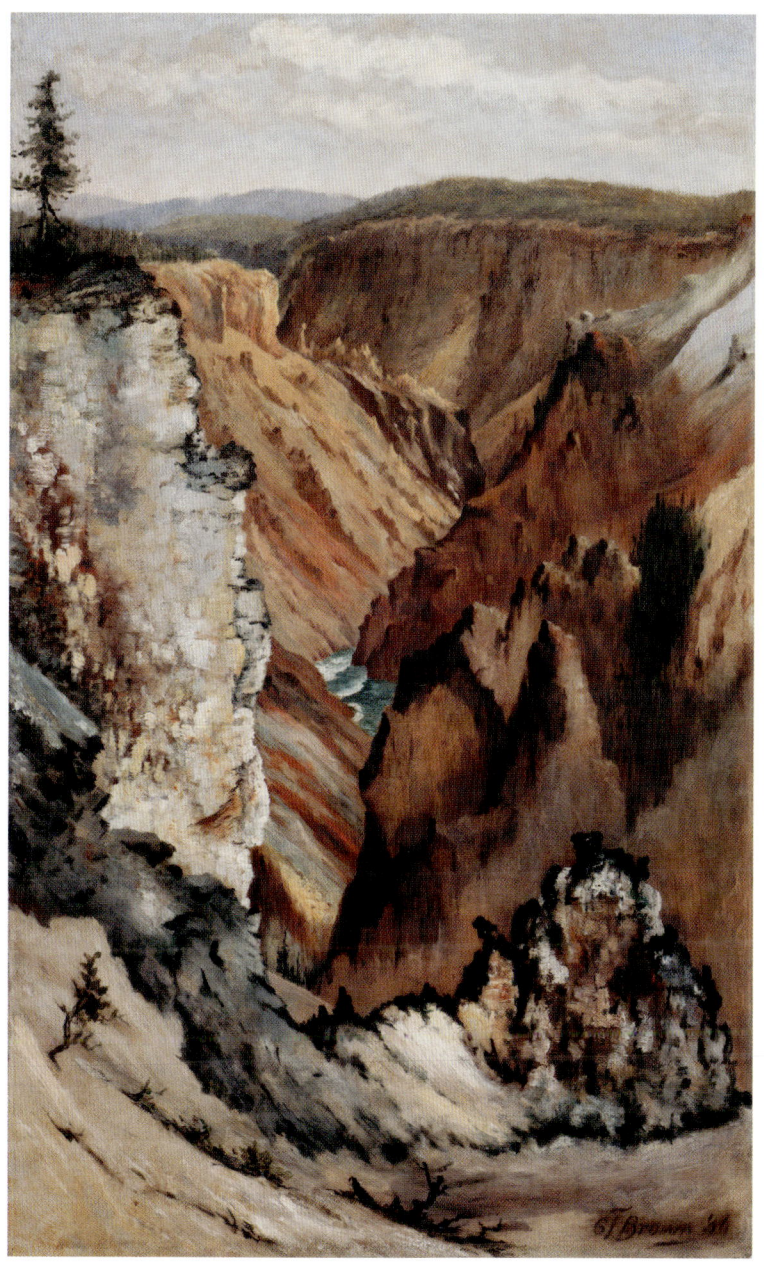
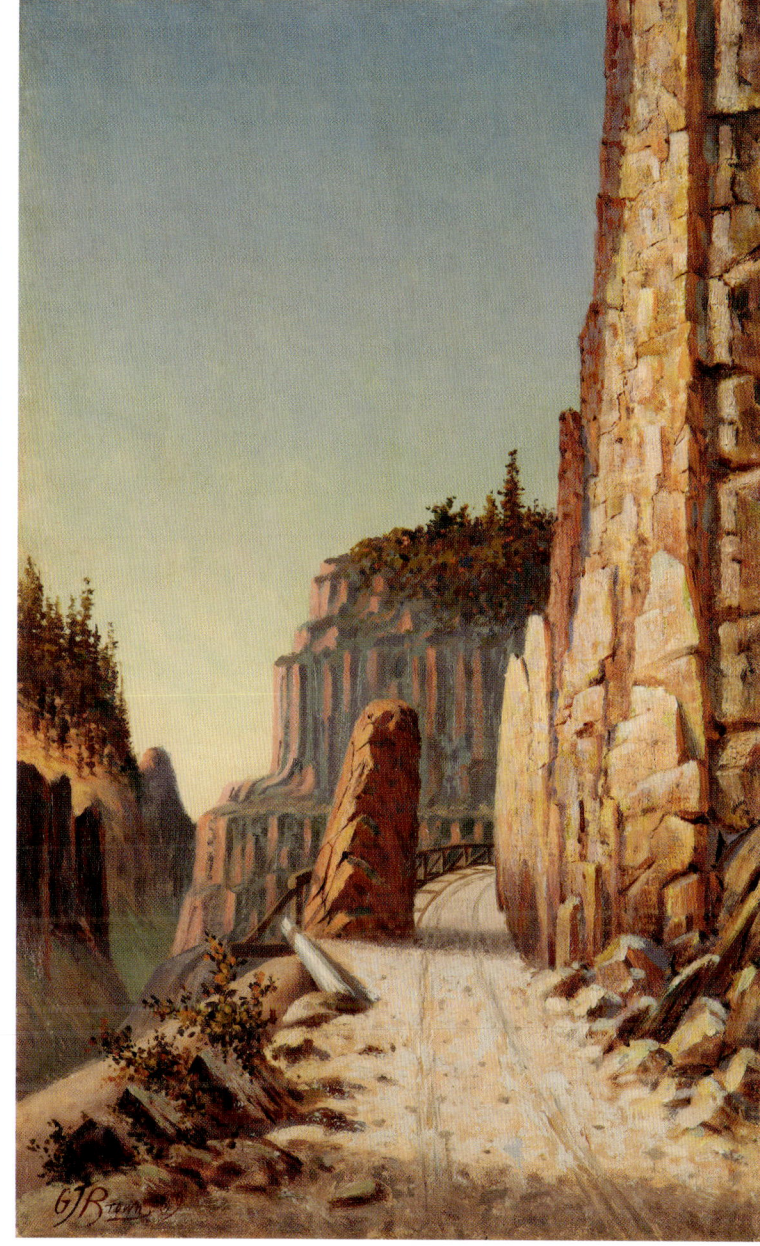

Grafton Tyler Brown
(American, 1841–1918)
Grand Canyon, Yellowstone, 1886

Oil on canvas, 29¾ × 17½ × 3⅞ in.
Gift of Milton and Nancy Washington, 2012.92
Provenance: Acquired by Michael Rosenfeld Gallery, by 1997; purchased by Milton and Nancy Washington, June 1997; donated, December 31, 2012.

Golden Gate, Yellowstone, 1889

Oil on canvas board, 19⁹⁄₁₆ × 13⁹⁄₁₆ × 1⁷⁄₁₆ in.
Gift of Charlynn and Warren Goins, 2022.42
Provenance: Prior to 1987, provenance not yet documented; 1987, purchased from an unidentified antique shop by Nancy Kuhn of Bakersfield, CA; between 1987 and 2003, provenance not yet documented; by 2003, acquired by Braarud Fine Arts, La Conner, WA; January 2003, purchased from Braarud Fine Arts by Charlynn and Warren Goins of New York, NY; donated, December 2022.

Radical Care

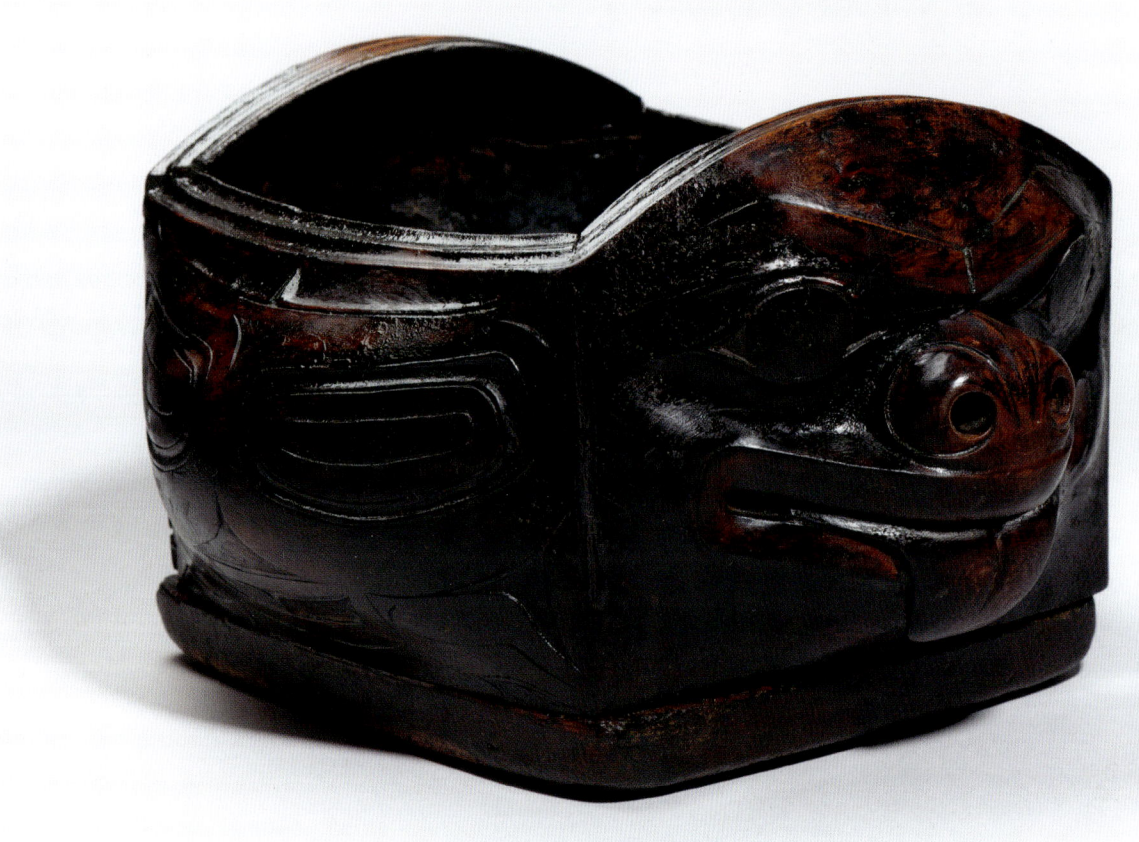

Haida artist
Bear Feast Bowl
Haida Gwaii, British Columbia, Canada, 19th century

Wood, plant fiber, twine, 8 × 13½ × 12 in.
Museum Expedition 1905, Museum Collection Fund, 05.251
Provenance: Acquired by the Brooklyn Museum, before 1930s.

Indigenous Community Perspective: Haida Carving

Master Haida carvers created these works with expert love and care, balancing both beauty and function for everyday use. Collected in the nineteenth century from Haida Gwaii, an archipelago off the coast of the Pacific Northwest of Canada, each work is adorned with intricate carvings in a style known as "formline." The two bowls display crests—one of a seal and the other of a bear—while the handle of the mountain-goat horn spoon shows three birds. Figures depicted throughout our art represent who we are and where our lineage comes from, as each clan within our nation has their own crests, songs, and stories.

Such pieces would be used in feast and potlatch ceremonies. Potlatches are integral in our culture—at such gatherings, we conduct business within our nation, celebrate important events, gift Haida names to clan members, and share cultural knowledge. Though the Christian church and government systems tried to strip our culture away from us, our treasures and cultural objects hold a high importance to this day. Although these items were not made to be displayed in a museum, Indigenous community members continue to build relationships with museums to reconnect with our cultural belongings and our history.

—SGidGang.Xaal (Shoshannah Greene), Haida artist

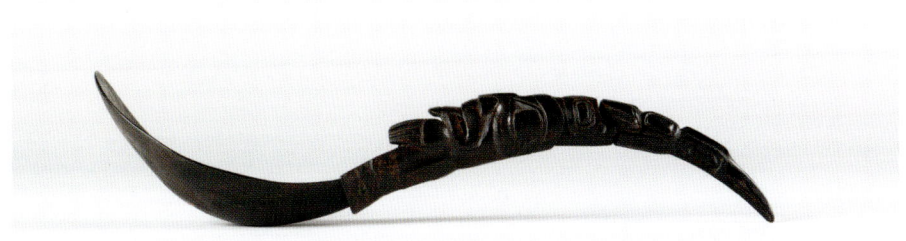

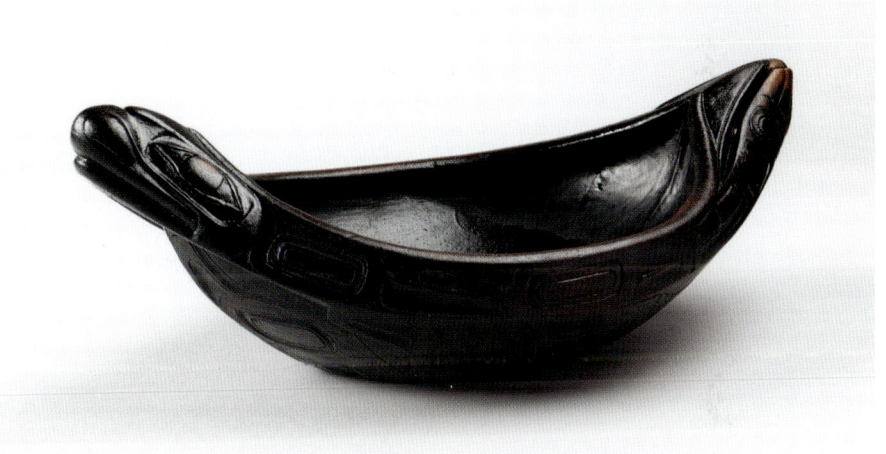

Haida artist
Spoon with Carved Handle
Skidegate, Haida Gwaii, British Columbia, Canada, 19th century

Mountain goat horn, copper alloy rivets, 11 × 2 9/16 × 1 in.
Museum Expedition 1905, Museum Collection Fund, 05.304
Provenance: Acquired by the Brooklyn Museum, before 1930s.

Haida artist
Seal Feast Bowl
Skidegate, Haida Gwaii, British Columbia, Canada, 19th century

Wood, 5¼ × 14¼ × 8½ in.
Museum Expedition 1905, Museum Collection Fund, 05.588.7321
Provenance: Acquired in Skidgate, Canada by Charles Frederick Newcombe, before 1905; purchased in Victoria, Canada by Stewart Culin for the Brooklyn Museum, August 13, 1905.

Radical Care

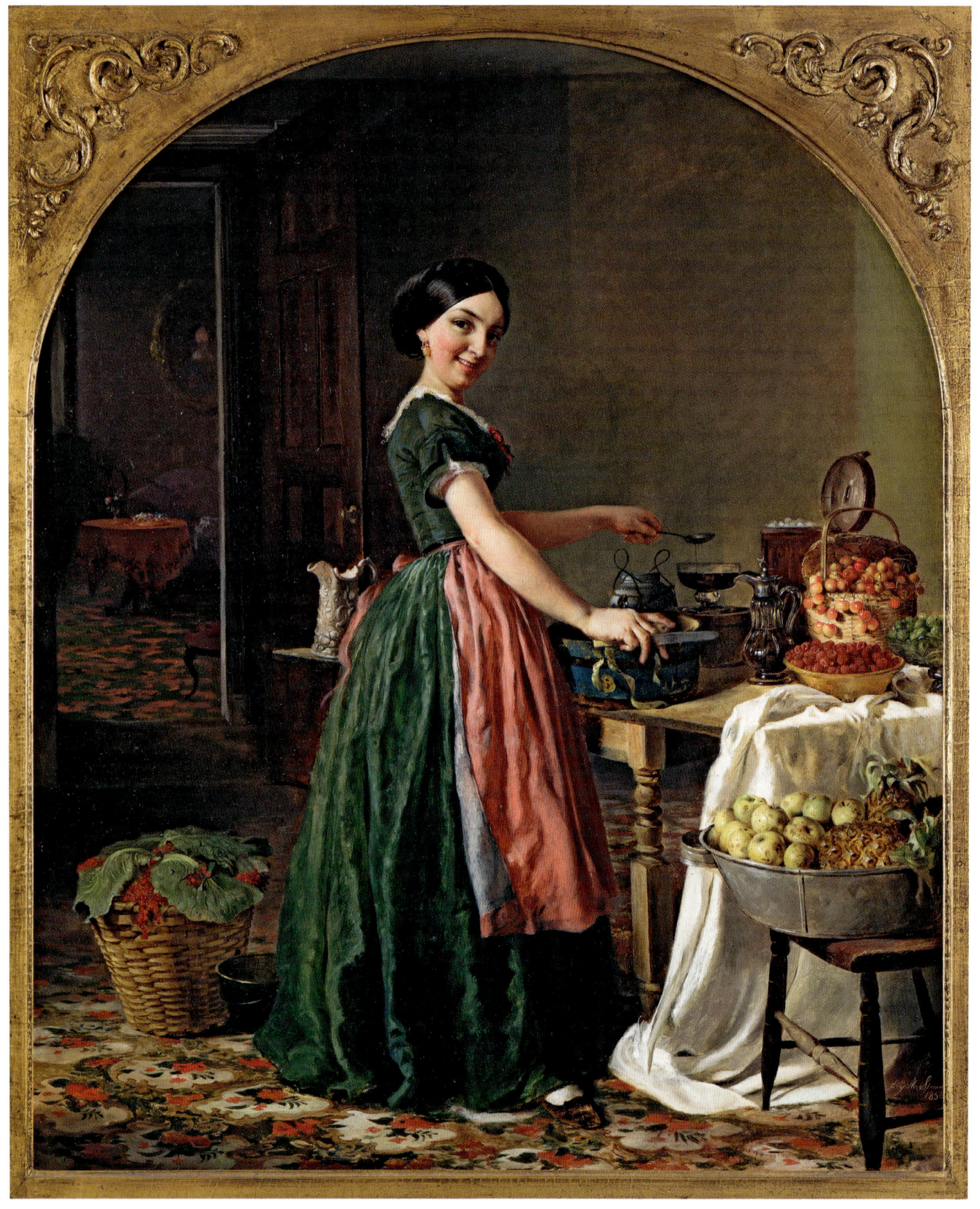

Toward Joy

Lilly Martin Spencer
(American, born England, 1822–1902)
Kiss Me and You'll Kiss the 'Lasses, 1856

Oil on canvas, 29¹⁵⁄₁₆ × 24¹⁵⁄₁₆ in.
A. Augustus Healy Fund, 70.26
Provenance: Commissioned from the artist by the Cosmopolitan Art Association, 1856. Acquired by E. A. Carman, 1857. Acquired by Bernard Danenberg Galleries, by March 3, 1970; purchased by the Brooklyn Museum, April 15, 1970.

In a rare exhibition of independence and industry, painter Lilly Martin Spencer established herself as a working artist in the early-to-mid-nineteenth century, as well as the sole economic provider for her husband and children. Best known for her genre scenes depicting women in the domestic sphere, Spencer's popularity coincided with the taste for displaying still lifes and genre scenes in middle-class American homes. Her niche focus distinguished her work in a market focused on the quotidian interactions of men.

In *Kiss Me and You'll Kiss the 'Lasses*, the artist depicts herself as an exuberant and playful housewife, taking pleasure in her task and company. She is smartly dressed in pink and green, a palette reflected in the luscious fruits that surround her, and in the richly colored rose and foliage patterned rug below her feet. Containers of apples, cherries, currants, gooseberries, pineapples, and raspberries abound around a table laden with syrups and a box of sugar cubes used for preserving or sugaring. As the title implies, this bold young woman promises a dose of molasses to the person advancing to kiss her. And while one might assume the flirtation is being received by a male viewer, Spencer's paintings are for women audiences, who likely saw in them favorable, empowered, and good-natured representations of themselves.

SSW

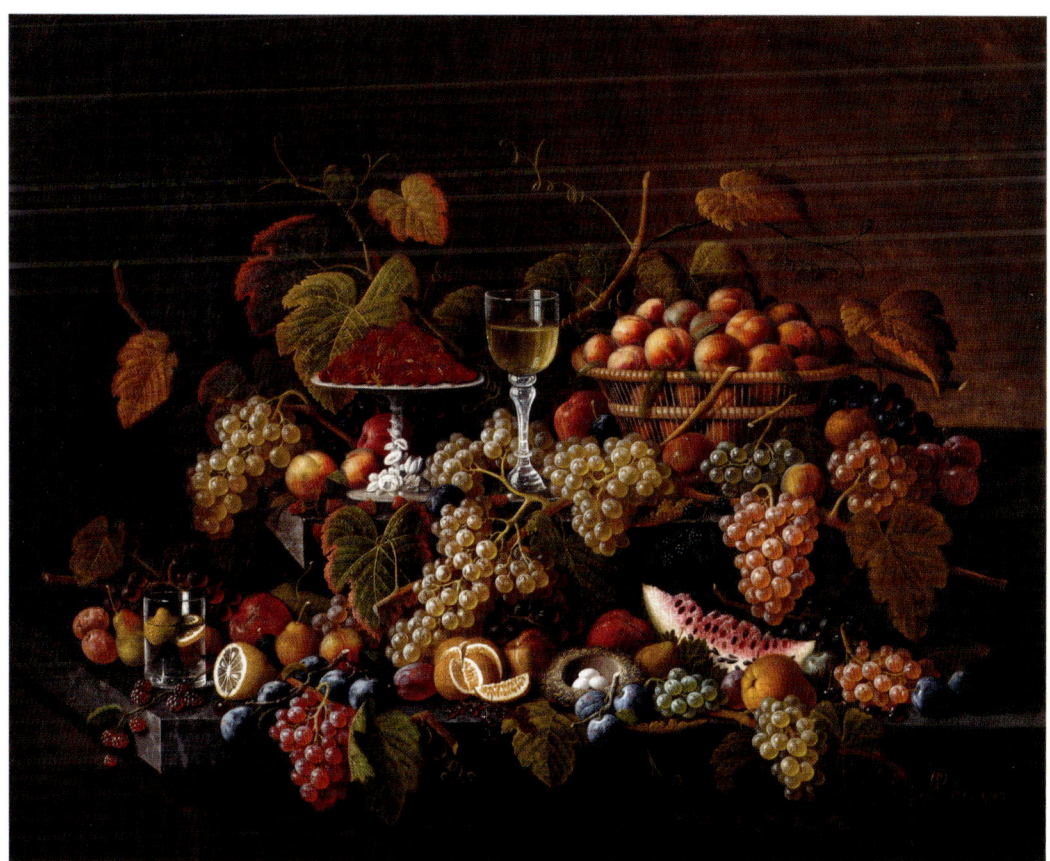

Severin Roesen
(American, born Germany, ca. 1815–after 1872)
Still Life with Fruit, ca. 1860

Oil on canvas, 40¹⁄₁₆ × 50⅛ in.
Dick S. Ramsay Fund, 67.9
Provenance: Acquired by Mrs. Gilbert Hitchcock, before 1966. Acquired by Robert G. Osborne, by December 23, 1966; purchased by the Brooklyn Museum, November 11, 1967.

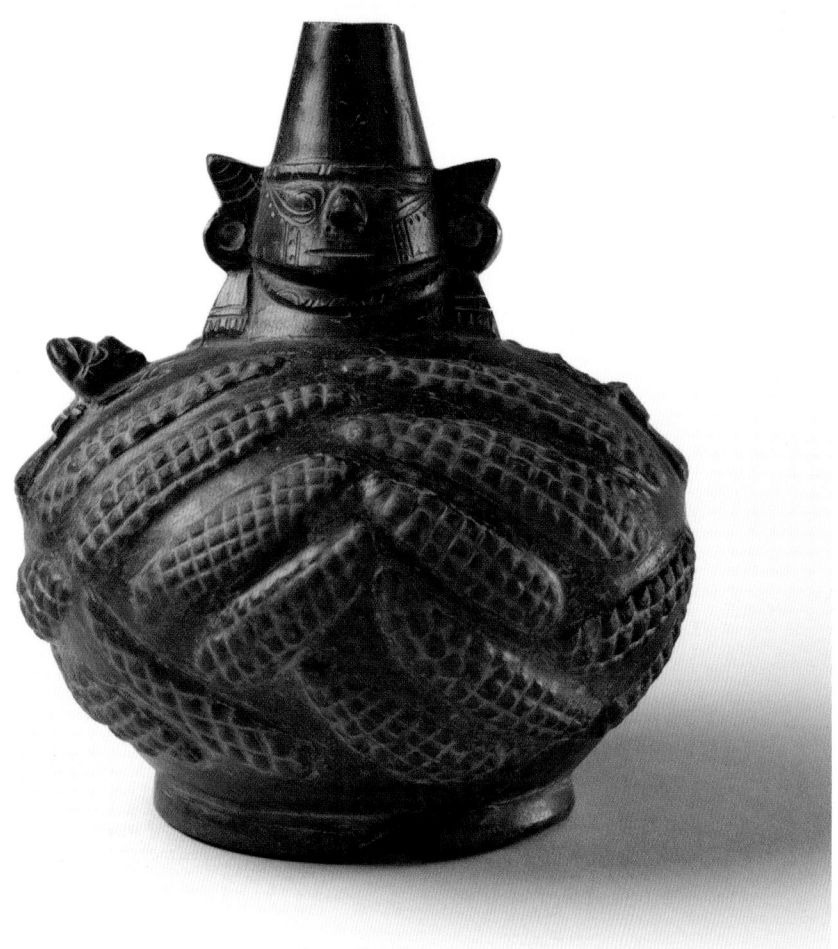

Sicán artist
Bottle with Sicán Deity
North Coast, Peru, 1000–1050

Ceramic, 6 5/16 × 5 3/4 × 6 1/2 in.
Gift of Mrs. Eugene Schaefer, 36.320
Provenance: Acquired by Mrs. Eugene Schaefer, by 1936; donated, July 1, 1936.

The ancient Sicán people, who inhabited the northern coast of Peru from 800 to 1375, practiced intensive irrigation agriculture and cultivated plants such as maize, a dietary staple. Mold-made ceramic vessels with lustrous black surfaces were among the hallmarks of this culture. This black, spouted bottle with a strap handle at the back depicts the culture hero known as the Sicán Deity, who is believed to have established an important ruling dynasty.[1] The god is depicted emerging from a pile of maize cobs that make up his body. The association of maize with the Deity reflects its sacred significance to the Sicán people. The Deity is accompanied by a prone human figure on the proper right (the left figure is lost), perhaps representing an attendant in the supernatural realm, and two birds, possibly parrots, standing beak-to-beak on the handle. Research by archaeologist Izumi Shimada reveals that parrots appear during the rainy season in coastal Peru, so their representation on this vessel may allude to the importance of water for a successful harvest.[2] Rain is further referenced in the rows of dots, interpreted as tears, below the Deity's eyes.[3] Together, these sustenance- and fertility-related elements demonstrate the Sicán people's desire to maintain cosmic order through veneration of the Sicán Deity in one of the most arid places on Earth, a region that is vulnerable to droughts, earthquakes, and flash floods.

1. Izumi Shimada, "The Sicán Culture: Its Development, Characteristics and Legacies," *Cultural Sicán: Esplendor Preinca de la Costa Norte*, ed. Izumi Shimada (Lima, Peru: Fondo Editorial del Congreso del Perú, 2013), 12–13, https://www.academia.edu/74657702/The_Sic%C3%A1n_Culture_Its_Development_Characteristics_and_Legacies.
2. Ibid., 14.
3. Ibid.

NR

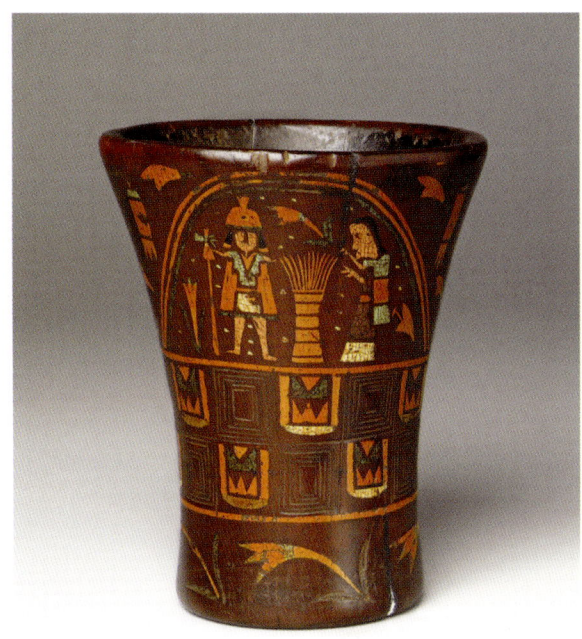
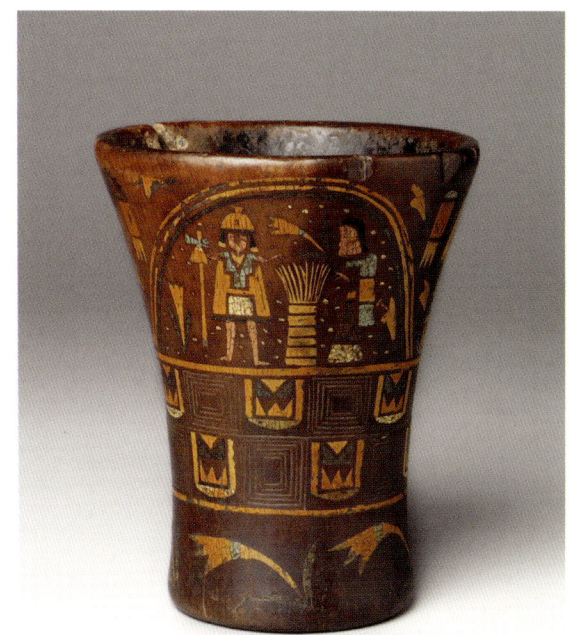

Quechua artist
Qero Cup
Peru, late 16th–17th century

Wood, resin, pigment, 7¹³⁄₁₆ × 6½ × 6½ in.
Gift of Dr. Werner Muensterberger, 64.210.2
Provenance: Acquired by Werner Muensterberger, by November 1964; donated, December 19, 1964.

Quechua artist
Qero Cup
Peru, late 16th–17th century

Wood, resin, pigment, 7¹³⁄₁₆ × 6½ × 6½ in.
A. Augustus Healy Fund, 1993.2
Provenance: Acquired by Fine Arts of Ancient Lands, Inc., by 1993; purchased by the Brooklyn Museum, January 21, 1993.

The ancient Inca of South America, who ruled a vast empire from 1438 to 1532, used *qeros*—paired wooden cups meant for fermented maize beer (*a'qa* in Quechua)—during ceremonial toasts that affirmed reciprocal social, political, and religious relationships. These cups were decorated with incised, geometrical designs that reflected the Inca aesthetic of uniform, non-figural abstraction.[1] After the Spanish conquest in 1532–33, Inca woodworkers known as *querocamayocs* (*qero*-makers), continued the tradition of incising and dividing the cup's decorative surface into two or more horizontal registers, but they added painted scenes of flora, fauna, and people influenced by European artistic styles.[2] This pair of *qeros* with three registers includes both decorative techniques. The upper register features an Inca king and a *coya*, or queen, standing under a rainbow, a symbol of rain and fertility.[3] The king wears a short tunic, rounded helmet, and holds a staff, while the *coya*, depicted in a long dress and shawl, holds a long-stemmed flower (*chiwanway*).[4] The grass (*ichhu*) bundle between them was used by the Inca to build house roofs and rope bridges.[5] Frontal feline heads between the rainbows symbolize openings in the earth from which rainbows were believed to emerge. The middle register is decorated with incised concentric squares and painted shields, and the lower register contains *chiwanway* flowers. The painted decoration was created by filling incised cavities in the wood with mopa mopa, a tree resin, colored with local mineral and plant pigments.[6] The Quechua makers of these *qeros* combined Inca subjects, Andean flora and fauna, and local materials and techniques with a European narrative style to create a uniquely Spanish American art form.

NR

1. Thomas B. F. Cummins, *Toasts with the Inca: Andean Abstraction and Colonial Images on Quero Vessels* (Ann Arbor: The University of Michigan Press, 2002), 25.
2. Ibid., 20–21, 121.
3. Ibid., 262.
4. Ibid., 190.
5. Jorge A. Flores Ochoa, Elizabeth Kuon Arce, and Roberto Samanez Argumedo, *Qeros: Arte Inka en Vasos Ceremoniales* (Lima, Peru: Banco de Crédito del Perú, 1998), 201–202; Ramiro Matos Mendieta and José Barreiro, *The Great Inka Road: Engineering an Empire* (Washington, DC: National Museum of the American Indian in association with Smithsonian Books, 2015), 168.
6. See Ellen J. Pearlstein, Emily Klaplan, Ellen Howe, and Judith Levinson, "Technical Analyses of Painted Inka and Colonial Qeros," *Objects Specialty Group Postprints*, Volume Six, 1999, 94–111, https://resources.culturalheritage.org/wp-content/uploads/sites/8/2015/02/osg006-07.pdf.

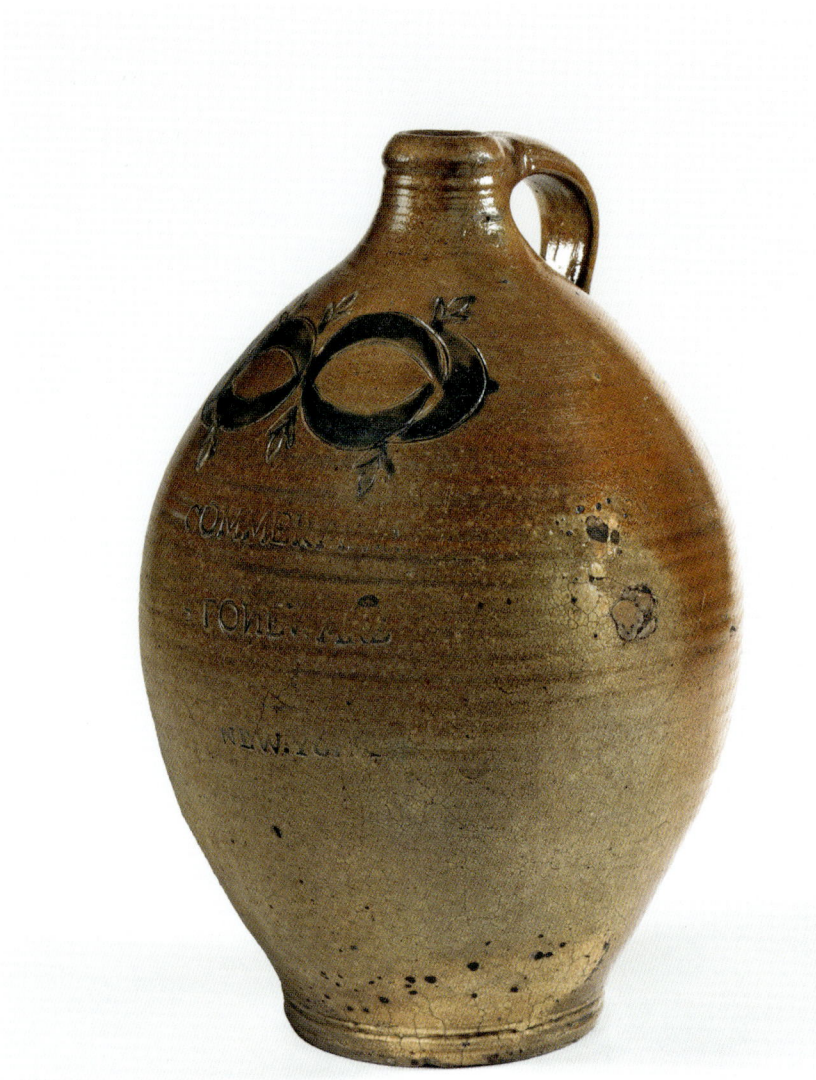

Thomas W. Commeraw
(American, ca. 1772–1823)
Jug, early 19th century

Glazed stoneware, 15 × 10 × 10 in.
Gift of Arthur W. Clement, 43.128.12
Provenance: Acquired by Arthur W. Clement, by 1942; donated, May 27, 1943.

Thomas Commeraw was an African American potter known for his stoneware vessels that came in a variety of shapes for storing liquids, as in this example, or foodstuffs like grain, oysters, and preservatives. This jug is typical of Commeraw's pottery: incised with Commeraw's name, the location of production, and floral decoration, all accented with cobalt blue pigment. Born enslaved, from the 1790s to 1819 he operated a kiln as a free business owner in the Corlears Hook neighborhood on Manhattan's Lower East Side. Until recently, Commeraw's racial identity had been suppressed. But historical documentation reveals that he wrote pamphlets engaging in national and local political debates, was active in the free Black community and his religious congregation, and was a powerful voice for abolition. In 1820 he traveled to Sierra Leone as an advocate for the American Colonization Society, which endorsed the return of free African Americans to Africa. He was initially optimistic about the colony's mission and success, describing the beauty and fertility of the land. However, the Society maintained rigid control over the freedoms of the inhabitants, and with the death of his second wife during a forced relocation of the settlement, Commeraw was motivated to return to the United States in about 1822.

LSG

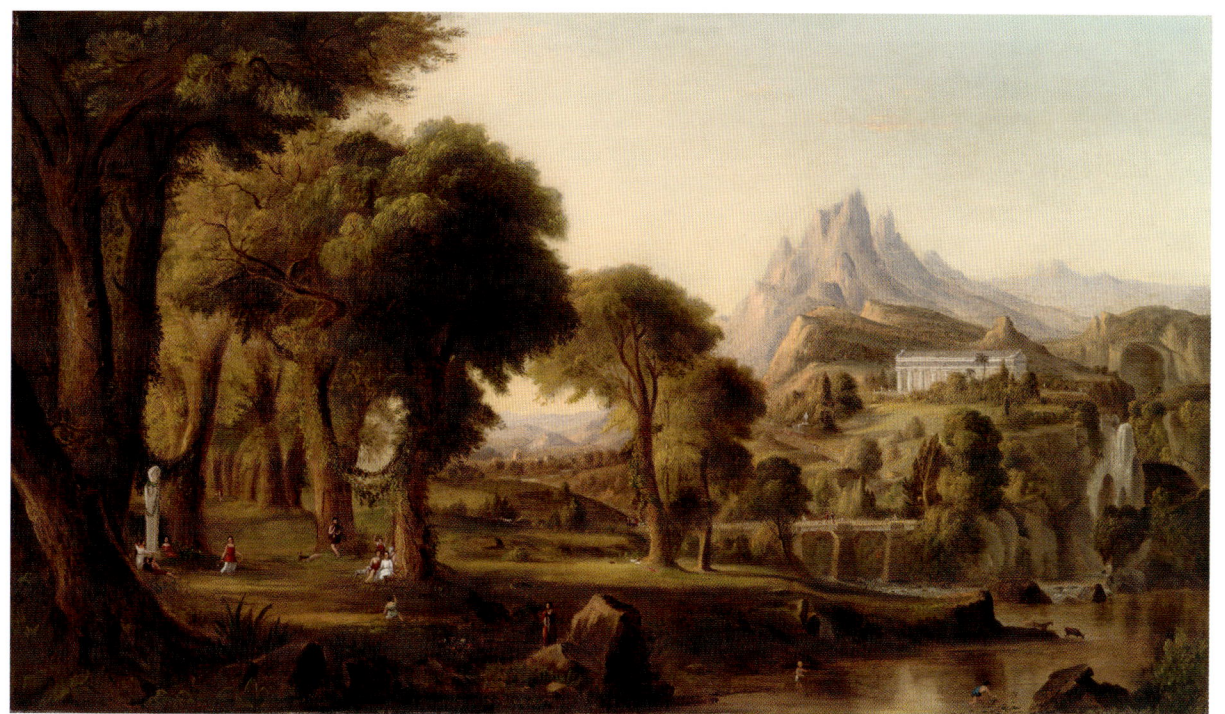

Robert Seldon Duncanson
(American, 1821–1872)
Copy after Thomas Cole's "Dream of Arcadia," 1852

Oil on canvas, 24 × 42 in. Gift of Charlynn and Warren Goins, 2020.13.1 Provenance: Before 1991, acquired by the Dinsmore family of Cincinnati, OH; by 1991, acquired by Cincinnati Art Galleries, Cincinnati; January 1991, purchased at Cincinnati Art Galleries by Charlynn and Warren Goins; 2020, gift of Charlynn and Warren Goins to the Brooklyn Museum.

Born into a family of free Black carpenters and house painters, Robert Seldon Duncanson excelled in the family business before traveling as an itinerant portrait painter and photographer.[1] After settling in the Cincinnati, Ohio, area in the early 1840s, he shifted his focus to genre scenes and landscapes, painting this iteration of Thomas Cole's *Dream of Arcadia* (ca. 1838).

Self-taught, Duncanson copied engravings of other artists' paintings, many of which were in the romanticized style of the Hudson River School. He was likely also exposed to the work of Cole and others in person in public exhibitions, where they were regularly shown, or in the homes of his local patrons. Many of the compositional features that appear in *Dreams of Arcadia* can be observed in landscapes the artist completed before and after his European grand tour in 1853. Elements like majestic mountain peaks (background), cascading falls (far right), tranquil and reflective waters (foreground), groupings of trees that often frame important vistas (middle-ground, center left), and the subtle or overt presence of humans. Duncanson was a central figure of the Ohio River Valley regional landscape painting school and was lauded by local media as one of the best in the West.[2]

One of the last paintings completed before his first trip abroad, *Dream of Arcadia* captures the classical Greek paradise, where humans live in harmony with nature. Though likely made for white patronage, in its subtle nod to the landscape of the North, the work's idea of a tranquil promised land undoubtedly resonated with Duncanson and other free and enslaved Black people in the United States. While a small number of scholars have given in-depth attention to Duncanson's trajectory as a significant nineteenth-century landscape painter, there is still much work to be done into the critical reception of his paintings, and the experience of the artist himself as a light-skinned Black man amid the polarizing tensions before and after the Civil War.

SSW

1. Joseph D. Ketner has completed the most extensive study of Duncanson's life and works to date, having published an important monograph in 1993, and amassing an impressive research archive and catalogue of known works by the artist. These resources along with Ketner's papers related to Duncanson are now housed with the Archives of American Art. See Joseph D. Ketner, *The Emergence of the African-American Artist: Robert S. Duncanson 1821–1872.* (Columbia: University of Missouri Press, 1993).
2. For more on Duncanson, the Ohio River Valley school, and the artist's acclaim and success as a landscape painter see Joseph D. Ketner "The Spiritual Striving of the Freedmen's Sons," in *Robert S. Duncanson: "The Spiritual Striving of the Freedmen's Sons"* (Catskill, NY: Thomas Cole National Historic Site, 2011).

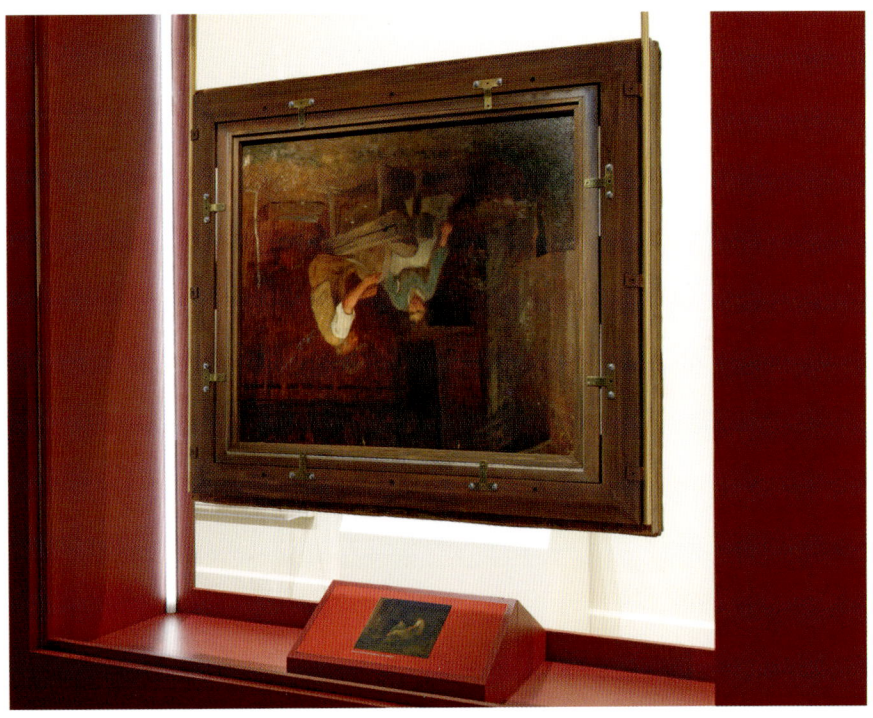

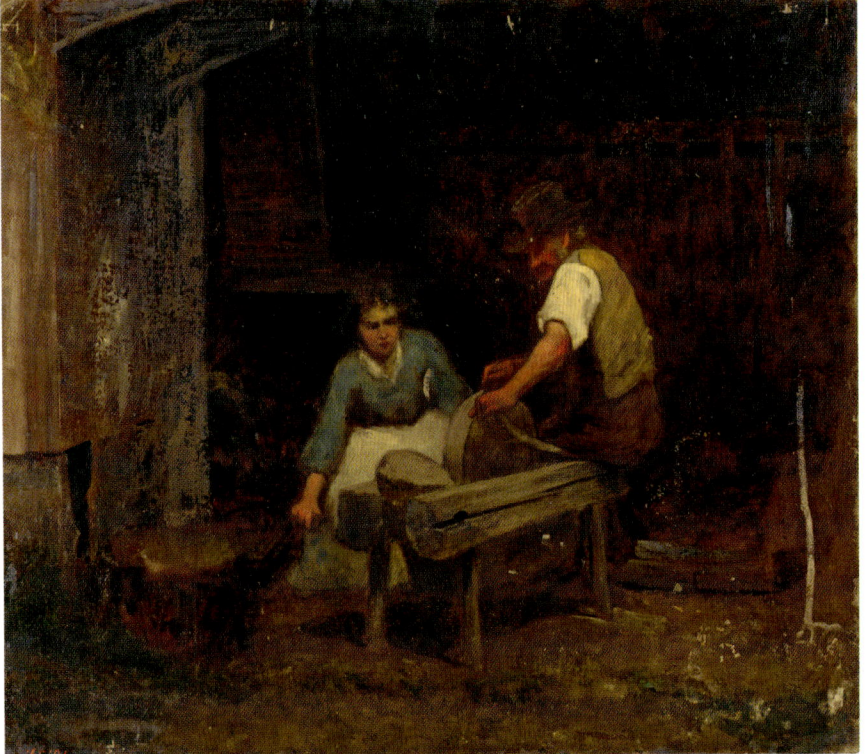

Eastman Johnson
(American, 1824–1906)
[Study for Sharpening the Scythe], ca. 1862

Oil on paperboard
Gift of Gwendolyn O. L. Conkling, 40.59a-b
Provenance: Inherited from the artist by Elizabeth Williams Buckley Johnson, 1906; inherited by Ethel Eastman Johnson Conkling, 1927; inherited by Gwendolyn O. L. Conkling, 1931; donated, February 26, 1940.

What am I looking at?
Shown here and in the galleries is the back (or verso) of *A Ride for Liberty—The Fugitive Slaves* (1862), an iconic painting by leading mid-nineteenth-century figure painter Eastman Johnson. At the center, a man and woman sharpen a scythe, a theme the artist would return to and fully realize in another of the Museum's paintings, *Sharpening the Scythe* (1865). Like many of his contemporaries and centuries of artists before him, Johnson recycled his painting supports.

What can we learn from the back of a painting?
Recycled supports are part of a body of evidence researchers collect to better understand an artist's studio practice. Artistic process, production dates, and even shifts in patron tastes can all be gleaned from the back of a painting.

The display of the painting in a suspended frame allows curators and visitors alike to study both sides of the piece.

Why display a discarded and upside-down picture on the back of an iconic painting?
Simple—to give audiences unique access to an important work in the collection. In turn, this provides a rare vantage into the practice of a significant American painter.

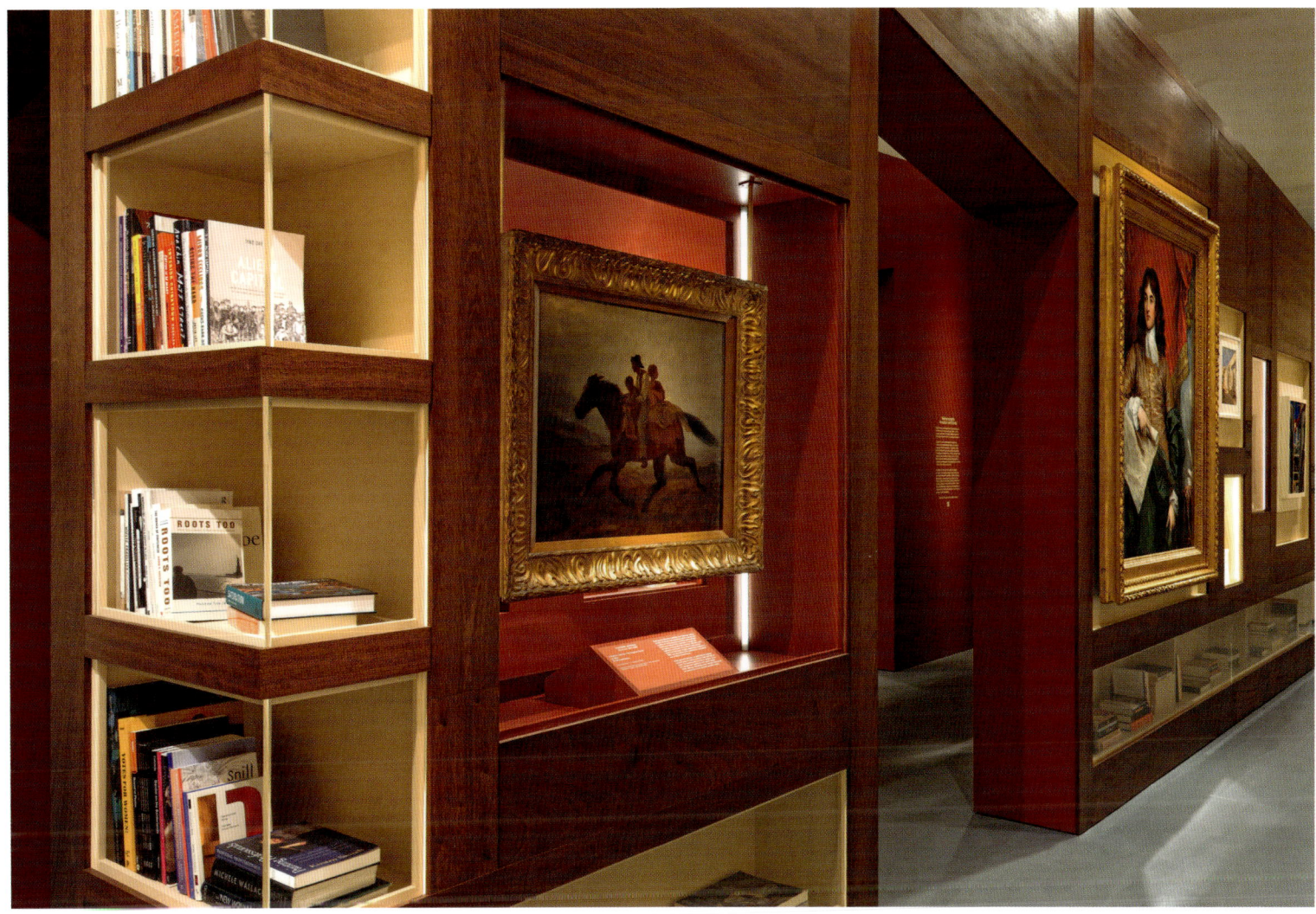

Eastman Johnson
(American, 1824–1906)
A Ride for Liberty—The Fugitive Slaves, ca. 1862

Oil on paperboard, 21¹⁵⁄₁₆ × 26⅛ in.
Gift of Gwendolyn O. L. Conkling, 40.59a-b
Provenance: Inherited from the artist by Elizabeth Williams Buckley Johnson, 1906; inherited by Ethel Eastman Johnson Conkling, 1927; inherited by Gwendolyn O. L. Conkling, 1931; donated, February 26, 1940.

During and after the American Civil War, few American artists undertook direct representations of the catastrophic conflict or of the experience of the enslaved Black Americans whose fate it decided. A remarkable exception is this painting by Eastman Johnson, who claimed the subject was based on an event he witnessed near the Manassas, Virginia, battlefield on March 2, 1862, just days before the Confederate stronghold was ceded to Union forces.

In this powerful composition, a family fleeing enslavement charges for the Union line in the dull light of dawn. The painting affirms that its subjects were the independent agents of their own freedom, and while it appears Johnson never exhibited this work, he painted the scene at least two other times.

SSW

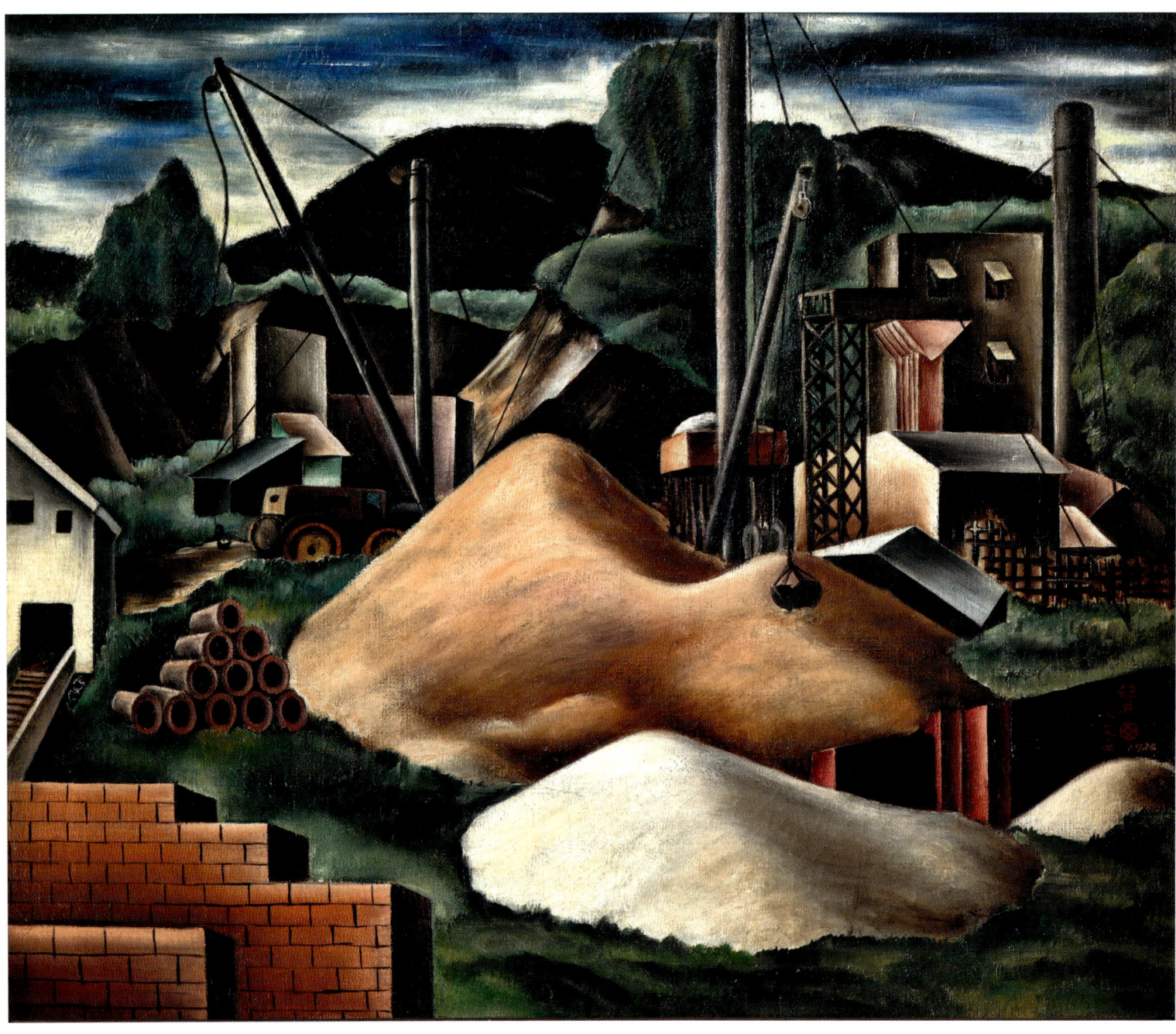

Bumpei Usui
(American, born Japan, 1898–1994)
Bronx, N.Y., 1924

Oil on canvas, 20¼ × 24¼ in.
Dick S. Ramsay Fund, 2022.35
Provenance: Acquired by Salander-O'Reilly Galleries, by 1992; purchased by Arthur Imperatore, Sr., 1992; donated to Stevens Institute of Technology, 1998; consigned to Gallery 511, 1998; purchased by the Brooklyn Museum, October 25, 2022.

In *Bronx, N.Y.*, Bumpei Usui explores industrial development in the Bronx, New York.[1] Between 1900 and 1929, rural land in the borough was rapidly transformed as manufacturing businesses were established and urban settlement expanded to accommodate the immigrant communities flocking to the area. In Usui's painting, a verdant landscape becomes a construction zone as raw materials overtake a composition devoid of human presence, drawing attention to transformations in the environment. Emphasis on the geometric shape of bricks and buildings and the exaggerated flattened angularity of the landscape demonstrates Usui's interest in American Modernist styles such as Precisionism. The stylistic influence of Yasuo Kuniyoshi (1889–1953), with whom Usui established a close friendship, is apparent in the expressive sky and green landscape.

Born in Nagano, Japan, Usui trained as a furniture maker before immigrating to the United States. He arrived in New York in 1921, and worked for a time at a furniture factory. Perhaps this experience sparked his interest in manufacturing businesses around the city. Usui was also an accomplished frame maker, and he carved frames for many of his artist contemporaries including Kuniyoshi and Reginald Marsh (1898–1954), as well as for collector Abby Aldrich Rockefeller (1874–1948).[2] Usui likely faced the pervasive xenophobia in the United States that led to the prohibition of Japanese immigration by the Johnson-Reed Act in 1924, the same year *Bronx, N.Y.* was painted. Yet despite this prejudice, Usui moved in Modernist artistic circles, and this painting affirms his stylistic contributions to American Modernism.

CG

1. *Bronx, N.Y.* was acquired in October 2022 as part of the American art department's Asian American Acquisition Initiative.
2. *American Art at the Virginia Museum of Fine Arts* (Richmond: Virginia Museum of Fine Arts; Charlottesville: In association with University of Virginia Press, 2008), 377; "Japanese Handy Man," *New Yorker* (January 5, 1935): 16; Greg Robinson, "Hidden in Plain Sight: Rediscovering the Life and Art of Bumpei Usui," *Discover Nikkei* (December 17, 2021), https://discovernikkei.org/en/journal/2021/12/17/bumpei-usui/.

Charles Sheeler
(American, 1883–1965)
Incantation, 1946

Oil on canvas, 24⅛ × 20⅛ in.
Ella C. Woodward Memorial Fund and John B. Woodward Memorial Fund, 49.67
Provenance: Probably acquired from the artist by The Downtown Gallery, ca. 1947; purchased by the Brooklyn Museum, March 14, 1949.

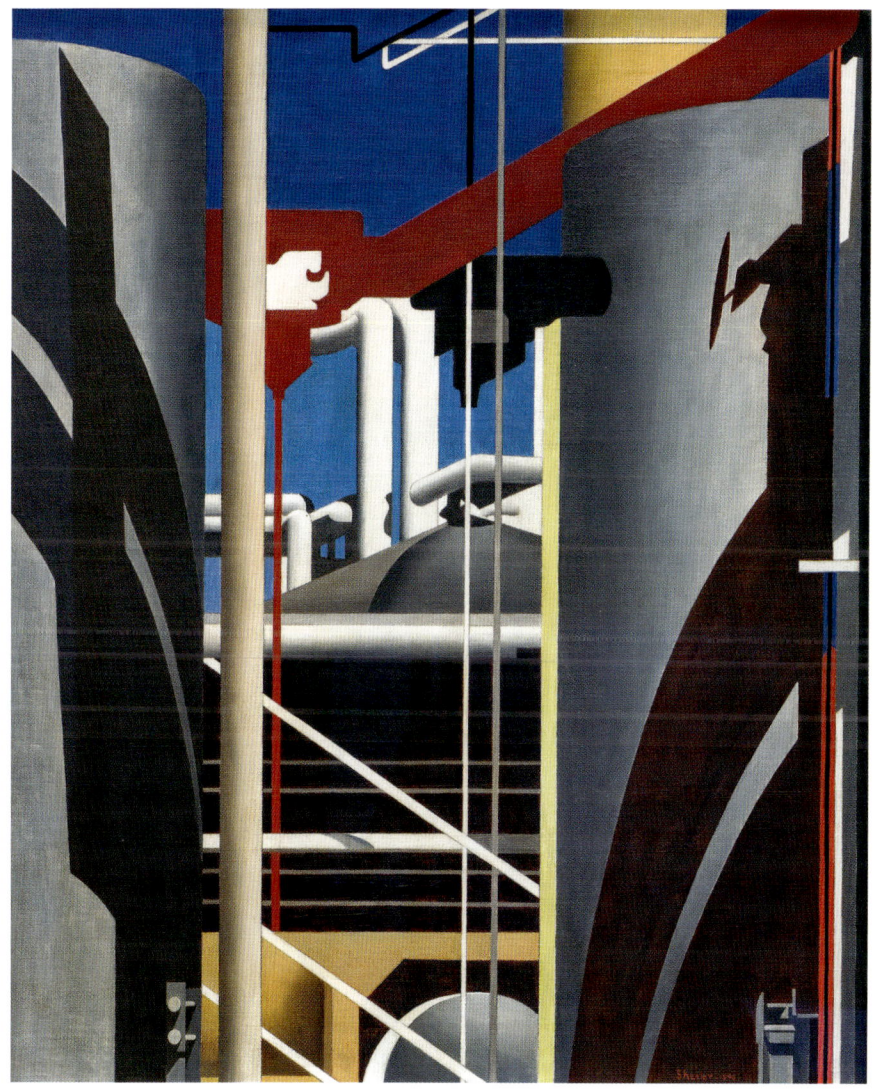

Peruvian artist
Atahualpa, Fourteenth Inca King, mid-18th century

Oil on canvas, 23⅝ × 21¾ in.
Dick S. Ramsay Fund, Mary Smith Dorward Fund, Marie Bernice Bitzer Fund, Frank L. Babbott Fund, gift of The Roebling Society and the American Art Council, purchased with funds given by an anonymous donor, Maureen and Marshall Cogan, Karen B. Cohen, Georgia and Michael de Havenon, Harry Kahn, Alastair B. Martin, Ted and Connie Roosevelt, Frieda and Milton F. Rosenthal, Sol Schreiber in memory of Ann Schreiber, Joanne Witty and Eugene Keilin, Thomas L. Pulling, Roy J. Zuckerberg, Kitty and Herbert Glantz, Ellen and Leonard L. Milberg, Paul and Thérèse Bernbach, Emma and J. A. Lewis, Florence R. Kingdon, 1995.29.14
Provenance: Acquired by Frederic De Peyster, before March 31, 1873; donated to the New-York Historical Society, 1873; purchased at Sotheby's, New York, "Americana and Decorative Arts, the Property of the New-York Historical Society," by the Brooklyn Museum, January 29, 1995.

One of fourteen portraits of Inca kings, this work depicts Atahualpa (1502–1533), the last Inca king, wearing an intricately patterned tunic with gilded jewelry, scepter, and crown of intertwining serpents.[1] The first thirteen portraits (1995.29.1-.13) are based on illustrations printed in an early seventeenth-century text that narrativized accounts of the Spanish conquistadors.[2] Atahualpa is not included in those illustrations; thus no known printed prototype for this painting exists. European portraiture conventions, such as three-quarter turned pose and orator's gesture, informed the compositions of this portrait series. The costly blue background pigment is another European-style treatment to elevate the subject. With greater economic stability in the early eighteenth century, portrait commissions in the viceroyalties of Peru and New Spain increased.[3] Portraits of Inca kings were often displayed in the homes of *caciques* (Indigenous noblemen) to indicate ancestral ties to Inca nobility, even centuries after Spanish conquest.[4]

In the Museum's series, each king is recognized by name and place in the succession. Rather than identifying Atahualpa as the "fourteenth Inca King," he is labeled "*el tirano bastardo*" (the bastard tyrant), referencing his illegitimate birth and ruthless triumph over his brother, Huáscar, in 1532 during the Inca Civil War.[5] Amid Francisco Pizarro's conquest the following year, Atahualpa was captured and executed. The Spanish avoided accusations of regicide by discrediting Atahualpa's reign, thereby legitimizing the colonial rule of Spanish King Philip II. Images typically depict Atahualpa defeated. Here, however, Atahualpa sits alert, holding his staff upright rather than in surrender. Despite this dignified depiction, the accompanying text reveals the controversial legacy of the last Inca king.

CG with DG

1. Diana Fane, ed., *Converging Cultures: Art and Identity in Spanish America* (New York: The Brooklyn Museum in association with Harry N. Abrams, 1996), 239. For more on portraits of nobles in colonial Peru see Thomas B. F. Cummins, "We are the Other: Peruvian Portraits of Colonial Kurakakuna," in *Transatlantic Encounters: Europeans and Andeans in the Sixteenth Century*, ed. Kenneth J. Andrien and Rolena Adorno (Berkeley and Los Angeles: University of California Press, 1991), 203–31; and Carolyn Dean, "Inka Nobles: Portraiture and Paradox in Colonial Peru," in *Exploring New World Imagery: Spanish Colonial Papers from the 2002 Mayer Center Symposium*, ed. Donna Pierce (Denver: Frederick and Jan Mayer Center for Pre-Columbian and Spanish Colonial Art, Denver Art Museum, 2005), 80–103.
2. Antonio de Herrera y Tordesillas, *Historia general de los hechos de los castellanos en las islas i tierra firme del mar océano* (Madrid: en la Emplenta Real, 1601–15).
3. Suzanne L. Stratton-Pruitt, "Paintings in the Home in Spanish Colonial America," in *Behind Closed Doors: Art in the Spanish American Home, 1492–1898*, ed. Richard Aste, (New York: Brooklyn Museum and Monacelli Press, 2013), 135.
4. Michael A. Brown, "Portraits and Patrons in the Colonial Americas," in *Behind Closed Doors*, 146.
5. King Huayna Capac appointed his two sons, Huáscar and Atahualpa, to rule different regions of the Inca Empire: Huáscar in Cusco and Atahualpa in Quito. Beginning in 1527, Atahualpa led his army against Huáscar to unite the empire under his rule. Huayna Capac is depicted in the twelfth portrait of this series, and Huáscar is the thirteenth (1995.29.13).

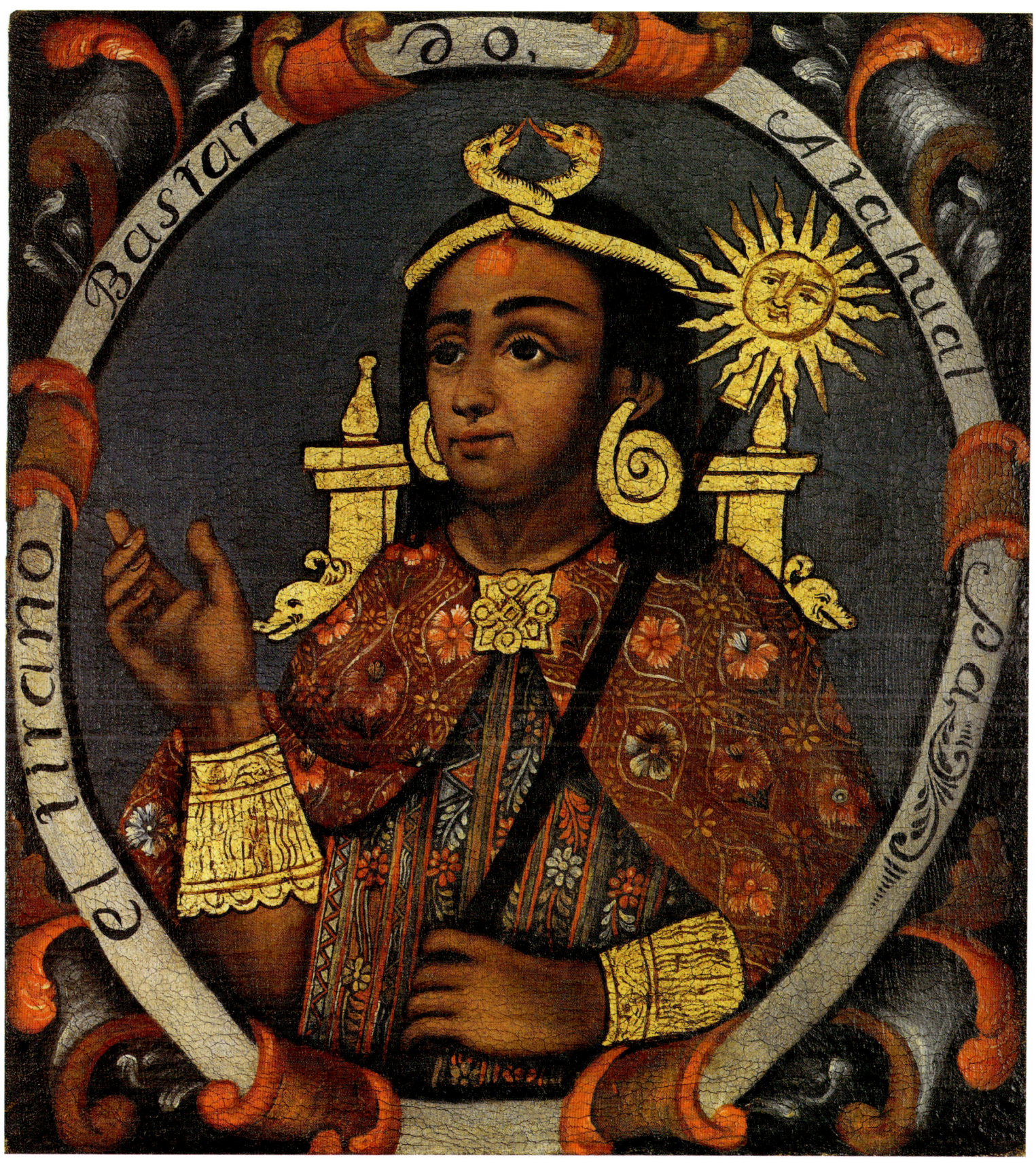

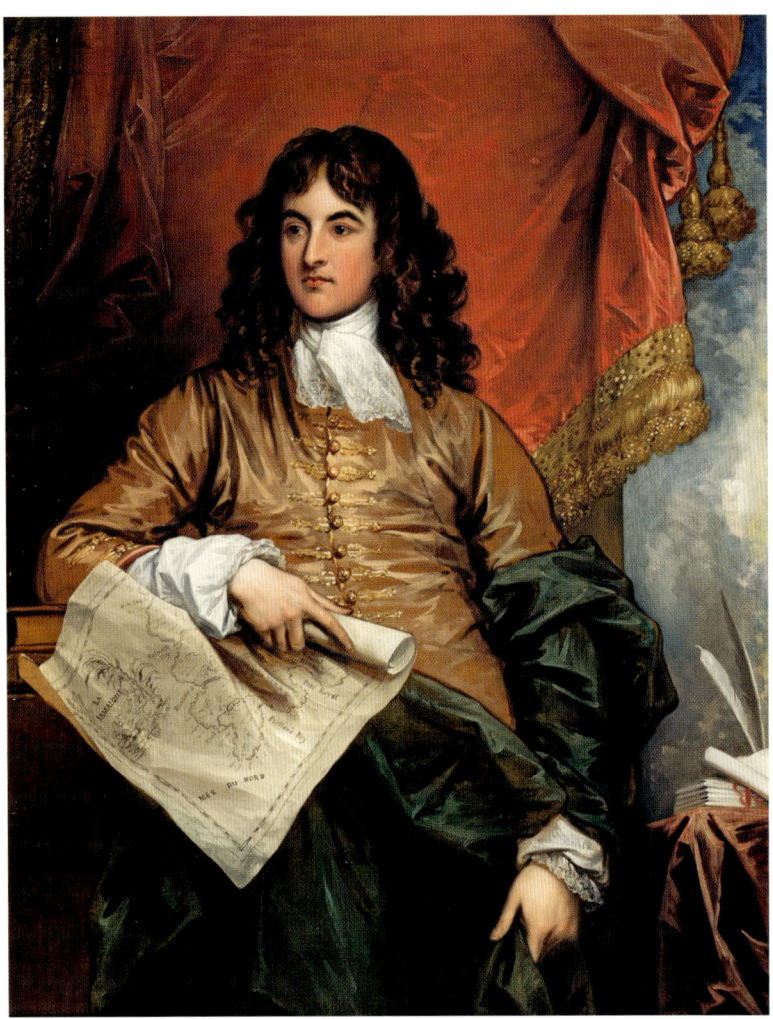

Benjamin West
(American, 1738–1820)
Peter Beckford, 1797

Oil on canvas, 57½ × 45⅜ in.
Gift of Lilla Brown in memory of her husband, John W. Brown, by exchange, 2012.44
Provenance: Commissioned from the artist by William Beckford, 1797; inherited by Susan Euphemia Beckford, 1844; inherited by William Hamilton, 1859; inherited by William Douglas-Hamilton, 1862; purchased from the Douglas-Hamilton estate at Christie's, by John R. Morron, November 6–7, 1919; bequeathed to the Metropolitan Museum of Art, 1950; purchased at Sotheby's, London, "Important British Pictures," by Derek Johns Ltd, November 24, 2005; purchased by the Brooklyn Museum, October 18, 2012.

Peter Beckford (1672/3–1735) appears here as a young man surrounded by indicators of his wealth and estate ownership.[1] The American-born artist Benjamin West began as a self-taught portraitist in Pennsylvania before moving to England, where he found success in London as a painter of historical scenes, even receiving royal patronage. Renowned for his Neoclassical painting style, he depicted Beckford richly dressed in satin and lace, and framed by luscious green, red, and gold fabrics. Books, documents, and quills allude to the sitter's intellectual and business endeavors. A map labeled "La Jamaique" unfurls from his hand, revealing the names of cities, ports, and bays, connecting Beckford to the island of Jamaica where he had inherited twenty sugar plantations from his father (also Peter Beckford). The eighteenth-century global sugar trade, centered around production in the Caribbean, created vast fortunes for European colonial families while exploiting the labor of enslaved people. Beckford expanded his family fortune in this industry, and by his death in 1735 was enslaving over 1,700 people at his sugar plantations.[2]

More than sixty years later, his grandson William commissioned this portrait. Considered "new money" by British aristocratic standards, the Beckford family could point to the portrait of William's grandfather as a sign of their family lineage and inheritance of wealth and property. West completed this painting in a moment when the Beckford plantations were in decline due to poor management and an absent estate owner; William never visited. Further, estates such as these were challenged by the strength of the political movement leading to Britain's 1807 abolition of the slave trade and 1838 abolition of slavery.

CG

1. For more about this painting, see Richard Aste, *Behind Closed Doors: Art of the Spanish American Home, 1492–1898* (New York: Brooklyn Museum and Monacelli Press, 2013), 39–40.
2. For more about the Beckford family, see Beckford's Tower and Museum, *Beckford and the Slave Trade: The Legacy of the Beckford Family and Slavery* (2007), retrieved July 22, 2024, https://beckfordstower.org.uk/wp-content/uploads/2024/06/Beckfords-and-Slavery-leaflet-2007.pdf.

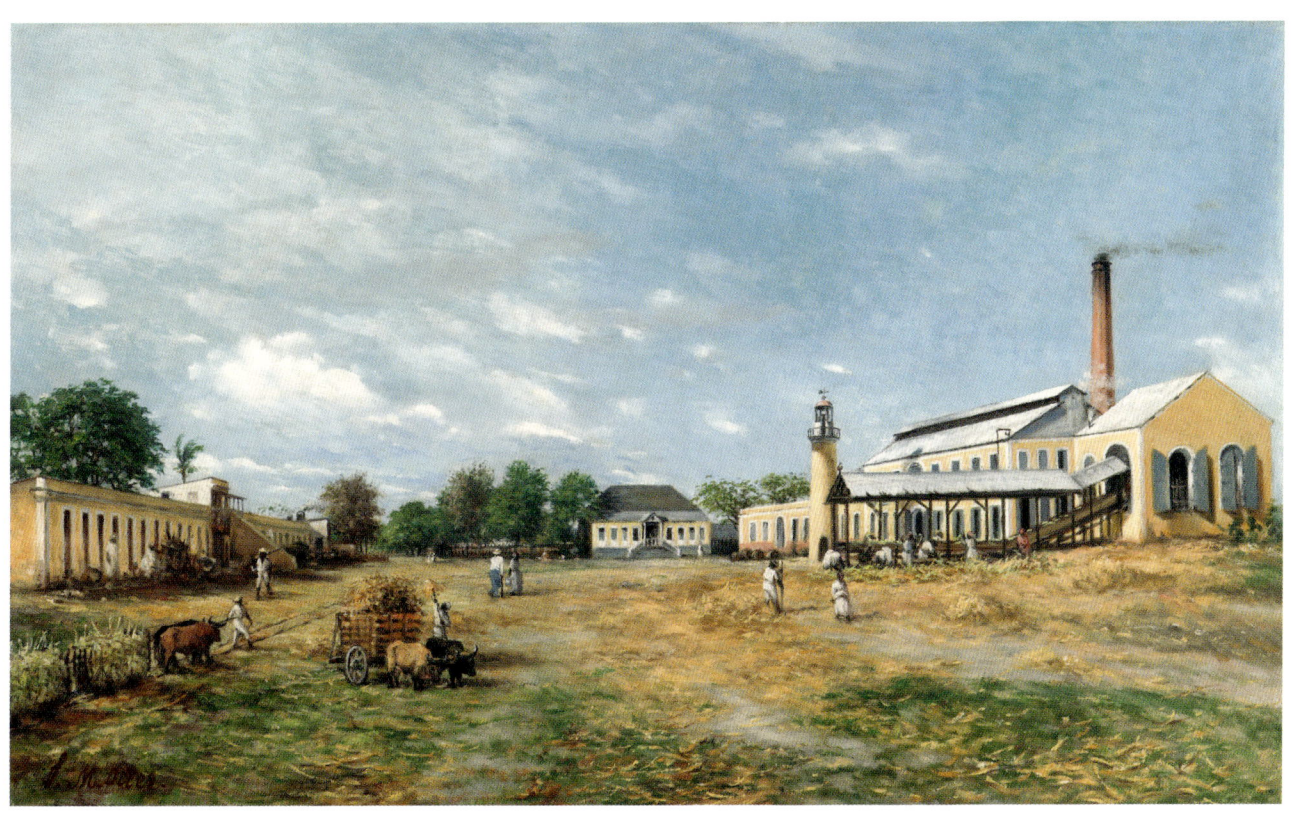

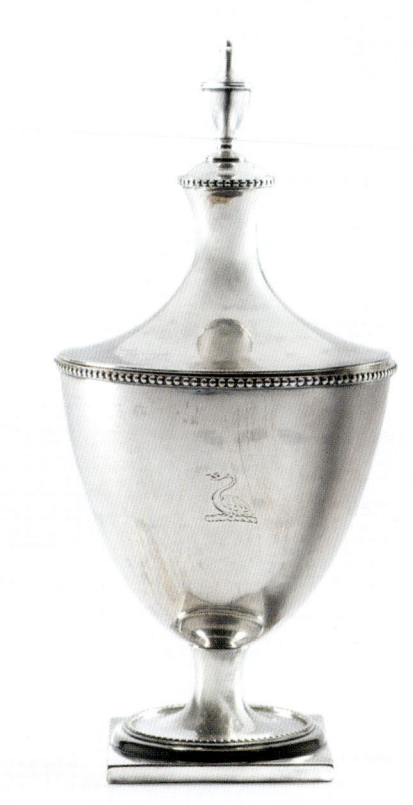

Previous page, above:
Francisco Oller
(Puerto Rican, 1833–1917)
Hacienda La Fortuna, 1885

Oil on canvas, 26 × 40 in.
Gift of Lilla Brown in memory of her husband, John W. Brown, by exchange, 2012.19
Provenance: Commissioned from the artist by José Gallart Forgas, 1885; inherited through the Gallart family, by 2004; purchased at Balcli's Auction, "Joyas, Antigüedades y Muebles: Pintura Catalana y Española de Colecciones Particulares," by Carmen G. Correa, March 2, 2004; purchased by the Brooklyn Museum, April 19, 2012.

Previous page, below:
Myer Myers
(American, 1723–1795)
Covered Sugar Bowl, ca. 1770–95

Silver, 9¼ × 4½ in.
Gift of Stephen Ensko, 52.154a-b
Provenance: Acquired by Stephen Guernsey Cook Ensko, by 1952; donated, 1952.

Opposite:
Whitfield Lovell
(American, born 1959)
Thursday, 2006

Charcoal on wood, silver sugar bowls, 64 × 45¾ in.
Gift in Memory of Lila Teich Gold by the Halpern and Sosnick Families, 2022.9
Provenance: Purchased from DC Moore Gallery by Lila Teich Gold, 2006; inherited by the Halpern and Sosnick families, 2016; donated, June 14, 2022.

In 1885 Spanish émigré José Gallart Forgas commissioned Puerto Rican artist Francisco Oller to paint his five *ingenios* (sugar mills) located on the island's southern coast. This was the only composition Oller completed for Forgas, although the artist painted other hacienda landscapes during his lifetime.[1] Hacienda owners like Forgas organized the *ingenios* into factory-like configurations to promote efficient production and easy surveillance.[2] Oller centered the structured courtyard of Hacienda La Fortuna in the composition rather than the sweeping fields of sugarcane. Laborers, enslaved prior to their 1873 emancipation, load sugarcane onto the steam-powered mill's conveyor belt, emphasizing the processing of the crop into raw sugar before it was exported.

The eighteenth century saw exports soar for luxury commodities like sugar and silver from the Caribbean and Latin America to markets in Asia, Europe, and the United States. These industries were environmentally damaging and relied upon the exploited labors of enslaved African and Indigenous people. Silver was also heavily mined in Central and South America and manipulated into serving containers for sugar as well as coffee and tea. As with this sugar bowl, made in New York City by the Jewish American silversmith Myer Myers, silver often housed these comestibles, with both the vessel and the commodity serving as a status symbol. Additionally, silver as a form of monetary exchange fueled global trade, allowing European and U.S. merchants and consumers to procure other fine global imports.

Whitfield Lovell's *Thursday* references the history of Black labor in the sugar industry, incorporating found silver sugar bowls, similar to the one created by Myers, into this portrait of two Black women. Lovell bases his figures on early twentieth-century photographs of unnamed Black Americans, whose anonymity he counters with imagined occupations. Here, the women appear as domestics, and the title *Thursday* references their one day off. The sugar bowls symbolize their domestic service, while also carrying the weight of centuries of exploited—and forced—Black labor in the American South and Caribbean.

CG/IA/LSG

1. For more on Oller and this painting, see Richard Aste, "Art of the Spanish American Home at the Brooklyn Museum," in *Behind Closed Doors: Art in the Spanish American Home, 1492–1898* (New York: Brooklyn Museum and Monacelli Press, 2013), 17–47; and Edward J. Sullivan, *From San Juan to Paris and Back: Francisco Oller and Caribbean Art in the Age of Impressionism* (New Haven, CT: Yale University Press, 2014).
2. Sidney Mintz notes that sugar plantations were "a synthesis of field and factory." Sidney W. Mintz, *Sweetness and Power: The Place of Sugar in Modern History* (New York: Penguin Books, 1985), 47.

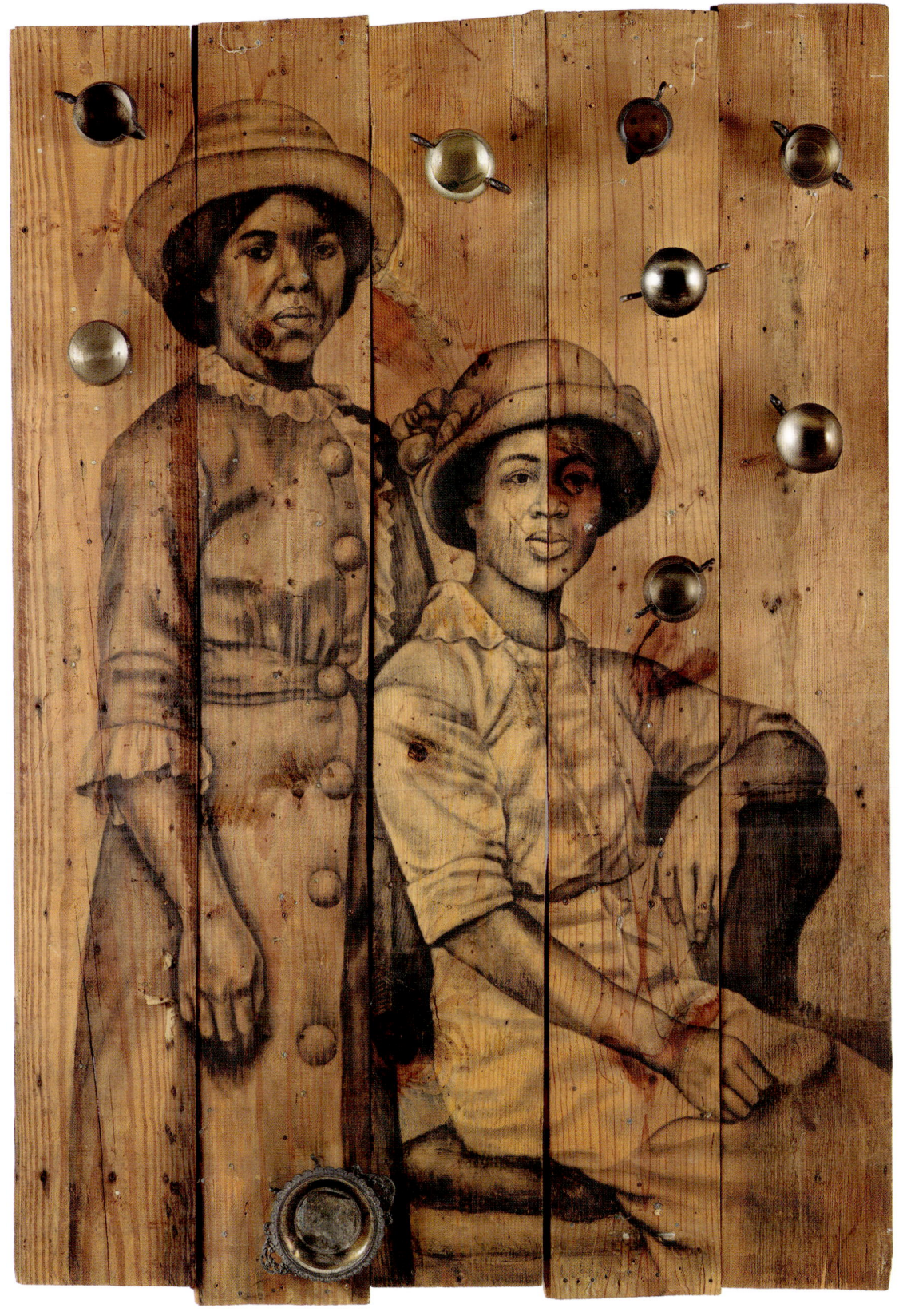

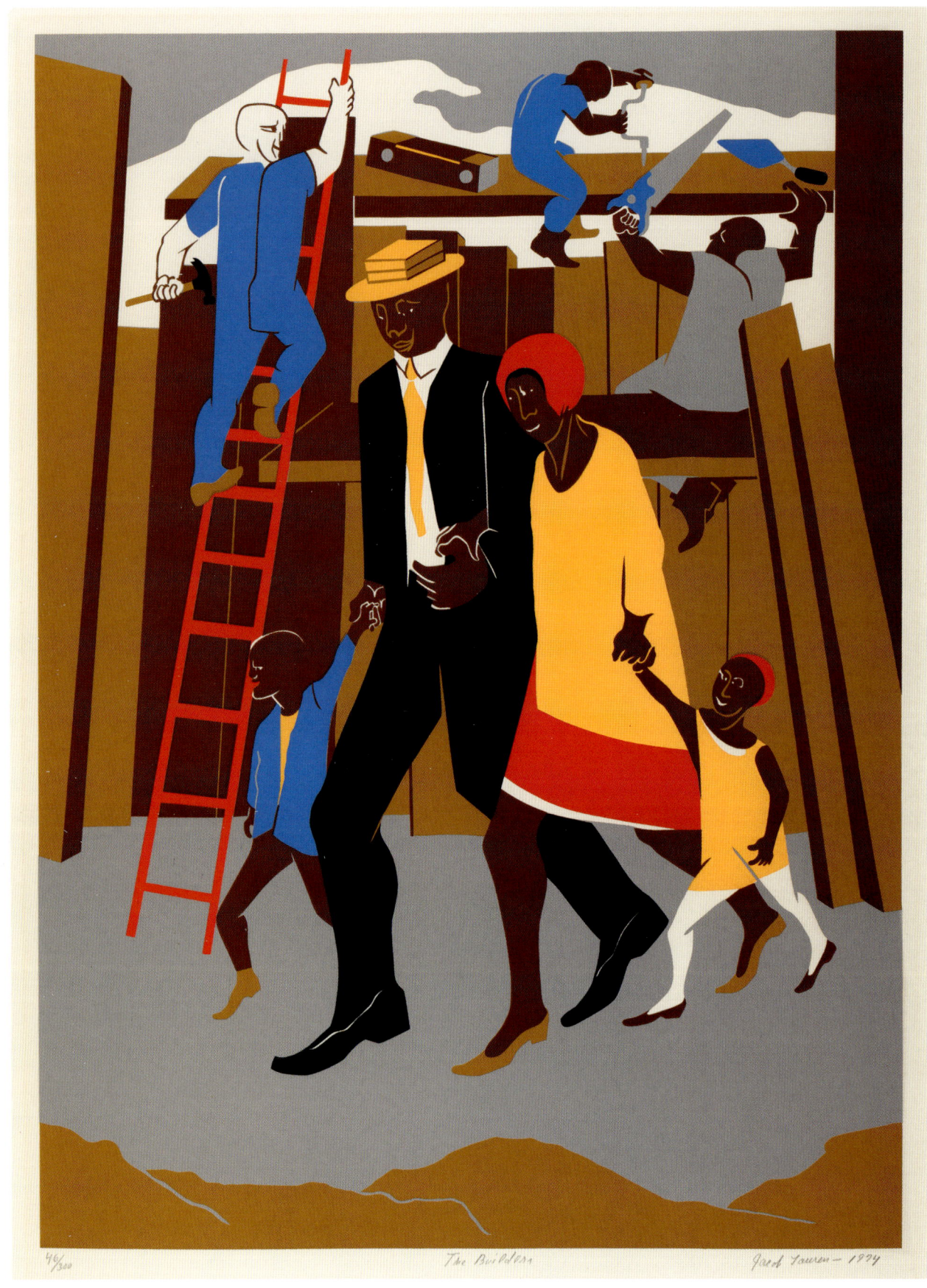

Toward Joy

Jacob Lawrence
(American, 1917–2000)
The Builders, 1974

Screenprint, 34 × 25¾ in. (sheet); 30 × 22⅛ in. (image)
Gift of Helen and Monte Getler, 84.23
Provenance: Acquired by Helen and Monte Getler, by 1984;
donated, February 16, 1984.

If at times my productions do not express the conventionally beautiful, there is always an effort to express the universal beauty of man's continuous struggle to lift his social position and to add dimension to his spiritual being.[1]

—Jacob Lawrence

Jacob Lawrence's long and prolific career celebrated and critiqued the everyday experiences of African American life within the twentieth century. One of the experiences he returned to over the decades was the skills of workers, especially those working in various trade jobs. Spanning cabinet makers to construction workers, street vendors, farmers, and gardeners, Lawrence presented these laborers as figures who were crucial in the developing American society. In two early works, *Cabinet Makers* (1946; Hirshhorn Museum and Sculpture Garden, Smithsonian Institution) and *The Builders* (1947; The White House Historical Association), the artist presents men in exaggerated poses, their bodies straining to perform their duties. They move tools across tables and lift and carry beams of timbers across scaffolding at construction sites. In both instances, Lawrence's skilled use of color to create patterns is visible. Blocks of red, uniforms of blue, and brown- and white-toned figures draw the eyes across the canvas, dividing an overall composition into smaller scenes. Though a static setting, viewers can easily imagine the actual movement of the figures, and the chaotic nature of dozens of individuals working together to produce a home, hospital, library, restaurant, or any of the numerous spaces needed to a build a neighborhood.

Lawrence continued to paint similar scenes in over sixty paintings throughout his *oeuvre*, including Brooklyn Museum's own *The Builders* (1974). Created thirty years after *Cabinet Makers*, this painting focuses not on the builders themselves, but those for whom they are building. In the foreground is a smartly dressed nuclear family, walking past several men constructing a structure. The close presence of the family, and their smiling faces, with the developing edifice suggests Lawrence is making a relationship between them. Both are necessary: shelter for a family and families to produce a community.

KG

1. Jacob Lawrence in Ellen Harkins Wheat, *Jacob Lawrence: The Frederick Douglass and Harriet Tubman Series of 1938–40* (Hampton, VA: Hampton University Museum, 1990), 46.

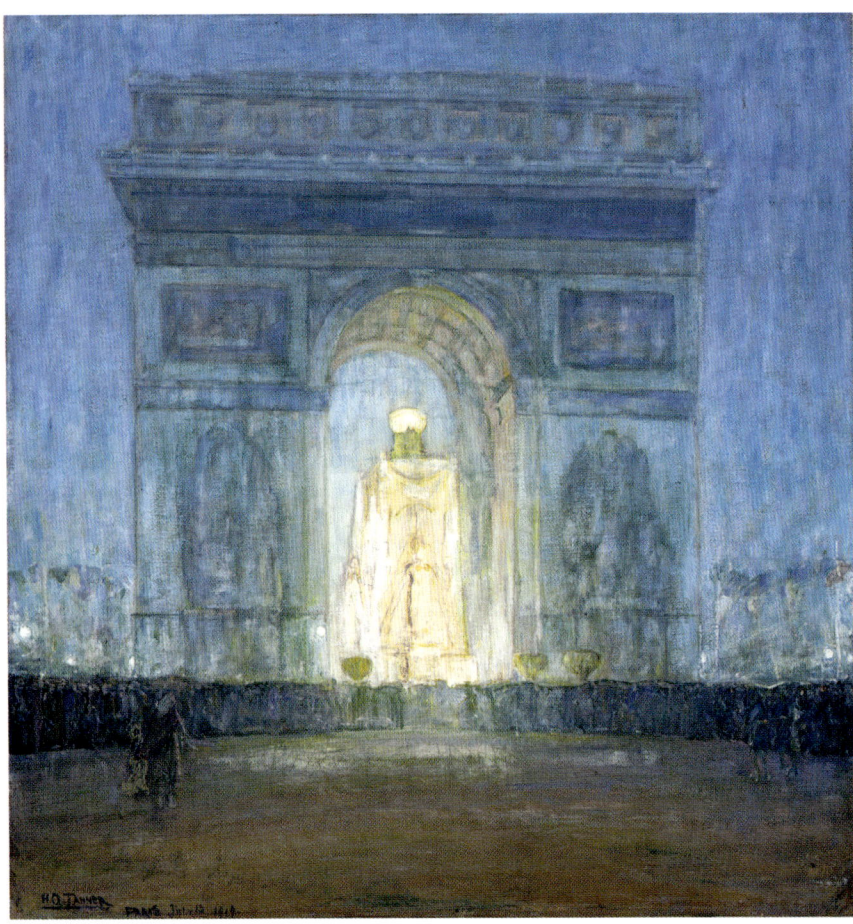

Henry Ossawa Tanner
(American, 1859–1937)
The Arch, 1919

Oil on canvas, 39¼ × 38³⁄₁₆ in.
Gift of Alfred W. Jenkins, 32.10
Provenance: Acquired from the artist by Grand Central Art Galleries, by 1929. Acquired by Alfred W. Jenkins, by 1932; donated, February 3, 1932.

Artists who were excluded from training or other opportunities in the United States on the basis of race and/or gender often found greater opportunity to explore their craft abroad. In the late nineteenth century and at the turn of the twentieth century, a large number Black American scholars, artists, writers, and performers traveled to cities like Amsterdam, Paris, and Venice.

Henry Ossawa Tanner, an expatriate artist of international renown, resided in Paris and in Brittany for most of his adult life. As was the case for many Black American artists, Tanner experienced less racial prejudice and greater artistic freedom and opportunity abroad. The French capital was a familiar subject to Tanner, and in this dramatic nocturnal scene, the artist recorded the Celebration of the Dead, held on July 13, 1919, in Paris to honor those who died defending France during World War I. Here, the crowd is rendered as a largely anonymous mass; the figures converge before a brilliantly illuminated cenotaph, or empty tomb, temporarily erected behind the Arc de Triomphe. As in many of Tanner's acclaimed religious nocturnes, the cool cerulean palette and muted tonalities evoke a solemn, even spiritual, mood.

For Emily Sargent, who was born in Italy to American parents, travel abroad was also the context in which she explored her own artistic freedom. Living most of her life in Europe, Sargent toured extensively through Italy, Spain, North Africa, and the Levant with her brother, the artist John Singer Sargent. She produced hundreds of watercolors depicting landscapes, architectural sites, and people. With Impressionist brushstrokes and attention to the effects of sunlight, such as the lavender shadows on the pale stone, Sargent represented the architectural details of a street scene in Tangier, Morocco. Her composition, one of twenty recently gifted to the Brooklyn Museum, includes the distinctive pointed horseshoe arches commonly found in Islamic architecture, as well as intricate tiling suggested through dappled blues and greens.

CG/SSW

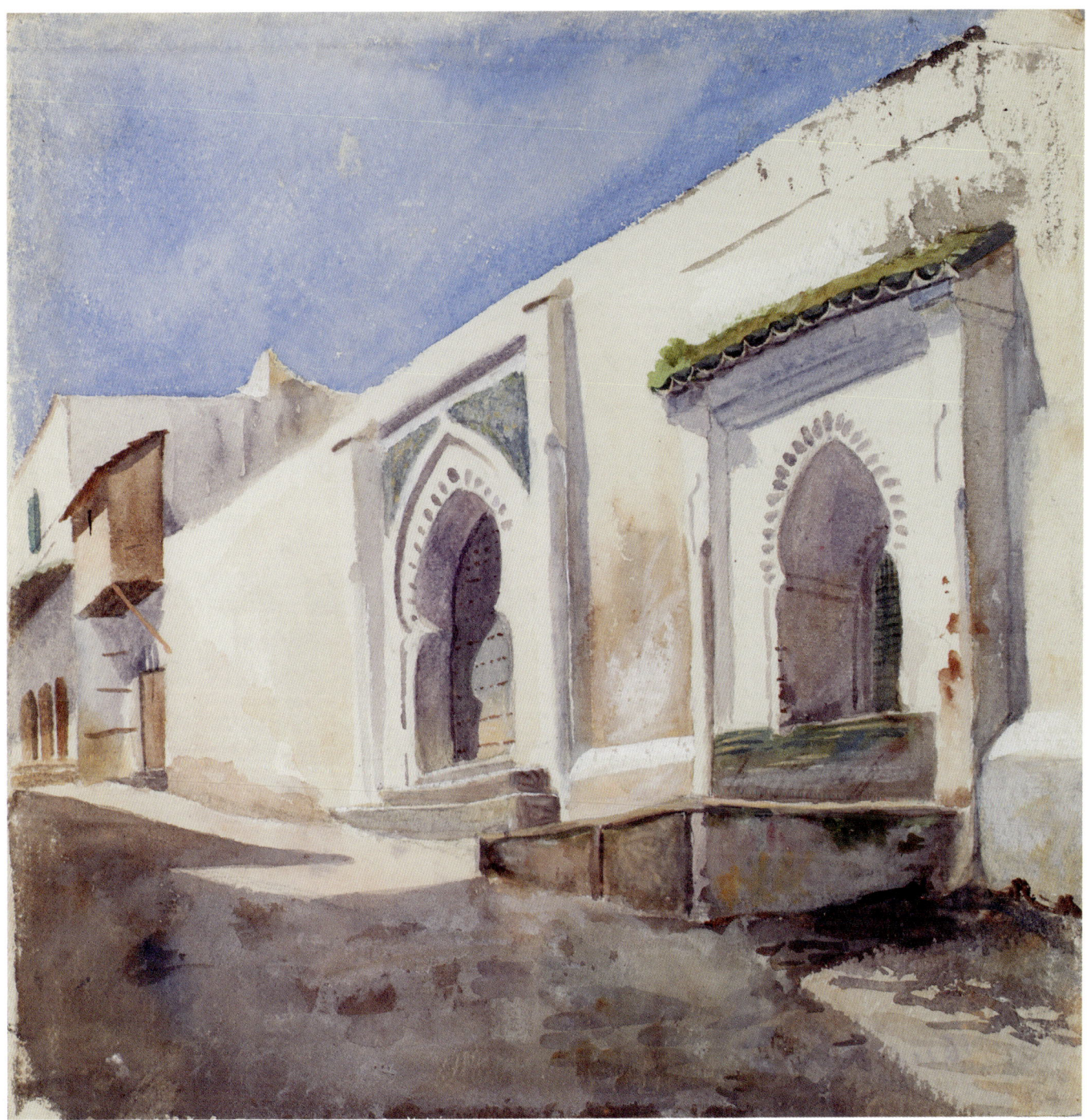

Emily Sargent
(American, 1857–1936)
Tangier, 1900

Graphite, watercolor, 12½ × 12½ in.
Anonymous gift, 2022.57.15
Provenance: Inherited from the artist by her family, 1936; transferred by the artist's family to an anonymous collector, 2022; donated, December 15, 2022.

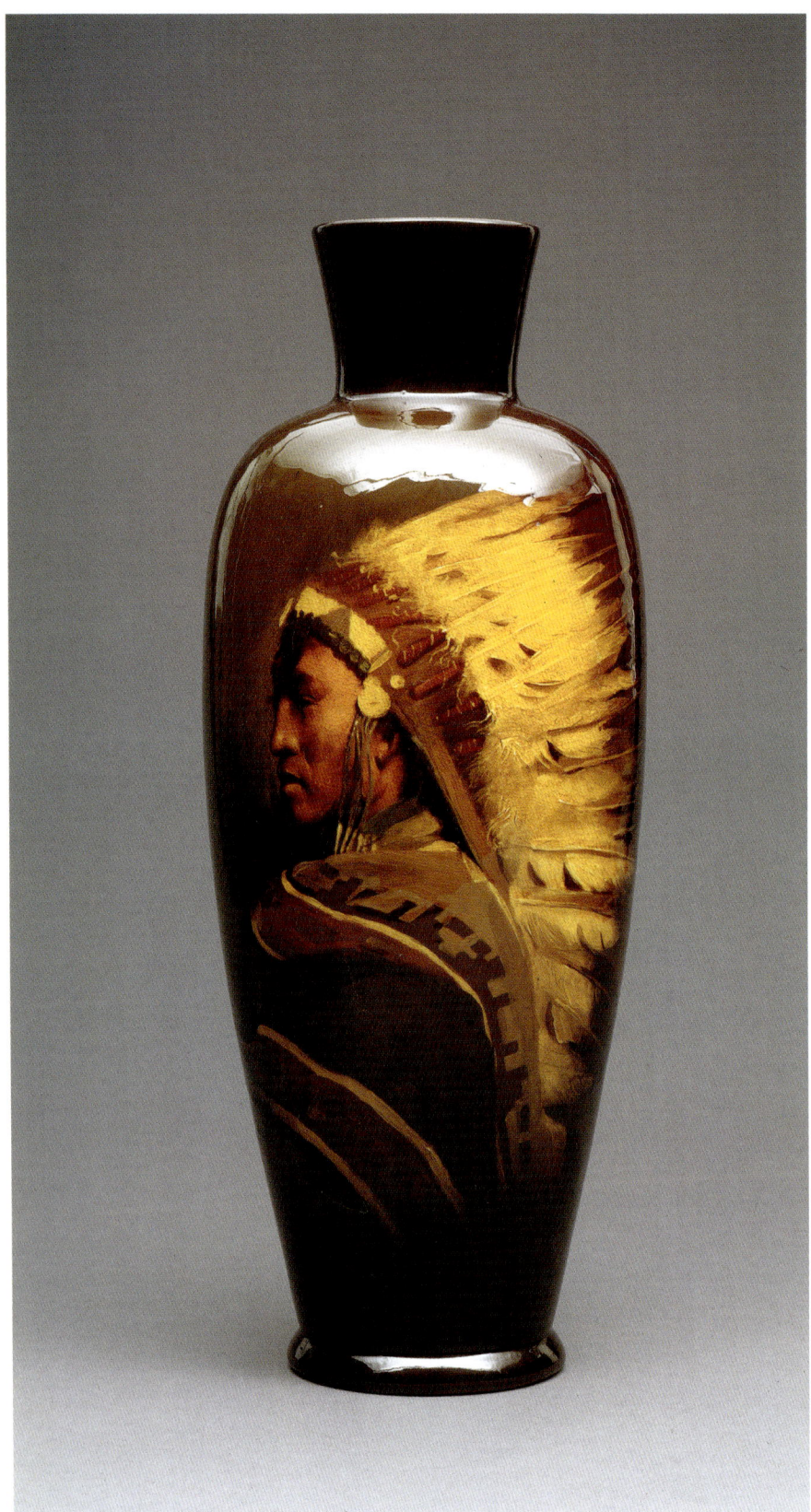

Grace Young, Decorator
(American, 1869–1947)
Rookwood Pottery Company
Manufacturer, Cincinnati, Ohio, founded 1880
Chief Shavehead Vase, ca. 1899

Glazed earthenware, 15½ × 6 × 6 in.
Gift of Mr. and Mrs. Jay Lewis, 84.176.4
Provenance: Acquired by Jay Lewis and Emma Lewis (Mrs. Jay Lewis), by 1984; donated, December 20, 1984.

In the late nineteenth century, while Indigenous peoples were displaced onto reservations and their cultural practices forcibly banned, non-Native manufacturers capitalized on romanticized likenesses of Indigenous peoples. Promoted by design journals, harmonious living rooms were shown filled with Native baskets, rugs, and ceramics, along with paintings, prints, and photographs produced by white artists of Native peoples.

Grace Young, one of the artists employed by the internationally renowned woman-owned Rookwood Pottery of Cincinnati, Ohio, was noted for her realistic portraits of Indigenous people. Despite being barred from the Cincinnati Art Club because of her gender, she found opportunities to decorate ceramics at Rookwood, becoming one of their most requested artists. Like her colleagues at the pottery, Young copied contemporary photographs and prints for her portraits of Indigenous people. Most of the photographs were taken of Indigenous delegation visits to Washington, DC, or at world's fairs, such as the 1893 Columbian Exposition, held in Chicago. These photographs were highly curated, and the subjects were encouraged to wear their traditional attire, but also to fulfill romanticized stereotypes of the passive "Vanishing Indian." This amber-hued vase bears the image of an Arapaho individual identified as "Shavehead," and portrays him as a dignified leader, a design that was particularly attractive to white consumers.

CF/MGP

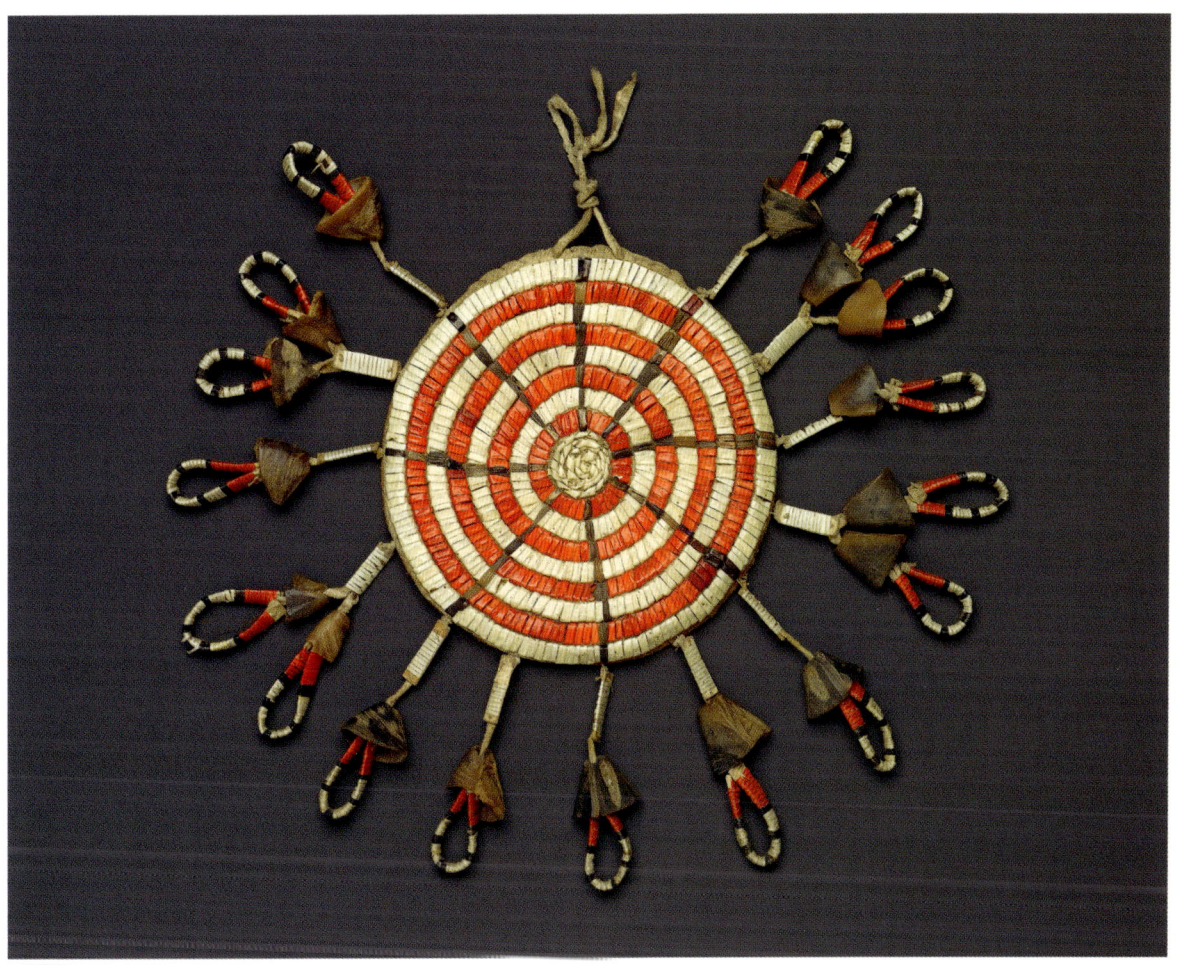

Arapaho artist
Pouch
Northern or Southern Plains, United States, late 19th or early 20th century

Hide, beads, porcupine quills, deer hooves, sinew, plant fiber, 5⅛ × 5⅛ in.
Brooklyn Museum Collection, 08.434
Provenance: Acquired by the Brooklyn Museum, before 1930s.

Historically, Arapaho communities constructed and lived in structures known as tipis that were well-suited to their nomadic lifestyle in the Great Plains region of North America. Derived from the Dakota word for "dwelling," tipis consist of a pole framework covered by stretched hide or canvas.[1] Male artists sometimes painted battle scenes on tipi covers to proclaim their war achievements, power, and high social status. A far greater number of tipis, however, were ornamented with quilled or beaded rosettes made by women. This quilled pouch is likely an "upcycled" tipi ornament.

The pouch features a design of alternating white and red circular bands of dyed porcupine quills bisected by eight black stripes and encircled with fringe made from quill-wrapped leather strips and carved deer hooves. The concentric circles radiating out from a central point reference both the sun and the form of the tipi itself.[2] Historically, four such ornaments hung on tipis facing the southeast, southwest, northwest, and northeast. According to the Southern Arapaho Knowledge Keeper Fred Mosqueda, "Our Father, when he created Mother Earth, put four Old Men in those directions. Their purpose is to take care of us . . . The four emblems in the directions represent the Whirlwind/Tornado Woman (Niiyooket) who helped create the world as we know it today. She blew the dirt and created the size of the Earth as she travels all over. These emblems helped the Whirlwind/Tornado Woman see or sense the Arapaho Camp and would go around them."[3] The concentric circle design illustrates Whirlwind Woman's movement, as it "evokes her circuit, while her occasional stops to rest are indicated by the radii, which interrupt the circles."[4]

While the tipi ornament was likely made by a female artist, a male Arapaho artist painted this miniature tipi that presents a dramatic battle scene in which Native warriors ride and lead horses while wielding weapons. Two enemy warriors—possibly Pawnee or Osage based on their hairstyle—have fallen in battle, and horse hoofprints encircle the scene, indicating movement. Former warriors crafted such miniature tipis with imagery that referenced their lost way of life for sale to white consumers.

The late nineteenth century saw a radical rupture in traditional Indigenous lifeways as the Early Reservation Period began, which is reflected in shifting art practices and materials alike. Instead of painting large tipis made of buffalo hide, men painted miniature tipis for sale and instead of creating adornment for their tipis, women repurposed traditional forms.

DT

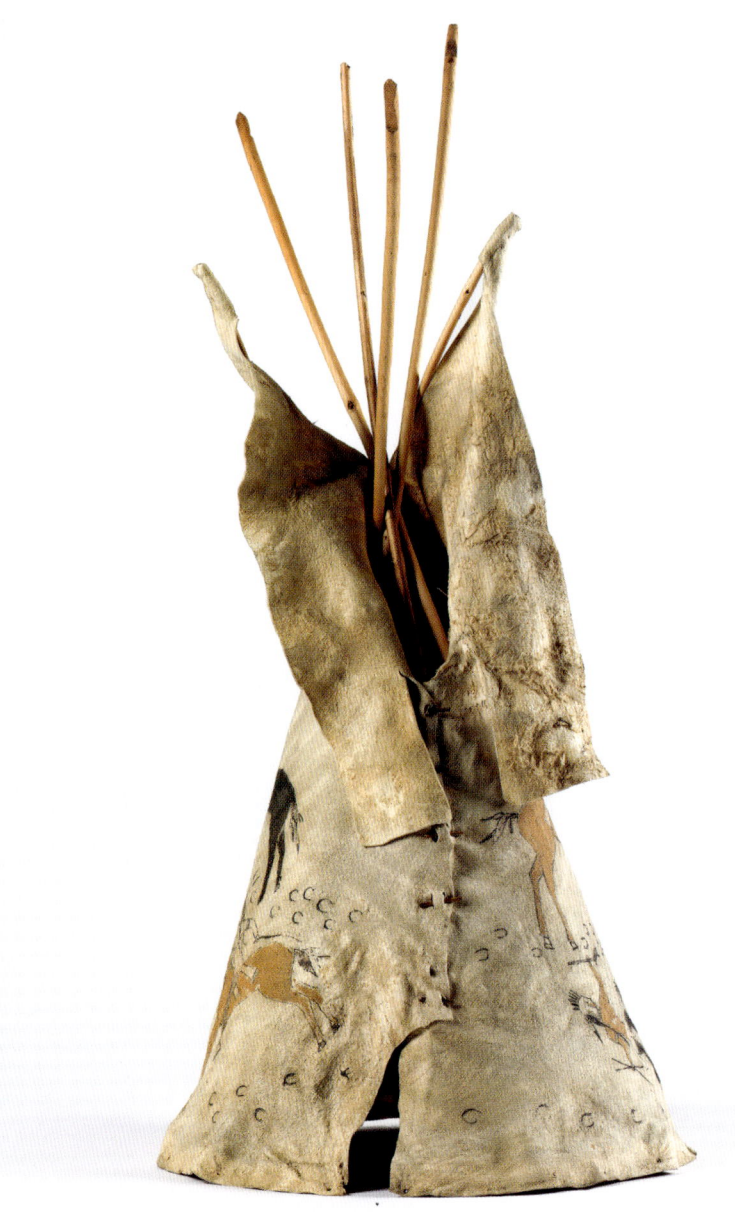

1. Nancy B. Rosoff, "Tipi: Heritage of the Great Plains," in *Tipi: Heritage of the Great Plains*, ed. Nancy B. Rosoff and Susan Kennedy Zeller (New York: Brooklyn Museum; Seattle: University of Washington Press, 2011), 3–35.
2. Adrianne Santina, "Recreating the World: Tipi Ornaments by Cheyenne and Arapaho Women," *Women's Studies* 33, no. 7 (October 2004): 951, https://doi.org/10.1080/00497870490503842.
3. Fred Mosqueda, email to author, February 23, 2024.
4. Santina, "Recreating the World."

Arapaho artist
Miniature Tipi with a Painted Battle Scene
Northern or Southern Plains, United States, late 19th century

Hide, pigment, wood, $22^{13}/_{16}$ × 13 × 13 in.
Dick S. Ramsay Fund, 63.201.8
Provenance: Acquired by George Terasaki, by November 20, 1963; purchased by the Brooklyn Museum, December 11, 1963.

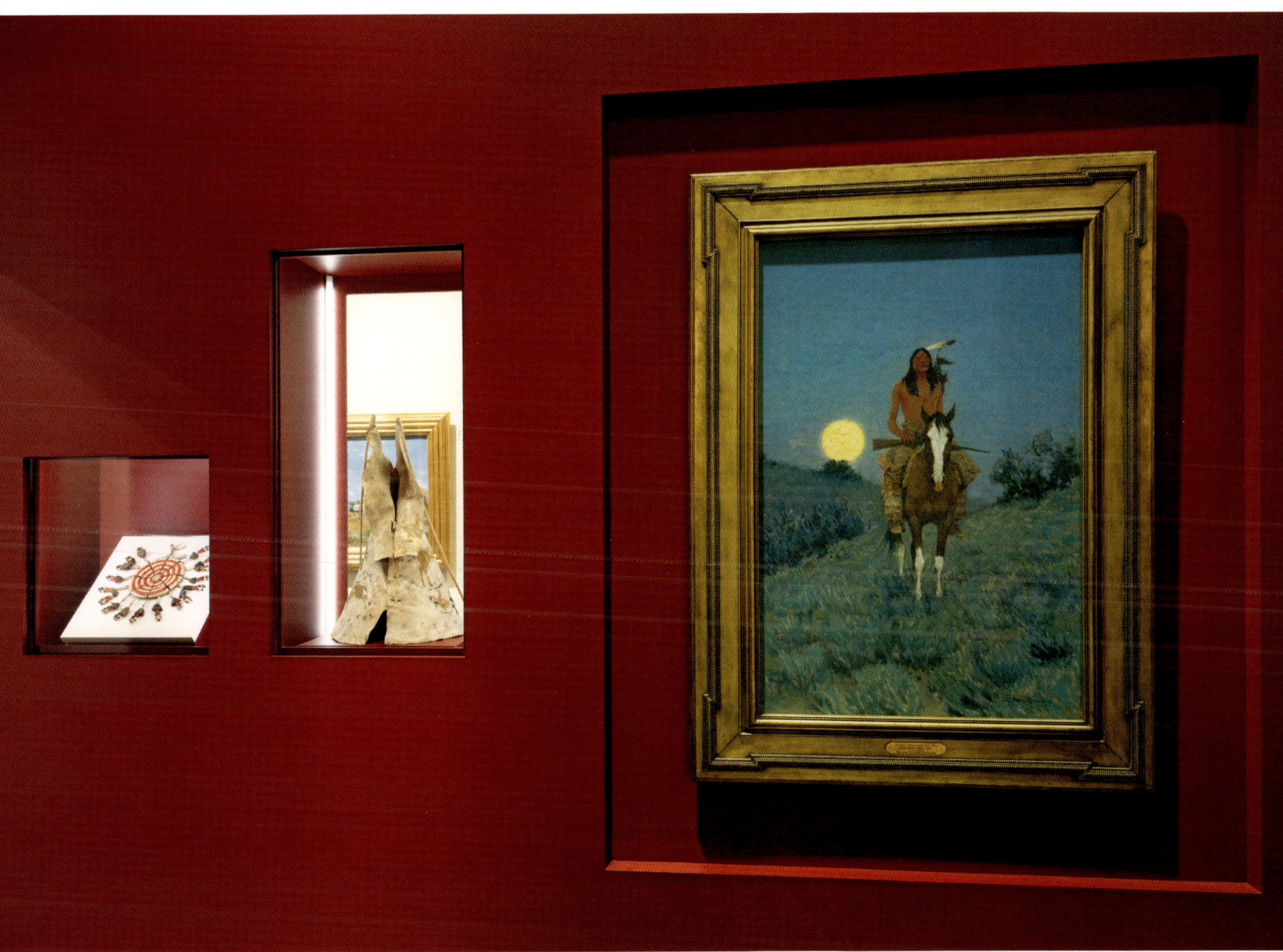

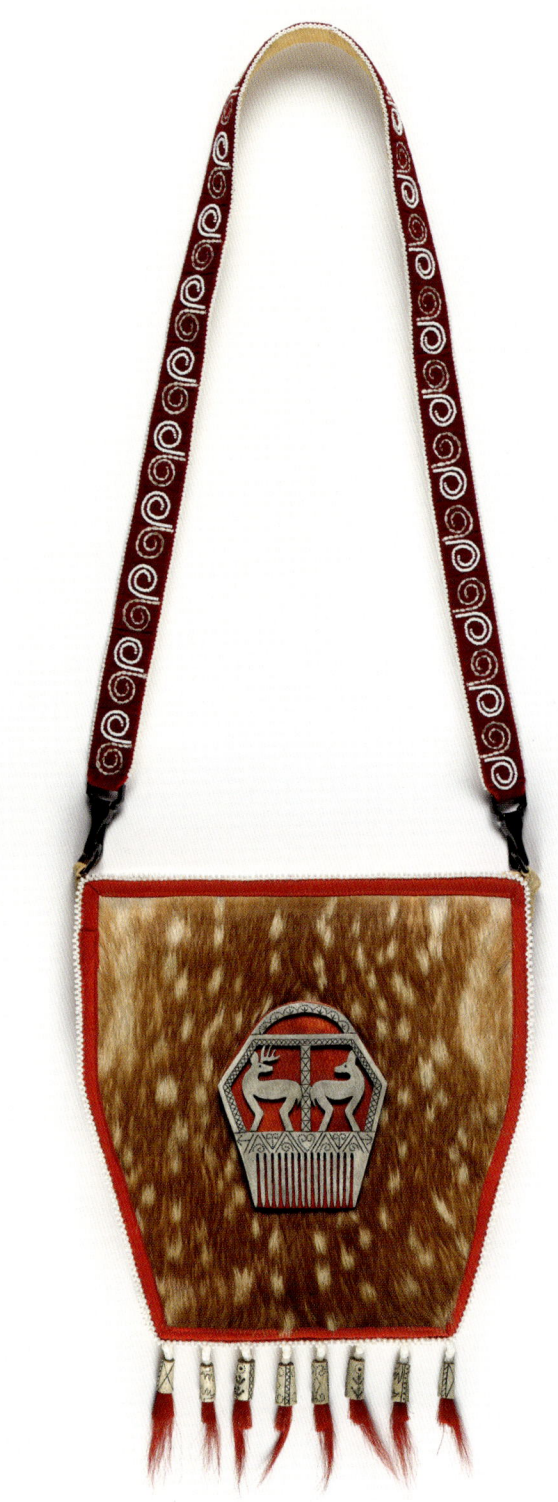

Hayden Haynes
(Onöndowa'ga:', Deer Clan, Seneca Nation of Indians, Cattaraugus Territory, born 1983)
Samantha Jacobs
(Turtle clan, Seneca Nation of Indians, born 1983)
New Beginnings, 2022

Fawn hide, brain-tanned buckskin, velvet, gunmetal hardware, mother of pearl, Czech beads, vintage German beads, moose hair, dyed deer hair, moose antler, and whitetail deer antler, 38 × 12½ × 1 in.; strap: 45 in.
Marie Bernice Bitzer Fund, 2024.13
Provenance: Purchased from the artist by the Brooklyn Museum in 2024.

New Beginnings blends historic artmaking practices with a contemporary aesthetic and serves as visual testament to the ways that Seneca people have maintained their culture in the face of the destructive forces of settler colonialism and cultural genocide. After discovering a fawn recently killed in a traffic accident, artist Hayden Haynes chose to honor the animal's life through the creation of this artwork with Samantha Jacobs. Jacobs constructed, beaded, and embroidered it, while Haynes carved the comb at the center and the beads at the bottom.

The bag's materials honor the Seneca people's nonhuman relatives and possess deep spiritual significance. The carving on the antler comb depicts a male and female deer facing each other. In one version of the Seneca's Creation Story, the first object mentioned was such a comb, which was associated with transformation, power, and healing.[1] The spirals of embroidered moose hair and commercial glass beads on the strap mimic the form of fiddlehead ferns, which grew abundantly within Seneca ancestral homelands. Jacobs's revitalization of animal hair embroidery honors her ancestors and reinforces the artists' partnership with the animals with whom they share their homelands. Through all of these elements, *New Beginnings* reclaims traditional Seneca narratives while also calling upon humans to recognize the interconnectedness of the natural world and to take responsibility for environmental stewardship.

DT

1. Hayden Haynes, email to author, October 1, 2023.

CRITICAL SHORT

Framing the World through Gratitude

Dare Turner

Our Creator made the whole world, the whole universe. And he made everything that grows. And every animal and every bird and every kind of water—everything. And when he finished that, then the last one he made were the human beings. . . . He instructed us about how the world goes, how it operates, and how you live here . . . that's what we call Ohén:ton Karihwatéhkwen.[1] It's *what we say before we do anything important.* . . . Our Creator gave us this miraculous life . . . and so we say to our Creator, "Thank you for the privilege that I can walk again today. And our mind is agreed."[2]
—Tom Porter (Sakokweniónkwas),
Bear Clan Elder of the Mohawk Nation

Every night around the dinner table, my family holds hands and each of us shares one thing we are grateful for that happened that day. My five-year-old usually mentions his favorite activity from school, while my husband often reflects on his teaching and writing practices, and my one-year-old smiles and throws some pasta. I most often express gratitude for the sort of work I am able to do in my role as a curator of Indigenous art. Though I doubt my youngest fully comprehends this practice, I like to imagine he absorbs our gratitude and that it shapes the way he receives the world as it does for the rest of the family.

As an Indigenous woman in a curatorial role, I am uniquely positioned to advocate for my community and ensure that museums make space for the brilliance that is Native art. Over the years, my work has assumed different forms. At times, I focused entirely on historical art and contextualized it within complex narratives about Indigenous sovereignty. In other moments, I have worked closely with Indigenous artists to create commissions that transformed galleries and the facade of the museum. Within the context of this project—in which we hope to radically disrupt the way the public understands American art—my curatorial practice has been deeply collaborative and rooted in gratitude.

The concept of gratitude helps us find a way of being in the world, because it generates inexhaustible wealth and contentment. It reminds us that everything needed to support life sustainably can be found in nature, and centers abundance rather than scarcity. This revolutionary idea reveals our potential to reciprocally connect with things outside of ourselves and build meaningful relationships. These complex and interconnected ideas served as the foundation of this framework, curation as an act of care.

This framework places a focus on both gratitude and rematriation, and centers the Hodinöhsö:ni' Thanksgiving Address, reproduced at the beginning of this chapter, as a pillar upholding the work of the gallery. The Hodinöhsö:ni' Confederacy includes six tribes who live in upstate New York and Canada: the Cayuga, Mohawk, Oneida, Onondaga, Seneca, and Tuscarora. For longer than memory, tribal members have spoken the Thanksgiving Address to establish gratitude as the highest priority and remind us that everything in our world is subject to the same forces. Reciting this every day, sometimes even before one's feet hit the ground in the morning, leads to a feeling of contentment and respect for everything in the natural world.

The Thanksgiving Address speaks to the idea of rematriation as well. Rematriation contains multitudes—it calls on all beings to respect and maintain kinship with ancestral homelands and recontextualizes humanity's responsibilities to center reciprocity instead of extraction. In doing so, it transforms and challenges our relationship to place. Within the space of the museums, rematriation reminds us that while institutions steward material culture in their collections, those artworks truly belong to the people and cultures who made them.

The entries in this chapter that consider Native art have gratitude and rematriation at their foundation. Bringing the artworks into conversation with voices from their Indigenous community members allows us to see rematriation in action and taking form.

When I sit around the dinner table with my family tonight, I will express gratitude for the ability to share these ideas with you. I hope you see these concepts as a gift or a lens that you can use to see all the art within this book in a new light. And I hope this way of understanding may transform your world as well.

1. This is the Mohawk term for the Thanksgiving Address.
2. Tom Porter, *And Grandma Said . . . Iroquois Teachings: As Passed Down through the Oral Tradition,* ed. Lesley Forrester (Philadelphia: Xlibris Corp, 2008), 10.

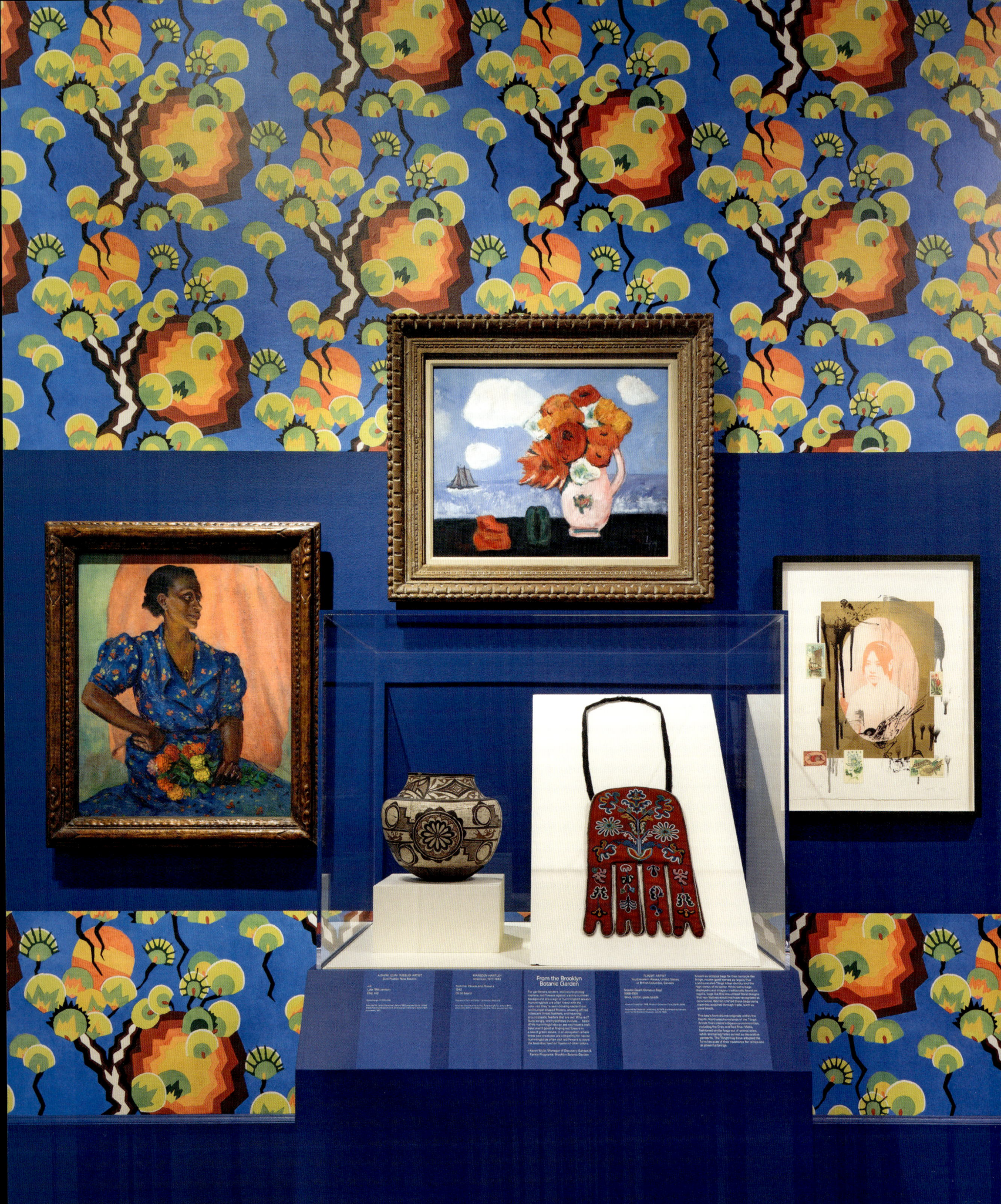

FRAMEWORK

To Give Flowers

This framework meditates on the adage "to give someone their flowers." Emerging from Black American funerary and gospel traditions, the saying encourages listeners to "give flowers" while the recipient can "smell them," asserting the importance of giving people their due credit while they are alive to receive it.

Flowers and floral motifs have been imbued with a breadth of meanings across global cultures, as seen from Anishinaabe bandolier bags and Japanese ikebana to Chinese painted porcelain and Mexican pottery. Discouraged from studying history and portrait painting, sculpture, and other subjects, early white European and American women turned to floral painting and design, acceptable artistic pursuits given flowers' feminine symbolism. Black Americans, in turn, saw their creative talents excluded from the fine arts and relegated to the production of furniture, quilts, pottery, and commercial design, in which floral patterns are prominent.

Loïs Mailou Jones, a celebrated painter, was lesser known for her work in design. Reproduced as wallpaper, her vibrant floral pattern (p. 106) is presented alongside an array of artworks featuring floral motifs to create a whimsical and immersive experience. Here Mailou Jones's design is a celebratory acknowledgement of the contributions of many unsung American creatives highlighted in this section and supports fresh points of entry and interpretation. Following are works by well-known artists, interpreted anew through the research and writing of Black and Indigenous scholars and the results of a partnership with the Brooklyn Botanic Gardens, whose teams offered specialized expertise on the botanical subjects within several works.

Here, we bear witness to the ways diverse—and often unsung—creatives practiced their craft, as well as love, spirituality, healing, and hope, amid historical and cultural erasure. Inspired by Alice Walker's canonical ode to Black feminist space-making, *In Search of Our Mothers' Gardens: Womanist Prose*, the Museum highlights and celebrates the trailblazers—those who charted *wayward* and oft-overlooked paths of creative expression and freedom.[1]

SSW

[1]. Here, "wayward" is understood as the persistence of a beautiful and creative existence in the face of overwhelming erasure and disregard. It is "the paradox of cramped creation, the entanglement of escape and confinement," the self-determined and "untiring practice of trying to live when you were never meant to survive," in the work of Saidiyda Hartman, *Wayward Lives, Beautiful Experiments: Intimate Histories of Riotous Black Girls, Troublesome Women, and Queer Radicals* (New York: W. W. Norton & Co., 2020), 227–28.

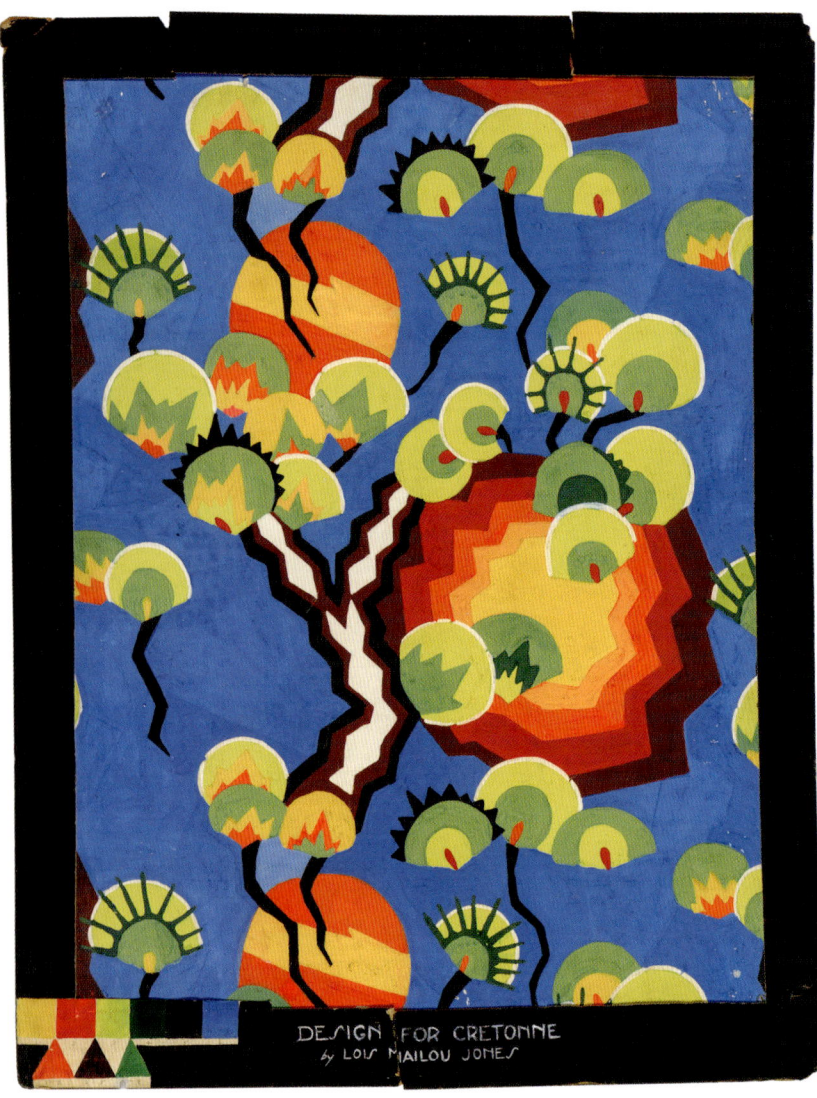

Loïs Mailou Jones
(American, 1905–1998)
Textile Design for Cretonne, 1928

Watercolor on paper, 28 × 21 in.
Smithsonian American Art Museum,
Bequest of the artist, 2006.24.10

Designed for drapery fabric, this electrifying modern floral pattern was likely never commercially reproduced. Loïs Mailou Jones, like many peers, created dozens if not hundreds of meticulously composed and expertly colored design swatches to sell to manufacturers of wallpaper, carpets, and fabrics. Research is ongoing into the sale and production of Jones's designs; however, as noted on the verso of this swatch, it was exhibited in Asniéres, just north of Paris, in the seventh annual Exhibition of Fine and Decorative Arts in 1937, nearly a decade after it was created.

Jones's creative trajectory can be observed in the designs she produced during her time at the School of the Museum of Fine Arts in Boston (SMFA), where she was the only Black American student enrolled.[1] During her tenure, she would supplement her coursework with evening design classes at Boston Normal Art School (now Massachusetts College of Art), in hopes of becoming a textile designer. She went on to win competitions that resulted in the purchase of her designs.[2] Upon graduating in 1927, Jones achieved some success—her designs were purchased and manufactured by F. A. Foster and Schumacher Company, the latter of which also produced the bold and popular Art Deco patterns of Austrian-born Swedish designer Josef Frank in the 1920s and '30s. The stylized floral pattern in this swatch echoes Frank's freewheeling and vibrant style.

In the same year she painted this pattern, Jones traveled between Boston and New York, where she was exposed to artists working in Harlem at the latter part of the New Negro Movement. This contact with artists looking to the African diaspora for inspiration may have led to her own explorations of African motifs by the early 1930s.[3] It can be argued that this and other textile designs from this period visually reflect this inspiration.

SSW

1. See Rebecca VanDiver, *Designing a New Tradition: Loïs Mailou Jones and the Aesthetics of Blackness* (University Park, PA: Penn State University Press, 2020), 30.
2. Ibid., 44; including the SMFA competition that resulted in the purchase of Jones's design by Nashua Manufacturing Company, and other competitions sponsored by Shepherd Stores and the Rayon Institute of America.
3. Ibid.

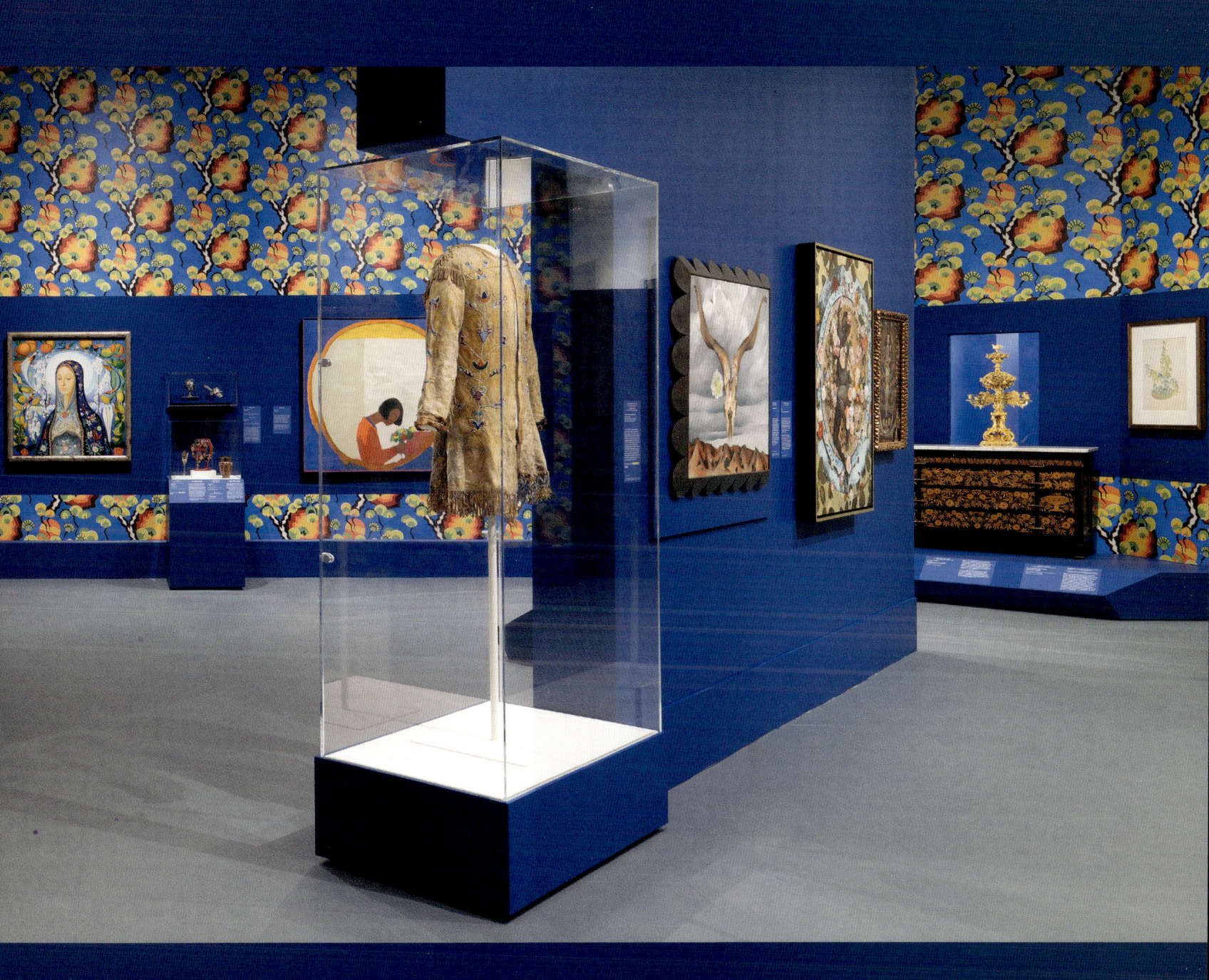

Maurice Brazil Prendergast
(American, 1858–1924)
Flowers in a Vase (Zinnias), ca. 1910–13

Oil on canvas, 23¼ × 25³⁄₁₆ in.
Gift of Frank L. Babbott, 39.53
Provenance: Acquired by Kraushaar Galleries, before 1926. Acquired by Frank Lusk Babbott, Jr., by 1939; donated, March 1939.

We love zinnias in Brooklyn Botanic Garden's Children's Garden. They are cheery, vibrant flowers that bloom from June through October.

Zinnias are an easy plant to try with kids, as the seeds germinate quickly, typically within four to seven days. We start the seeds indoors and then transplant them outdoors once the soil has warmed up. Zinnias also attract pollinators, and they make a wonderful cut flower. It makes sense that Maurice Prendergast used zinnias for this still life; with their sturdy stems, they can last a week or more in a vase.

Like Prendergast, students in the Children's Garden work with flowers as artistic inspiration. We often use zinnias and other blooms for activities like watercolor painting and flower pressing. We also use flowers to support scientific inquiry and observation; students collect data and learn about how the color, scent, and shape of flowers help determine which pollinators are attracted to them.

—Ellen McCarthy, former Children's Garden Co-ordinator, Brooklyn Botanic Garden

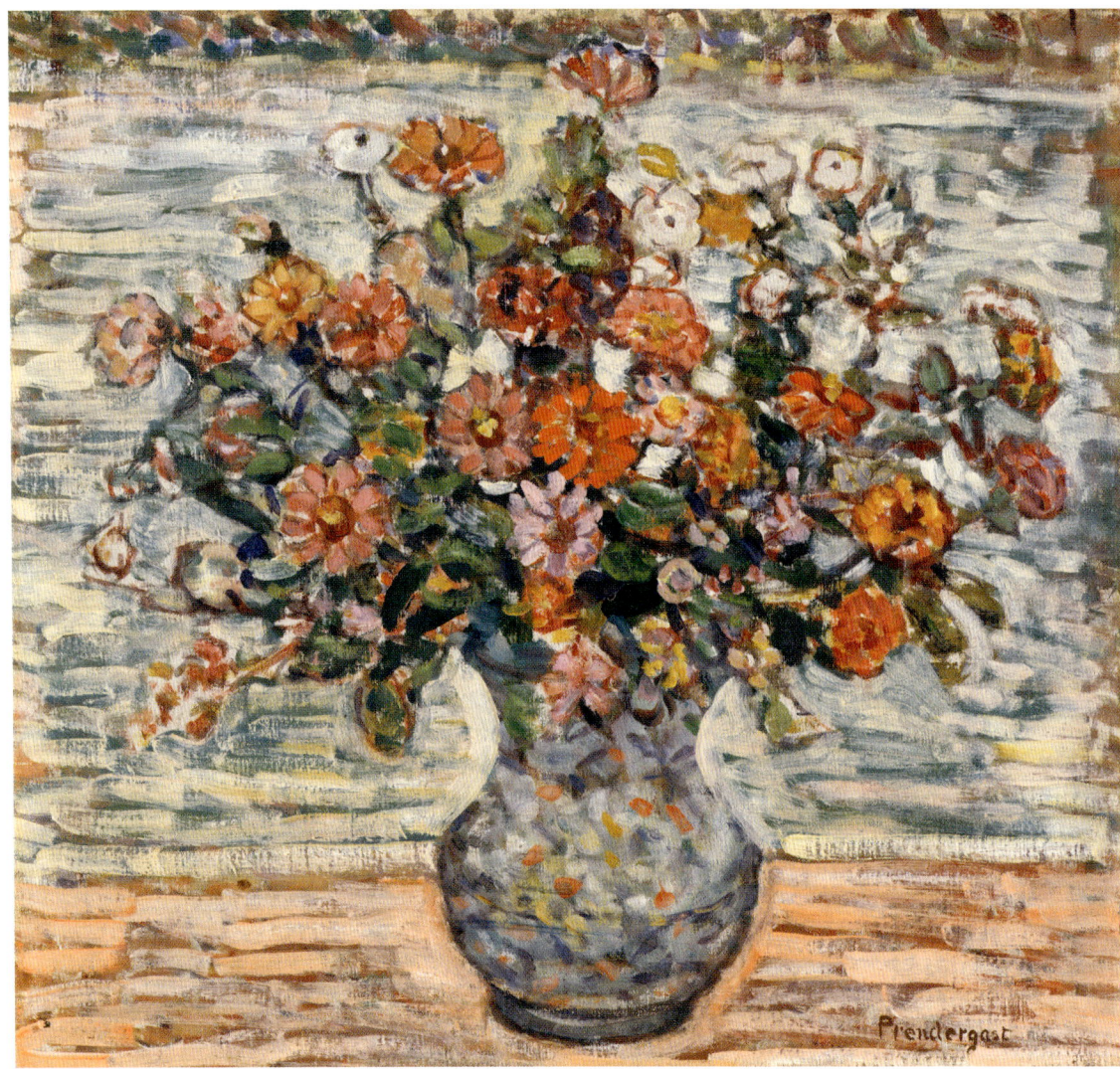

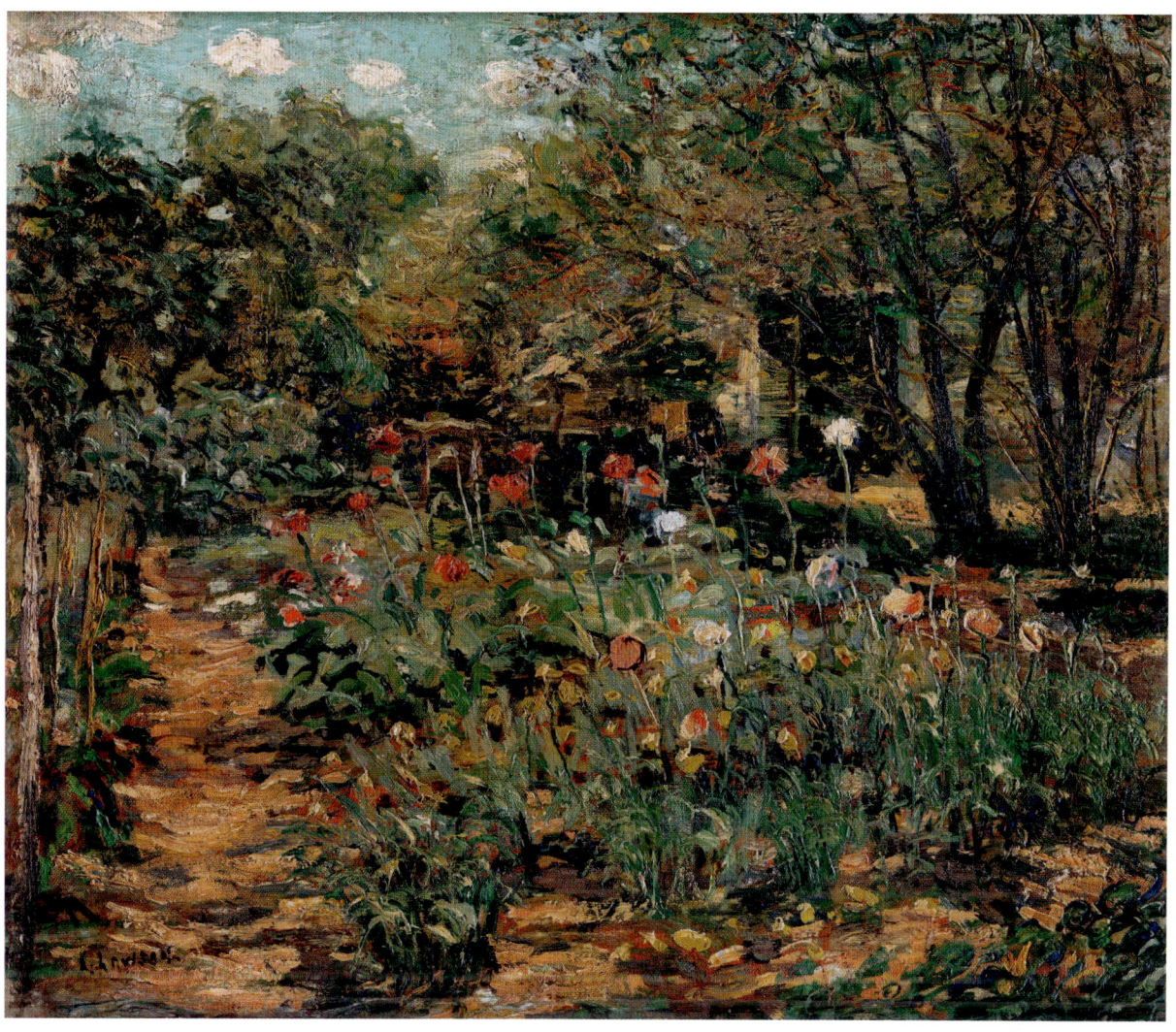

Ernest Lawson
(American, 1873–1939)
Garden Landscape, ca. 1915

Oil on canvas, 19 15/16 × 23 7/8 in.
Bequest of Laura L. Barnes, 67.24.10
Provenance: By 1966, acquired by Laura Leggett Barnes of Merion, PA; March 8, 1967, bequeathed by Laura Leggett Barnes to the Brooklyn Museum.

The flower bed in this painting looks a bit wild at first glance, but I see the deliberate hand of a gardener here: simultaneous blooms of various colors, arranged in vertical layers, observable all at once from close range. This takes planning! Given enough time and space, a similar scene might occur naturally, but it's less likely that an artist with easel, brushes, and oils would happen upon such a concentrated bloom.

The loose, Impressionist technique Ernest Lawson uses here emphasizes the relationship of the plants to each other and their environment. Without the distraction of sharp detail, it's easier to experience the glory of a midsummer's day. This is an increasingly popular approach in contemporary garden design, whether in Brooklyn Botanic Garden's mixed-bed plantings or the Brooklyn Museum's pollinator garden. The whole is greater than the sum of its parts.

—Jesse Brody, Belle's Brook Gardener, Brooklyn Botanic Garden

To Give Flowers

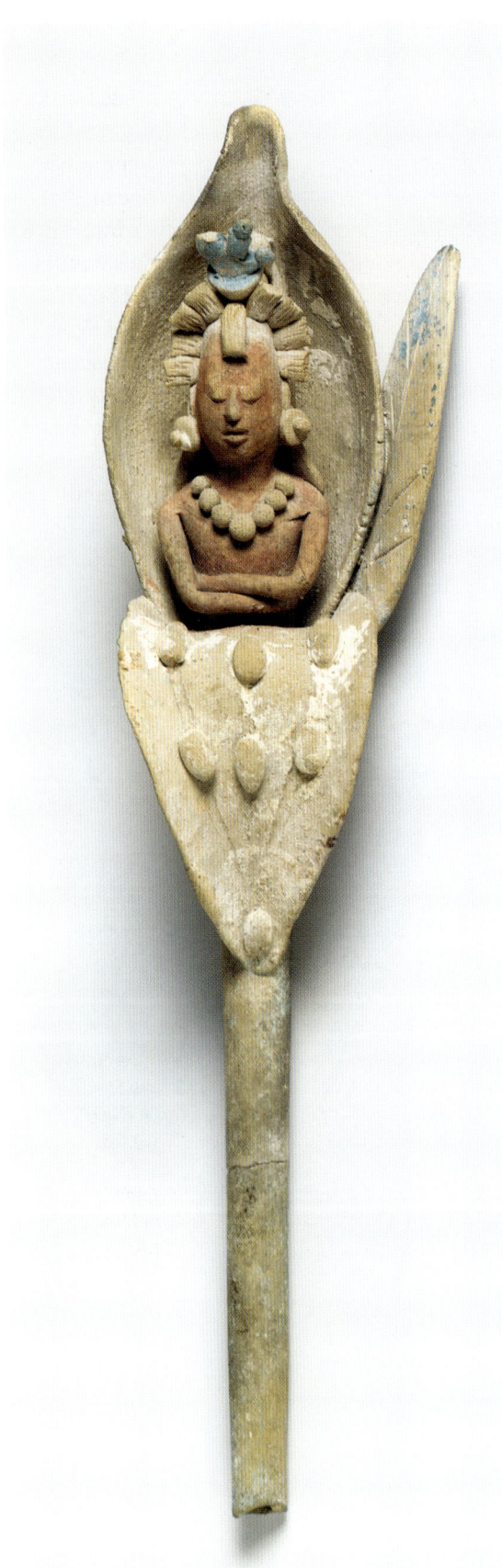

Maya artist
Whistle with the Maize God Emerging from a Flower
Campeche, Mexico, 600–900

Ceramic, pigment, 8¼ × 2⅛ × 1¹¹⁄₁₆ in.
Dick S. Ramsay Fund, 70.31
Provenance: Prior to 1970 undocumented; acquired by Alphonse Jax, New York City, before 1970; purchased in 1970 by the Brooklyn Museum.

This delicately modeled ceramic whistle features a young and bejeweled Maize God emerging from a flower. Venerated across the Maya region for millennia, the Maize God is often depicted as a metaphor for new growth and regeneration. He is identified by an elongated head, reminiscent of an ear of corn, and the idealized features of a beautiful young man. He wears a beaded necklace and ear spools, ornaments that were made of jade, a precious stone that likely referred to the green and vital qualities of the living maize plant.[1]

In Maya creation stories, the Maize God dies, descends into the underworld, and is reborn, a metaphor for the corn seed that is planted underground and emerges with new life as a maize plant. Thus, the god is symbolic of agricultural fertility, abundance, and renewal. According to Maya worldview, ancestors and deities, particularly the Maize God, reside in Flower Mountain, a paradise full of beautiful and fragrant flowers and music.[2] This paradise is also permeated by *ch'ulel*, or breath soul, a vitalizing force also present in the ethereal qualities of scent and sound. Among the ancient Maya, music and copal incense were both the food and essence of gods and ancestors, and they were used to summon deities and ancestors during rituals.[3] This whistle, which was likely played during special ceremonies, references the concepts of flowers as residing places for divine beings, and music and the fragrance of flowers to bring them to life.

DR/NR

1. Karl Taube, "The Classic Maya Maize God: A Reappraisal," in *Fifth Palenque Round Table, 1983*, ed. Virginia M. Fields (San Francisco: The Pre-Columbian Art Research Institute, 1985), 174, https://www.mesoweb.com/pari/publications/RT07/Maize-OCR.pdf.
2. Karl A. Taube, "Flower Mountain: Concepts of Life, Beauty, and Paradise among the Classic Maya," *RES: Anthropology and Aesthetics*, no. 45 (Spring 2004): 69, https://www.jstor.org/stable/20167622.
3. Ibid., 72.

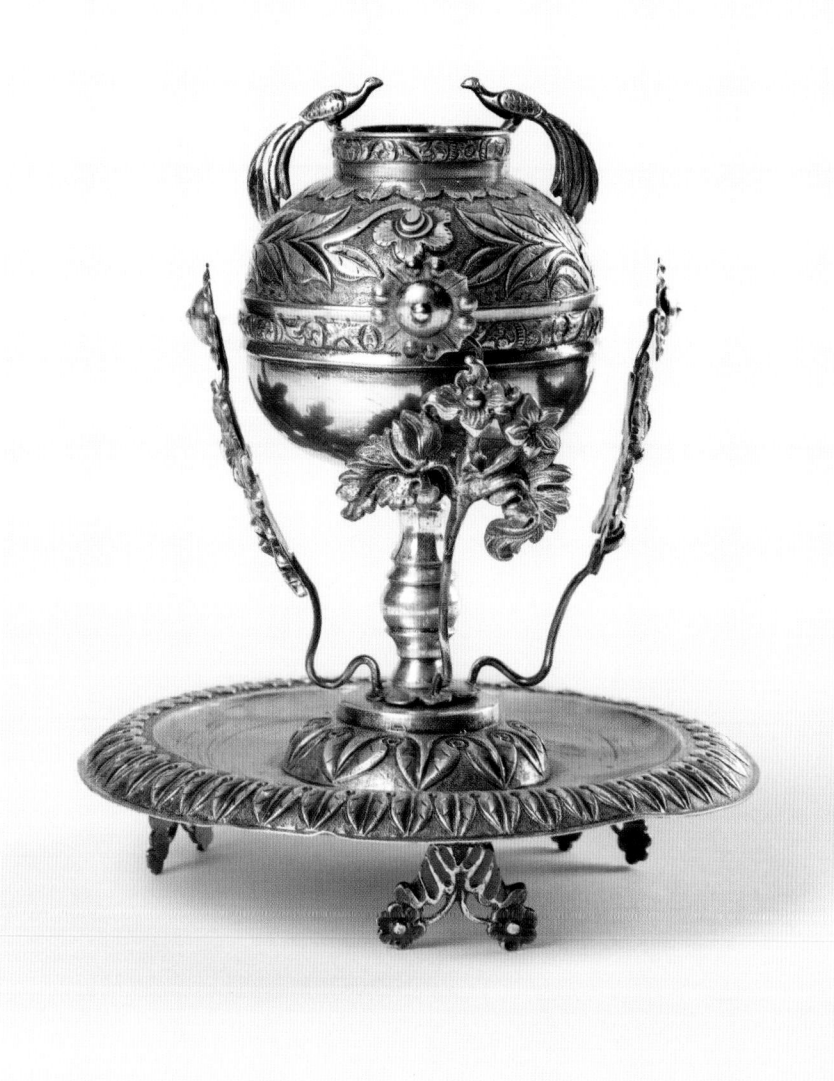

Chilean artist
Maté Cup and Saucer
Chile, 19th century

Silver, 7 × 6 3/16 × 6 3/16 in.
Gift of Mary Ann Krotzer, 2003.50.1
Provenance: Ca. 1925, acquired, probably in Chile, by Henry Wiley Krotzer of New Orleans, LA; before 2003, inherited from Henry Wiley Krotzer by Mary Ann Krotzer; 2003, gift of Mary Ann Krotzer to the Brooklyn Museum.

Silverworking was a highly developed art form in South America before the arrival of Spanish colonizers, and Indigenous craftsmen continued to play an important role in the production of silver objects throughout the colonial era. Due to silver mining, cattle ranching, and trade in the lucrative markets of tobacco, cacao, sugar, and red cochineal insect dye, Spanish colonists were among the world's wealthiest people. In the Viceroyalty of Peru, one of Spain's South American colonies, their homes and those of the Indigenous elite, who traced their descent from Inca kings, showcased the finest luxury goods such as silver trays, plates, bowls, candlesticks, and flatware.[1] During banquets and other social occasions, these precious objects were flamboyantly displayed in the formal reception room, on a special piece of furniture shaped like a flight of stairs called a *mostrador*, which was covered with rich textiles.[2] This silver cup, made to drink Andean yerba maté (herb) and coca-leaf teas, features intricate European floral designs. The globular form is modeled after the gourd and coconut-shell cups that were traditionally used prior to colonization. The tea was made by pouring hot water over dried leaves, and the infusion was sipped through a silver filtering straw called a *bombilla*. Silver maté cups were sometimes ornamented with gold, indicating how thoroughly this Indigenous beverage was accepted by the wealthy upper classes.[3]

NR

1. Jorge F. Rivas Pérez, "Domestic Display in the Spanish Territories," in *Behind Closed Doors: Art in the Spanish American Home, 1492–1898*, ed. Richard Aste (New York: Brooklyn Museum and Monacelli Press, 2013), 75.
2. Ibid., 74.
3. Diana Fane, ed., *Converging Cultures: Art and Identity in Spanish America* (New York: The Brooklyn Museum in association with Harry N. Abrams, 1996), 263.

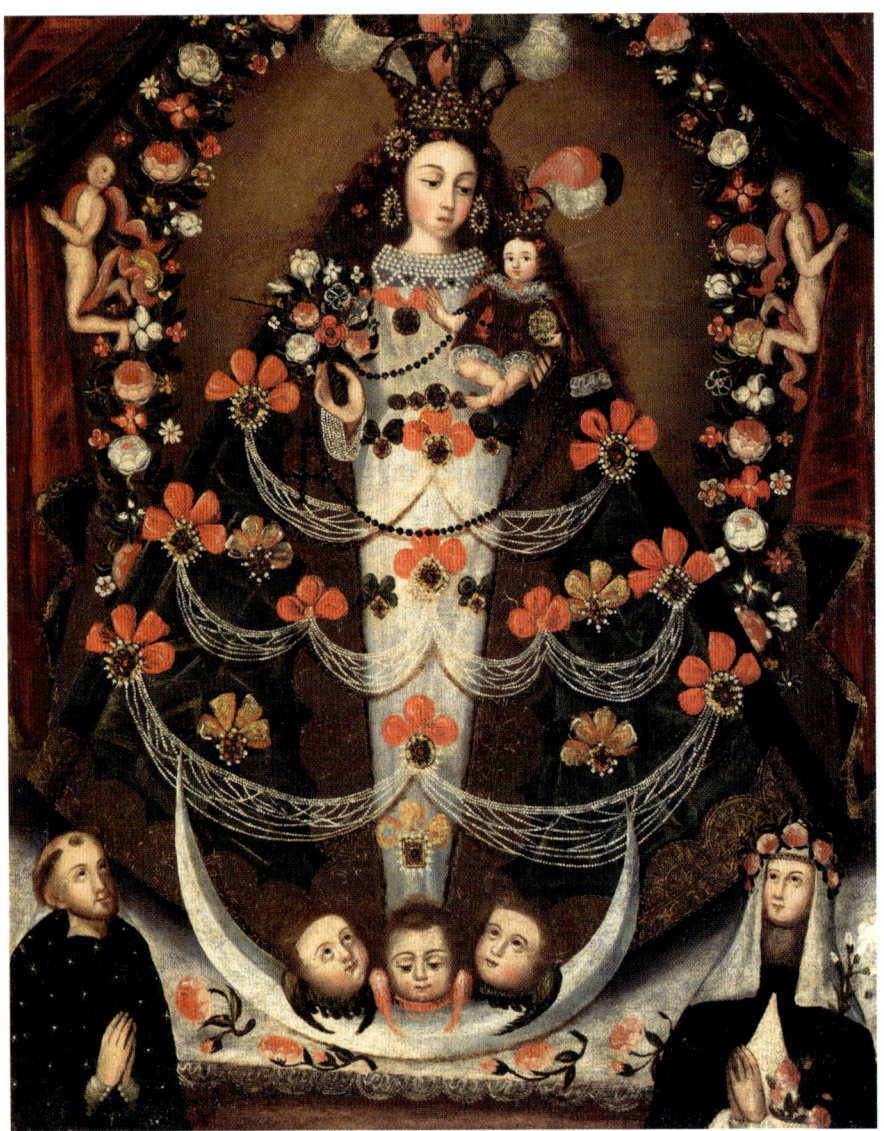

Peruvian artist
Virgin of Pomata with St. Nicholas Tolentino and St. Rose of Lima, 1700–1750

Oil on canvas, 26 × 21 in.
Museum Expedition 1941, Frank L. Babbott Fund, 41.1275.400
Provenance: Acquired in Peru by Herbert Spinden for the Brooklyn Museum, 1941.

Joseph Stella
(American, born Italy, 1877–1946)
The Virgin, 1926

Oil on canvas, 39 11/16 x 38 3/4 in.
Gift of Adolph Lewisohn, 28.207
Provenance: Acquired by Adolph Lewisohn, by June 1928; donated, June 11, 1928.

Roses and lilies have long symbolized the Virgin Mary, they were incorporated as embellishment and imbued with meaning in artworks such as this eighteenth-century Peruvian painting and another made in 1926 by Joseph Stella. In each, Mary is centralized and surrounded by a vibrant profusion of iconographic blossoms that enhance the splendor of the Virgin. Both artists looked to Renaissance representations of Mary, adapting European styles and iconography to their own distinct artistic approaches.

In colonial Peru, understandings of the Virgin Mary often combined Christian and Indigenous Andean beliefs, and artistic representations likewise united symbolism from both traditions.[1] In this painting, the symbolism of the flowers was significant to both Indigenous and Spanish viewers. For European Christians, red and white Marian roses were associated with the Virgin. In Indigenous traditions, flowers were used in ceremonial offerings, scattered on the ground, added to headdresses, and adorned canopies that protectively covered the Inca (king), much like their varied use in this painting.[2] This particular painting depicts the miracle-working statue of the Virgin of the Rosary in Pomata, Peru, which was a popular pilgrimage destination.[3] Floral motifs were also represented in tunics and Inca *qero* cups as indicative of their many ceremonial and

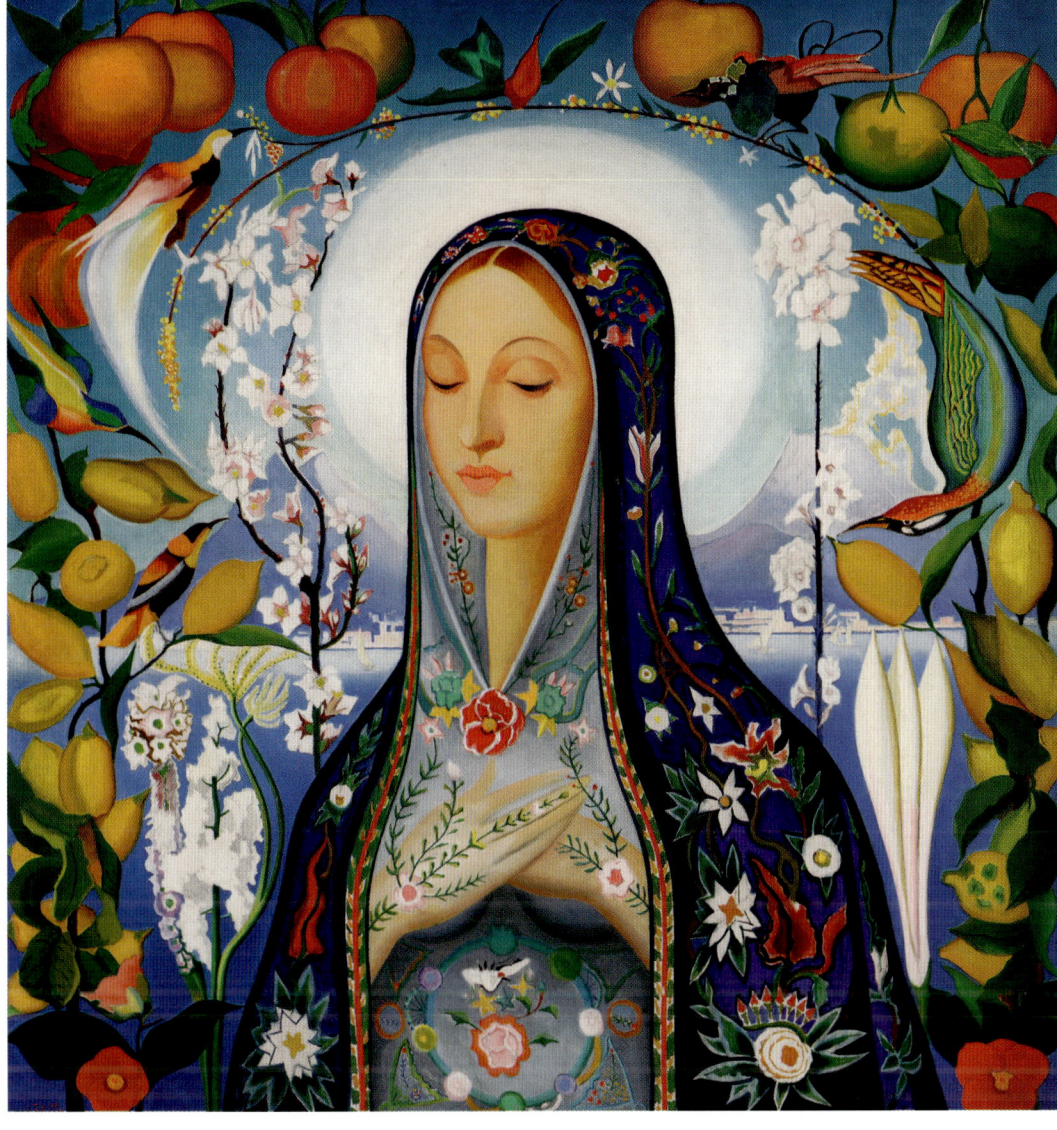

medicinal uses (p. 81).⁴ Flowers and headwear with feather plumes unite Inca traditions with European Christian iconography in this composition, which is characteristic of the Cusco School of painting.⁵ Centered in the former Inca capital of Cusco and led by Indigenous artists who had been trained in European Mannerist and Baroque painting styles, Cusco School artists also incorporated bold colors, gilding, and flatter forms.

Similarly, Stella was inspired by the historic artworks of Christian and ancient mythological subjects he viewed during a visit to his native southern Italy in 1922. His paintings from this moment focus on religious and literary topics. They exemplify Stella's bold and modern vision for these subjects while still honoring the inextricable links between ancient Roman subjects and Christianity in the artwork and culture of his homeland.⁶ In this painting, Stella sets Mary amid a kaleidoscope of vibrant flowers, birds, and fruits, including vines laden with succulent oranges and lemons and adorned with delicate orange blossoms. Because they produce fruit and flowers at the same time, citrus plants signify both the Virgin's purity and fertility.⁷ A rich abundance of flowers, including lilies, white lotuses, and a rose, symbolize her inherent femininity and beauty.

CG with DG

1. Carol Damian, "The Virgin of the Andes: Queen, Moon and Earth Mother," *Southeastern College Art Conference Review* 14, no. 4 (2004): 303–13; and Maya Stanfield-Mazzi, *Object and Apparition: Envisioning the Christian Divine in the Colonial Andes* (Tucson: The University of Arizona Press, 2013).
2. Eleonora Mulvany, "La Flor en el Ciclo Ritual Incaico," *Boletín de Arqueología PUCP* 9 (2005): 376–82, 384. Mulvany notes that red, white, and yellow flowers were commonly used by the Inca.
3. For more on this painting, see Diana Fane, ed., *Converging Cultures: Art & Identity in Spanish America* (New York: Harry N. Abrams, 1996), 218.
4. Eleonora Mulvany, "Motivos de Flores en Keros Coloniales: Imagen y Significado," *Chungara: Revista de Antropología Chilena* 36, no. 2 (July–December 2004): 407–19; Thomas B. F. Cummings, *Toasts with the Inca: Andean Abstraction and Colonial Images on Quero Vessels* (Ann Arbor: University of Michigan Press, 2002).
5. Regarding the iconography of the *Maskapaycha* (feathered crown), see Carolyn Dean, *Inka Bodies and the Body of Christ: Corpus Christi in Colonial Cuzco, Peru* (Durham, NC: Duke University Press, 1999), 100–109, 128, 130.
6. Irma B. Jaffe, *Joseph Stella's Madonnas and Related Work* (New York: Snyder Fine Art, 1993), 2–5; Irma B. Jaffe, *Joseph Stella's Symbolism* (San Francisco: Pomegranate Artbooks, 1994), xiv–xv.
7. Christina Mazzoni, *Golden Fruit: A Cultural History of Oranges in Italy* (Toronto: University of Toronto Press, 2018), 55.

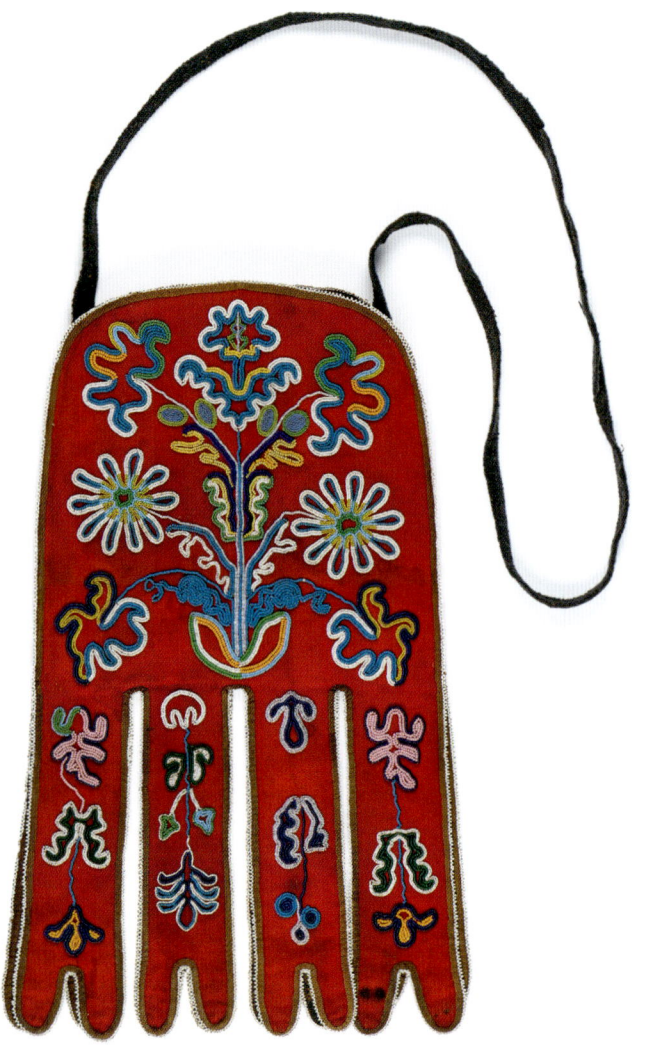

Tlingit artist
Naakw gwéil (Octopus Bag)
Southeastern Alaska, United States
or British Columbia, Canada, 1868–1901

Wool, cotton, glass beads, 17 11/16 × 7/16 in.
Museum Expedition 1908, Museum Collection Fund,
08.491.8896
Provenance: Acquired by Frederick Landsberg, by 1908; purchased by Stewart Culin for the Brooklyn Museum, July 15, 1908.

The life of the white man came over the Tlingit people like a great thunderstorm. . . . An invader may satisfy himself in saying that the native customs and habits have about disappeared, but could the lid of the true Tlingit woman's mind be thrown wide open there would be seen the mystic veneration of her art still alive and active.[1]

—Stoowukháa (Louis Shotridge),
Tlingit Knowledge Keeper

Known as octopus bags because of their tentacle-like fringe, *naakw gwéil* served as regalia that communicated Tlingit tribal identity and the high status of its owner. Framed with delicate beadwork around the edge, the design elements take form with evenly spaced seed beads, which lay flat against the surface of the bag—a hallmark of masterful technical execution.[2] Though select *naakw gwéil* were adorned with crest imagery traditionally found on ceremonial attire, pieces like this one embrace "foliate or floral designs that would not have been recognized by non-Natives as ceremonial."[3] They allowed for the continuation of cultural practices outlawed by colonial authorities and stand in contrast to the visual designs traditionally employed on items like the *Thunderbird Transformation Mask* (p. 238).

Octopus bags did not originate with the Tlingit; rather, artists from inland Indigenous communities like the Cree and Red River Métis first fashioned them from animal skins and utilized animal leg hides to create decorative pendants. Tlingit women artists adopted the form—perhaps due to their reverence for powerful octopuses—utilizing fabric and seed beads acquired through extensive trade networks. While the use of floral designs illustrates the interconnectedness of tribal nations, the beadwork style here is distinctively Tlingit.

DT

1. Louis Shotridge, "Tlingit Woman's Root Basket." *The Museum Journal* XII, no. 3 (September 1921): 162–78, https://www.penn.museum/sites/journal/936/.
2. Megan A. Smetzer, *Painful Beauty: Tlingit Women, Beadwork, and the Art of Resilience* (Seattle: Bill Holm Center for the Study of Northwest Coast Art, Burke Museum: University of Washington Press, 2021), 10.
3. Aaron Glass, "Bag, Object Gallery, Objects of Exchange," Bard Graduate Center, accessed April 11, 2024. https://www.bgc.bard.edu/object-exchange-bag.

Cover, pp. 10, 104:
Laura Wheeler Waring
(American, 1887–1948)
Woman with Bouquet, ca. 1940

Oil on canvas, 30 × 25 in.
Brooklyn Museum Fund for African American Art
in honor of Teresa A. Carbone, 2016.2
Provenance: Acquired by Milton Morriss James, by 1947. Acquired by Michael Rosenfeld Gallery, by January 2002; purchased by the Brooklyn Museum, April 14, 2016.

Laura Wheeler Waring was an artist and educator best known for her academic portraits of Black American subjects. Born in Hartford, Connecticut, she trained at the Pennsylvania Academy of the Fine Arts. Upon graduating, Waring was granted the A. William Emlen Cresson Memorial Travel Scholarship—the first Black woman to receive the award—allowing her to study in Paris in 1914.[1] She also completed quiet landscapes and vibrant still lifes inspired by both Impressionist and Social Realist techniques. Her early illustrations for the National Association for the Advancement of Colored People's journal *The Crisis*, founded by W. E. B. DuBois, also exemplified the Modernist styles of the period, and an interest in the African themes proliferated by the New Negro Movement.[2] In 1927, Waring participated in the first exhibition of works by Black Americans organized by the Harmon Foundation and received the Harmon Gold Award, the highest prize granted by the organization.

In *Woman with Bouquet*, Waring's effortlessly poised sitter holds a bouquet of zinnias, their vibrant colors echoing the dabs of red, yellow, and orange in her dress. Painted in the latter part of her career, the depiction of the casual elegance and understated beauty of the woman, as well as the floral iconography, are enhanced by adept brush and color work. A single pink bloom peeks out, a flash of pigment mirrored in the portrait's makeshift backdrop of draped fabric. Although often associated with friendship and long-standing affection, zinnias sometimes symbolized the absence or loss of a companion. The woman's distant gaze and her locket pendant suggest a deeper meaning lies behind the portrait, a testament to the dignity, complexity, and humanity Waring afforded her subjects, and for which the artist's portraits of Black Americans are celebrated.

SSW

1. "Laura Wheeler Waring," Connecticut Women's Hall of Fame, accessed May 5, 2024, https://www.cwhf.org/inductees/laura-wheeler-waring.
2. This movement gave rise to the Harlem Renaissance. For more, see Denise Murrell, ed., *The Harlem Renaissance and Transatlantic Modernism* (New York: Metropolitan Museum of Art, 2024).

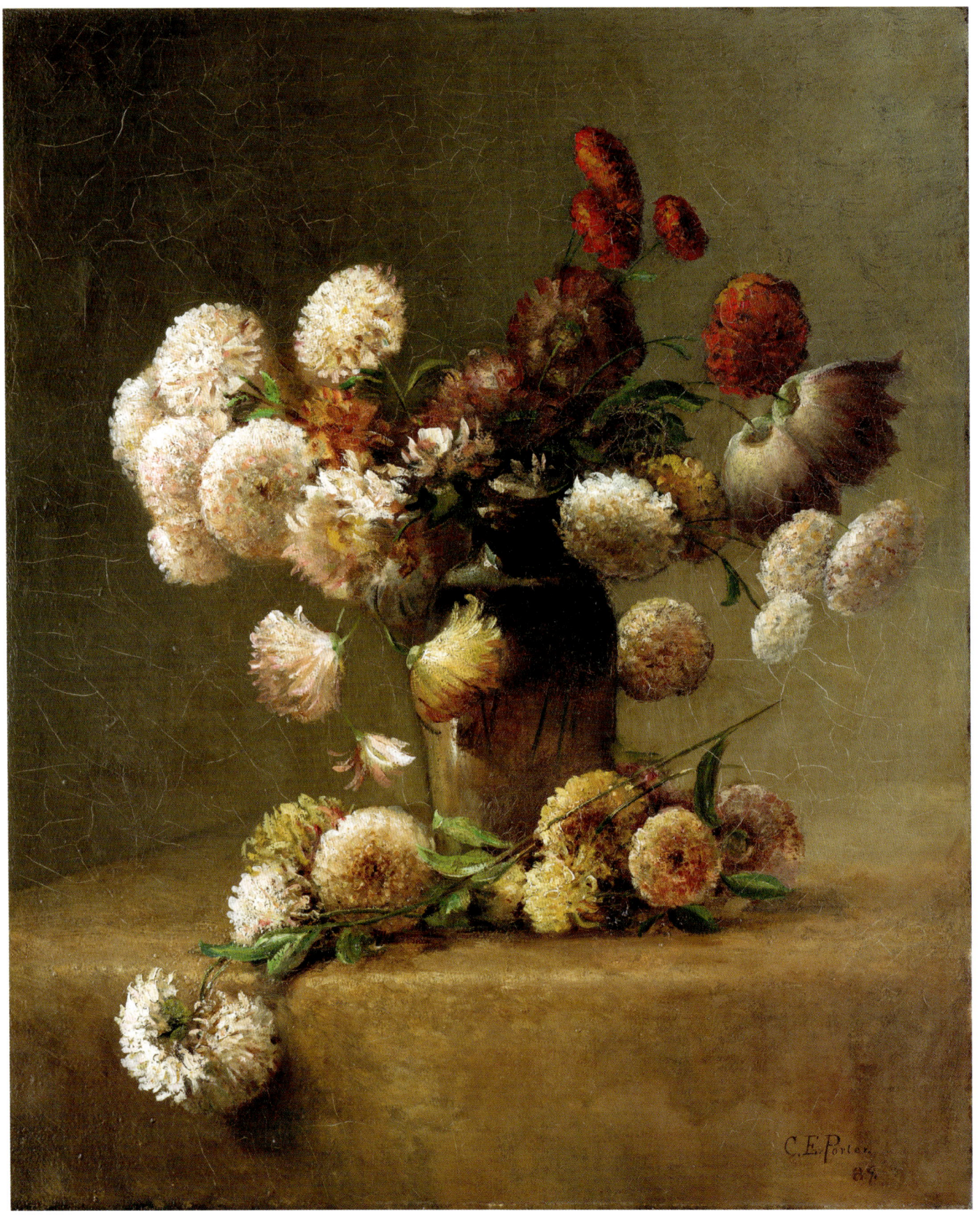

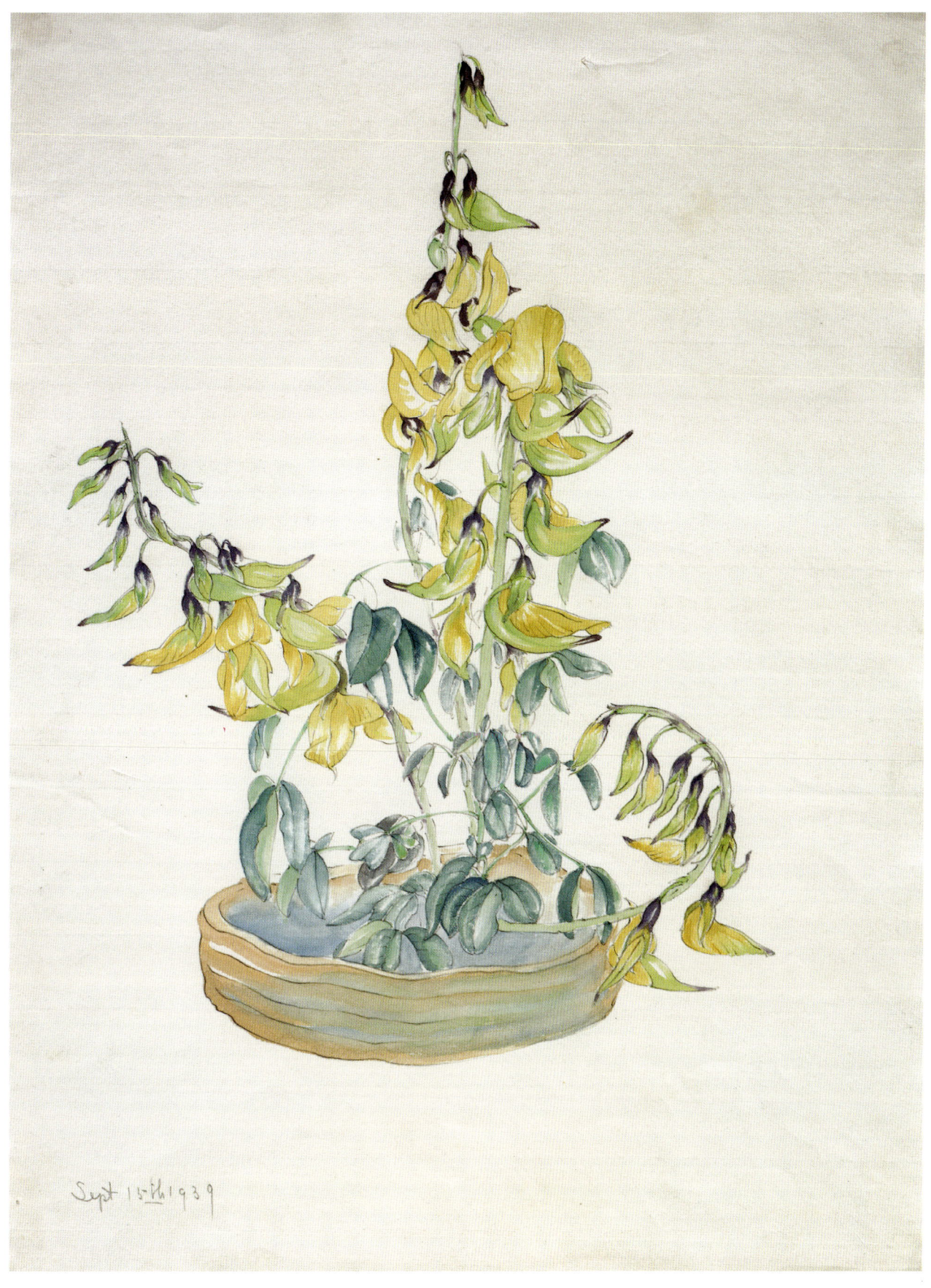

To Give Flowers

117

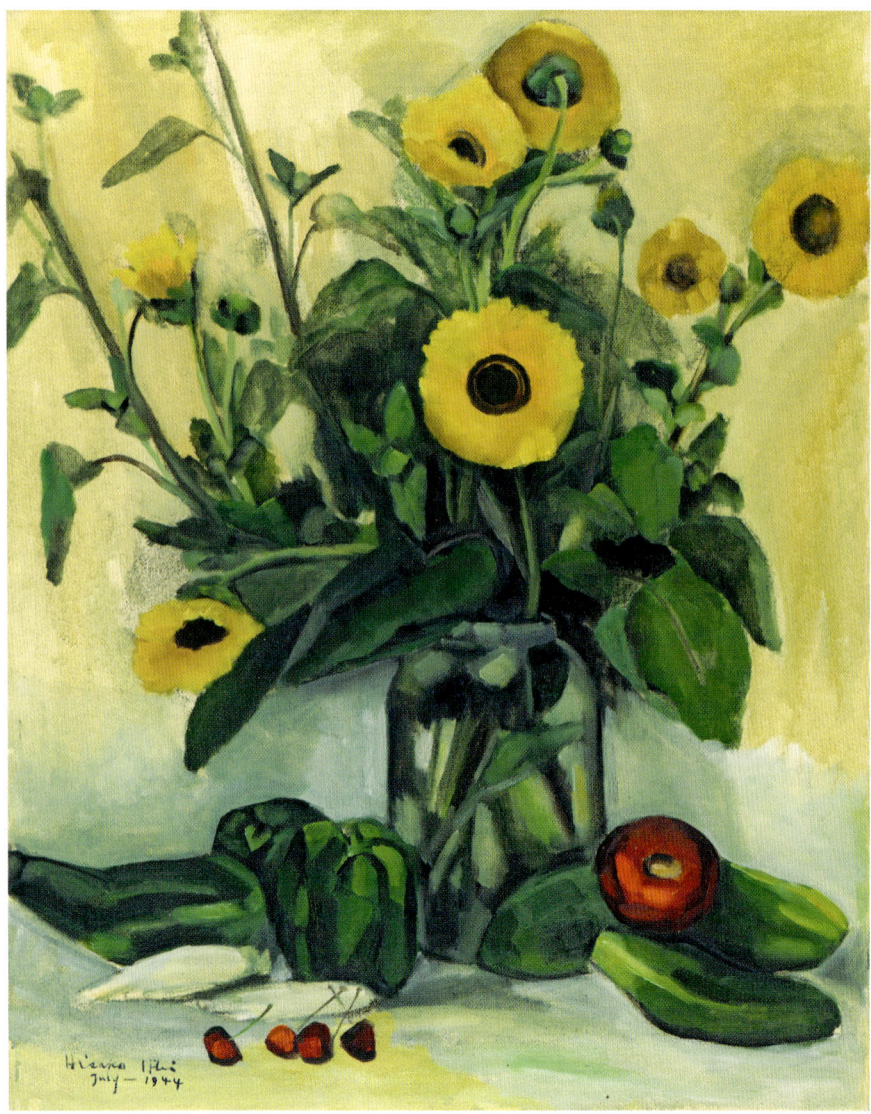

Page 116:
Charles Ethan Porter
(American, 1847–1923)
Chrysanthemums, 1888

Oil on canvas, 23 × 19½ in.
Gift of Charlynn and Warren Goins, 2023.46.1
Provenance: Acquired by Cal Smith, before 1990; purchased at Pleasant Valley Auction House by Charlynn and Warren Goins, 1990; donated, October 24, 2023.

Page 117:
Chiura Obata
(American, born Japan, 1885–1975)
Flower Arrangement, Yellow, 1939

Watercolor on paper, 20¾ × 15½ in.
Gift of the Estate of Chiura Obata with additional support from the Alfred T. White Fund, 2023.16.7
Provenance: Donated by the artist's estate, April 4, 2023.

Hisako Hibi
(American, born Japan, 1907–1991)
Topaz Sunflowers, July 1944

Oil on canvas, 22 × 18 in.
Gift of Ibuki Hibi Lee, 2023.26.2
Provenance: Purchased from the artist's estate by the Brooklyn Museum, June 14, 2023.

Groupings of inanimate objects from daily life, or still lifes, are found across art history, spanning culture, medium, and subject. The ubiquity of still lifes in art across the globe, particularly floral renditions, speak to the ways the genre and its manifestations reflect a reverence for the natural world and the human experience. In some contexts, this regard is purely practical, or studious, and in others deeply aesthetic and spiritual, transcending many of the national and societal barriers more generally imposed across other, namely, Western, art traditions.

Charles Ethan Porter, one of the first Black American painters to work professionally and experience commercial success as a painter and arts educator, is best known for his still life paintings. *Chrysanthemums* is a spectacular display of the artist's handling of color and texture in this representation of an overflowing flower vase. The work is characteristic of the artist's engagement with Impressionism after traveling to Paris in the 1880s, demonstrated through the thicker dabs of paint and the play of light and colors that bring depth and greater vibrancy to the blooms, particularly the white petals. Despite segregation and racialized discrimination, Porter was celebrated within the vibrant art scene of Hartford, Connecticut, where he enjoyed glowing art reviews and the patronage of notable figures such as artist Frederic Edwin Church and writer Mark Twain.

Though still life painting was included within a rigorous academic art training, those who would go on to pursue it commercially were often disparaged by their peers, intellectuals, and critics for lacking the power to "elevate and enlighten" their audiences through their paintings.[1] For artists who were already marginalized within the social fabric of the United States, floral paintings, in particular, took on their own power, resonance, and indeed edifying effects. To Japanese American Hisako Hibi, sunflowers were the symbol of resilience and power par excellence, as discussed in Grace Billingslea's essay, "From Our Mothers' Gardens" (pp. 124–25). For Billingslea, Hibi's *Topaz Sunflowers*, a still life of bright yellow sunflowers, boldly arranged with squash, bell peppers, and cherries, represented the resilience of unjustly imprisoned Japanese Americans during World War II. While incarcerated at the Topaz War Relocation Center in central Utah, Hibi celebrated with brush and paint the cheerful harvest she and fellow inmates cultivated in the harsh desert soil. The fresh fruits and vegetables seen in Hibi's paintings supplemented government rations and brightened residential barracks.

The centuries-old Japanese art of flower arranging, ikebana, a similar symbol of cultural resilience, continues to be practiced today. The graceful arrangement seen in *Flower Arrangement, Yellow* was created by accomplished *kado-ka* (ikebana artist) Haruko Obata and skillfully rendered in watercolor by her husband, Chiura Obata. An example of the formal *seika* style, Haruko's arrangement models the three core elements of ikebana: Heaven, Man, and Earth.[2] The tallest central branch represents Heaven, the branch bending left represents Man, and the lowest branch represents Earth. When all three are in harmony, a perfect *seika* ikebana is achieved. Made of branches from a birdflower plant (*Crotalaria cunninghamii*), the arrangement highlights the plant's distinctive flowers, which resemble birds hanging by their beaks from the central stem.

Historically, artists of diverse backgrounds working in the United States have had varying and inequitable access to the modes of creative production. The drive and inspiration to create flower pictures reflects both the cultural significance of particular blooms and their arrangements, as well as a market in which beautification through domestic decoration offered socially acceptable means through which artists who may have been excluded from formal training could find wide-ranging appreciation for their creative work. In this way, too, the still life genre is central for understanding early American cultural consumerism and likewise recognizing that the paintings themselves also "manifest frameworks of knowledge and experience shared by artist and audiences."[3] Moreover, still lifes thus are imbued with historically situated knowledge and meaning, much like a time capsule, as noted by scholar and curator Mark D. Mitchell;[4] a layered and nuanced appreciation of still life takes into account the cultural, social, political, and economical contexts in which any given work emerges.

SSW with GB

1. Still life painting was often disdained because it focused on quotidian objects. See Carol Troyen, "Fruit, Flowers, and Lucky Strikes: The Still Life in American Culture," in *The Art of American Still Life: Audubon to Warhol,* ed. Mark DeSaussure Mitchell (Philadelphia: Philadelphia Museum of Art, in association with Yale University Press, 2015), 23.
2. Haruko Obata. *Japanese Flower Arrangement: An Illustrated Handbook* (Berkeley, CA: Obata Studio, 1953), 5.
3. Mark DeSaussure Mitchell, "Philadelphia Still Life and American Art," in *The Art of American Still Life: Audubon to Warhol,* ed. Mark DeSaussure Mitchell (Philadelphia: Philadelphia Museum of Art, in association with Yale University Press, 2015), 1.
4. Ibid. Mitchell goes on to assert that in still life, "the selection and juxtaposition of objects—sometimes mysterious to us now—were 'perfectly logistical and overtly significant,'" quoting Alfred Frankenstein in Alfred Frankenstein, *After the Hunt: William Harnett and Other American Still Life Painters, 1870–1900* (Berkeley: University of California Press, 1953), 9.

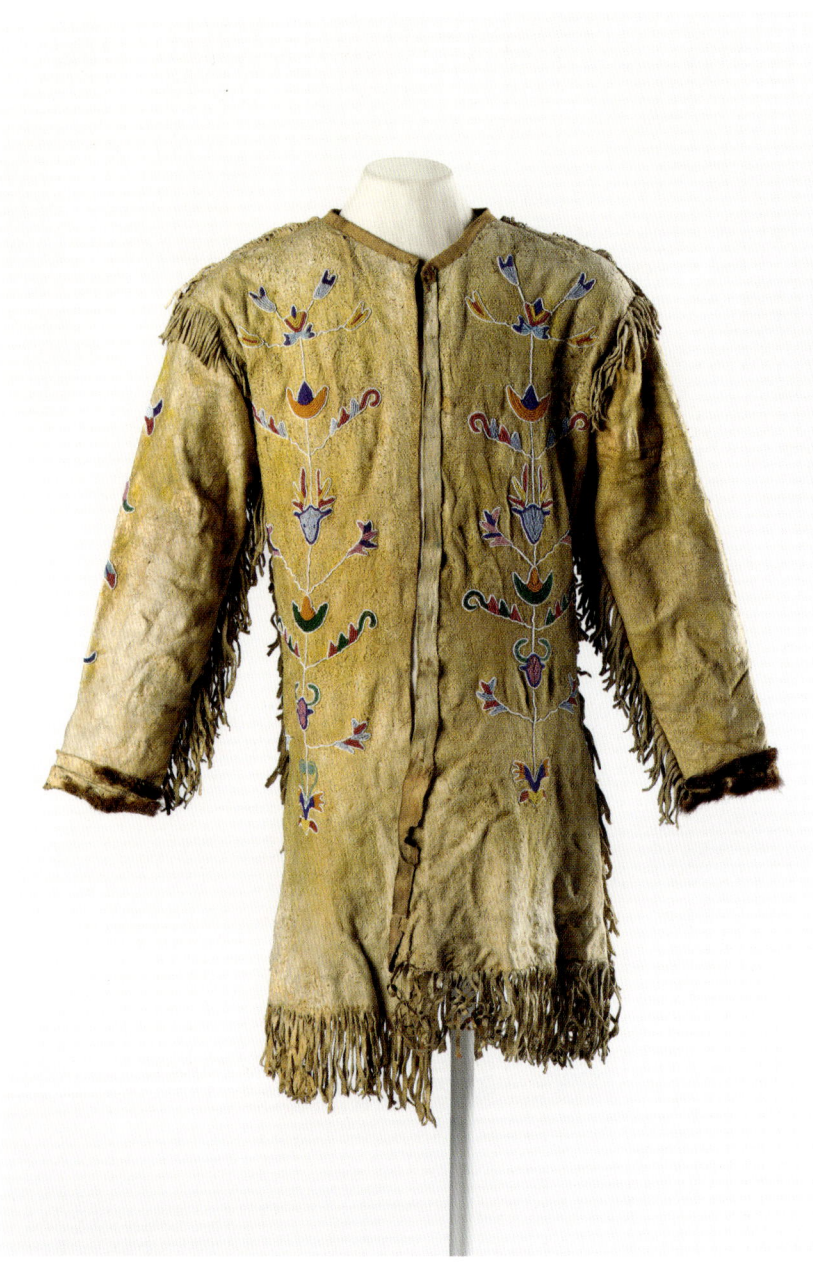

Red River Métis artist or Eastern Dakota artist
Man's Shirt Cut in European Style
Manitoba, Canada or Northern Plains,
United States, late 19th century

Buckskin, pigment, fur, glass beads, cotton,
53 3/16 x 35 1/2 in.
By exchange, 41.866
Provenance: Acquired by Wendell Ter Bush, before 1935; donated to the Department of Religion, Columbia University, ca. 1935; purchased by the Brooklyn Museum, by exchange, September 13, 1941.

Women's artistic work gives evidence to the critical role they played in integrating new materials and ideas, while simultaneously maintaining a certain stable and continuous core of ancient knowledge. Collectively, the objects tell a story . . . that recounts the important roles women played in communicating visual information to an audience of humans, animals, and spirits; these women who clothed their families, negotiated change, and contributed to the economic survival of their communities.[1]
—Sherry Farrell Racette, Métis/Timiskaming Algonquin/Irish scholar and artist

Known as the "flower beadwork people," Red River Métis artists used trade goods, including European-made glass beads and silk thread, to adorn clothing. Made by a woman likely from the Métis or Eastern Dakota tribal community, this shirt is adorned with intricate floral designs, and fringe along the sleeves and hem. Cut from buckskin in a European-style tailored fit, this garment departs from the loose-fitting shirts traditionally worn by Indigenous men from this region. Its blend of aesthetics reflects a history of settler–Indigenous entanglement.

Dating to the seventeenth century, French, Scottish, and British fur traders often married Indigenous Cree and Anishinaabe women to build strategic alliances. The resulting families became a distinct cultural group: the Métis. According to historian Susan Sleeper-Smith, such marriages "transformed French fur traders into friends, family, and allies [and] kinship transformed the impersonal exchange process characteristic of capitalism into a socially accountable process."[2] Many Métis girls attended mission schools in the nineteenth century where nuns taught them embroidery styles and floral motifs informed by European tastes. Those students indigenized such techniques to create the distinctive style exemplified here.

DT

1. Sherry Farrell Racette, "Looking for Stories and Unbroken Threads: Museum Artifacts as Women's History and Cultural Legacy," in *Restoring the Balance: First Nations Women, Community, and Culture*, ed. Gail Guthrie Valaskakis, Madeleine Dion Stout, and Éric Guimond (Winnipeg: University of Manitoba Press, 2009), 285–86.
2. Susan Sleeper-Smith, *Indian Women and French Men: Rethinking Cultural Encounter in the Western Great Lakes* (Amherst: University of Massachusetts Press, 2001), 4.

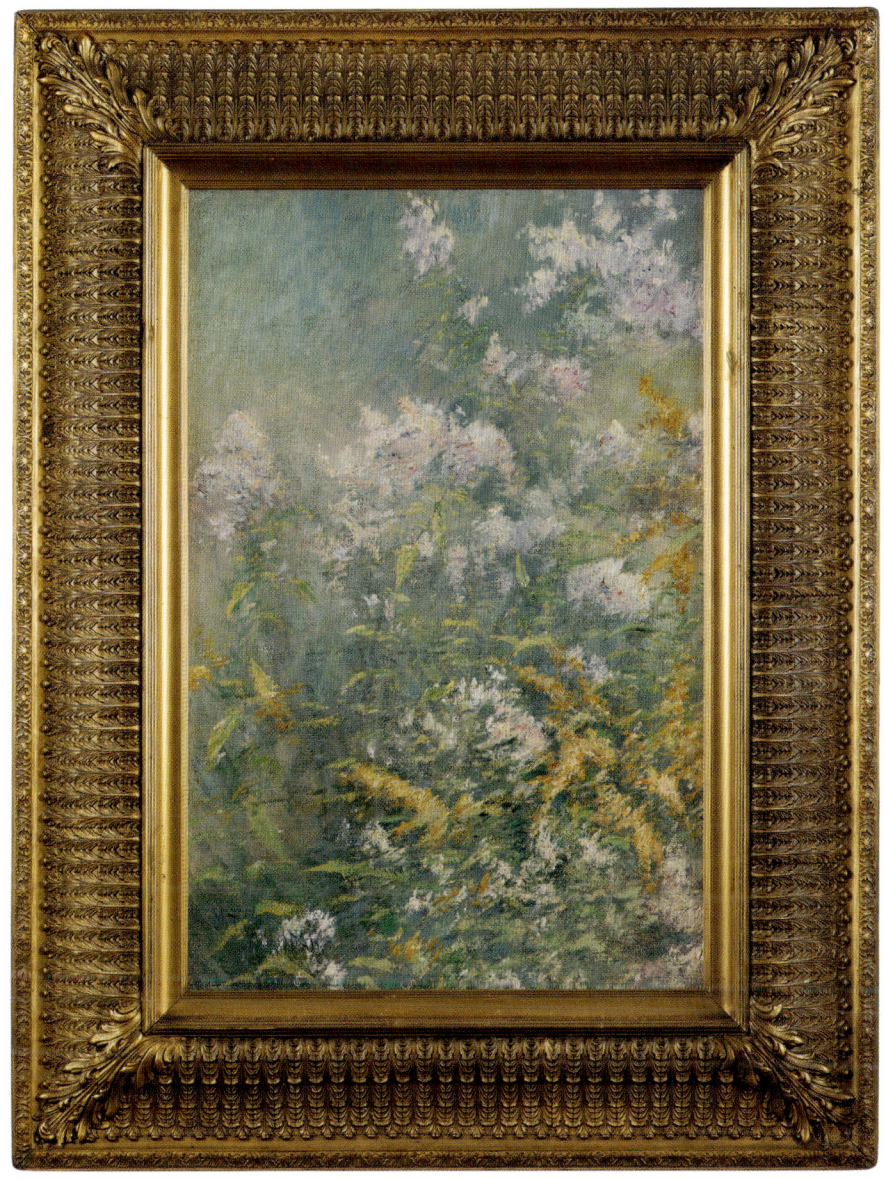

John Henry Twachtman
(American, 1853–1902)
Meadow Flowers (Golden Rod and Wild Aster), ca. 1892

Oil on canvas, 33 5/16 × 22 3/16 in.; frame (designed by Stanford White): 47 × 36 1/4 × 2 1/4 in.
Caroline H. Polhemus Fund, 13.36
Provenance: Inherited from the artist by Martha Scudder Twachtman (Mrs. John Henry Twachtman), 1902; purchased by William T. Evans, by 1908; purchased at American Art Association, William T. Evans sale, by the Brooklyn Museum, April 1, 1913.

John Henry Twachtman was an American Impressionist, who, while popular among his artist peers, saw limited commercial success during his lifetime. Throughout his thirty-year career, Twachtman created paintings characterized by a skillful mastery of color, light, and mood.[1] While traveling and training in Europe between 1875 and 1886, Twachtman experimented with several of the approaches he encountered, including the soft color palette and atmospheric effects attributed to Tonalist painters. Several landscapes from this period are considered among his strongest. His painting style shifted following his move to Connecticut, where he purchased a farm in Greenwich in 1890. There Twachtman painted colorful spring garden compositions, dozens of picturesque streams and waterfalls, and snowy winter landscapes, all in his unique personal technique that coalesce light, color, and subject matter into diffuse scenes that disorient and enchant equally.

Greenwich was once known for its profusion of wild aster and goldenrod at summer's end. In this painting, Twachtman documented their showy effects in a meadow near his home. Asters and goldenrods are often found growing together, forming wisps of golden yellow and clusters ranging from pale pink to deepest purple. The flowers have evolved to grow together to attract pollinators. Photoreceptor cells in the eyes of both humans and bees respond to complementary color combinations—particularly yellow and purple—making these flowers visually compelling to both species. Thus, more pollinators visit when the two flowers bloom together.[2] Twachtman paints the floral pair in what became his later signature Impressionistic style—lively colors and brushstrokes—enhanced by an opulent gilded frame designed by the architect Stanford White.

SSW

1. For more on Twachtman's life and work, see Lisa Peters's collection of essays, produced for the 1999 traveling exhibition of the artist's work organized by the High Museum of Art in Atlanta. Her essays trace the development of Twachtman's art from his early years in Cincinnati (1853–75) through his death in Gloucester, MA, in 1902. Lisa Peters, *John Henry Twachtman: An American Impressionist* (New York: Hudson Hill, 1999).
2. Plant biology adapted from the research and writing of Potawatomi scientist Robin Wall Kimmerer. See Robin Wall Kimmerer, *Braiding Sweetgrass: Indigenous Wisdom, Scientific Knowledge, and the Teachings of Plants* (Minneapolis, MN: Milkweed Editions, 2013).

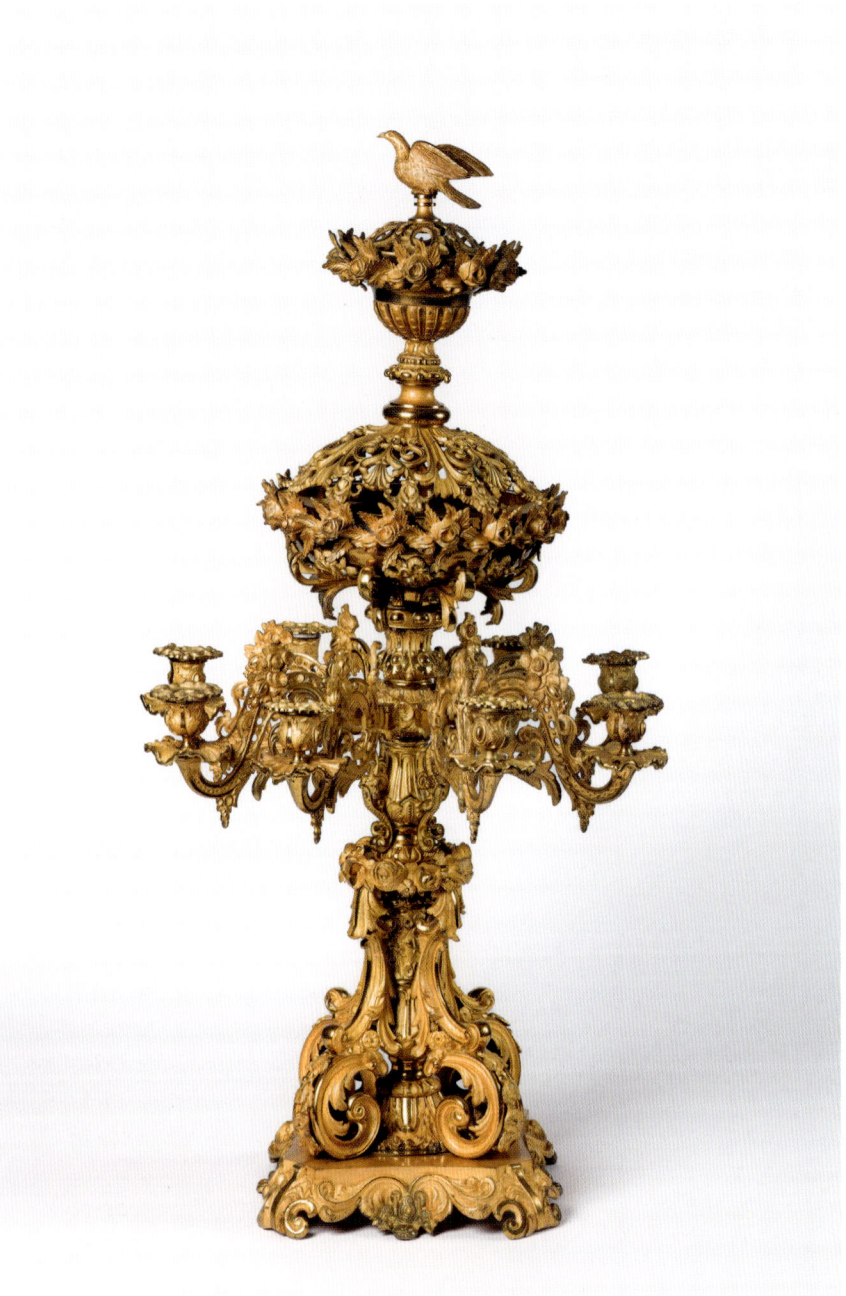

Cornelius & Baker
Manufacturer, Philadelphia, Pennsylvania, 1853–1869
Candelabrum, ca. 1853

Gilded bronze, 34 × 18½ × 18½ in.
Marie Bernice Bitzer Fund, 1998.89
Provenance: Acquired by Galleria Hugo, by 1998; purchased by the Brooklyn Museum, October 15, 1998.

Lighting has always been an integral element in interiors, and designers and manufacturers over the millennia have focused on creating works that coordinate with fashionable tastes. Cornelius & Baker of Philadelphia—the leading nineteenth-century manufacturer of lighting devices for wax candles, oil, gas, kerosene, and electricity—produced metal fixtures in myriad styles to harmonize with American upper-middle-class domestic spaces.

As opposed to the static lighting of electric lightbulbs, other means of illumination—such as candle or gas flames—produced variable brilliance that animates the surfaces of objects in a way more akin to that of natural light, which shifts with the passing of a cloud over the rays of the sun. Designers sought to manipulate lighting to create the sensation of movement. Cornelius & Baker's robust candelabrum encrusted with leaves and flowers, topped by an eagle, must have appeared alive when the light from the candle flames danced across the gilded metal surface.

The American Cornelius & Baker's prominence was internationally recognized when it participated in the first world's fair, held in London in 1851, and, in 1853, in the first American world's fair the company won critical acclaim with a monumental version of this remarkable candelabrum. Employing over five hundred men, women, and children in its Cherry Street factory, the company manufactured not only lighting devices but also decorative sculptures made of zinc, a low-cost metal, which was patinated, or covered in gold or bronze, so as to be more affordable to American consumers.

CF

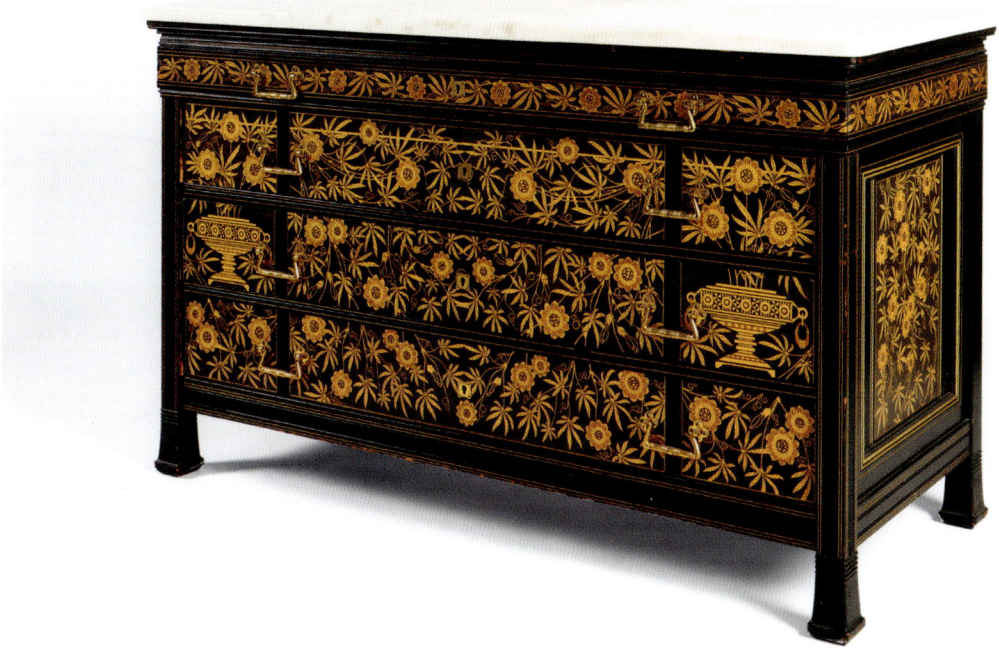

Herter Brothers
Manufacturer, New York, New York, 1864–1906
Chest-of-Drawers, ca. 1880

Ebonized cherry, other woods, modern marble top, brass, 30 1/16 × 52 1/16 × 22 in.
Modernism Benefit Fund, 1989.69
Provenance: Acquired, possibly commissioned from the artist, by Darius Ogden Mills, ca. 1880. Reportedly purchased at an antiques market in New Orleans, LA, by Garrison Kingsley, before 1989. Acquired by Neal's Auction, before 1989; purchased by Richard and Eileen Dubrow Antiques, by 1989; purchased by the Brooklyn Museum, June 28, 1989.

Part of a large suite of bedroom furniture, this densely decorated, late nineteenth-century chest of drawers would have been part of a completely integrated interior. Designed by Christian Herter of Herter Brothers, the most fashionable American furniture and design firm of this period, this elegant and innovative chest displays two stylistic trends in mid- and late-nineteenth-century decorative arts and interiors: the natural world and Japanese art and design.

Mid-nineteenth-century decorative arts featured realistic carved and painted renderings of plants and animals. The U.S. government's forced opening of Japan in 1853 to compel Japanese manufacturers and consumers to participate in international trade, however, produced a greater awareness of the art and culture of this formerly isolated country. European and American artists and designers were particularly drawn to the Japanese aesthetic that flattened space and floral and animal motifs, as seen here with the melding of European-style vases and flowers and Asian bamboo, abstracted and rendered in light-colored wood marquetry. In addition, American designers began to imitate Japanese black-ground lacquer work, ebonizing, or staining in black, the background of this chest. The firm of Herter Brothers fulfilled commissions, with such suites of florally decorated furniture, for some of the most well-known and notorious industrial and railroad developers of the nineteenth century, ironically despoiling the nature they seemed to cherish at home.

CF

CRITICAL SHORT
From Our Mothers' Gardens

Grace Billingslea

Artist Hisako Hibi carefully tended sunflowers that grew in vivid contrast to the dull desert soil and wooden buildings of Topaz War Relocation Center in central Utah. She planted the cheerful blossoms along the entrance of the tar-papered barrack her family shared with up to five other Japanese American families while wrongfully imprisoned during World War II.[1]

In May 1942, after the signing of Executive Order 9066, Hibi, her husband and fellow artist George Matsusaburo Hibi (1886–1947), and their two young children, Satoshi and Ibuki, were ordered to pack what they could carry and leave their home in Hayward, California.[2] Photographer Dorothea Lange captured this liminal moment of forced relocation in an image of Hibi and her daughter at a bus stop against a backdrop of stacked luggage. In September 1942, the Hibi family was transferred from Tanforan Assembly Center, a repurposed racetrack in San Bruno, California, to Topaz War Relocation Center.

Despite being uprooted, Hibi increased her artistic output while at Topaz.[3] Usually working from an initial sketch, she painted quickly, finishing paintings in one or two days and completing well over seventy oil paintings during her imprisonment.[4] Hibi captured landscapes and scenes of everyday life ranging from the debilitating dust storms that swept through camp to fellow inmates sharing meals or washing clothes. Still lifes featuring flowers, or foliage accompanied by seasonal fruits and vegetables

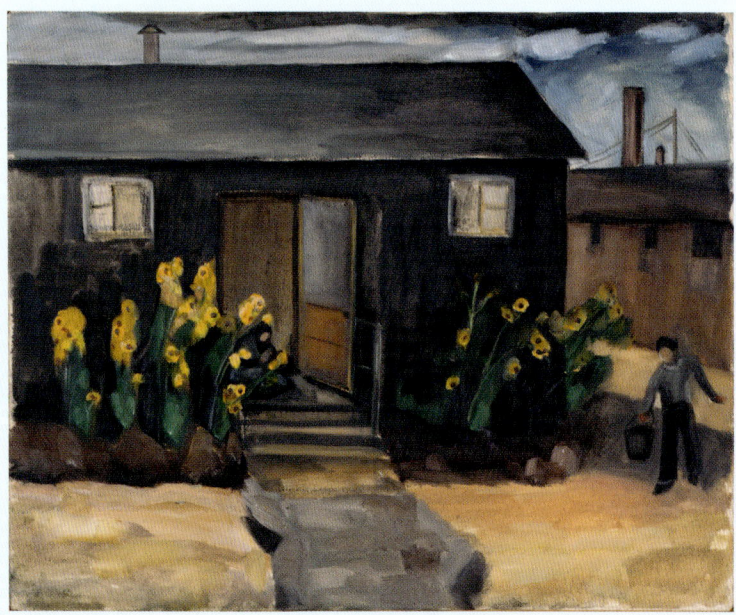

Hisako Hibi (American, born Japan, 1907–1991), *In front of my apt.*, 1944. Oil on canvas, 16 x 10 inches. Japanese American National Museum (Gift of Ibuki Hibi Lee, 96.601.41).

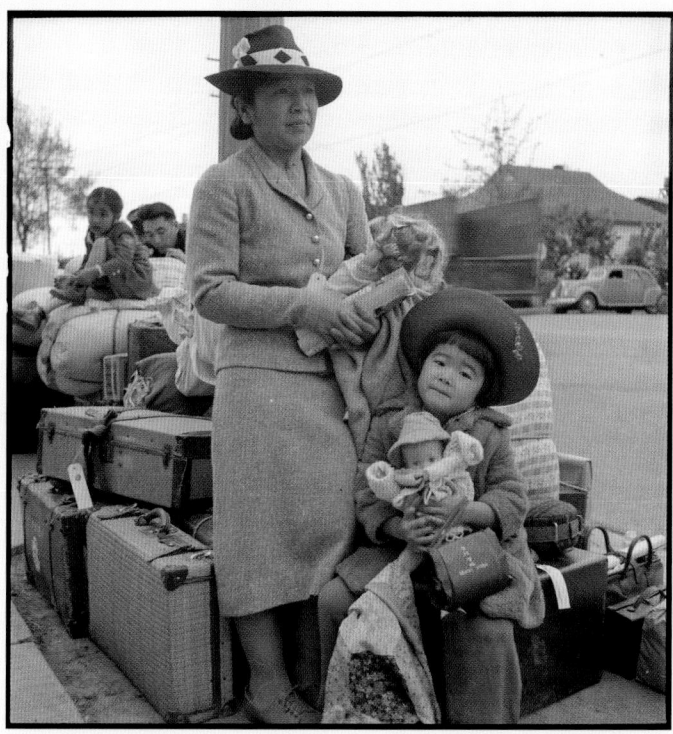

Dorothea Lange (American, 1865–1965). [Untitled], 1942. National Archives and Records Administration, Records of the War Relocation Authority, 1941-1989, NAID 537522.

grown in the camps, such as *Topaz Sunflowers* (1944), were a favorite subject of the artist (p. 118). These pieces make up nearly a fifth of the paintings Hibi completed while incarcerated.

Sunflowers held special significance to Hibi. She reflects in her memoir:

> They bloomed firmly in the white heat of the summer, as though a symbol of existence in their desert life, like the Issei immigrants who had endured the heat and cold and the stormy, political weather.[5]

To Hibi, the robust flower's ability to flourish in harsh environments represented the resilience of Japanese Americans.

Ibuki Lee, who was just five years old when incarcerated, has spent her life preserving her mother's artistic legacy, archiving her mother's papers, and publishing Hibi's memoir, *Peaceful Painter: Memoirs of an Issei Woman Artist* (Heyday Books, 2004). The mother and daughter exchanged hundreds of letters throughout Hibi's lifetime, with the artist often writing about her Buddhist beliefs and personal philosophies centered around nature and peace. Lee recalls her mother's oft-repeated adage, "Life is transitory. Yesterday's flower is tomorrow's dream. Everything changes in time and condition."[6]

Lee passed her mother's art and words to her daughter, Amy Lee-Tai, who wrote a children's book titled *A Place Where Sunflowers Grow* (Lee & Low Books) in 2015. In this touching narrative, a young girl named Mari, incarcerated at Topaz, discovers moments of joy in planting sunflowers with her mother, attending art classes, and making friends despite her circumstances. Incorporating imagery from Hibi's paintings into the illustrations, Lee-Tai's book memorializes her grandmother's art as well as her belief in flowers as metaphors for hope and resilience.

In her seminal essay, "In Search of Our Mothers' Gardens" (1974), writer Alice Walker recounts memories of her own mother, Minnie Tallulah Grant Walker, and her spectacular flower garden, which she planted in front of every "shabby house [they] were forced to live in."[7] This impulse to cultivate splendor out of nothingness, particularly in marginalized communities, is an under-recognized tradition in the American artistic landscape. Hibi's legacy comes to us preserved and honored by her daughter and granddaughter, a mission that Walker, too, understands and takes up as she discovers her own mother's art in the form of her garden.

In nurturing flowers, Hibi and Minnie Walker culled beauty out of chaos, grace out of degradation. In their subtle yet self-determined acts of creation and refusal in the face of oppression, these women passed on to their children "the creative spark, the seed of the flower they themselves never hoped to see."[8] Hibi's sunflowers and Walker's dahlias, towering proudly over their caretakers, were sown in the barren ground of American racism. Rooted in an insistence on life and joy and tended with care, the result is an enduring resplendence of which generations of daughters are able to meditate on, cherish, and emulate today.

1. Between 1942 and 1945, the United States wrongfully incarcerated 120,000 Japanese Americans in ten prison camps across the West Coast and the Southwest. People of all ages and professions, regardless of their citizenship, were detained in remote "Relocation Centers" due to racially fueled fears after the Japanese attack on Pearl Harbor and the U.S. entry into World War II. https://densho.org/catalyst/how-many-japanese-americans-were-incarcerated-during-wwii/.
2. Signed by President Franklin D. Roosevelt on February 19, 1942, Executive Order 9066 provided the legal authorization for the United States military to forcibly remove people deemed a threat to national security from the West Coast and relocate them inland.
3. Ibuki Lee, oral history by author, November 16, 2023, San Francisco, CA.
4. Ibid.
5. Hisako Hibi and Ibuki Lee, *Peaceful Painter: Memoirs of an Issei Woman Artist* (Berkeley, CA: Heyday Books, 2004), 23.
6. Lee, oral history.
7. Alice Walker, "In Search of Our Mothers' Gardens," in *Within the Circle: An Anthology of African American Literary Criticism from the Harlem Renaissance to the Present*, ed. Angelyn Mitchell (Durham, NC: Duke University Press, 1994), 408.
8. Ibid, 407.

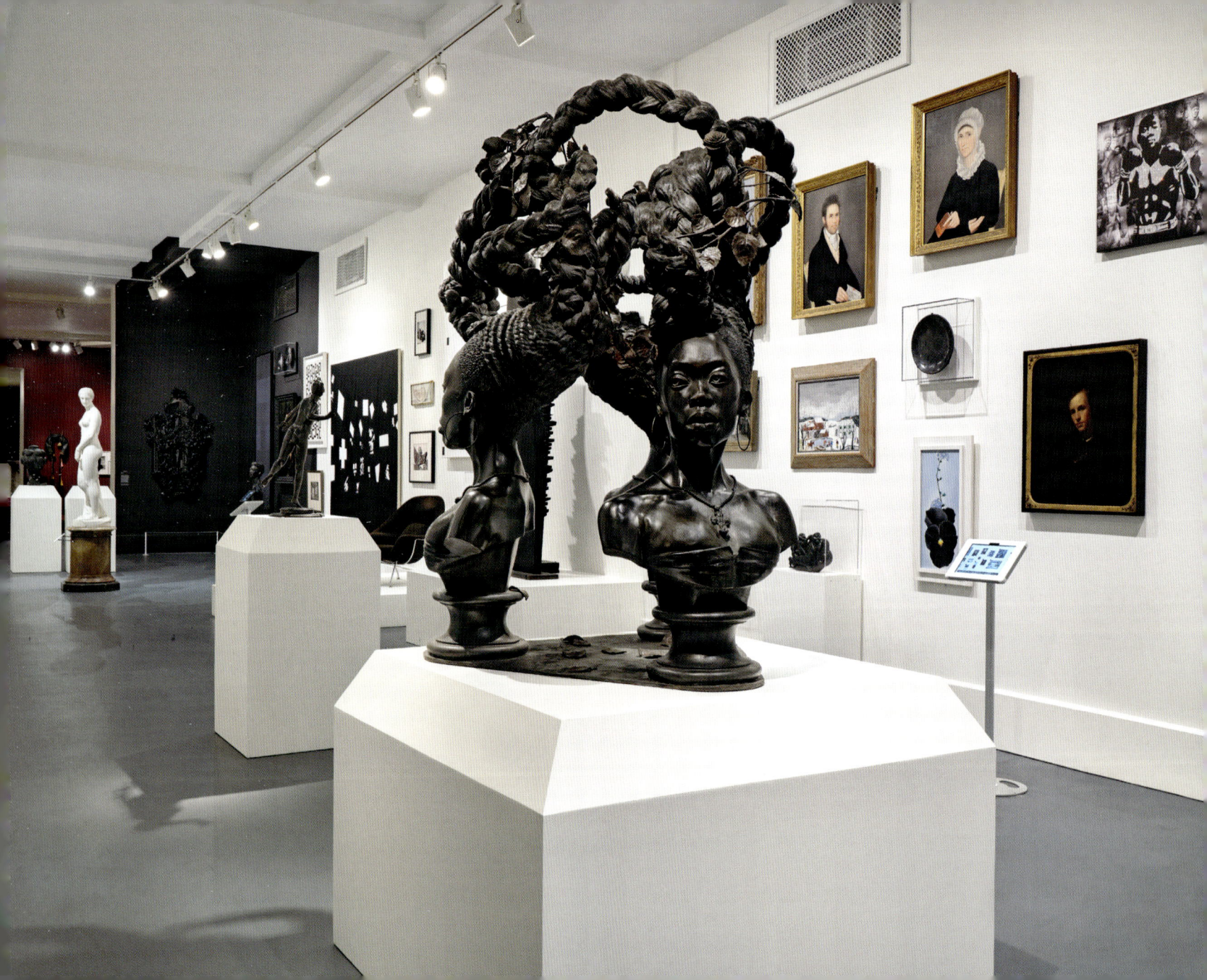

FRAMEWORK

Counterparts

How is meaning made through contrast? Can contrast be complementary?

Emphasizing form and materiality, this framework creates a space for daring conversations and dramatic discoveries. Black squares, shadows, chairs, dresses, photographs, bronzes, lines, matte black frames. White marble, garments, clay, paper, prayers, porcelain, gesso, blue-white snow. Here, black and white are not opposite—but rather coequal and counterpart. This framework brings together disparate artworks typically segregated by time, culture, and medium in a display that heightens similarities and recontextualizes differences. Together, the works in this section reverberate with infinite connections across their shared palette.

 This curatorial approach was inspired by two past exhibitions, both in New York. In 1965, the Black artist collective Spiral mounted *FIRST GROUP SHOWING (works in black & white),* and in 1983, Black feminist conceptual artist Lorraine O'Grady curated *The Black and White Show*, where Black and white artists submitted works in black and/or white. Critiquing the persistently segregated art world, these exhibitions challenged the ways art by Black artists was displayed and interpreted as separate from their white artistic counterparts.

 Here, we both build on and depart from the racial considerations of these earlier projects. In its achromatic display, both the in-gallery experience and the sampling of artworks included here destabilize the art historical categories that have traditionally signified value and determined what—and who—is included in American fine art.

 This is visualized when a limestone sculpture by William Edmondson is presented next to a photograph by Graciela Iturbide. Or when paintings by Emil Fuchs, Ad Reinhardt, Ilya Bolotowsky, and Kyohei Inukai are printed here side-by-side. Or when colonial portraits by Ammi Phillips are exhibited between an Impressionist canvas by Childe Hassam and a work by street art pioneer Fred Brathwaite (b. 1954, also known as Fab 5 Freddy). This new proximity to and commingling of disparate mediums, styles, and forms occasions a shift in our looking, a recalibration in our focus.

SSW

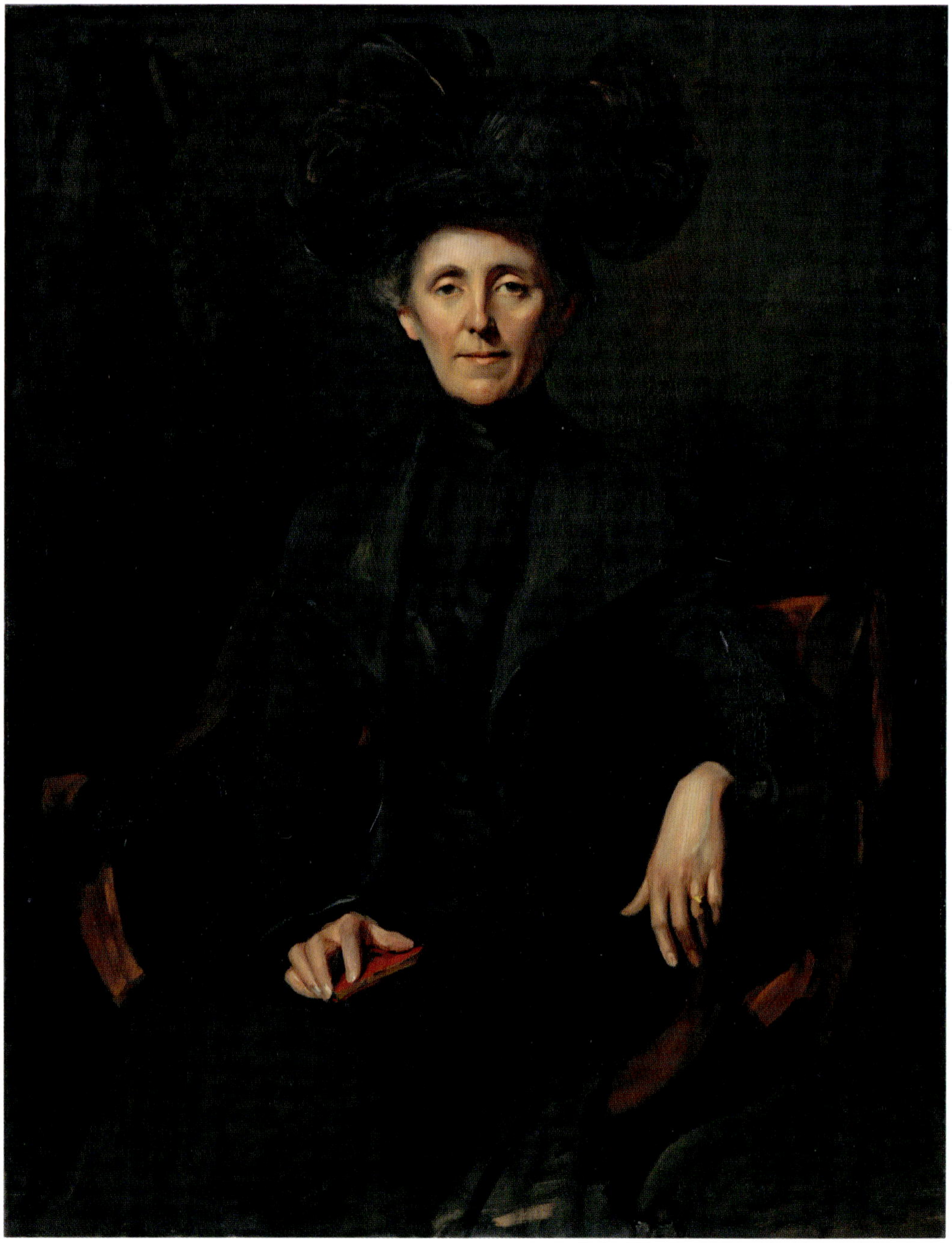

Toward Joy

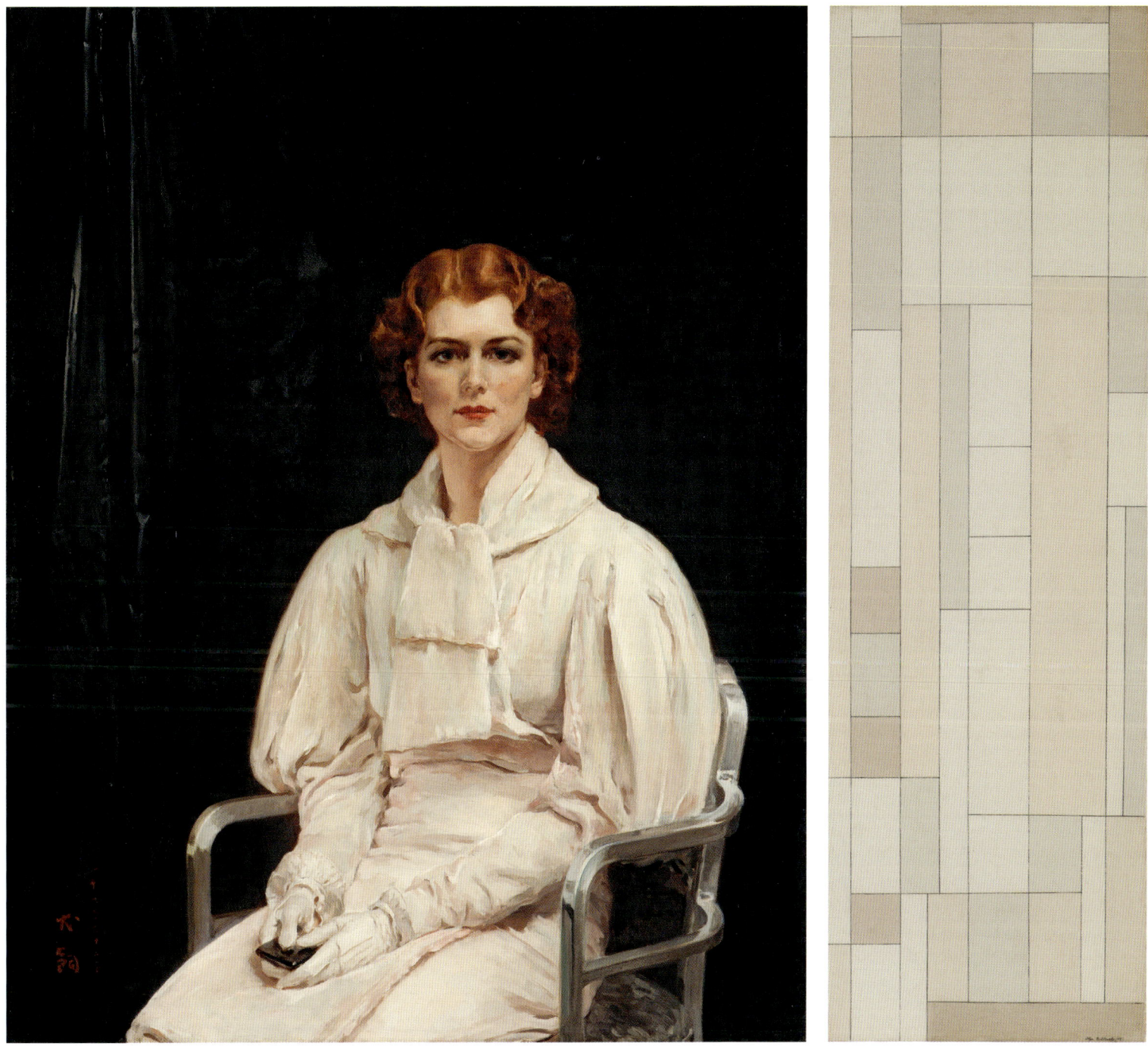

Counterparts

Page 128, left:
Ad Reinhardt
(American, 1913–1967)
Untitled (Composition #104), 1954–60

Oil on canvas, 110¾ × 42¾ × 2½ in.
Gift of the artist, 67.59
Provenance: Donated by the artist, 1967.

Page 126, right:
Emil Fuchs
(American, born Austria, 1866–1929)
Lady in Black, 1901

Oil on canvas, 46¹⁵⁄₁₆ × 36¹⁵⁄₁₆ in.
Gift of the Estate of Emil Fuchs, 32.199.7
Provenance: Donated by the artist's estate, July 12, 1932.

Previous page, left:
Kyohei Inukai
(American, born Japan, 1886–1954)
Dorothy, 1933

Oil on canvas, 50 × 40 in.
Gift of John and Miyoko U. Davey, 2024.1.4
Provenance: Acquired, probably from the artist, by Nancy Kunze Inukai, before 2023; purchased by John and Miyoko Davey, before 2023; donated, April 16, 2024.

Previous page, right:
Ilya Bolotowsky
(American, born Russia, 1907–1981)
Opalescent Vertical, 1955

Oil on canvas, 34 × 11 in.
Gift of Mr. and Mrs. Warren Brandt, 78.265
Provenance: Acquired from the artist by Warren Brandt and Grace Borgenicht Brandt (Mrs. Warren Brandt), by 1978; donated, December 1978.

Aesthetics then is more than a philosophy or theory of art and beauty; it is a way of inhabiting space, a particular location, a way of looking and becoming.[1]
—bell hooks

Before me—blackness: an inky-black sky studded with stars that glowed but did not twinkle; they seemed immobilized. Nor did the sun look the same as when seen from Earth. It had no aureole or corona; it resembled a huge incandescent disc that seemed embedded in the velvet black of the sky of outer space. Space itself appeared as a bottomless pit. It will never be possible to see the cosmos the same way on Earth.[2]
—Aleksei Leonov, the first man to walk in space, March 18, 1965

When artworks from across the collection are brought together on the pages of this catalogue and within the context of the installation, these groupings offer new ways of looking. These curatorial decisions move toward more expansive modes of seeing and becoming in relationship to historic American art. *Lady in Black* by Emil Fuchs, *Dorothy* by Kyohei Inukai, *Untitled (Composition #104)* by Ad Reinhardt, and *Opalescent Vertical* by Ilya Bolotowsky, four paintings by one U.S.-born and three émigré artists, span the first half of the twentieth century and represent disparate styles and approaches to working in oil on canvas.

Best known for his "black" or "ultimate" paintings, abstract artist Reinhardt was also a prolific writer, lecturer, and activist.[3] Painted during his time teaching at Brooklyn College, *Untitled (Composition #104)* first appears uniformly black, though it actually consists of blocks of nuanced pigment. Through these abstract meditations on the visual phenomenon that is "black," Reinhardt, as astronaut Aleksei Leonov articulates in the epigraph, posits black as a critical mode through which the world (and the cosmos) might be seen more clearly. In describing the depth and breadth of blackness in painting he explained, "There is a black which is old and a black which is fresh. Lustrous black and dull black, black in sunlight and black in shadow."[4]

Lady in Black was painted only a few short years after Fuchs spent time in John Singer Sargent's Kensington studio in 1897, marking a turn in his practice toward painting, which included portraits of English elite.[5] In preparation for its installation debut, the original frameless painting is boldly paired with an upcycled frame painted a deep matte black by artist Jan Dickey (p. 157). The visual effect of the layered black surfaces—the black wall, black frame, and the painter's subject in black—allows audiences to better see the artist's skilled brushwork, marks that have been previously dismissed as lacking in detail and "painterly flash."[6] This curatorial move experimentally extends the ideas of artists like Reinhardt and Fred Wilson, who, through their artwork, demonstrate the powerful impact of the concept and materiality of Blackness on sight and perception.

Like *Lady in Black*, Inukai's portrait of his lover and muse Dorothy Hampton offers a meditation on a single color: white. Inukai explored the many colors the eye perceives in Dorothy's white garment, which includes pink, yellow, and green. With a virtuosic Impressionist style that has been likened to that of Sargent, Inukai captured the textures of her satin dress, silky red hair, and the chrome chair in which she sits. When exhibited in 1934, the *New York Herald*

Tribune identified this "stunning" portrait as "among the best of [Inukai's] works."[7] After immigrating from Japan, Inukai built a successful career as a portraitist in New York and lived with Dorothy for many years in Greenwich Village.[8]

Bolotowsky, known for his geometrically abstract paintings, was influenced by Dutch painter Piet Mondrian's use of horizontal and vertical lines to create geometric patterns. *Opalescent Vertical* is pure abstraction without subject matter, using straight lines to divide the canvas into rectangular areas of differing sizes. The title also refers to the artist's exploration of various white and beige tones, reminiscent of an opal's shimmery surface. According to Bolotowsky, his search for "ideal harmony and order" through abstraction was a response to the childhood traumas he experienced living through World War I and the Russian Revolution in Saint Petersburg, Russia, before immigrating to the United States.[9]

These works were displayed apart from one another in the gallery; the exceptions are the Reinhardt and Fuchs paintings, which were exhibited adjacent to Wilson's *Iago's Mirror* (p. 35, 149). Their striking proximity on the preceding page allows for their resonate and diverging styles and color palettes to amplify one another, an effect repeated throughout the framework, and resulting in a kind of engagement that allows for each person's sense of exploration and amplifies individual perspectives. Taking a cue from bell hooks, this curatorial approach understands the question of aesthetics as moving beyond reflections on the merits of art to how one engages in looking, and through that looking is reoriented or transformed. Black outer space served as that context for Leonov's sight, and we offer these four paintings—and the artworks and belongings within *Counterparts* framework—to catalyze similarly rare encounters and discoveries.

SSW/CG

1. bell hooks, "An Aesthetics of Blackness—Strange and Oppositional," *Lenox Avenue: A Journal of Interarts Inquiry* 1 (1995): 65–72.
2. The *Unesco Courier,* June 1965; as quoted in "A Tribute to Ad Reinhardt" in *artscanada*, no. 113 (October 1967): 19.
3. Ad Reinhardt wrote and lectured extensively on abstraction and painting and pursued his Black Paintings until his death in 1967. He regarded these paintings as the final, absolute, "ultimate" expressions of the medium, resulting in "the strictest formula for the freest artistic freedom." Barbara Rose, ed., *Art As Art: The Selected Writings of Ad Reinhardt* (New York: The Viking Press, 1975), 52.
4. Reinhardt quoting Japanese artist Hokusai in a lecture. Transcribed conference call between Aldo Tambellini, Michael Snow, Cecil Taylor, Ad Reinhardt, Arnold Rockman, Stuart Broomer, and Harvey Cowan, connected by phone between New York and Toronto, appeared in *artscanada* no. 113 (October 1967): 2–19.
5. Emil Fuchs, *With Pencil, Brush and Chisel: The Life of an Artist* (New York and London: G. P. Putnam's Sons, 1925). In addition to the gift of art to the Museum's collection by the artist's estate, the Museum's Archives contain his papers. See "Emil Fuchs Papers, 1880–1931," Brooklyn Museum Archives.
6. Teresa A. Carbone, "Emil Fuchs," in *American Paintings from the Brooklyn Museum: Artists Born by 1876*, Teresa A. Carbone, Barbara Dayer Gallati, and Linda S. Ferber (New York: Brooklyn Museum; London: D. Giles Limited, 2006), 1: 533.
7. Carlyle Burrows, "An Exhibition of Kyohei Inukai," *New York Herald Tribune,* May 13, 1934, D10.
8. For a biography of Inukai, see Miyoko and John Davey, eds., *Kyohei Inukai (1886–1954)* (New York: 46 WSS Press, 2014).
9. Quoted in Louise Averill Svenson with Mimi Poser, "Interview with Ilya Bolotwosky," in *Ilya Bolotowsky* (New York: The Solomon R. Guggenheim Foundation, 1974), 32.

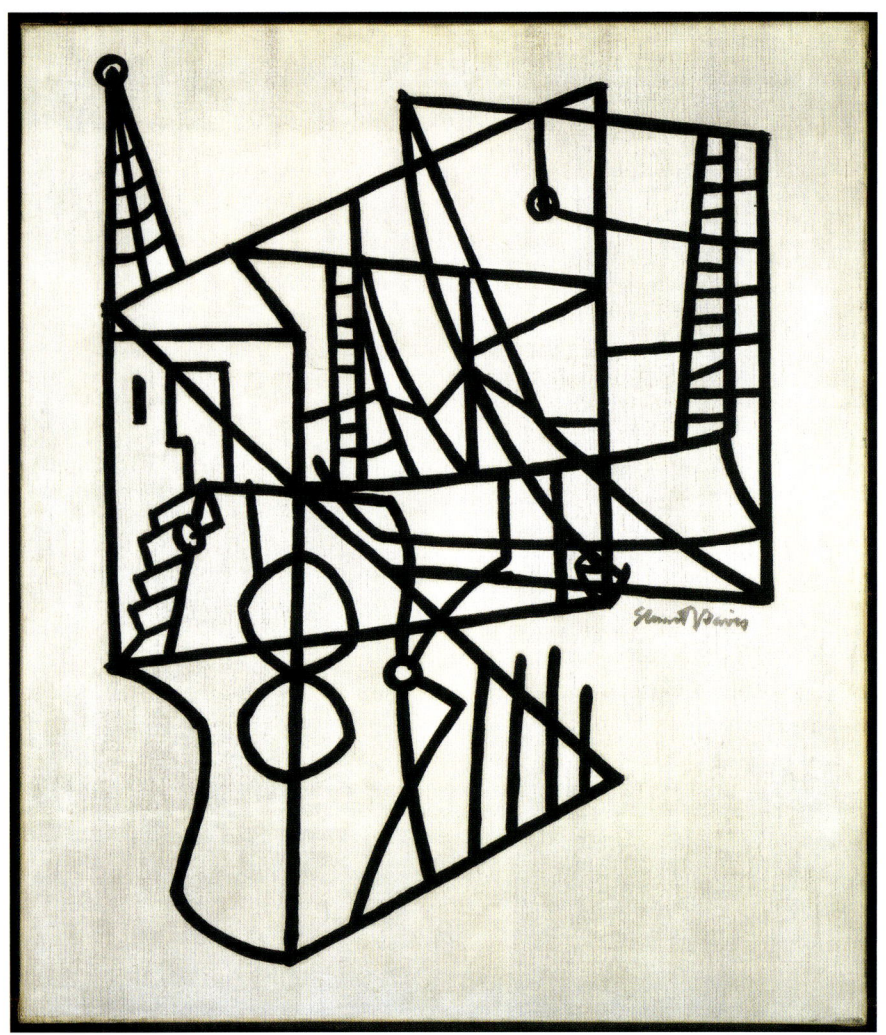

Stuart Davis
(American, 1892–1964)
Landscape, 1932 and 1935

Oil on canvas, 25 × 22 in.
Gift of Mr. and Mrs. Milton Lowenthal, 73.150
Provenance: Possibly acquired by The Artist's Gallery, before 1973. Acquired by Edith and Milton Lowenthal, by 1973; donated, December 11, 1973.

In *Landscape*, Stuart Davis's bold black lines intersect and dart across the composition to frame fractured spaces of white canvas. The result evokes streets, buildings, and a tower along the waterfront in Gloucester, Massachusetts, as the lively crisscrossing of lines conveys the energy of the wharf. Rather than relying upon illusionistic techniques like perspective, Davis began juxtaposing flat geometric planes in solid colors to create structure and spatial relationships in his abstractions of the 1920s, a theory he later termed "color-space."[1] In this painting, however, he worked in monochrome, focusing only on shapes and lines to define space and suggest abstracted objects.

Davis's early training in New York City was with Robert Henri, the leader of the group of Urban Realists known as the Ashcan School, which informed his study of city street scenes. He exhibited at the 1913 Armory Show where he was inspired by European Modernists including Pablo Picasso and Fernand Léger. By the 1920s, Davis had developed a distinct form of abstraction he felt was uniquely American, uniting his study of Cubism with his interests in advertising design, jazz music, and the modern city.[2] Works such as *Landscape* capture a sense of bustling movement, uniting the flat planes and fractured surfaces of analytic Cubism with a hard-edged style inspired by commercial advertising.

CG

1. Many scholars have discussed Davis's color-space theory. For a brief discussion of this concept and some of Davis's own words, see Lloyd Goodrich, "From the Archives: Stuart Davis on Painting," *Art in America* (June 14, 2016), https://www.artnews.com/art-in-america/features/from-the-archives-stuart-davis-on-painting-63171/.
2. For more on Davis, see for instance the retrospective exhibition catalogue, Barbara Haskell and Harry Cooper, *Stuart Davis: In Full Swing* (New York: Prestel Publishing, 2016). For more on this painting, see Lisa Mintz Messinger, *American Art: The Edith and Milton Lowenthal Collection* (New York: Metropolitan Museum of Art, 1996), 21.

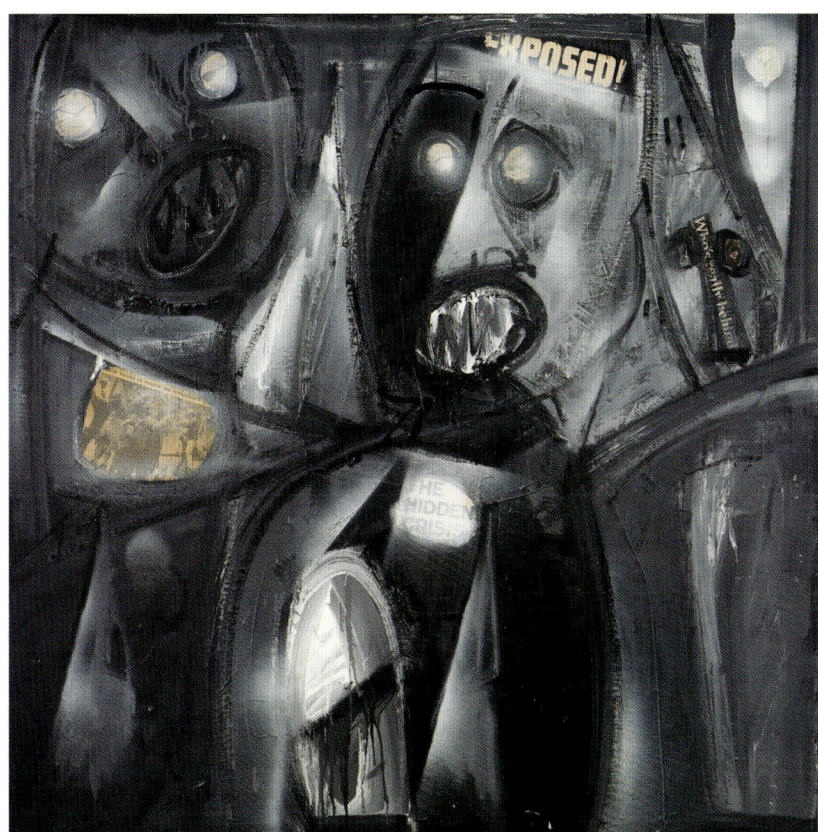

Merton D. Simpson
American, 1928–2013
U.S.A. '65, 1965

Oil, paper collage on canvas
Dick S. Ramsay Fund, 2011.28
Provenance: Purchased from the artist by the Brooklyn Museum, June 23, 2011.

Merton D. Simpson enjoyed a wide-ranging and successful career as a painter and African art collector and dealer, achieving global renown in both fields. While the artist ultimately developed an Abstract Expressionist style and produced politically inflected art, he began his career as a portraitist in the U.S. Air Force and painted portraits of commanders still on view in the Pentagon today.

Simpson, who was part of the Black artist collective Spiral, exhibited *U.S.A. '65* in the group's only exhibition, which ran from May 14 to June 5, 1965 and was titled *FIRST GROUP SHOWING (works in black & white)*. In addition to generating critical dialogue around their work, members of Spiral pointedly debated the role of the Black artist, particularly amid the struggle for civil rights in the United States. The black-and-white theme, which inspired this framework, was a response to the segregated artworld and addressed the collective's formal and sociopolitical concerns.

Keen to evoke a "signature" or "thumbprint" that would formally link the members, Spiral often discussed the qualities found in jazz, which grew out of grassroots Black American culture.[1] In their efforts to decenter traditional Western ideas from their conversations, the group studied African intellectuals and aesthetic ideas. Simpson lectured on African sculpture and guided the group in their study of tribal designs found on Zulu shields, textile patterns, and furnishings.[2] Despite members' varying positions on the association of their art with social protest, Simpson's style was deeply reflective of the prevailing tensions in the struggle for civil rights. The work he created as part of Spiral's black-and-white installation was a precursor to the artist's "Confrontation" series, which emerged from Simpson's experience of the Harlem riot of 1964 and featured achromatic black and white overlapping faces in violently expressive brush strokes that set off their pairing.

1. Jeanne Siegel, "Why Spiral?" *Nka: Journal of Contemporary African Art,* no. 29 (Fall 2011): 78–85, originally published in *ARTnews*, 1966.
2. Ibid.

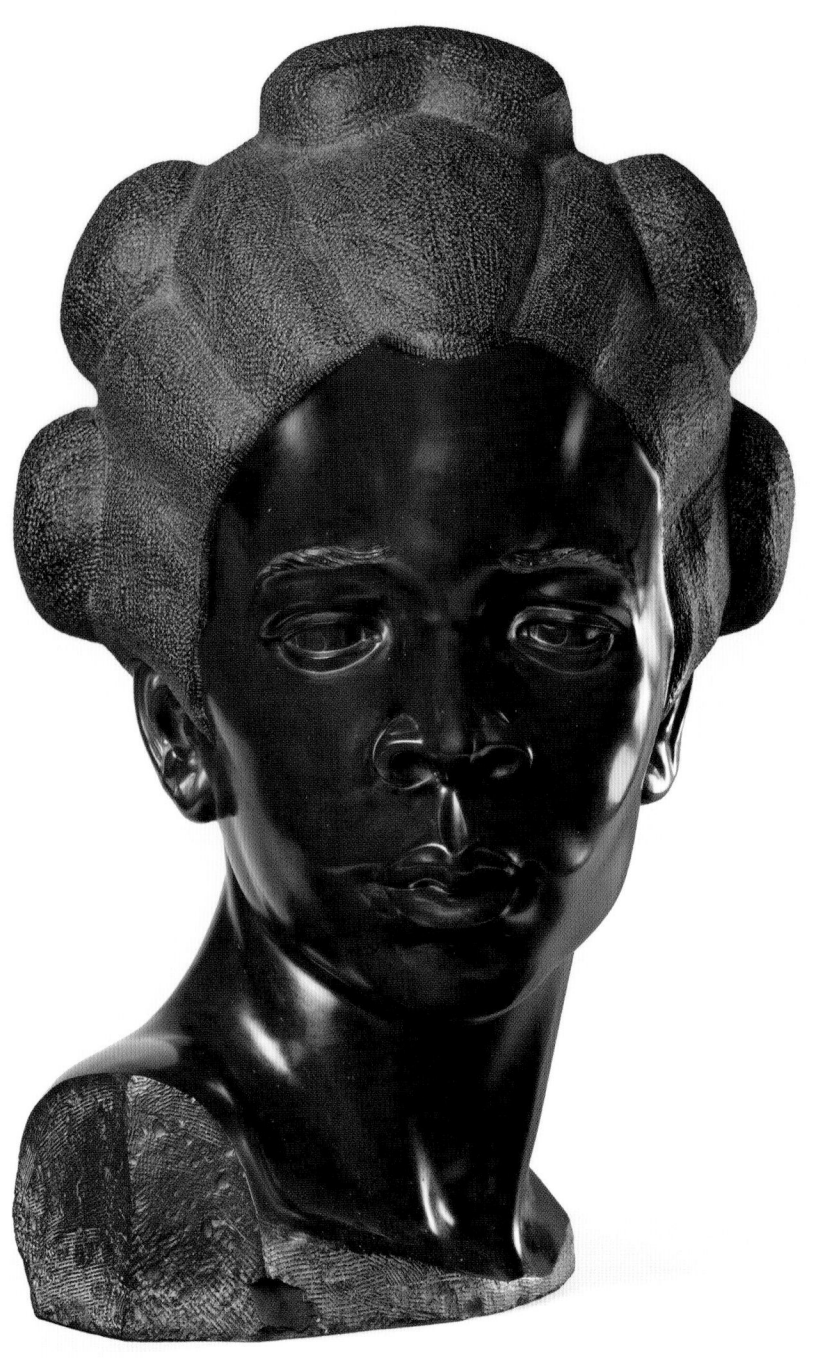

Malvina Hoffman
(American, 1885–1966)
Martinique Woman, 1928

Black Belgian marble, 22 × 14¼ × 15¼ in.
Dick S. Ramsay Fund, 28.384
Provenance: Purchased from the artist by the Brooklyn Museum, December 10, 1928.

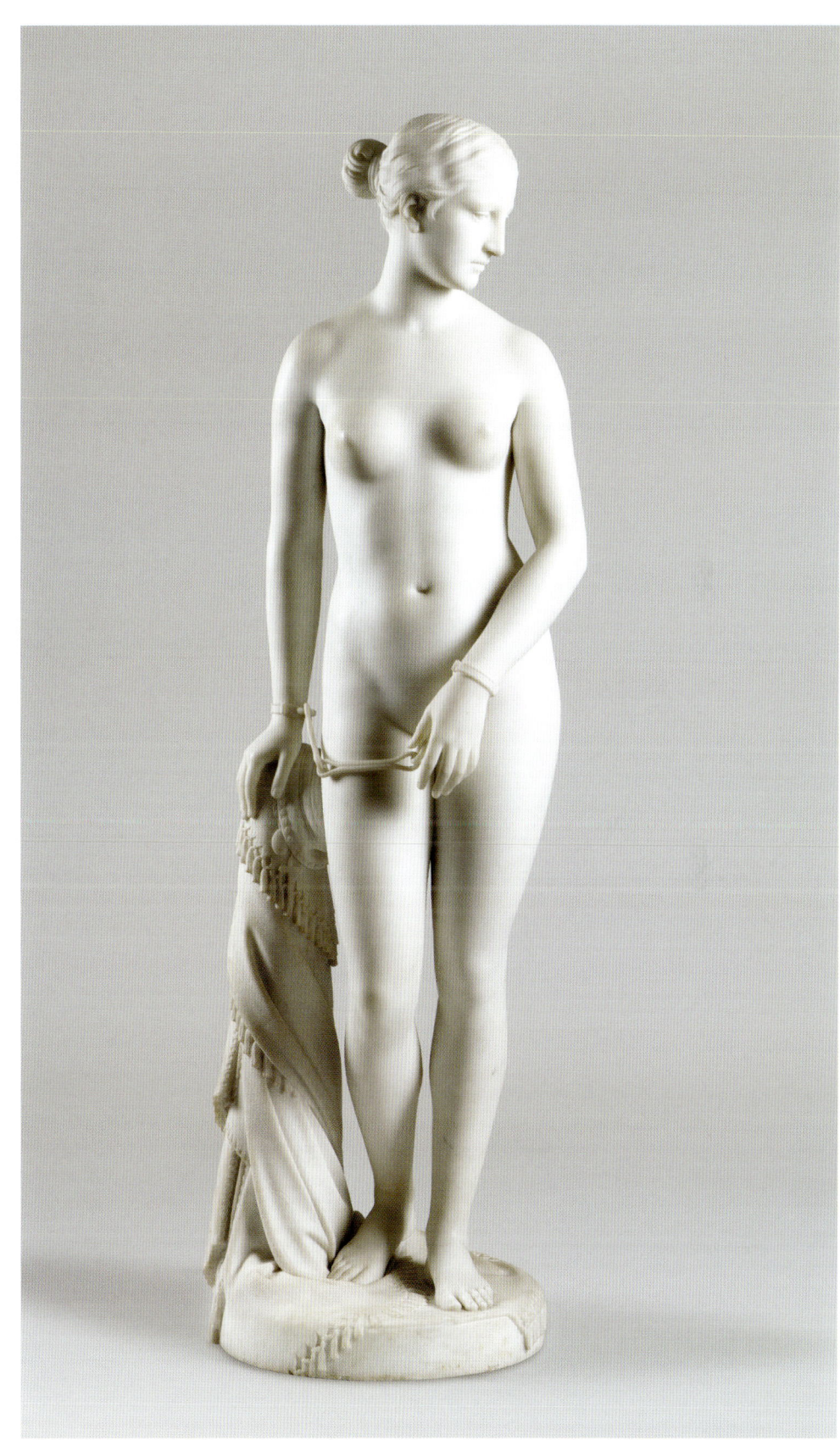

Hiram Powers
(American, 1805–1873)
The Greek Slave, 1866

Marble, 65½ x 19¼ x 18¾ in.
Gift of Charles F. Bound, 55.14
Provenance: Acquired by Charles Fiske Bound, by May 27, 1919; inherited by Josephine R. Bound (Mrs. Charles Fiske Bound), by May 26, 1925; donated, January 12, 1955.

Counterparts

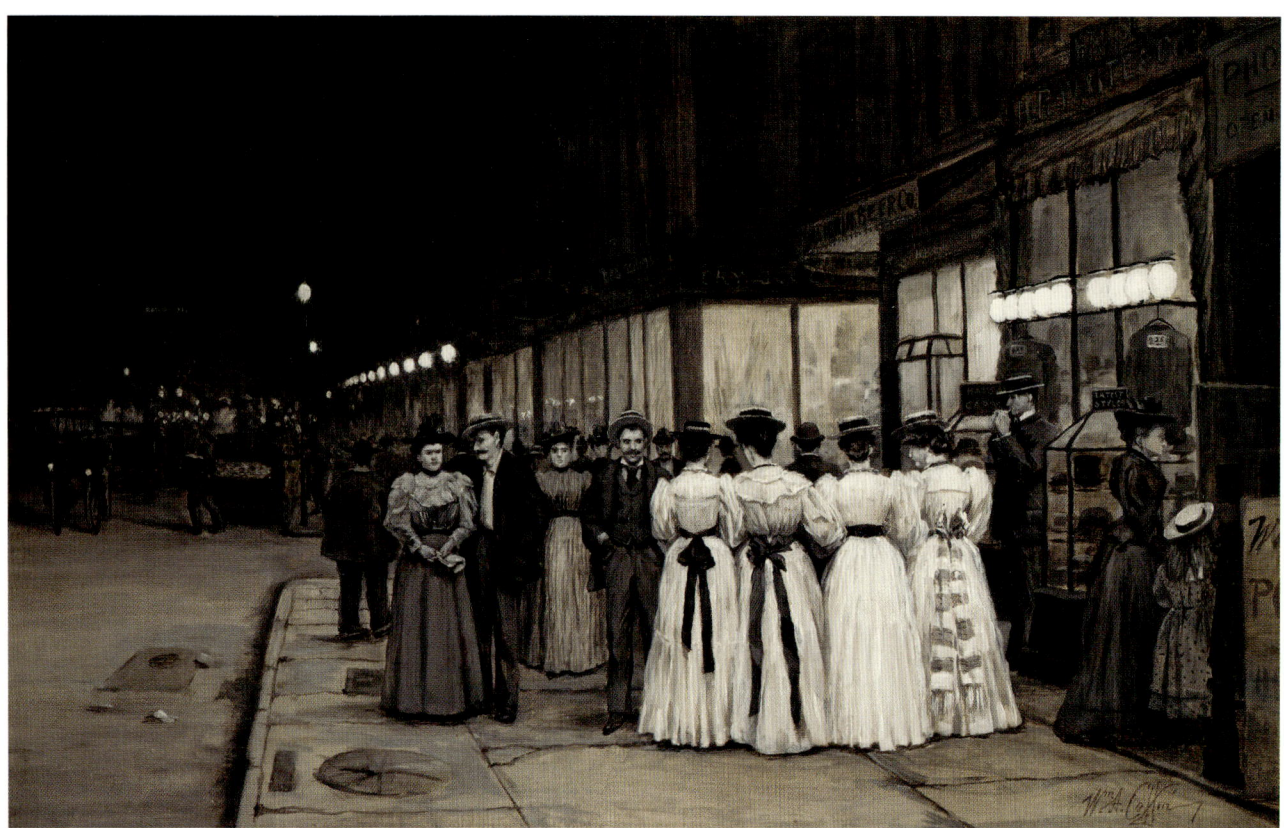

William Anderson Coffin
(American, 1855–1925)
Saturday Night in August—Eighth Avenue,
ca. 1900

Oil on canvas, 16⅛ × 26 in.
Gift of Mr. and Mrs. Stuart Feld, 74.207
Provenance: Acquired by Stuart Feld and
Sue Kessler Feld (Mrs. Stuart Feld), by 1974;
donated, December 31, 1974.

Painting in grisaille or shades of gray, William Anderson Coffin depicts a nighttime scene along Manhattan's Eighth Avenue near 42nd Street.[1] Electric lights illuminate the candid, street-level view, offering a documentary glimpse into the nightlife of this area. Men and women dressed in typical early 1900s Edwardian fashion stroll along this commercial strip, made slightly grittier by the presence of curb trash and the cracked pavement around manhole covers.

By the turn of the twentieth century, New York City's theater district was shifting northward into the area around 42nd Street and Broadway, now called Times Square. In addition to businesses—such as the hat store, beer company, and dry goods shop that Coffin paints—the neighborhood was home to newly popular roof garden theaters, many of which hosted variety entertainment (or vaudeville).[2] One such establishment was the American Theatre Roof Garden at Eighth Avenue and 42nd Street, which had an electric marquee that is partially visible in the upper left of Coffin's painting.

After receiving a fine arts degree from Yale University, Coffin studied in Paris and later established a portrait studio in New York City in 1882. In addition to painting, Coffin wrote for various publications as an art critic and art editor. This urban street scene was a departure from his typical work in portraiture and landscapes, and the monochrome palette is unusual for his *oeuvre*. Grisaille is a method long used for underpainting or sketching prior to a finished composition, and it is possible that Coffin may have been planning this as a black-and-white newspaper or magazine illustration.

CG

1. For more on this painting, see Teresa A. Carbone, "William Anderson Coffin," in *American Paintings from the Brooklyn Museum: Artists Born by 1876*, Teresa A. Carbone, Barbara Dayer Gallati, and Linda S. Ferber (New York: Brooklyn Museum; London: D. Giles Limited), 1: 380.
2. Vance Thompson, "The Roof-Gardens of New York," *The Cosmopolitan* 27, no. 5 (September 1899): 503–14.

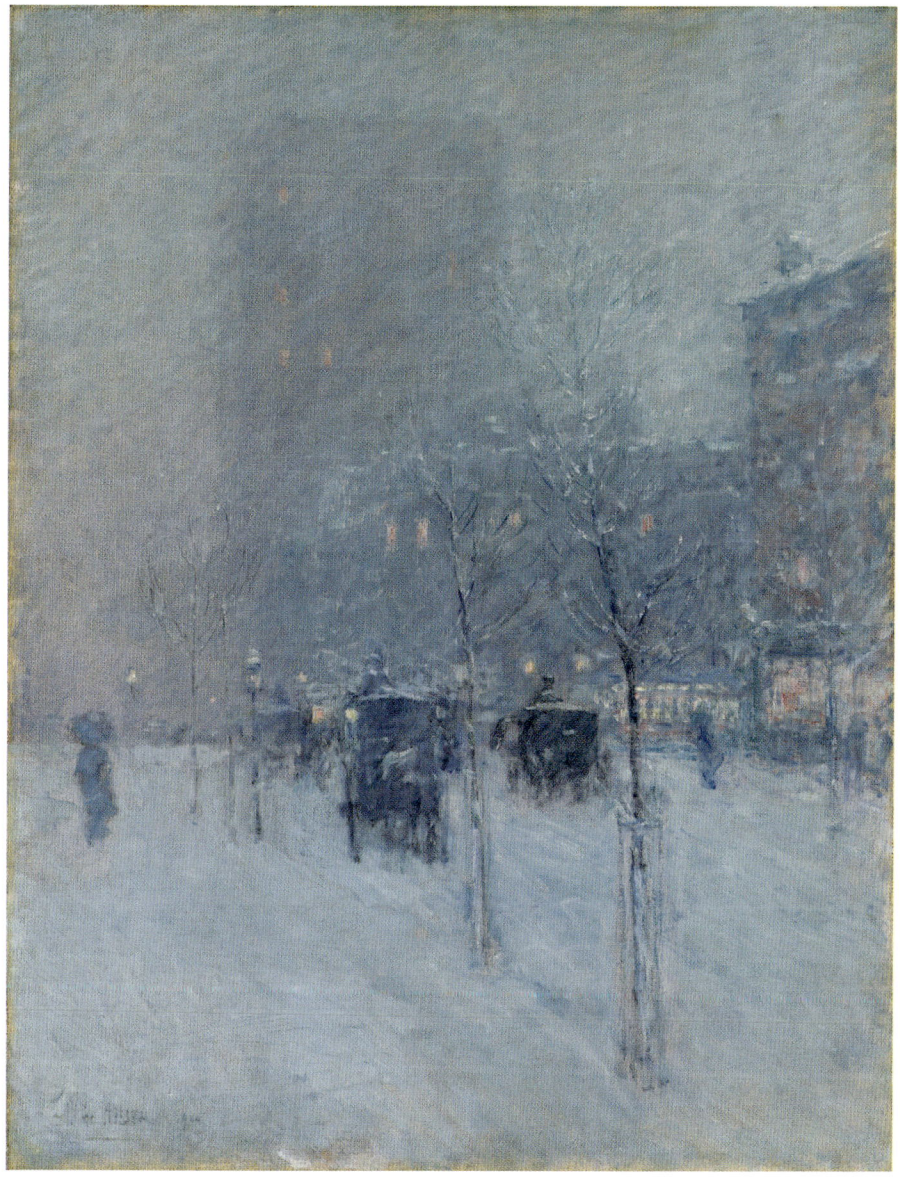

Frederick Childe Hassam
(American, 1859–1935)
Late Afternoon, New York, Winter, 1900

Oil on canvas, 36¹⁵⁄₁₆ x 29 in.
Dick S. Ramsay Fund, 62.68
Provenance: Acquired from the artist's estate by the American Academy of Arts and Letters, before 1953. Acquired by Milch Gallery, before 1960. Acquired by John Fox, before 1960. Acquired by Babcock Galleries, by 1960; purchased by the Brooklyn Museum, May 10, 1962.

Through a veil of falling snow, spectral forms of pedestrians and carriages emerge along a New York City street as shadowy buildings rise above them. Influenced by French Impressionism, Childe Hassam painted this wintry scene with a flurry of loose brushstrokes, interpreting his experience of being enveloped in a snowfall shimmering with transient shifts in the light. He rendered the atmosphere not simply in white, but in tints of blue, purple, pink, and yellow, capturing varied hues cast by the late afternoon sun and the glow of lamps reflecting off snowflakes.

Hassam spent time in Paris, including a three-year residency from 1886 to 1889, where he studied the atmospheric and tonal landscapes of the Barbizon School and the Impressionists' experiments in representing fleeting light effects.[1] He settled in New York City in 1889, and became known for urban scenes that were likened to the Impressionists' views of Paris. This painting may represent Central Park South near Seventh Avenue, already an upscale neighborhood of residences and hotels.[2] Unlike the Urban Realists who embraced the grittiness of New York, Hassam's approach aestheticized city views and presented the artist's personal impression of the scene.[3]

CG

1. For more on Childe Hassam, see, for instance, Ulrich Hiesinger, *Childe Hassam, American Impressionist* (New York and Munich: Jordan-Volpe Gallery and Prestel-Verlag, 1994) and H. Barbara Weinberg, *Childe Hassam, American Impressionist* (New Haven, CT: Yale University Press, 2004).
2. Teresa A. Carbone, "Frederick Childe Hassam," in *American Paintings from the Brooklyn Museum: Artists Born by 1876,* Teresa A. Carbone, Barbara Dayer Gallati, and Linda S. Ferber (New York: Brooklyn Museum; London: D. Giles Limited), 2: 613–15.
3. A. E. Ives, "Talks with Artists: Mr. Childe Hassam on Painting Street Scenes," *The Art Amateur* 27, no. 5 (October 1892): 116–17.

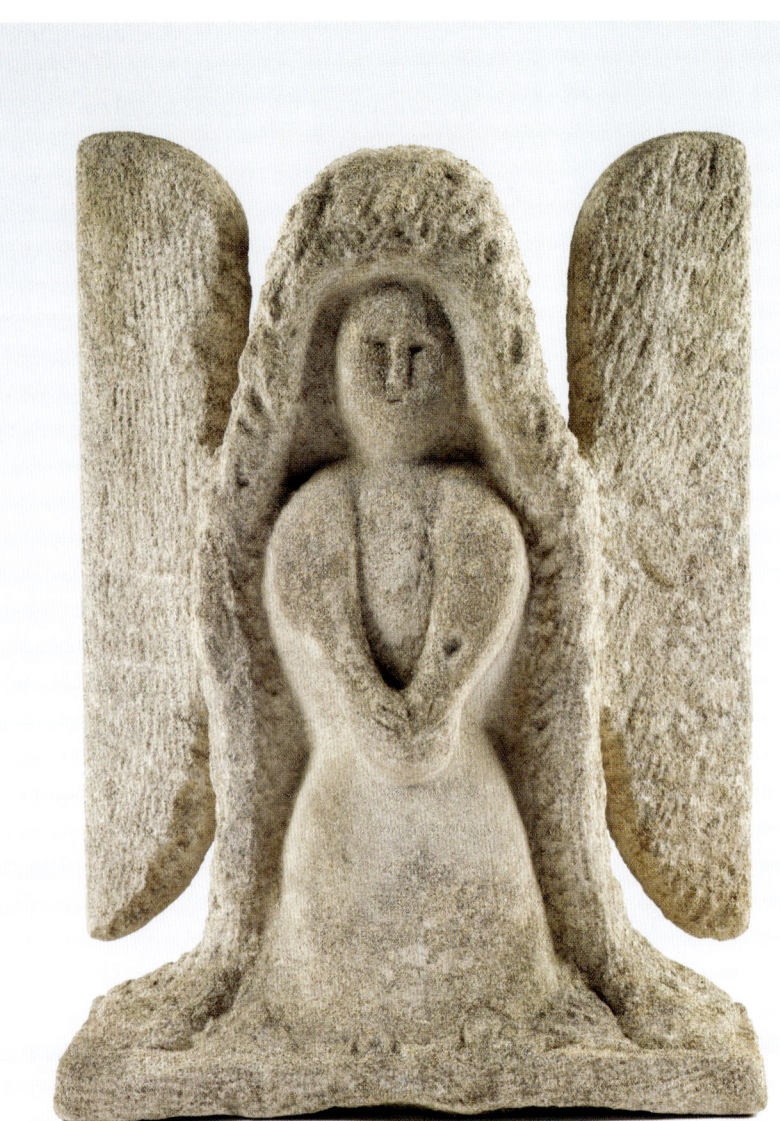

William Edmondson
(American, 1874–1951)
Angel, ca. 1930s–40s

Limestone, 18½ x 13½ x 7 in.
Gift of Mr. and Mrs. Alastair B. Martin, the Guennol Collection, 87.28
Provenance: Acquired by Doris Lee, by 1973; acquired by Edmond L. Fuller, 1978. Acquired by Edith Park Martin (Mrs. Alastair Bradley Martin), before February 16, 1987; donated, April 16, 1987.

Carved from found limestone, William Edmondson's *Angel* is the striking result of the artist's submission to divine instruction. According to Edmondson, in a vision, God commanded him to carve tombstones: "Jesus . . . planted the seed of carving in me."[1] The sculptor began carving when he was nearing his sixties, after he retired from his job as a day laborer. Born to formerly enslaved parents in Tennessee, Edmondson regarded his sensitive renderings of religious subjects as "miracles." These included free-standing figurative sculptures, gravestones, and garden ornaments chiseled from modified railroad spikes. Edmondson's secular subjects included portraits of Nashville school teachers, Eleanor Roosevelt, and animals, and his work dovetailed with the 1930s revival of direct carving in stone. Still, unaware of this trend, the artist remained steadfast in his calling, historically and culturally linking him to other Black Americans whose spirituality also provided the critical impetus for their art, music, and literature.

Separated by time, geography, and culture, the frontal pose and formal simplicity of Edmondson's *Angel* is echoed in Mexican photographer Graciela Iturbide's stunning image of a Oaxacan sponge vendor, taken in 1974 during a visit to southern Mexico.

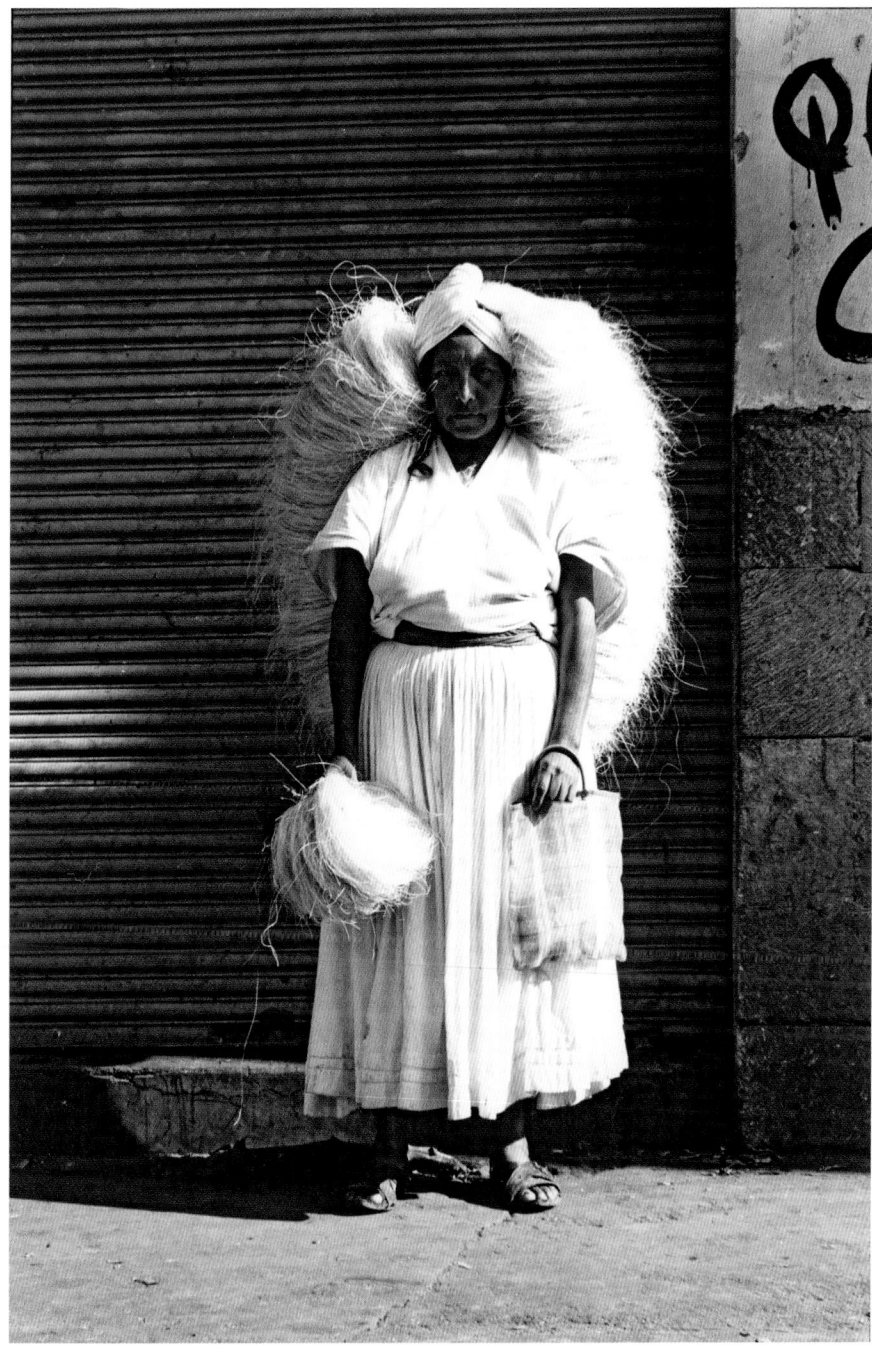

Graciela Iturbide
(Mexican, born 1942)
Vendedora de Zacate, Oaxaca (Sponge Vendor, Oaxaca), 1974

Gelatin silver print, image: 12 x 8 in.; sheet: 14 x 10⅞ in.
Gift of Marcuse Pfeifer, 1990.119.39
Provenance: Acquired by Marcuse Pfeifer, by 1990; donated, 1990.

Much like the limestone angel, the woman is framed by a white textured arch; hers consisting of dozens of dried sea sponges strung together, and reminiscent of the holy arches that encircle depictions of the Virgin Mary. Both Edmundson and Iturbide got their artistic start in and around cemeteries. Iturbide took up photography after the death of her six-year-old daughter in 1970, and some of her earliest work involved documenting *angelitos*—children who recently died, and their burial. Edmundson in white stone and Iturbide in black-and-white photography, each in their own poetic ways, commemorated those who passed away.

Iturbide composed *Vendedora de Zacate, Oaxaca* during one of her trips to the region in the years directly following her work as the assistant to Mexican Modernist photographer Manuel Álvarez Bravo. The word *zacate* comes from the Nahuatl "zacatl," which means grass. It is also commonly used in Mexico to describe a scouring pad, particularly those created from the plant "luffa acutangula"; its zucchini-shaped fruit is dried for nearly six months to produce the white fibrous sponge. Also known as *estropajo*, the flattened scrubber the vendor is selling would last over three months, an ecological household staple used to clean everything from bodies, dishes, floors, and other surfaces. Iturbide would return to the state in 1979 at the invitation of artist Francisco Toledo to photograph the Juchitán people who form part of the Zapotec culture native to Oaxaca.

SSW

1. "Art: Mirkels," *TIME*, November 1, 1937, https://time.com/archive/6820159/art-mirkels/.

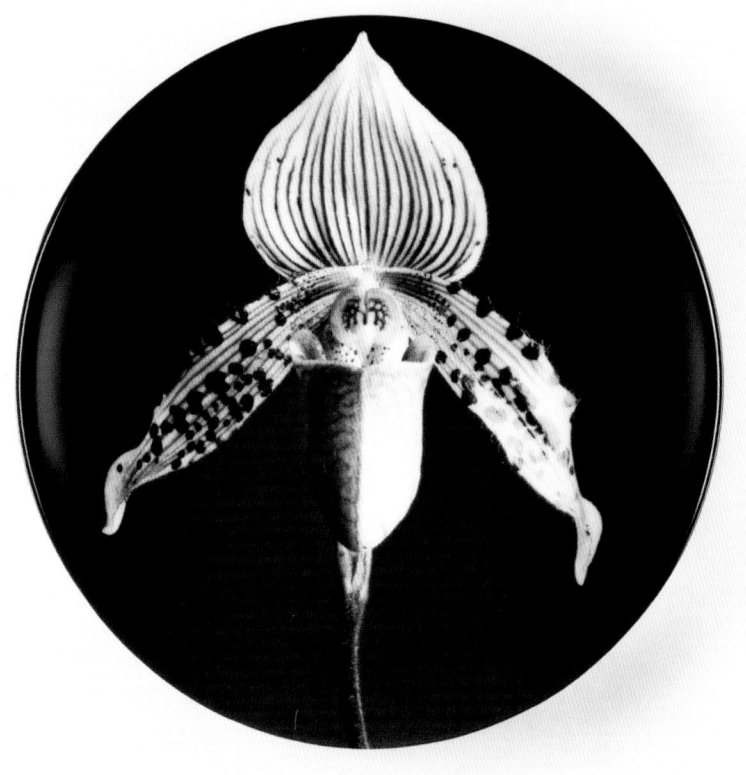

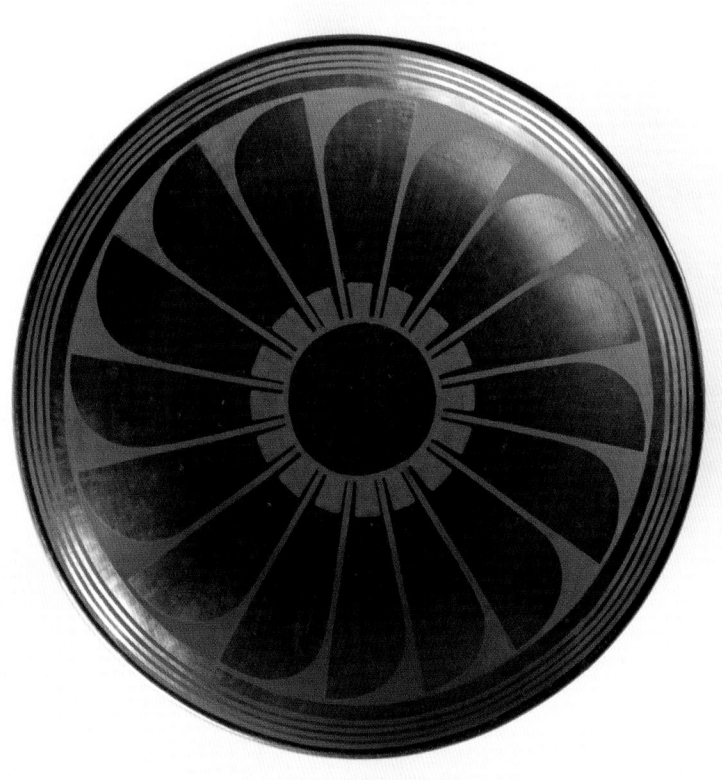

Robert Mapplethorpe
(American, 1946–1989)
Swid Powell, Manufacturer, New York, New York, 1983–90
Orchid Plate, 1989

Porcelain, 1⅜ × 12 × 12 in.
Gift of Swid Powell, 1990.34.6
Provenance: Donated by the manufacturer, 1990.

Photographer Robert Mapplethorpe is esteemed for his black-and-white photographs of highly eroticized male and female nudes, celebrity portraits, and still lifes of flowers. All share the same aesthetic: simple compositions, high black-and-white contrast, and a cool detachment from the subject. Mapplethorpe's works are precise, leading the viewer to explore the subtleties of form rather than probe for emotion.

In 1988, the year before his death from AIDS-related illness, Mapplethorpe designed three plates, featuring his commanding floral images, including *Orchid*, 1987, for the New York–based tableware firm of Swid Powell. Established in 1982 by Nan Swid and Addie Powell, the company embarked on a series of collaborations with internationally renowned architects and designers to capture the aesthetics of Postmodernism. This style of architecture and design used historical precedents, especially early twentieth-century modern designs, as reference points to manipulate and play into new forms of buildings and functional objects. Swid Powell wanted to bring the design of a skyscraper to the dining room table. From the success of Swid Powell's partnerships with architects came the collaboration with Mapplethorpe. As with the architect series, the tableware allowed those interested in photography to afford and enjoy something that might have been unreachable otherwise. Although the architect-designed tableware were intended for use, those produced from Mapplethorpe's photographs were probably destined for decoration, not function.

CF

Opposite, below:
Maria Martinez
(San Ildefonso Pueblo, ca. 1887–1980)
Julian Martinez
(San Ildefonso Pueblo, 1885–1943)
Circular Shallow Bowl, ca. 1943

Clay, slip, 2⅜ x 13¼ in.
Anonymous gift in memory of Dr. Harlow Brooks, 43.201.198
Provenance: Acquired by Henry Harlow Brooks, before 1936; acquired by an anonymous collector, by 1943; donated, 1943.

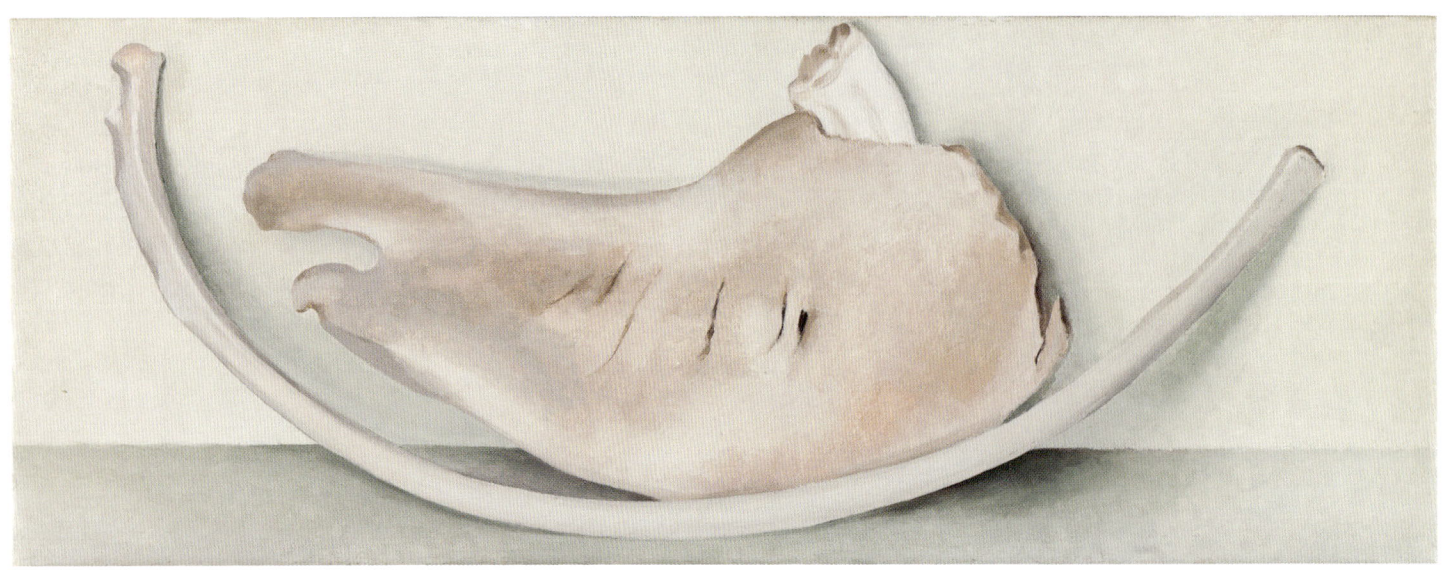

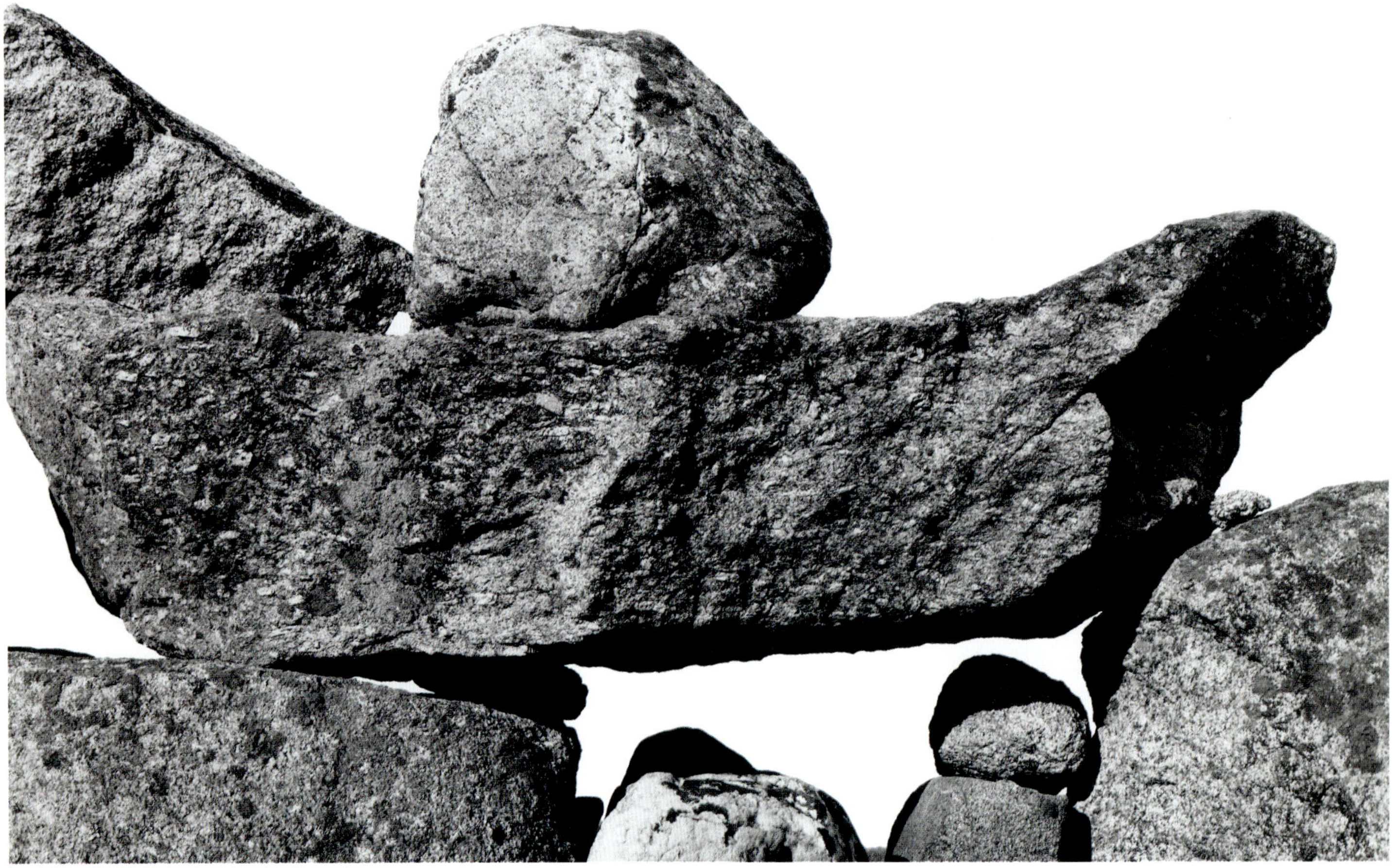

Toward Joy

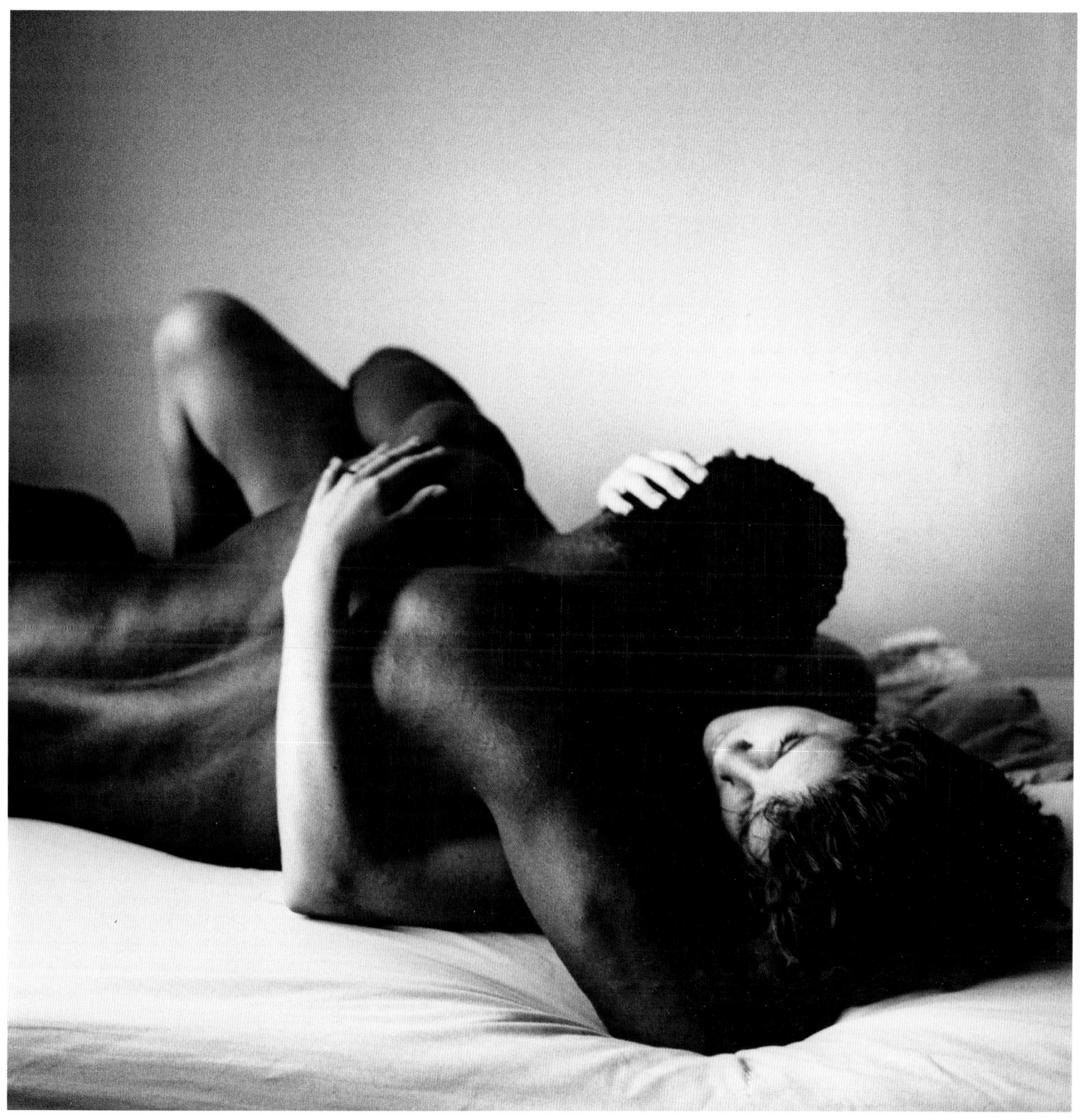

Page 142, above:
Georgia O'Keeffe
(American, 1887–1986)
Rib and Jawbone, 1935

Oil on canvas, 9 x 24 in.
Bequest of Georgia O'Keeffe, 87.136.5a-b
Provenance: Bequeathed by the artist, October 29, 1987.

Page 142, below:
Aaron Siskind
(American, 1903–1991)
Martha's Vineyard 4, 1950

Gelatin silver print, image: 13¼ x 17¾ in.; sheet: 16 x 19¾ in.
Gift of Robert L. Smith and Patricia L. Sawyer, 1999.127.7
Provenance: Acquired by Robert L. Smith and Patricia L. Sawyer, by 1999; donated, 1999.

Previous page:
Susan Rubin
(American, born 1965)
Suzanne and Lance, 1999

Gelatin silver print, 14 x 10⅞ in.
Gift of Lillian Rubin, 2000.121
Provenance: Acquired from the artist by Lillian Rubin, by 2000; donated, 2000.

Eero Saarinen, Designer
(American, born Finland, 1910–1961)
Knoll International, Inc., Manufacturer,
New York, New York, founded 1938
Womb Chair and *Ottoman*, Models No. 70 and No. 74, designed 1946, manufactured ca. 1959

Chrome-plated steel, fiberglass, plastic, wood-particle shell, latex foam, original fabric upholstery, chair: 36 × 40 × 34 in.; ottoman: 16 × 25½ × 20 in.
Gift of Sandra Sheppard Rodgers, Gail Sheppard Moloney, Lynn Sheppard Manger, John W. Sheppard, Jr. from the Estate of their mother, Rose Jackson Sheppard Milbank, by exchange, 2001.37.1, 2001.37.2
Provenance: Acquired by Phillips, by 2001; purchased by the Brooklyn Museum, June 21, 2001.

Conceived about 1946, the *Womb Chair* was one of the first works architect and designer Eero Saarinen produced for Knoll International, a high-end design company founded in 1938 and famed for its radical collaborations with emerging mid-century designers. Although Saarinen was trained as an architect, his early success resulted from his experiments with industrial design and materials, first with molded plywood and then fiberglass. While stronger adhesives developed in World War II led to improvements in dynamically bending plywood, Saarinen found new possibilities for intricate structures with fiberglass. A single sheet of this type of plastic could be worked into greater complex curves, creating unique and lively shapes. Saarinen developed the concept for the *Womb Chair* from the idea that most people had not felt safety or security since they left the womb due to the adversities and burdens of contemporary life. The *Womb Chair* had a distinctly modern form that diverged from more mass-market easy chair designs with heavy padding and rigid shapes. Covered in a soft woven wool fabric, the chair exudes a soothing and warm feeling to touch. Its sloped, high back and curved sides establish a relaxed posture that envelops the sitter, giving them a sense of comfort and embrace.

LSG

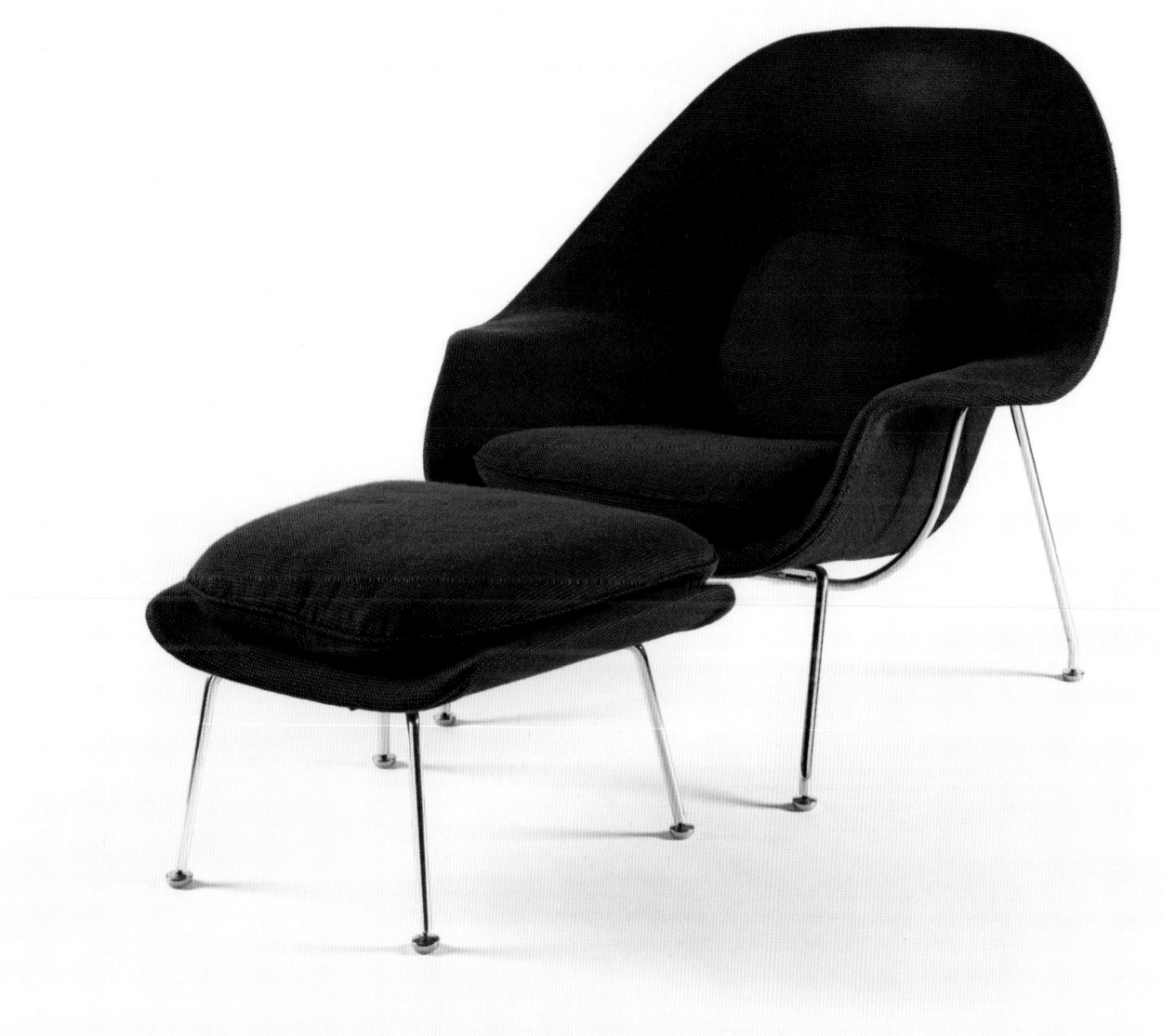

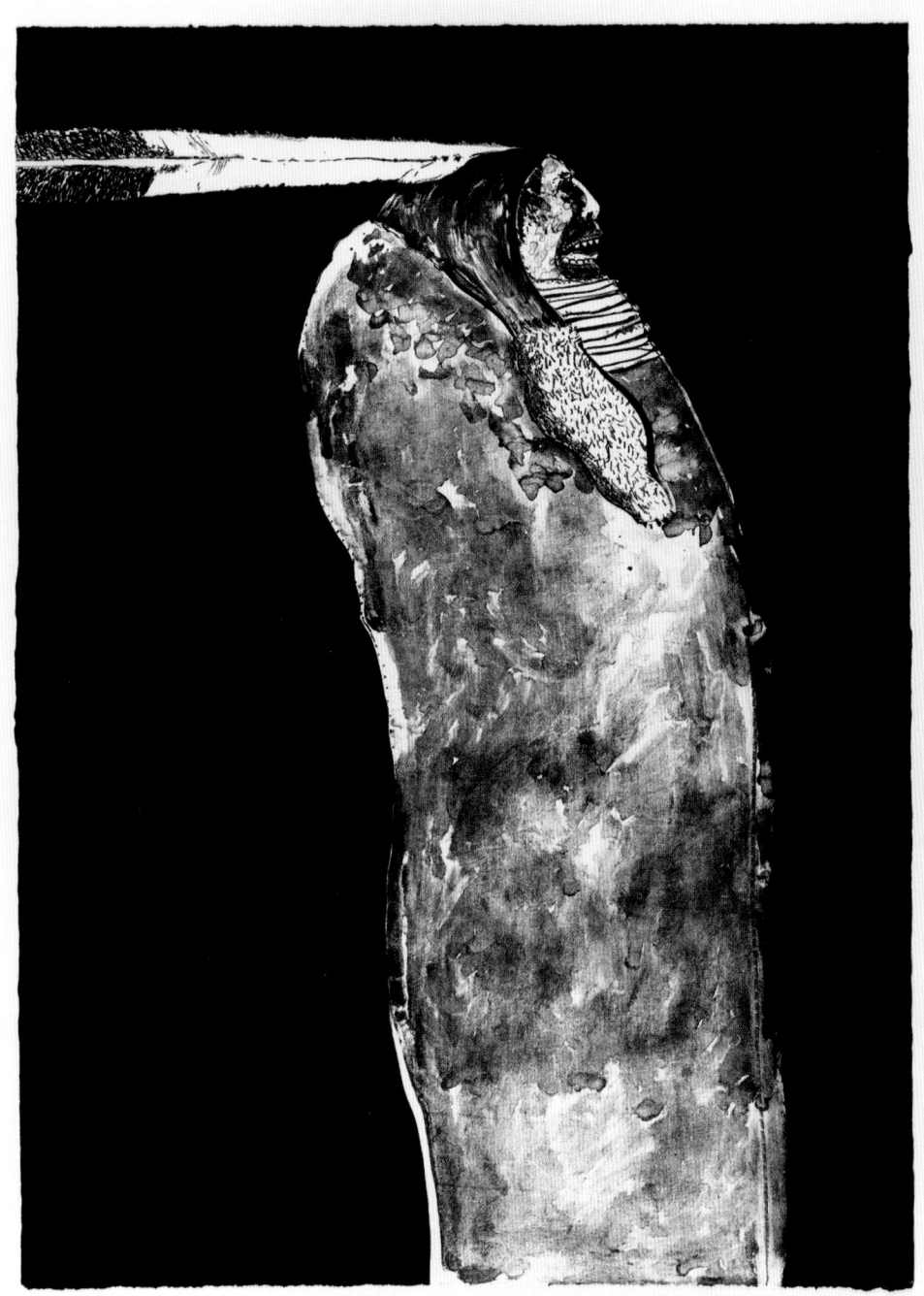

Fritz Scholder
(Luiseño, 1937–2005)
Tamarind Institute, Publisher, Los Angeles, CA, founded 1960
Indian with Feather, 1970–71

Lithograph, 30¼ x 22 in.
Bristol-Myers Fund, 71.134.2
Provenance: Acquired by Janus Gallery, by August 1971; purchased by the Brooklyn Museum, October 19, 1971.

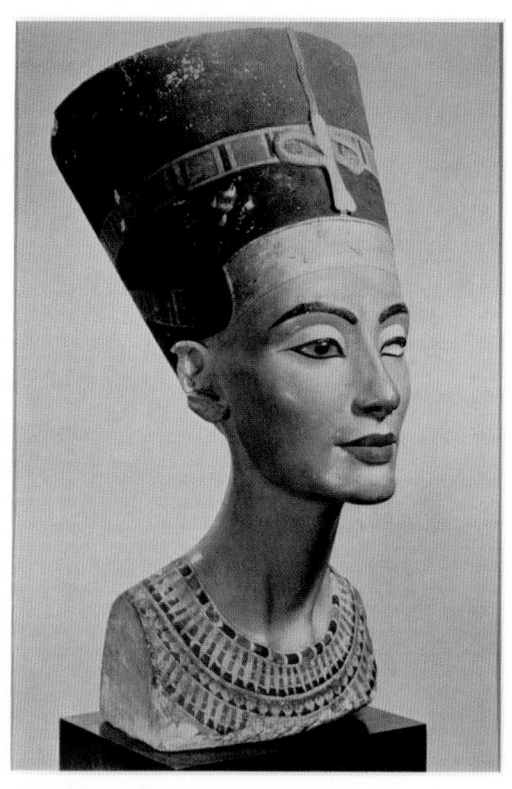
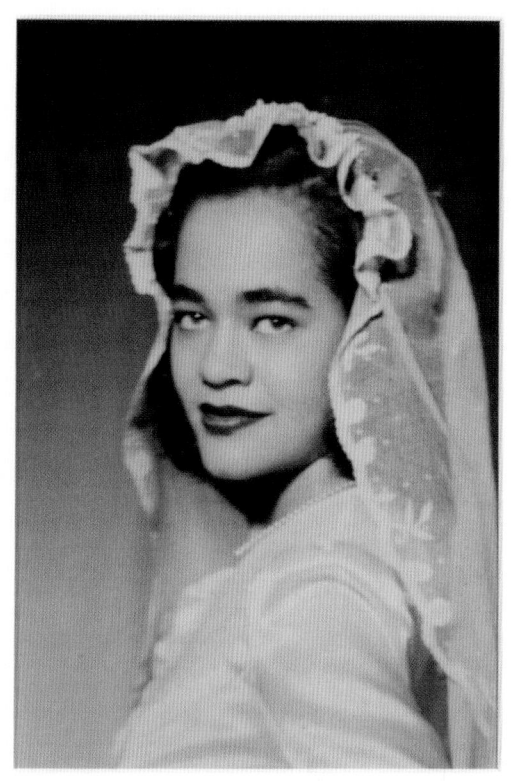

Lorraine O'Grady
(American, 1934–2024)
Miscegenated Family Album
(Sisters I) and *(Sisters III)*, 1994

Silver dye-bleach print, 20 × 16 in. Purchased with funds given by John and Barbara Vogelstein and Shelley Fox Aarons and Philip E. Aarons and bequest of Richard J. Kempe, by exchange, 2008.80
Provenance: Purchased from Gracie Mansion Gallery by the Brooklyn Museum, December 11, 2008.

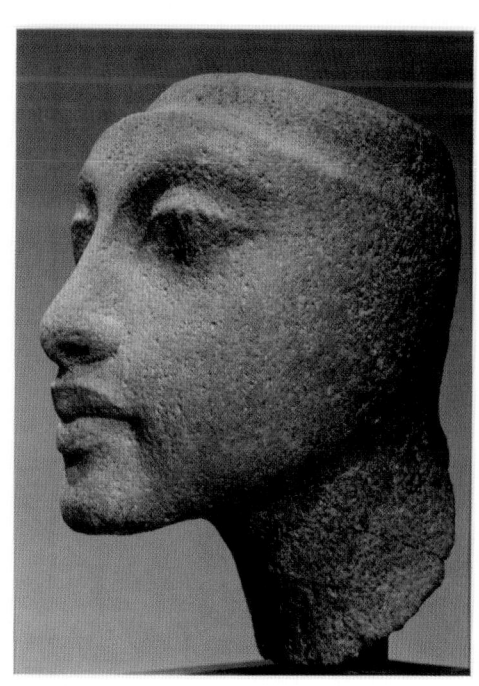
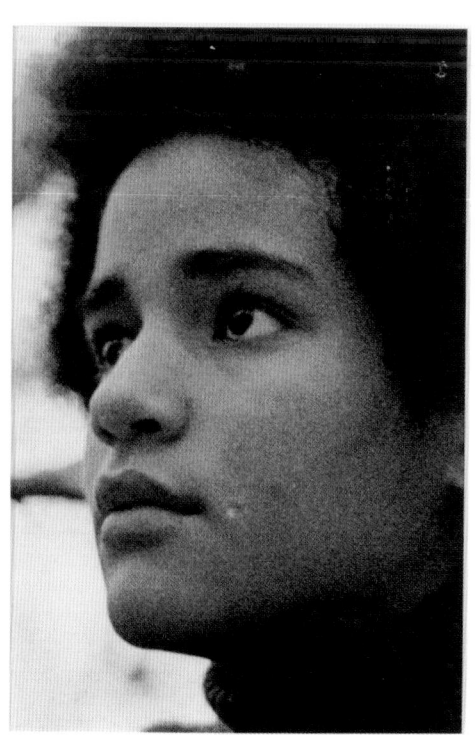

Counterparts

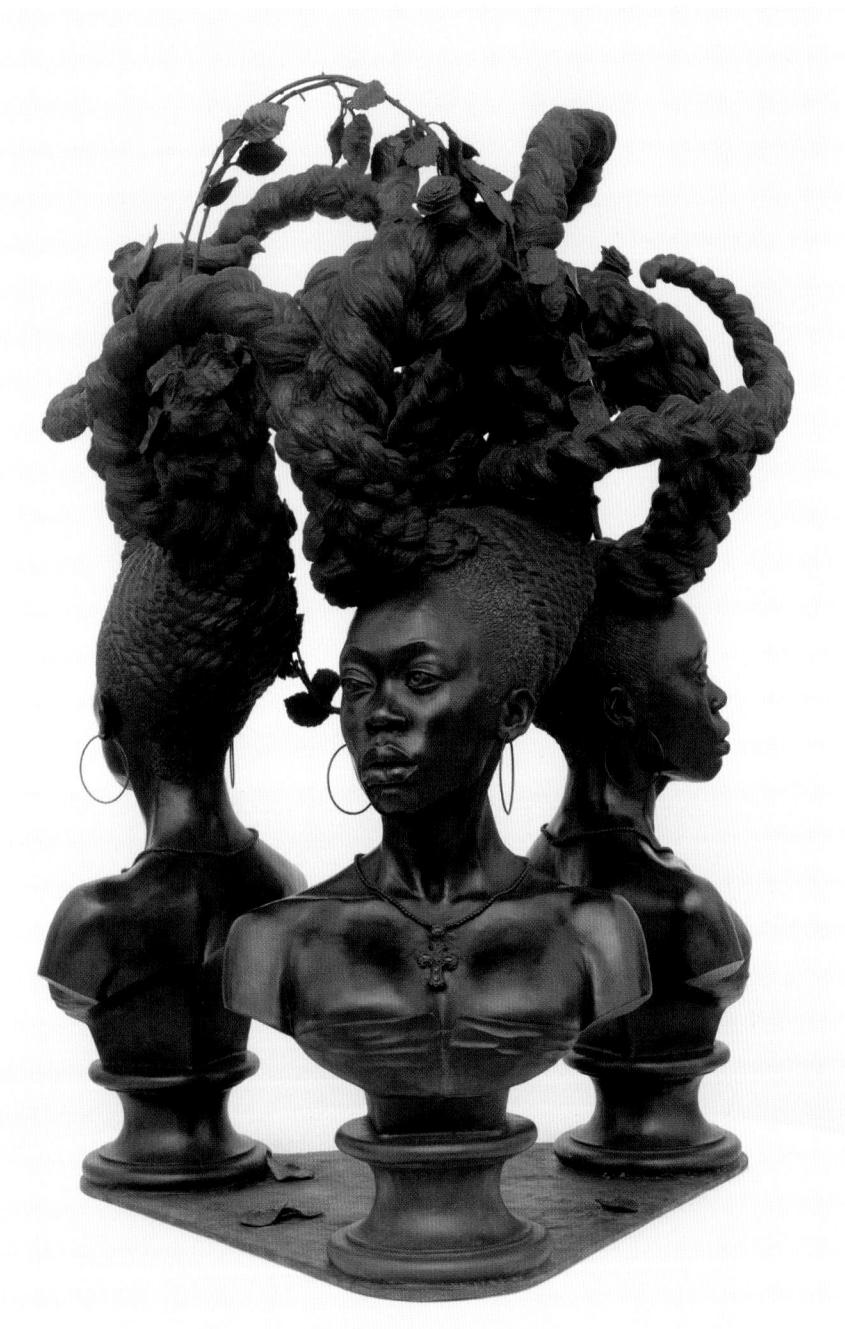

In the hands of Kehinde Wiley and Fred Wilson, history is as fundamental a medium as bronze or glass. Both artists draw heavily upon the grandeur, ornamentation, scale, and techniques of eighteenth- and nineteenth-century European art to amend historical visual records that exclude images and narratives of Black people.

In Wiley's *Bound*, this approach culminates in a trio of lofty, bronze busts. Each rests atop a plinth that occupies the rounded tip of a flat, triangular base, a physical elevation that, alongside the artist's choice of medium, mirrors the sense of exaltation historically signaled through similar sculptural portraits. Such works would not typically depict a Black subject, let alone a Black woman—or three; that *Bound* appropriates symbols of power to subvert expectations around race is emblematic of Wiley's broader practice. The subjects are nearly identical, wearing large, thin hoop earrings, ornate cross necklaces, and piercing expressions that simultaneously see through and look beyond the viewer. With heads turned slightly to their right, they face away from one another; yet, as the title indicates, they are inseparably bound by a heavy tangle of braids that floats overhead. Tight plaits weave around their scalps, becoming looser and wilder as they coil over, around, and under one another. Adorned with leaves, flowers, and birds, this shared, whimsical updo appears to defy gravity, though its physical and emotional weight, with respect to the ongoing

Kehinde Wiley
(American, born 1977)
Bound, 2014

Bronze, 65 x 45½ x 44 in.
Gift of Kehinde Wiley and Sean and Mary Kelly in honor of Arnold Lehman, 2015.59
Provenance: Donated by the artist, Sean Kelly, and Mary Kelly, June 11, 2015.

politicization of Black women's hair, is undeniable. Nonetheless, the unwavering grace of each subject suggests the unbowed heads that wear this crown lie easy.

While Wilson similarly employs historical aesthetics to engage past depictions of Blackness, or the lack thereof, *Iago's Mirror* notably lacks a figurative subject. The work takes the form of a Venetian mirror made in the tradition of Murano glassmakers, with whom Wilson worked to realize his extravagant design. Rococo in its dramatic composition, with stacked panels of etched glass, Wilson's work is trimmed with floral decorations, its solid-black patina a stark departure from its typically silver-backed, gilt, and pastel-embellished predecessors. To look at *Iago's Mirror* is to confront an unavoidable reflection of Blackness girded in ornate beauty. In doing so, the viewer is also faced with the artist's assertion that Black people are as much a part of the historical landscape as the decorative art traditions first expressed through such works. Specifically, this mirror stands among a larger grouping of black Murano glass works by Wilson that engage the underrepresented presence of African and African-descended peoples in Venice. This correlation becomes even clearer when the work's title is taken into consideration: Iago is the villain of Shakespeare's Venice-based tragedy *Othello* (1603), whose machinations against the play's title character are inextricable from Othello's Blackness.

IA

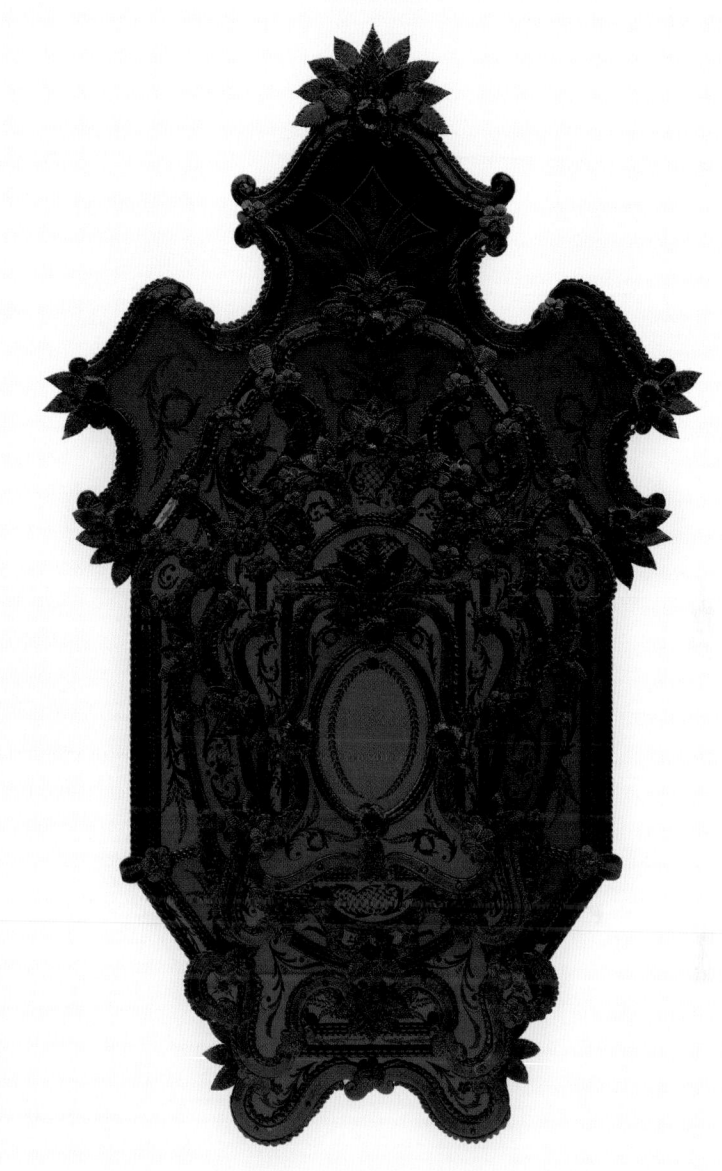

Fred Wilson
(American, born 1954)
Iago's Mirror, 2009

Murano glass, 80 x 48¾ x 10½ in.
Purchased with funds given by John and Barbara Vogelstein, purchase gift of Stephanie and Tim Ingrassia, Arline and Norman Feinberg, Beverly and Steven A. Newborn, Sheila and Richard J. Schwartz, Leslie L. and Alan Beller, Barbara and Richard W. Moore, and Carla Shen, 2011.11
Provenance: Purchased from Pace Gallery by the Brooklyn Museum, April 28, 2011.

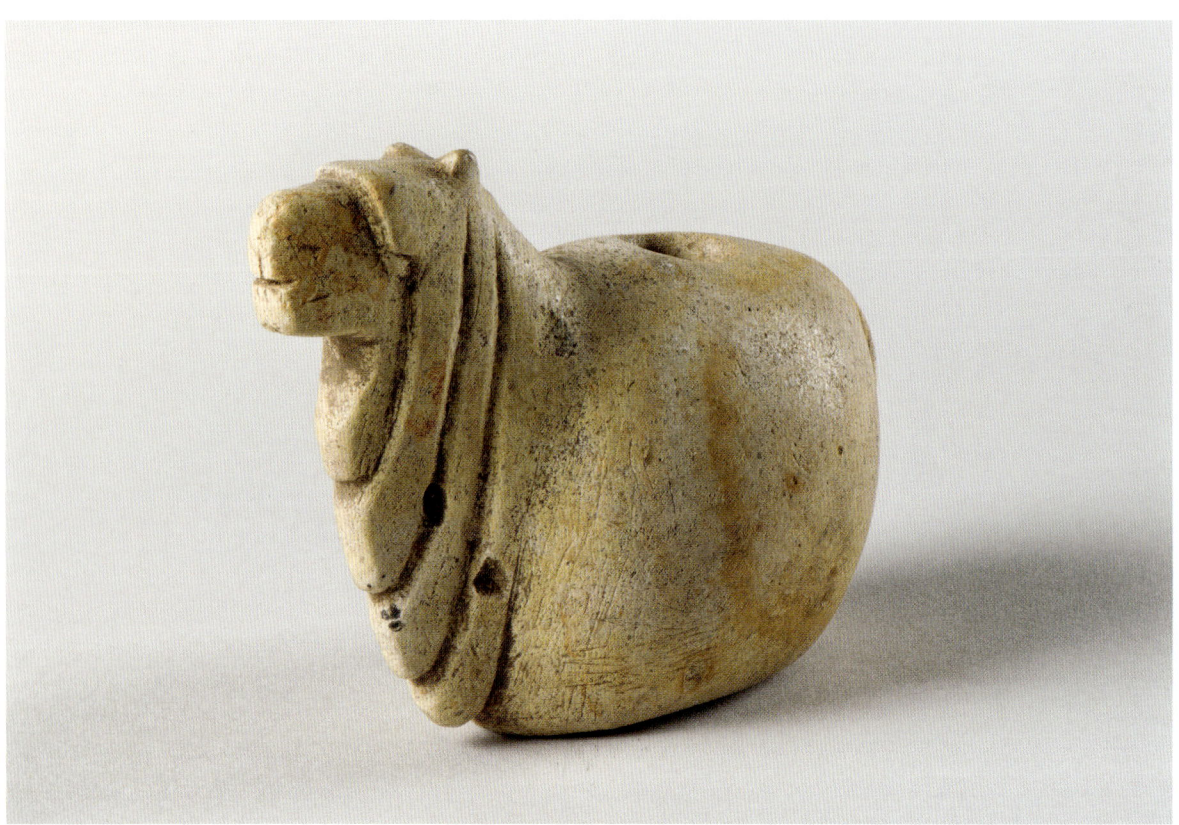

Inca artist
Alpaca Conopa
Peru, 1470–1532

Stone, 2½ × 3¼ × 1½ in.
Promised gift of Georgia and Michael de Havenon, L1996.5.7
Provenance: Prior to 1995 undocumented; by 1995, Joerg Haeberli, Morris Plains, New Jersey; promised gift of Georgia and Michael de Havenon.

Stone figurines, or *conopas* in Quechua, were the most common naturalistic stone carvings produced by Inca artists. They depict stylized camelids (members of the camel family, such as llamas and alpacas) that often conveyed the essence of the animal. The color of stone was chosen to relate to the animal's physical appearance.[1] For example, this *conopa* likely depicts a creamy-white, long-haired suri alpaca known for its lustrous fleece, which was shorn and spun into thread to weave cloth for textiles. As with other alpaca *conopas*, the animal is shown with orderly hair folds draped around the neck, a short tail, open mouth, slightly upturned ears, and a small cavity in its back. When the cylindrical cavity was filled with a sacred mixture of animal fat, coca leaves, maize kernels, and seashells, the figurine became a ceremonial offering to ensure the health and fertility of the herds.[2]

The Inca state (1438–1532) controlled vast pastures and herds of domesticated llamas and alpacas in the Andean high plain (*colla* in Quechua), which had extensive high-altitude grasslands that were ideal for camelid herding.[3] Numbering in the millions, llamas and alpacas were the heart of the Inca state's economy.[4] They provided meat for food, fleece for warmth and cloth, and dung for fuel. In addition, llamas served as pack animals and played an important ceremonial role: they were often placed in high-ranking burials, sacrificed during ceremonies, and were considered intermediaries with the gods.[5]

NR

[1] Richard L. Burger and Lucy C. Salazar, ed. *Machu Picchu: Unveiling the Mystery of the Incas* (New Haven, CT, and London: Yale University Press, 2004), 170.
[2] Ibid., 170, 171.
[3] Ramiro Matos Medieta and José Barreiro, ed. *The Great Inka Road: Engineering an Empire* (Washington, DC, and New York: National Museum of the American Indian in association with Smithsonian Books, 2015), 100.
[4] Terence N. D'Altroy, "Funding the Inka Empire," in *The Inka Empire: A Multidisciplinary Approach*, ed. Izumi Shimada (Austin: University of Texas Press, 2015), 107–108.
[5] Matos Mendieta and Barreiro, *The Great Inka Road*, 72.

Chimú-Inca artist
Jar with Feline Design
North Coast, Peru, 1470–1532

Ceramic, 9 × 7¼ × 7 in.
Museum Expedition 1941, Frank L. Babbott Fund, 41.1275.83
Provenance: Prior to 1941 undocumented; purchased in Peru, 1941.

This black jar with stylized felines from Peru's north coast was made after the Inca conquered the Chimú Empire in 1470, and introduced new features such as the flared rim and strap handles. The vessel was likely used by local elites for storing chicha, a fermented maize beer. The Chimú culture arose on the north coast around 900, and during its 570-year history, the Chimor Kingdom dominated an over six-hundred-mile territory. The Chimú state built roads and irrigation systems, established imperial administrative centers, and developed a system of mass-produced pottery where clay was pressed into molds—the technique used to make this vessel and its low-relief decoration of felines surrounded by stippling. The Inca utilized this existing imperial infrastructure, and sometimes shared rule with local conquered Chimú elites.[1]

According to archaeologist Izumi Shimada, the glossy black finish on this vessel is rare among Chimú and Chimú-Inca vessels, and was likely produced by the descendants of Sicán potters. When the Chimú conquered the Sicán people around 1375, they relocated the potters to the capital of Chan Chan near the present-day city Trujillo so they could produce lustrous black vessels for the Chimor Kingdom.[2] The felines probably represent the wild cats who inhabited the region and were likely revered for their ferocity and hunting skills.

NR

1. Frances M. Hayashida and Natalia Guzmán, "Reading the Material Record of Inka Rule: Style, Polity, and Empire on the North Coast of Peru," in *The Inka Empire: A Multidisciplinary Approach*, ed. Izumi Shimada (Austin: University of Texas Press, 2015), 288–89.
2. Izumi Shimada, communication with author, April 1, 2024.

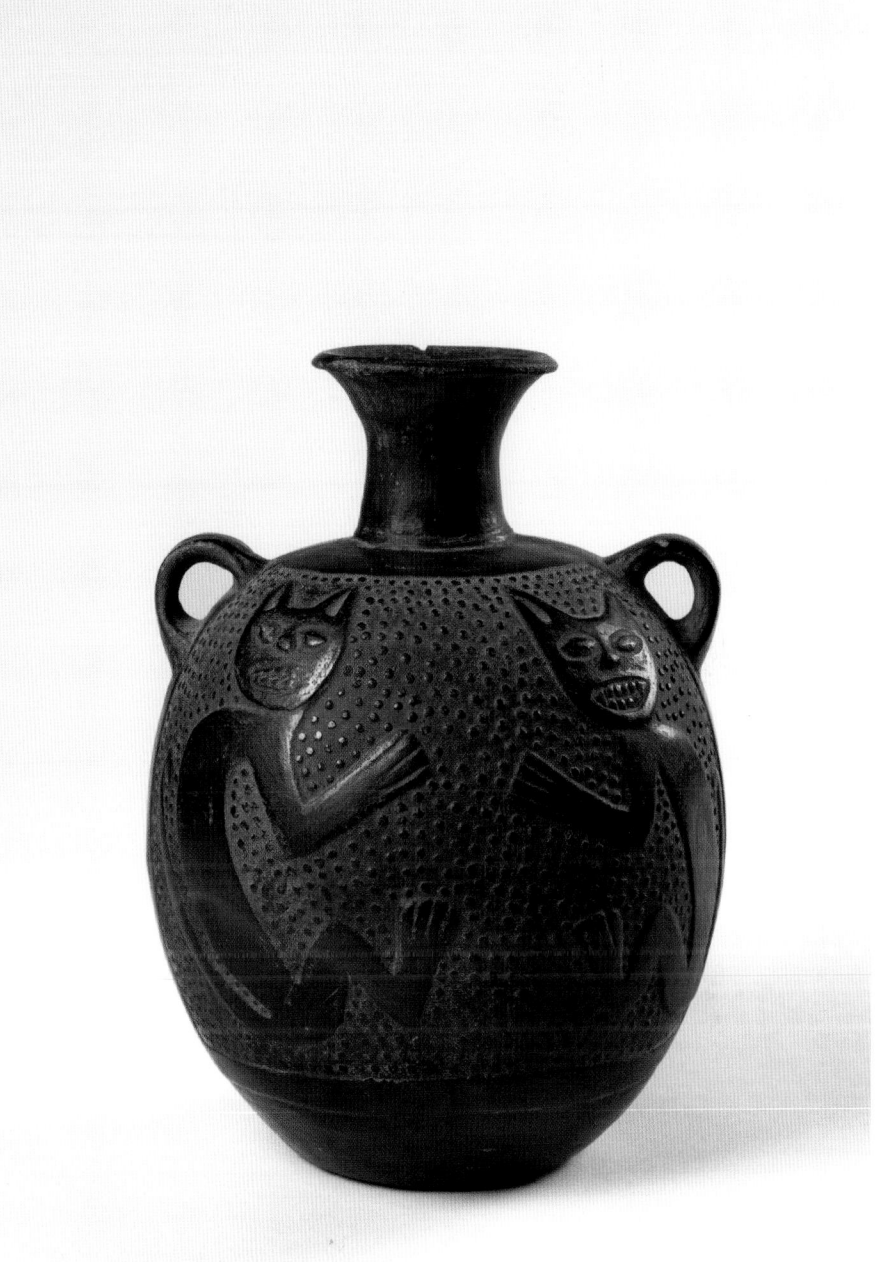

Helen Shupla
(Kha'p'o Owingeh [Santa Clara Pueblo], 1928–1985)
Melon Bowl, 1970–80

Clay, slip, 8 × 16 in.
Gift of The Roebling Society, 87.63
Provenance: Purchased from Mudd-Carr Gallery by the Brooklyn Museum, June 18, 1987.

Pottery vessels can outlast us; often their remnants are around long after the people who made them are no longer with us. These living elements of clay are gifts from our ancestors. For us, the current inhabitants of Mother Earth, these vessels serve as signposts of the past, of our ancestors' hands and work. They are inspirations not only to their descendants but also to people with no knowledge of their culture.[1]
—Tony R. Chavarria, Santa Clara Pueblo curator

This melon jar possesses vertical ribs reminiscent of those found on casaba melons grown in the American Southwest. Recognized as a preeminent master of her craft, Helen Shupla created this sculptural vessel through an innovative and labor-intensive approach. She hand-formed the pot then carefully pushed the wet clay from the inside with her hands to create ribs that can be felt on both the interior and exterior.[2] This technique contrasts with vessels created by carving out sections of their exterior and required great care; if she pushed too hard and created a hole, it could not be repaired. By taking advantage of the plasticity of clay collected from the Hopi lands on which she lived, Shupla made impressively large works; this piece is among the biggest she ever made.[3]

Shupla combined the melon jar form with the famous Santa Clara Pueblo artistic tradition of polished blackware. The vessel's black surface is the result of the artist smothering flames in an outdoor kiln during the final stage of the pot's firing.[4] Its highly stone-polished, undulating surfaces cast shadows and manipulate light.

DT

1. Tony Chavarria, "Pueblo Pottery: Meditations on Clay Mother's Gift," in *Water Wind Breath: Southwest Native Art in the Barnes Foundation*, ed. Lucy Fowler Williams (Philadelphia: The Barnes Foundation, 2022), 69.
2. Susan Kennedy Zeller, *Brooklyn Museum Highlights* (Brooklyn, NY: Brooklyn Museum, 2014), 130.
3. *Brooklyn Museum of Art* (Brooklyn, NY: Brooklyn Museum of Art in association with Scala Books, 1997), 80.
4. Ibid.

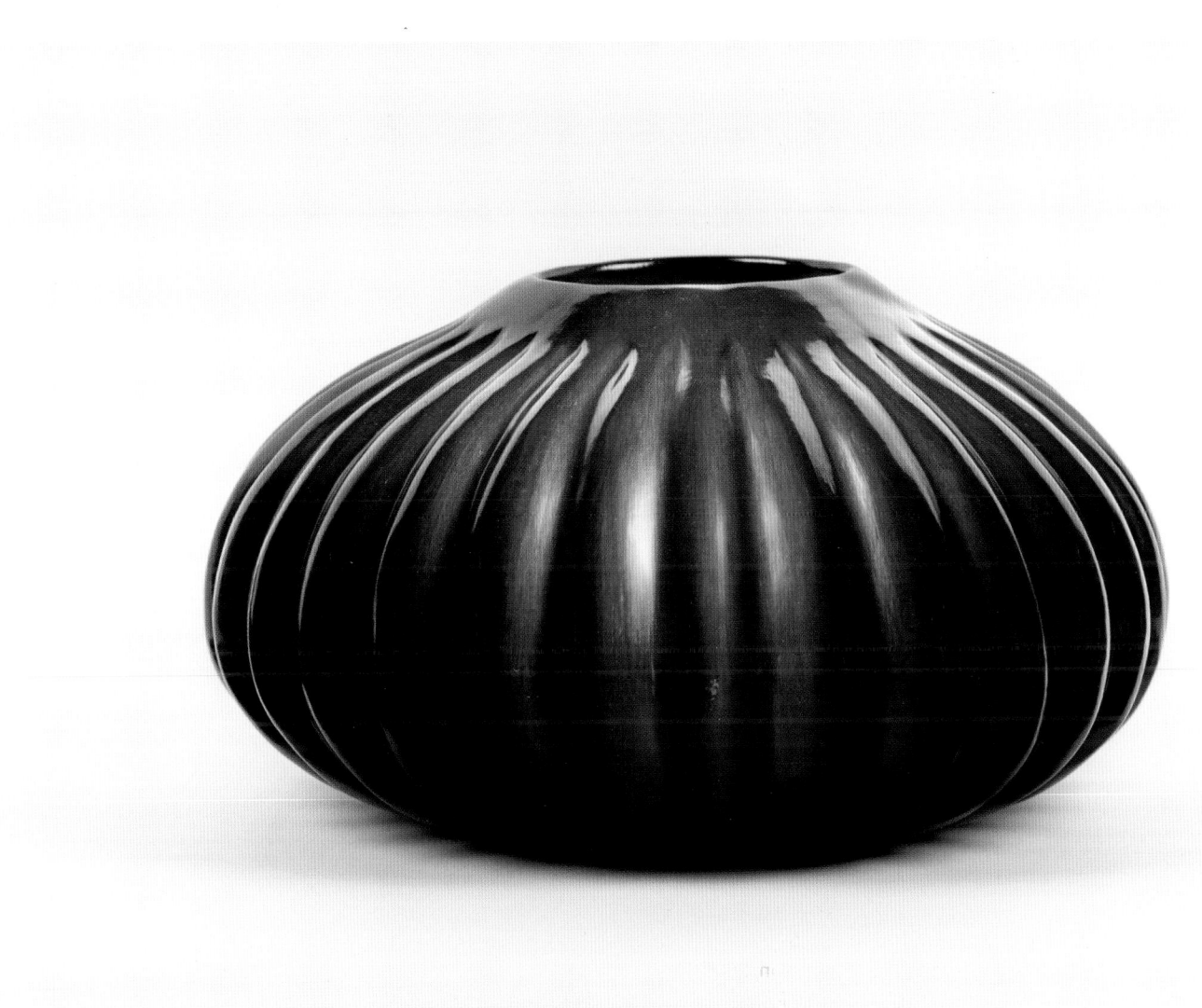

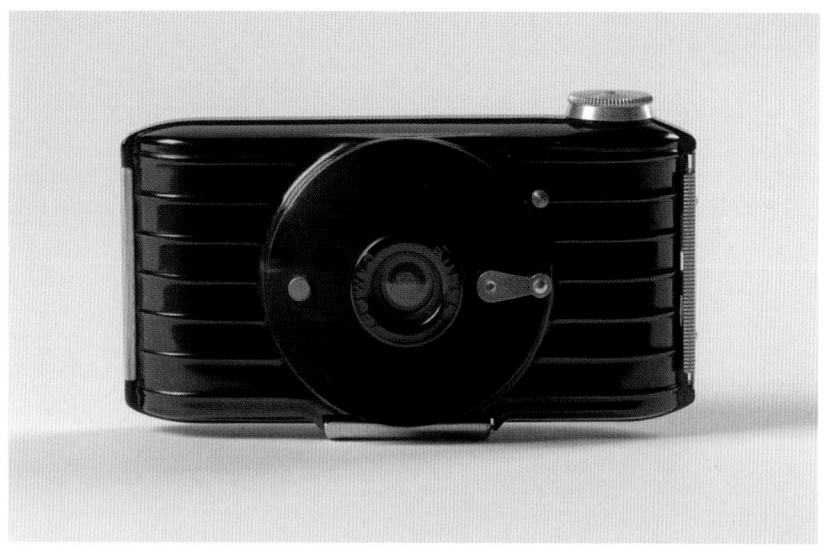

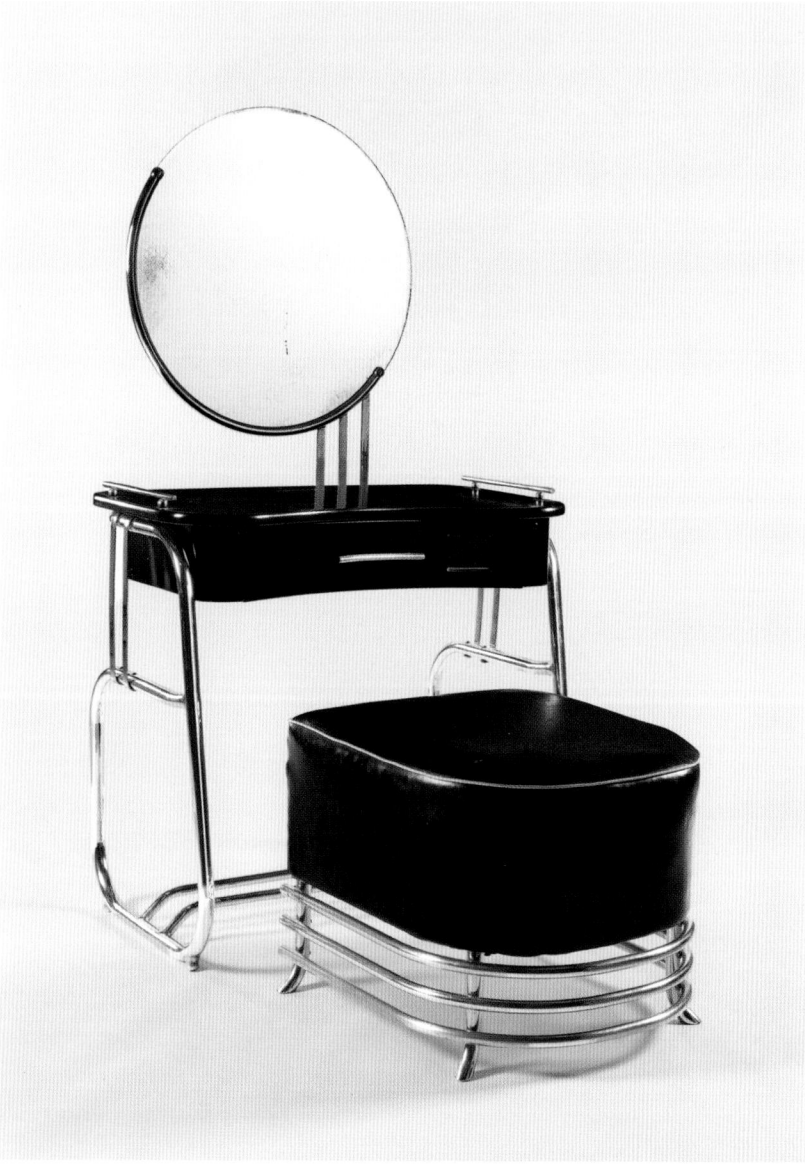

Walter Dorwin Teague
Designer (American, 1883–1960)
Joseph Mihalyi
Designer (born Hungary)
Chester W. Cumrine
Designer (American, 1889–1952)
Eastman Kodak Company, Manufacturer, Rochester, New York, founded 1888
Bullet Camera, 1936–42

Bakelite, glass, aluminum, paper, 2¾ × 4⅞ × 1⅞ in.
Gift of Eva, Alan, and Louis Brill, 1998.143.4
Provenance: Acquired by Eric Brill, by 1998; donated, 1998.

Kem Weber
Designer (American, born Germany, 1889–1963)
Lloyd Manufacturing Company
Manufacturer, Menominee, Michigan, 1906–1921
Vanity and Stool, 1934

Chrome-plated tubular steel, wood, glass; vanity: 55 × 33 × 19½ in.; stool: 17½ × 21 × 22½ in.
Modernism Benefit Fund, 87.123.1a-b, 87.123.2
Provenance: Acquired by Dyan Economakos, by 1987; purchased by the Brooklyn Museum, January 1, 1987.

Undecorated with curving lines, Kem Weber's vanity and stool are excellent examples of a visual style known as Streamlining, popular in the United States during the late 1920s and 1930s. Streamlining was inspired by groundbreaking research in aerodynamics, or an object's interaction with air as it moves through space. This design approach communicated, through everyday things, a hopeful belief that technology would spur positive cultural growth and change. In this example, Weber reinvented the concept of a vanity, an item historically marketed to women that served a practical purpose in the dressing ritual. Vanities were typically made of natural woods, and, depending on the price point, could have expensive inlays, carving, or other design elements. This work made with chromed tubular steel, a new technology developed for furniture in the early 1920s, had a distinctive modern look and was also well-suited to mass production. Its contemporary appearance appealed to consumers looking for innovation that rejected tradition in both lifestyle and fashion.

LSG

Earl Hooks
(American, 1927–2005)
Vessel, 1957

Thrown and hand-built glazed stoneware, 17 × 8 × 8 in.
Museum Collection Fund, 2022.44
Provenance: Acquired by an unidentified collector, before 2022; acquired by Swann Galleries, by 2022; purchased by the Brooklyn Museum, December 15, 2022.

While this artwork may be used as a vase, its bold composition and cantilevered structure are reminiscent of sculpture and dissolve the distinction between art and functionality. Its fluid and meandering lines point to Earl Hooks's interest in biomorphism—an abstract style popularized in the mid-twentieth century that evokes the organic shapes of plants and animals—and reflect his formal experimentation with representing both the human body and emotions. Hooks is most known for innovating in form. Here the vessel's thick, pitted black glaze creates depth, absorbing light and generating lively shadows across its surface.

    Trained as a ceramicist and sculptor, Hooks received an arts education from Howard University and Catholic University in Washington, DC. He also attended the School of American Craftsmen at the Rochester Institute of Technology in New York. In 1955, Hooks was the founder of Studio A in Gary, Indiana, one of the first Black-owned and operated fine arts galleries in the United States, which remained open for only one year. Subsequently he worked as a teacher and art consultant in the Gary public school system. From 1967 to 1997, Hooks served as professor and later as chair of the art department at Fisk University in Nashville, Tennessee.

LSG

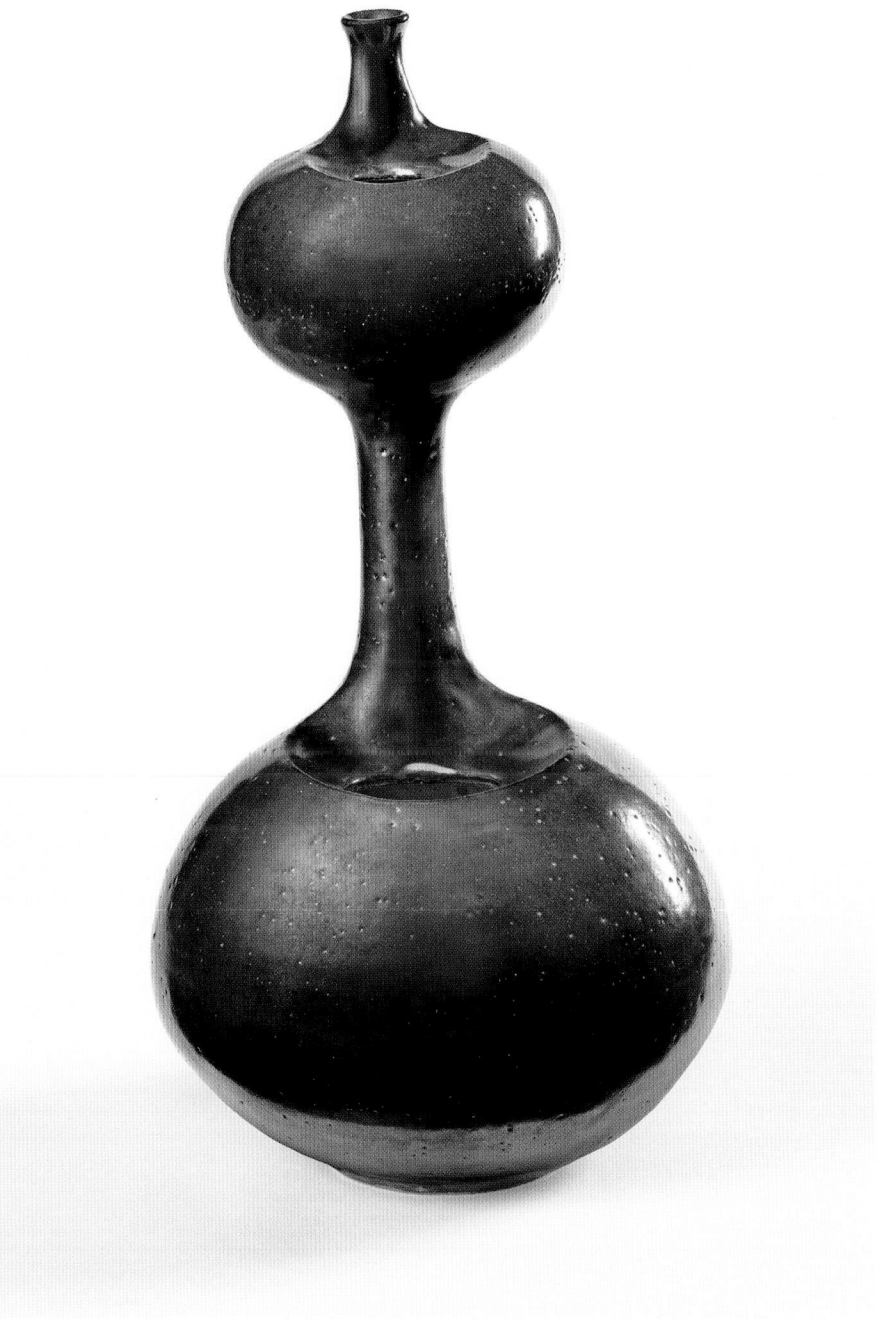

CRITICAL SHORT

In Dialogue

Camille Bacon and Leslie Wilson

Adapted from the responses Camille Bacon and Leslie Wilson provided within the context of the Black Feminist Roundtable, a series of conversations staged around each framework in the reinstallation for the purpose of peer review. Bacon and Wilson facilitated the session on the framework then titled *The Black and White Show*, which took place over Zoom on September 1, 2023.

black/white
absorption/reflection
presence/absence
light/dark
pressure
night/day
density/dissemblance
everything/nothing
black holes
compression/expansion
(im)possibility
coequal
counterparts

How might we think about the powerful associations that black and white—as achromatic colors, as metaphors, as symbols—hold on the historical, material, formal, and sociopolitical registers of our visual imaginations? In a collection of disparate artworks, how might new connections be found by focusing on so-called opposites in relation? *Counterparts* takes its inspiration from two historic exhibitions staged by Black American artists to invoke and disrupt the kind of binaristic— "this or that"—thinking endemic in our everyday lives and often reinforced by cultural institutions.

Hung in a salon-style arrangement, visitors experience nearly one hundred artworks through varying degrees of physical proximity. Their achromaticity offers viewers a unique vantage from which to examine the materiality of the objects themselves. In this space, distinctions like line, form, scale, shape, and sheen come into sharper relief and solicit close looking, which encourages expansive interpretative frames and, in turn, a new kind of play becomes possible between the artworks themselves as well as between the artworks and the viewer.

There is a love and care for historical precedent in this framework, carrying forward an avant-garde curatorial philosophy that extends the ethos of Sankofa, a lens explored in the framework Radical Care (pp. 68–69). Here, as always, history, and our attentiveness to the past, propels us forward into the future. The Spiral collective, a convening of Black artists in the mid-1960s, sought to build up the critical dialogue around their work. Pointedly, they asked: what is the role of the Black artist? Their first and only exhibit—*FIRST GROUP SHOWING (works in black & white)*—was invested in developing a thorough lexicon to apprehend both the formal and conceptual dimensions of their members' work. They proposed embracing "limitation" to open up a wider range of "feelings and approaches to art."

Black feminist conceptual artist Lorraine O'Grady also sought to produce discourse between artists segregated by race in the 1980s. The result was *The Black and White Show*, curated by her alter ego Mlle. Bourgeoise Noire. The dialogical nature of O'Grady's and Spiral's achromatic projects posed questions that permeate the Brooklyn Museum's display decades later such as: How can art, or curatorial practice, take more risks? What curatorial strategies might emphasize relationships between seemingly disparate artworks within the collection to propose alternative ways of looking, feeling, and relating? And finally, what is the function of the collection, or even the function of American art in the contemporary moment?

What, then, are the useful terms for reckoning with our experiences of American art, in its vastness and complexity, when an idea or a language of color is being offered? And from here: what interpretive tools might viewers pick up in this framework that can be helpful along a journey of transformation and, thus, be carried beyond the Museum's walls and into the world?

This framework centers "black and white" in pursuit of their complexities, subtleties, and range. Informed by the provocations of the Spiral Group and O'Grady, we want to consider the relations of black and white through the term "counterpart"—peer, complement, parallel, fellow, coequal. "Counterparts" suggest familiarity even at distance, intimacy even in tension.

Whether looking closely at individual artworks in this gallery, or meandering through the overwhelming whole, how might this space, in its errant and experimental approach as grounded in the legacy of the Black avant-garde, assist us in reconsidering the fundamental entanglement between counterparts?

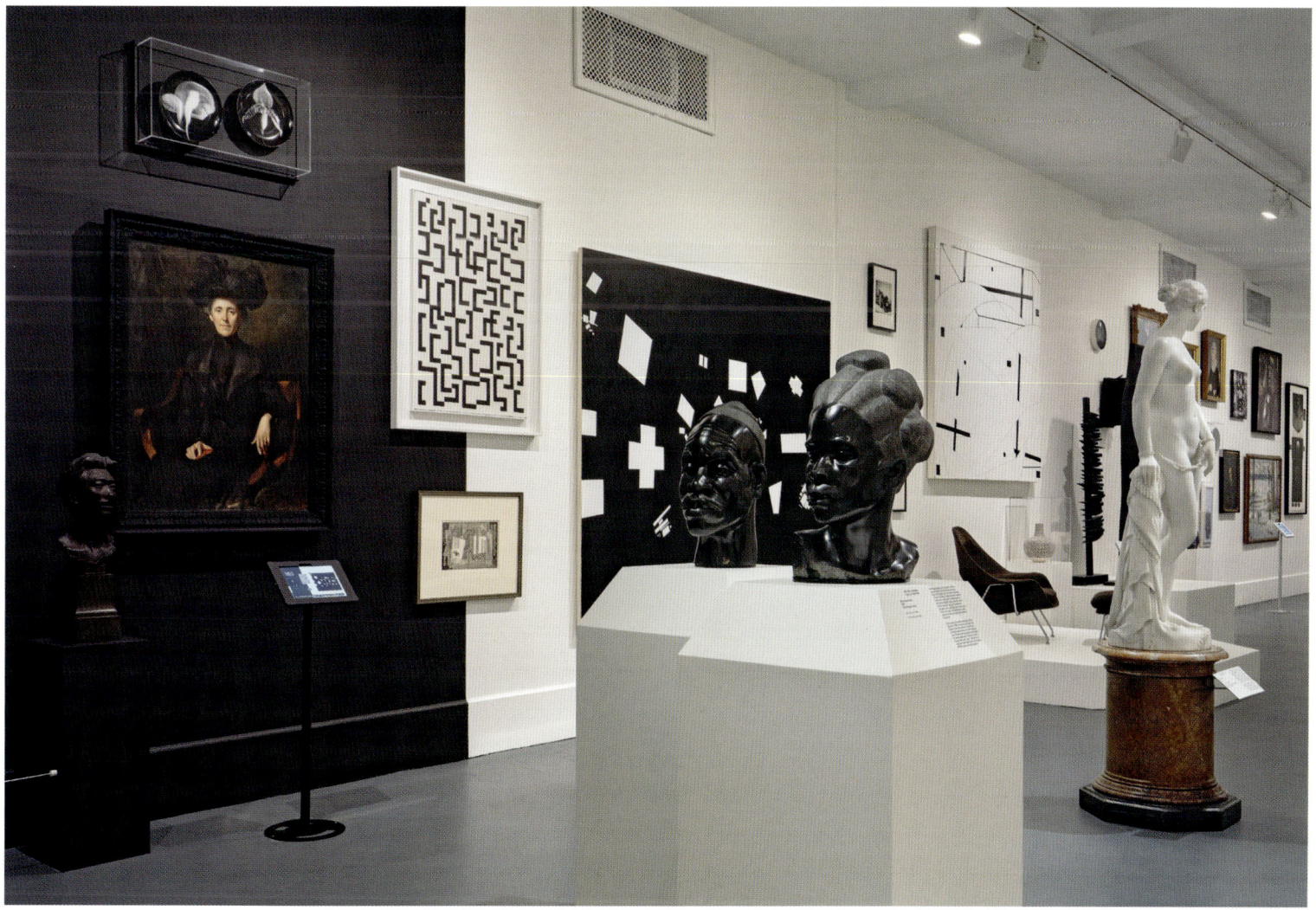

Counterparts

157

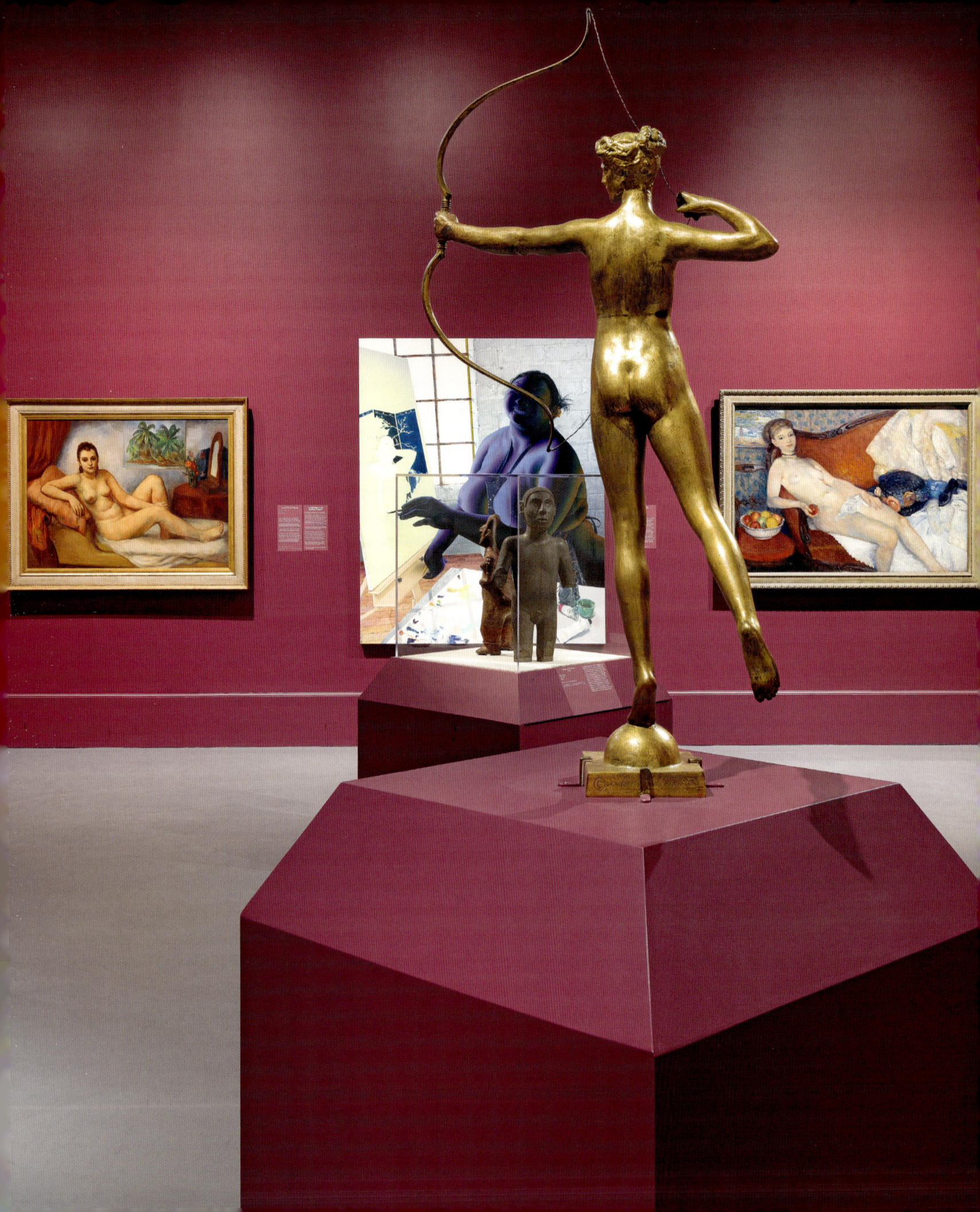

FRAMEWORK

Surface Tension

The Nude is not the subject of art, but a form of art.[1]

—Kenneth Clark

In a time of heightened visibility and contentious control over human bodies, this framework brings together and celebrates the nude figure in art, an impressive stronghold across the collections represented. Culture, religion, and society have always shaped how artists depict the human form—and dictated whose bodies are worthy of artistic study. This section illuminates masterpiece depictions of the human form and sets them in conversation with contemporary questions of power, agency, and embodiment.

These themes are explored across the installation, sampled in this chapter, and will continue to be studied in greater depth in rotating spotlights of light-sensitive works over the next several years. Artists Renee Cox, Gaston Lachaise, and a Nayarit sculptor champion powerful standing female figures. Laura Aguilar and Sarah Paxton Ball Dodson pose the reclining nude in distinct settings, while Bernard Karfiol, Mickalene Thomas, and others enlist desire in their confrontations of the viewer's gaze. Daniel Huntington and Augustus Saint-Gaudens celebrate the body in motion, while Thomas Eakins, John Koch, and Sasha Gordon complicate views of the artist and their muses at work. And finally, with a keen attention to surface, Senga Nengudi, Edwin Scheier, and Beatrice Wood use various materials, textures, styles, and mediums in work in abstract and functional art inspired by the human body.

This framework hosts our ongoing cross-departmental collaboration around this ubiquitous form, across time and culture. Future investigations will examine areas of the collection through the lenses of cultural difference, sex work, performance, and body positivity. Rather than critique historical art, however, the framework model brings these works into the present by inspiring timely links between representations of the human form and the concerns and curiosities of modern audiences and readers.

SSW

1. Kenneth Clark, *The Nude: A Study in Ideal Form*, The A. W. Mellon Lectures in the Fine Arts (Princeton, NJ: Princeton University Press, 1972), 5.

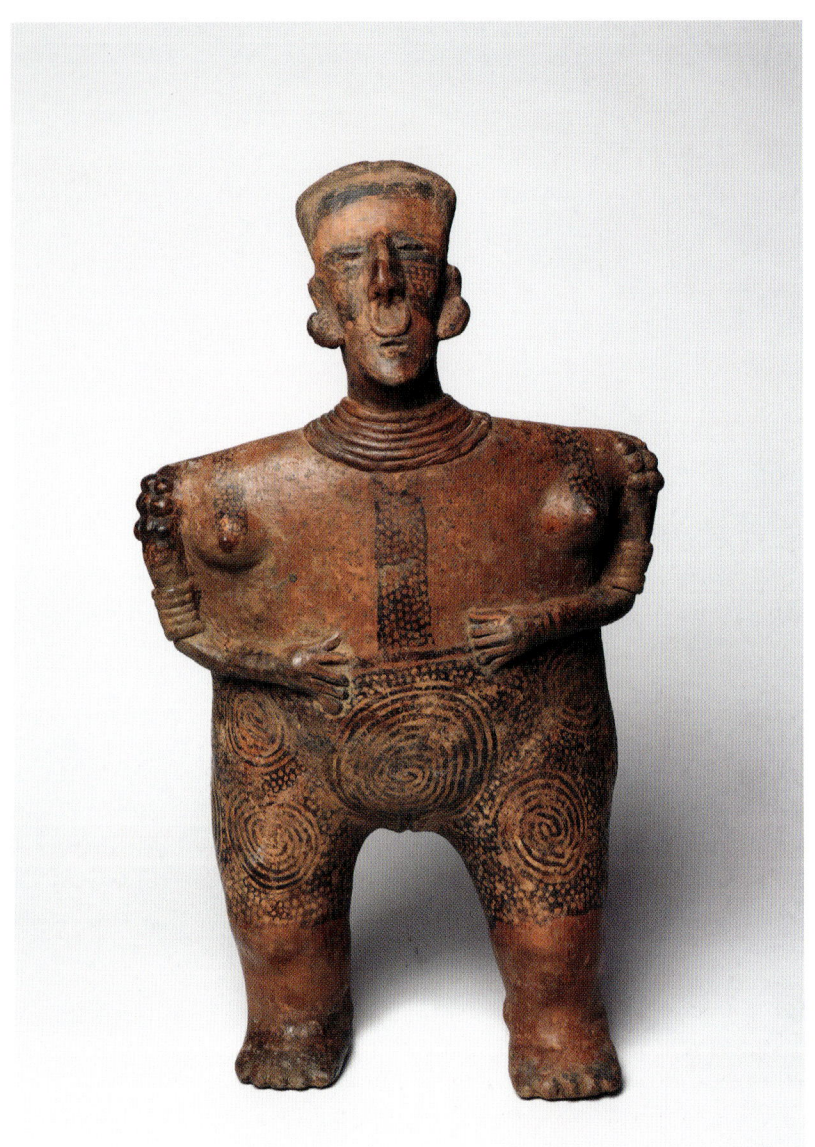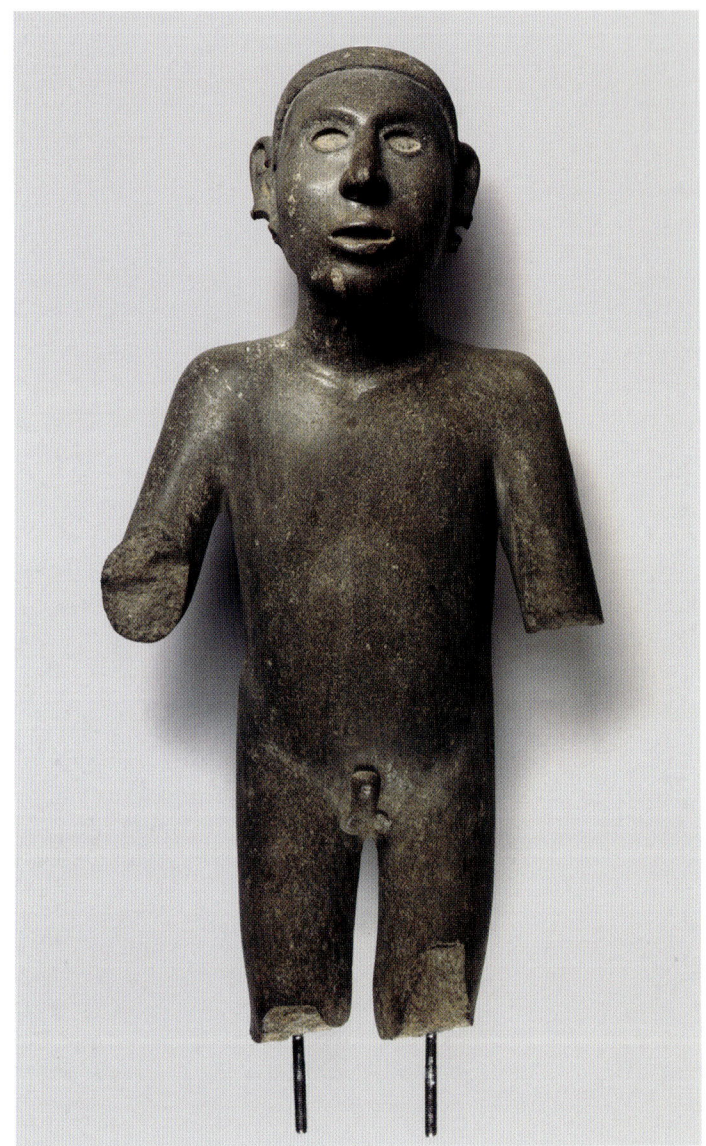

Toward Joy

Nayarit artist
Female Figure
Nayarit, Mexico, 200 B.C.E.–200 C.E.

Ceramic, pigment, 23⁵⁄₁₆ × 14 × 8¹¹⁄₁₆ in.
Carll H. de Silver Fund, 45.127
Provenance: Acquired by Stendahl Art Galleries, before 1945; purchased by the Brooklyn Museum, November 13, 1945.

Mexica (Aztec) artist
Male Figure
Mexico, 1440–1521

Stone, 27¼ × 14⅝ × 7½ in.
Gift of the Estate of Alice M. Kaplan, 2001.28.1
Provenance: Acquired by Edward H. Merrin Gallery, 1973. Acquired by Alice M. Kaplan, before 1980; donated by the Estate of Alice M. Kaplan, June 21, 2001.

Representations of the human body are found in almost every ancient culture in the Americas. They can be naturalistic, abstracted, or possess supernatural features that connect to the spiritual realm. The two-thousand-year-old ceramic sculpture of the nude woman was likely a funerary offering, discovered in a shaft-tomb in Nayarit, western Mexico. Adorned with ornaments on her ears, nose, neck, and arms, the figure has a sizable torso and legs, which gives her a powerful presence.[1] The intricately painted spirals and dots may represent ancient practices of body painting or tattooing, and the prominent spiral on her abdomen hints at her reproductive power as a giver of life.

In the Mexica sculptural tradition, completely nude figures are rare. The polished sculpture of a young man epitomizes the Mexica ideal of the human body. He possesses graceful yet strong features, such as an aquiline nose, eye and mouth depressions that may have held light-catching shell or obsidian inlays, and large, stylized ears with perforated lobes for ornaments. The subtle collarbone and faintly undulating muscles of the chest imbue the statue's rigid pose with vitality. Despite the broken arms and legs, the right arm appears as if it was once raised, perhaps holding a staff. During ceremonies, sculptures like this were dressed and adorned.[2]

NR

1. Richard Townsend, "Before Gods, Before Kings," in *Ancient West Mexico: Art and Archaeology of the Unknown Past*, ed. Richard Townsend (Chicago: The Art Institute of Chicago, 1998), 116.
2. Michael D. Coe, "Sculpture of a Naked Man," in *The Aztec Empire: Catalogue of the Exhibition* (New York: The Solomon R. Guggenheim Foundation, 2004), 31–32.

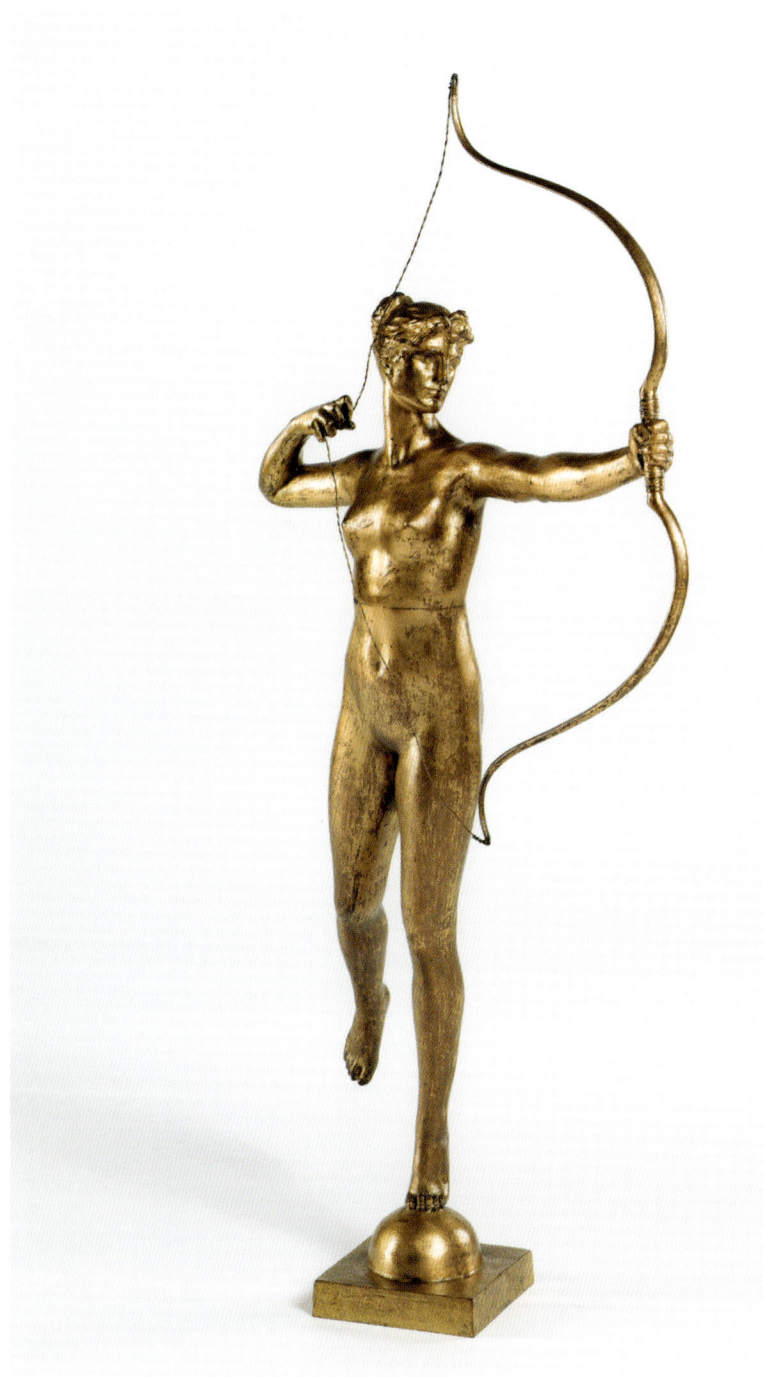

Augustus Saint-Gaudens sculpted Diana, the Roman goddess of the hunt, poised on one foot, with her arrow nocked and drawn in her bow.[1] Popular artist's model Julia Baird (1872–1932) posed for Diana's body, while Saint-Gaudens modeled the face on his 1886 bust-length sculpture of his longtime model and lover Davida Johnson Clark (1861–1910). This sculpture is one of several he produced based on his initial 18-foot-tall version, which was installed as a weathervane atop Madison Square Garden in 1891. Commissioned by Stanford White, renowned architect of the building, Saint-Gaudens's first Diana sculpture was designed with drapery that would catch the wind, and her arrow acted as a pointer. However, it was too heavy to spin as intended and was replaced with a 13-foot-tall version in 1893.

For a time, Diana was the tallest point in New York City. Her gilded bronze surface glistened in sunlight and reflected the electric light with which she was illuminated at night. Diana's nudity was shocking to many, including members of the New York Society for the Suppression of Vice. Their vociferous objections led Saint-Gaudens to wrap fabric around the statue for modesty—an addition that quickly blew away, once again revealing Diana's lithe body.

Saint-Gaudens was an influential sculptor whose extensive work on public monuments and memorials aligned with the Gilded Age–era American Renaissance ideals and the "City Beautiful" reform movement that sought to beautify urban spaces. He was known for his naturalistic sculptures, often representing military heroes or allegorical figures, rendered with great vitality that depart from the more static Neoclassical traditions. Saint-Gaudens's statues of Diana are the only nude female figures the artist depicted.

CG

Augustus Saint-Gaudens
(American, born Ireland, 1848–1907)
Diana of the Tower, 1895

Gilded bronze, 40⅞ x 20⅞ x 15¾ in.
Robert B. Woodward Memorial Fund, 23.255
Provenance: 1907, inherited from the artist by Augusta Fisher Homer Saint-Gaudens (Mrs. Augustus Saint-Gaudens) of Windsor, VT; December, 1923, purchased from Augusta Fisher Homer Saint-Gaudens to the Brooklyn Museum.

1. For more about Saint-Gaudens's sculpture versions of Diana, see Kathryn Greenthal, *Augustus Saint-Gaudens, Master Sculptor* (New York: Metropolitan Museum of Art, 1985), 136–40; Thayer Tolles, ed., *American Sculpture in The Metropolitan Museum of Art* (New York: Metropolitan Museum of Art, 1999–2000), 1: 305–309; and Thayer Tolles, "Augustus Saint-Gaudens in The Metropolitan Museum of Art," *The Metropolitan Museum of Art Bulletin* 66, no. 4 (Spring 2009): 72.

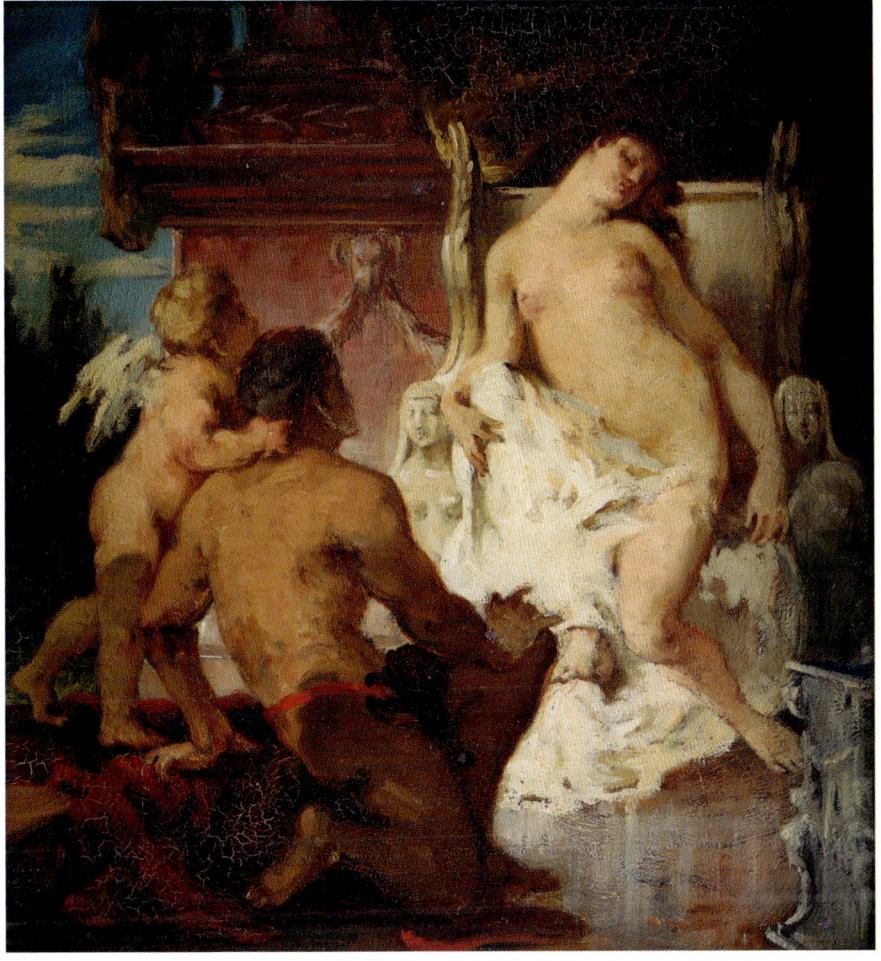

Sarah Paxton Ball Dodson
(American, 1847–1906)
Pygmalion and Galatea, ca. 1880

Oil on canvas, 13⅞ × 12¹⁵⁄₁₆ in.
Gift of R. Ball Dodson, 25.523
Provenance: Inherited from the artist by Richard Ball Dodson, 1906; donated, May 27, 1925.

Philadelphia-born Sarah Paxton Ball Dodson was a well-respected painter of biblical and mythical subjects, and produced large-scale history paintings during her time studying in Europe from 1873 to 1885.[1] This work is smaller in scale and exhibits a looser paint application, suggesting it was created as a preliminary study of the subject. The composition depicts the Greek myth of Pygmalion and Galatea, in which the sculptor Pygmalion falls in love with the idealized figure he has created. Here, the kneeling Pygmalion gazes up at Galatea, whose pale complexion reflects her metamorphosis from white marble to animated flesh. The elegant, sinuous curve of the nude body reflects Dodson's early commitment to late eighteenth-century French Rococo styles, while the rich colors are informed by her study of Italian Renaissance masters, influences likely gained during her studies in Paris and Italy.

In 1885 Dodson moved to New York City, and finally settled in Brighton, England, by 1891. Her works were exhibited widely during her lifetime including at the Paris Salon, and later at the Pennsylvania Academy of the Fine Arts, National Academy of Design, and at the 1893 World's Columbian Exposition in Chicago. The catalogue for a posthumous exhibition of her work at the American Art Association in 1911 celebrates her aptitude in many styles, stating that the exhibited collection "emphasizes more strongly than can any written word the variety of artistic impulse of the painter, her sympathetic understanding of many schools and her continuing purity of vision and felicity of imagination."[2]

CG

1. For more on Dodson and *Pygmalion and Galatea*, see Barbara Dayer Gallati, "Sarah Paxton Ball Dodson," in *American Paintings in the Brooklyn Museum: Artists Born by 1876*, Teresa A. Carbone, Barbara Dayer Gallati, and Linda S. Ferber (New York: Brooklyn Museum; London: D. Giles Limited, 2006), 1: 464–66; and Barbara Gallati, "The Paintings of Sarah Paxton Ball Dodson 1847–1906," *The American Art Journal* 15 (Winter 1983): 69–70.
2. *Exhibition of Paintings by Sarah Ball Dodson* (New York: American Art Galleries, 1911), unpaginated.

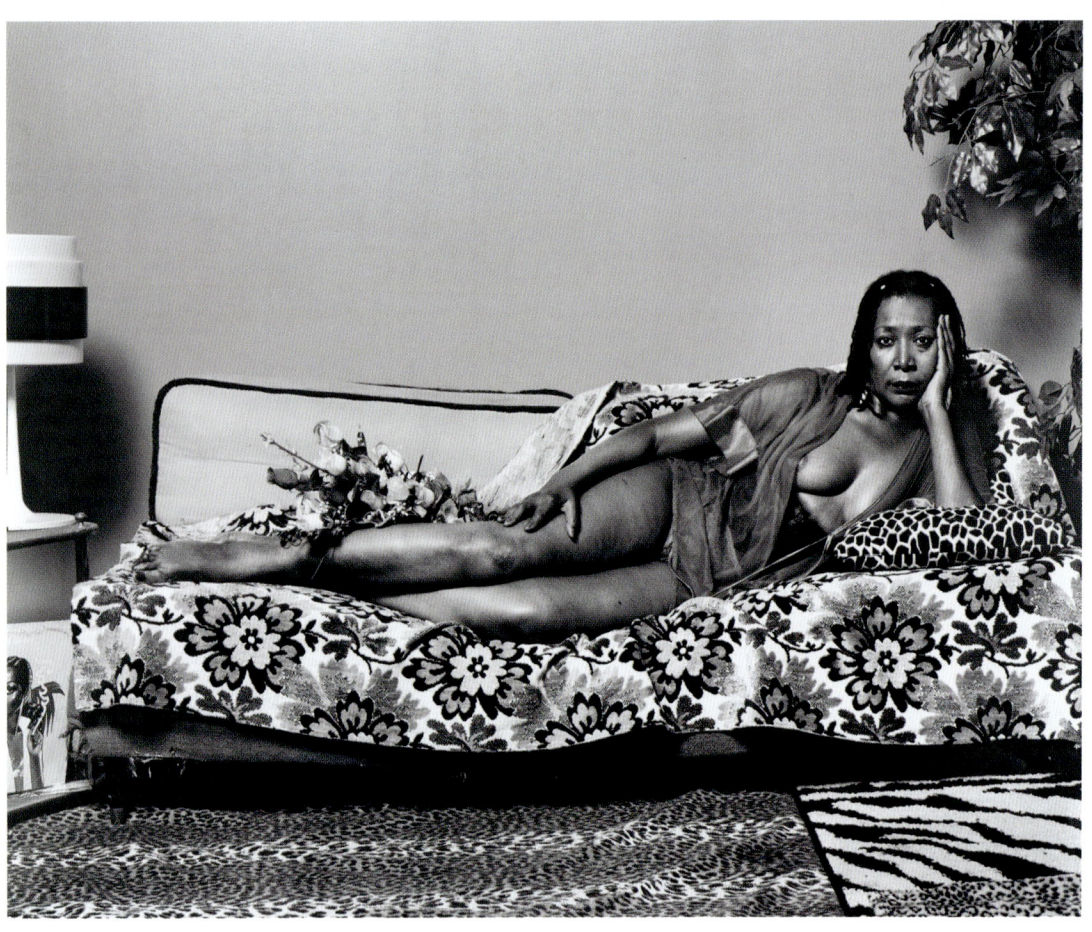

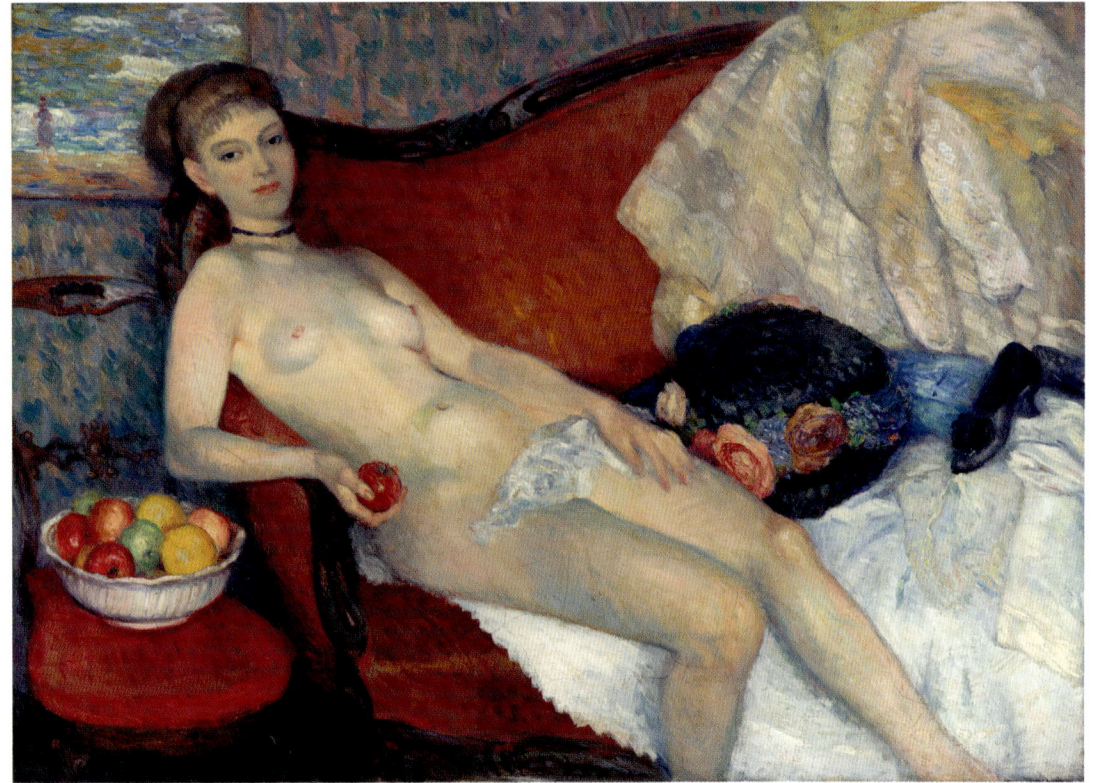

Mickalene Thomas
(American, born 1971)
Madame Mama Bush in Black and White, 2007, printed 2011

Chromogenic print, 16 × 20 in.
Gift of Mickalene Thomas, 2011.26
Provenance: Donated by the artist, April 28, 2011.

William James Glackens
(American, 1870–1938)
Girl with Apple, 1909–10

Oil on canvas, 39 7/16 × 56 3/16 in.
Dick S. Ramsay Fund, 56.70
Provenance: Inherited from the artist by Edith Dimock Glackens (Mrs. William J. Glackens), 1938. Acquired, probably from the estate of Edith Dimock Glackens, by Kraushaar Galleries, by 1956; purchased by the Brooklyn Museum, April 11, 1956.

The reclining female nude, such as the sexualized odalisque, or female attendant or courtier, is a common subject in Western iconography. Spanning one hundred years, William James Glackens, Bernard Karfiol, and Mickalene Thomas take on this trope to produce artworks that respond to and challenge status-quo sensibilities of their respective periods.

Cradling an apple, a biblical symbol for knowledge and the original sin of Adam and Eve, the model in Glackens's painting *Girl with Apple* glances suggestively at the viewer—will she take a bite? With a ribbon around her neck and her hair drawn back, this model bears a striking resemblance to the subject of Édouard Manet's 1863 painting *Olympia*, revealing one of Glackens's inspirations for this departure from his typical subject and styling.[1] Her liveliness and self-possession are heightened by William Glackens's tactile application of paint and the full palette of color with which she is rendered. Though no record of her name or background remains, the model exudes dignity and confidence in her gesture, gaze, and adornment.

In Karfiol's *The Awakening*, the model props herself on a settee, grasping her calf with one hand and flexing her feet into the cushion. Her posture and gestures are strong and stable, rather than languorous or submissive, and her gaze is directed out to the viewer. The painting's title suggests the woman is experiencing a liberation of her sexual feelings and energy, embodied by her alert and active position. Karfiol presents the classical subject of the nude figure, whose skin is rendered in an Impressionist style. Her dark-rimmed gaze is similar to Henri Matisse's exoticized depictions of women who appear to wear kohl makeup around their eyes. The palm trees and colorfully patterned textile under the pillow suggest tropical locales, likely informed by Karfiol's travels in the Caribbean and Mexico.

Part of a body of work responding to the race and gender norms of "the muse," Thomas's photograph reclaims sensuality, beauty, and, as the artist explains, "ownership [over] Black erotica."[2] Thomas's muse here is her mother, Sandra Bush, who volunteered to be her first nude sitter. Bush gazes directly into the camera—like the models who posed for Glackens and Karfiol, she appears self-possessed and aware of the viewer's presence. This powerful act of looking might be also interpreted as an act of defiance, what Black feminist theorist bell hooks termed the "oppositional gaze."[3] The lushly patterned textiles are a nod to the 1970s interiors Thomas grew up with that were prevalent during the Black is Beautiful movement. Riffing on traditions by white portraitists and sitters, as seen in Glackens's and Karfiol's work, Thomas creates a resplendent Black space for her muse, one that is empowered and self-determined.

CG/ML/SSW

1. For more on this painting by Glackens and the influence of Manet's *Olympia*, see Teresa A. Carbone, "William J. Glackens," in *American Paintings in the Brooklyn Museum: Artists Born by 1876*, Teresa A. Carbone, Barbara Dayer Gallati, and Linda S. Ferber (New York: Brooklyn Museum; London: D. Giles Limited, 2006) 1: 558–60.
2. Mickalene Thomas, "Mickalene Thomas on Black Female Sexuality and Her Artistic Process Behind 'je t'adore'," *ARTnews*, September 27, 2023, video of interview, 3:43, https://www.youtube.com/watch?v=DTMWnqE6p-E&rco=1.
3. bell hooks, "Oppositional Gaze: Black Female Spectators," in *Black Looks: Race and Representation* (Boston: South End Press, 1992), 115–31.

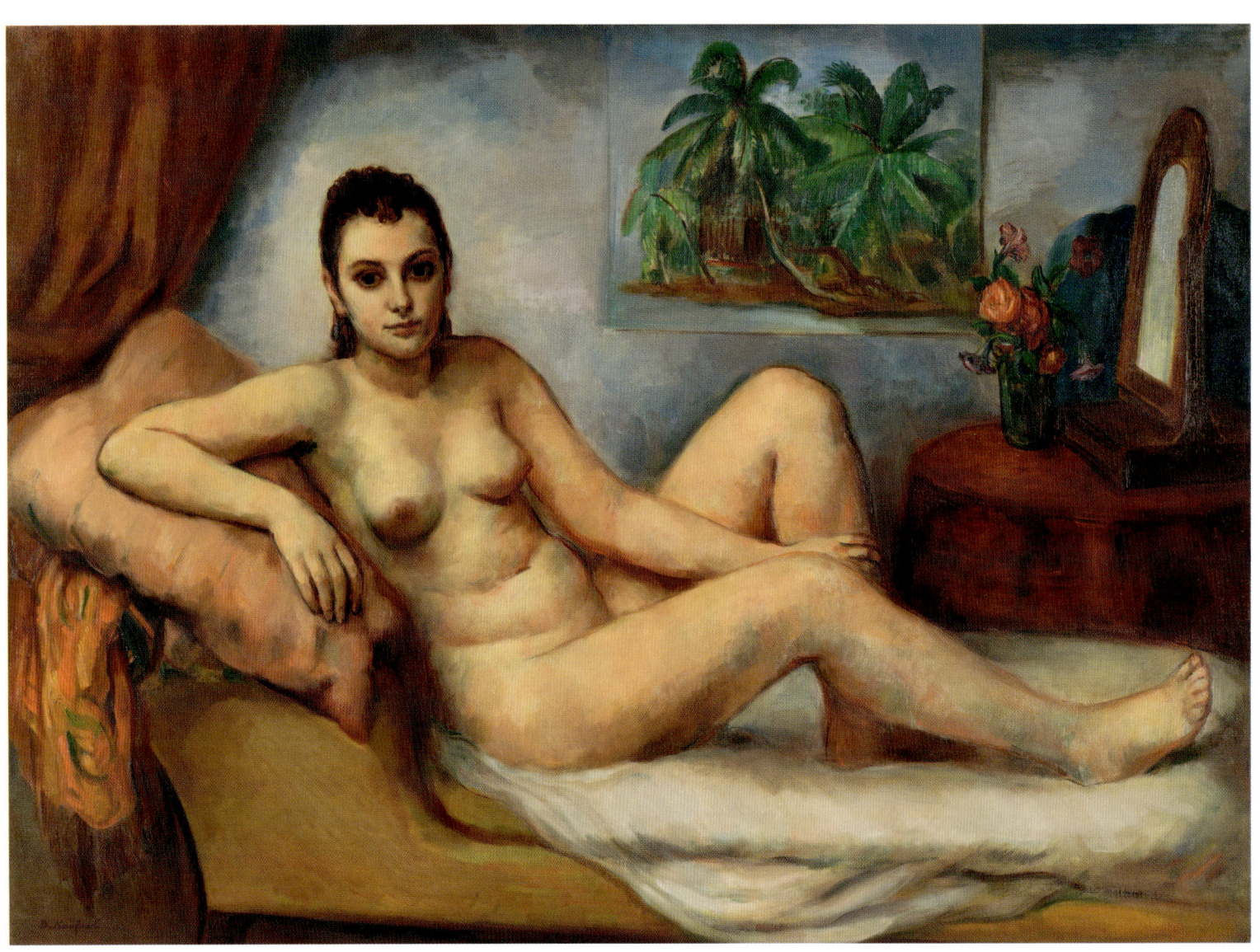

Bernard Karfiol
(American, born Hungary, 1886–1952)
The Awakening, ca. 1940

Oil on canvas, 36 × 50 in.
John B. Woodward Memorial Fund, 41.680
Provenance: Probably consigned by the artist to The Downtown Gallery, by 1941; purchased by the Brooklyn Museum, May 8, 1941.

CONSERVATOR'S EYE: Surface Tension
This artwork by Bernard Karfiol is a perfect example of surface tension in a paint film. Oil paint shrinks slightly as it dries, and various colors and paint thicknesses do so at different rates. This shrinkage causes tension within the paint film, and it may pull apart at the surface, exposing the layers below and forming drying cracks. You can see an example of this in the brown mirror frame and red tablecloth at the right where the lighter ground is exposed. These cracks are stable, but their appearance is a bit distracting, so they have been addressed by minimal retouching to allow the viewer to focus on the image as a whole.

Paintings on canvas also need even tension across the structure to maintain a planar, or flat, surface. However, poor stretching technique, a weak stretcher, or fluctuating environmental conditions can cause canvas deformations, as was the case with this painting. There are a few ways conservators can treat this, such as expanding the corners of a stretcher to increase canvas tension. Conservators can also carefully humidify and flatten the canvas, and/or re-stretch the canvas, which involves removing and remounting the canvas to the stretcher with more even tension.

EN

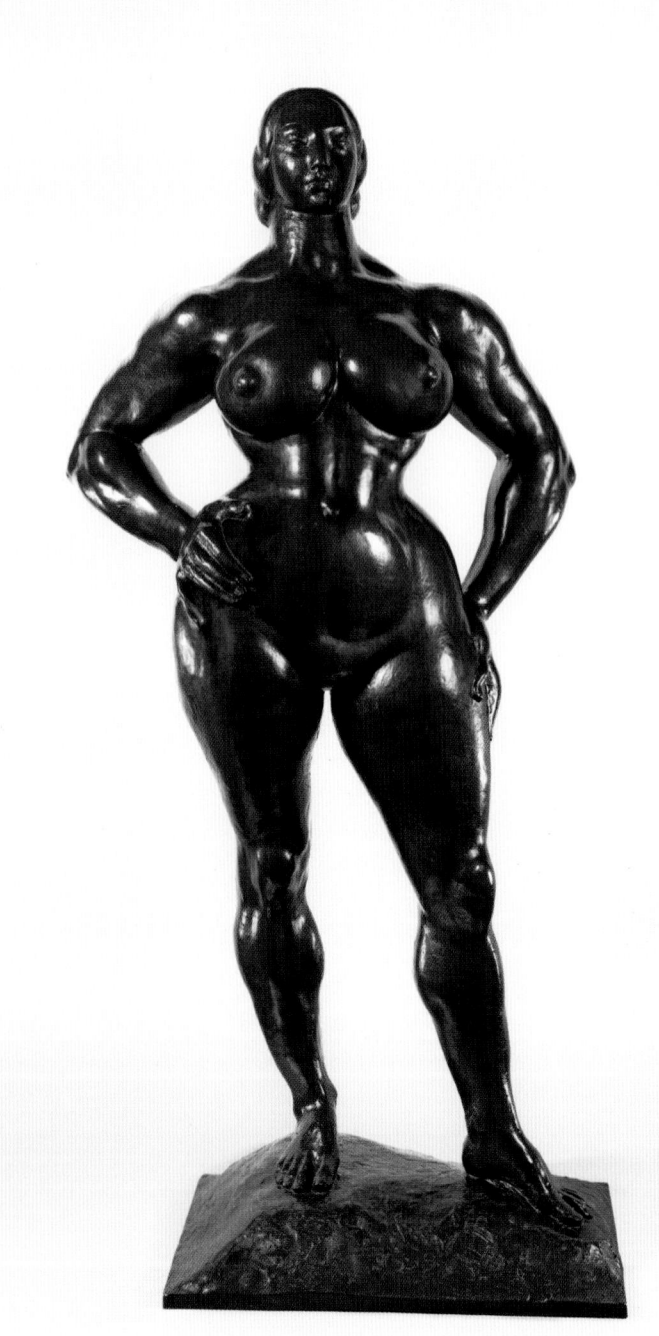

Gaston Lachaise
(American, born France, 1882–1935)
Standing Woman, 1955–56

Bronze, 88½ × 44⅜ × 24¹¹⁄₁₆ in.
Frank Sherman Benson Fund, A. Augustus Healy Fund, Alfred T. White Fund, and Museum Collection Fund, 56.69
Provenance: Acquired by Weyhe Gallery, by April 1956; purchased by the Brooklyn Museum, April 11, 1956.

"I worked from you all afternoon, expressing your body—expressing your thoughts—your body is your thought . . . It has been burning hot in the studio . . . I am all aflame—a flame that burns of You . . ."[1]

Gaston Lachaise wrote these impassioned words in a letter to Isabel Nagle, an accomplished poet, Lachaise's career-long muse, and, by 1917, his wife. In his eyes, Nagle embodied the essential traits of womanhood, inspiring and informing Lachaise's approach to representing the nude female form. He referred to her in artwork titles as simply "woman." Here Nagle poses in a self-assured and powerful stance, her hands on her hips emphasizing the muscularity and vitality of her figure. This depiction of *Standing Woman*—a later casting after the artist's death—celebrates the curvature of Nagle's body and her proudly displayed FUPA ("fatty upper pubic area").

While Lachaise adopted the contrapposto stance seen in this work from ancient Greek statues, he also sought to depart from classical proportions and idealized naturalism. With Nagle as his model, Lachaise developed an innovative approach to representing the female form: he embraced her proportions with slight exaggeration, incorporated smooth contours around breasts and belly, and often used graceful curvilinear lines informed by his early apprenticeship with Art Nouveau designer René Lalique. Lachaise's contributions to American Modernism and the influence of his wife as model were recognized by his contemporaries, including a reviewer of his 1935 retrospective at the Museum of Modern Art who noted that, in regard to the artist's distinct approach to the female nude, "he is indeed fortunate, he himself recognizes, to have found in his wife the embodiment of everything he needs in this respect."[2]

CG/SA

1. Letter to Isabel Lachaise, ca. 1913–14, YCAL MSS 434, Beinecke Library, Yale University, New Haven, CT. Also quoted and translated from the French in Paula Rand Hornbostel, "Alain Kirili/Gaston Lachaise: Flesh in Ecstasy," in *Alain Kirili & Gaston Lachaise* (New York: Ed. Salander-O'Reilly Galleries, 2007), 8.
2. Laurie Eglington, "Lachaise Survives Current Retrospective with Honor," *The Art News* 33, no. 19 (February 9, 1935): 3.

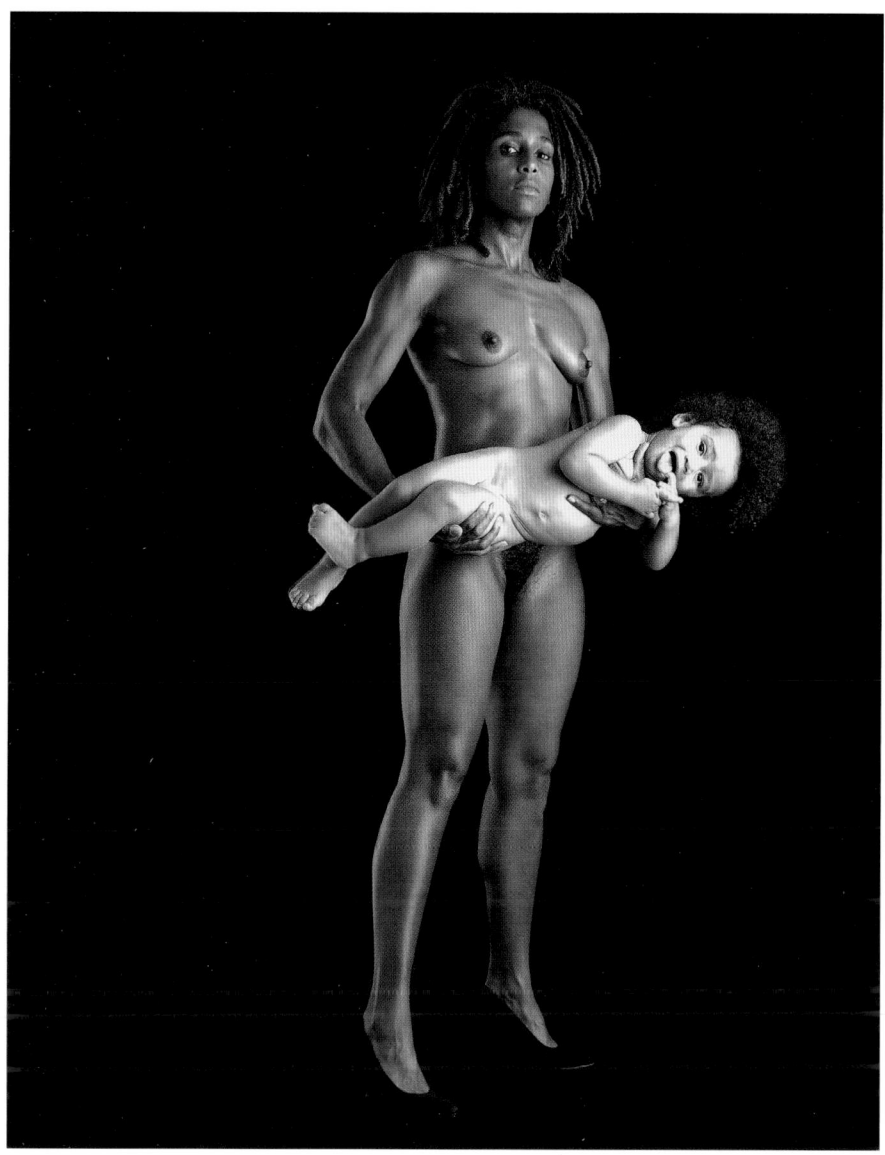

Renee Cox
(American, born Jamaica, 1960)
Yo Mama, 1993

Gelatin silver print, sheet: 83 × 47 in.
Gift of the Carol and Arthur Goldberg Collection, 2009.82.3
Provenance: Acquired by Carol and Arthur Goldberg, by 2009; donated, December 10, 2009.

I don't care if Christ is depicted as a black man and black woman . . . There would be no problem if you had kept your clothes on.[1]
—William Donohue, president of the Catholic League for Religious and Civil Rights

The installation of Renee Cox's *Yo Mama's Last Supper*, from her *Yo Mama* series, at the Brooklyn Museum sparked a cultural frenzy in 2001. In it, a nude Cox stands in as Jesus at the Last Supper, surrounded by all Black disciples. In this work from the same series, Cox embodies another icon of Christianity: the Mother of Christ. Challenging the traditional view of a submissive Virgin Mary, Cox reimagines her as unflinching and self-aware. The artist poses with her child, calling attention to her own maternal power and the child's purpose-filled future.

The self-portrait is a response to the criticism Cox received from her graduate school professors and peers when she announced her pregnancy. For decades, women artists were expected to forgo having children in favor of their careers. Instead of hiding her motherhood, Cox titled this work *Yo Mama* to celebrate her ability to be both artist and mother—all while wearing stilettos, a fraught symbol of beauty, poise, and desirability.

SSW

[1]. William Donohue quoted in Monte Williams, "'Yo Mama' Artist Takes on Catholic Critic," *New York Times*, February 21, 2001.

Both Daniel Huntington and John Koch took inspiration from ancient Greek mythological subjects as well as from the male nude form. In a suite of three drawings, Huntington peels back the layers of the body, examining the skeletal framework, muscular build, and supple fleshiness of a youthful man in motion.[1] Based on a Hellenistic Greek statue of a dancing satyr, or faun, Huntington's drawings reveal his training in anatomy and study of ancient sculpture and plaster casts. The rear view allowed the artist a closer study of the satyr's exaggerated S-curve body and the tautness of his back muscles. Arms lifted animatedly, the satyr holds a pair of cymbals in his hands, while his right foot keeps time on a kroupezion (a percussive clapper), accentuating his contrapposto stance.

Koch also captures the backside of a male model—Ernest Ulmer—posed in an elegant contrapposto in a quiet moment in his studio.[2] Koch's sensual depiction of Ulmer moves beyond traditional displays of heroic athleticism, becoming charged with homoerotic tension. The viewer's gaze is drawn along the model's muscular shoulders, past a thin loin cloth string, to his upturned foot. Koch represents himself leaning toward Ulmer lighting his cigarette, suggesting their easy familiarity with one another. The cigarette blaze and beak-like calipers in Koch's hand allude to the Greek myth of Prometheus. After lovingly forming humankind from mud, the titan Prometheus defies Zeus and illicitly gifts fire to humans. Koch's sculpture in the painting's background depicts Zeus punishing Prometheus with a vulture that viciously devours his liver.[3] Ulmer likely also modeled for the sculpture. Highlighting the powerful connection between sculptor and creation, the myth underscores the intimacy between artist and model in Koch's studio scenes.

CG/SA

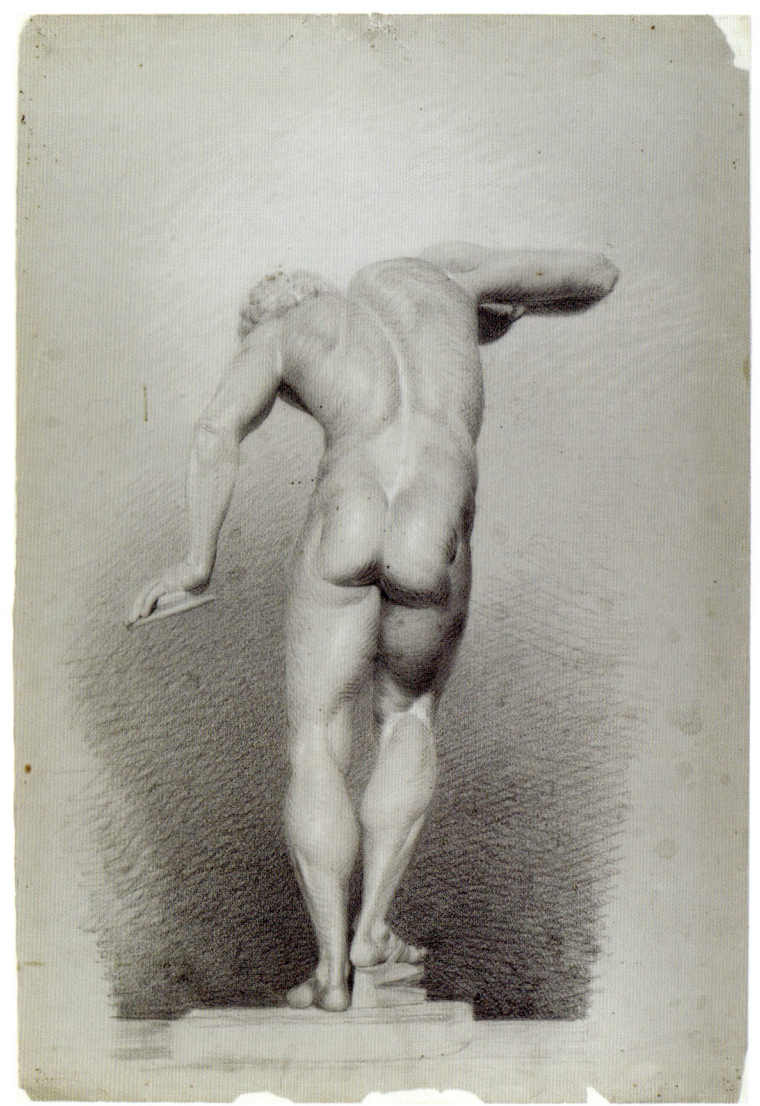

Daniel Huntington
(American, 1816–1906)
Nude Study, ca. 1848

Crayon on paper, sheet: 21¾ × 15⅛ in.
Gift of The Roebling Society, 68.167.5
Provenance: Acquired by Spanierman Gallery, by 1968; purchased by the Brooklyn Museum, November 12, 1968.

John Koch
(American, 1909–1978)
The Sculptor, 1964

Oil on canvas, 80 × 59⅞ in.
Gift of the artist, 69.165
Provenance: Donated by the artist, 1969.

1. Karen A. Sherry, *Fine Lines: American Drawings from the Brooklyn Museum* (New York: Brooklyn Museum; London: D. Giles Limited., 2013), 20.
2. *John Koch: Painting a New York Life* (London: Scala, 2001).
3. For Koch's discussion of the myth and its connection with this painting, see John Koch, interviewed by A. Jacobowitz, February 15, 1968, transcript, page 2, curatorial file for object 69.165, Brooklyn Museum.

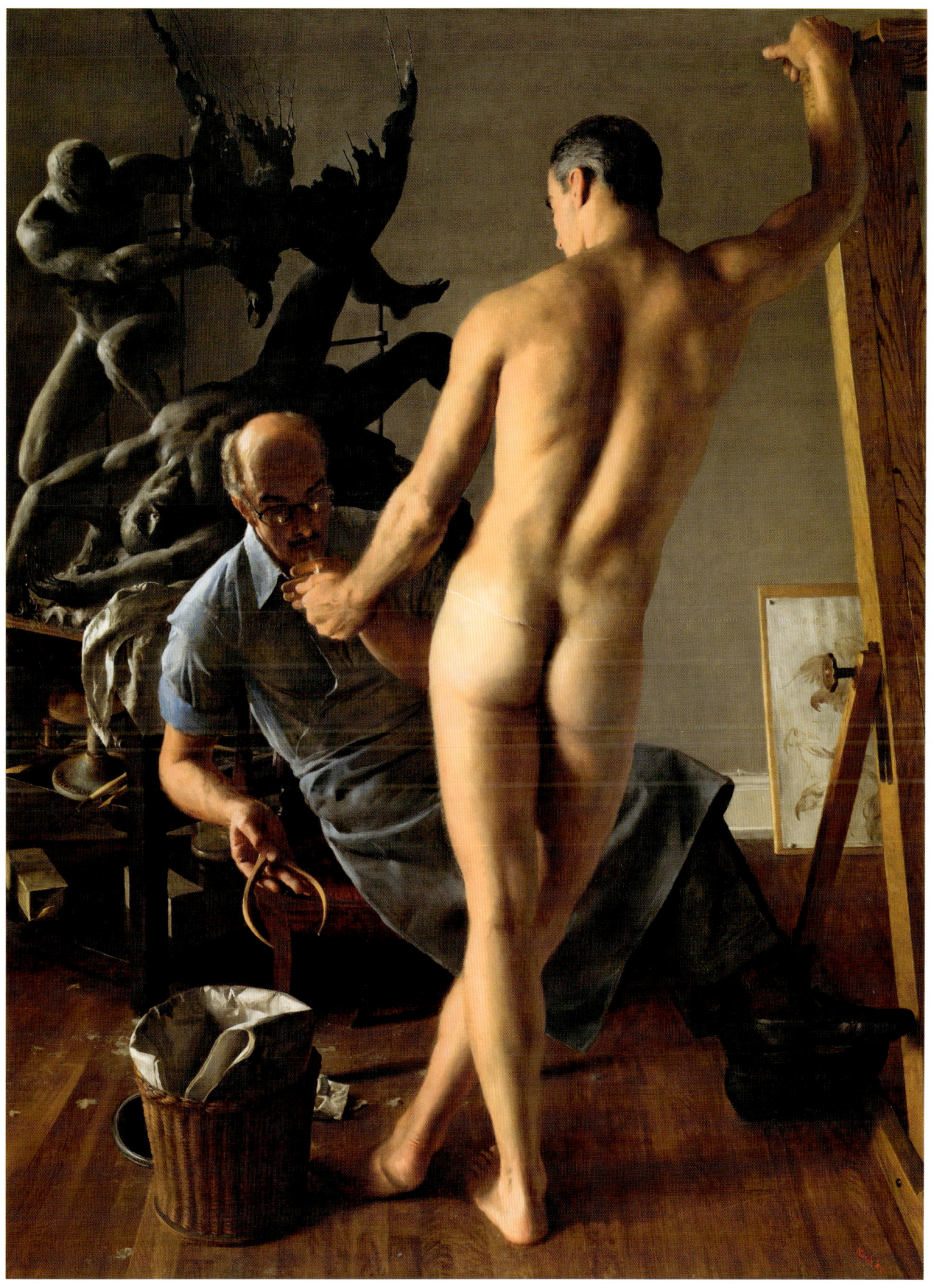

Surface Tension

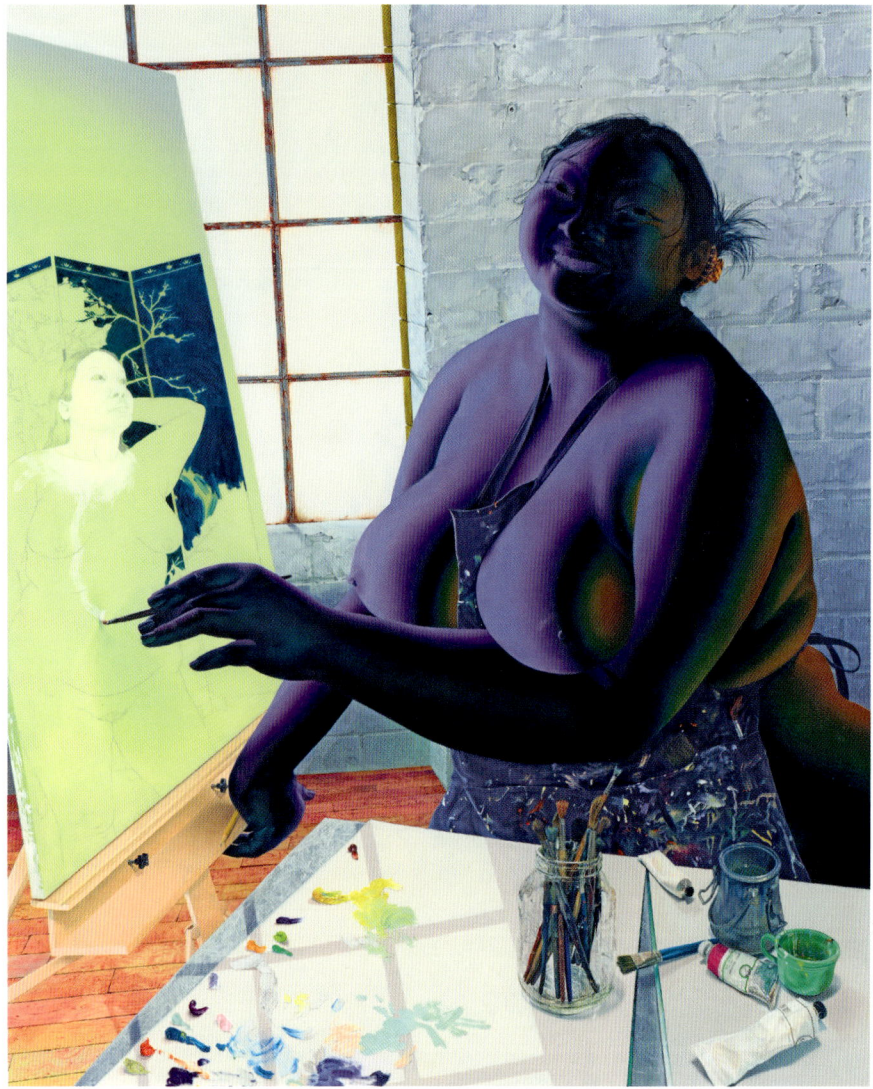

Sasha Gordon
(American, born 1998)
My Friend Will Be Me, 2022

Oil on canvas, 72 × 60 × 1½ in.
Promised gift of Carla Shen and Christopher Schott, L2024.8.1

In this large-scale painting, Sasha Gordon depicts herself in the nude with lustrous purple and blue skin, casually leaning on her easel and grinning widely at the viewer. Wrapped in a paint-streaked smock, she works on a study of herself, applying white pigment to the yellow underpainting of her outlined bare skin—a suggestively racialized choice. In her work, Gordon often grapples with her Polish-Jewish and Korean American mixed-race identity. Growing up in the majority-white town of Somers in Westchester County, New York, Gordon was bullied and felt compelled to assimilate.[1] During her training at the Rhode Island School of Design, Gordon began painting her doppelgängers, and with them, embracing her identity as a queer Asian American artist.

In *My Friend Will Be Me* Gordon engages in—and challenges—Western traditions of self-portraiture, complicating the relationship between herself as an Asian American woman and her viewers. While her pose—paintbrush aloft, at the easel—is reminiscent of historic self-portraits by iconic women artists such as Artemisia Gentileschi (1593–1653), Judith Leyster (1609–1660), and Élisabeth Louise Vigée Le Brun (1755–1842), Gordon's enlarged features and technicolor skin tone grounds viewers in the present. Her bold formal choices reflect a psychological depth Gordon is keen to explore in her art, particularly regarding her own racial identity and mental health—struggles the artist makes visible through narrative, expression, and gesture within her work.[2] Defying white and gender normative expectations, Gordon's indigo-skinned persona stares confidently from the canvas and the page, inviting and enjoying our attention.

GB

1. Dodie Kazanjian, "By Painting Herself, Sasha Gordon Found True Perspective," *Vogue*, March 2023, 132.
2. For more on identity and mental health in Gordon's paintings see Katie White, "'I Want to Show the Conflict I Experience Within My Brain': Young Painter Sasha Gordon on Her Tender and Menacing Self-Portraits," *Artnet*, June 24, 2022, https://news.artnet.com/art-world/sasha-gordon-deitch-interview-2135400.

Senga Nengudi
(American, born 1943)
Inside/Outside, 1977

Nylon, mesh, rubber, 60 × 24 in. approx.
Gift of Burt Aaron, the Council for Feminist Art, and the Alfred T. White Fund, 2011.21
Provenance: Acquired by Thomas Erben Gallery, by September 2003; purchased by the Brooklyn Museum, April 28, 2011.

After giving birth to my own son, I thought of black wet-nurses suckling child after child—their own as well as those of others, until their breasts rested on their knees, their energies drained. My works are abstracted reflections of used bodies—visual images that serve my aesthetic as well as my ideas.[1]
—Senga Nengudi

Senga Nengudi's affinity for nylon and rubber stems from their elasticity and resemblance to the "tender, tight beginnings to sagging end" of the human body. In this sculpture, the deflated tubing and thin drooping fabric, heavy with sand, invoke distended fleshy parts, as well as the impact of labor on Black women's bodies.[2] As with many of her sculptures, Nengudi activated *Inside/Outside* through live performance, blurring the formal boundaries of sculpture as static and autonomous objects. Referencing ritual objects and costumes resonant across the African diaspora, the artist would don the curving plastic, transforming the sculpture into a colorful headdress during her performances.

ML/SSW

1. John Perreault, "The Whitney Counterweight: Stretching It," *Soho Weekly News* 4/25 (March 1977): 22–27. Reviews of shows at Yu and Just Above Midtown Galleries. Photo with *RSVP No. 10*.
2. Ibid.

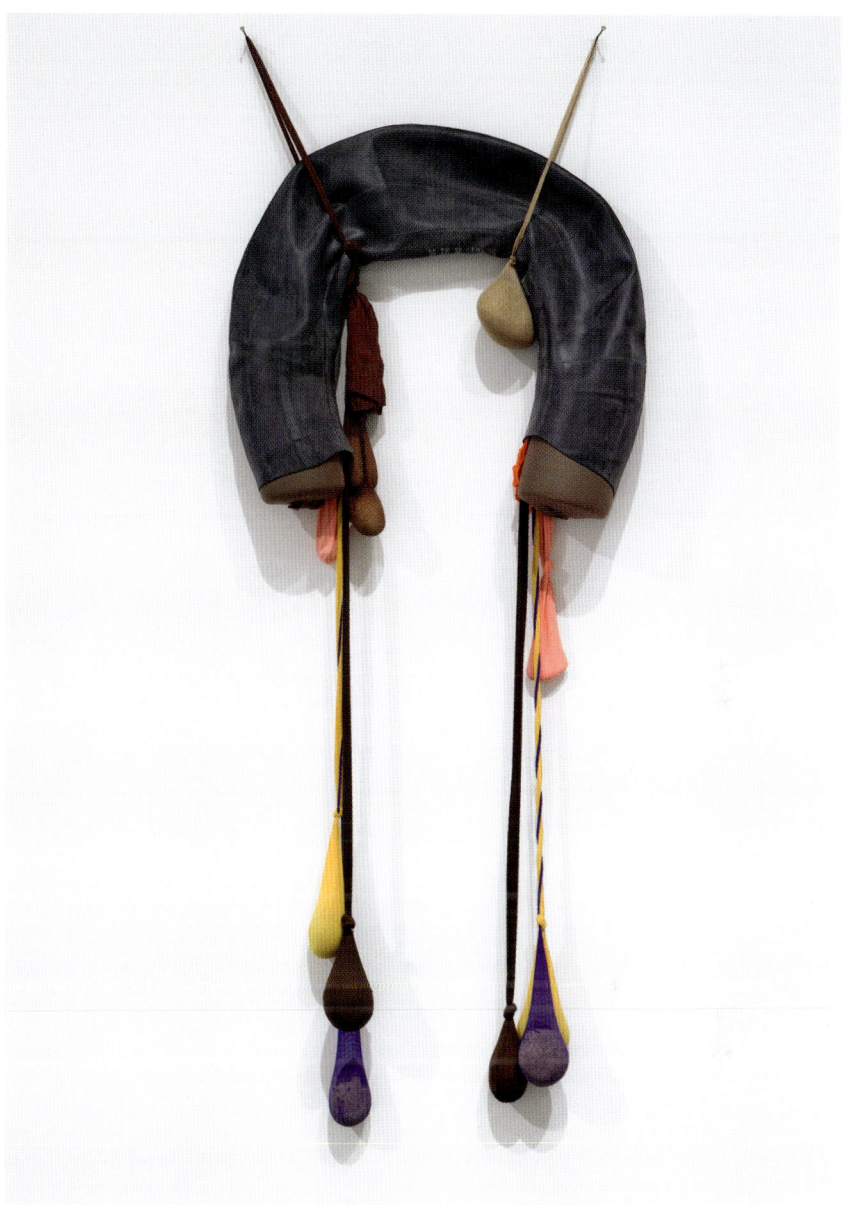

CONSERVATOR'S EYE: The Science of Stretch
First available in 1959, pantyhose were a relatively new invention when Senga Nengudi began using them in her art. Their elasticity—the ability to stretch and expand—and connection to the human body are what drew the artist to the material. These properties are due to the durability and pliancy of synthetic fibers such as nylon and Lycra, which were developed in the twentieth century in large part due to the demands of the women's hosiery and underwear market. While they represent technical advancements in strength and flexibility, pantyhose are composed of very thin plastic fibers that are vulnerable to deterioration from light, heat, stress, and strain. To preserve these fragile materials, this work is exhibited for short lengths of time and stored flat in a custom box.

KWT

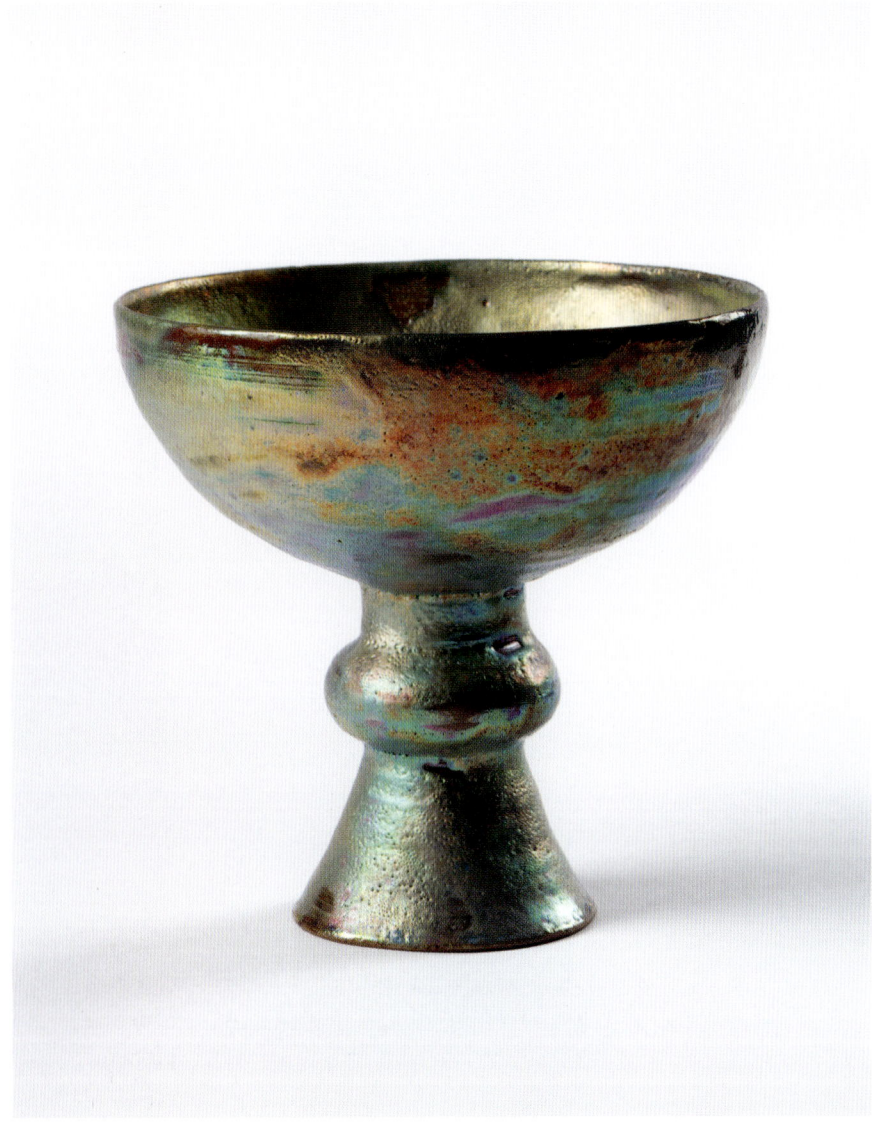

Beatrice Wood
(American, 1893–1998)
Chalice, ca. 1975

Luster-glazed earthenware, 7½ × 7¹¹⁄₁₆ × 7¹¹⁄₁₆ in.
Denis Gallion and Daniel Morris, 1992.165.1
Provenance: Gift of Denis Gallion and Daniel Morris, by 1992; donated, 1992.

Known as the "Mama of Dada," Beatrice Wood had a long (105 years), eccentric, and illustrious life. Today, she is recognized as an artist who worked primarily in clay, creating vessels and sculptures of figures, often covered with sumptuous, shimmering iridescent glazes.

Born to a wealthy family in San Francisco, Wood moved to New York when she was thirteen. Determined to be an artist, she convinced her family to allow her to travel to France. It was there that she studied acting and painting. Upon returning to New York, she continued to act, although her interests turned more and more to art, as she associated with avant-garde writers, composers, and artists. In the mid-1910s, she collaborated with the Dada artist Marcel Duchamp on publications and exhibitions while he was in New York, starting the first American publications devoted to the performance and visual art movement that rejected reason and logic as well as middle-class values. It was Duchamp who encouraged Wood to focus on drawing. Wood's interest in the scintillating luster glaze—achieved through the application of metallic salts on the surface of the work—coating the clay vessels came later in life after she purchased a set of plates and wanted to make a teapot to match. While Wood produced many different forms, she created dozens of chalices, probably due to their connection to ceremonial uses, although she was more interested in the reflective and changing surfaces than their contents. For Wood, "It is truly marvelous to create, for thus we touch divinity."[1]

CF

1. Beatrice Wood, "Color, Light and Art." *The Star* 1, no. 3 (1928): 38–40.

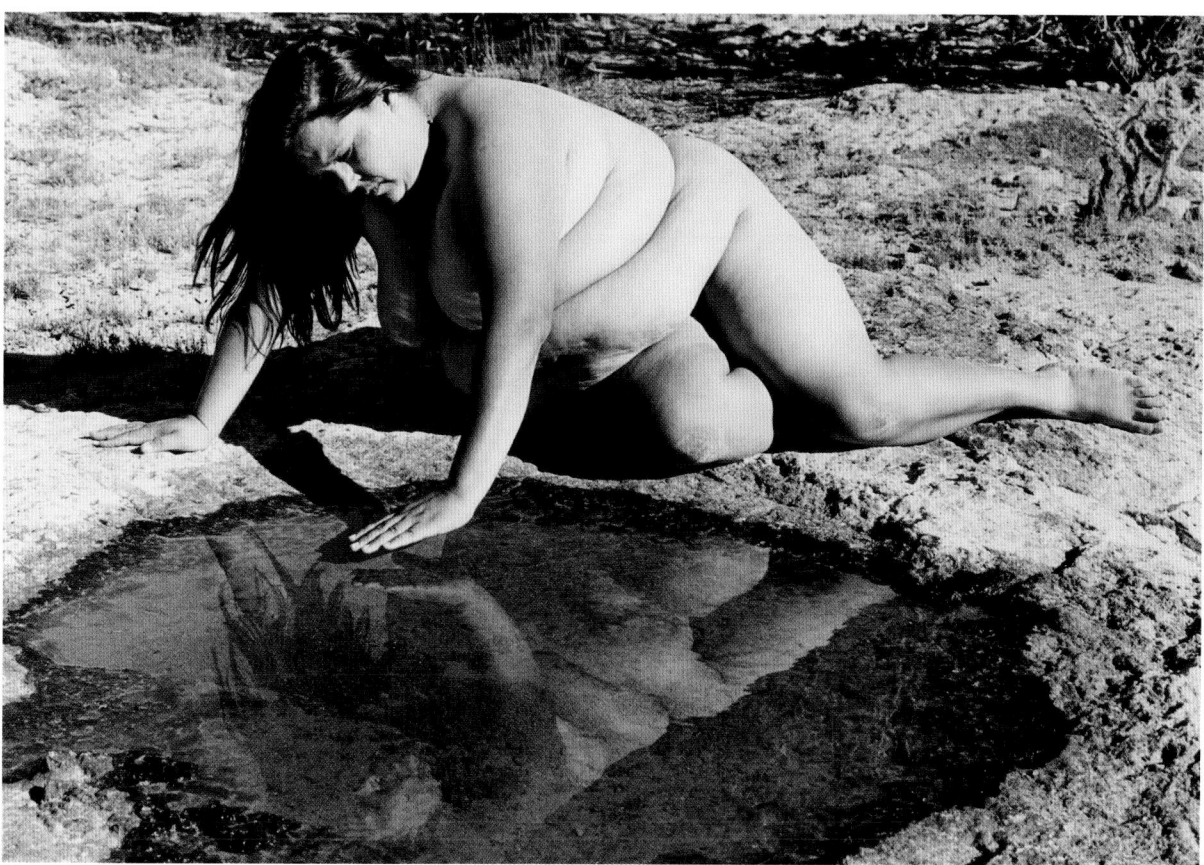

Laura Aguilar
(American, 1959–2018)
Nature Self-Portrait #14, 1996

Gelatin silver print, 16 × 20 in.
Purchased with funds given by the Charina Endowment Fund, 2021.37.2
Provenance: 2016, gift of the artist to the Laura Aguilar Trust of 2016; October 29, 2021, purchased from the Laura Aguilar Trust of 2016 by the Brooklyn Museum.

Laura Aguilar self-identified as a Chicana lesbian artist and spent her entire career examining these identities through her photography, decades before it would become commonplace to do so. An important figure in the Chicanx and queer art scenes in Los Angeles, the artist made images that centered on working-class women, and addressed issues like mental health, disability, and access. In the late 1990s, Aguilar began experimenting with nude self-portraits, using her large body to challenge what has historically been considered inappropriate in artwork. Often shooting herself in the landscape, Aguilar confronted traditions of western landscape photography alongside those of the nude, two artistic forms often associated with white male pioneers.

In this striking self-portrait, Laura Aguilar carefully stages her own body in nature. Part of a larger series titled *Nature Self-Portraits*—her first body of work shot in the landscape—the artist contorts her brown, full-figured form into shapes that mimic her environment: rounded boulders, extended tree limbs, a sloping hillside. Here, Aguilar positions herself at the edge of a small pool. Her reflected shape on the water's surface mirrors the ridges of the surrounding landscape. The sublime composition hints at the story of Narcissus, the character in Greek mythology who falls in love with his own reflection in a pool of water. An allegory on self-love, the piece disrupts traditional presentations of the nude female form. It also reveals Aguilar's interest in mythology and her understanding of art history, exemplifying the ways the artist used her photography practice to challenge both.

SSW

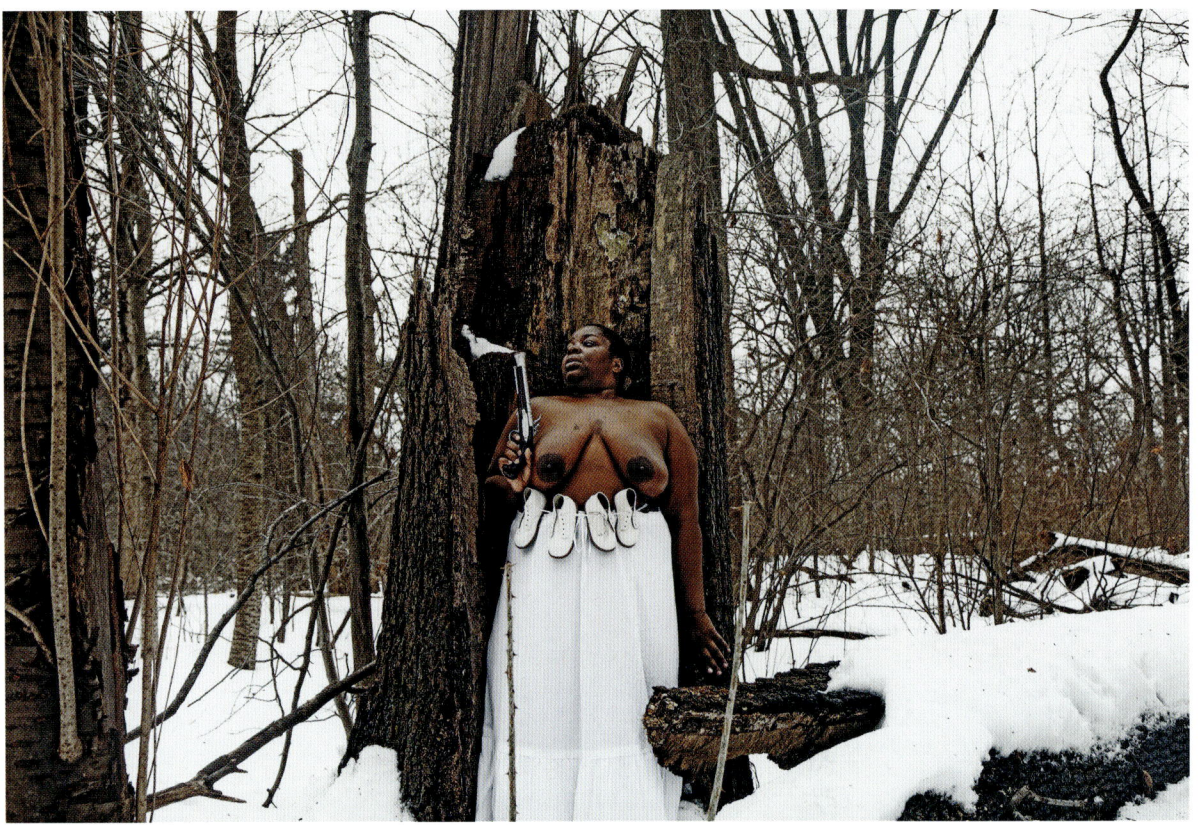

Nona Faustine
(American, born 1977)
Lobbying The Gods For A Miracle, Brooklyn, 2016

Chromogenic print, sheet: 27 15/16 × 42 in.;
image: 26 9/16 × 40 in.
Emily Winthrop Miles Fund, 2017.41c
Provenance: Purchased from the artist by the
Brooklyn Museum, December 19, 2017.

Nona Faustine's *oeuvre* intersects conceptual photography, public history, and Black feminist art historical intervention. *Lobbying the Gods For A Miracle* exemplifies this taxonomy. Part of a series of over forty self-portraits titled *White Shoes* (2013–21), each photograph acknowledges the history and legacies of United States chattel slavery between 1626 and 1827, when enslaved African labor built the scaffold for present day New York City.[1]

Faustine uses her own body, often fully or partially nude, to memorialize sites significant to the history of enslavement across all five boroughs of New York. Throughout the series, the artist dons a pair of white "church lady" shoes that symbolize the confining symptoms of Whiteness and colonialism deployed through interlocking systems of power and oppression Black women must daily navigate, including social respectability and white hegemonic beauty standards.

In *Lobbying The Gods For A Miracle*, Faustine poses apprehensively in the cavity of a decayed tree trunk while wielding a prop flintlock pistol that mimics smoke when held against the snow of a wintry Prospect Park, where slave-holding Dutch families once resided.[2] Faustine collapses time by grounding historical allusions of Black women fleeing in her own body, illustrating a shared, resilient lineage of navigating safety, resistance, and self-possession. Wearing only a petticoat belted by four white children's shoes, Faustine acknowledges the children stolen from Black mothers through past and contemporary systems of anti-black violence. She also emphasizes how Black motherhood has continuously been entangled with the hope—in fact the right—to raise their children safely as a tenet of reproductive justice.

CSF

1. For more on Faustine and this photographic series, see Nona Faustine, *White Shoes* (London: Mack Books, 2021); Jonathan Jones, "The Scars of America: Why a Nude Artist Is Taking a Stand at Slavery Sites," *The Guardian*, August 5, 2015, https://www.theguardian.com/artanddesign/jonathanjonesblog/2015/aug/05/the-scars-of-america-nude-artist-slavery-sites-nona-faustine; and Demi Kim, "New York Artist Nona Faustine Exposes the City's Slaveholding Past," *Artsy*, December 26, 2016, https://www.artsy.net/article/artsy-editorial-new-york-artist-nona-faustine-exposes-city-slaveholding-past. For additional context on the history of slavery in New York City, see Leslie M. Harris, *In the Shadow of Slavery: African Americans in New York City, 1626–1863* (Chicago: University of Chicago Press, 2004).
2. For more on the Lefferts family, their role as enslavers, and the activism of the African people they enslaved, see "History of Lefferts Historic House," Prospect Park Alliance, accessed August 16, 2024, https://www.prospectpark.org/visit-the-park/places-to-go/lefferts-historic-house/lefferts-historic-house-history/.

Mary Scheier (American, 1908–2007)
Edwin Scheier (American, 1910–2008)
Vase, ca. 1966

Glazed earthenware, 20⅛ × 7 × 7 in.
H. Randolph Lever Fund, 67.76.4
Provenance: Purchased from the artists
by the Brooklyn Museum, June 7, 1967.

Married ceramic artists Edwin and Mary Scheier explored human bodies, faces, and skins through vessel forms and surfaces. Mary threw the clay vases and bowls, while Edwin, who supposedly wanted to be an army tattoo artist during World War II, decorated them with unique glazes and patterns. While treating the clay surface as skin, Edwin stated, "Tattooing is a decorative art fitted to individual personalities as much as a special design is appropriate for a certain piece of pottery."[1] The glaze and texture on this vase call to mind layers of skin and cracks and damage, signs of aging and wear, that appear on the surface, highlighting fragility and resilience.

The Scheiers met in 1937, when they were both in Virginia working for the Federal Works Progress Administration, part of the New Deal, that employed artists during the Great Depression. After marrying, they traveled the country as puppeteers, ending up in Tennessee, where the director of the Tennessee Valley Authority's Ceramic Laboratory suggested they try working with clay. It was here, using the lab's facilities in exchange for tending the kilns at night, that the Scheiers began to learn their craft through experimentation and visiting local, traditional potters. They returned to Virginia in 1939, after opening their own pottery business, but a year later they were offered positions in the Department of Arts at University of New Hampshire: Edwin as an instructor and Mary as artist-in-residence. Important teachers of ceramics for the next twenty years, they were integral to the interest in handmade pottery by artists who built on ceramic traditions to produce a uniquely American style.

CF/MGP

1. Mylinda Woodward, "Feats of Clay," *UNH Today*, July 10, 2015, https://www.unh.edu/unhtoday/2015/07/feats-clay.

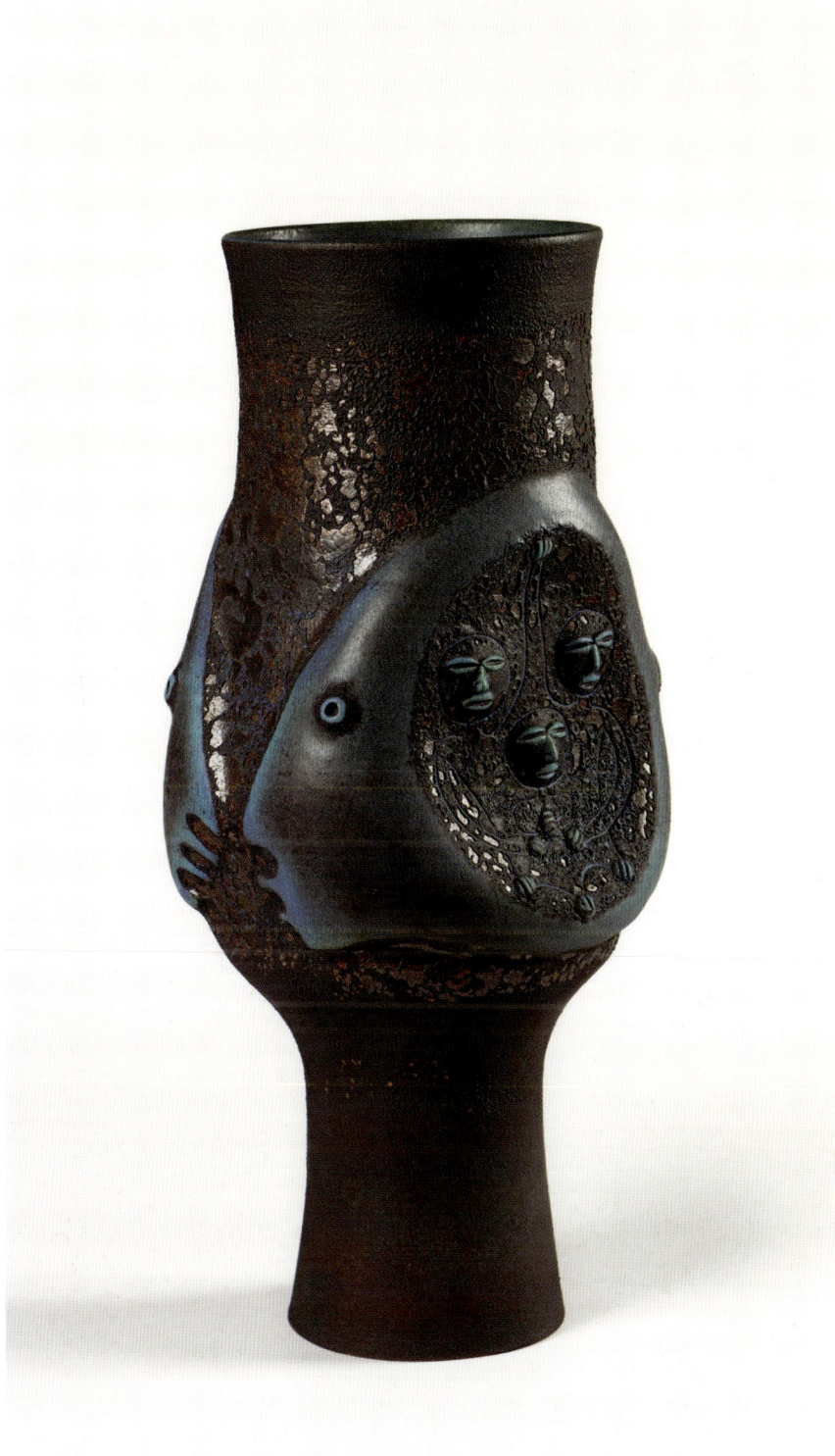

Surface Tension

CRITICAL SHORT

The Dorsal View

Stephanie Sparling Williams with Sena Amuzu and Madeleine Levinsohn

Part of an ongoing commitment to share even more of the museum's collection and aligned with our efforts to maintain dynamic galleries that continue to surprise and delight audiences, the reinstallation project prioritizes and systematizes regular in-gallery rotations. Within the framework *Surface Tension*, a selection of drawings, paintings, photographs, and prints are presented for more focused and in-depth looking that engages with novel, pertinent, or timely themes. The first of these spotlights is "The Dorsal View," which playfully engages with the prominence of the backside in nude figure art.

Etymology and Origins

The human backside has been known by many names across cultures and languages. In Old English, the nether region of livestock and humans was referred to using the Germanic and Old French-derived "haunches," which combined the buttocks and thighs. In the late eighteenth century, this area was euphemized as the French *derrière* for "back part, rear."

Today, one might hear ass, backside, batty, booty, bottom, bum, bumper, buns, butt, heinie, rump, seat, tush, tuchus, and the list continues. As many words for this body part exist as the emotions it evokes, a reflection of an undeniable societal fixation.

The rear end has featured prominently in art since ancient times. In 300 B.C.E., the philosopher Aristotle, who sought to define the "highest good," claimed the sphere to be the perfect and most beautiful form. This set the stage for images of dorsal views to come, including a Greek bronze and later Roman marble statue titled *Venus Callipyge*, or "Venus of the beautiful buttocks" in Greek. The dorsal view continues to capture artists' attention, their interests ranging from anatomical study to aesthetic allure.

The Collection

Out of the representations of nude figures in the Brooklyn Museum's American Art and Arts of the Americas collections, nearly a quarter feature the human backside. From ancient Americas ceramic figurines and nineteenth- and twentieth-century works on paper to sculptures, photographs, and paintings made in the last twenty years, the dorsal view has been a vital presence in visual culture.

Marking a departure from medical, ethnographic, and anatomical studies, with the incorporation of figure drawing into American art academy curricula in the early nineteenth century, nude representations became more prominent. Sixty percent of the Museum's dorsal views date to the first half of the twentieth century.

Even as styles shifted, the subjects largely remained the same: white women make up 95 percent of the collection's nudes. Out of the hundreds of artworks, only three depict models of color, five are by women-identified artists, and six are by artists of color. Today, contemporary artists, as seen in this framework, are working with—and against—these legacies.

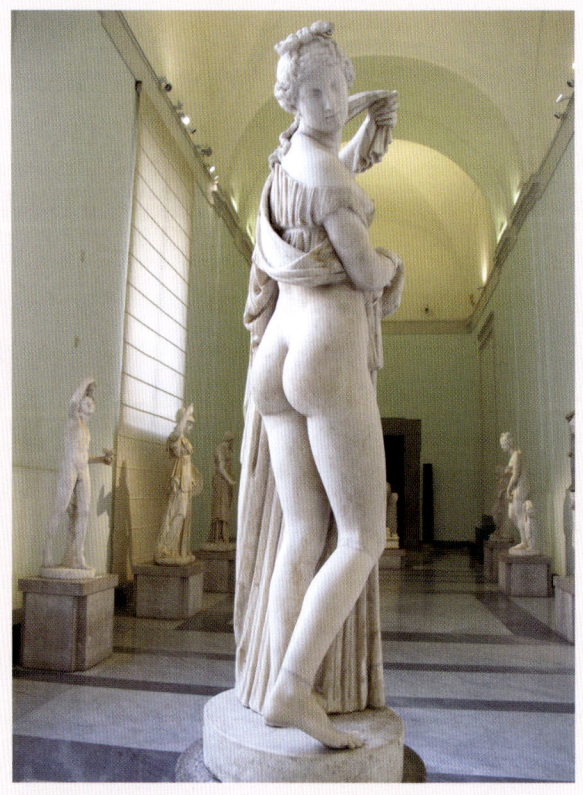

Venus Callipyge, 1st or 2nd century B.C.E. White marble. National Archaeological Museum, Naples.

The Politics of Being Seen

There's an art to this business. There's a hell of a lot more to it than skin and bones. It's very difficult work. You find muscles you didn't know you had. Just when you think you're relaxed, the sweat starts running—and then you itch. The strain is tremendous.
—Florence "Flo" Wysinger Allen (1913–1997), artist's model

Life models, and their posing bodies, have fueled creativity for hundreds of years. Historically overlooked, models were often considered passive conduits for artistic expression while the work they inspired risked criticism of obscenity.

Nude model activists of the 1950s and '60s, such as Florence "Flo" Wysinger Allen, challenged these stereotypes through protests, writing, and interviews. Allen reframed modeling as an art form of its own, offering opportunities for self-representation—as well as sexual, artistic, and economic liberation.

Whether positioning themselves out of anonymity, modesty, or confrontation, the subjects here embody their desires to be seen or to be hidden. Some turn to reveal and others to obscure. This gesture redirects, and at times deflects, the viewer's gaze, bringing the agency of nude models to the fore.

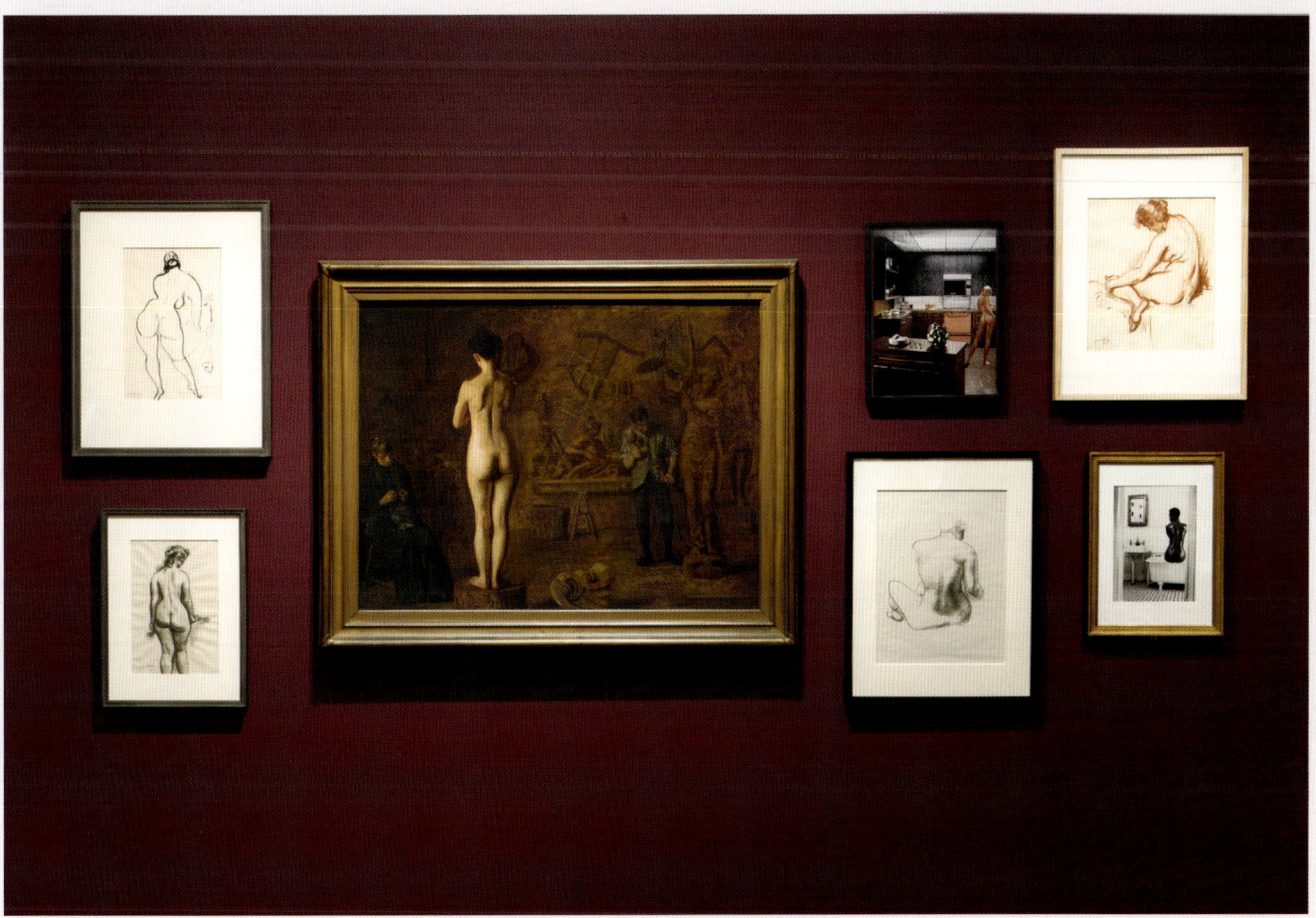

Surface Tension

FRAMEWORK

Several Seats

One of the most popular art forms in the early Americas, portrait painting was inextricably tied to projects of nation-building, to sitters' real or aspirational relationship to power, and to their attempts at control over the historical record. Examining seated portraiture and historical seating, this framework offers a lively context in which to engage with the questions and challenges such canonical art forms present. While these portraits represent a major holding of the collection, visitors have rightfully called out the harm caused by uncritical presentations of a "sea of white faces." Similarly, opulent, ornamented chairs may signify the access and cultural experiences of a select few, raising questions about what design traditions museums have historically valued over others.

Rather than remove these works from view, this framework takes its cue from the expression "have several seats." Originating in Black and Latinx ballroom culture, the rebuke is directed at someone monopolizing space and informs the curatorial decision to hang these portraits just off the ground in the gallery, at or below the level of most seating.[1] As with each framework, the display is a critical aspect of viewers' engagement with the collection. Here, in addition to a line-up of low-hanging portraits and a striking display of chairs, the in-gallery experience provides three additional points of interaction. The first is a set of newly refurbished New York City park benches that offer a perch from which to gaze eye-to-eye with the portraits' sitters as well as democratizing counterpoints to the exclusivity reflected in the chairs and paintings.

The second is the bold and experimental interpretation that accompanies several of the portraits provided by a group of NYC-based performers.[2] Inspired by the expression "my T"—first used by transgender actress and performer Lady Chablis to stand for her "truth" and often expressed as "the tea"—this section answers calls from viewers to present the "truth" about artworks presented in museum galleries. The performers "spill the T" on the artists and sitters of these portraits, examining their biographies and social status—as well as the ways they present themselves through clothing and accessories.

By embodying new identities—often exaggerated gender expressions, whether masculine or feminine—drag queens and kings liberate themselves from oppressive societal standards and norms. Offering art, entertainment, and cultural critique, ballroom and drag artists engage in creative self-fashioning. Historically, portrait traditions across the Americas served a similar purpose. With the help of the artist, many sitters amplified or performed aspects of their identity they wished to highlight for viewers, such as showing off their wealth and position in society.

The final feature is the inclusion of a painted runway that spans the length of the gallery, and creates another visual focus for those seated on the park benches. In 1860s Paris, designers used live models to showcase their fashion, and "fashion parades" soon spread to London and New York. Around the same time, ballroom culture quietly emerged in Washington, DC, following emancipation. At secret parties, attendees—primarily men wearing imaginative gowns and elaborate womenswear—performed popular dances. The first to call themselves a "drag queen," William Dorsey Swann, a formerly enslaved Black American, hosted many of these events at home. In the early twentieth century, these soirees spread to Baltimore, Chicago, New Orleans, New York, and Philadelphia. Parodying fashion runway shows and debutante ball traditions such as "coming out," the practice of parading in front of "high society" was widely adopted. For trailblazers of early ballroom culture, the runway itself became a symbol of empowerment, liberation, and survival.

These display aspects, along with discussions of the paintings and chairs, also present critiques of art historical traditions that privilege white, wealthy individuals. Together, these works prompt conversations about personal wealth and privilege within societies built on displacement, colonialism, and enslavement.

SSW

1. Ballroom, ball, or house culture is an LGBTQ+ subculture with origins dating back to Black American performance in the antebellum U.S. South and later to balls hosted in New York City's Harlem neighborhood. Ballroom and the formation of family-like units called houses have been significant for Black and Latinx queer and transgender communities. Participants find liberation and self-expression through ballroom competitions during which they might embody, exaggerate, and even parody different genders, occupations, or social classes.
2. For an example of these unique readings, see entries for paintings by Joshua Johnson and William Merritt Chase by Miss Peppermint (pp. 188–89) and Emi Grate (p. 193), respectively.

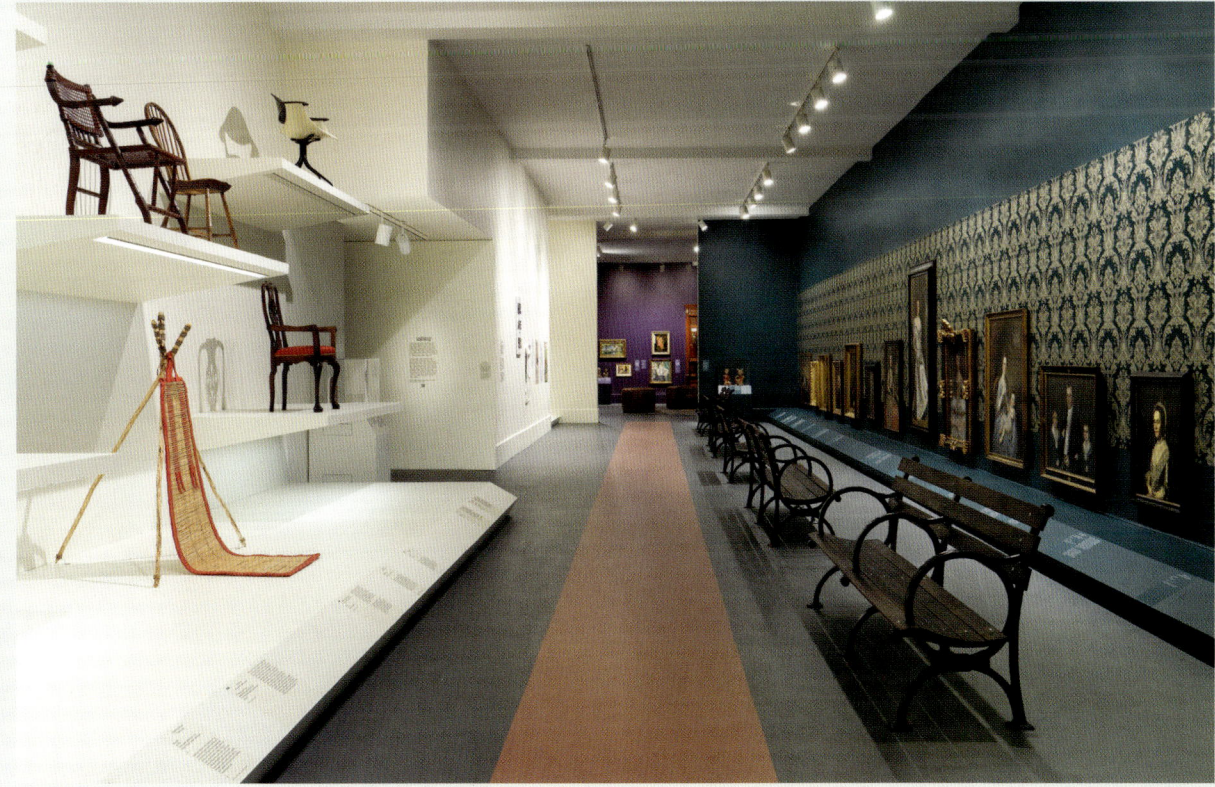

Several Seats

Thomas Thompson
(American, born England, 1776–1852)
Portrait of Augustus Graham, ca. 1842

Oil on canvas, 34⅛ × 26¹⁵⁄₁₆ in.
Transferred from the Brooklyn Institute of Arts and Sciences to the Brooklyn Museum, 97.2
Provenance: Probably commissioned from the artist by Augustus Graham, ca. 1842; probably inherited by Mrs. Robert Sherwell, 1851; probably inherited by Robert Sherwell, by 1872; acquired by the Brooklyn Institute of Arts and Sciences, by 1879; donated, 1897.

Brooklyn philanthropist Augustus Graham (born Richard King, 1775–1851) poses here surrounded by books including the catalogue for the Brooklyn Apprentices' Library—the predecessor to the Brooklyn Museum—which Graham helped found in 1823. This lending library provided free access to books, maps, pictures, tools, drawing courses, and more to educate and socially elevate working-class Brooklynites. Graham eventually commissioned local painters to produce artworks for the collection.[1] The artist Thomas Thompson initially specialized in portraiture while living in England, and his *oeuvre* expanded to focus on maritime views by the early 1800s. He immigrated to the United States by 1829, and moved to Brooklyn around 1840–41. This portrait was likely commissioned to celebrate Graham's 1842 purchase of the Lyceum Building, which accommodated the Library's transformation into the Brooklyn Institute.

A successful business owner, Graham led a nontraditional social and entrepreneurial life.[2] By 1808, he and his business partner, John Graham (born John Bell, 1784–1853), established a lumber business in Delhi, New York, leaving Augustus's wife and children in Brooklyn. The two men returned to Brooklyn in 1815 where they operated a distillery and, later, the Brooklyn White Lead Company. Having adopted the same surname, they went by the "Graham Brothers," despite no relation, and shared a residence until John's marriage in 1842. However, by 1844, the Grahams resumed living together until the end of their lives, also residing with their housekeeper who likewise took the last name Graham. Speculation into the true nature of their relationship has continued to the present day.[3]

CG

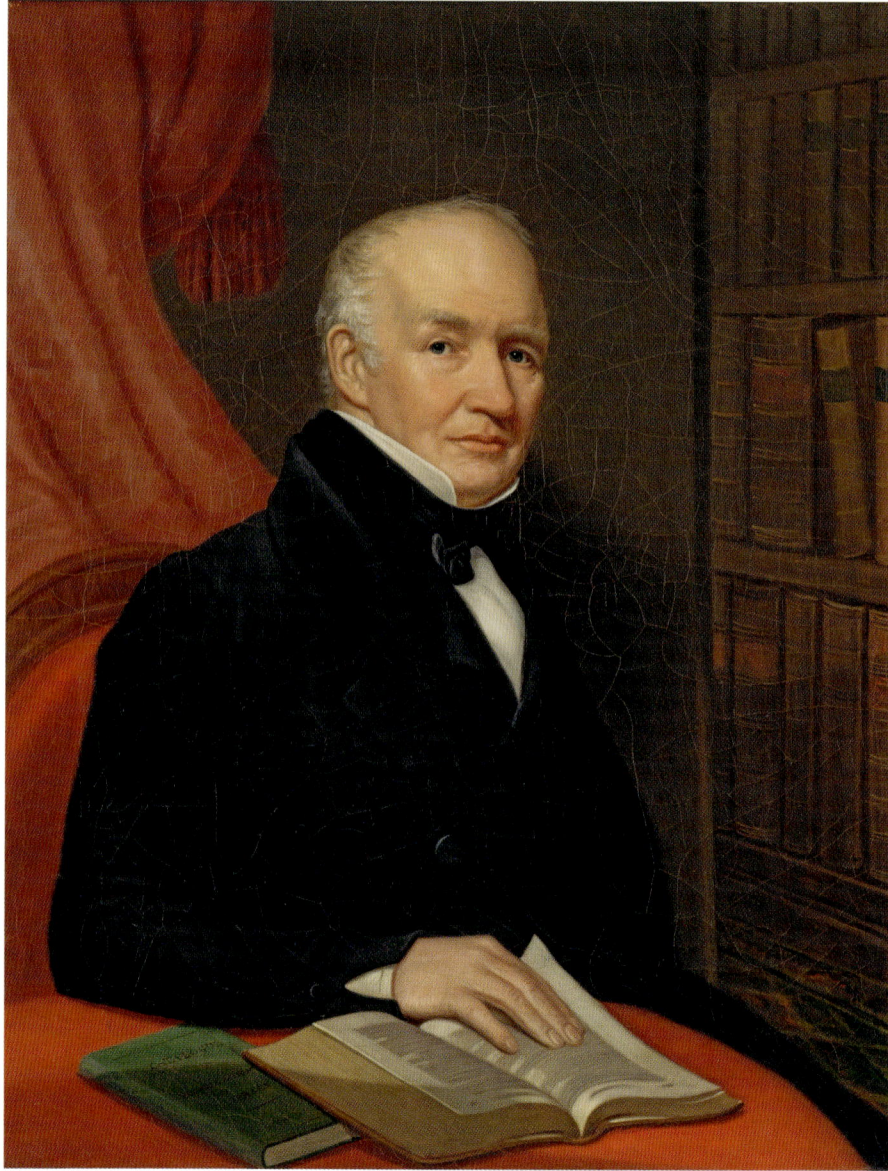

1. The Brooklyn Apprentices' Library became the Brooklyn Institute in 1843. By 1890 it was known as The Brooklyn Institute of Arts and Sciences, and then the Brooklyn Museum in 1897.
2. For more biographical details and information about this painting see Teresa A. Carbone, "Thomas Thompson," in *American Paintings in the Brooklyn Museum: Artists Born by 1876*, Teresa A. Carbone, Barbara Dayer Gallati, and Linda S. Ferber (New York: Brooklyn Museum; London: D. Giles Limited, 2006), 1: 1003–4.
3. Julius Chambers, "An Unsolved Brooklyn Mystery," *The Brooklyn Daily Eagle*, March 4, 1906, 13.

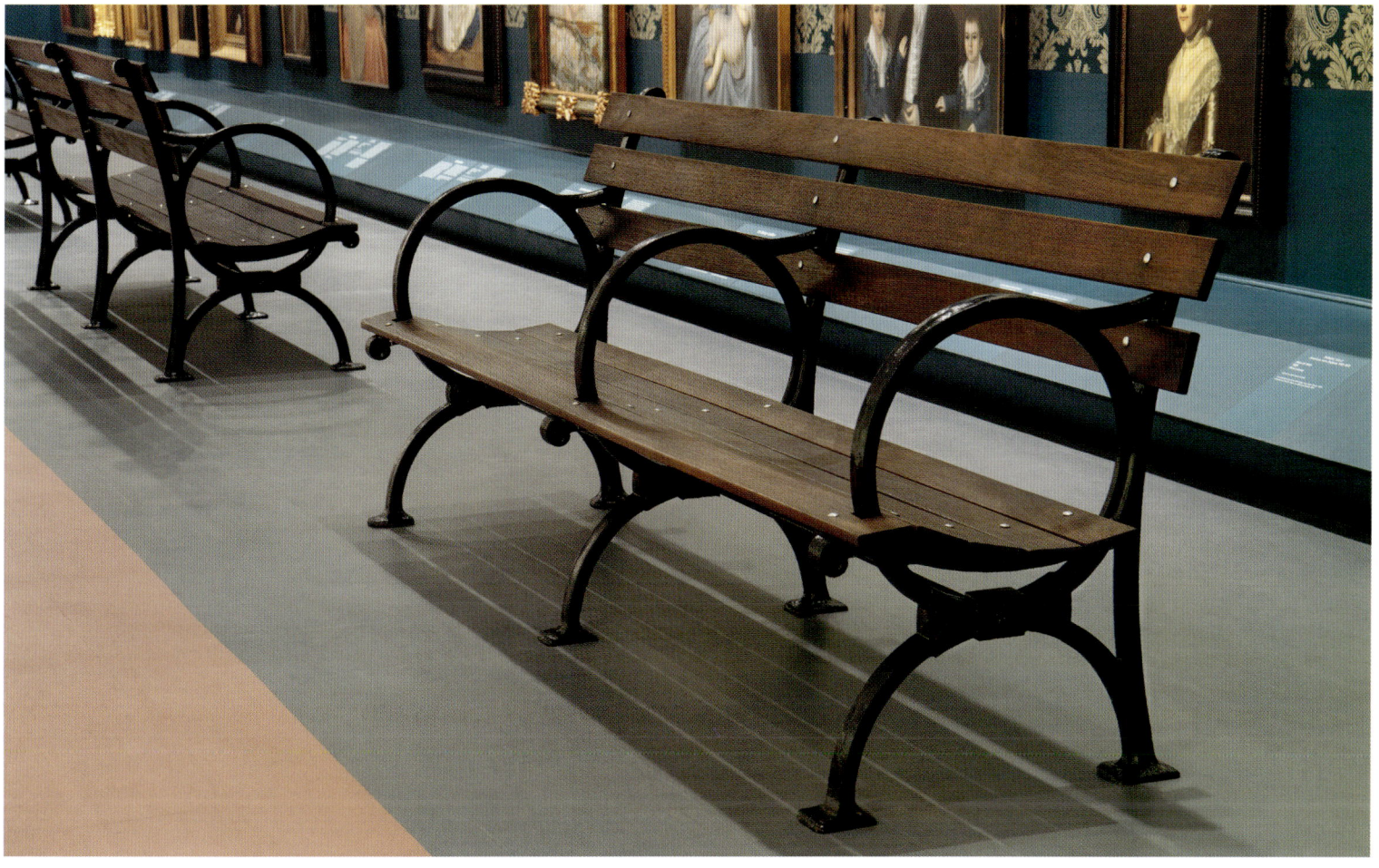

New York City Park Benches, ca. 1930

Wood, cast iron, paint, each: 95 1/2 × 34 1/2 × 21 in. Gift of New York City Parks Department, 85.20.1-.3

Unlike classroom desks, plush sofas, or seats at a boardroom table, where access is limited to a select few, city park benches offer a moment of relief for people from all walks of life. Omnipresent in New York City public spaces, benches provide a space to rest, a vantage from which to see and be seen, a spot to wait for transportation, a gathering point, and often a place to sleep. In the gallery, they provide similar functions; visitors are invited to sit and relax, look more closely at the collection, enjoy an impromptu runway show, or simply check their phone.

The benches in the Brooklyn Museum's collection were gifted by the Department of Parks & Recreation and come from across the city, including Central Park, Coney Island, and Eastern Parkway. Designed by urban planner and former Parks Commissioner Robert Moses for the 1939 New York World's Fair, they have a sleek, modern profile compared to earlier, more ornate models. Before entering the Museum's collection, these modest seats provided decades of opportunities for New Yorkers to savor moments of solitude or engage with their surroundings from these perches.

BT

Several Seats

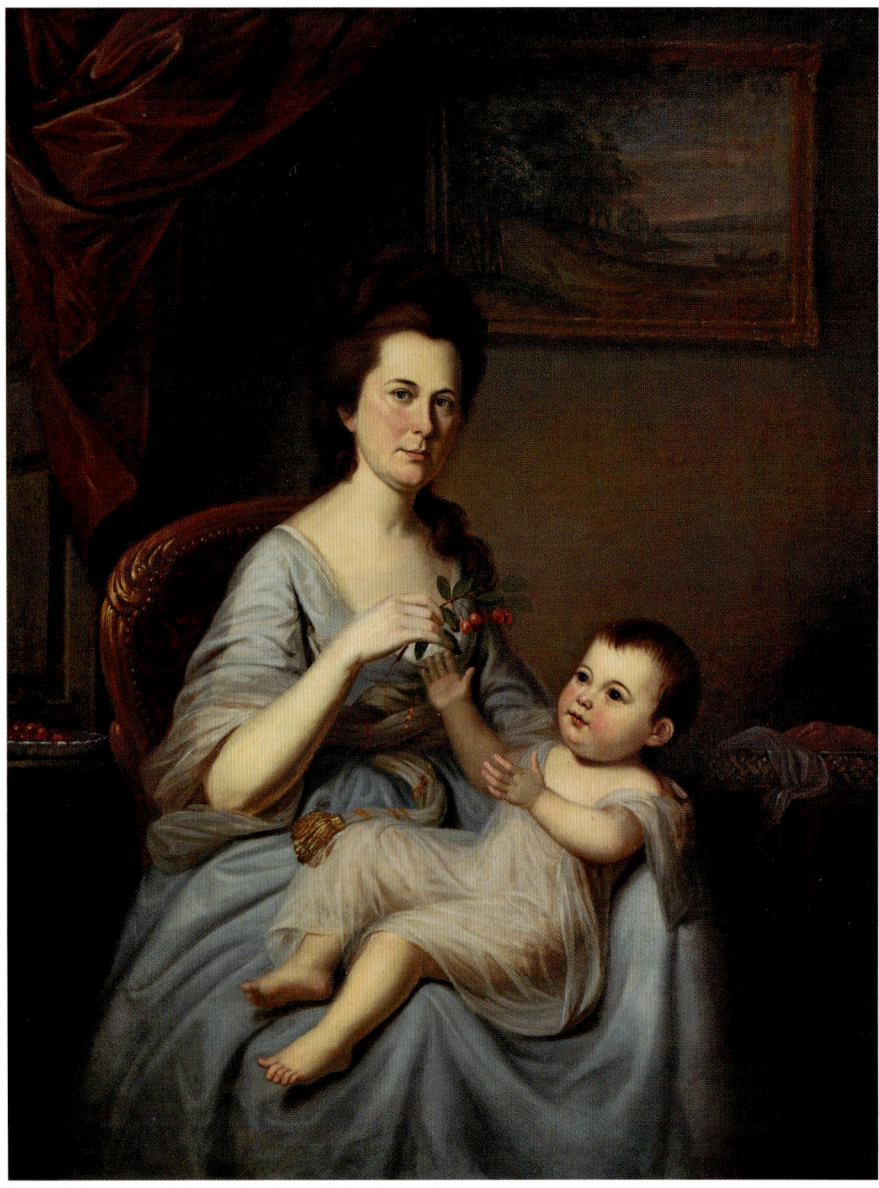

Charles Willson Peale
(American, 1741–1827)
Mrs. David Forman and Child, ca. 1785

Oil on canvas, 51 × 39⅜ in.
Carll H. de Silver and Museum Collection Fund, 23.51
Provenance: Commissioned from the artist by David Forman and Ann Marsh Forman (Mrs. David Forman), ca. 1785; inherited by Malvina Forman, 1798. Acquired by George Latham Fletcher, before 1913; purchased by M. Knoedler & Co., May 6, 1913; purchased by the Brooklyn Museum, January 20, 1923.

Early Republic idealization of motherhood and nationhood are entangled in Charles Willson Peale's portrait of Ann Marsh Forman. Mrs. Forman is dressed in a blue silk gown, surrounded by fine furnishings and a landscape painting, which indicates her family's elevated social standing and cultured life.[1] Having borne eleven children, she appears in this portrait in the role of nurturing mother. The active and alert child on her lap reaches playfully for a branch of cherries, which symbolize the future promise of love and matrimony. Peale's representation of Mrs. Forman as raising the future of the young nation conveys ideals of white womanhood and the common interest held by mothers and the nation in the elevation of offspring.[2] Her husband, David Forman, was appointed to colonel in the Continental Army. Even as they supported independence during the American Revolution, the Formans enslaved people at their Monmouth County, New Jersey, estate. They expanded their land holdings in 1789 with the purchase of a tobacco plantation in Mississippi where Mr. Forman sent sixty enslaved men, women, and children to forcibly labor at this new property.[3] Despite their status as enslavers, Mrs. Forman's portrait exhibits Peale's commitment to expressing the ideals of a nation through portraits of elite families and Revolutionary heroes.

CG

1. For more on the Formans and this portrait, see Teresa A. Carbone, "Charles Willson Peale," in *American Paintings in the Brooklyn Museum, Artists Born by 1876*, Teresa A. Carbone, Barbara Dayer Gallati, and Linda S. Ferber (New York: Brooklyn Museum; London: D. Giles Limited, 2006), 2: 839–40, 844–45.
2. Margaretta M. Lovell, "Reading Eighteenth-Century American Family Portraits," *Winterthur Portfolio* 22 (Winter 1987): 256–57. Lovell notes that after 1760, portraits of children and families in America such as this attested to the interest and investment in the social elevation of both children and their mothers.
3. Samuel S. Forman, *Narrative of a Journey down the Ohio and Mississippi in 1789–90* (Cincinnati: Robert Clarke and Co., 1888), 19.

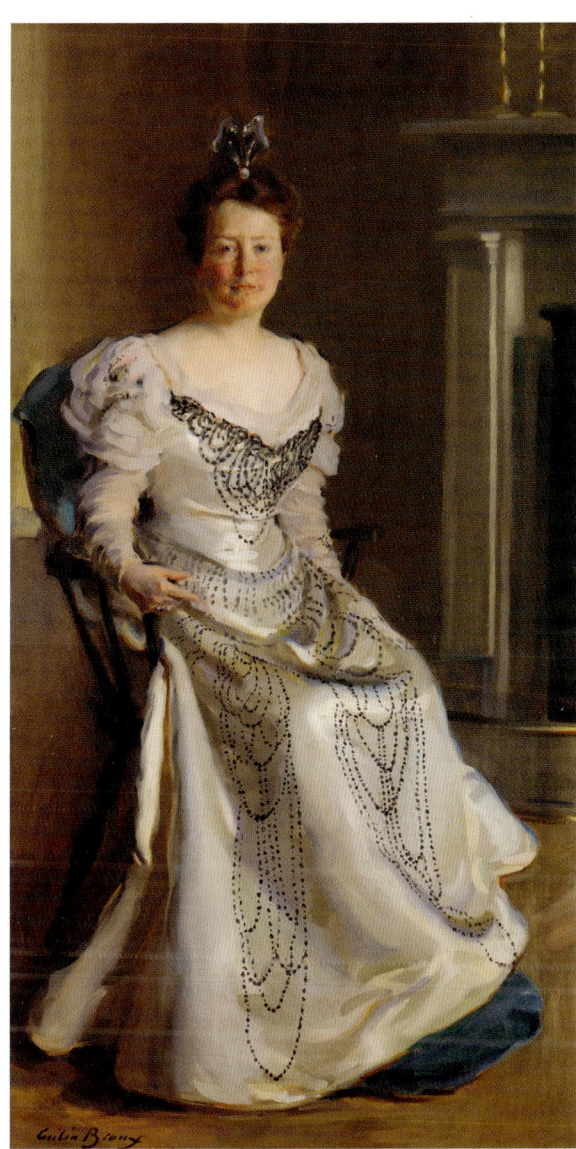

Cecilia Beaux
(American, 1855–1942)
Mrs. Robert Abbe (Catherine Amory Bennett), 1898–99

Oil on canvas, 74 × 39 in.
Gift of Mr. and Mrs. M. R. Schweitzer, 1999.113
Provenance: Commissioned from the artist by Robert Abbe and Catherine Amory Bennett Abbe (Mrs. Robert Abbe), ca. 1898; inherited by Courtland Palmer III, 1928; acquired, possibly from the estate of Courtland Palmer III, by the City History Club, by 1951. Sold at Sotheby's, New York, "American Paintings, Drawings, and Sculpture," March 10, 1993. Acquired by Mac R. Schweitzer and Frederik Serruya Schweitzer, by 1993; donated, 1999.

In a white gown adorned with black beading, Catherine Abbe embodies her position as a wealthy New York socialite.[1] Her hair is elegantly swept up and ornamented with a headpiece. In contrast, her surroundings are less reflective of Gilded Age opulence, and more akin to colonial and early Republic era aesthetics, which perhaps speaks to her commitment to championing U.S. colonial history and morality. While devoted to the cause of women's suffrage, Abbe was also a member of the National Society of the Colonial Dames of America and founded the City History Club of New York.[2] The Club sought to assimilate immigrant children by educating them in local New York history, believing this would transform them into upstanding citizens.

Abbe likely commissioned this work upon the incorporation of the Club in 1897, selecting the Philadelphia-based Cecilia Beaux, an ambitious and successful portraitist, as the artist.[3] The artist's depiction of Mrs. Abbe is typical of her fluid, loose handling of the paint, creating a sense of immediacy and life. Beaux, who never married so as to not jeopardize her career, often surrounded herself with other women artists who supported one another in professional advancement.

CG

1. For more on this portrait and artist, see Barbara Dayer Gallati, "Cecilia Beaux," in *American Paintings in the Brooklyn Museum: Artists Born by 1876*, Teresa A. Carbone, Barbara Dayer Gallati, and Linda S. Ferber, (New York: Brooklyn Museum; London: D. Giles Limited, 2006), 1: 264–67.
2. Clifton Hood, "Journeying to 'Old New York': Elite New Yorkers and their Invention of an Idealized City History in the Late Nineteenth and Early Twentieth Centuries," *Journal of Urban History* (September 2002): 17–20.
3. For more on Cecilia Beaux, see Sarah Burns, "Under the Skin: Reconsidering Cecilia Beaux and John Singer Sargent," *The Pennsylvania Magazine of History and Biography* 124, no. 3 (2000): 317–47; Tara Leigh Tappert, *Cecilia Beaux and the Art of Portraiture* (Washington, DC: Smithsonian Institution Press, 1995).

Miguel Cabrera
(Mexican, 1695–1768)
Doña María de la Luz Padilla y Gómez de Cervantes, ca. 1760

Oil on canvas, 43 × 33 in.
Museum Collection Fund and Dick S. Ramsay Fund, 52.166.4
Provenance: Ca. 1760, commissioned from the artist for María de la Luz Padilla y Gómez de Cervantes; 1789, probably inherited from María de la Luz Padilla y Gómez de Cervantes by Ygnacio Leonel Gómez de Cervantes; 1813, probably inherited from Ygnacio Leonel Gómez de Cervantes by Jose María Cervantes y Velasco Padilla y Obando; by 1889, probably inherited from Jose María Cervantes y Velasco Padilla y Oband by Ana María de Cervantes Ozta y de Velasco; by 1952, inherited from Ana María de Cervantes Ozta y de Velasco by Ángel Algara Romero de Terreros de Cervantes of New York, NY; 1952, purchased from Ángel Algara Romero de Terreros de Cervantes by the Brooklyn Museum.

In a portrait by Miguel Cabrera, Doña María de la Luz Padilla y Gómez de Cervantes dons quintessential eighteenth-century luxury fashion, including a silk brocade dress likely imported from Valencia, Spain. Five *chiqueadores*, which are false beauty spots typically made of tortoiseshell, silk, or velvet, adorn her face to cover blemishes or other skin conditions.[1] She is laden with jewelry—earrings, necklace, pearl bracelets, and rings—which were expressions of wealth and opulence.

Descended from colonizers who arrived amid the Spanish Invasion of the Mexica (Aztec) capital of Tenochtitlan in 1521, Doña María was from a prominent family in New Spain (present-day Mexico).[2] Family lineage to the original conquistadors indicated status in the colonial caste system. In his chronicles, Doña María's ancestor Gonzalo Gómez de Cervantes (ca. 1537–ca. 1599) argued, "One of the most important things that His Majesty ought to do in this New Spain is to mandate a general and perpetual distribution [of land grants] to the . . . descendants of the conquistadors and early settlers of New Spain."[3] The Spanish crown indeed granted the Gómez de Cervantes family colonized land through a practice known as *merced*.

A leading painter in eighteenth-century New Spain, Cabrera was of mixed Spanish and Indigenous ancestry. Born in Oaxaca, he later moved to Mexico City to pursue art training and helped establish the second Academy of Painting in Mexico City in 1753. In addition to portraits of New Spain elite, Cabrera was known for his Casta paintings (familial scenes depicting racial classifications) and altarpieces for churches, having found favor with the Archbishop of Mexico at the time.

TC with CG

1. Some information on *chiqueadores* is derived from Rachel Kaplan, "Beauty is in the Eye of the Beholder: Fashion in 18th Century Mexico," *LACMA*, February 1, 2018, https://unframed.lacma.org/2018/02/01/beauty-eye-beholder-fashion-18th-century-mexico.
2. Richard Aste, ed., *Behind Closed Doors: Art in the Spanish American Home, 1492–1898* (New York: Brooklyn Museum and Monacelli Press, 2013), 136–38.
3. Translated by Tiziana Capizzi. Gonzalo Gómez de Cervantes, *La Vida Económica y social de Nueva España, al finalizar el siglo XVI* (Mexico: Antigua Librería Robredo, de José Porrúa e Hijos, 1944), 77.

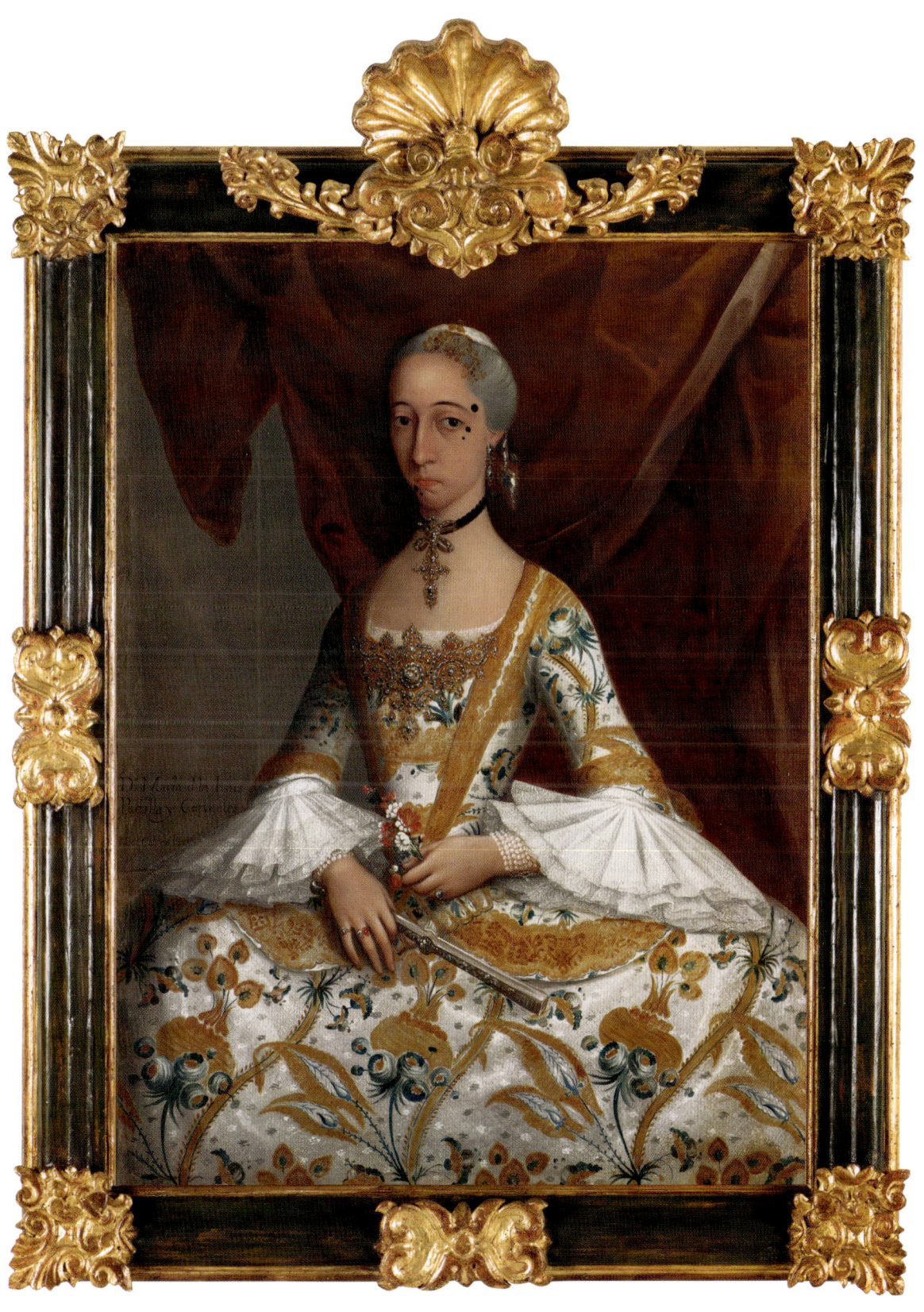

Several Seats

Joshua Johnson
(American, active ca. 1795–1825)
John Jacob Anderson and Sons, John and Edward, ca. 1812–15

Oil on canvas, 30⅛ × 39¹¹⁄₁₆ in.
Dick S. Ramsay Fund and Mary Smith Dorward Fund, 1993.82
Provenance: Commissioned from the artist by John Jacob Anderson, ca. 1812; inherited by Edward Anderson, ca. 1890; inherited through the Anderson family by Fanny Anderson Hyslop (Mrs. John T. B. Hyslop) and Sarah Young Anderson, before 1966; donated to the Eastern Shore of Virginia Historical Society (now Shore History), 1966. Acquired by Washburn Galleries, before 1987. Acquired by Kathryn and Robert Steinberg, by 1987. Acquired by James Graham & Sons, by June 1993; purchased by the Brooklyn Museum, June 21, 1993.

Portraitist Joshua Johnson is considered to be the first Black American artist to work professionally and to receive public recognition in the United States.[1] Born into slavery in Baltimore, Maryland, he was the son of George Johnson, a white man, and a Black woman enslaved by William Wheeler, Sr. After obtaining his freedom in 1782, Johnson began working as a portrait artist and resided on Nelson Street, in the Old Town neighborhood of Baltimore.[2] This was the same historic neighborhood in which the Anderson family portrayed in this portrait lived, alongside other middle-class white sitters whom Johnson also painted.[3] Marketing his services in the *Baltimore Intelligencer*, Johnson described himself as a "self-taught genius having experienced many insuperable obstacles in the pursuit of his studies."[4]

    Grocer John Jacob Anderson and his sons, John and Edward, are depicted wearing the typical fashion of the time. Anderson dons a black overcoat and white waistcoat beneath with a cravat tied at his neck. His sons wear "skeleton suits," which were short jackets worn over a white shirt with open collar and looser fitting pants. Anderson appears as a devoted father and stabilizing force at the center. Johnson painted his sitters in a crisply delineated and somewhat stiff style against a plain backdrop, emphasizing the details of their clothing and the intimate familial connections indicated by gestures. The portrait records family lineage for the sake of inheritance, and the Andersons, in collaboration with Johnson, fashion themselves as part of Baltimore's middle class.

CG

1. Lisa E. Farrington, "Black Or White?: Racial Identity in Nineteenth-Century African-American Art," *Source: Notes in the History of Art* 31, no. 3 (Spring 2012): 5. An early source on Johnson is J. Hall Pleasants, "Joshua Johnston, the First American Negro Portrait Painter," *Maryland Historical Magazine* 37 (June 1942).
2. Regarding the conditions of Johnson's manumission, see Jennifer Bryan and Robert Torchia, "The Mysterious Portraitist Joshua Johnson," *Archives of American Art Journal* 36, no. 2 (1996): 3.
3. William Fry, *Fry's Baltimore Directory, for the Year 1812* (Baltimore: B.W. Sower, & Co., 1812), 6.
4. "Portrait Painting," *Baltimore Intelligencer*, December 19, 1798; and quoted in Farrington, "Black or White?," 6. Pleasants also suggests Johnson's familiarity with artworks by members of the Peale family, who were well known in Baltimore. Pleasants, *Joshua Johnston*, 127.

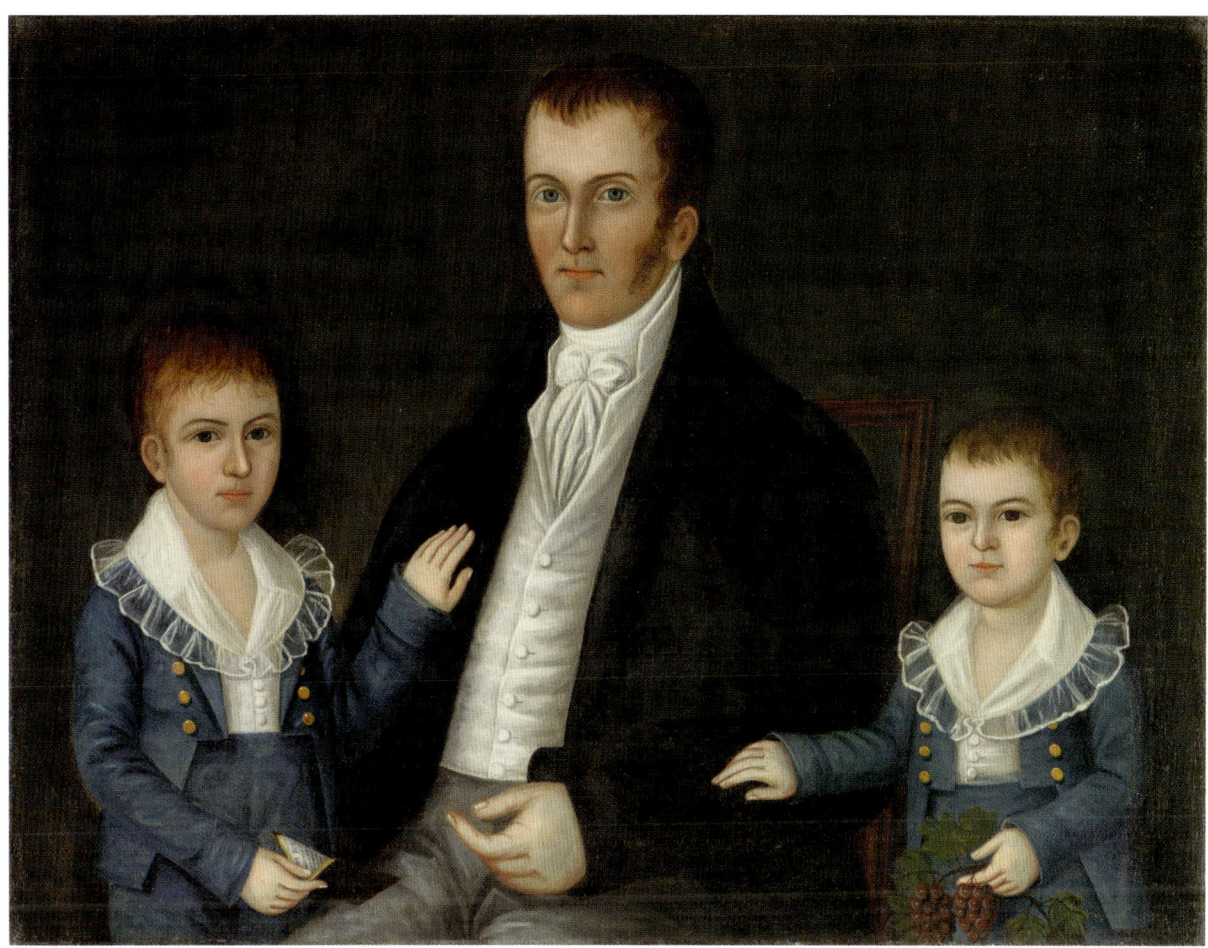

It's Giving Cotillion

Joshua Johnson's portrait shows a tenderness between John Jacob Anderson and his kids. I can see the family resemblance, and they're saying something! These are some say-something outfits, for sure! The fact that they were commissioning a portrait must mean that they had access to some money—and these kids are FAN-CY. The ruffles are ruffling for the painting on Sunday! "Look at our silk ruffles that are extending past the shoulder." It's giving cotillion. Through a 2024 lens, this looks like a dad who is very supportive of his genderqueer, nonbinary, ruffly children.

This is also a family bragging about how well-read they are and how much they can afford with these exotic grapes. What it says to me is this family is putting on an air of upper-crustedness, whether it's warranted or not. And the painter must have been able to move in these circles, too. But Johnson was a Black artist so I'm curious whether they paid top dollar . . . I hope they paid him fairly, at least.

Johnson was born enslaved and worked as a portraitist after being freed. This really highlights the utility that Black men served in different industries. White European artists may have had more freedom to paint what they wanted or refuse commissions. I'm wondering what Johnson's thoughts were about his subjects, and what he would've really wanted to paint if he had been born into different circumstances. Who and what would he have captured if he hadn't had to rely on this grocer's dime? We may never know. But given what we *do* know, this family portrait sparks many more questions and conversations around power, privilege, and artistic freedom.

—**Miss Peppermint**

Several Seats

Samuel Lovett Waldo
(American, 1783–1861)
William Jewett
(American, 1792–1874)
Mrs. James K. Bogert, Jr., 1819

Oil on canvas, 32 13/16 × 25 13/16 in.
Gift of Kittie A. Doolittle, 18.39
Provenance: Commissioned from the artist by Elizabeth Benezet Bogert and James K. Bogert, Jr., 1819; probably inherited by Lawrence Kimball Bogert, 1858; probably inherited by Katherine Augusta Bogert Dolittle, 1873; inherited by Kittie A. Doolittle, before 1918; donated, September 5, 1918.

Although due for a "glow-up" in 2024, Elizabeth Benezet Bogert's fashion was in vogue in 1819. Her black dress with Empire waist and frilly lace ruff around her neck were typical of the 1810s in Europe and America, and other stylish accessories signaled her cosmopolitan fashion sense. Influenced by a growing fascination with the Ottoman Empire, the draped turban entered French fashion by the 1770s and gained popularity in England and the United States through the early nineteenth century. The floral textile draped around her likely takes inspiration from Kashmiri shawls and was often paired with a turban, uniting "classical" European fashion with details regarded as more exotic.[1]

CG

1. Charlotte Jirousek and Sara Catterall, *Ottoman Dress and Design in the West: Visual History of Cultural Exchange* (Indianapolis: Indiana University Press, 2019), 201; Joan Hart, "Kashmir Shawls: The Perfect Exemplar of a Textile Shaping and Being Shaped," *Textile Society of America Symposium Proceedings* (2016), accessed May 21, 2024, http://digitalcommons.unl.edu/tsaconf/1020.

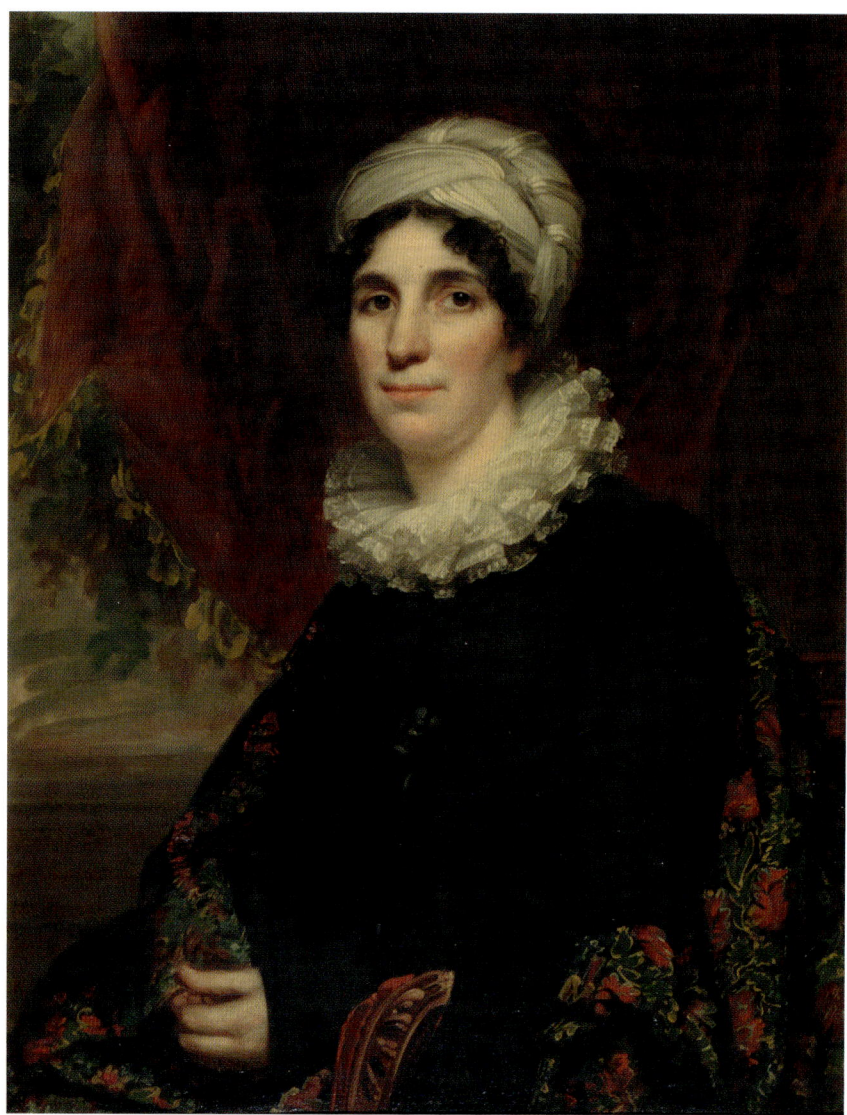

Before treatment

CONSERVATOR'S EYE: GLOW UP

Just like us, painting materials age and change over time. This was the case for the varnish on a portrait of Mrs. James K. Bogert. A varnish is a coating that saturates the paint film and modulates gloss. Over time, natural resin varnishes darken and yellow, shifting the perceived color palette and diminishing the tonal range. After more than one hundred years, Mrs. Bogert's portrait was cloudy and difficult to appreciate behind a layer of old, yellowed varnish. Indeed, she was due for a much-needed refresh. Using carefully tested solvents, the discolored varnish was removed without disrupting the paint layer, giving Mrs. Bogert a well-deserved glow-up.

AB

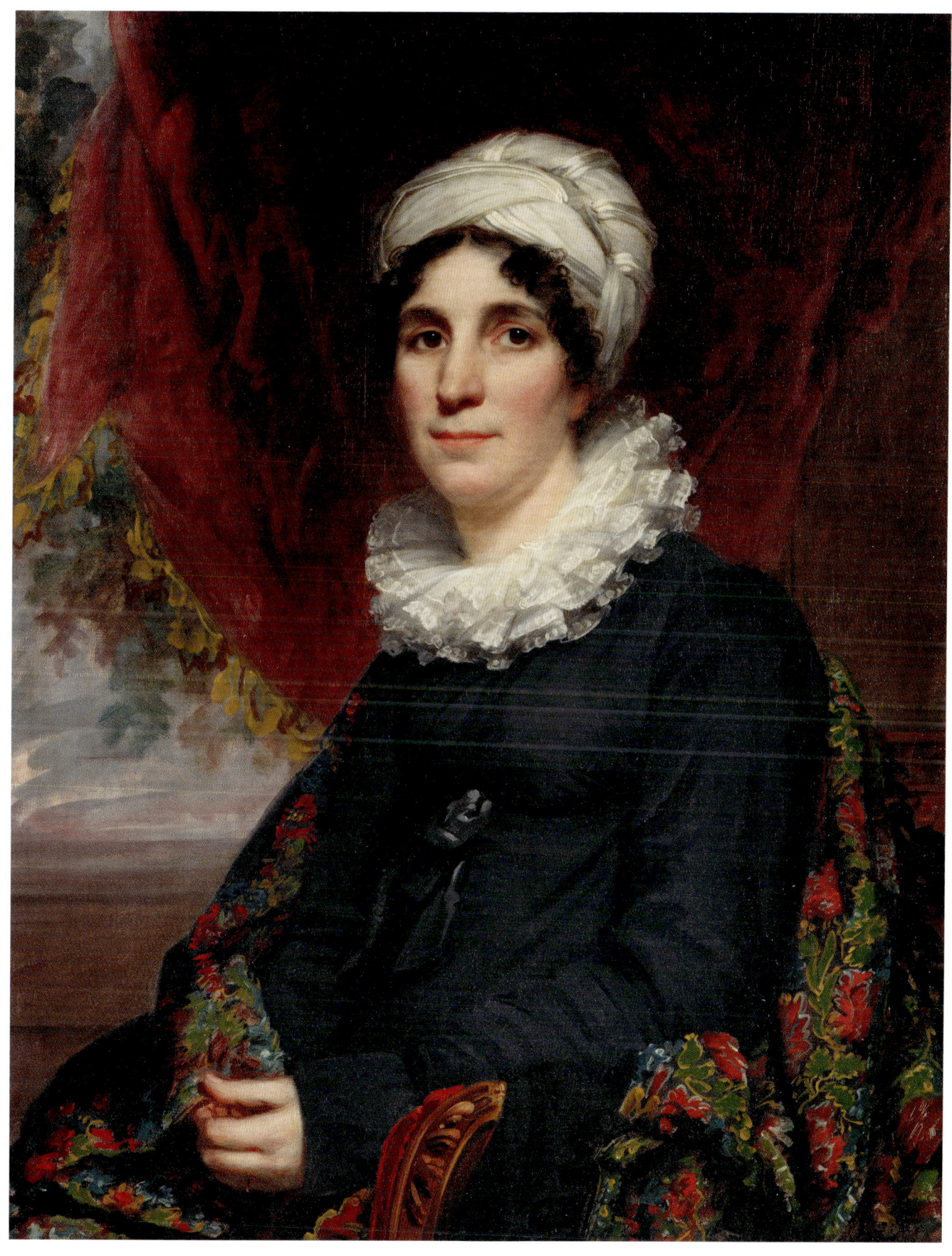

Several Seats

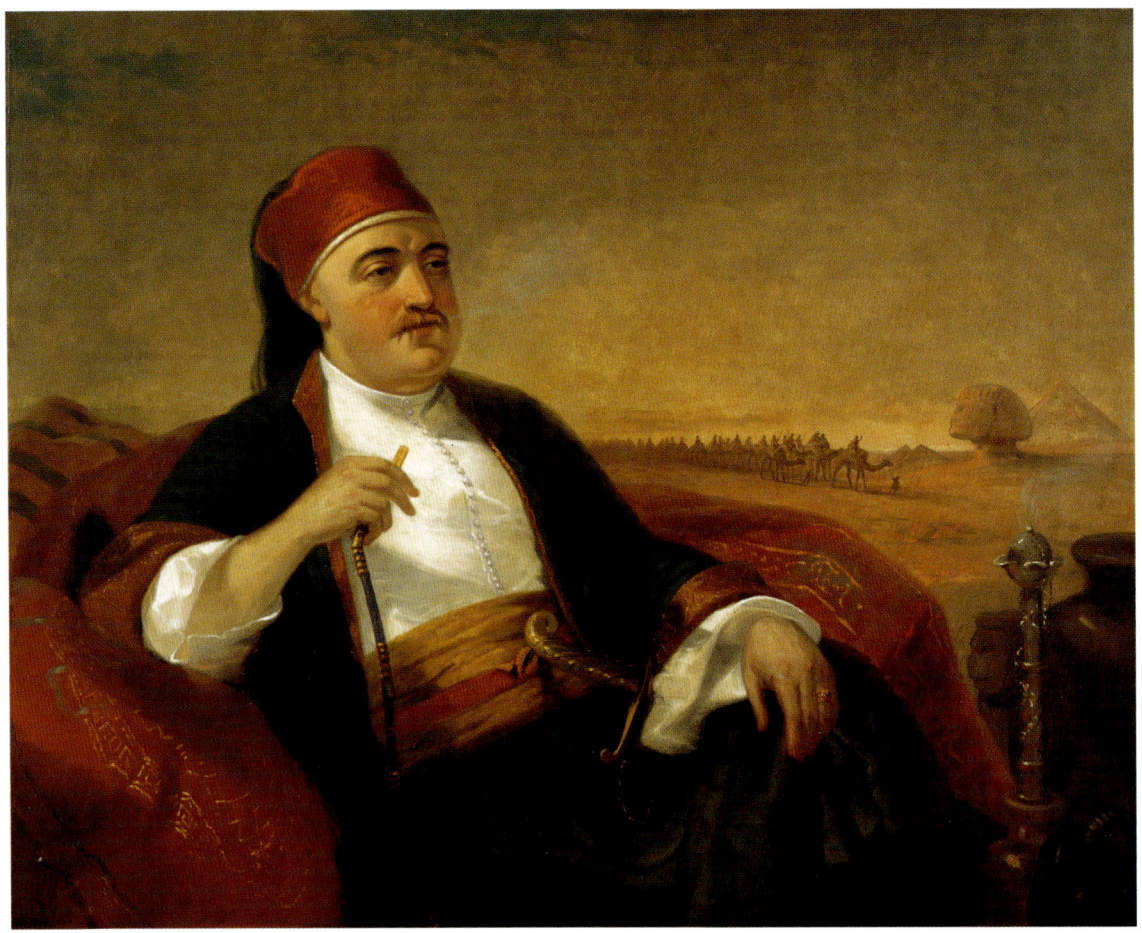

Thomas Hicks
(American, 1823–1890)
Portrait of Henry Abbott, ca. 1861

Oil on canvas, 39¾ × 50¼ in.
Gift of the New-York Historical Society, 48.191
Provenance: Commissioned from the artist by the New-York Historical Society, 1863; purchased by the Brooklyn Museum, November 17, 1948.

William Merritt Chase
(American, 1849–1916)
Girl in a Japanese Costume, ca. 1890

Oil on canvas, 24⅝ × 15¹¹⁄₁₆ in.
Gift of Isabella S. Kurtz in memory of Charles M. Kurtz, 86.197.2
Provenance: 1863, commissioned from the artist by the New-York Historical Society, New York, NY; November 17, 1948, gift of the New-York Historical Society to the Brooklyn Museum.

An unidentified woman, possibly a family member of the artist, gazes out at the viewer (opposite).[1] She wears a Japanese kimono secured with a red obi around her waist—garments likely from William Merritt Chase's collection of imported items. Japanese textiles that Chase appropriated—referred to simply as "costume" in the title—were in vogue, along with other Japanese objects and aesthetics, across Europe and the Americas. Rendered in Chase's Impressionist style, the kimono's pattern is mostly illegible, obscuring its natural motifs and potential significance, though the loose brushstrokes suggest birds and flowers. The virtuosic flourish of his paint handling, however, still highlights the beauty of the kimono's color and method of fashioning.

CG

[1]. Past Brooklyn Museum curators have suggested the family connection. See Teresa A. Carbone, "William Merritt Chase," in *American Paintings in the Brooklyn Museum: Artists Born by 1876*, Teresa A. Carbone, Barbara Dayer Gallati, and Linda S. Ferber (New York: Brooklyn Museum; London: D. Giles Limited, 2006), 1: 368–69.

Japonaiserie[1]

We may recognize the "Japanese costume" in the painting as a kimono. Traditionally, kimonos are worn in layers. The inner layers are often white or a solid color, and visible around the neckline, and the outer ones bear more intricate and elaborate designs. Birds, trees, and flowers are common visual motifs. The front closure goes left over right, and the kimono is tied at the waist with an obi (sash). There is also an unlined, casual variation on the kimono called the *yukata*, which is worn in the summer, at bathhouses, and without undergarments. Here, the model wears no undergarment, and the closure goes right over left, which is more standard in Western clothing. Despite the indication of the kimono and obi having details, they are indiscernible due to the nature of Chase's Impressionist brushstrokes.

And who is this "girl"? Even though her features incorporate more detailed brushstrokes and are therefore clearly recognizable, she remains unidentified.

For me, this painting is more than an Impressionist rendering of some girl in some Japanese costume. There were imperial expansions, international trade negotiations, currency exchange, tariffs, and transportation across water and land—all before the kimono and obi arrived at Chase's Greenwich Village studio to join the collection of foreign artifacts he loved showing off to his patrons. And of all the women Chase may have known, he chose this particular "girl," who is speculated to be a family member, to model with the "Japanese costume." Yet, despite this familial knowing, she became a mere visual spectacle wrapped in another. We do not know her name and we don't see the details on her outfit— both have been subjected to exotification and the male gaze.

Now, I leave you with this: do you think she was sitting on a stool or bench, as a model would in an art studio, or was she on the floor or a tatami (grass mat), as the Japanese would sit? Does it matter?

—Emi Grate

1. "Japonaiserie" is a term for "using Japanese objects as props for conjuring up fanciful visions of Japan." This was a trend that emerged in European and American art after the reopening of Japan to international trade in 1853. See Elisa Evett, *The Critical Reception of Japanese Art in Late Nineteenth Century Europe* (Ann Arbor, MI: UMI Research Press, 1982), viii.

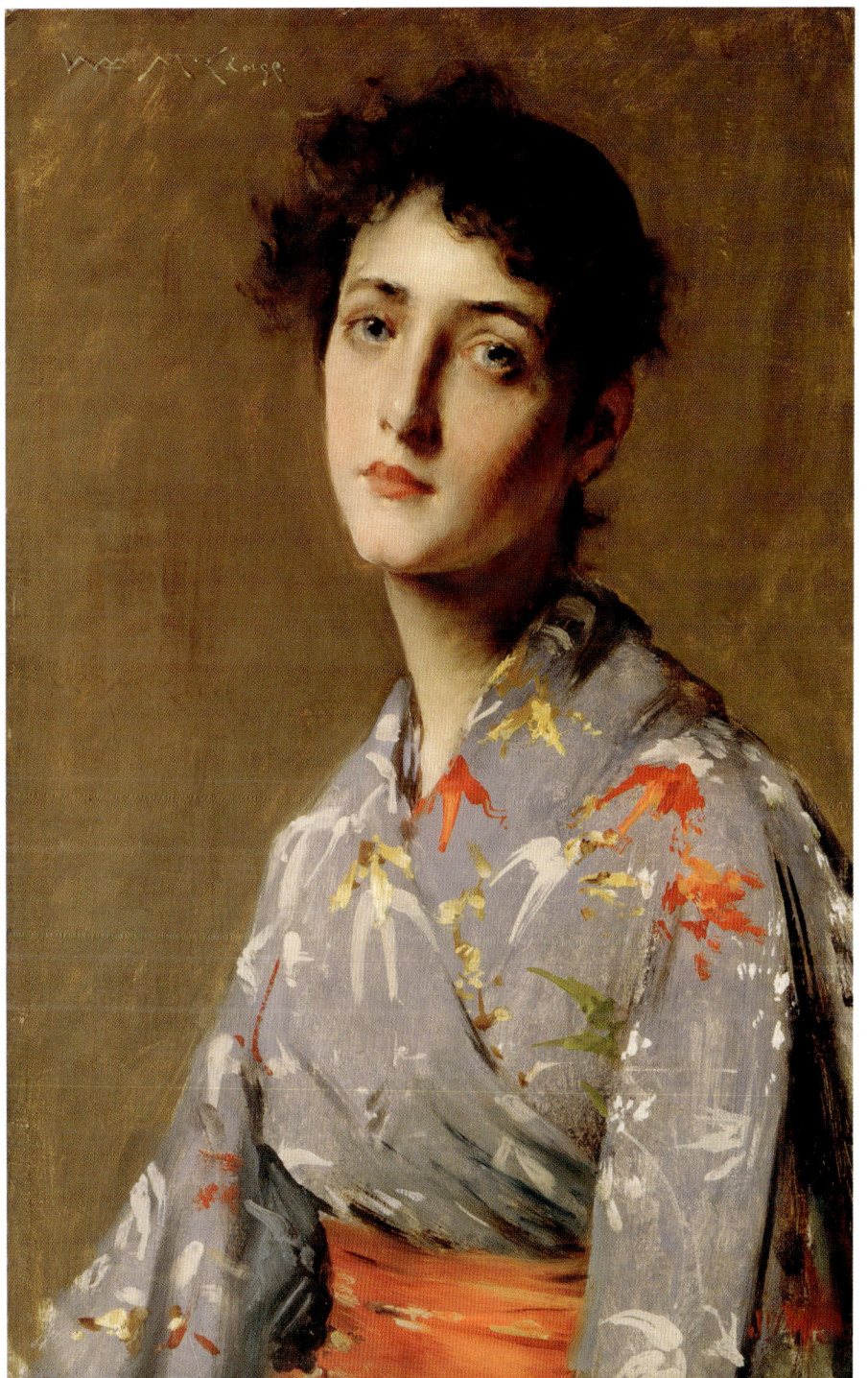

Several Seats

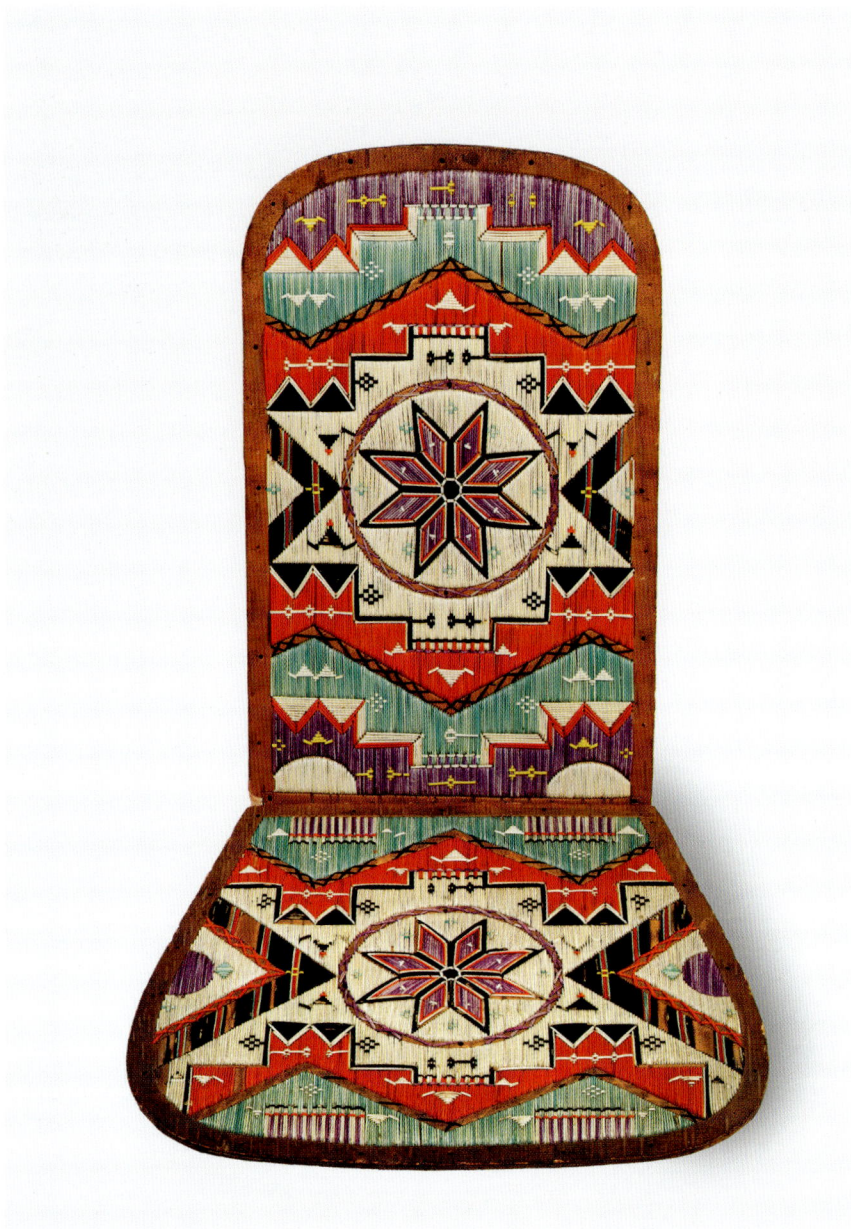

Mi'kmaw artist
Quilled Chair Seat and Back, 19th century
Nova Scotia, New Brunswick, or Newfoundland, Canada or Maine, United States

Porcupine quills, birchbark, back: 15½ × 9¾ × ¼ in.; seat: 12¹³⁄₁₆ × 14³⁄₁₆ × ¼ in.
Brooklyn Museum Collection, 09.867a-b
Provenance: Acquired by the Brooklyn Museum, before 1996.

Expertly crafted by a Mi'kmaw woman, this quilled chair seat and back reflect generations of knowledge passed down within Indigenous artistic communities. To craft this item, the maker collected, processed, and dyed porcupine quills before applying them to birch bark, which had been sustainably harvested. In doing so, the artist celebrated the lives of the plants and animals whose materials were used to fabricate the piece.

DT

This quillwork originally adorned a settler-made chair, now lost. While chairs featuring Mi'kmaw quillwork could be viewed as an example of settler recognition of Mi'kmaw artistry, they are more reflective of how Christian settlers of European descent viewed themselves as superior to the Mi'kmaw people as a Nation. This perspective extended to art. Because settlers believed they could dictate the form and medium of quillwork, Mi'kmaw artists were stymied from developing art according to their values. Instead, they incorporated more intricate details reflective of European needlework. The market also required Indigenous art to be affixed to items desirable to settlers, such as calling-card cases, place mats, and trinket boxes, to be valuable. By featuring quillwork on the seat of a chair, settlers were literally and figuratively placing themselves above the Mi'kmaw.

—**Melissa Peter-Paul and Cheryl Simon, Mi'kmaw quill artists)**

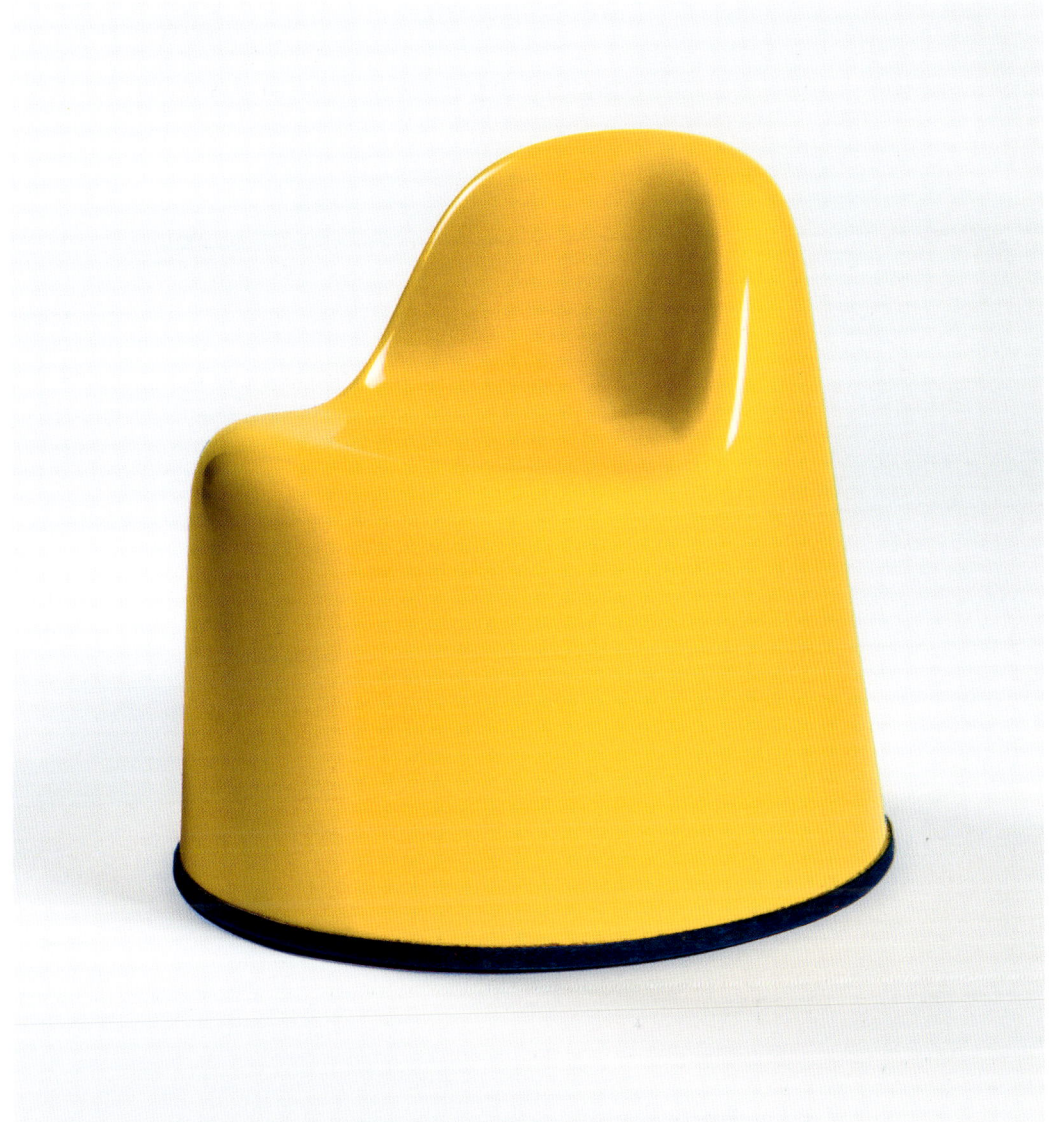

Wendell Castle, Designer
(American, 1932–2018)
Baby Molar chair, 1971

Gel-coated, fiberglass-reinforced plastic,
17 × 19 × 18 in.
Gift of R & Company, New York, 2018.15
Provenance: Acquired by R & Company,
by 2018; donated, June 19, 2018.

Rochester, New York–based furniture designer Wendell Castle experimented with materials, styles, and fabrication techniques to create some of the most distinctively sculptural seating and cabinet forms of the 1960s through late 2010s. For Castle, furniture was functional sculpture, occupying the same space and tackling concepts of the relationship of the human form to a work of art. Works by Castle, such as the *Baby Molar* chair, also reflect his playfulness and sense of humor. While parents could have a single seat chair or a three-seat settee, a youngster could have its own special, child-sized version.

As one of the founders of the American Studio Furniture movement, Castle was always experimenting and innovating. In 1963, inspired by the fabrication of nineteenth-century duck decoys carved from stacks of wood, Castle formed large blocks of stack-laminated wood that could be hand-, machine-, or robot-carved. Building on innovations in the use of fiberglass, he created plastic and fiberglass seating furniture. Later in life, following his attraction to cars—Castle was a gearhead—he experimented with high-gloss automotive paint finishes. Always designing, several of Castle's designs can be found in the collection of the Brooklyn Museum.

CF

Several Seats

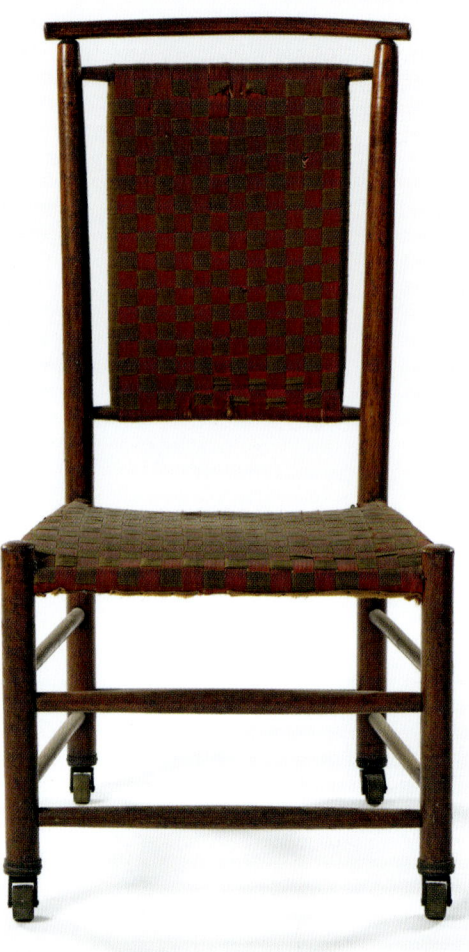

Unknown craftsperson
American, Shaker (United Society of Believers in Christ's Second Appearing) community
Side Chair, ca. 1880

Beech, shellac, 33¾ × 18¼ × 21¼ in.
Anonymous gift, 66.111.1
Provenance: Acquired by an anonymous collector, by 1966; donated, 1966.

Commonly called the Shakers, the United Society of Believers in Christ's Second Appearing, founded in England in about 1747, and established in Watervliet, New York, in 1776, are frequently celebrated for their simple, well-made, and utilitarian furniture. The Shakers maintain egalitarian ideals, with both women and men leading spiritual worship, and practice a celibate, simple, and communal way of life. In the mid-nineteenth century, there were about two to four thousand Shakers, living in eighteen communities. Today, there is only one active community remaining, at Sabbathday Lake in Maine.

During the peak of the sect's popularity, the Shakers were entrepreneurial and innovative in technology and marketing. They supported their communities by producing a large line of goods for sale, all characterized by care for the land, animals, and other human beings, from chairs and tables to woven textiles and seeds. The furniture, constructed of inexpensive, lightweight, undecorated wood, is functional and elegant. Shaker furniture could be easily moved, as with the casters on the end of the legs on this model, and stored by hanging on wall pegs to make room for spiritual meetings. Even today, Shaker furniture is valued for and epitomizes the essence of simplicity and function.

CF

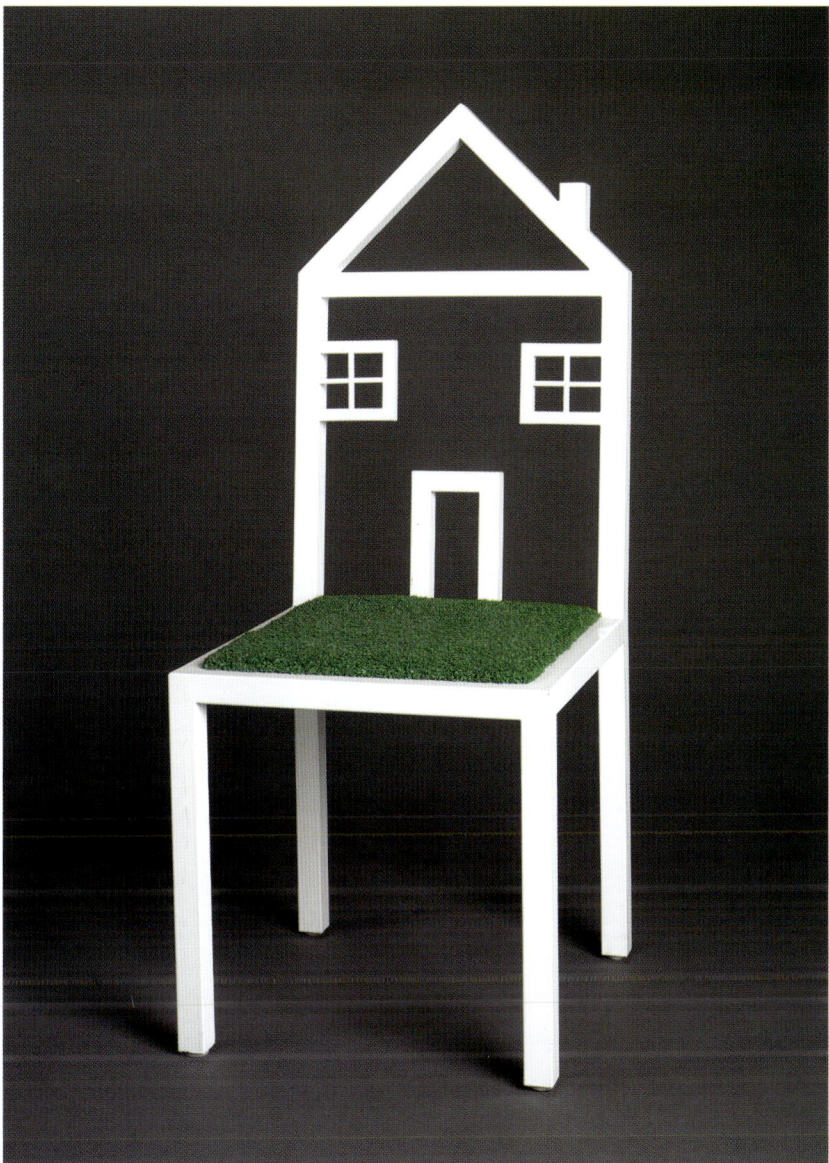

Kate Loye, Designer
(American, life dates unknown)
One Family House Chair, designed 1984, manufactured 1986

Steel tubing, electrostatic paint, Astroturf, plywood, 42½ × 17 × 17 in.
Gift of Riane Eisler, 86.240
Provenance: Acquired by Riane Eisler, by 1986; donated, December 1986.

Kate Loye's chair is a charming example of Postmodernism, a diverse approach to design globally fashionable in the 1980s that referenced emotion, popular culture, wit, and history in its visual forms. This work is not inventive in its materials or production techniques, but rather in the affection and critical viewpoints evoked by the archetypal image of a single-family American home with a green, well-manicured lawn. On one hand, this chair could be an endorsement of the conservative post–World War II American Dream that advocated for the heterosexual nuclear family, monetary stability, material wealth, and suburban home ownership. In many social spheres, this conventional vision is still desired. However, this piece could also take on a more cutting interpretation if viewed in the context of today's social and economic realities, with high inflation and stagnant earnings, particularly the minimum wage. Indeed, it is now challenging to contemplate this chair without considering the narrowness and impossibility of this aspiration. Many Americans can no longer afford to buy a single-family home and new attitudes on family, community, and housing have emerged. Whatever the perspective, Loye's work is layered with cultural references and meanings that conjure a spectrum of feelings depending on the viewer's lived experience.

LSG

Several Seats

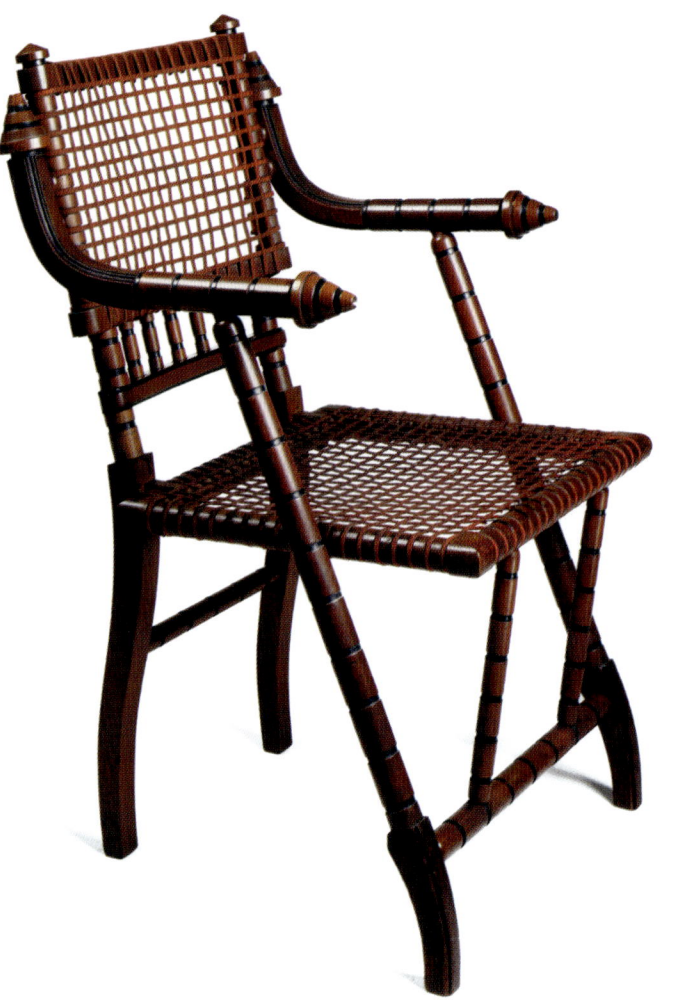

New York City–based George Jacob Hunzinger was probably the most idiosyncratic yet innovative American furniture designer and maker of the nineteenth century. He was a pioneer inventor, marketer, and, even, proto-Modernist. Trained in Geneva, Switzerland, in 1855 Hunzinger joined New York's rapidly growing German community. He first settled in Brooklyn where he began manufacturing his furniture before moving to Manhattan in 1860.

Hunzinger's specialty was patent furniture; by incorporating new materials and technology in construction, he secured twenty-one patents for innovative table, chair, and bed designs. His designs appealed to middle-class American requirements for adaptability and affordability, and also fulfilled a desire for invention. Hunzinger offered consumer choice over a wide economic range, attracting customers of different tastes and budgets. The nineteenth-century prices for his wares, ranging from $10 to $70 for a chair, depended on finishes, such as the quality of upholstery, staining, or gilding. This chair retains its original woven steel seat and back, which was probably covered by upholstered cushions to provide some comfort to the sitter.

CF

George Jakob Hunzinger
(American, born Germany, 1835–1898)
Armchair, ca. 1876

Walnut, steel mesh, fabric, 33⅜ × 21 × 18½ in.
Brooklyn Museum, H. Randolph Lever Fund, 83.27
Provenance: Acquired by Down the Road Antiques, by 1983; purchased, 1983.

Unknown craftsperson
Mexican
Armchair, 1750–1800

Mahogany, upholstery, 40¼ × 25¼ × 17¾ in.
Gift of Robert W. Dowling, 64.243.6
Provenance: Acquired by Ashley Chanler, by 1950; purchased by Robert W. Dowling, by April 1964; donated, April 1964.

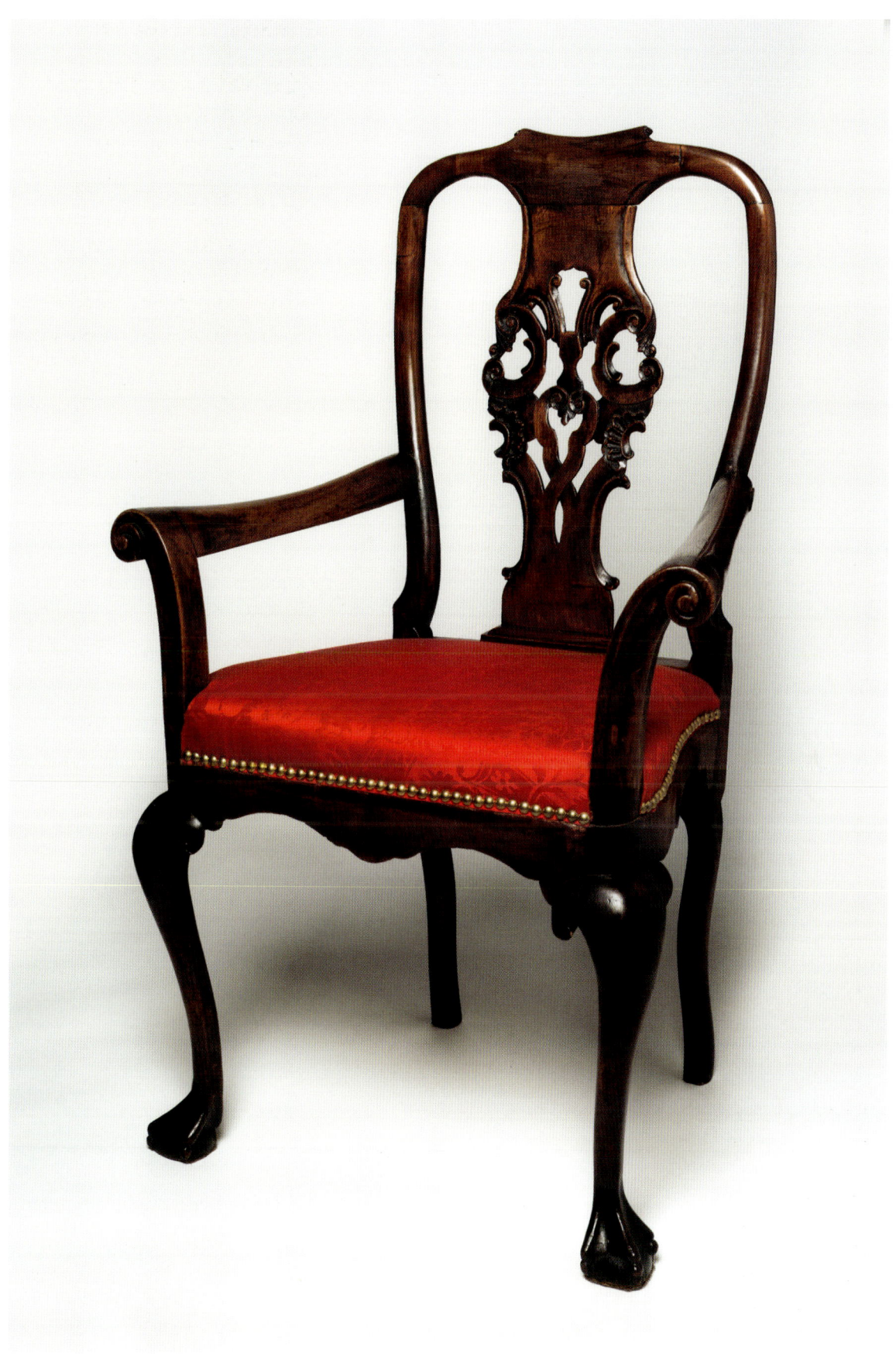

Several Seats

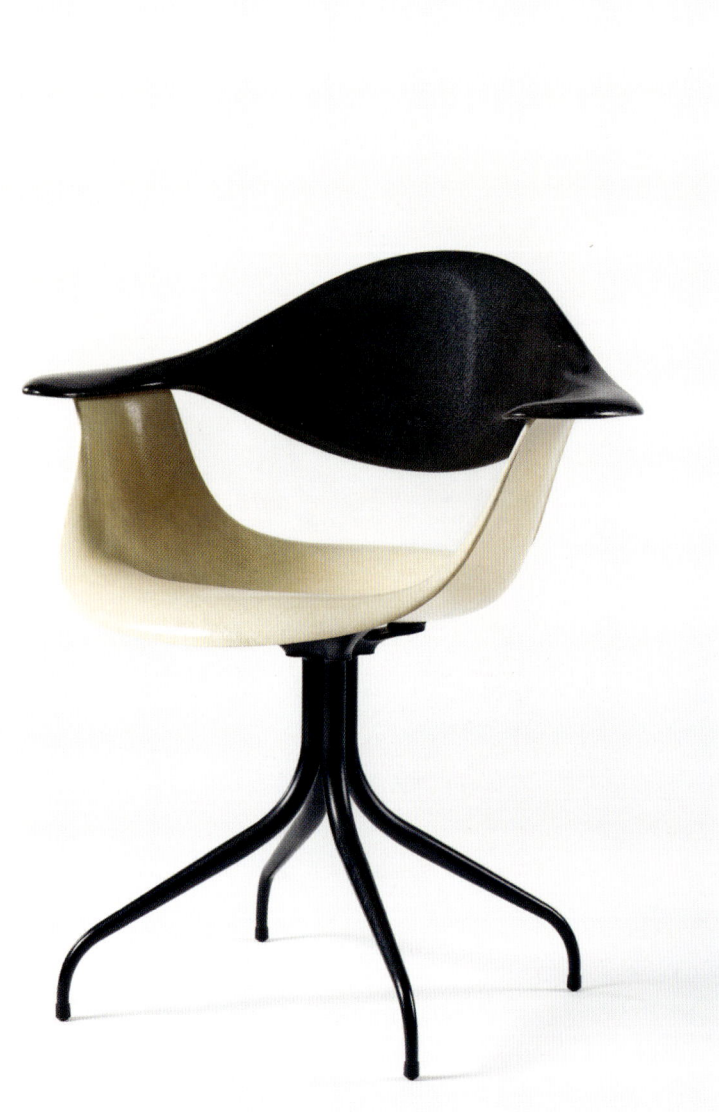

Charles Pollock, Designer
(American, 1930–2013)
George Nelson, Designer
(American, 1908–1986)
Herman Miller, Manufacturer
(American, est. 1905)
Armchair, *Model DAF*, ca. 1956

Fiberglass, steel, rubber, 31½ × 28½ × 21¾ in.
Gift of Barry Friedman, 84.275.5
Provenance: Acquired by Barry Friedman, by 1984; donated, 1984.

Likely in collaboration with famed mid-twentieth-century designer George Nelson, Charles Pollock conceived an updated version of the office chair, a typology he would reenvision throughout his career. During the 1950s, many major corporations mobilized modern design to organize office spaces and make them feel more relaxed to encourage longer working hours. This is probably best evident in the interior design section of Florence Knoll Bassett (1917–2019), the Knoll Planning Unit (founded 1946), which established these concepts through grid layouts, flexibility, visually dynamic shapes, and bold pops of color and monochromatic juxtapositions. Working in Nelson's forward-thinking studio, Pollock would have been aware of these trends and clearly integrated them into his armchair. The white dyed seat and black backrest are in two separate curved pieces and made of fiberglass, a new lightweight material for furniture that was in common usage during the 1950s. This dual color scheme gave the chair a lively appearance and the fiberglass made the piece easy to move. Embodying casual comfort, Pollock's armchair is a fine example of innovative approaches to office arrangement and attitudes towards work during the 1950s.

LSG

Unknown craftsperson
Italian or American
Armchair, ca. 1875

Ebony, various woods, ivory, mother-of-pearl, modern upholstery, 39 × 25⅞ × 26⅜ in.
Gift of Mr. and Mrs. George N. Richard, 71.95
Provenance: Acquired by George N. Richard and Mrs. George N. Richard (possibly Helen Menken Richard), by 1971; donated, 1971.

Expensive materials, such as ebony, ivory, and mother-of-pearl, signify that this monumental throne-like chair was destined for a luxurious interior for a wealthy patron. Although likely fabricated in Milan, Italy, it was probably marketed and intended for an American client who could convey status and wealth, as well as sophistication, with such a grand, almost ostentatious, chair in a richly appointed room. This chair exhibits the form and motifs derived from ancient Roman and Italian Renaissance sources, such as the intricate, entwined flowers and vines and the hippocamps, or horses with fish tails for their lower bodies. Other examples incorporated figures of Native Americans and American family coats of arms, their decoration indicating that the owner of the chair wanted to communicate their position and prestige.

CF

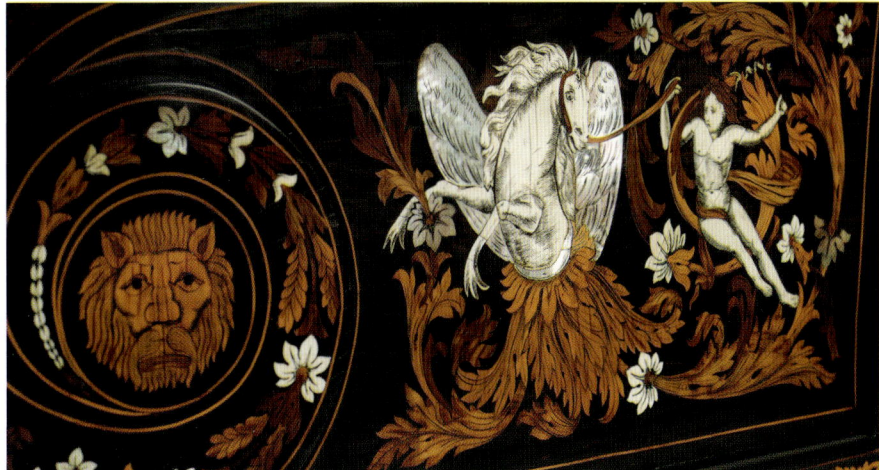

Several Seats

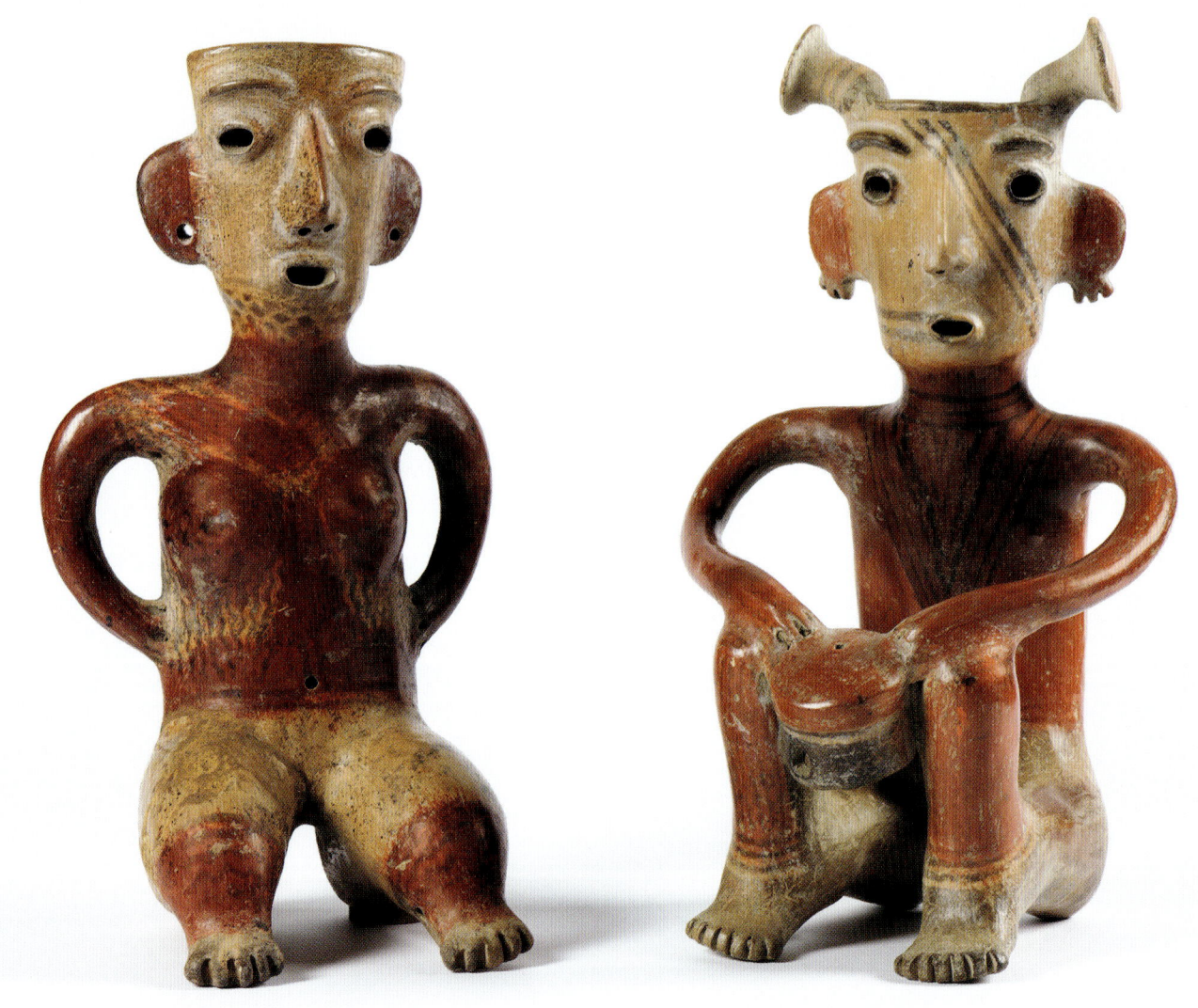

Jalisco artist
Pair of Ancestral Figures
Jalisco, Mexico, ca. 200

Ceramic, slip, female: 15½ × 9 × 6¾ in.; male: 16 × 9 × 8 in.
Gift of Mr. and Mrs. Arnold Maremont, 69.132.1 and 69.132.2
Provenance: Acquired by Stendahl Galleries, before 1969;
purchased by Arnold and Eileen Maremont, 1969; donated, 1969.

These seated Zacatecas-style figures from Jalisco, in western Mexico, may represent a married couple or founders of an ancestral lineage.[1] The figures are hollow with highly burnished red and tan clay slips applied to the surface. Patterns of black straight and wavy lines adorn their nude bodies. These elaborate markings may represent body painting or tattooing, which possibly signals the couple's high social status. The man wears the typical Zacatecas-style male "headdress," made by wrapping hair around a spool-like support, as well as fan-shaped earrings and bands around his ankles. The holes in his partner's earlobes suggest that she may have worn perishable earrings, perhaps of feathers or plant fibers, that did not survive. The woman's hands rest near her abdomen, a possible sign of fertility and the birth of their family line, while her mate plays a drum as they both sing. These sculptures of ancestors were made to be funerary offerings, placed together with other grave goods in shaft-and-chamber tombs to accompany high-ranking individuals in the next life.[2] Kristi Butterwick proposes that these tombs, and their location near homes, served to establish the ancestors' and their descendants' territorial rights to productive lands that continued to support the family and their high social status.[3] These 1,800-year-old portraits therefore serve as a window into the lives of ancient peoples and their powerful connections to land and community.

NR

1. Kristi Butterwick, *Heritage of Power: Ancient Sculpture from West Mexico, The Andrall E. Pearson Family Collection* (New York: Metropolitan Museum of Art and New Haven and London: Yale University Press, 2004), 31–32.
2. This style of tomb had a slanted or vertical shaft leading to one or more burial chambers. Ibid., 13, 29, 56–58.
3. Ibid., 13.

CRITICAL SHORT

To Be Real!

Caroline Gillaspie

A crowd has congregated at a hall on 125th Street in Manhattan, the unadorned blue walls interrupted by orange beams that flank a long narrow aisle—a runway. The audience sits on folding chairs or stands on either side of the runway, and a panel of judges awaits the first contestants who compete, or "walk," in categories at this House Ballroom competition.[1]

Wearing a pink knee-length dress, a white flower in her hair, bold earrings, and perfectly applied makeup, Pepper LaBeija announces into a microphone:

We are gonna start... *right*... *now*. Oh, no. I'll introduce myself. *I* am Pepper LaBeija.

It is 1982, and Pepper, the Mother of the House of LaBeija, is emceeing the "Harlem Fantasy Ball." For the category Realness, the first contestant is Margo, from the House of Princess.[2] The first few bars of Cheryl Lynn's 1978 disco anthem "Got to Be Real" fill the hall. Margo struts into view wearing a white patterned shirt and shorts set with black pumps, one hand on her swinging hips.

The crowd responds enthusiastically—clapping, cheering, leaping to their feet, and yelling words of encouragement.

As Lynn belts "to be real!" over the speakers, Margo tilts her head way back, shimmies her shoulders, and sensuously draws her hand down her neck and torso. She continues her strut and is joined by Erica, wearing a flowing knee-length green dress. The two work the crowd, Margo soliciting cheers with raised arms, and Erica striking poses along the runway. One by one, competitors join them. Pepper exclaims, "Give her what she wants! She's real!"

As is typical of the early 1980s Ballroom scene, the categories continue: Best Body, Nostalgia, Punk Rock vs. New Wave, Face, Ethnic Effect, 2001 Models Effect... The energy builds as dance battles are sparked and increasingly elaborate costumes—works of art and craftsmanship—are flaunted before an energized audience. Characterized by the struts, poses, dancing, expression, style, and radiating joy, Ballroom and its adaptation of glamor, opulence, fantasy, realness, self-fashioning, and freedom has set it apart in histories of performance and cultural criticism. Within the safe space of the Ball, Ballroom and drag artists embody identities freed from societal constraints, often mimicking genders, cultures, or social classes different from their own.

In fostering a sense of empowerment and belonging against societal exclusion, LGBTQ+ community leader, activist, and

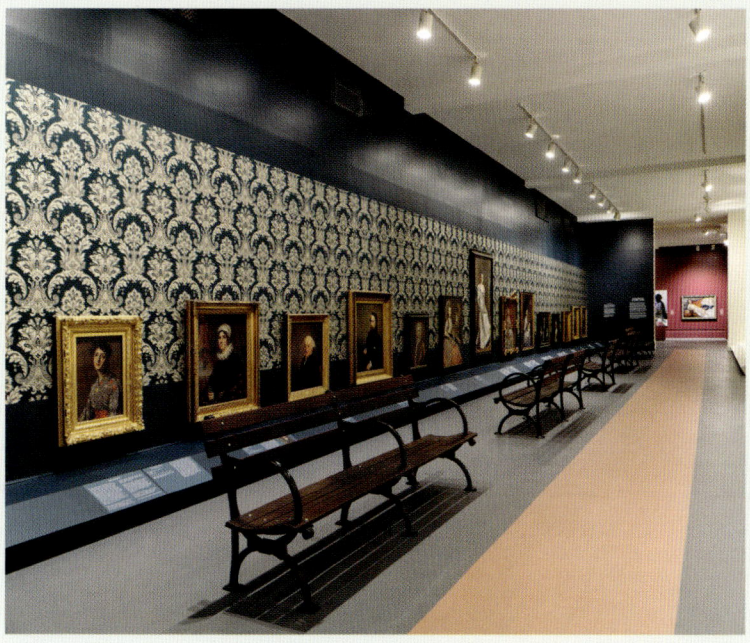

social status, material possessions, or lineage. In the context of this framework, Ballroom and drag's incisive criticism of status quo society is instructive. By reclaiming and sometimes parodying historical affluence and elite cultural traditions such as debutante balls, Ballroom performers and scholars inspire fresh interpretive lenses from which to engage these historic American portraits anew. As an art form equal to the works in this framework, Ballroom informs an interrogation of their public display.[7] In this new way of experiencing the collection, visitors are empowered to strut, prance, and sashay; to be playful and self-expressive in the face of cultures of gender, race, and class supremacy.

1. The description of this Ball is based on footage from Michele Capozzi and Simone de Bagno's 1982 documentary *T.V. Transvestite*.
2. In Ballroom culture, Houses are a chosen family, formed among members to create a support system and sense of belonging. At House Balls, "Realness" is a category in which performers blend in with heteronormative ideas of gender identities, imitating the appearance of being "female" or "male."
3. Michael Roberson, "The Enduring Legacy of Ballroom," TEDResidency, May 2019, https://www.ted.com/talks/michael_roberson_the_enduring_legacy_of_ballroom. Roberson evokes Martin Luther King, Jr.'s description of the "Beloved Community" centered around care and compassion.
4. As we celebrate House/Ballroom culture as a rigorous art form and form of liberation, we acknowledge its rich history and the writing, scholarship, and documentary photography that has been produced, including: Marlon M. Bailey, *Butch Queens up in Pumps: Gender, Performance, and Ballroom Culture in Detroit* (Ann Arbor, MI: University of Michigan Press, 2013); George Chauncey, *Gay New York: Gender, Urban Culture, and the Making of the Gay Male World, 1890–1940* (New York: BasicBooks, 1994); Gerard H. Gaskin, Deborah Willis, and Frank Leon Roberts, *Legendary: Inside the House Ballroom Scene* (Durham, NC: Duke University Press, 2013); Ricky Tucker, *And the Category Is...: Inside New York's Vogue, House, and Ballroom Community* (Boston, MA: Beacon Press, 2021); Chantal Regnault and Stuart Baker, *Voguing and the House Ballroom Scene of New York City 1989–92* (London: Soul Jazz Books, 2022). Regarding Marcel Christian LaBeija's extensive archive of material related to the history of Ballroom ("Idle Sheets"), see Sydney Baloue, "Marcel and Me: How Ballroom's First Historian Made My Life Possible," *Them*, February 28, 2024, https://www.them.us/story/marcel-christian-labeija-ballrooms-first-historian-essay.
5. Crystal LaBeija and Lottie LaBeija were the cofounders of the House, with Pepper LaBeija succeeding them as House Mother.
6. Voguing is a stylized and improvisational dance form widely performed in Ballroom culture in which dancers imitate the poses of models in fashion magazines. Some credit Paris Dupree, Mother of the House of Dupree, with originating the form as early as the 1970s, and it was popularized by the late 1980s.
7. Google Arts & Culture now has a segment celebrating Ballroom as an art form. https://artsandculture.google.com/project/ballroom.

speaker Michael Roberson has said that "Ballroom creates a new home... created out of love, created out of care, even when it's faced with brutality."[3] The self-expressive form cultivates liberatory spaces and kinship bonds, particularly among Black and Latinx queer and transgender individuals who have been socially ostracized, and who often experience violence.[4] Pepper LaBeija, an icon, led her House for over twenty years until her death in 2003. Pepper and other House mothers offered familial support to many without it elsewhere.[5] Their generation ushered in the era of House Balls and the artistry and performance they mastered, including creative self-fashioning and voguing, which would have been at odds with fine art included in museums at the time.[6]

However, decades later, on January 5, 2023, two members of the cast of *RuPaul's Drag Race* season 15 spontaneously strutted their stuff through one of the Brooklyn Museum's American art galleries during a visit to the exhibition on the work of French fashion designer and creative director Thierry Mugler. In bold ensembles, Anetra and Luxx Noir London confidently walked along a wall of Gilded Age portraits. What if we could recreate this face-off of style and opulence for our Museum visitors within the framework: *Several Seats*? Could they, too, feel empowered to playfully take up space and engage differently with the portraits?

Recalled by generations of House Ball performers, the gold, glitz, and opulence of María de la Luz's ornately embroidered gown enabled the colonial diva to fashion an identity for herself, completing her look with stylish *chiqueadores*, or applied beauty marks (p. 186). Art historically, portraits such as hers are often read and presented in ways that privilege the iconography of

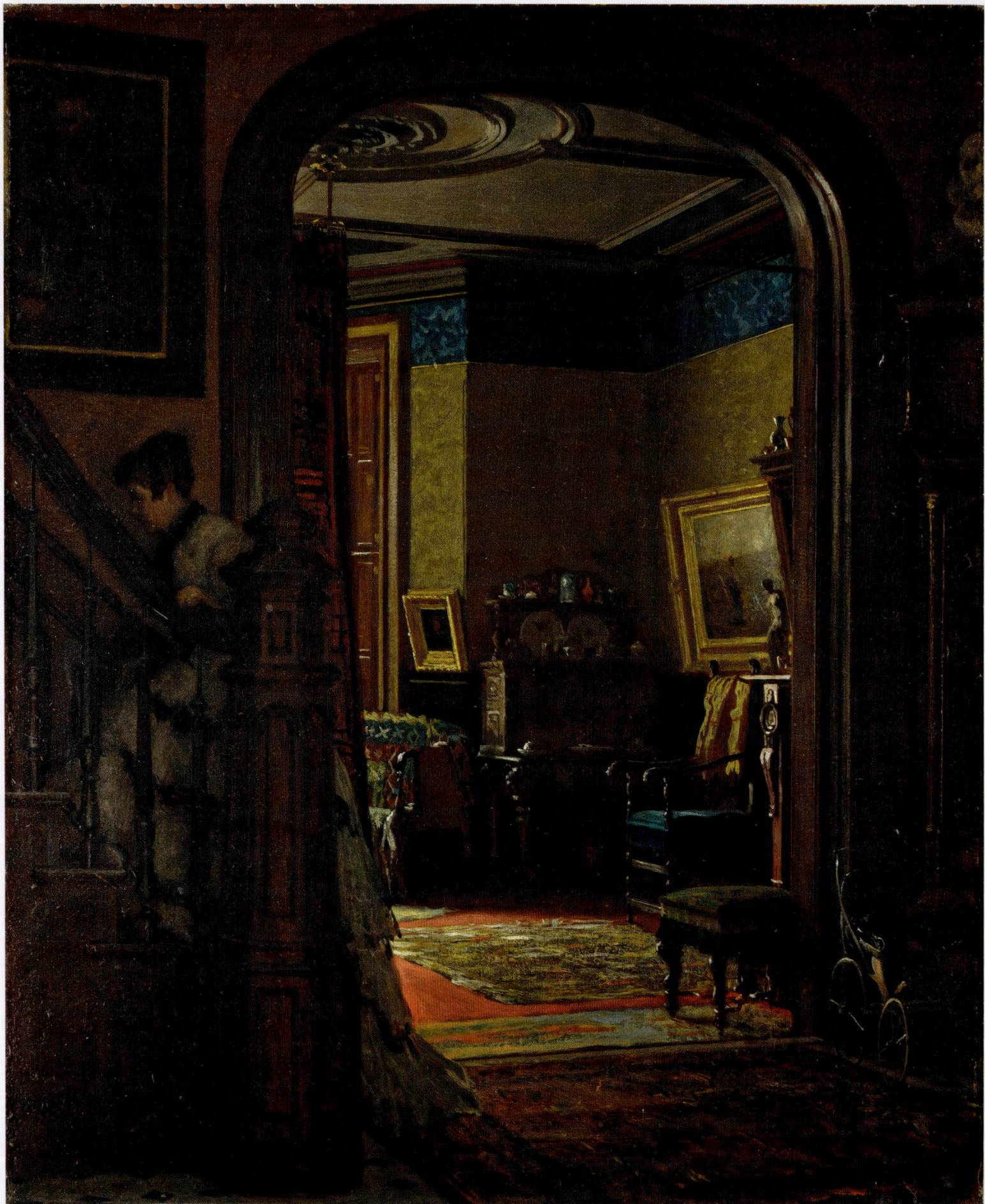

FRAMEWORK

A Quiet Place

Eastman Johnson
(American, 1824–1906)
Not at Home, ca. 1873

Oil on laminated paperboard, 26⁷⁄₁₆ × 22⁵⁄₁₆ in.
Gift of Gwendolyn O. L. Conkling, 40.60
Provenance: Estate of the artist, to his wife Elizabeth Buckley Johnson; to her daughter Ethel Johnson Conkling; to her daughter Gwendolyn O. L. Conkling; to the Brooklyn Museum.

Who has access to rest? . . . to peace and quiet?

There is a subtle refusal in Eastman Johnson's painting, *Not at Home*. His wife, Elizabeth, climbs the stairs in their Manhattan residence on West 55th Street, perhaps to draw a bath or to retire with their then three-year-old daughter, Ethel, for a nap. Sunlight pours into the parlor suggesting midday, and making the couple's quiet retreat seem particularly luxurious. Historically, the phrase "not at home" indicated the occupants of the house were unavailable to receive visitors—a common practice given the Johnsons' popularity, wealth, and the artist's success. Amid the bustle of daily life, Johnson captures the timeless act of reclaiming one's time and personal space.

Inspired by the ways American artists have sought quietude through their art, this framework is designed to inspire reflection and rest. Together, images of leisure and sleep, peaceful meditations on the landscape, and belongings that promote restfulness capture experiences of silence, repose, tranquility, and spaciousness. The work of Black feminist creatives and cultural critics, such as Tricia Hersey of the Nap Ministry and Cole Arthur Riley of Black Liturgies, deeply inform this framework.[1] Hersey and Riley call for individuals and communities to slow down, practice introspection, and move with intention through the world. Speaking to contemporary experiences of fatigue, including "museum fatigue," they foreground the need for care and rest-centered communion with the artworks on view.

In her work on African diaspora photography, art historian and cultural theorist Tina Campt entreats readers to "listen to images" that may not be fully discernible to the eye.[2] She offers tools for mining the subtle ways artworks resist the oppressive forces around them. Building on Campt's approach, this framework invites visitors to engage the "lower frequencies" within the art through close looking. To pause the scroll; look carefully. What do you see? Look again. What do you see that makes you say this? Look again . . . and again.

These slow-looking practices may reveal creative refusals in the works sampled here in this chapter and promote well-being for those inspired to move at a different pace. We invite you to sit down, to savor each color reproduction, to breathe a little more deeply—to rest.

SSW

1. For more on the Nap Ministry and the power of rest, see Tricia Hersey, *Rest Is Resistance: A Manifesto* (New York: Little, Brown Spark, 2022). Black Liturgies is a project space created by Cole Arthur Riley, embedded in the Center for Dignity and Contemplation. See *Black Liturgies: Prayers, Poems, and Meditations for Staying Human* (New York: Convergent Books, 2024).
2. Tina Campt, *Listening to Images* (Durham, NC: Duke University Press, 2017).

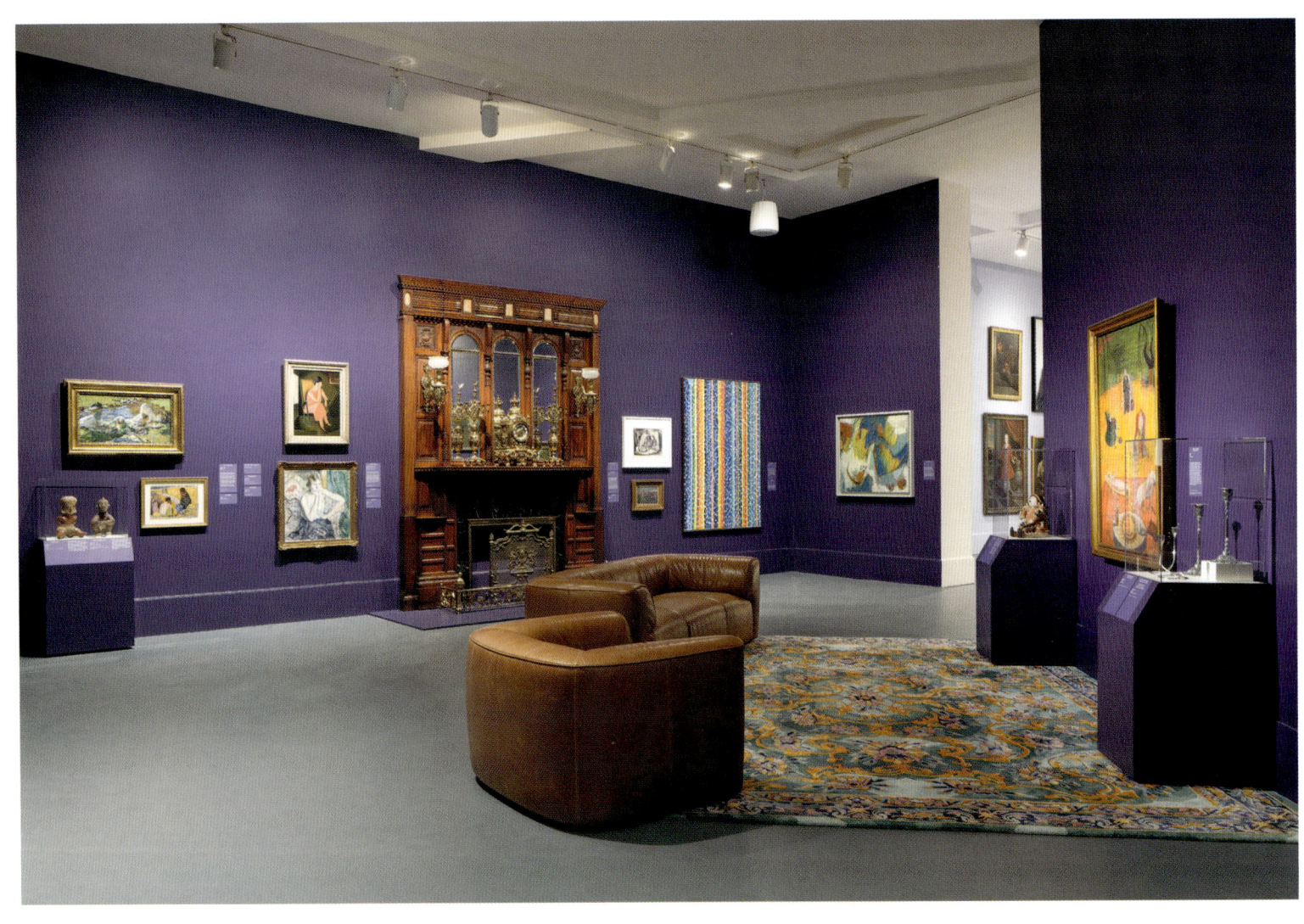

Anna Russell Jones
(American, 1902–1990)
Design No. 326, ca. 1924–28

Watercolor and gouache on paper
Collection of the African American Museum in Philadelphia
Photograph by Andrea Nunez

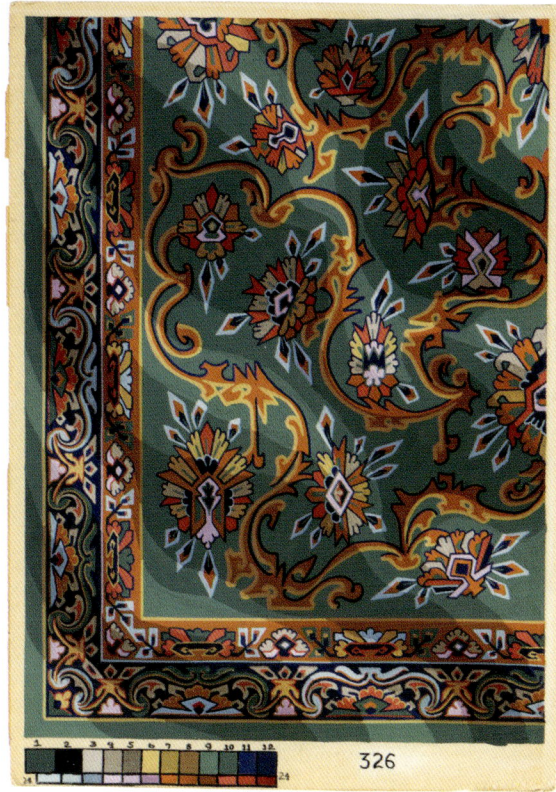

A civil-service illustrator and artist, Anna Russell Jones is largely recognized for her carpet and wallpaper design. With a degree in Theoretical and Practical Design, she is celebrated as the first Black American graduate of the Philadelphia School of Design for Women (now Moore College of Art and Design). In her four years at the institution, she was the only Black student enrolled, and completed studies in "geometric construction, nature—convention and application, historic ornament, perspective, composition, theory of color, history of art, charcoal, posters, and other areas of design."[1]

Russell Jones went on to work as an in-house rug designer at the James G. Speck Design Studio in Philadelphia from 1924 to 1928.[2] She then established her own studio, selling design sketches to carpet and rug manufacturers across the United States and Canada. In the center of the gallery, visitors to the Brooklyn Museum can enjoy an area rug reproduced from an original hand-painted swatch from Russell Jones's archives, housed in the African American Museum in Philadelphia. Russell Jones often incorporated myriad stylistic influences, experimenting with color and technique to accomplish designs with "tweed effects, self-tone, contrasting colors, and other modern trends."[3]

The artist often stressed: "I had three strikes against me: I was a woman, Black, and a freelancer," acknowledging the challenges she and other Black women designers faced throughout their careers. In the midst of the Great Depression, Russell Jones transitioned away from design work to pursue her political interests and commitments, which focused on "concerns for Black life in the United States."[4]

SSW

1. "Anna Russell Jones: The Art of Design," African American Museum in Philadelphia, 2021, https://onlineexhibits.aampmuseum.org/anna-russell-jones/home/.
2. Ibid.
3. Ibid.
4. Huewayne Watson, "Anna Russell Jones and Archives of African American Art and Life" (lecture, African American Museum in Philadelphia, May 26, 2021), https://www.facebook.com/AAMPMuseum/videos/anna-russell-jones-and-archives-of-african-american-art-and-life/287198512984899/.

Alma Thomas
(American, 1891–1978)
Wind, Sunshine and Flowers, 1968

Acrylic on canvas, 71¾ × 51⅞ in.
Gift of Mr. and Mrs. David K. Anderson, 76.120
Provenance: Acquired from the artist by Martha Jackson Gallery, before 1976; purchased by David K. Anderson and Rebecca Reed Anderson (Mrs. David K. Anderson) for the Brooklyn Museum, October 20, 1976.

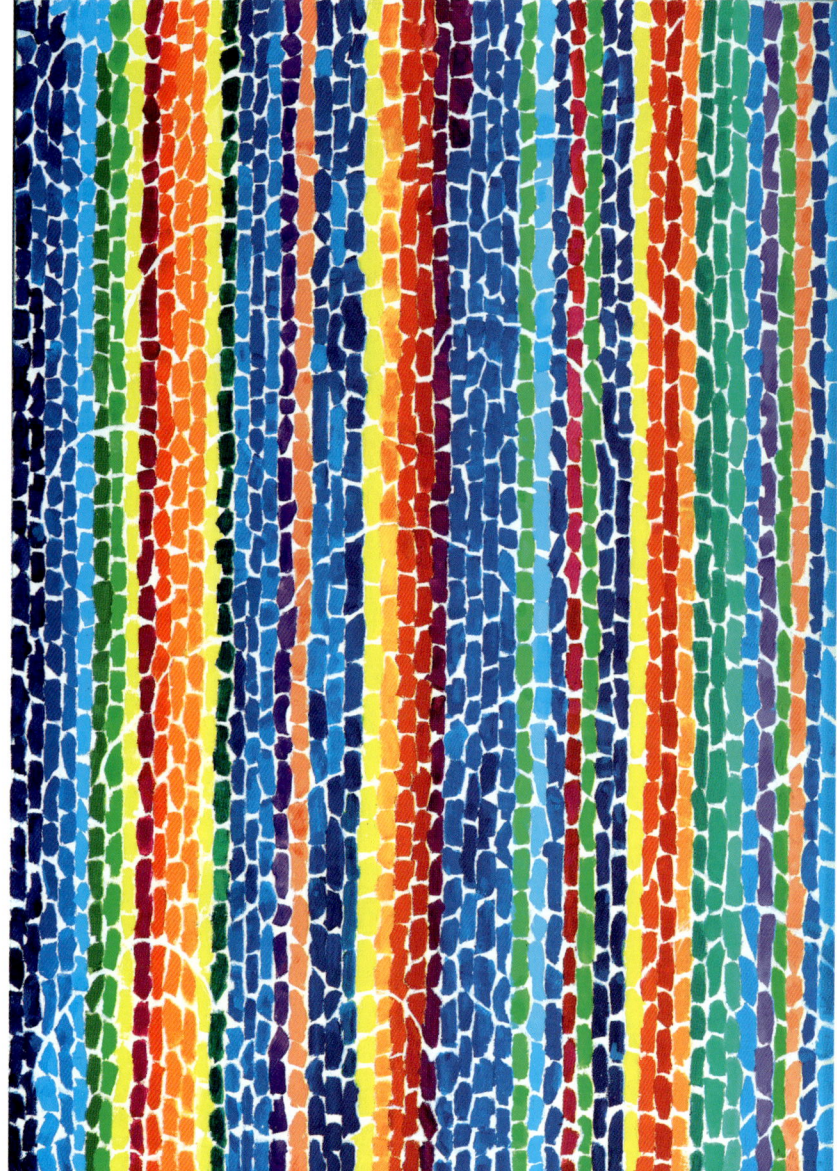

In 1971, artist Alma Thomas declared that *Wind, Sunshine and Flowers* should be the title of the book about her life.[1] For Thomas, nature was a perfect muse. It was also a perfect escape. Captivated by the color of petals and the dance of light over moving leaves, Thomas found respite from the racial biases that shaped her experiences as a Black woman in the lush realm of natural phenomena. Of her vibrant palette she wrote, "Color is life. Light is the mother of color. Light reveals to us the spirit and living soul of the world through colors."[2]

Bridget R. Cooks notes that in Thomas's work, color is also form, and that the artist "used color to construct her impressions" of the natural world.[3] In her signature style, the painting *Wind, Sunshine and Flowers* exemplifies Thomas's application of vertical bands of color to create rainbow canvases that mimic "the dispersion of the sun's light into colors."[4] In what she called her "earth paintings," the artist captured a bird's eye view looking out of her Fifteenth Street home in the Shaw district of Washington, DC. Nikki A. Greene has posited that the Brooklyn Museum's painting may in fact map "a specific site: the undulating hills and meandering pathways of the United States National Arboretum, as seen from high above, making *Wind* an homage to what was clearly a special place. . ."[5]

Thomas's *oeuvre* of vibrant non-figurative color-field paintings associated her with the Washington Color School, a stylistic movement that emerged from abstract painters working in Washington, DC, in the 1950s through the '70s. She was engaged in many creative circles, including the Little Paris Salon, co-led by another of Brooklyn's Collection artists, Loïs Mailou Jones, alongside French artist Céline Tabary, in the early 1940s.

In the same year Thomas completed *Wind, Sunshine and Flowers*, artist Hale Woodruff was also transforming nature's power and majesty into abstract landscapes. Through flattened perspective, bold use of color, and improvisational brushstrokes, *Blue Landscape* epitomizes the artist's embrace of Abstract Expressionism, which allowed him to explore his unconscious and emotional response to the land through sweeping, gestural brushstrokes. Woodruff believed an artwork's form should embody the artist's personal "sensibility," and stated that, "more important to the work of art are the energies, the efforts, and the deep insights that come from the artist as he works through what he has experienced in life."[6]

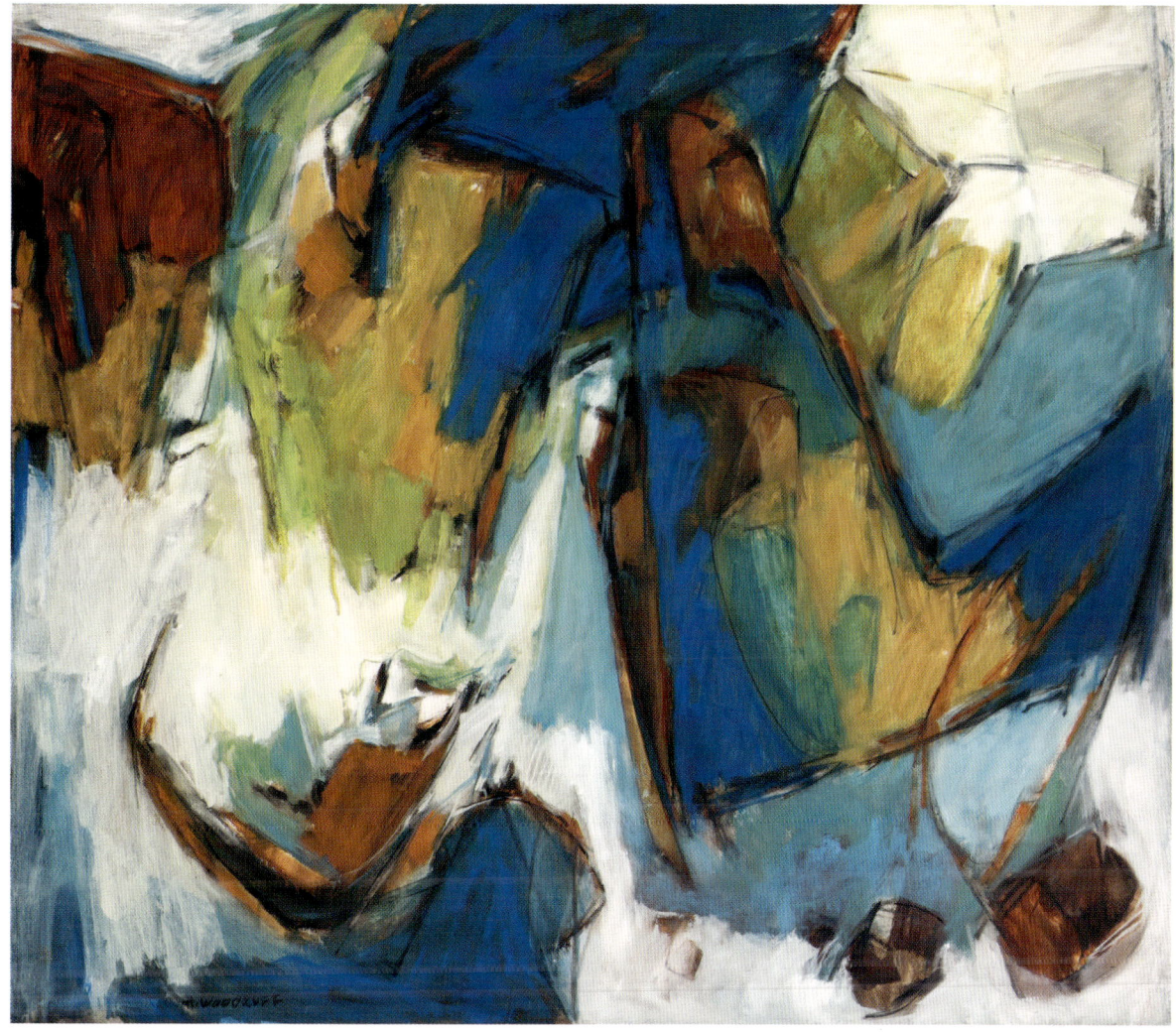

His long and successful career of nearly six decades as an artist and educator took him from Nashville to Paris and Mexico City via Atlanta, and finally on to New York City. When he arrived in New York in the late 1940s, he began to transition away from his figurative style of the decade prior, and the murals for which he was wellknown. Throughout his *oeuvre*, Woodruff integrated influences as wide ranging as African art and Mexican muralism, Abstract Expressionism, and Cubism. Like Thomas, he was involved in several important artistic communities, including Spiral, a Black artists collective he helped to found with fellow artists Romare Bearden, Charles Henry Alston, and Norman Lewis. Spiral was originally formed in response to the March on Washington for Jobs and Freedom in August 1963.

SSW with CG

Hale Woodruff
(American, 1900–1980)
Blue Landscape, 1968

Oil on canvas, 36 × 42¼ in.
Gift of Mr. and Mrs. E. Thomas Williams, Jr., 87.86
Provenance: Inherited from the artist by Theresa A. Woodruff, by 1980; purchased by Edgar Thomas Williams, Jr. and Auldlyn Higgins Williams (Mrs. E. Thomas Williams, Jr.), before 1987; donated, 1987.

1. Ida Jervis, "Magic Windows of Alma Thomas," *Art Scene I,* no. 3 (Summer 1971): 15.
2. "Alma Thomas," *Free Within Ourselves: African-American Artists in the Collection of the National Museum of American Art* (Washington, DC: Smithsonian Institution, 1992), 167.
3. Bridget R. Cooks, "The Nature of Color," in *Alma Thomas,* ed. Ian Berry and Lauren Hayes (New York: DelMonico Books, 2016), 154.
4. Nikki A. Greene, "'Wind, Sunshine and Flowers': The Visual Cadences of Alma Thomas's Washington, DC," in *Alma Thomas,* ed. Ian Berry and Lauren Hayes (New York: DelMonico Books, 2016), 53.
5. Ibid., 57.
6. Romare Bearden, Sam Gilliam, Jr., Richard Hunt, Jacob Lawrence, Tom Lloyd, William Williams, and Hale Woodruff, "The Black Artist in America: A Symposium," *The Metropolitan Museum of Art Bulletin* 27, no. 5 (January 1969): 253.

When people ask me what it is, I tell them it's my grandfather... he was a really wise man. He knew so much and he was a really good storyteller. There were always lots of us grandchildren around him, and we're all in there, in the clay. All my potteries come out of my heart. They're my little people. I talk to them and they're singing. If you're listening, you can hear them.[1]

—Helen Cordero, Ko-Tyit (Cochiti Pueblo) artist

This storyteller figure, hand modeled from clay by Helen Cordero, represents the artist's grandfather. The strong male figure—rendered in Cordero's preferred color palette of black, cream, and warm rust—wears a headband like that seen in a photograph of her grandfather from around 1906.[2] Cordero crafted fourteen grandchildren with distinct attire and varying forms, then appliquéd them on top of the larger figure. They envelop the grandfather as he closes his eyes and shares Ko-Tyit narratives and customs through song. Many Indigenous communities revere the act of storytelling, which ensures the continuance of tradition, and children are expected to be respectful and careful listeners.

While Pueblo artists made figurative sculptures for personal use within religious contexts for hundreds of years, they began selling them to tourists at white-owned trading posts after the introduction of the railroad in the late nineteenth century.[3] Many such pieces represented singing women holding a child or pottery. Cordero built upon that artistic legacy by pioneering the Storyteller figure in 1964.[4] Her efforts garnered acclaim and established a new artistic category for which Ko-Tyit Pueblo artists have become renowned.

DT

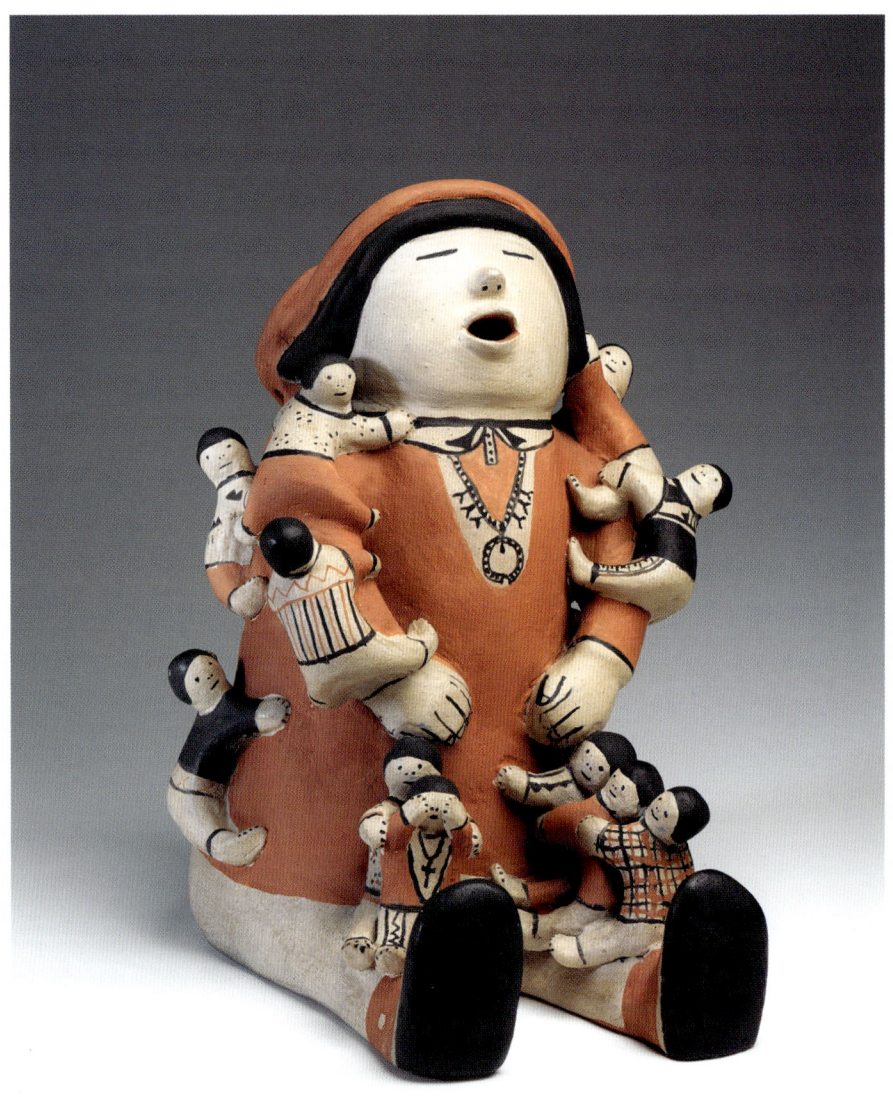

Helen Cordero
(Ko-Tyit, Cochiti Pueblo, 1915–1994)
Storyteller Pottery Sculpture
Cochiti Pueblo, New Mexico, 1987

Clay, pigment, 12 × 8¼ × 10 in.
Gift of Joann and Sidney Rosoff, 2012.26.1
Provenance: Purchased from the artist by Joann and Sidney Rosoff, May 22, 1987; donated, June 21, 2012.

1. Barbara A. Babcock, Guy Monthan, and Doris Monthan, *The Pueblo Storyteller: Development of a Figurative Ceramic Tradition* (Tucson: University of Arizona Press, 1997), 97.
2. Ibid., 22.
3. Ibid., 11.
4. Ibid., 3.

Florine Stettheimer painted the luxurious lifestyle of New York City's elite, including scenes of her own family at their summer retreat in Bedford Hills, New York. The artist and her sisters were well known for their eclectic personal styles and involvement in the art world. In *Heat*, they enjoy a moment of rest as they celebrate their mother's birthday. Rosetta sits as if enthroned at the top of the composition surrounded by her daughters in a vibrant yellow and orange setting that evokes the sweltering heat of July. Overcome by the weather, Stella and Carrie abandon their knitting at the compositional center. Ettie and Florine recline on lounge chairs in the foreground, mimicking the wilting tree branches, as Florine stretches her arm toward a playful cat.

Stettheimer's highly idiosyncratic style has been described as Rococo—an eighteenth-century French style that is often considered dramatic and decorative—and emerges in this painting in her depiction of elongated bodies and ornate details. Art historian Linda Nochlin argued that Stettheimer, while academically trained at the Art Students League, also encapsulated camp sensibility through theatrical and playful compositions rendered with her distinct stylization of distorted forms.[1] Stettheimer and her family lived in the luxurious Alwyn Court apartment building in Manhattan, although she successfully navigated the bohemian avant-garde art world and remained engaged in social activism. *Heat* foregrounds Stettheimer's upper-class access to leisure, while also subverting these things through the highly exaggerated—even absurd or humorous—poses and forms that defy patriarchal artistic traditions.

CG

1. Linda Nochlin discusses Stettheimer's style in the context of Susan Sontag's definition of camp as a sensibility that embraces artifice, stylization, and exaggeration. See Linda Nochlin, "Florine Stettheimer: Rococo Subversive," *Art in America* 68 (September 1980): 64–83; Susan Sontag, "Notes on 'Camp'" (1964), in *Against Interpretation and Other Essays* (New York: Farrar, Straus and Giroux, 1966).

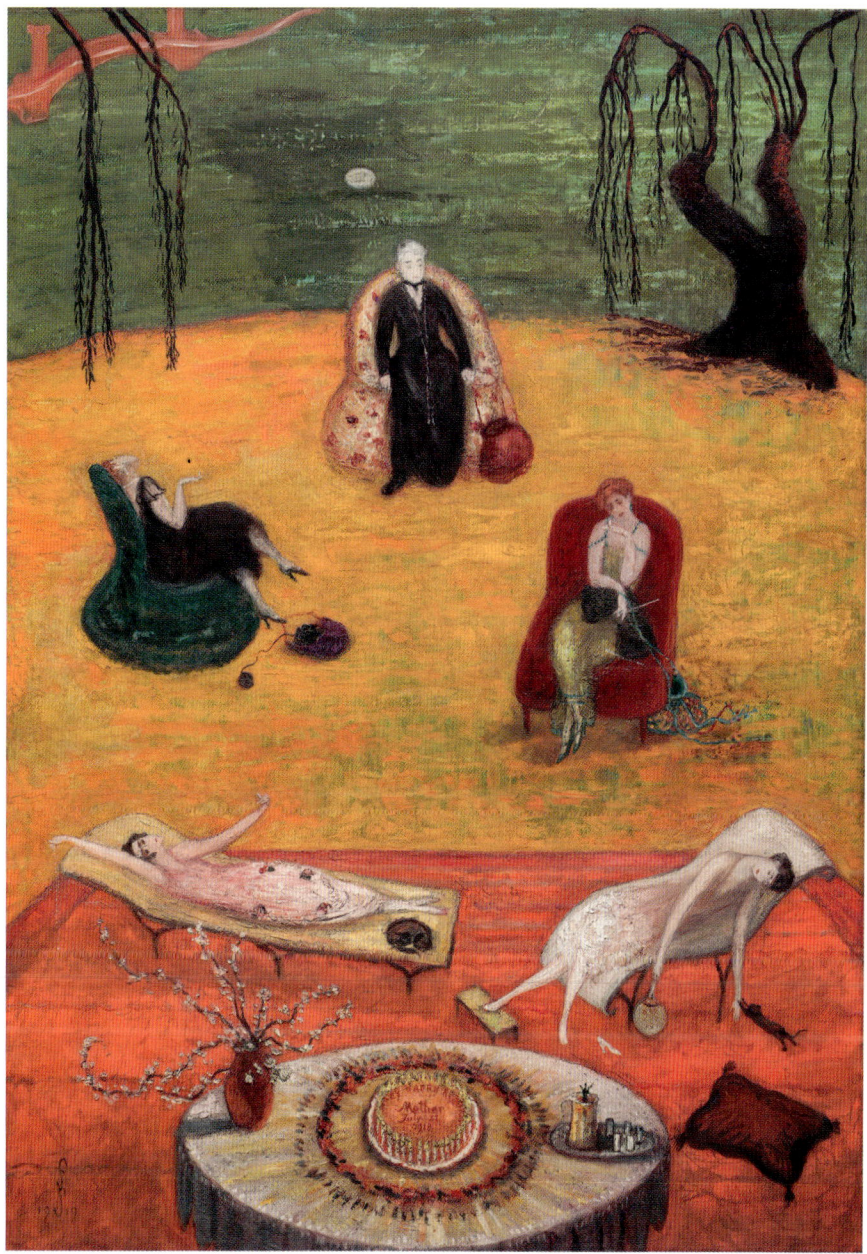

Florine Stettheimer
(American, 1871–1944)
Heat, 1919

Oil on canvas, 50 × 36½ in.
Gift of the Estate of Ettie Stettheimer, 57.125
Provenance: Inherited from the artist by Ettie Stettheimer, 1944; donated by the estate of Ettie Stettheimer, June 12, 1957.

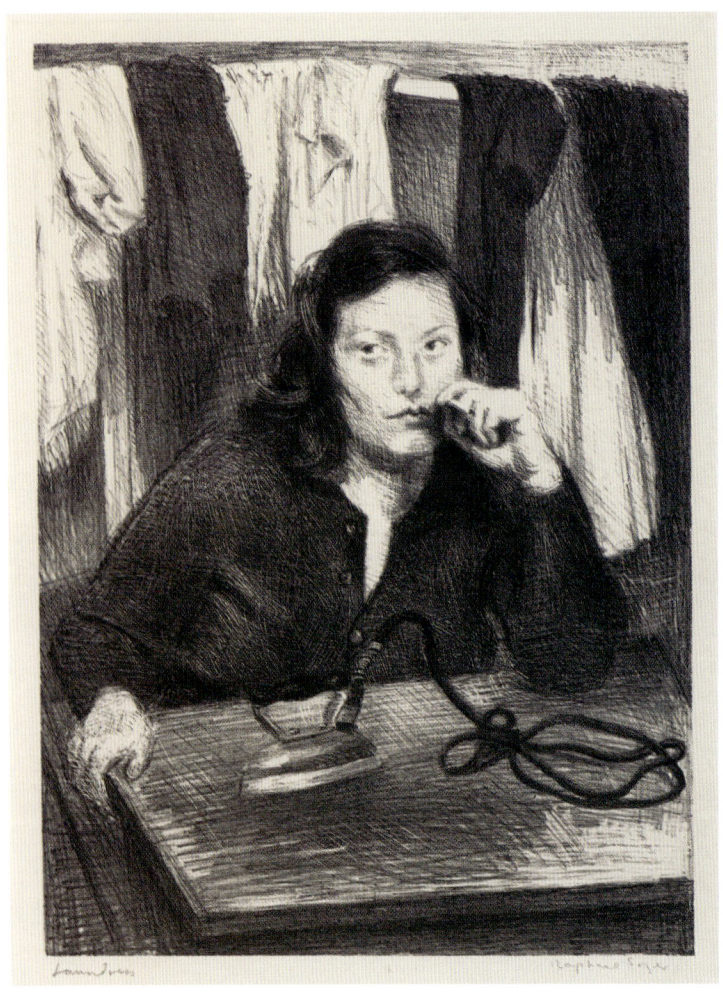 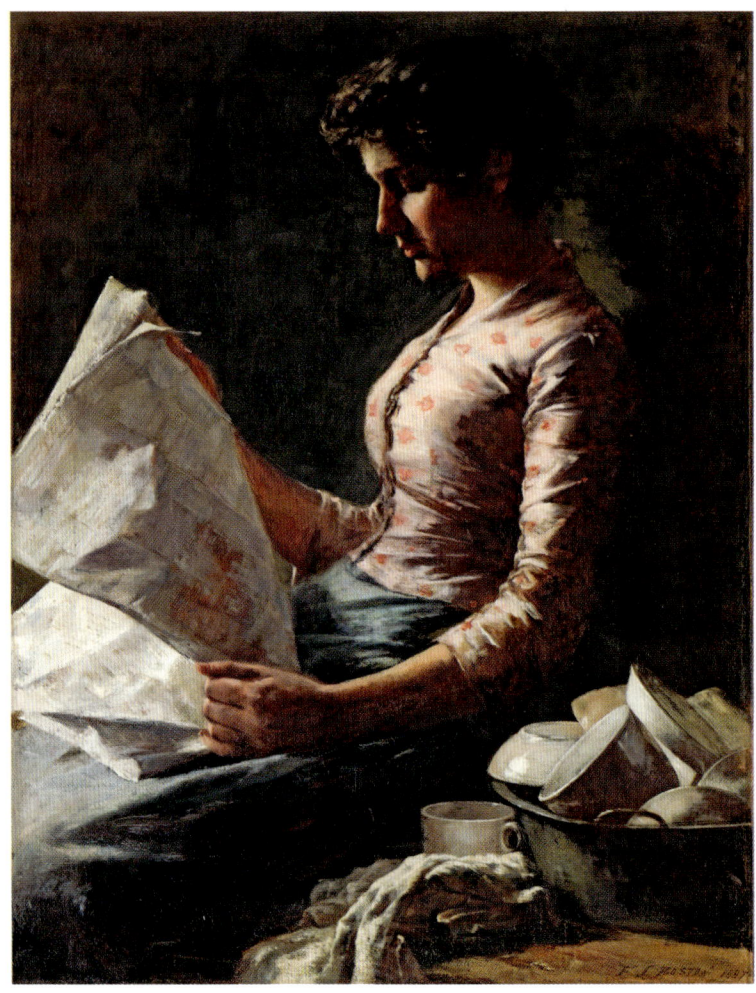

Raphael Soyer
(American, born Russia, 1899–1987)
Laundress, ca. 1941–42

Lithograph on paper, sheet: 23¾ × 16 in.
Gift of Samuel Goldberg in memory of his parents, Sophie and Jacob Goldberg, and his brother, Hyman Goldberg, 79.299.15
Provenance: Acquired by Samuel Goldberg, by 1979; donated, 1979.

Frederick James Boston
(American, 1855–1932)
The Morning News, 1887

Oil on canvas, 28 × 22 in.
Gift in loving memory of Mildred M. Lowe, 2013.24
Provenance: Purchased by Edith Price Golden Ruckert, before 1945; inherited by Mabel Ruckert Knapp Marshall, 1945; inherited by Mildred Knapp Marshall Lowe, 1951; purchased from the estate of Mildred Lowe by Linda Lowe Asmar, ca. 2012; donated, June 20, 2013.

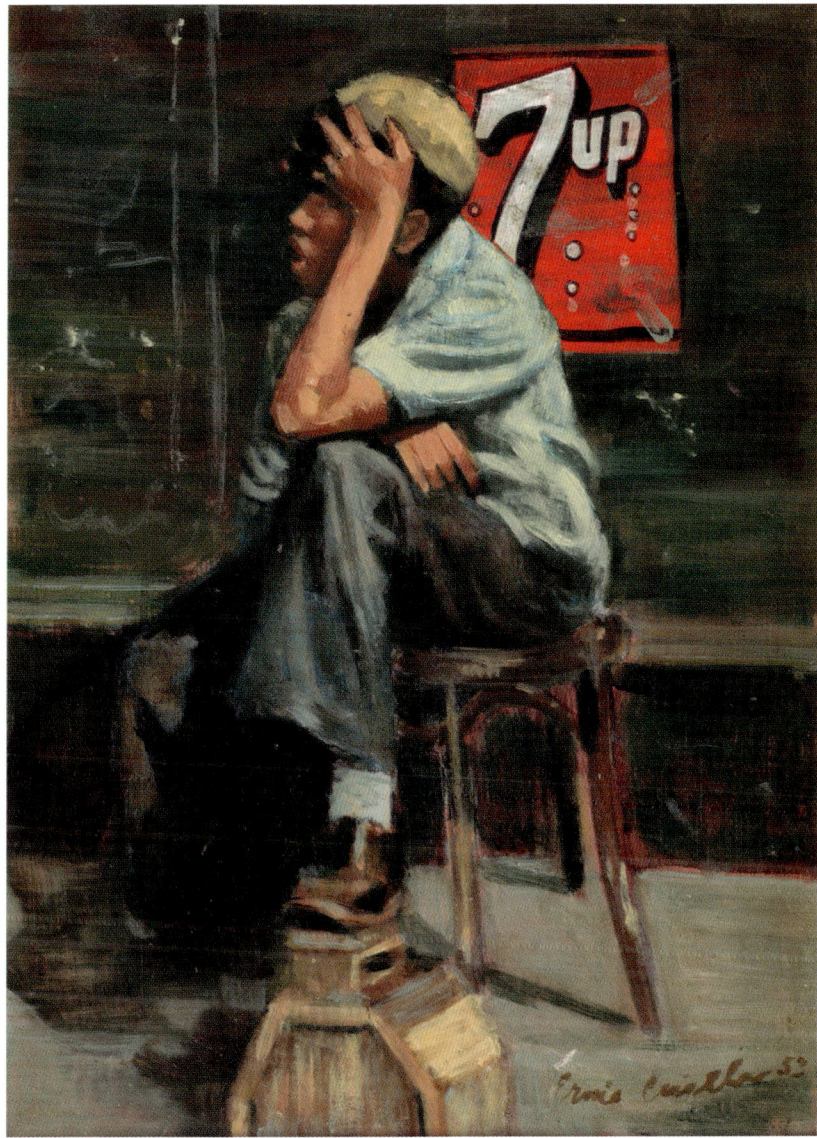

Ernest Crichlow
(American, 1914–2005)
Shoe Shine, 1953

Oil on Masonite, 16 1/16 × 12 1/16 in.
Gift of Daniel and Rita Fraad, Jr., 65.204.3
Provenance: Acquired by Barbara Marks, before December 1955; purchased by Daniel Fraad, Jr., and Rita Rich Fraad, December 2, 1955; donated, December 8, 1965.

Made over fifty years apart, the Frederick James Boston and Ernest Crichlow paintings depict two working-class individuals of different ages, races, and genders stealing a moment of respite from their respective toil. A young shoeshiner slumps against his propped knee, perched on a stool presumably in a high trafficked thoroughfare; a woman rests against a dark wall in a quiet interior.

By the late nineteenth century, literacy rates for women had grown exponentially, and depictions of women reading further contributed to shifting ideas around agency and gender roles. Reading not only asserted a woman's intellectual capacity but also served as a form of "portable privacy," as art historian Kathryn Brown notes.[1] Here, Boston captured a woman turning her attention away from dirty dishes to read a newspaper. Indeed, for both women and Black Americans, literacy offered a pathway to emancipation and greater self-determination.

First-generation Caribbean immigrant artist Crichlow represented the experiences of Black Americans at the height of segregation, which were characterized by limited opportunities and access to housing, education, and work. Both Brooklyn-based artists, Boston and Crichlow infused their compositions with a quiet dignity that animates, rather than flattens, the complex social and cultural contexts from which their subjects emerge.

SSW

1. Kathryn Brown, *Women Readers in French Painting 1870–1890* (Farnham, UK: Ashgate, 2012), chapter 1.

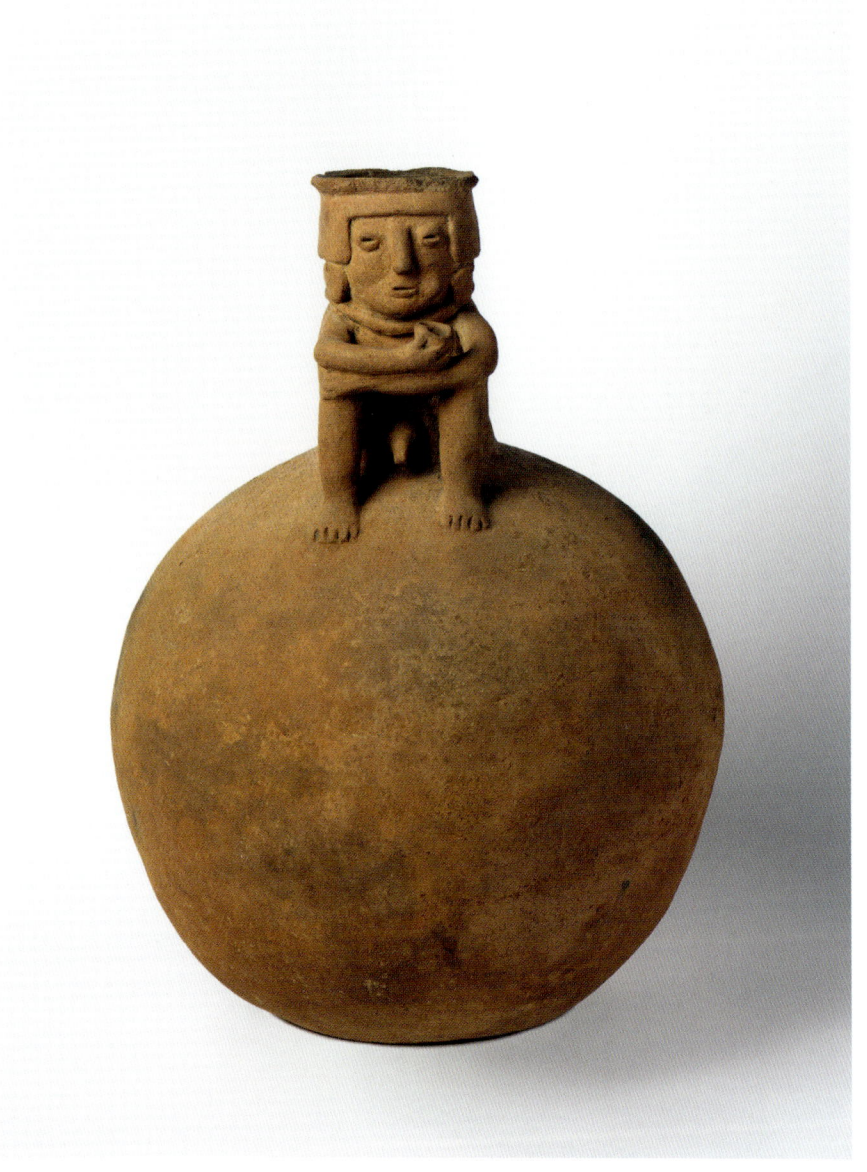

Possibly Carchi artist
Jar Decorated with a Seated Figure
El Angel, Carchi, Ecuador, 1000–1500

Ceramic, 16½ × 12⅛ × 3¼ in.
Museum Expedition 1938, Dick S. Ramsay Fund, 39.282
Provenance: Purchased in Colombia, Ecuador, or Peru by Herbert Spinden for the Brooklyn Museum, 1938.

A modeled human figure forms the mouth and neck of this large storage jar from the northern sierras of Ecuador. The male figure sits calmly while chewing a quid, or wad, of coca leaves in his left cheek. Coca leaves are chewed by Indigenous people in the Andean region to increase energy and alleviate hunger. The figure holds a cup in his right hand, perhaps representing a beverage or powdered lime. The latter is used to activate the stimulant properties of the coca leaves. The jar was possibly used for storing water or *chicha*, a fermented maize beverage.

The ceramic sculpture of a seated nude woman, with hands resting on hips and closed eyes, conveys a relaxed, meditative state. Its highly polished red and cream surface is characteristic of the Nayarit-Lagunillas style of Mexico's Pacific coast. In some variants of the style, female figures are rendered abstractly with heads and faces enlarged and flattened, legs splayed outward, and special designs to accentuate the hips and genital area. Her flattened head, a sign of beauty, reflects the practice of cranial deformation in which an infant's skull was shaped by applying pressure to padded boards strapped on opposite sides of the head. Typical of the Lagunillas style, the woman's hair is represented by parallel incised lines, and she wears large fan-shaped, multiple-hoop earrings. The sculpture would have been one of many offerings placed in a shaft-and-chamber tomb to honor and accompany the dead.[1]

NR

1. Kristi Butterwick, *Heritage of Power: Ancient Sculpture from West Mexico, The Andrall E. Pearson Family Collection* (New York: Metropolitan Museum of Art; New Haven, CT, and London: Yale University Press, 2004): 30, 34–35, and 89.

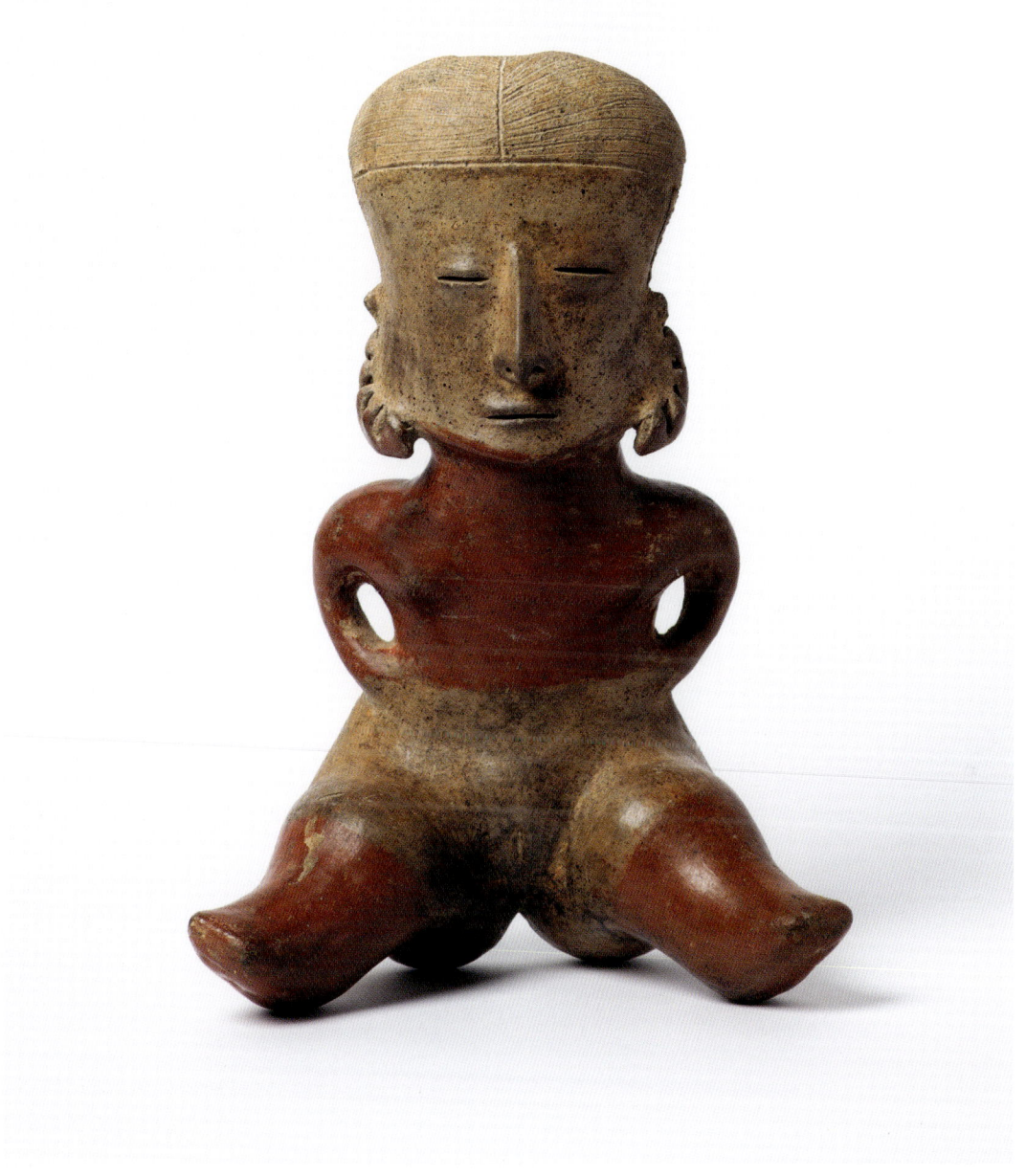

Nayarit artist
Female Figure
Nayarit, Mexico, 100–300

Ceramic, 13 × 9½ × 5½ in.
Purchased with funds given by Joseph F. McCrindle, 64.12
Provenance: Acquired by John Stokes, by February 1964; purchased by the Brooklyn Museum, February 5, 1964.

A Quiet Place

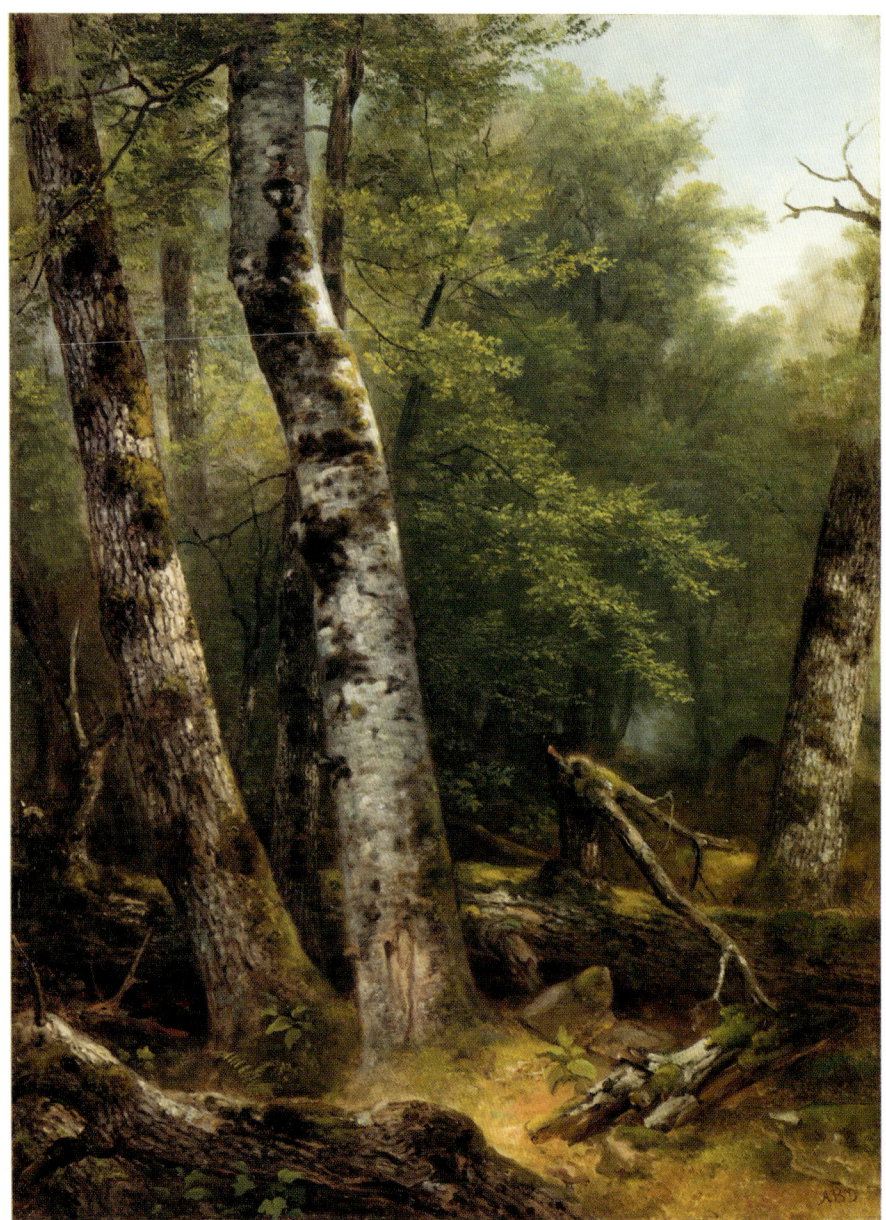

Asher Brown Durand
(American, 1796–1886)
Landscape (Birch and Oaks), ca. 1855–57

Oil on canvas, 23 15/16 × 17 7/8 in.
Bequest of Charles A. Schieren, 15.326
Provenance: Acquired by Charles Adolph Schieren, before December 31, 1912; bequeathed, April 5, 1915.

Thomas Cole
(American, born England, 1801–1848)
A View of the Two Lakes and Mountain House, Catskill Mountains, Morning, 1844

Oil on canvas, 35 13/16 × 53 7/8 in.
Dick S. Ramsay Fund, 52.16
Provenance: Acquired from the artist by Henry S. Mulligan, by 1845; inherited through the family by Mr. Cox, by 1952. Acquired by Victor Spark, by 1952; purchased by the Brooklyn Museum, by exchange, February 15, 1952.

Mosses were the first plants to blanket the Earth. I wouldn't be surprised if they are also the last.[1]
—Robin Wall Kimmerer

Mosses are as ancient as they are adaptable. They evolved to grow on land since the continents first emerged from the ocean floor. Having no roots, mosses can thrive even when growing on inorganic surfaces, flourishing where other plants may not survive.[2] A witness to the passage of time, these hearty and primordial plants are harbingers of decay and archives of resilience. Yet the presence of moss is also protective and indicates new life amid perpetual change.

    In Thomas Cole's *A View of the Two Lakes and Mountain House*, a hiker—possibly the artist himself—stands in the foreground on Sunset Rock in the Catskill Mountains. He looks toward the popular Catskill Mountain House, established in 1824 for tourists seeking respite from urban centers. The hotel sat on a tree-cleared ledge that offered visitors a panoramic view of New York's Hudson River Valley. At the composition's right are two lakes, today joined as one called North-South Lake. Under the hiker's feet and covering the craggy rocks and trees around him is a layer of moss. A sign of an ancient landscape, the moss underscores the mountain's timelessness and magnitude, even in the face of

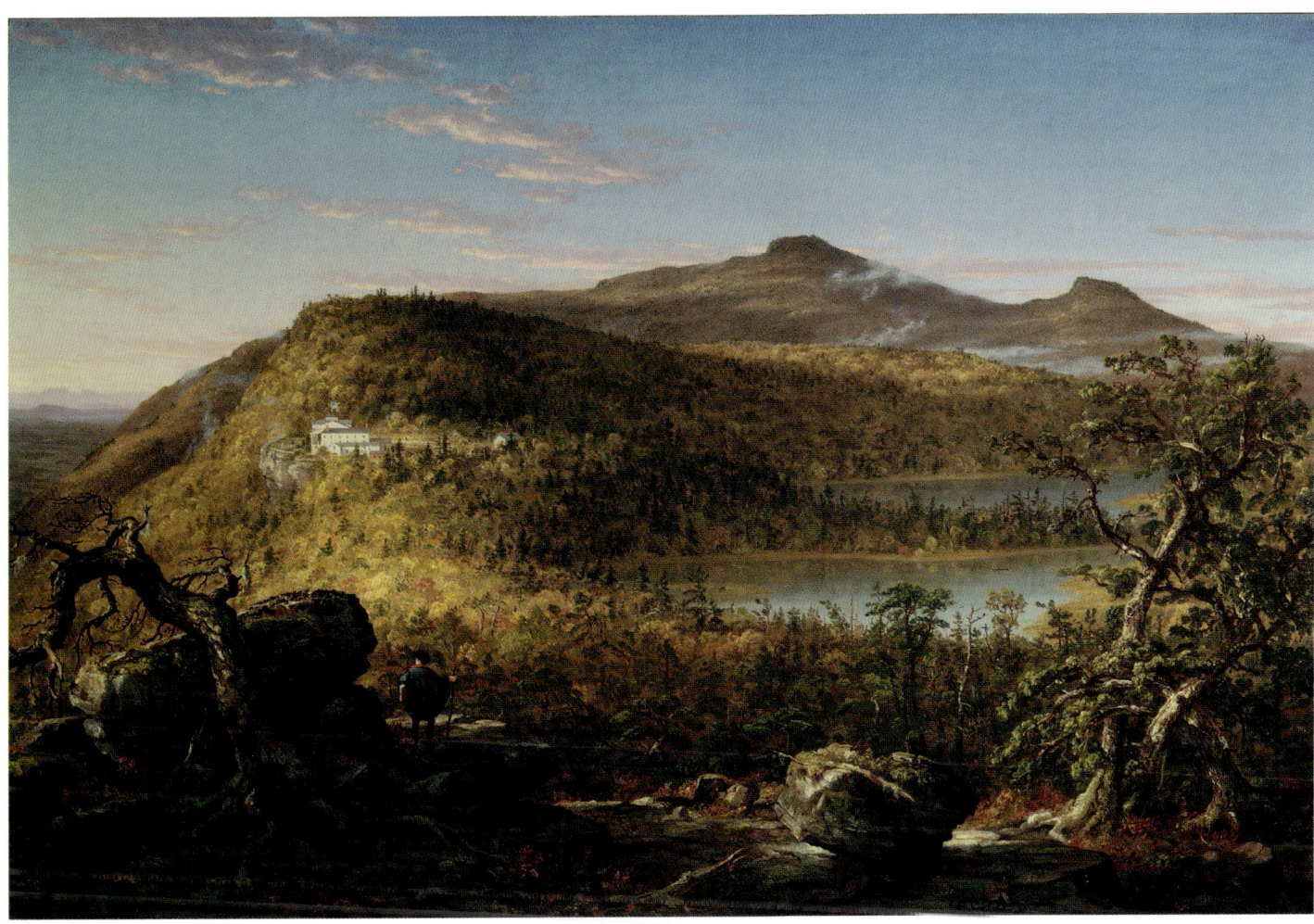

settler presence and intervention. According to Potawatomi botanist and scholar Robin Wall Kimmerer, "in the Anishinaabe languages of Skywoman, our words for moss, *aasaakamig* and *aasaakamek*, carry the meaning 'those ones who cover the earth.'"[3] Amid transformations in the Hudson Valley and Catskills caused by tourism and industry, the moss-covered expanse is where Cole sought rest and reflection, visually asserting the power of the natural world and rejecting expansionist policies that fueled rapid development in the region.[4]

The presence of moss also looms large in paintings by Asher Brown Durand, who, like Cole, revered the woods as an inherently spiritual place, where truth and beauty are the rewards of close study. Mosses stretch out their spongy leaves, blanketing every surface in deep green, yellow, and earthy brown patches. Their presence and biodiversity suggest the cool dark wetness of their preferred habitat, creating the painting's mood as much as any brushwork. Indeed, Durand mastered a state of quietude in his signature forest interior scenes, and *Landscape (Birch and Oaks)* exemplifies the artist's distinctive style. Compressed, vertical, and painted with a precision that reveals the artist's careful study of nature, the composition of mossy logs and lush foliage creates an intimate sanctuary.

CG/SSW

1. Robin Wall Kimmerer, "Ancient Green: Moss, Climate, and Deep Time," *Emergence Magazine*, April 20, 2022, https://emergencemagazine.org/essay/ancient-green/.
2. Ibid.; and Robin Wall Kimmerer, *Gathering Moss: A Natural and Cultural History of Mosses* (Corvallis: Oregon State University Press, 2003).
3. Kimmerer, "Ancient Green."
4. Angela Miller, "Thomas Cole and Jacksonian America: *The Course of Empire* as Political Allegory," *Prospects* 14 (October 1989): 65–92.

I always had taken me some quilt pieces in the fields when I was working there, and when I knock off work at twelve to eat, I make me a block or so till I go back to the fields. When the field days ended, I went to making quilts most all the time when I wasn't sewing and making clothes for my children to wear.[1]

—Lucy T. Pettway

Through the act of creating objects for everyday use, a community develops and expresses its visual and material culture. For centuries, Indigenous people and those descended from Africans in the Americas have innovated their creative traditions in response to genocide, forced migration, enslavement, and displacement. Historically made by women, quilts were often created for protection against unpredictable winters in unheated shacks, and for relaxation at day's end after backbreaking labor. In the last two decades, Southern Black quilting practices have been recognized for their beauty, intricacy, and ingenuity.

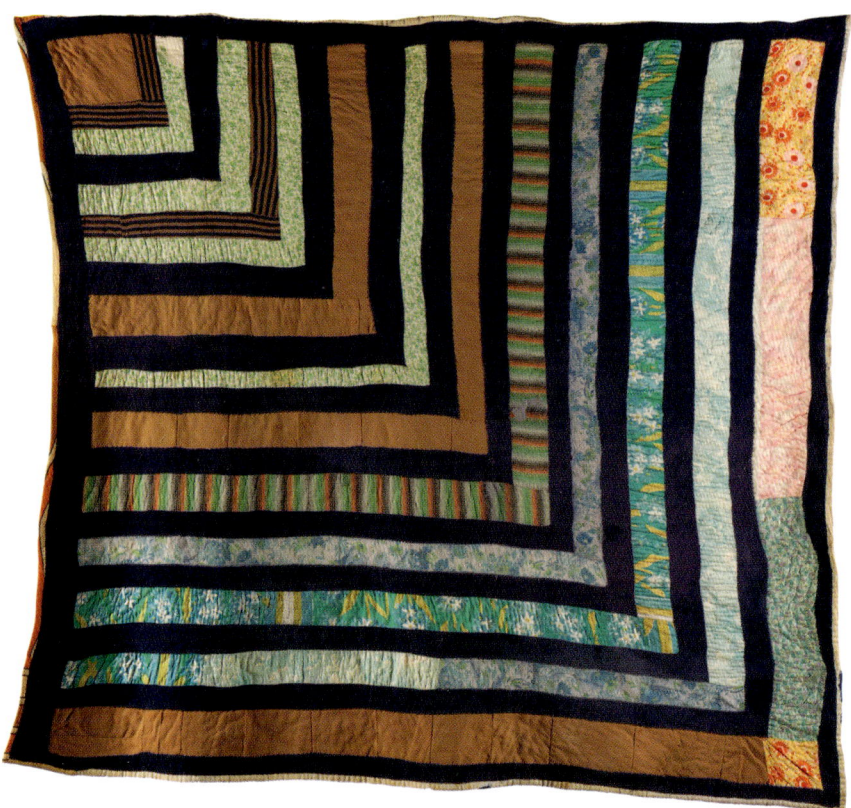

> I started piecing quilts when I was probably about twelve. I loved to sew. I watched my mama, and got me some cloth, and went to piecing. The first quilt I ever made was a "Lazy Gal." I was thirteen. Then a "Nine Patch." Then I went to string quilts, just sewing pieces together. Old clothes we didn't wear no more, that's what we made them out of then.[2]

A southern Black woman from a rural Alabama hamlet known as Gee's Bend, Lucy T. Pettway mastered innumerable complex patterns and techniques in her more than seventy-year career, including those represented here. While other quilters often stuck to and mastered one or two patterns or styles, Pettway, her mother, and aunts were renowned for their experimentation based on patterns sourced from books, visual phenomena observed in nature or riffed on compositions made by other quilters in the community. This quilt is an exceptional example of one of the most popular patterns in Gee's Bend. Dominated by concentric squares, the *Housetop* pattern is typically pieced from a starter square, with an improvisational pattern then formed by adding strips and additional squares.

SSW

Lucy T. Pettway
(American, 1921–2004)
Quilt, Housetop Pattern, ca. 1945

Cotton, 73 ¼ × 83 ¾ × ¼ in.
Gift of the Souls Grown Deep Foundation from the William S. Arnett Collection, 2018, 2018.37.2
Provenance: Acquired by William S. Arnett, before 2018; transferred to the Souls Grown Deep Foundation, by 2018; donated, October 23, 2018.

1. "Lucy T. Pettway," interview, Souls Grown Deep Foundation, accessed August 12, 2024, https://www.soulsgrowndeep.org/artist/lucy-t-pettway.
2. Ibid.

So much of Lakota artwork is related to either the adornment of an individual or of your relatives. Creating a fully beaded cradleboard that you're going to carry your newborn in means you're surrounding them with beauty. It is an act of love, it's an act of honoring, it's an act of bringing your love for a person into physical form, and wrapping them in it.[1]

—Dyani White Hawk, Sičáŋǧu Lakota artist

For countless generations, Indigenous women from the Great Plains have lovingly crafted cradleboards like this before the birth of a newborn. Here, a buffalo hide carrier adorned with thousands of tiny seed beads attaches to a lattice of painted wooden boards ornamented with metalwork. This embellishment demonstrates the family's adoration of the child. Traditionally, artists used dyed and manipulated porcupine quills to decorate such objects. However, once they were forced onto reservations, many artists lost access to porcupine quills and others looked for new media, so they acquired beads in bulk through trade with white settlers to sustain their creative practices.

Viewed as protection for the beginning of life, cradleboards comforted babies by mimicking the snug embrace of their loved ones. Carefully swaddled within, they rested peacefully in a tipi or while in transit, riding on a horse or a mother's back. Trinkets often hung from the top of the hood to delight babies. These miniature versions of objects used by adults, like the teapot used here, reflected the responsibilities of adulthood. To this day, artists make cradleboards to envelope their communities in warmth, beauty, and protection.

—DT

1. Victoria Ahmadizadeh Melendez and Dyani White Hawk, "Victoria and Dyani on Beads, Re(writing) and Relations," November 20, 2023, in *GEEX Talks Q&A Podcast*, 1:15:48, https://geex.glass/programming/geextalks/.

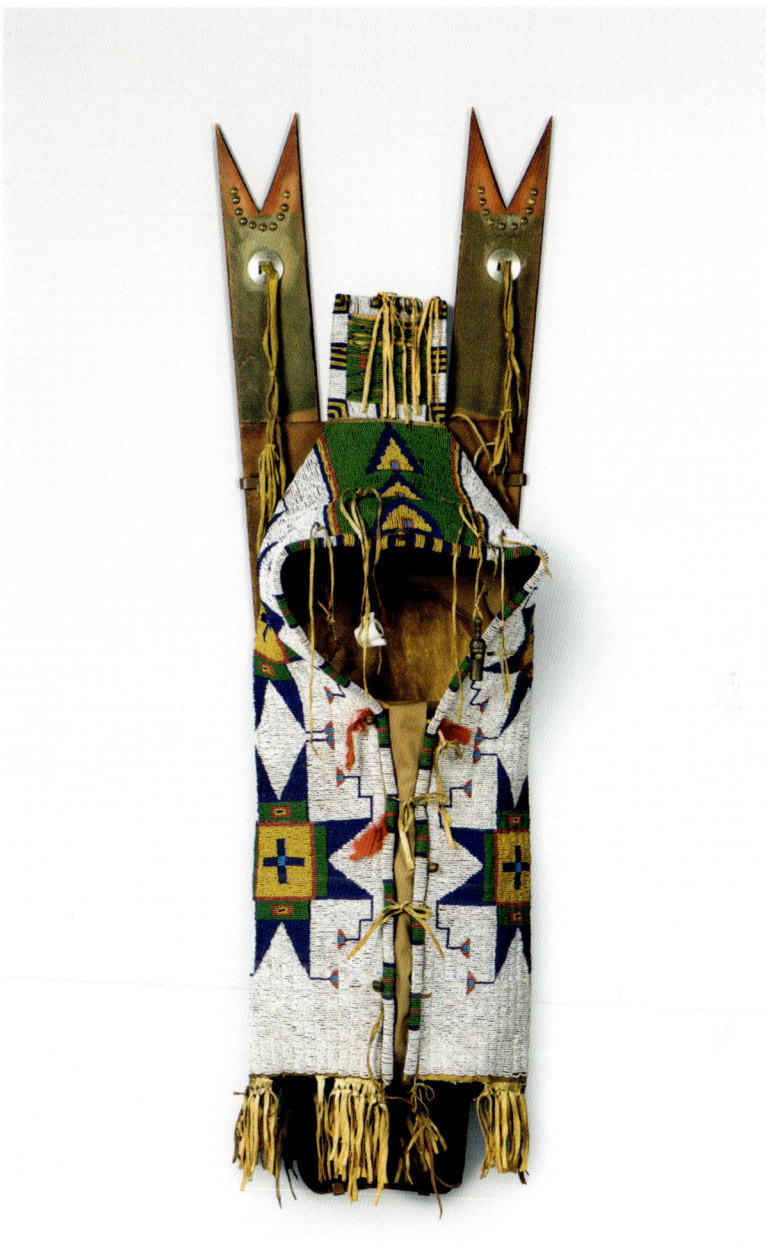

Očhéthi Šakówiŋ artist
Cradleboard with Attached Toys
Northern Plains, 1870–1900

Buffalo hide, wood, glass beads, metal, ceramic, porcupine quills, brass nails, pigment, 32 5/16 × 12 3/16 × 7 in.
Dick S. Ramsay Fund, 38.630
Provenance: Acquired by M. William Bradley, before 1938; purchased at Samuel T. Freeman & Co., "The Unusual Collections of American Indian Rarities from the Estate of the late M. William Bradley," by the Brooklyn Museum, November 21 or 22, 1938.

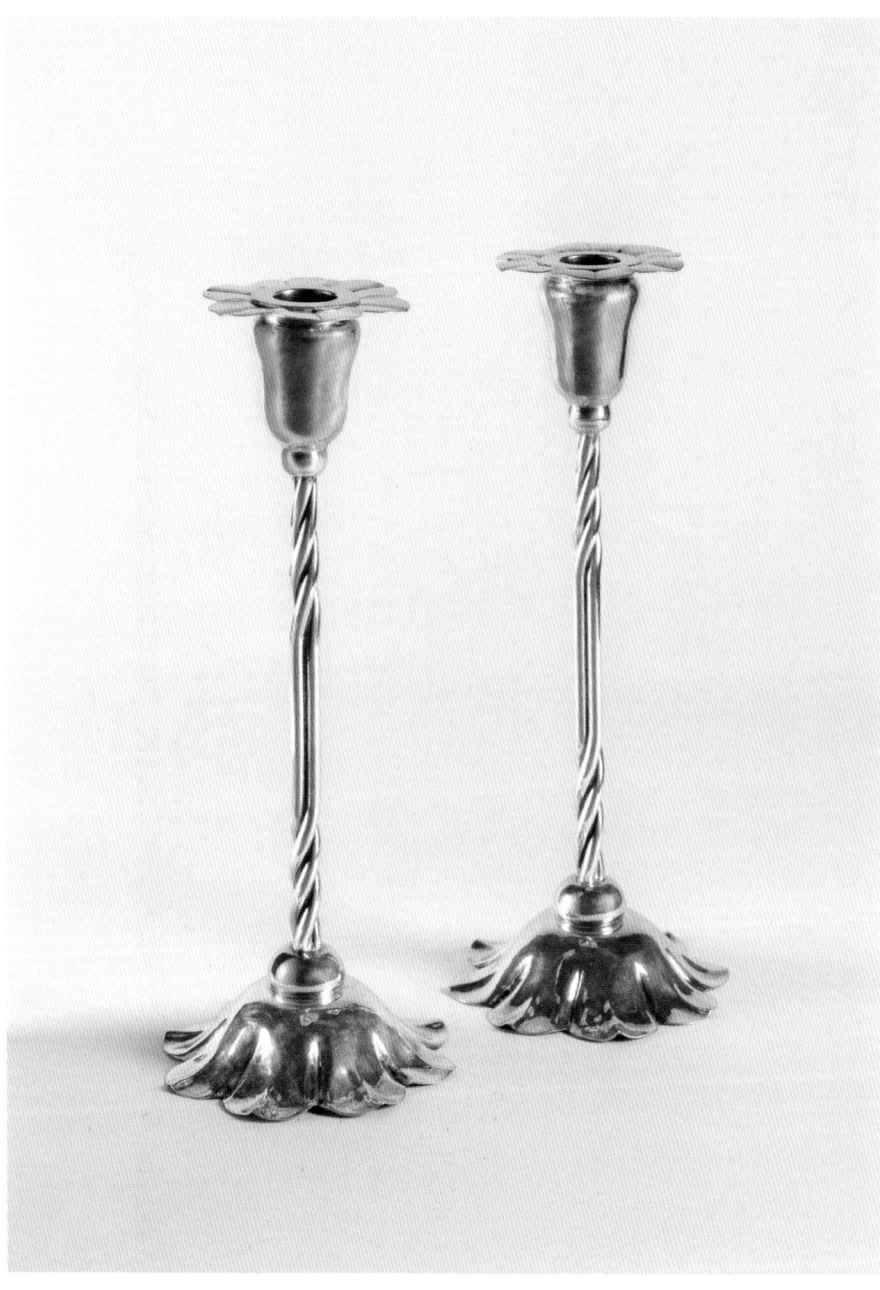

Marie Zimmermann
(American, 1879–1972)
Candlesticks, 1921–25

Sterling silver, 12½ × 5¼ in. each
Alfred T. and Caroline S. Zoebisch Fund, 2015.25.1a-b, 2015.25.2a-b
Provenance: Acquired by an unidentified collector, by 1997; sold at Christie's, New York, December 12, 1997. Acquired by Max Palevsky, before May 5, 2010, until at least December 15, 2010. Acquired by Robert Mehlman, by 2015; purchased by the Brooklyn Museum, April 9, 2015.

Herter Brothers
New York, New York, 1864–1906
Architectural Elements from the Sloane-Griswold House, 883 Fifth Avenue, New York, ca. 1881

Mahogany, marble, brass, glass: 14¾ × 100¼ × 7 in.
Gift of Mrs. William E. S. Griswold in memory of her father, John Sloane, 41.980.15, 41.980.16, 41.980.17.1-3, 41.980.72a-e
Provenance: Purchased from Herter Brothers by John Sloane, 1882; inherited by Adela Berry Sloane (Mrs. John Sloane), 1905; probably inherited by Evelyn Sloane Griswold (Mrs. William E. S. Griswold), 1911; donated, September 9, 1941.

American nineteenth-century upper-middle-class homes often had rooms, such as libraries, dedicated to specific activities, with the interior woodwork, lighting, and decorative objects reinforcing not only style and taste, but also function. Libraries could be refuges from the bustle and stresses of daily life in grand New York residences, and, therefore, were often paneled with dark woods, hung with luxurious textiles, and furnished with comfortable upholstered seating. This created a private refuge, or a sanctuary away from public or social events.

This mahogany mantelpiece is a component from an entire room; the paneling and contents of the library from the New York City residence of John Sloane, that once stood at 883 Fifth Avenue, at 69th Street, in Manhattan. The room was designed by the foremost American nineteenth-century interior decorating and furniture manufacturing firm of Herter Brothers, suppliers to some of the wealthiest American industrialists, or "robber barons." The New York firm of W. & J. Sloane, purveyors of textiles for curtains, carpets, and upholstery, frequently collaborated with Herter Brothers, to supply the "soft goods" for the interiors. Here, Herter Brothers supplied the furnishings for the library of John Sloane, president of W. & J. Sloane.

The Sloane library was paneled in woodwork inspired by English seventeenth-century examples, yet decorated with Japanese mixed metal and enameled vases and chargers, or large plates, Italian ceramics, South Asian metalwork, luxurious embroidered silk curtains, and American paintings, all still retained in the Museum's collection.

CF

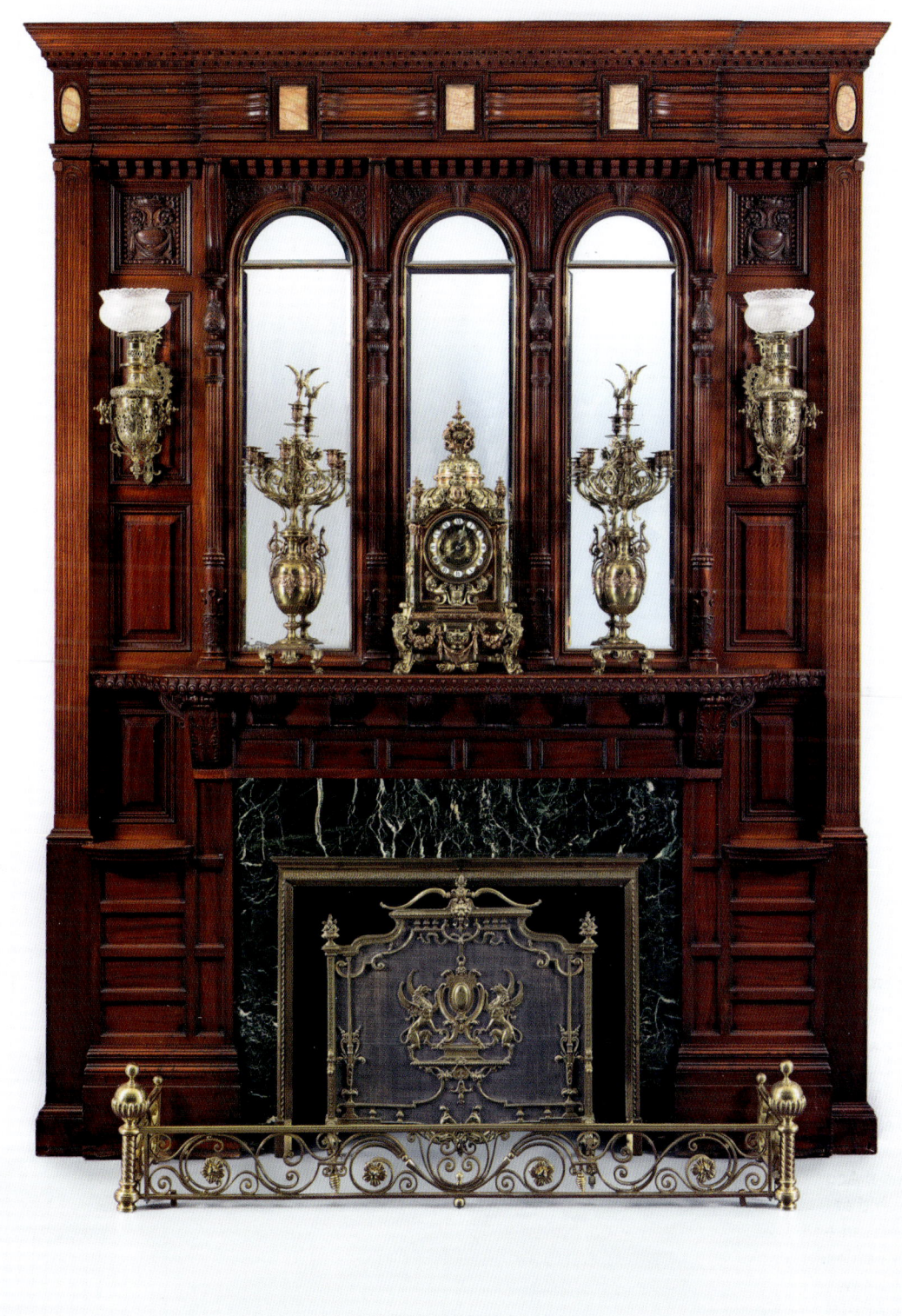

A Quiet Place

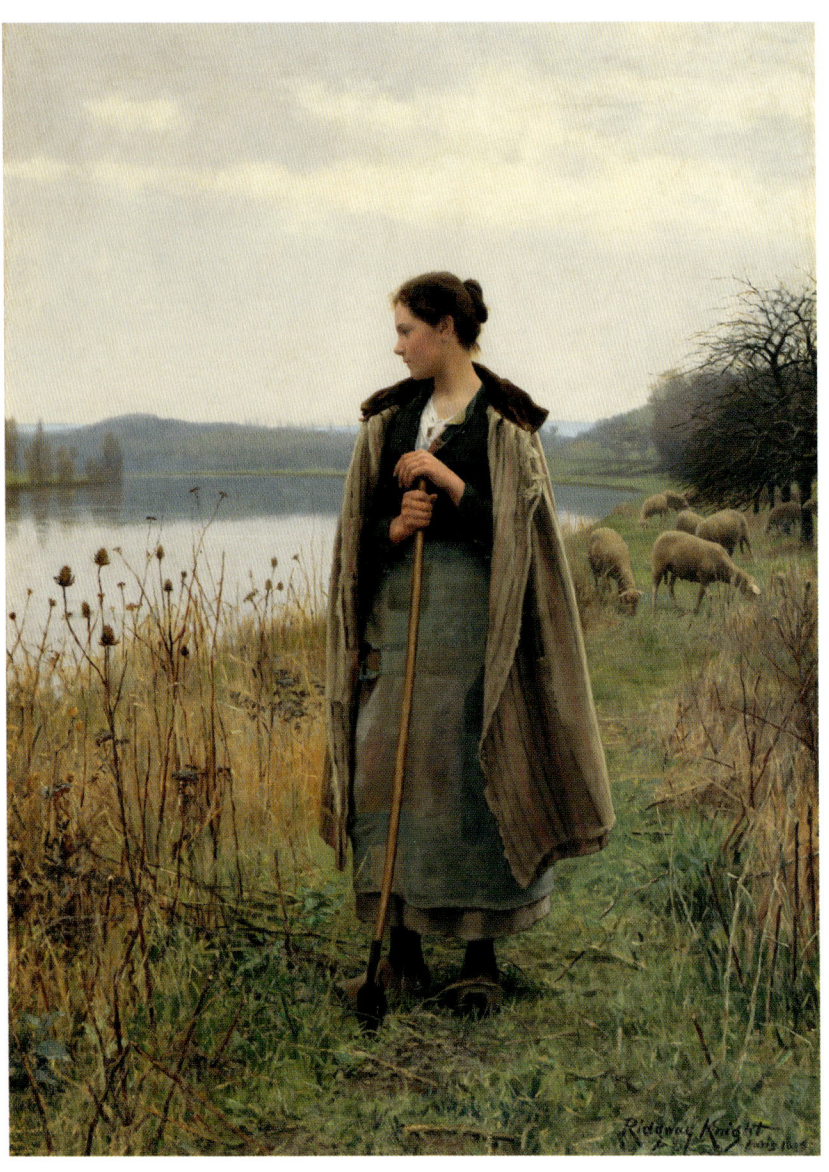

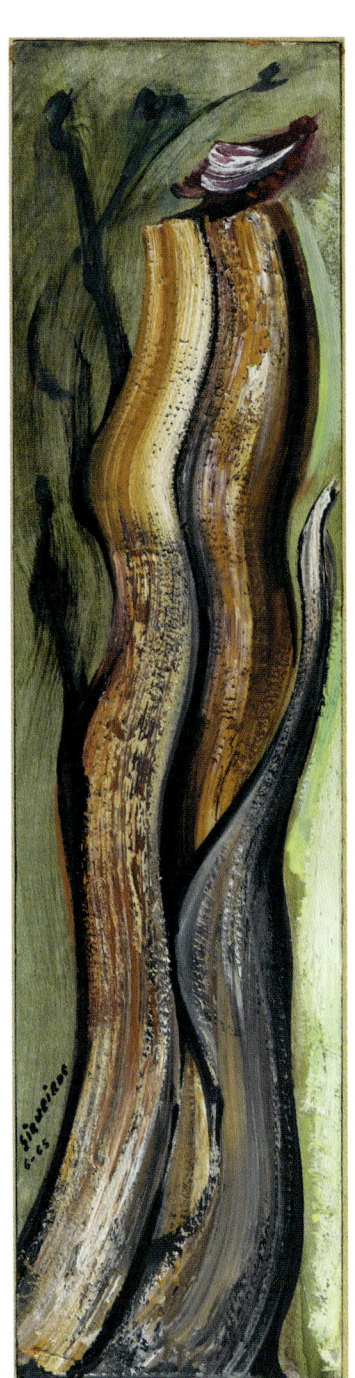

Daniel Ridgway Knight
(American, 1839–1924)
The Shepherdess of Rolleboise, 1896

Oil on canvas, 68 × 50½ in.
Gift of Abraham Abraham, 98.14
Provenance: Purchased, probably from the artist, by Abraham Abraham, ca. 1896; donated, 1898.

David Alfaro Siqueiros
(Mexican, 1896–1974)
Arbol Fondo, 1965

Oil on panel, 47½ × 12 in.
Gift of the Beatrice and Samuel A. Seaver Foundation, 2004.30.20
Provenance: Acquired by Beatrice and Samuel A. Seaver, by 1992; donated by the Beatrice and Samuel A. Seaver Foundation, 2004.

Toward Joy

CRITICAL SHORT

Rest Life

Tricia Hersey

You can rest

You can rest

You can rest

You can rest

Welcome to the Dream Space

This is a transmission

A download

A daydream

Breathe in

Breathe in your imagination

Stay here

Stay in rest

Stay in the dream space

Our collective rest will save us

Welcome to the Dream Space

Another world is possible

You are enough

Our dreams are enough

This is imagination work

Imagine you have everything you need

Imagine a world with justice

Imagine a world where capitalism doesn't exist

Poverty is no longer created

Welcome to your Dream Space

A portal opens when we rest

When we nap

When we stop

When we sleep

When we have silence

Stay here

You can daydream

You can daydream

Welcome to the Dream Space

Daydream you have everything you need

You have everything you need

You have everything you need

This is a transmission

Daydream

Daydream

Stay here

This is imagination work

This is dream work

Welcome to your Dream Space

You can just be

You can just be

**RELEASED NOVEMBER 2021
BY THE NAP MINISTRY**

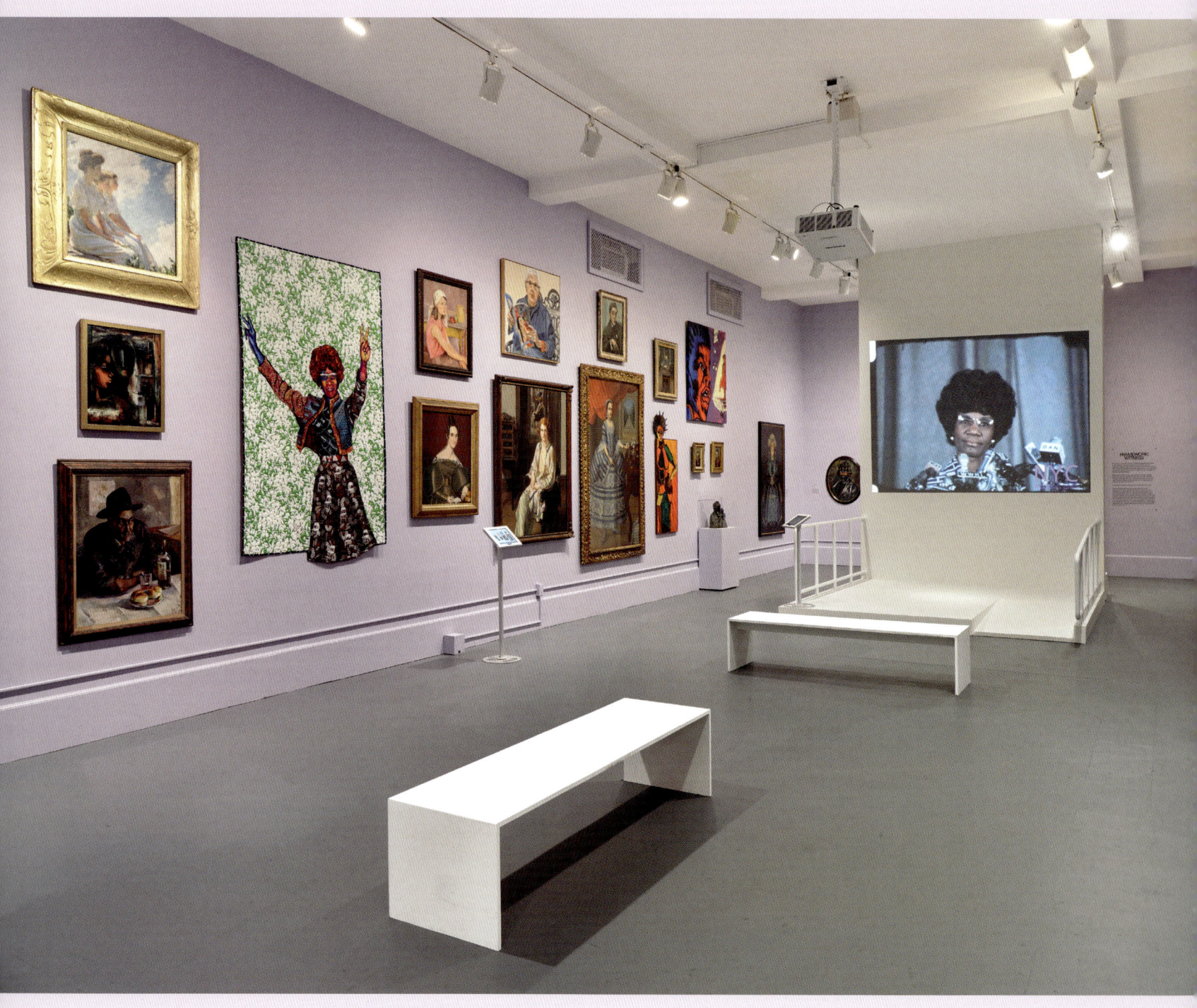

FRAMEWORK

Witness

For many communities, the act of bearing witness holds deep social, political, and spiritual significance. Subverting the language of legal systems that have historically disenfranchised them, these communities adopted and redirected "witnessing" and "testifying" to express personal and communal suffering and subjugation—but also joy and liberation.

Witnessing is distinct from merely looking. To bear witness means you are accountable to what you have seen. Whether in fast-paced, high-tech, high-consumption environments, or a quiet gallery in a large art museum, we sometimes take the act of looking, and of witnessing culture, for granted.

This framework is about seeing, but it is also about being seen.

Historically, making portraits has been an essential tool of visual self-determination. Commissioned portraits let sitters determine how they present themselves and are seen, as well as fundamentally affirming their existence and significance. These representations influenced self-identity and countered overtly racist and dehumanizing imagery even while images of and by white people dominated the narrative of the genre, particularly in the Americas.

Portraits made in the American colonies were linked to projects of nation-building, as European settlers strove to define themselves anew, often using the artistic traditions and visual vocabularies of past civilizations, as well as the societies from which they strove to extract and distinguish themselves. Thus, representing oneself moved beyond a mere status gesture to one that drove identity formation on a national scale, and produced an early popular culture rooted in pictures.

Artists have always invoked the power of witnessing within their art, and the presentation of this framework in the galleries emphasizes this notion. With depictions of subjects with distinct and direct gazes, facing out at the viewer—and in-person, directed toward an in-gallery stage—the artworks formally bear witness to the present. Whether visitors direct their attention to the stage—where performance, teaching, or political action is taking place—take selfies, or deliver their own impromptu verse, their very presence, as your attention here, activates the relationships embedded in the installation and in these pages, challenging and complicating what American art is and how it should be experienced.

SSW

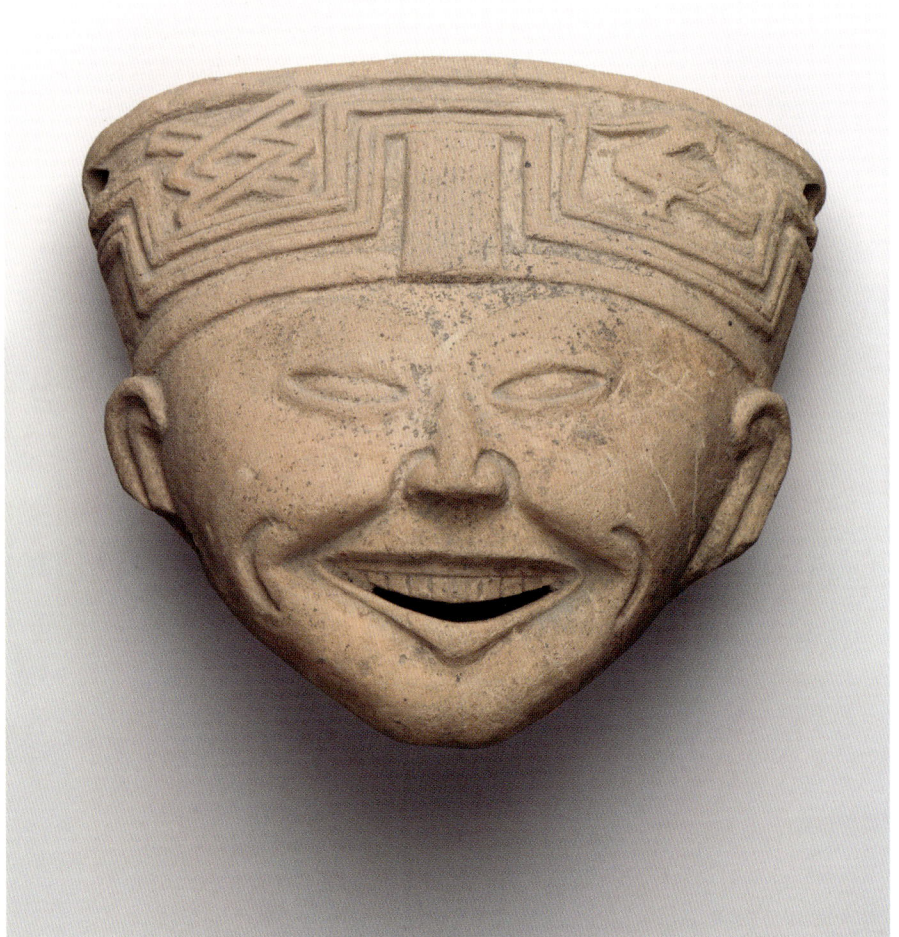

South Central Veracruz artist
Head of a Laughing Man
Veracruz, Mexico, 600–900

Ceramic, 6 × 6¾ × 4¼ in.
Gift of Princess Gourielli (Mme Helena Rubinstein), 53.149.2
Provenance: Possibly acquired by Julius Carlebach Gallery, before 1953. Acquired by Helena Rubinstein, by 1953; donated, 1953.

This smiling ceramic head of a laughing man was once attached to a complete figurine. The expressive face has modeled features including a naturalistic nose. Laugh lines frame the open mouth in which a row of teeth is visible below the upper lip. The headdress is decorated with a geometric step pattern surrounding two twined chevrons and a bird, which resembles a pelican.

The complete figurines often wear elaborate garments, headdresses, and ornaments, and have their hands raised as if in supplication. Called *sorientes* (smiling figures), the ceramic sculptures have been found at the archaeological site of El Zapotal in south-central Veracruz. One of the site's ceremonial mounds, Mound 2, contains an elaborate funerary complex that provides a ritual context for understanding the function of these figurines.

Smiling figures, and hundreds of other offerings, were discovered associated with two hundred human burials in the vicinity of an earthen structure dedicated to Chane, the God of Death. One of the figurines has its hands raised in homage, and is depicted wearing a headdress adorned with a heron, a waterbird commonly found in the rivers and estuaries of the region.[1] The pelican depicted on this smiling head also frequents Veracruz's coastal waters. Based upon this ritual context, these smiling figures served as guardians and companions to the human dead.

NR

1. Cherra Wyllie, "The Mural Paintings of El Zapotal, Veracruz, Mexico," *Ancient Mesoamerica* 21, no. 2 (Fall 2010): 209–27, 214.

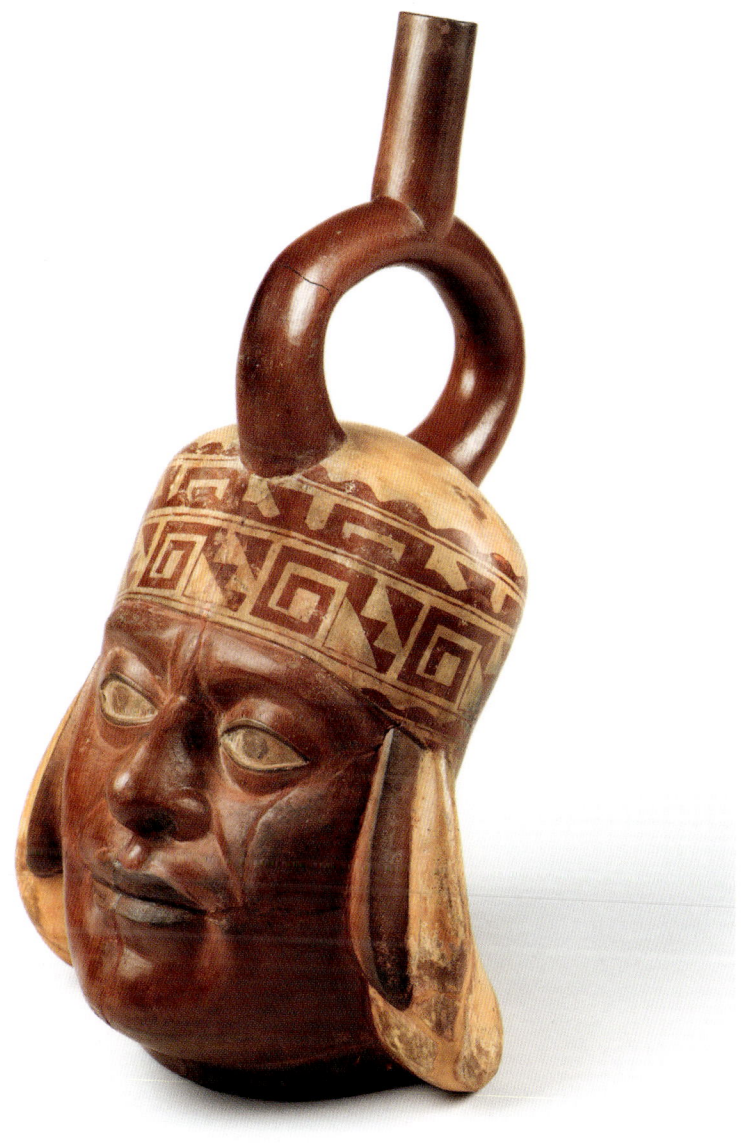

Moche artist
Portrait Vessel of Man
North Coast, Peru, 100–800

Ceramic, pigment, 13 x 7¾ x 9 in.
Gift of Mrs. Eugene Schaefer, 36.331
Provenance: Acquired by Mrs. Eugene Schaefer, by 1936; donated, July 1, 1936.

The Moche culture, which flourished on the northern coast of present-day Peru from 100 to 800 C.E., was one of the ancient civilizations in the Americas to perfect true portraiture.[1] Moche potters skillfully captured the distinctive facial features of specific individuals, almost always adult men, on elaborately modeled and painted ceramic vessels.[2] In some instances, these lifelike portraits commemorated an important person, probably a community leader, who is represented from childhood to adulthood.[3] This vessel depicts a mature man with expressive features and a direct gaze. He wears a white cloth over his head that is further adorned with a woven tapestry headband with bold geometric designs. While we do not know who he is, his powerful presence suggests an esteemed member of the community.

Moche portrait vessels, with or without stirrup-spout handles, were made in two-part clay molds that fit snugly together to create a hollow chamber by joining the front and back of the head. After the molds were removed, the seam on the exterior was smoothed and a stirrup-spout handle, if used, was added. The vessel was then painted with colored slips of clay mixed with water. For this vessel, red and white slips were used and burnished (polished) with a smooth stone or bone implement before the piece was fired in a shallow earthen pit.[4]

Portrait vessels were likely used in the home to hold liquids, based upon signs of wear such as abrasions, chips, and mended breaks. Most vessels in museum collections lack provenience, an archaeological context, but it is likely that they came from burials, placed there after domestic use. Vessels excavated archaeologically have been found almost exclusively in high-status graves of both males and females, suggesting that they may not have been available to commoners.[5]

NR

1. Christopher B. Donnan, *Moche Portraits from Ancient Peru* (Austin: University of Texas Press, 2004), 3.
2. Ibid., 9.
3. Ibid., 1. While each vessel depicts a single person, multiple vessels showing the same individual at different stages of life have been found.
4. For a detailed description of how Moche portrait vessels were made, see ibid., 21–41.
5. Ibid., 10.

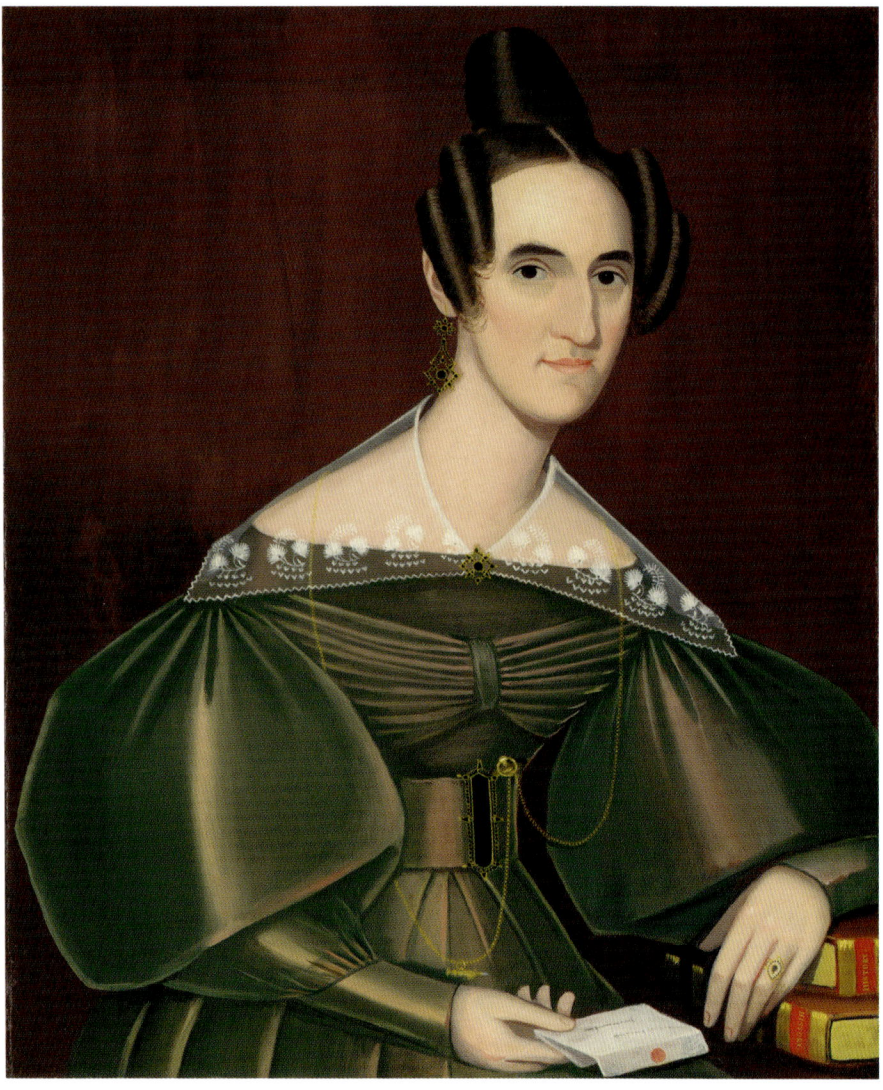

Ammi Phillips
(American, 1788–1865)
Jeannette Woolley, later Mrs. John Vincent Storm, ca. 1838

Oil on canvas, 33 × 27 15/16 in.
Gift of Mrs. Waldo Hutchins, Jr., 69.7
Provenance: Commissioned from the artist for Jeanette Woolley Storm, ca. 1838; inherited through the family by Jeanette Southard, by 1948; donated to Sara S. A. Hutchins (Mrs. Waldo Hutchins, Jr.), 1948; donated, February 5, 1969.

The portrait of Jeannette Woolley captivates the viewer with her striking presence and directed gaze. Accentuated by the voluminous sleeves of her green satin dress, her angular frame is adorned with a sheer lace fichu over her shoulders. Pink and red highlights reflect the satin's sheen, suggesting volume and emphasizing the pleating at her bust and waist. Itinerant portraitist Ammi Phillips posed his subjects against plain backgrounds, with attention focused on clothing, accessories, and props that provide insight into the identity of the individual.[1] Details such as Woolley's delicate gold watch chain with decorative ornament in the shape of a hand, the opened letter she holds, and two volumes of *History* under her arm add interest and character. Typical of Phillips's stylization, Woolley's geometric figure appears rigid, and the lace and jewelry are reduced to basic patterning.

In the late 1830s, Phillips was living in Dutchess County, New York, when he met the Woolley family. A prolific artist, Phillips supported himself entirely through portrait painting, having spent more than twenty-five years pursuing commissions in New York, Massachusetts, Connecticut, and Vermont. He successfully won the favor of the communities into which he moved, which often led to him painting portraits of entire extended families.[2] Around the same time Phillips painted Jeannette Woolley, he also completed portraits of her brother, Henry Peter Pells Woolley, and sister, Sarah Woolley Haxtun, as well as likenesses of Sarah's husband, children, and family cat.[3] Shortly after these portraits were completed, Jeannette married John Vincent Storm, although no Phillips portrait of him has yet been found.

CG

1. Stacy C. Hollander, "Revisiting Ammi Phillips: Fifty Years of American Portraiture," *Folk Art* (Spring 1994): 42–45.
2. Ibid. Hollander suggests that Phillips may have painted as many as 2,000 portraits. Also see Barbara and Lawrence B. Holdridge, *Ammi Phillips: Portrait Painter 1788–1865* (New York: Clarkson N. Potter, 1969) and Stacy C. Hollander, ed., *Revisiting Ammi Phillips: Fifty Years of American Portraiture* (New York: Museum of American Folk Art, 1994).
3. David R. Allaway, *My People: The Works of Ammi Phillips* (2022), 1: 104–105, 205–206; https://issuu.com/n2xb/docs/ammi_phillips_-_abstract_thumbnail.

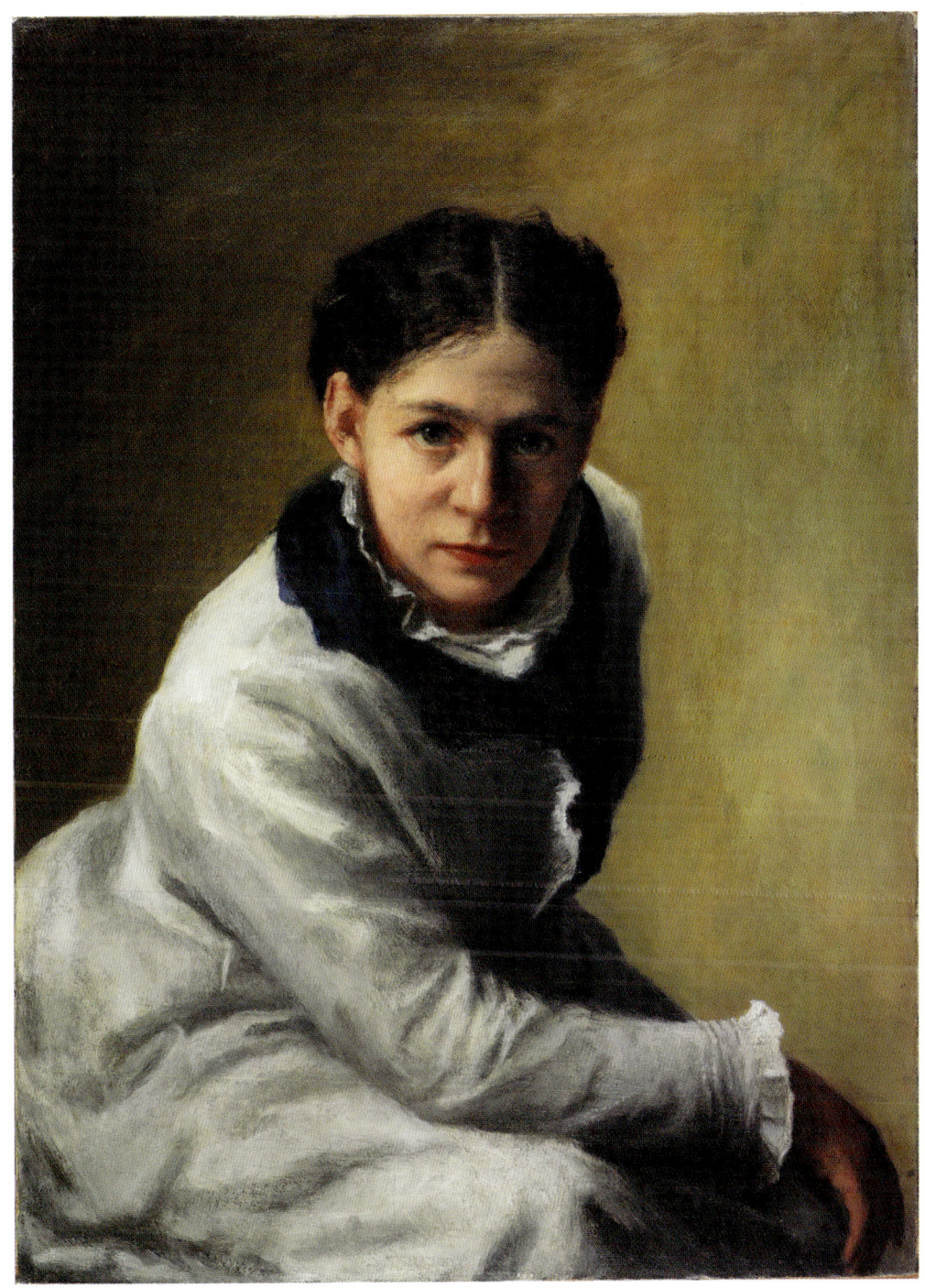

Jane E. Bartlett
(American, active ca. 1872–1899)
Sarah Cowell LeMoyne, 1877

Oil on canvas, 30 1/16 × 22 1/16 in.
Gift of Mrs. A. Augustus Healy, 24.84
Provenance: Acquired from the artist by Mary Theodosia Currier (later Mrs. Aaron Augustus Healy), before 1924; donated, December 10, 1924.

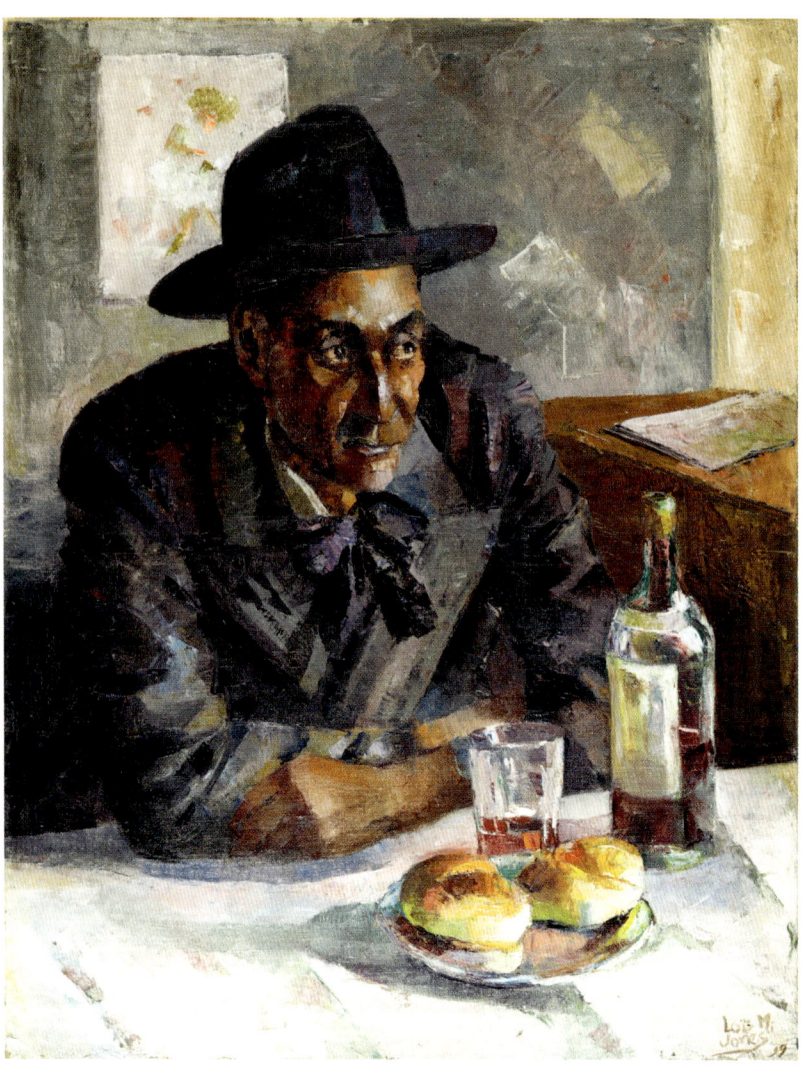

Loïs Mailou Jones
(American, 1905–1998)
Dans un café à Paris (Leigh Whipper), 1939

Oil on canvas, 36 × 29 in.
Brooklyn Museum Fund for African American Art and gift of Auldlyn Higgins Williams and E. T. Williams, Jr., 2012.1
Provenance: With the artist, until 1982. Acquired by Edgar Thomas Williams, Jr., and Auldlyn Higgins Williams, by 2012; donated, January 19, 2012.

Painted within a year of one another and at the advent of World War II, artists Loïs Mailou Jones and Raphael Soyer position their sitters in solitary café scenes that reflect the mood of modern urban life in the wake of the Great Depression. Engaging in a genre scene tradition made popular by European painters like Paul Cézanne (1839–1906), Edgar Degas (1834–1917), Édouard Manet (1832–1883), and Vincent van Gogh (1853–1890), Jones and Soyer use the café scene decades later to similarly reflect the friction between morality, progress, and social isolation.

Leigh Whipper, a Broadway and Hollywood actor, posed for *Dans un café à Paris* at Jones's studio in Washington, DC, the same year he played Crooks in the film adaptation of John Steinbeck's *Of Mice and Men*. Jones's decision to situate Whipper in Paris rather than DC, or New York where he lived, is meaningful. Bringing together Impressionist and Post-Impressionist styles that were popular in France in the decades prior, Jones paints the sitter with hunched posture, in solitude, conveying a sense of wistfulness for a city many Black Americans at the time associated with cosmopolitanism and self-determination.[1]

Jones's portrayal of a pensive Whipper answered Alain LeRoy Locke's call for Black artists to create ennobling representations of Black Americans.[2] "The representational paintings of African Americans that Jones produced at the end of the 1930s and into the 1940s," including the Brooklyn Museum's painting, are "considered part of her 'Locke period,' with their careful, realistic portrayals of Black subjects."[3]

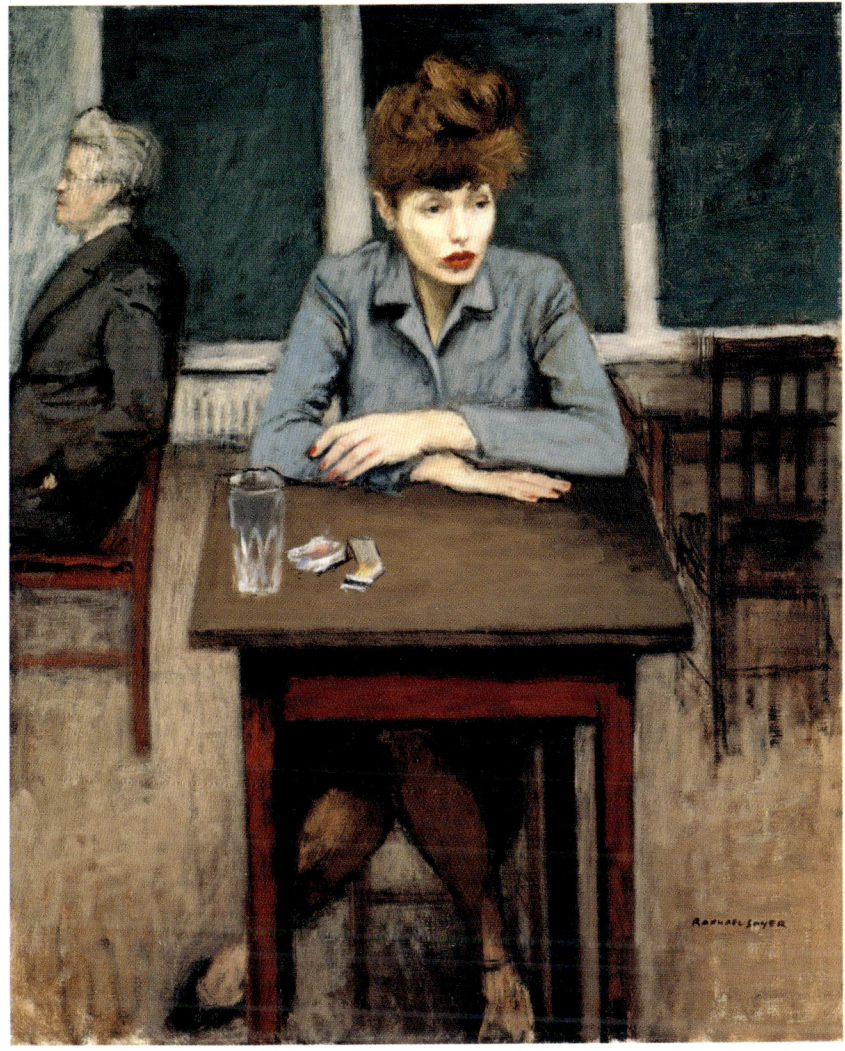

Raphael Soyer
(American, born Russia, 1899–1987)
Cafe Scene, ca. 1940

Oil on canvas, 24 × 20 in.
Gift of James N. Rosenberg, 46.15
Provenance: Purchased from the artist by Julius Zirinsky, by November 30, 1945. Acquired by James Naumburg Rosenberg, by January 2, 1946; donated, January 9, 1946.

Another champion of representational art who was associated with parallel impulses seen in Social Realism and the Fourteenth Street School of artists, Soyer nurtured a lifelong interest in capturing the daily lives of working-class New Yorkers. Painted as though lost in thought, the lone woman in *Cafe Scene* bears a striking resemblance to Soyer's wife, Rebecca Letz, who may have sat for this composition. Stylishly dressed, her weary expression and pose reflect both the strain of absent loved ones and the tension and fatigue women undoubtedly experienced as they entered the workforce en masse during World War II.

The artist observed a significant pattern in his work; despite the pressures he felt to modernize his style toward abstraction, he remained committed to picturing "the life that I have known."[4] He continued: "the emphasis in my work has been on content and mood. I think I have consistently retained [an] enduring quality of frankness of outlook and technique."[5] Less engaged than his peers in social protest, his portrayals of the stark reality most faced during the Depression reveal a poignant vision of the human condition.[6]

Lethargic, lonely, and with empty or half-empty glasses, the sitters in Jones's and Soyer's paintings demonstrate a sensitivity the artists shared for their respective subjects—Jones with the experience of Black Americans and Soyer with largely white working-class New Yorkers—as they are positioned in an iconic space of public sociability in the midst of great sociopolitical tumult.

SSW

1. Rebecca VanDiver, *Designing a New Tradition: Loïs Mailou Jones and the Aesthetics of Blackness* (University Park: The Pennsylvania State University Press, 2020), 96.
2. Locke was an intellectual during the Harlem Renaissance, a movement of the 1920s and '30s that resulted in a blossoming of African American culture.
3. Tritobia Benjamin, *Life and Art of Loïs Mailou Jones,* 50, as cited in VanDiver, *Designing a New Tradition,* 96.
4. Autobiographical notes, Raphael Soyer. Box 2, Folder 13: Articles, Essays, and Lectures, circa 1946–1987. Archives of American Art, accessed June 30, 2024, https://www.aaa.si.edu/collections/raphael-soyer-papers-9465.
5. Ibid.
6. Virginia M. Mecklenburg, *Modern American Realism: The Sara Roby Foundation Collection* (Washington, DC: Smithsonian Institution Press for the National Museum of American Art, 1987), 130.

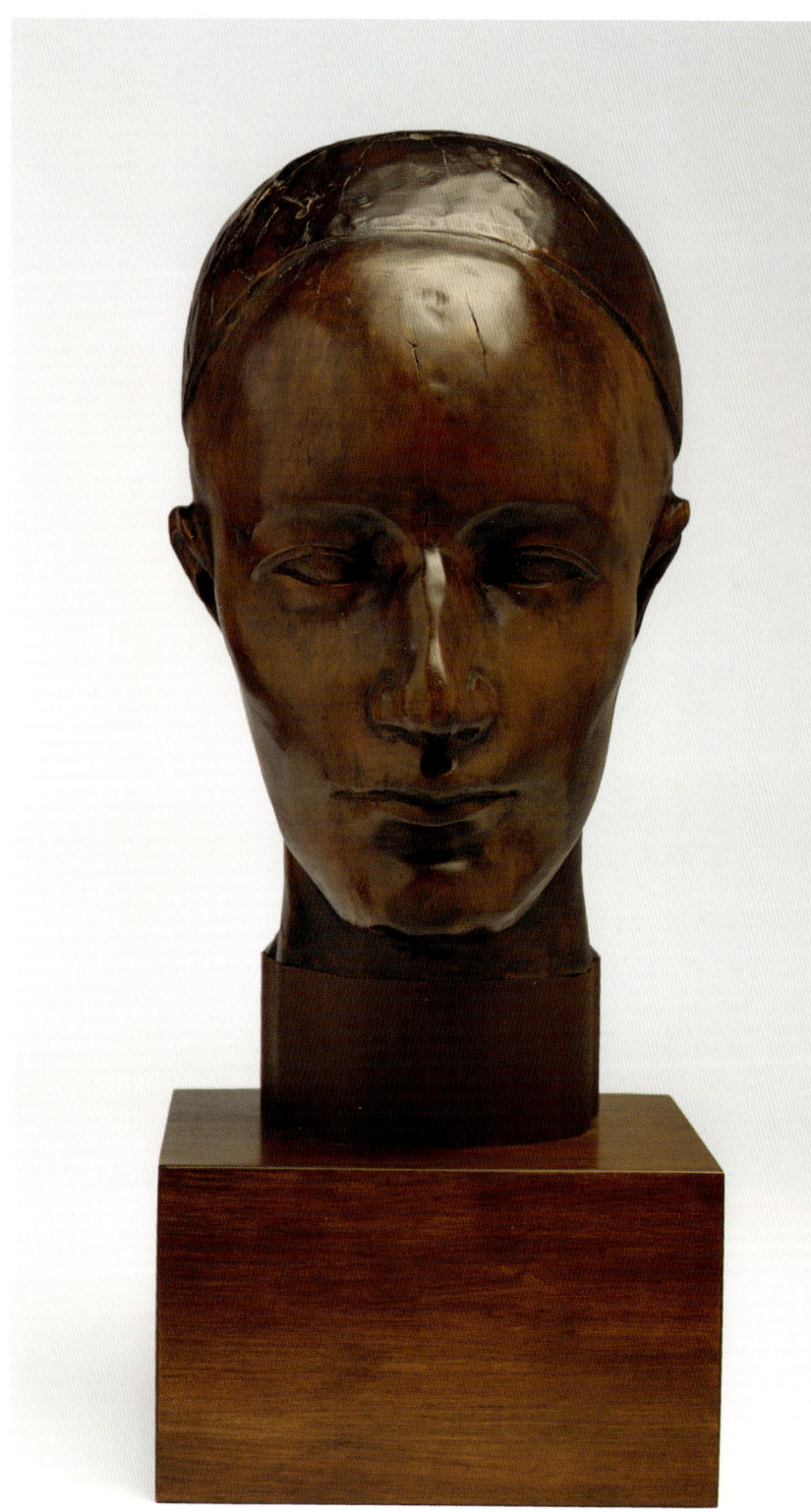

Nancy Elizabeth Prophet
(American, 1890–1960)
Youth (Head in Wood), ca. 1930s

Wood, head: 12¾ × 8¼ × 10¼ in.
Brooklyn Museum Fund for African American Art in honor of Saundra Williams-Cornwell, 2014.3
Provenance: Purchased at an estate sale in Providence, RI, by an unidentified Massachusetts collector, before 1970; purchased at Swann Galleries, "Shadows Uplifted: The Rise of African-American Fine Art," by the Brooklyn Museum, February 13, 2014.

Nancy Elizabeth Prophet's most acclaimed sculptures are celebrated for their ability to convey deep affective meaning, and *Youth (Head in Wood)* is a prime example. Carved from fruitwood, *Youth* is mounted to a separate wooden base, a departure from other similar head sculptures with complete necks. Together with the variation on Prophet's signature, this could suggest the evolution of the artist's intent, or the purpose of the sculpture. There is some speculation around when the work was made, though, if created during her time teaching at Spelman College, *Youth* may have originally served a pedagogical function.

Listed as "Untitled (Head)" at Swann Auctions in 2014, *Youth* is reportedly the first of Prophet's sculptures to come up at auction in the United States. Prior to entering the market, the work had been in private collections, having been sold by Prophet when she returned to Rhode Island in 1944, after leaving her post at Spelman. Upon its arrival at the Brooklyn Museum, Prophet's wooden head underwent extensive conservation treatment for several serious cracks and losses, abrasions, and deteriorating fills, and for the degradation of its original base system. Stabilizing and fill treatments brought *Youth (Head in Wood)* back nearer the sculpture that left the artist's studio, a truly stunning testament to the work of Brooklyn Museum's conservation lab. In form and trajectory, *Youth* reflects the spirit and determination with which Prophet approached her practice, and the finesse and sensitivity with which she treated her materials.

SSW

Raphael Soyer
(American, born Russia, 1899–1987)
Portrait of Eitaro Ishigaki, ca. 1941–43

Oil on canvas, 13 × 10 in.
Augustus Graham School of Design Fund, 2022.41
Provenance: Acquired by Rabin & Krueger Gallery, before 1970; purchased by Franklin Simon, by 1970. Acquired by Pook & Pook Inc., by 2022; purchased by Jarrett McCusker, 2022; purchased by the Brooklyn Museum, December 15, 2022.

Committed to Social Realism, artist Raphael Soyer was best known for representing everyday scenes of people in New York City as well as for his portraits of family members and friends, several of which are in the Brooklyn Museum's collection. One such work depicts his friend and fellow artist Eitaro Ishigaki. Typical of his portraits of artists, Soyer placed Ishigaki against a neutral background, bringing focus to his features, including the thick hair swept back from his face, slightly furrowed brow, direct gaze, and full lips. The rough brushstrokes and heightened colors and shading are characteristic of Soyer's realism.

Both immigrants, Japanese-born Ishigaki and Russian-born Soyer met in New York City. Ishigaki had first moved to California from Japan where he worked as a migrant laborer while pursuing his first formal artistic training. In New York, he continued studying at the Art Students League under John Sloan, a member of the Ashcan School group of Urban Realist artists. Soyer, likewise, pursued artistic training in New York City and was influenced by depictions of gritty urban scenes. Ishigaki became increasingly interested in socialism and communism, and in 1929 was a founding member of the John Reed Club, a communist group where Soyer taught the following year. The two men were aligned in their interest in working-class Americans, which informed the subjects of much of their art.

CG

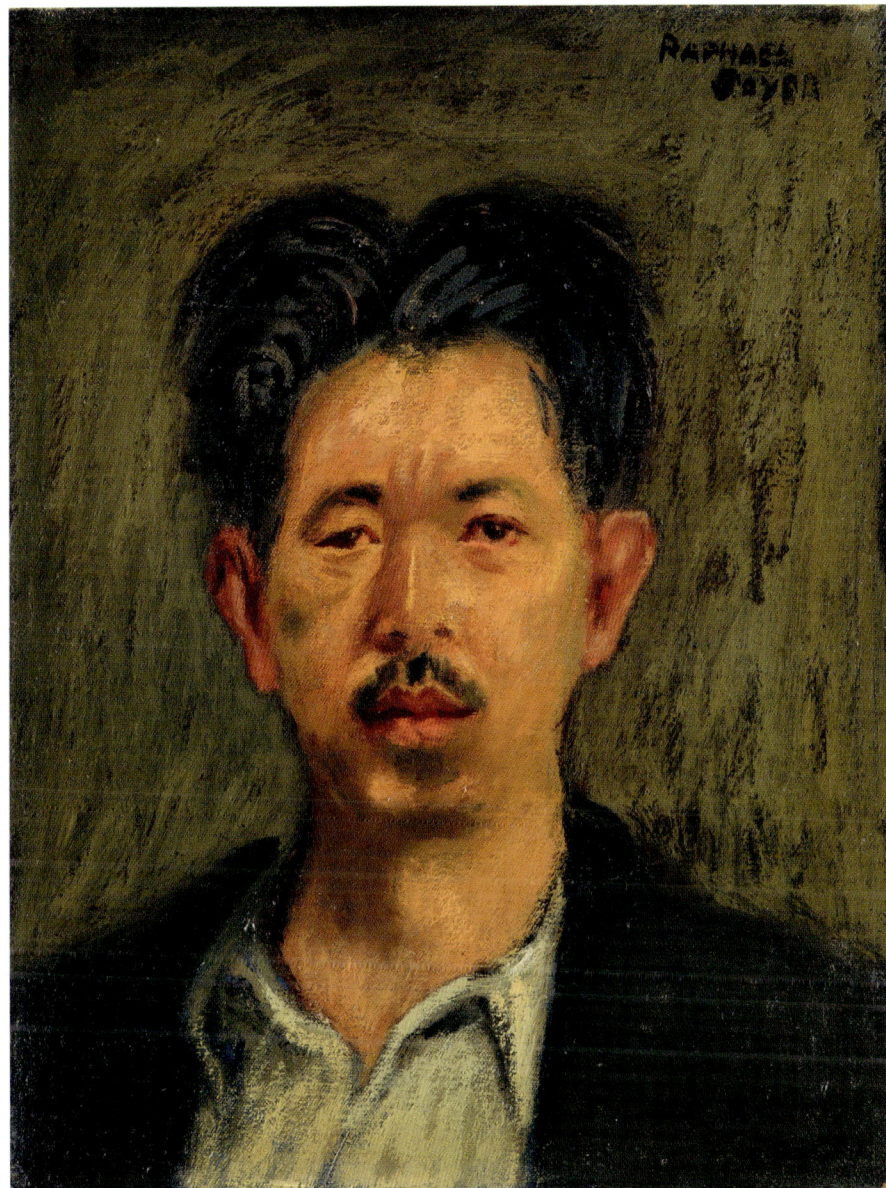

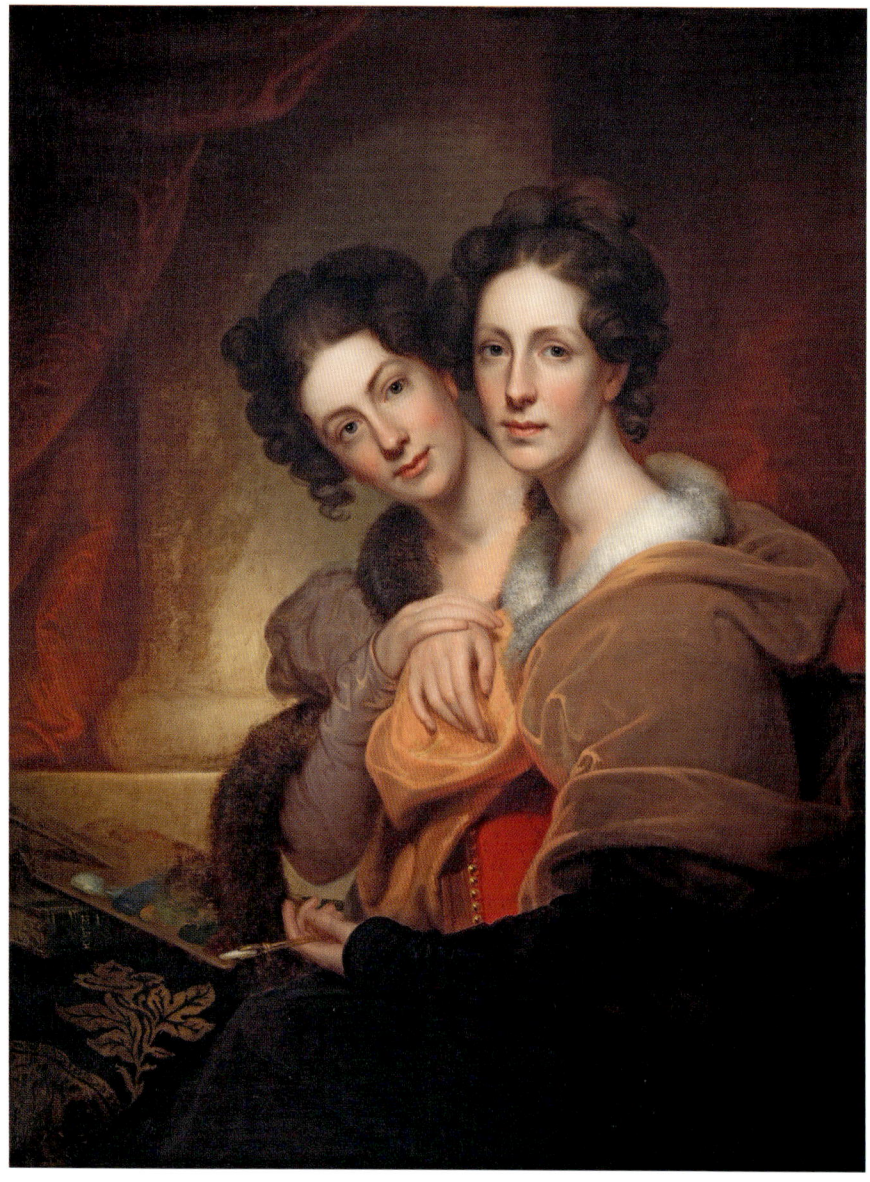

Rembrandt Peale
(American, 1778–1860)
The Sisters (Eleanor and Rosalba Peale), 1826

Oil on canvas, 42⅛ × 32¹¹⁄₁₆ in.
A. Augustus Healy Fund, 67.205.3
Provenance: Gift of the artist to Eleanor May Short Peale, 1826; inherited by Eleanor Peale Jacobs, 1836; inherited by Mary Clare Jacobs Wirgman, 1877; inherited by Grafton Bowly Wirgman, by 1903. Possibly acquired by James Graham & Sons, by 1941. Acquired by Millicent Rogers, by 1947; sold at Sotheby's, New York, May 8, 1947. Acquired by Russell J. Hoyt, before October 19, 1955; sold at Sotheby's, New York, May 19, 1956. Acquired by Franklin Palmer Hart and Mildred Paulina Humphrey Hart (Mrs. F. Palmer Hart), by January 1967. Acquired by Hirschl & Adler, by December 4, 1967; purchased by the Brooklyn Museum, December 13, 1967.

Oscar yi Hou
(British, born 1998, active in New York)
The Arm Wrestle of Chip & Spike; aka: Star-Makers, 2020

Oil on canvas, 55½ × 43 in.
Purchase gift of Scott Rofey and Olivia Song, 2021.45
Provenance: Purchased from James Fuentes Gallery by the Brooklyn Museum, December 14, 2021.

Oscar yi Hou's approach to portraiture prioritizes multidimensional recognition over what he calls "representationalism." As such, he often paints what he knows best; that is to say, those whom he knows best. Works like *The Arm Wrestle of Chip & Spike; aka: Star-Makers* offer intimate depictions of the artist alongside his closest friends, many of whom, like yi Hou, are queer, Asian diasporic creatives. Identified by the nicknames they use when playing poker, Chip and Spike stand side by side, hands clasped in a tentative battle of strength, eyes firmly fixed on the viewer. They stand amid a dizzying, encoded kaleidoscope of symbols, some referring to the subjects' identities and relationship, others alluding to a broader conversation around what it means to be part of the Asian diaspora in the United States. Collectively referred to by the artist as "Chinese cowboy" iconography, these images and words are as representative of the subjects as the figures themselves. Notably, the artist does not provide a key to his cipher, leaving viewers to make out for themselves that the all-American sheriff stars scattered throughout the work are inscribed with the artist's age at the time he painted this work, as well as the jumbled initials of yi Hou and his companion. Likewise, it is only through close looking that one sees a patch of graffiti-like poetry about Chip and Spike's friendship that lends its title, "Star-Makers," to the painting. In this way, the artist crafts an image of genuine relation, not mere representation, whose visual complexity correlates to an equally layered emotional heft.

IA

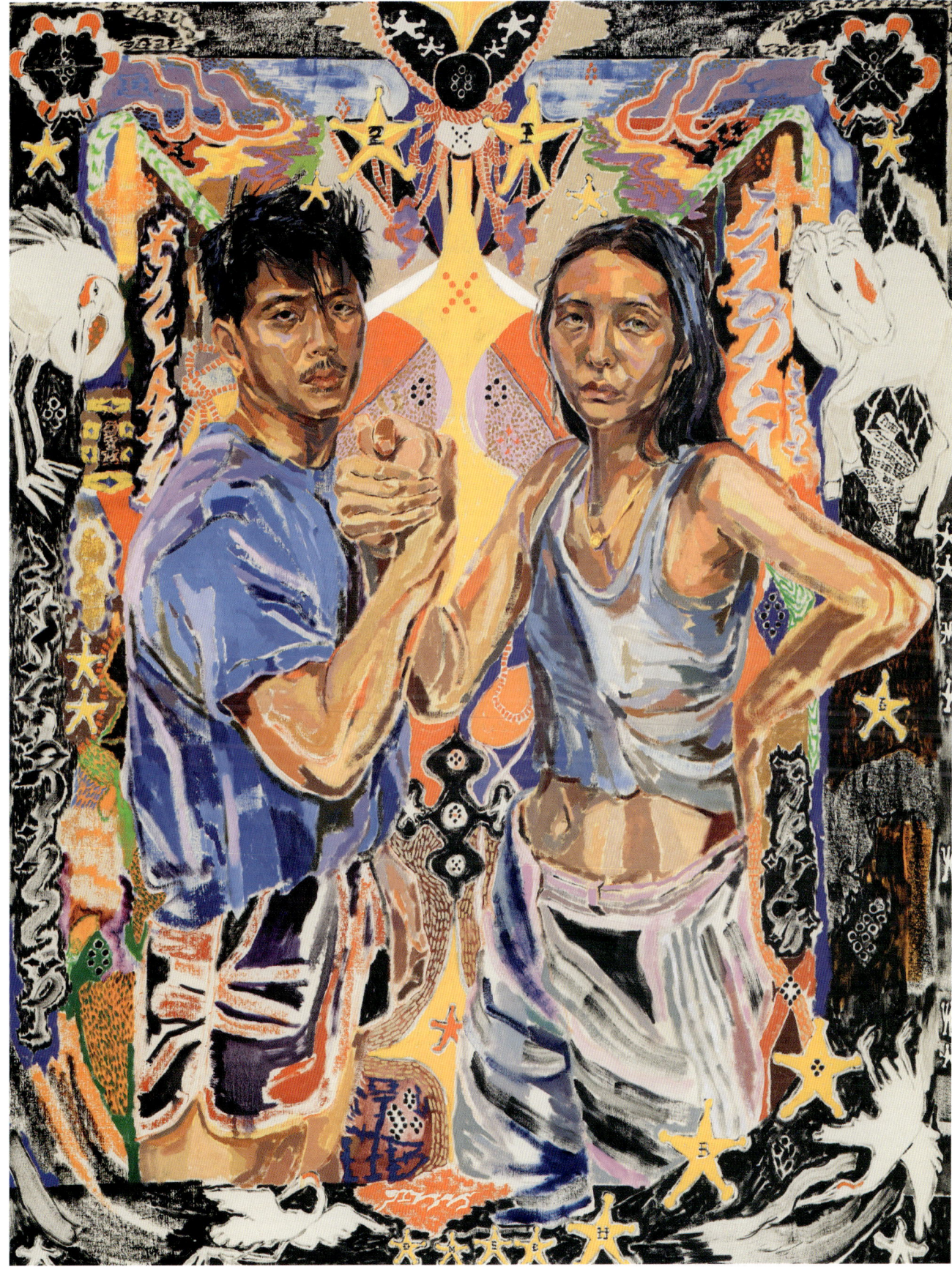

Witness

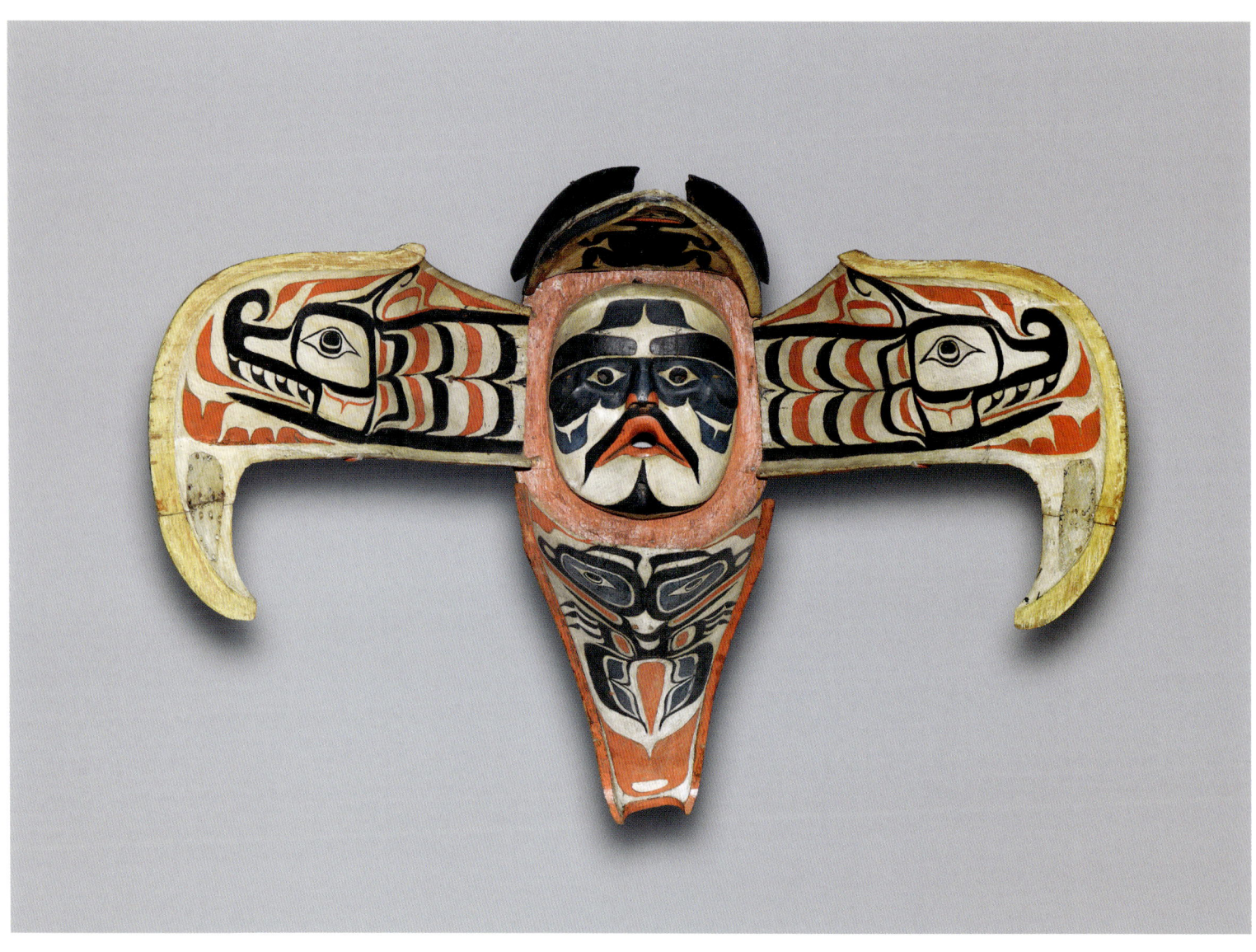

'Na̱mgis Kwakwa̱ka'wakw artist
Thunderbird Transformation Mask
Alert Bay, Vancouver Island, British Columbia, Canada, 19th century

Cedarwood, pigment, hide, metal nails, metal plate, 31 × 45 × 47 in. (open); 20½ × 17 × 29½ in. (closed)
Museum Expedition 1908, Museum Collection Fund, 08.491.8902
Provenance: Acquired by an unidentified member of the Gigilgam lineage, before 1905; acquired in Alert Bay, Canada by Charles Frederick Newcombe, by 1905; purchased in Victoria, Canada by Stewart Culin for the Brooklyn Museum, July 15, 1908.

The masks of Indigenous peoples of the Pacific Northwest Coast are powerful objects that assist us in defining our place in the cosmos. In a world of endless change and complexity, masks offer a continuum for Native people to acknowledge our connection to the universe.... Every mask is quintessential to our desire to embrace wholeness, balance and harmony.[1]

—Robert Joseph, Hereditary Chief of the Gwawa'enux̱w First Nation of the Kwakwa̱ka̱'wakw people

This mask represents Kwankwanxwalige', or Thunderbird, the mythical ancestor of the 'Na̱mgis clan of the Kwakwa̱ka̱'wakw people. Said to create lightning with his eyes and thunder with his beating wings, Thunderbird features prominently in oral traditions, which maintain that he lives in the celestial realm and can assume human form.[2] During potlatch ceremonies, a dancer emerged wearing this mask in its closed state, showing Thunderbird's head with its penetrating eyes and elongated beak. The mask transformed when the dancer pulled internal strings to reveal images within: a human face flanked by *sisiutl* (a double-headed lightning snake), with a human figure above and bird below.[3] Rendered in a curvilinear style known as formline, the mask's symmetrical motifs comprise u-shapes, s-shapes, and ovoids (rounded rectangles)[4] in the classic colors of black, red, and blueish green.

The Kwakwa̱ka̱'wakw and other Indigenous communities in the Pacific Northwest hold potlatches to commemorate milestones, including marriages, naming of clan members, transference of rights, and mourning the deceased. Hosts demonstrate their power and generosity by giving many gifts to attendees. Although potlatches were outlawed by colonial governments for decades, Indigenous communities maintained the tradition, which thrives to this day.

DT

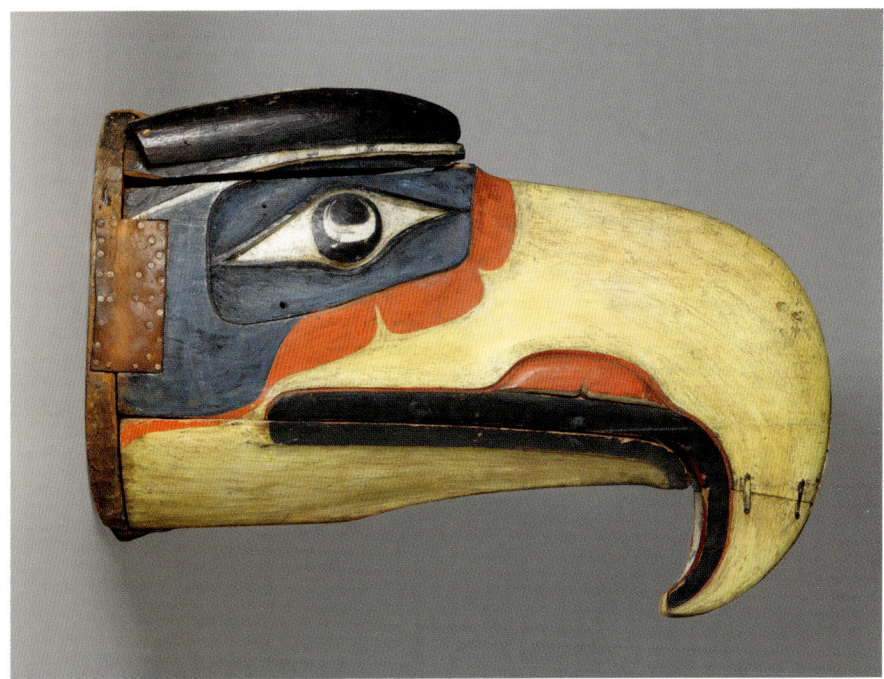

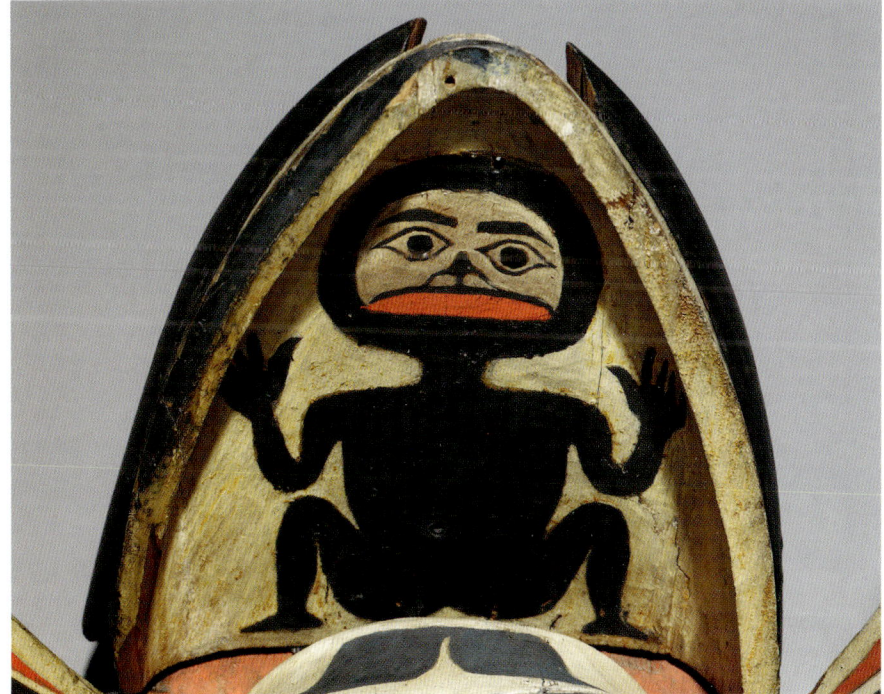

1. Robert Joseph, "Behind the Masks," in *Down from the Shimmering Sky: Masks of the Northwest Coast*, eds. Peter Macnair, Robert Joseph, and Bruce Grenville (Vancouver, BC: Douglas & McIntyre, 1998), 18–19.
2. Susan Kennedy Zeller, *Brooklyn Museum Highlights* (Brooklyn, NY: Brooklyn Museum, 2014), 126.
3. Ira Jacknis, "Thunderbird Transformation Mask," in *Objects of Myth and Memory: American Indian Art at the Brooklyn Museum*, eds. Diana Fane, Ira Jacknis, and Lise M. Breen (Brooklyn Museum in association with University of Washington Press, 1991), 270.
4. Bill Holm, *Northwest Coast Indian Art: An Analysis of Form* (Seattle: University of Washington Press, 1965), 29.

Witness

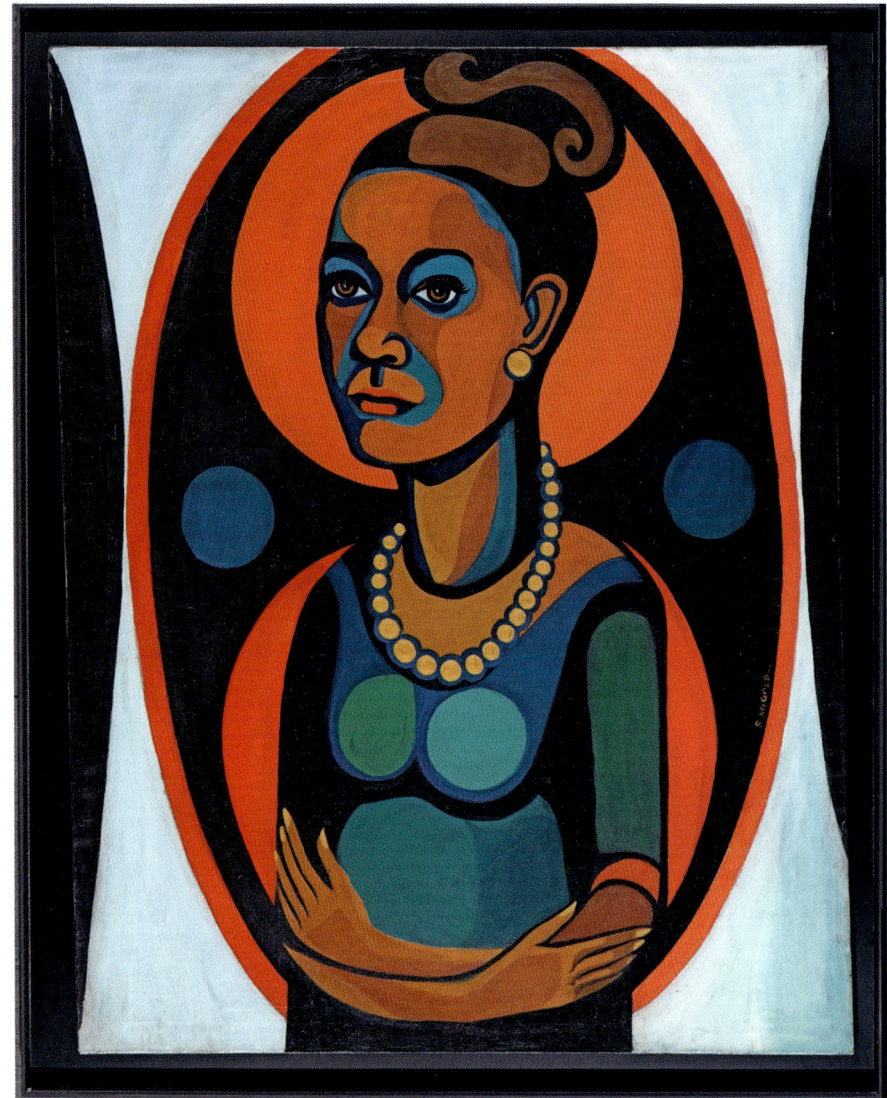

Faith Ringgold
(American, born 1930)
Early Works #25: Self-Portrait, 1965

Oil on canvas, 50 × 40 in.
Gift of Elizabeth A. Sackler, 2013.96
Provenance: Acquired, probably from the artist, by ACA Galleries, before March 4, 2007. Acquired, probably purchased from ACA Galleries, by Elizabeth A. Sackler, by December 20, 2010; donated, December 12, 2013.

Faith Ringgold altered the fabric of New York's art world and Western art histories through her concerted art and activism. Departing from curricula that centered European Old Masters, Ringgold took inspiration from Modernism, rejecting traditional chiaroscuro (shading to express lights and darks), believing it insufficient for rendering Black subjects' skin tones.

Ringgold finessed a distinct style, exemplified in *Early Works #25: Self Portrait*, that integrates flat composition, contrasting saturated colors, thick outlining, geometric forms, and patterning to articulate a semi-abstracted Black figuration. Through self-portraiture, a genre historically used to assert the identities of white male European painters, Ringgold lays claims to a tradition that scarcely represented Black women artists. She adopts an austere expression, while tracing a historicized regal pose and adornment. As she gazes beyond the frame, her folded arms create a barrier between her and the viewer, and a cautious distance between herself and the art histories she is implicating—perhaps for her own protection. This painting, in its determined self-assertion and subversive self-fashioning, insists on the value of the artist's voice and vantage point amid the tumult of sociopolitical tensions in the wake of the Civil Rights Movement, the burgeoning Black Arts Movement, and the percolating Feminist movement(s).

In 1971, Ringgold co-chaired a forum for feminist art workers to air grievances called "Are Museums Relevant to Women?" at the Brooklyn Museum. Through her institutional indictments and unapologetic arts practice, Ringgold created space for herself and future generations of Black artists, specifically Black women artists, to proclaim belonging and witness their presence within canonical lineage.

CSF

Wadsworth Jarrell
(American, born 1929)
Revolutionary (Angela Davis), 1971

Acrylic and mixed media on canvas, 64 × 51 in. Gift of R. M. Atwater, Anna Wolfrom Dove, Alice Fiebiger, Joseph Fiebiger, Belle Campbell Harriss, and Emma L. Hyde, by exchange, Designated Purchase Fund, Mary Smith Dorward Fund, Dick S. Ramsay Fund, and Carll H. de Silver Fund, 2012.80.18 Provenance: Acquired from the artist by David Lusenhop and M. M. Azzi Fine Art & Design, by 2008; purchased by the Brooklyn Museum, December 13, 2012.

The work of Wadsworth Jarrell exemplifies the intersection of visual culture and political thought that guided the Black Arts Movement (BAM) of the 1960s and '70s. *Revolutionary (Angela Davis)* is perhaps his most quintessential piece, with vibrant, Kool-Aid colors, compositional fluidity, text-based imagery, and commitment to figurative representation. These approaches had come to define the "Black aesthetic" that he and his peers developed within AfriCOBRA (the African Commune of Bad Relevant Artists), a Chicago-based collective associated with the sprawling, interdisciplinary efforts of BAM. As one of the group's cofounders, Jarrell was central to crafting its philosophy of foregrounding the cultural specificity of contemporary Black art through creating and promoting empowering images of Black people. Here, the artist applies the AfriCOBRA-delineated aesthetic to a depiction of—and tribute to—activist and scholar Angela Davis, in honor of her preeminent role as a vocal advocate for Black liberation. Its composition is based on a black-and-white photograph of Davis in a moment of fervent oration. The words "revolution," "resistance," "Black," and "beautiful" in orange, pink, purple, and yellow compose Davis's body and surroundings, punctuated by a rhythmic but erratic staccato of brushstrokes. Additionally, a single, powerful phrase drapes across Davis's chest and down her arm in bands, echoing the ladderlike placement of bullets slung across her shoulder and contextualizing her reputation as a bona fide revolutionary: "I have given my life to the struggle. If I have to lose my life in the struggle, that's the way it will have to be."

IA

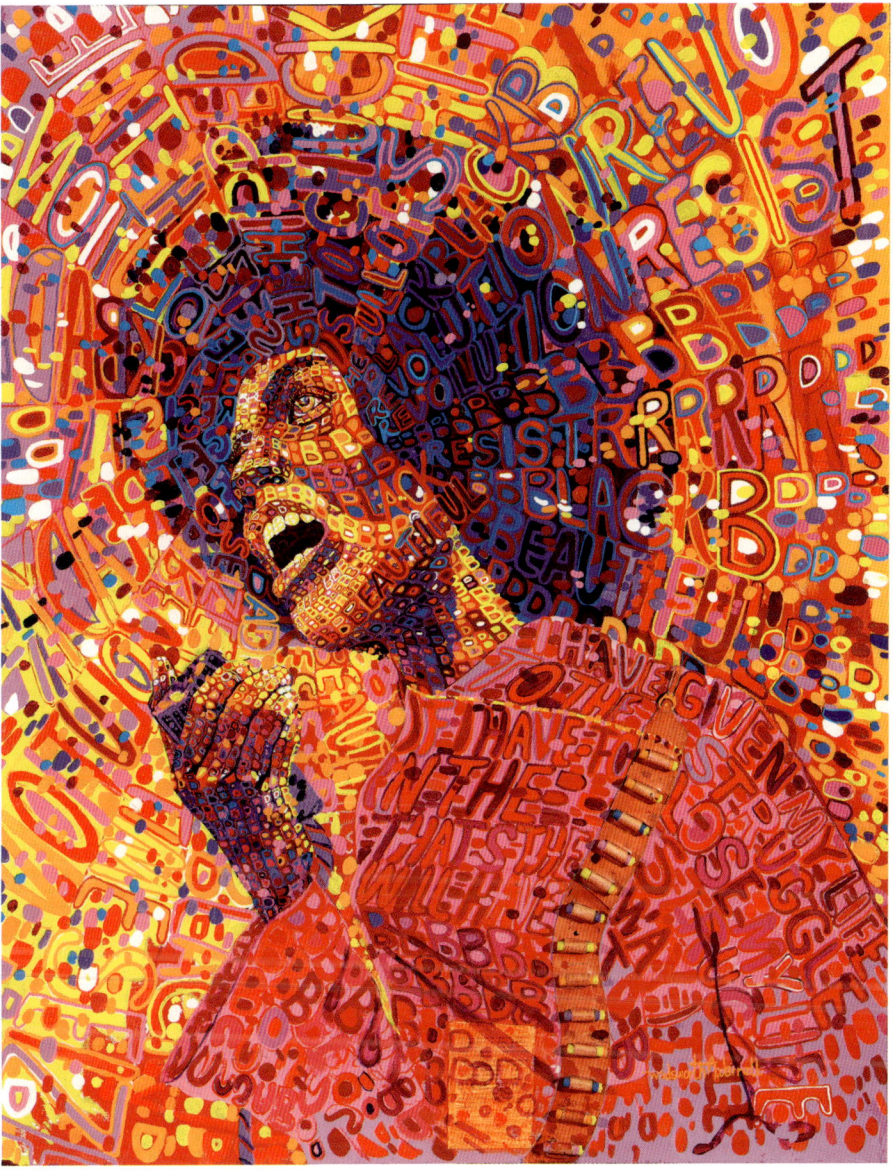

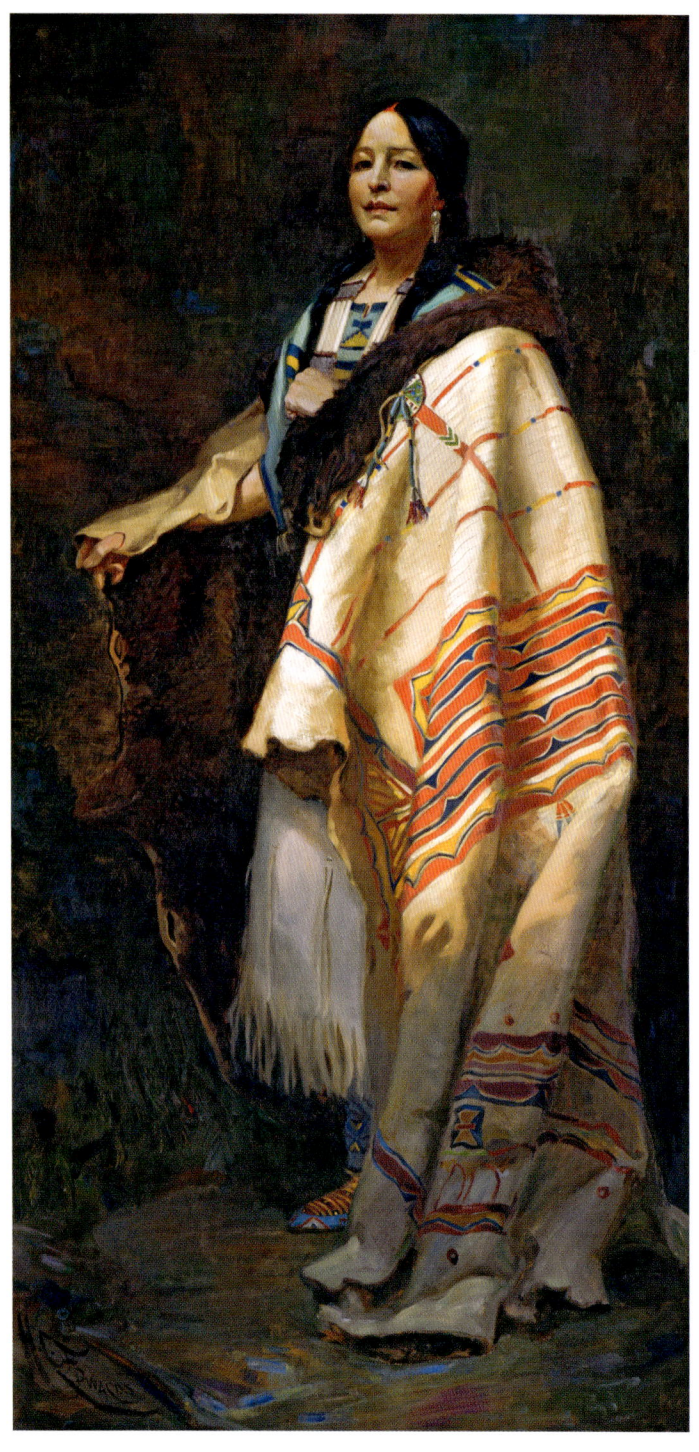
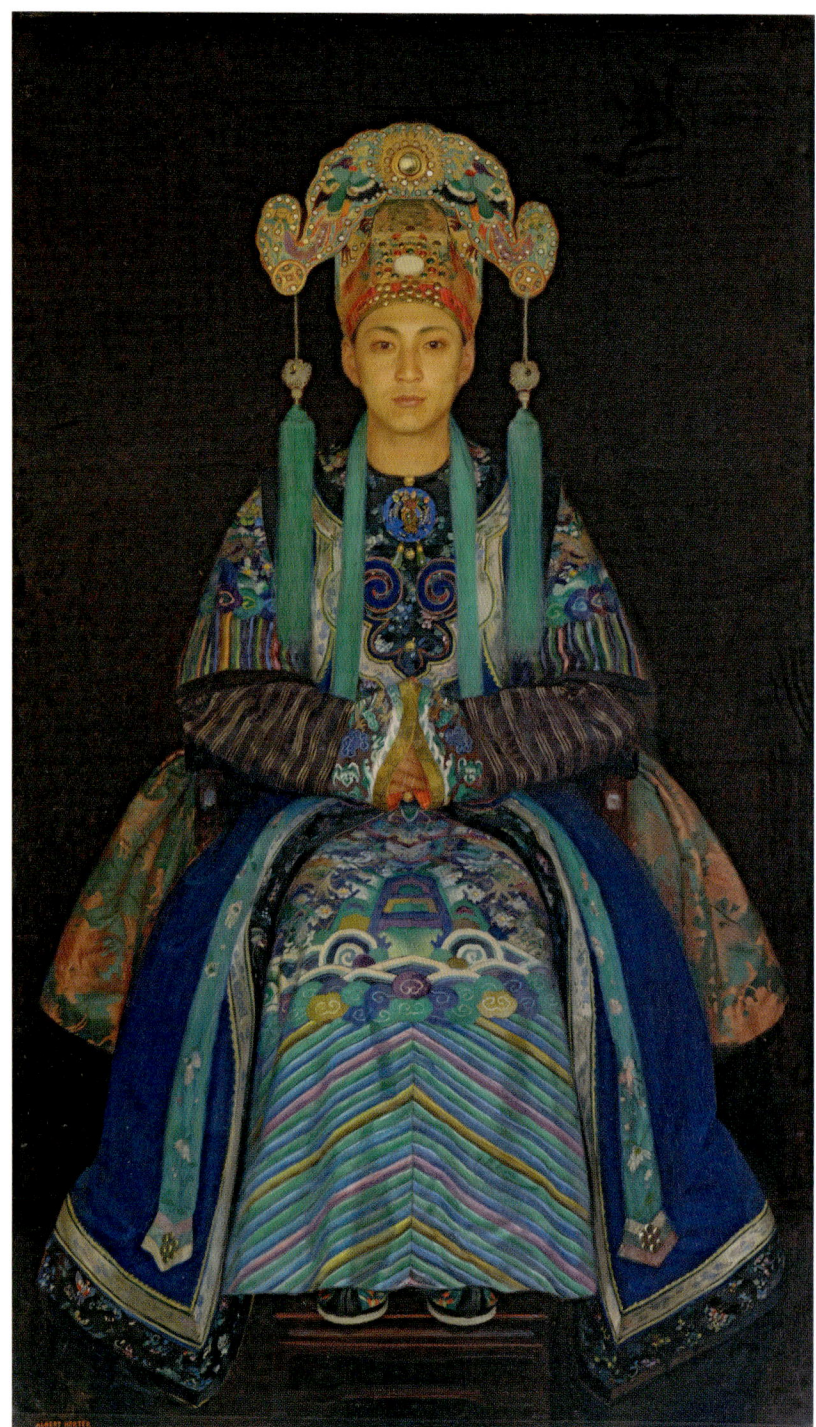

Toward Joy

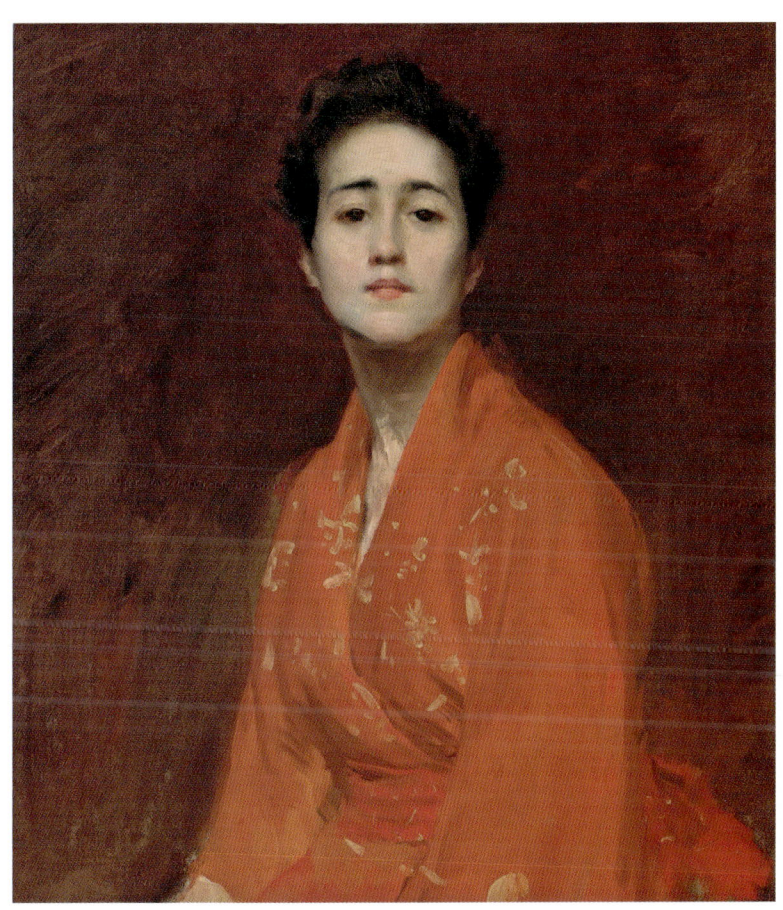 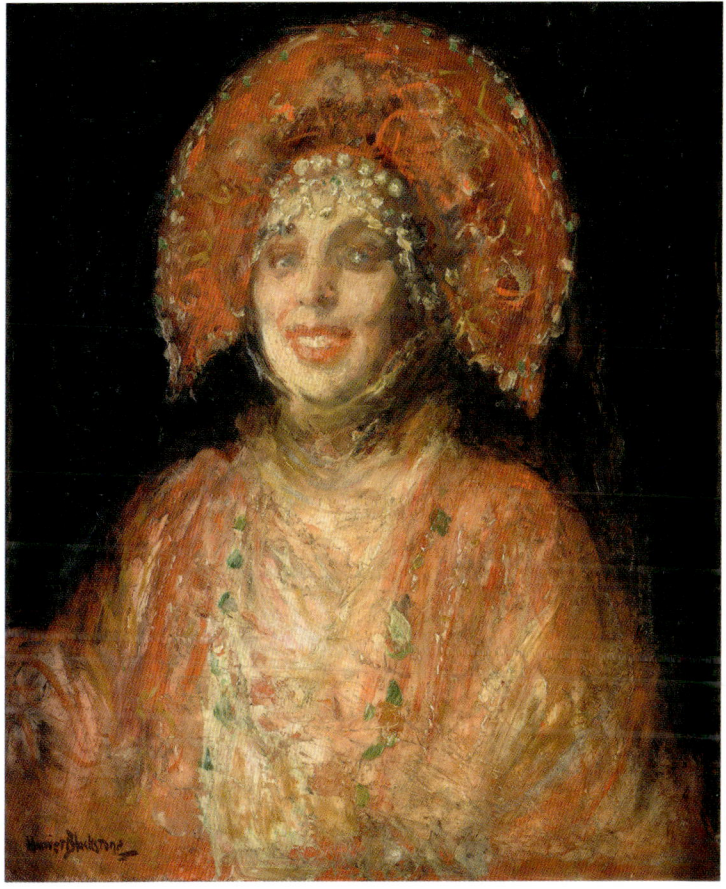

Page 242, left:
Harry C. Edwards
(American, 1868–1922)
Handsome Morning—A Dakota, 1921

Oil on canvas, 72 1/16 × 36 1/16 in.
Gift of the Estate of Grace C. Edwards, 26.149
Provenance: Inherited from the artist by
Grace C. Edwards, by 1922;
donated by the estate of Grace C. Edwards,
February 23, 1926.

Page 242, right:
Albert Herter
(American, 1871–1950)
Pilgun Yoon, ca. 1923

Oil on canvas, 70 1/8 × 41 1/4 in.
Gift of Mrs. Frederic B. Pratt, 32.68
Provenance: Purchased from the artist by the
Brooklyn Museum, by exchange, April 12, 1932.

Previous page, left:
William Merritt Chase
(American, 1849–1916)
Study of a Girl in Japanese Dress, ca. 1895

Oil on canvas, 28 1/8 × 25 3/16 in.
Gift of Mrs. Leon Griffiths, 51.60
Provenance: Acquired by Leon Griffiths, before 1951;
inherited by Mrs. Leon Griffiths, by 1951; donated,
March 6, 1951.

Previous page, right:
Harriet Blackstone
(American, 1864–1939)
Madame Plevitzskaia, ca. 1927

Oil on canvas, 28 × 24 1/8 in.
Museum Collection Fund, 29.1193
Provenance: Purchased from the artist by the
Brooklyn Museum, October 1, 1929.

This quartet of portraits indulges a late nineteenth-century taste for theatricality and reveals a fascination with exoticized difference. Though Americans have long had an interest in those considered foreign, including landscapes and objects, the rampant colonial incursions and resulting world's fairs and economic globalization in the second half of the nineteenth century saw this fascination reinvigorated. These paintings by William Merritt Chase, Albert Herter, Harriet Blackstone, and Harry C. Edwards, who all worked in and around New York City during the early twentieth century, rely primarily on clothing to signal Otherness and capture the imagination of their viewers.

Chase and Herter both looked eastward for inspiration. After the United States compelled the opening of Japan's trade ports to the world in 1853, Americans developed a fanaticism for Japanese culture, objects, and garments like the kimono, which was quickly adopted into Western fashion. Chase, a voracious collector of exotic goods, was drawn to the kimono for its finely woven fabric and collected many in his studio.[1] In *Study of a Girl in Japanese Dress*, an unknown model wears a bright red kimono and obi with nondescript gold embellishments. Styled incorrectly with the right side folded over the left and in a way that reveals more of her chest than is traditional, Chase made no attempt to represent the kimono as it would be worn in Japan.[2] Instead, the artist appropriated the garment and its cultural context to add visual interest to his portrait.

A richly patterned Chinese opera costume is the object of Herter's fascination in his striking portrait of Korean actor Pilgun Yoon.[3] In character as Aladdin from the popular turn-of-the-century pantomime *Aladdin and the Wonderful Lamp*, Yoon wears an outer garment inspired by Qing dynasty robes with tripart sleeves ending in horse-hoof-shaped cuffs and slits in the front and back.[4] His elaborate headdress, featuring heraldic phoenixes, gold rivets, and long silk tassels, is a standard attention-grabbing feature of Chinese opera ensembles. A muralist and the son of Christian Herter, the president of the renowned furniture and decorating company Herter Brothers, the younger Herter was likely drawn to the intricate detailing of Yoon's costume, which echoes the Japanesque inlays favored by his family's company. In depicting Yoon enthroned and in a rigid frontal pose, the artist also emulates Qing dynasty imperial portraiture. With this mix of inspiration, Herter flattens Yoon's portrait into decoration and suspends this dynamic stage actor in the past.

Russian folk singer Madame Nadezhda Plevitzskaia and her bold ensemble are the subjects of Blackstone's portrait. Using the direct painting technique encouraged by her instructor, William Merritt Chase, Blackstone animatedly paints her sitter's beaded *kokoshnik*, a traditional Russian headdress, and matching voluminous orange open robe.[5] Though only visible from the waist up, the straight lines of Plevitzskaia's embellished overgarment could be a seamless blend of the fashionable 1920s tubular silhouette with the traditional *sarafan*, a long A-line sleeveless dress worn by women in the Russian countryside, usually over a blouse and paired with a *kokoshnik*. The inability of Americans and Western Europeans to fit Russia cleanly into the East–West dichotomy meant that the nation's folk clothing—with its exceptionally ornate embellishments—would have certainly fascinated them. Plevitzskaia's international reputation as a performer and her highly publicized ties to the anti-Communist Russian White Army would have added further intrigue.[6] Though it is not known how Blackstone and the singer became acquainted, they likely met during one of Plevitzkaia's American tours through New York. Blackstone seized the opportunity to capture the performer's dramatic life and style on canvas, presumably to the delight and entertainment of an American audience following news of the celebrity in tandem with the Russian Civil War.

The clothing and culture of the Dakota and other Native American people of the Great Plains were no less foreign in the minds of many early twentieth-century Americans. In painting his life-size portrait of actress Handsome Morning, Edwards identifies his sitter as Dakota Sioux. An actor himself, Edwards was deeply involved in the theater and, like Blackstone and Herter, found elaborately dressed performers to be ideal subjects. Here, the artist capitalized on the public's interest in Native American subjects, which was drummed up by the staged documentary-style photographs, romanticized nostalgic paintings, and burgeoning Native American theater popular in this period.[7] Reflecting the taste for stereotyped images of Native people, dramatic spectacle, and perceived "authenticity," as defined by non-Natives, Edwards took great care in depicting Handsome Morning's dignified pose and multi-element ensemble that likely combines material culture from several Plains tribes, possibly including the Dakota, Cheyenne, and Blackfoot.[8] She wears a buffalo-hide robe painted with the traditional colorful box-and-border design executed by Plains women artists, as well as a fringed hide dress with a beaded yoke, tubular bone-bead necklace, beaded leggings, and quilled or beaded moccasins.

Using actors and models, all four painters constructed visions of people and traditions outside of their own experiences to increase the breadth of their *oeuvres* and appeal to the tastes of their patrons.

GB

1. For more on William Merritt Chase's biography, as well as those of Albert Herter, Harriet Blackstone, and Harry C. Edwards, see Teresa A. Carbone, Barbara Dayer Gallati, and Linda S. Ferber, *American Paintings in the Brooklyn Museum: Artists Born by 1876*, (London: Brooklyn Museum; London: D. Giles Limited, 2006), vols. 1 and 2.
2. In Japan, kimonos are always styled with the left side folded over the right, unless dressing the deceased.
3. "Chinese opera" is a blanket term for any Chinese stage performance. Traditionally, all Chinese stage performances involved singing. For more on Chinese opera's influence on visual culture, see Judith T. Zeitlin and Yuhang Li, *Performing Images: Opera in Chinese Visual Culture* (Chicago: Smart Museum of Art and the University of Chicago Press, 2014).
4. The original story of *Aladdin and the Wonderful Lamp*, recorded by French author Antoine Galland and published in his 1710 translation of *One Thousand and One Nights*, was set in China. For more context see Lauren Lee and Jenny Ghose, "Aladdin," University of Michigan Library Online Exhibits, https://apps.lib.umich.edu/online-exhibits/exhibits/show/seven-fantasy-classics/aladdin.
5. Carbone, Gallati, and Ferber, *American Paintings in the Brooklyn Museum*, 1: 297.
6. In the decade after Blackstone completed her portrait, Madame Plevitzkaia (also known as Nadia Skobline) was implicated in the kidnappings of important Russian political exiles in Paris and, in 1938, she was sentenced to twenty years of hard labor in a French prison. For more on the biography of Madame Plevitzskaia, see ibid., 297–98.
7. For more on Native American theater, see Christy Stanlake, *Native American Drama: A Critical Perspective* (Cambridge, UK: Cambridge University Press, 2009).
8. See research by Susan Kennedy Zeller, curatorial file for object 26.149, Brooklyn Museum.

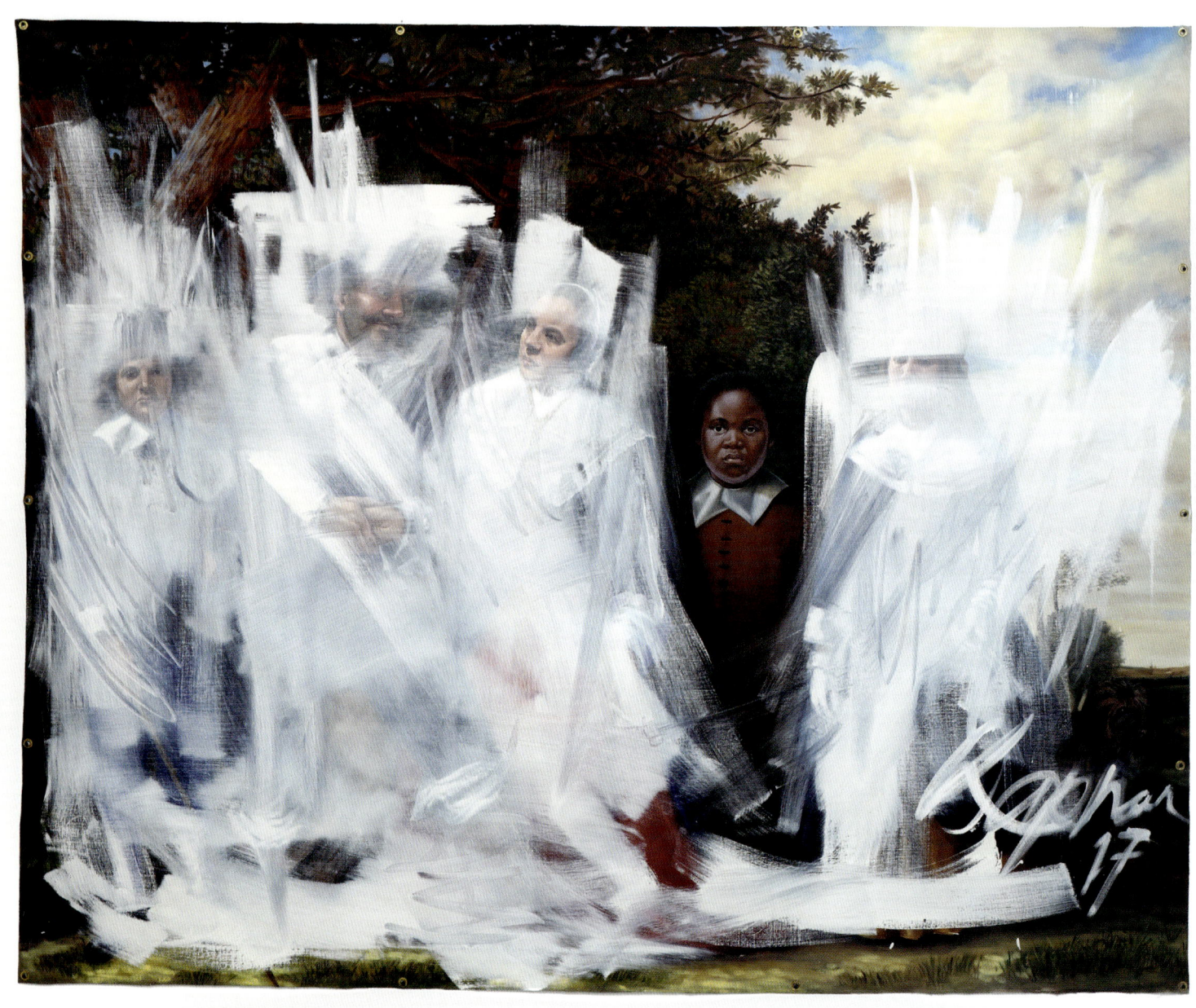

Titus Kaphar
(American, born 1976)
Shifting the Gaze, 2017

Oil on canvas, 83 × 103¼ in.
William K. Jacobs Jr., Fund, 2017.34
Provenance: Purchased from Jack Shainman Gallery
by the Brooklyn Museum, December 19, 2017.

Titus Kaphar's monumental painting *Shifting the Gaze* was produced as an instructive example of what it means to challenge and subvert exclusionary histories. The work was completed during Kaphar's 2017 TED Talk, titled "Can art amend history?," which addressed the perspectives reflected in art historical study, and those traditionally excluded. In the middle of his presentation, Kaphar unveiled a painting: his semi-faithful copy of Dutch artist Frans Hals's *Family Group in a Landscape* (ca. 1645–68). Among the group portraits for which Hals gained renown are a number that depict upper-class Dutch families; notably, this family portrait was considered unique for its open-air setting and for its inclusion of one of Haarlem's exceedingly few Black residents—likely the family's servant.

    According to Kaphar, it was not the sort of painting discussed in his art classes, which caused him to seek out works like this in museums instead. With didactic flourish, Kaphar called attention to the details: gold, lace, and silk adornments—the aspects art history is most keenly interested in—and their indication of affluence or status of the white family depicted. As he spoke, he applied white paint in large, loose brushstrokes over each white figure, leaving the sole Black figure unobscured. In this way, Kaphar trained his audience's focus on a subject historically ignored, a critical strategy emblematic of his practice. This often involves isolating the few Black subjects that do appear in historical artworks, whether through the use of a literal whitewash, as in *Shifting the Gaze*, or other interventions such as cutting canvas and juxtaposing images. The resulting artworks both conceal and reveal, forcing viewers to confront what is familiar and query what is not.

IA

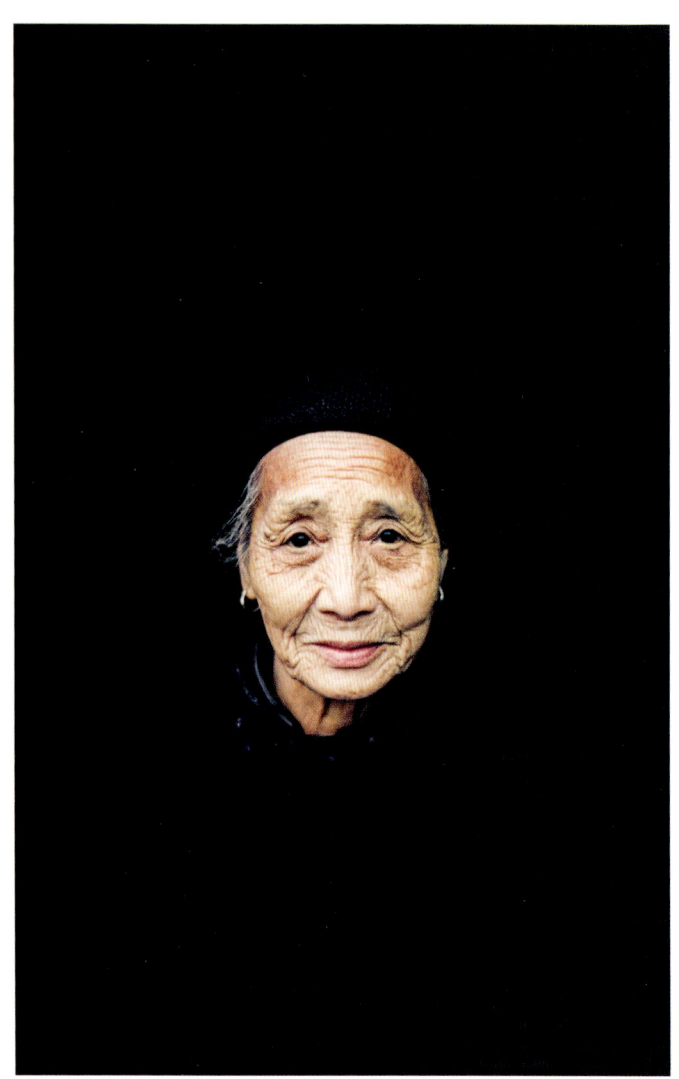
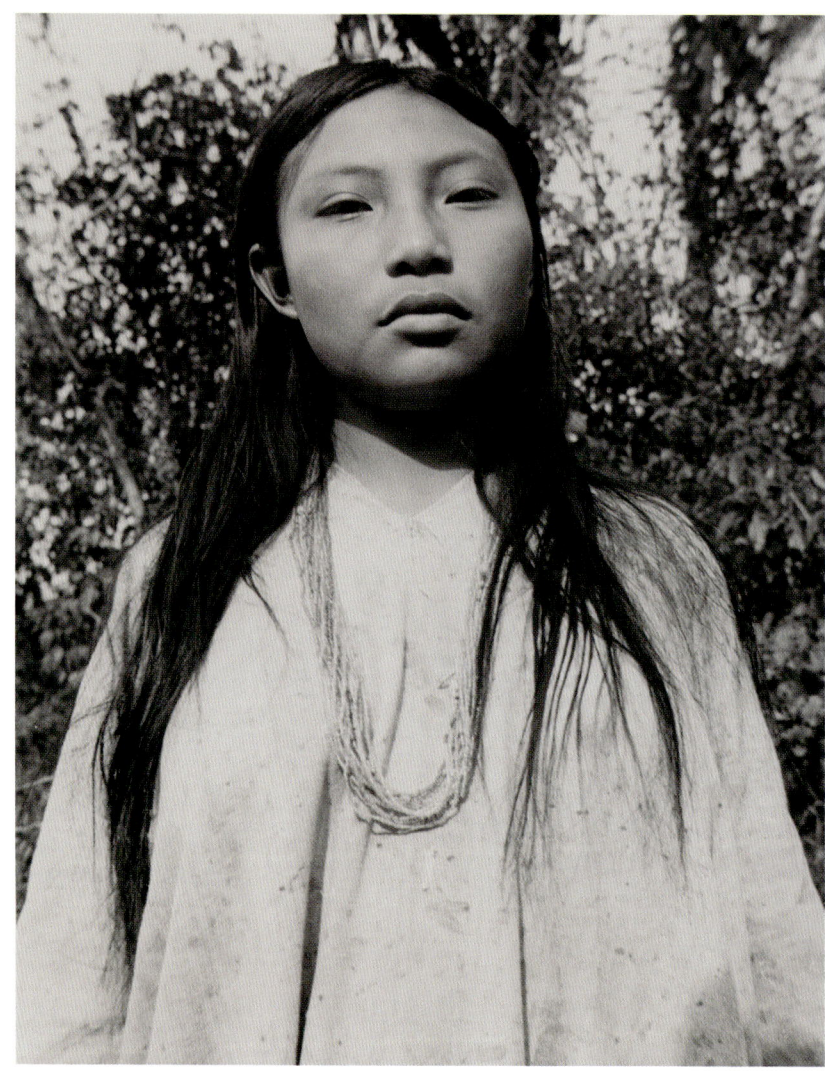

Eve Arnold
(American, 1912–2012)
Retired Worker, 1979

Dye transfer chromogenic print, 18¼ × 11¹⁵⁄₁₆ in.
Gift of the artist in memory of Gene Baro, 83.128.17
Provenance: Donated by the artist, 1983.

Manuel Álvarez Bravo
(Mexican, 1902–2002)
Margarita de Bonampak, 1949

Gelatin silver print, 9½ × 7½ in.
Gift of William Berley, 79.294.7
Provenance: Acquired by William Berley, before 1979; donated, 1979.

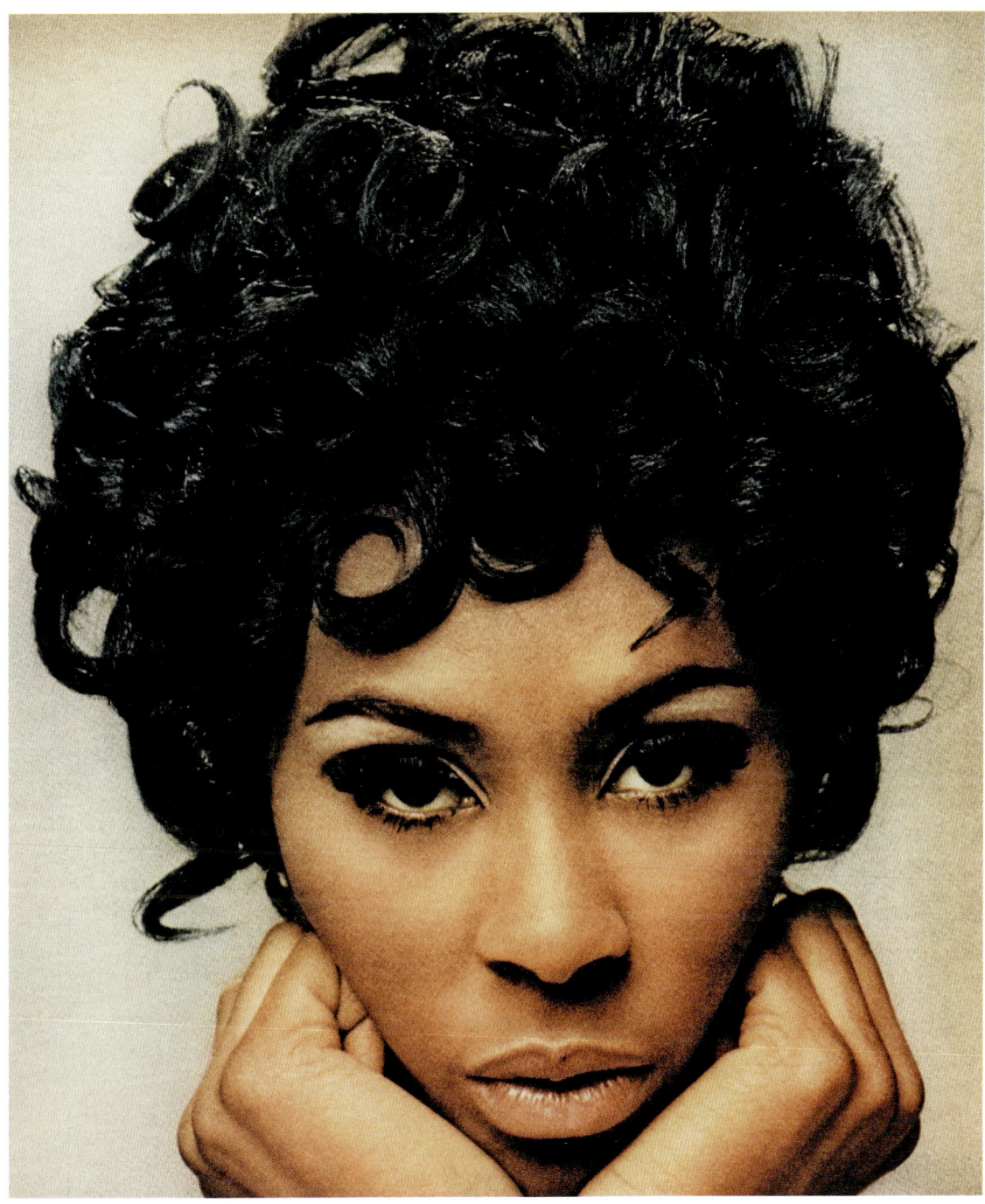

Hank Willis Thomas
(American, born 1976)
Why Wait Another Day to Be Adorable? Tell Your Beautician "Relax Me" 1968/2007

Digital print, 34⅛ × 30 in.
Mary Smith Dorward Fund and gift of Robert Smith, by exchange, 2010.18.1
Provenance: Acquired by Charles Guice Contemporary, by 2009; purchased by exchange, 2010.

Witness

CRITICAL SHORT

Showing Our Work

Stephanie Sparling Williams

What does it mean to bear witness, to mark this moment through a curatorial practice? Or through one's work with a collection?

Emerging from a series of workshops with the Brooklyn Museum's Education and Public Programs teams, the ideas that inform this framework honor this gallery's additional roles as a favored gathering space, a classroom, or a stage and forum for spoken-word poetry or other public programs. As curators, we want to amplify and uphold the democratic, subversive, and collective ways a gallery may be activated. By building an accessible stage, and filling the walls with art, as with the portraits from the gallery pictured here, we shift focus—literally—to the communities who gather *in* this space to produce creative work alongside the collection.

While always in progress, we endeavor toward a principle of elaboration and a politics of articulation. Full of presence, this gallery offers up space for our communities to be seen and heard.

What does it mean to bear witness, to create a mark for another?

Museums are their most rigorous when they are dialogical; their most sincere when they are transparent. Despite their exclusionary and problematic history, they remain critical sites for articulating cultural values and belonging into our present moment. Museums are never neutral. Representation within museums, then, is by definition a kind of witnessing, a set of practices that hold space in the cultural landscape for individuals and communities to be seen.

In each of the frameworks across this project, experiments in representation move away from a focus on "diverse" individuals and how their creative products fit within existing paradigms for American art. Though, expanding the collection to represent the breadth and depth of the North American cultural landscape *is* a central priority within the American art department at the Brooklyn Museum. In our efforts to promote richly layered experiences and conversations with and between our collections, and to be open and honest about the artwork in our care today, we had to extend the concept of representation beyond our collection's composition to the historically and strategically undervalued lenses and worldviews that now free us up to see or our holdings in new lights. Witnessing became a way to imagine a collection display outside of European American art historical canon formation, where representation is centered around ideas and action versus select heroic individuals and their creative accomplishments.

This final framework does, however, take up representation that visually centers individual people as depicted through manifold artists, cultural lenses, and media. The gallery and this book each stage and promote a powerful act of collective witnessing—an exchange of gazes—between a collection and its communities. The rotating salon of peopled pictures reflects the strength and diversity of the museum's figurative works. Here, the curatorial implication is that the people on the walls and those who enter the gallery, or turn each page, together constitute the museum itself. Each is no less present, no less significant. This is a proliferation of belonging, where, in taking up our own charge, the department will continue to expound and reflect our audiences in the collection's development and display over time.

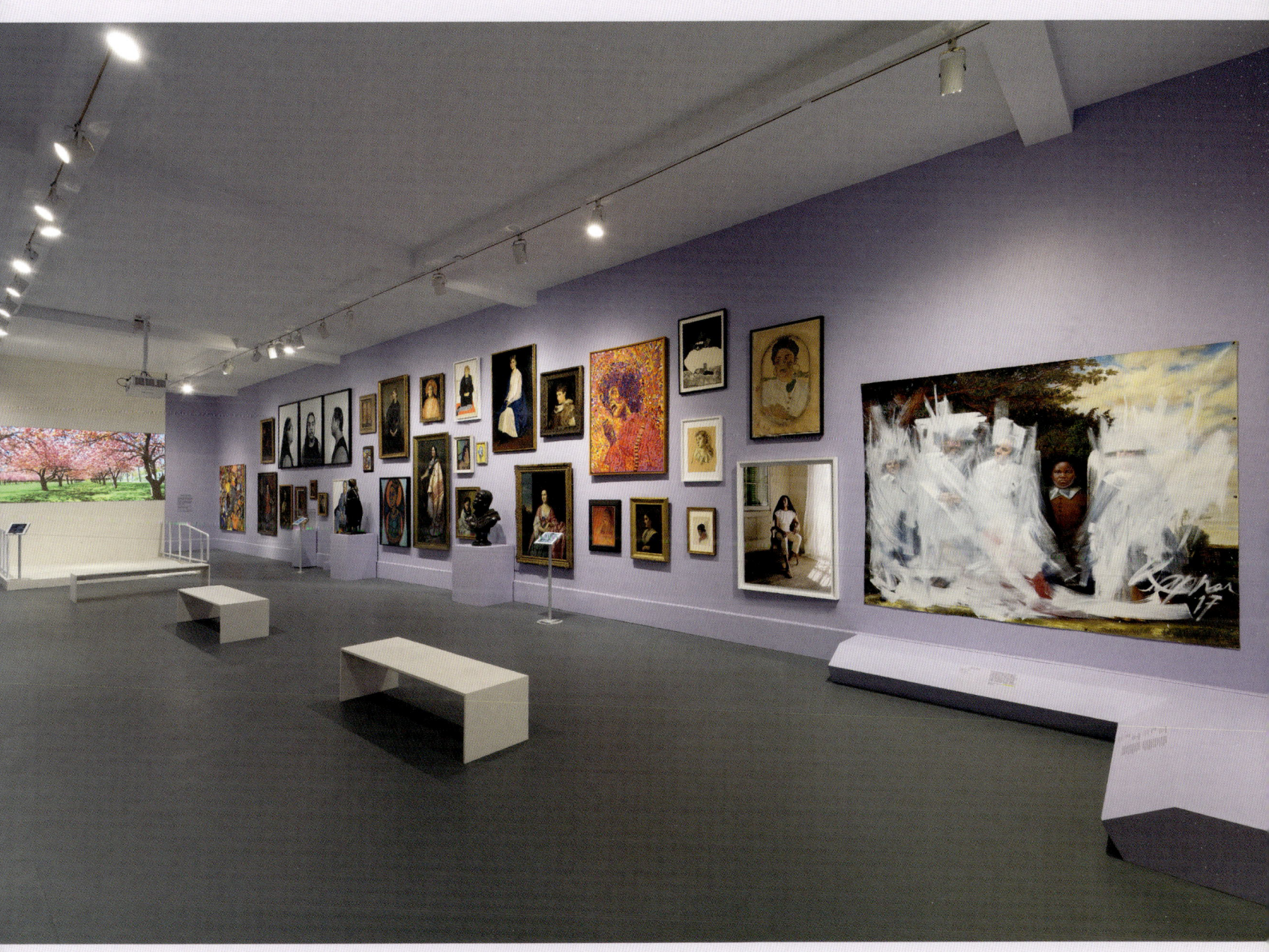

Witness

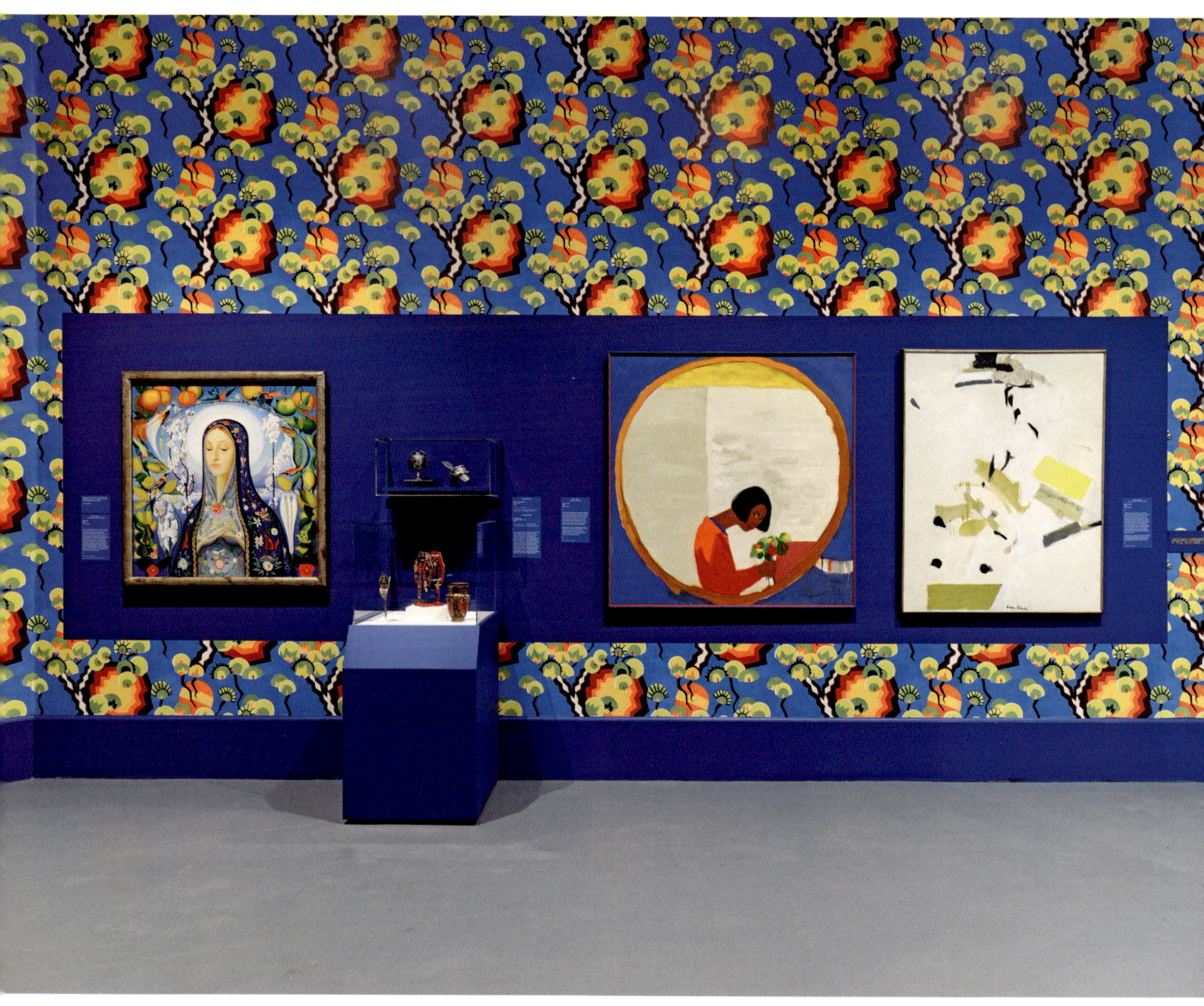

Contributor Biographies

Indira Abiskaroon (IA), Curatorial Assistant, Modern and Contemporary Art, Brooklyn Museum

Sena Amuzu (SA), former American Art intern, Brooklyn Museum

Adriana Benavides (AB), former Conservation intern, Brooklyn Museum

Grace Billingslea (GB), Curatorial Assistant, Arts of the Americas and American Art, Brooklyn Museum

Lauren Bradley (LB), Associate Paintings Conservator, Brooklyn Museum

Jesse Brody, Belle's Brook Gardener, Brooklyn Botanic Garden

Tiziana Capizzi (TC), former American Art intern, Brooklyn Museum

Carla S. Forbes (CSF), Curatorial Assistant, Elizabeth A. Sackler Center for Feminist Art, Brooklyn Museum

Catherine Futter (CF), PhD, Director of Curatorial Affairs and Senior Curator of Decorative Arts, Brooklyn Museum

Kimberli Gant (KG), PhD, Curator of Modern and Contemporary Art, Brooklyn Museum

Michael Gibson-Prugh (MGP), Curatorial Assistant, Decorative Arts and European Art, Brooklyn Museum

Caroline Gillaspie (CG), PhD, Assistant Curator of American Art, Brooklyn Museum

Emi Grate, Brooklyn-based drag artist

Domenica Guaman (DG), former Esther and Louis Scher American Art Research Associate, Brooklyn Museum

Tricia Hersey, performance artist, writer, activist, and founder of The Nap Ministry

Sará Yafah King, PhD, Postdoctoral Fellow in Neurology at Oregon Health Science University, Executive Director of Peace in Schools, and founder of MindHeart Consulting

Madeleine Levinsohn (ML), former American Art intern, Brooklyn Museum

Ellen McCarthy, former Children's Garden Co-ordinator, Brooklyn Botanic Garden

Tiffany Momon, PhD, Assistant Professor of History, University of the South

Kelli Morgan, PhD, Founding Executive Director, Black Artists Archive

Ellen Nigro (EN), Assistant Paintings Conservator, Brooklyn Museum

Miss Peppermint, New York City–based drag artist

Melissa Peter-Paul, Mi'kmaw quill artist

Leigh Raiford, PhD, Professor of African American Studies, University of California, Berkeley

Diana Cristina Rose, PhD, Independent Scholar of Pre-Hispanic and Contemporary Maya Art

Nancy Rosoff (NR), Andrew W. Mellon Senior Curator of Arts of the Americas, Brooklyn Museum

SGidGang.Xaal (Shoshannah Greene), Haida artist

Cheryl Simon, Mi'kmaw quill artist

Xiao Situ, PhD, Independent Scholar of Global Art History and Womanist and Liberation Theologies

Stephanie Sparling Williams (SSW), PhD, Andrew W. Mellon Curator of American Art, Brooklyn Museum

Jonathan Michael Square, PhD, Assistant Professor in Black Visual Culture, New School

Liz St. George (LSG), Assistant Curator of Decorative Arts, Brooklyn Museum

Briana Thompson (BT), former American Art intern, Brooklyn Museum

Dare Turner (DT), Curator of Indigenous Art, Brooklyn Museum

Brittany Webb, PhD, Evelyn and Will Kaplan Curator of Twentieth-Century Art and the John Rhoden Collection, Pennsylvania Academy of the Fine Arts

Kate Wight Tyler (KWT), Conservator, Brooklyn Museum

Leslie Wilson, PhD, Associate Director for Academic Engagement and Research, Art Institute of Chicago

Brooklyn Museum Board of Trustees

(as of May 30, 2024)

Chairman
Barbara M. Vogelstein
Vice Chair
Stephanie Ingrassia
Treasurer
Neil Simpkins
Secretary
Saundra Williams-Cornwell

Members
Regina Aldisert
Sasha Bass
Tamara C. Belinfanti
Adele Bernhard
Thomas Brodsky
Deenie Brosens
Rona Citrin
Jonathan Donnellan
Nikola Duravcevic
Sylvana Durrett
Henry B. Elsesser
Sharon Fay
Norman M. Feinberg
Michael Field
J.A. Forde
Amanda Fuhrman
Jeffrey Gibson
Steven Guttman
Jane Halt
Jeanine Heriveaux
Dan Houser
Kerby Jean-Raymond
Alan Jenkins
Michi Jigarjian
Ruth Jurgensen
Elizabeth Kahane
Titus Kaphar
Karen Kiehl
Susana Torruella Leval

Marley B. Lewis
Lynne M. Maguire
Joel Mallin
Todd Moscowitz
Vik Muniz
Asahi Pompey
Leslie A. Puth
Tracey G. Riese
Victoria Rogers
Jonathan Rosen
Carla Shen
Robert Soros
Ellen N. Taubman
Mickalene Thomas
Fred Tomaselli
Colleen Tompkins
Amanda Waldron
Sean Ward
Susan Weber
Kelly Williams
Matthew Wilson

Trustees Emeriti
Constance L. Christensen
Barbara Knowles Debs
Richard W. Moore
Otis Pratt Pearsall
Elizabeth A. Sackler
John S. Tamagni

Photography and Copyright Credits

© Laura Aguilar Trust of 2016, 175; © Eve Arnold/Magnum Photos, 248; © 2024 Artists Rights Society (ARS), New York / SOMAAP, Mexico City, 224; Photo by Thomas Barratt, 25, 40, 126, 226; Photo by Adriana Benavides, 190; © 2024 The Estate of Ilya Bolotowsky / Licensed by VAGA at Artists Rights Society (ARS), NY, 129; © Brooklyn Museum, 50, 142; Photo by Brooklyn Museum, 10, 20, 37, 42, 44, 45, 48, 40-54, 56-66, 72, 73, 76-79, 81, 82-84, 86, 87, 89-91, 93, 94, 96-100, 102, 106, 108-114, 116-118, 120-23, 128, 129, 132-40, 142, 143, 145-47, 150-52, 154, 155, 160, 162, 163, 164, 166, 168, 169, 170-77, 182, 184, 185, 187, 189, 192-202, 206, 210, 211, 212-24, 228-43, 248, 249, 251; © Eldzier Cortor, 59; © Renee Cox, 169; © 2024 Estate of Stuart Davis / Licensed by VAGA at Artists Rights Society (ARS), NY, 132; © Adama Delphine Fawundu, photo courtesy of the artist, 44; Photo by Christine Gant, 20; © Sasha Gordon, courtesy Matthew Brown, 172; © Estate of Albert Herter, 242; © Hisako Hibi, 24, 118, 124; © Chester Higgins. All Rights Reserved. Courtesy Bruce Silverstein Gallery, photo courtesy of the artist, 44; ho visto nina volare, 178; © Estate of Malvina Hoffman, 134; © Oscar yi Hou, 237; © Kyohei Inukai The Elder, 129; © Graciela Iturbide, 139; Courtesy of Jack Shainman Gallery, 246; © Wadsworth Jarrell, 241; © Estate of Loïs Mailou Jones, 56, 106, 232; © Titus Kaphar, 246; © Estate of John Koch, 62, 171; © Courtesy of the Lachaise Foundation, 168; © 2024 The Jacob and Gwendolyn Knight Lawrence Foundation, Seattle / Artists Rights, 94; © Courtney Leonard, 65; © Whitfield Lovell. Courtesy of DC Moore Gallery, 93; © 2024 Robert Mapplethorpe Foundation, 140; Photo by Kerry Ryan McFate, courtesy The Pace Gallery, 35, 149; © Senga Nengudi, 173; Photo by Andrea Nuñez, 209; © Chiura Obata, 117; © 2024 Lorraine O'Grady / Artists Rights Society (ARS), New York, 147; © 2024 Estate of Lucy T. Pettway / Artists Rights Society (ARS), New York, 220; Photo by Paula Abreu Pita, 30, 70, 71, 84, 85, 101, 104, 107, 157, 158, 179, 182, 183, 208, 251; © 2024 Anna Reinhardt / Artists Rights Society (ARS), New York, 128; © 2024 Faith Ringgold / Artists Rights Society (ARS), New York, 240; © Susan Rubin, 143; © Estate of Fritz Scholder, 146; © Nona Faustine Simmons, 176; © Aaron Siskind Foundation, 142 (below); © Estate of Raphael Soyer, 214, 235; © 2024 Estate of Alma Thomas (Courtesy of the Hart Family) / Artists Rights Society (ARS), New York, 210; © Hank Willis Thomas, 249; © Mickalene Thomas, 164 (above); © Colette Urbajtel/Asociación Manuel Álvarez Bravo, 248; © Estate of Laura Wheeler Waring, cover, 10, back cover; © Kehinde Wiley, 148; © 2010 Fred Wilson, courtesy Pace Gallery, 35, 149; © 2024 Estate of Hale Woodruff / Licensed by VAGA at Artists Rights Society (ARS), NY, 211; Max Yawney photo, courtesy of Sean Kelly, New York, 148.

Published on the occasion of the collection installation *Toward Joy: New Frameworks for American Art* at the Brooklyn Museum.

Made possible through support from the Terra Foundation for American Art.

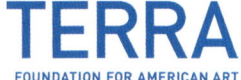

Leadership support is provided by Tracey and Phillip Riese. Major support is provided by American International Group, Inc.; Saundra Williams-Cornwell and W. Don Cornwell; Pfizer, Inc.; and the Brooklyn Museum Council for African American Art. Generous support is provided by Lizanne Fontaine and Robert Buckholz, the Hasso Philanthropic Foundation, the National Endowment for the Humanities, and Nkonye Okoh.

This edition © Scala Arts Publishers, Inc., and Brooklyn Museum, 2025
Text © Brooklyn Museum 2025

First published in 2025 by
Scala Arts Publishers, Inc.
c/o CohnReznick LLP
10th floor, 1301 Avenue of the Americas
New York, NY 10019, USA
www.scalapublishers.com
An imprint of B. T. Batsford Holdings Ltd.

In association with Brooklyn Museum

ISBN 978-1-78551-584-2

Library of Congress Control Number: 2025932896

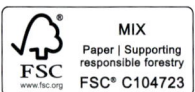

Edited by Erin Barnett
Designed by Anjali Pala

For the Brooklyn Museum
Director of Publications, Interpretation, and Editorial Services: Audrey Walen (former)
Director of Exhibition Planning: Dolores Farrell
Director of Digital Collections and Services: Sarah DeSantis
Image Licensing Specialist: Taylor Catalana
Photographer: Paula Abreu Pita

Printed in China

10 9 8 7 6 5 4 3 2 1

Scala is represented in UK and Europe by Abrams & Chronicle Books, 1 West Smithfield, London, EC1A 9JU and 57 rue Gaston Tessier, 75166 Paris, France.

All rights reserved. No part of this book may be reproduced, stored in a retrieval system or transmitted in any form or by any means electronic, mechanical, photocopying, recording or otherwise, without the written permission of the Brooklyn Museum and Scala Arts Publishers, Inc.

Every effort has been made to acknowledge correct copyright of images where applicable. Any errors or omissions are unintentional and should be notified to the Publisher, who will arrange for corrections to appear in any reprints.

Front cover: Laura Wheeler Waring. *Woman with Bouquet*, 1940.
Back cover: Laura Wheeler Waring. *Woman with Bouquet*, 1940. (detail)